Pregnancy and Childbirth

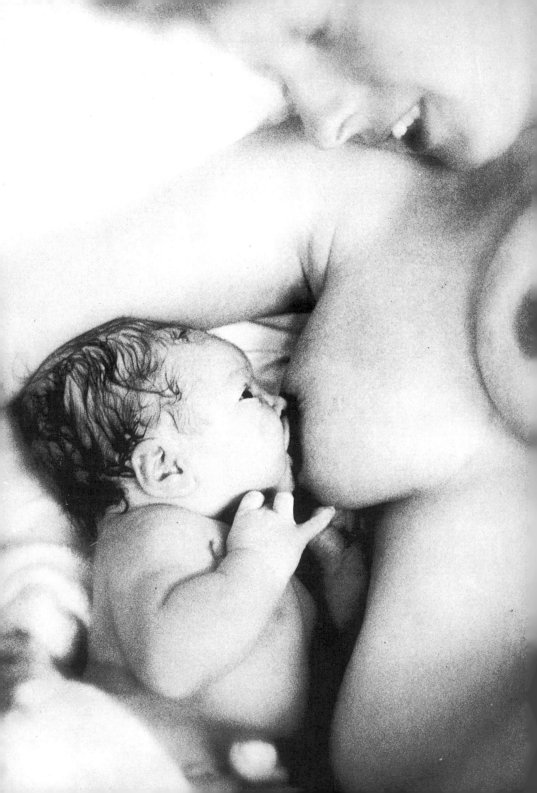

SHEILA KITZINGER

Pregnancy and Childbirth

REVISED EDITION

PHOTOGRAPHY BY CAMILLA JESSEL
& NANCY DURRELL McKENNA

Michael Joseph
LONDON

MICHAEL JOSEPH LTD

Published by the Penguin Group
27 Wrights Lane, London W8 5TZ, England
Viking Penguin Inc., 375 Hudson Street, New York, New York 10014, USA
Penguin Books Australia Ltd, Ringwood, Victoria, Australia
Penguin Books Canada Ltd, 10 Alcorn Avenue, Suite 300, Toronto, Ontario,
Canada, M4V 3B2
Penguin Books (NZ) Ltd, 182-190 Wairau Road, Auckland 10, New Zealand

Penguin Books Ltd Registered Offices: Harmondsworth, Middlesex, England

Pregnancy and Childbirth was conceived, edited and designed by
Dorling Kindersley Limited, 9 Henrietta Street, London WC2 8PS

First published in Great Britain November 1980
Revised edition May 1989
Second impression March 1992

Printed and bound in Great Britain by
William Clowes, Beccles, Suffolk

A CIP catalogue record for this book is available from the British Library

ISBN 0 7181 3171 1

CONTENTS

Introduction

When I first started to teach and counsel pregnant women back in the sixties, there was little birth education around. For a small minority of women there were breathing and relaxation exercises taught by physiotherapists (who then had no training for helping women in childbirth), and talks by midwives about "what to expect".

There was a handful of books written by the pioneers: Grantly Dick-Read, Kathleen Vaughan, Minnie Randall, Helen Heardman, Vevovsky and Lamaze. Though some of them discussed the fear of childbirth, there was nothing about the socially inculcated lack of confidence we felt in our bodies and in ourselves, nor about the pressure on women by a powerful medical system to surrender themselves to it as passive patients. It seemed that all we could hope for in labour was to put on as good a performance as possible and to be told "well done".

After the birth of my first child, when I started teaching for what is now the National Childbirth Trust, I remember talking to obstetricians from the USSR who had introduced psychoprophylaxis (a system of training based on breathing techniques) into some of their bigger hospitals and were proud because "there is now no noise in the labour ward". A great achievement—to silence women!

When psychoprophylaxis was first introduced into Britain from France a woman told me that the day after a gruelling labour involving drugs and the use of forceps, her antenatal teacher had shown up at her bedside and commented: "You didn't do too well!" In those days, if you needed pain-killing drugs or help with the birth, you were made to feel that you had failed. The choice was between having doctors take over completely, and putting on a solo performance without support or encouragement from professionals.

Remarkable changes have taken place since then—largely due to women in the childbirth movement who have joined together internationally and across continents. It is now acknowledged, almost everywhere, that women have a right to full and accurate information about their bodies and to participate in all decisions made about them. I doubt whether this could ever have occurred if we had left doctors, nurses and midwives to challenge the system.

This new edition of *Pregnancy and Childbirth* (first published in 1980) reflects the many changes that have come about because women refuse to remain ignorant of their bodies and about what doctors are doing to them. It is an expression of women's courage and growing self-confidence, and of the many ways in which we have reached out to each other to explore and understand those experiences in our lives which we share, which can reveal more about who we are, and which can help us realize our full potential as women.

◻In order to take an active part in giving birth rather than submit passively to delivery, you need to prepare yourself well in advance, understanding how to adapt to the work being done by your uterus, using breathing, relaxation, change of position, massage and focused concentration to "get in tune with" contractions. So there is a good deal of practical material in the book on how to do this. It is not just a matter of learning exercises. There is a harmony and rhythm about a natural labour: with the wave of each contraction you are swept on towards the birth of the baby in a pattern which makes labour into a process greater than all its separate parts, one in which all the techniques you have practised are submerged by the total satisfying experience.

The book describes the choices which are available so that you can decide how you would like to have your baby, the kind of setting and care you prefer, and how you wish your baby to be welcomed into the world. I include suggestions on talking with your doctor, how to ask about all the things that worry you, and how you can share in the decisions about yourself and your baby. The book also sets out to give a map of the route through pregnancy and labour and out the other side, explaining who does what to you and why, and what happens when things are not straightforward. In doing this I have used some of the words and phrases that you may see written on your medical chart or hear used by doctors or midwives, so that you will understand them when you meet them.

The book is threaded through with recognition of the father's importance for his partner and baby and suggestions as to how he can help most effectively during pregnancy, labour and the time after the birth. A baby is bound to change a couple's way of life, their feelings about each other and the kind of partnership they have. The man, as well as the woman, often faces emotional challenges, and this is rarely acknowledged in our society. So another thing that I have done is to focus on the experience of childbirth for him.

Most new parents gain confidence and find it easiest to have "conversations" with their baby when there are no rules to be obeyed and no standards to live up to, when they can explore their baby, take it into bed with them and stroke, hold and cuddle it as much as they wish. In this book I hope to show how a couple can create the kind of setting and atmosphere for birth, whether at home or in hospital, that nourishes relationships in the family.

Pregnancy and childbirth are normal life processes, not illnesses. You feel the incredible surge of life moving inside you, the ripening of your body heavy with fruit deep inside it, and then at last the flood of vitality as labour starts and your uterus contracts in wave after wave, bringing your baby into your arms. It is exciting, awe-inspiring and deeply satisfying. At the same time you grow up a bit, learn more about yourself and your partner, develop in understanding and awareness. I hope that this book will help you to savour the intense reality of the experience of childbearing and enjoy it to the full.

Notes to the reader

It is always difficult when writing about babies to know whether to use "he" or "she". By convention they are usually called "he", and this is often easiest in practice as it distinguishes the baby from the mother. Although I sometimes call the baby "it", I have mainly used a mixture of "he" and "she", since babies are people with their own budding personalities right from the start. I hope that the reader will not find this too awkward, and if there is a bias towards "she", note that my five babies were all girls, so it comes naturally to me.

Throughout the text references to research are marked with an asterisk (*); this indicates that the works in which the research findings have been published are given in Appendix 2, page 378, under the appropriate page number.

Author's acknowledgments

I should like to thank all those women who have helped me understand more about the experience of childbirth and how it was for them. From every couple I have taught I have learned something new or seen things in a different light. I have learned far more than I have ever taught.

My husband, Uwe, and our five daughters, Celia, Nell, Tess, Polly, and Jenny, are generous in their acceptance of my work, the time I give to couples having babies and the inevitable phone calls punctuating family get-togethers and meals. Knowing that Uwe values what I am doing and gives me his full emotional support generates fresh strength in me to carry on when the going gets rough.

Murray Enkin, Associate Professor of Obstetrics at McMaster, read every single word of the text for the first edition of this book and looked at it from a medical point of view, but often commented too as a warm and caring human being. I have learned a great deal about human relations in the hospital from him.

Sybil del Strother proved a skilled and understanding editor in preparing the book for its first publication. Lesley Riley dealt expertly with the second edition. I know readers will enjoy the photographs by Camilla Jessel, who also studied very carefully my approach to birth so that she could express this in her work. My thanks also to Nancy Durrell McKenna, who took the photographs that appear on page 211, between pages 232 and 257 and on page 319 specially for this revised edition.

The new edition was typed by Judith Schroeder, my secretary, on whose enthusiasm and hard work I rely heavily.

Giving birth

*One birth . . . not especially difficult, nor
especially easy . . . not a formula, not a
blueprint . . . just some moments during a
labour and the beginnings of a new life.*

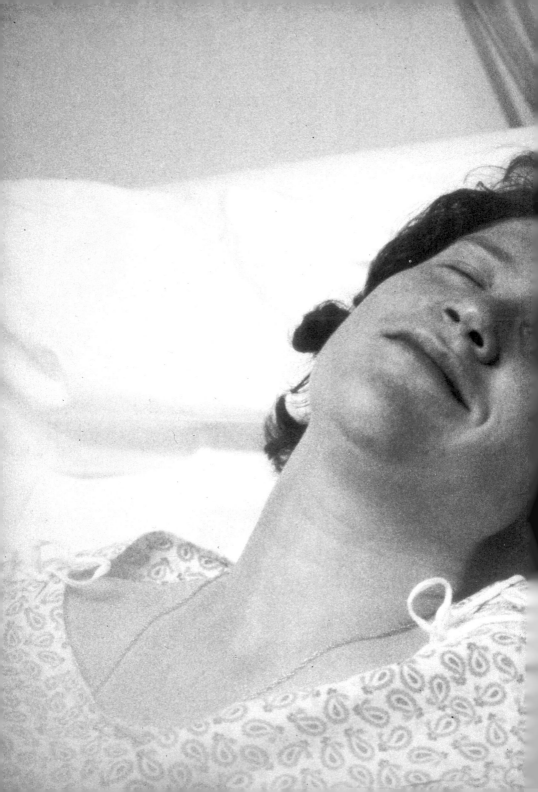

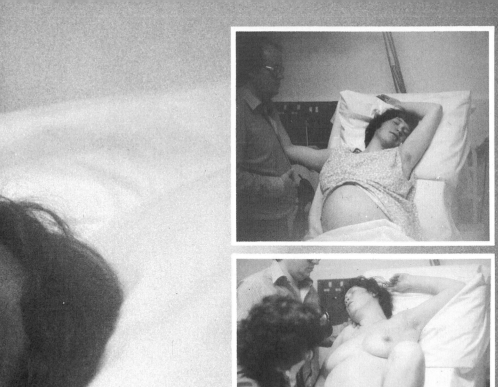

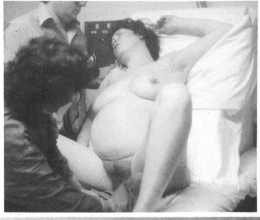

. . . in the first stage the contractions of the uterus dilate the cervix . . .

. . . in the second stage the head is being pressed down through the birth canal . . .

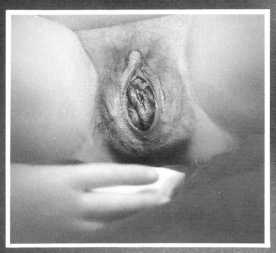

... then the baby's
head crowns and
slides out face down ...

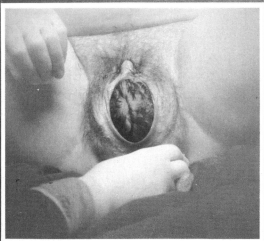

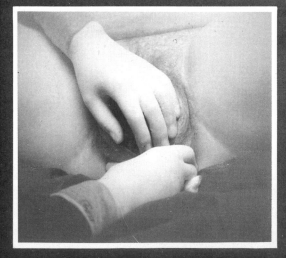

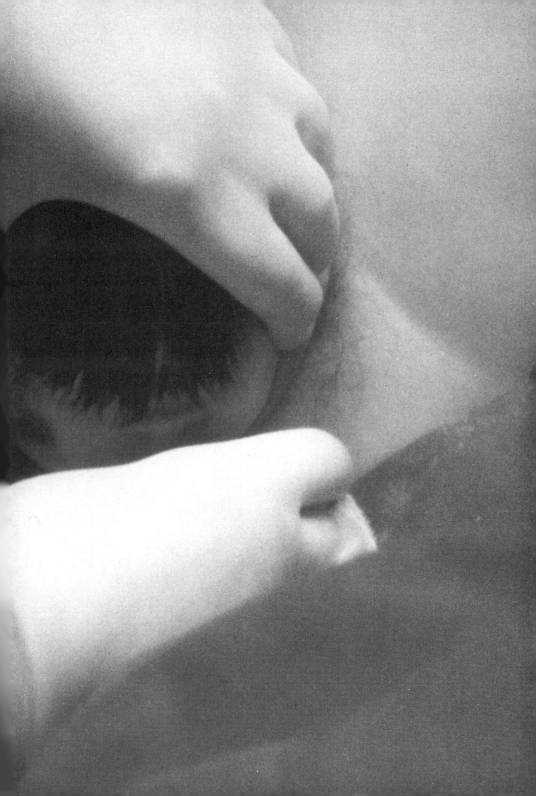

... the head rotates ...

*... the mother reaches down
to touch her baby before
it is born ...*

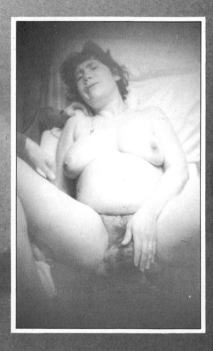

. . . the moment of birth . . .

. . . gently, quietly, the baby is lifted and placed in close, warm contact with her skin . . .

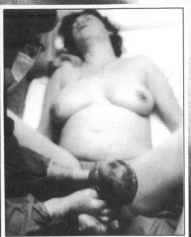

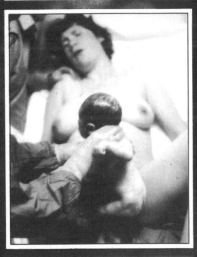

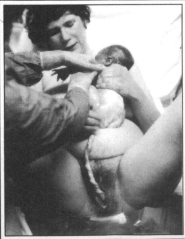

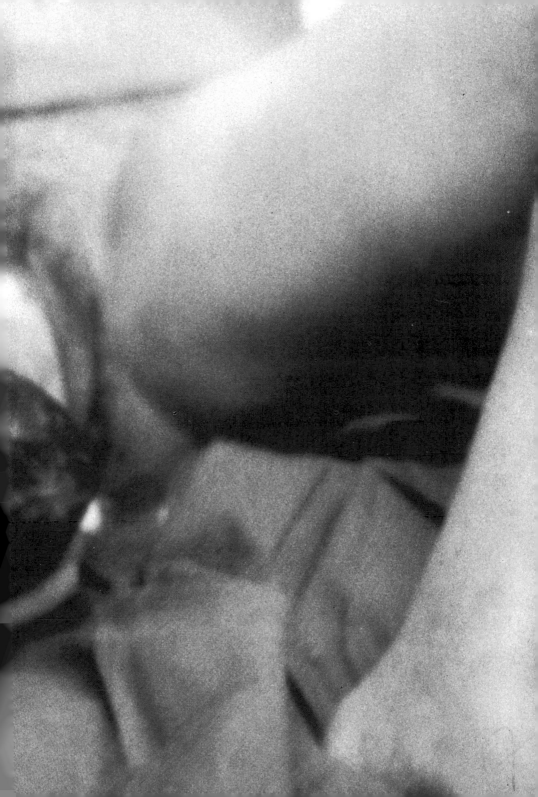

*. . . she takes his hand to tell him that all
is well in this world of new sensations . . .*

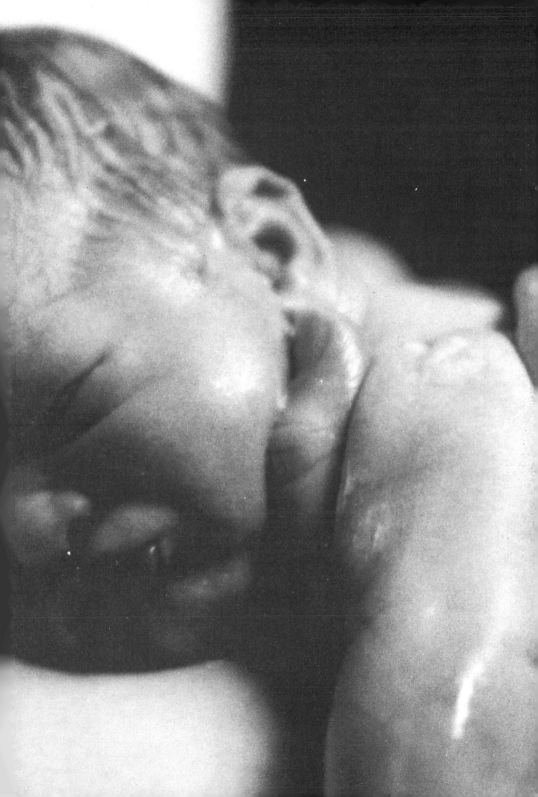

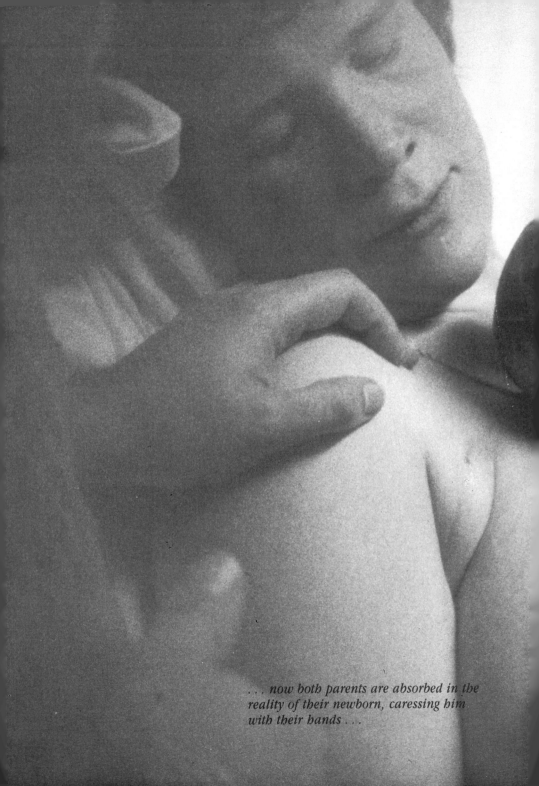

... now both parents are absorbed in the reality of their newborn, caressing him with their hands ...

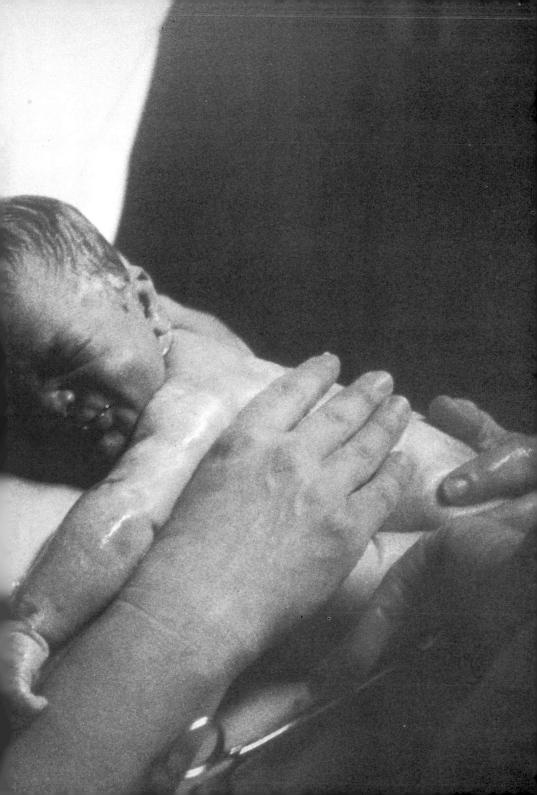

. . . when the baby is ready he will fasten on to his mother's breast . . .

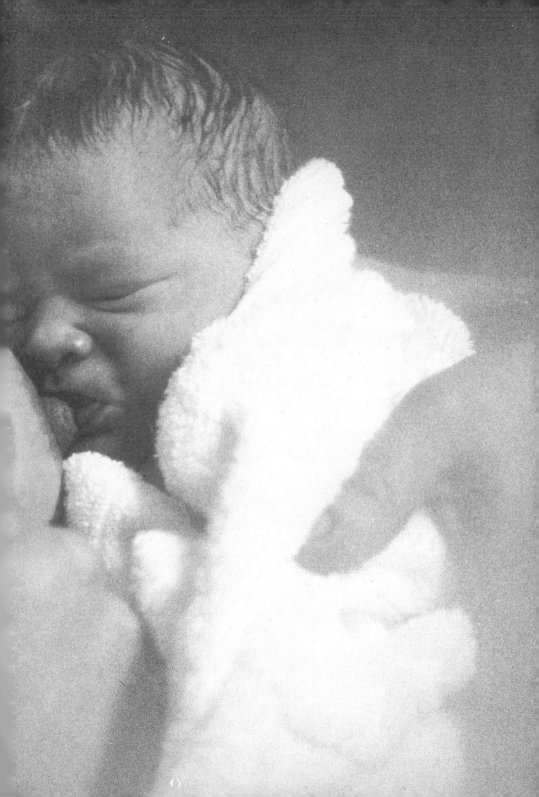

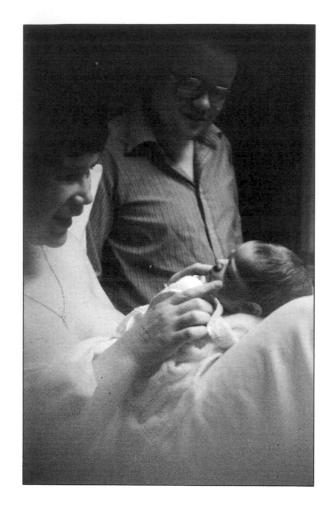

. . . not only a new baby is born,
but a new family too.

PREGNANCY

The early weeks

Finding out you are pregnant
Planning and preparation

Finding out you are pregnant

Some women are convinced that they are pregnant from the moment of conception; others have such irregular periods that a long gap in between does not alert them to the possibility of pregnancy. But for most women the first sign of pregnancy is a missed period.

Perhaps it is five days since the day when you expected it, but then you start wondering if your dates were wrong. Perhaps you usually make a note in your diary, but last time you forgot. You lie in bed, unable to sleep, trying to fix the dates firmly in your mind by finding some useful landmark, like your mother's visit or the end of a particular work assignment. Still another three days go by and the reality gradually dawns: you might be pregnant. You might not be, but it does seem quite possible that you are. When is it sensible to go to the doctor and how early can you know for certain?

You may have mixed feelings when you realize you are pregnant.

When to diagnose

Until recently it was usual to visit the doctor after missing two periods. Nowadays there is a strong case for finding out if you are pregnant before two periods have been missed. It is during these few weeks, while the embryo is still no larger than a hazelnut, that the major organs of the body and the brain itself are being formed; the sooner you know that you are pregnant the sooner you can start caring for yourself and for the baby.

An early confirmation of pregnancy is also important if you take any medicines. You will want to avoid taking drugs which could harm the developing baby (see page 93). It is also useful to know early for social reasons—you may be planning to go abroad or move house at the time the baby is due.

If there is a possibility that you may want a termination it is essential to diagnose pregnancy early: a termination at eight weeks is much safer and less upsetting than one after ten weeks. Bear in mind that if you go to your general practitioner for a urine pregnancy test, the GP very often has to wait for two weeks before the results come from the laboratory. Delays of this kind make an early termination less likely.

How to diagnose

Pregnancy can now be diagnosed on the day your period should have started, though you are likely to get more accurate results if you wait at least another four days—which can be difficult if you are feeling anxious or excited. When you are pregnant, the embryo releases the hormone human chorionic gonadotrophin (HCG) into your bloodstream. This can first be detected in your urine about six days after conception, but then the level builds up rapidly, doubling every two or three days until it reaches a peak about 60 days after conception—24 days after your period should have started.

The presence of this hormone can be detected in your urine by a simple test. You can take a urine sample either to your local GP or to a chemist who does pregnancy testing, or you can use one of the do-it-yourself kits that are available from chemists. Whichever method you choose, you should test urine passed first thing in the morning, when you have not drunk anything during the night, since it is at this time that urine contains the highest concentration of pregnancy hormone. Store the urine in an absolutely clean jar or bottle, free from any traces of soap or detergent.

Do-it-yourself tests There are a number of different kits on the market, but they all involve mixing a drop or two of urine with the chemicals provided. If you are pregnant, the presence of HCG in your urine will, depending on the test, either prevent the mixture from coagulating (ring test), or change the colour of the chemical in the test tube or on the dipstick (colour test). Depending on the kit, you can use these tests when your period is between one and four days late, but you do need to be sure of when your period was due.

Occasionally a woman notices a little spotting (light bleeding) 10–12 days after fertilization. This is not really a period and the dating of pregnancy can start from your last actual period.

If the result is negative, but your period still has not come a few days later, do the test again. It is possible that you conceived later than you thought likely and that at the time of the first test there was not enough HCG in your urine to indicate that you were pregnant. If your periods are irregular or far apart, the chances of a false result are increased. After perhaps one conception in every ten, the fertilized egg does not manage to embed itself in the lining of the uterus. In this case, a pregnancy test will give you a positive result, but a second test a few days later will produce a negative result. Some packs recommend that you always wait three to five days and then re-test, and they contain two tests so that you can do this.

Going to the doctor If you take a specimen of urine with you, the doctor can have it tested; as an alternative you may be given an internal examination. He or she introduces two gloved fingers into your vagina as far as they will go, while pressing with the other hand into your abdomen where the top of the uterus lies. If it is more than six weeks since the first day of your last period the doctor can feel the already softened lower part of the uterus, which is also slightly enlarged. The neck of the uterus, or cervix, which protrudes into the vagina, is felt as firmer than the lower part of the uterus, and it is about the same consistency as the tip of your nose. The internal change is known as "Hegar's sign".

◆

The examination may be uncomfortable but will not be painful. As the examining fingers are introduced, give a long, slow breath out through your mouth and continue breathing as slowly as you can.

Dating

Once the pregnancy is confirmed by your doctor it will be dated from the first day of your last menstrual period (LMP). If you cannot recollect this date with accuracy the doctor will probably ask you to make a guess at it. This means that from then on the length of your pregnancy is reckoned in terms of so many weeks, including the weeks from the beginning of your last period to the time when conception occurred. Since ovulation is most common midway between two periods, the usual medical way of dating pregnancy adds an extra two weeks to its length. The length of the average

Do-it-yourself pregnancy tests

There are two main kinds of test available—the ring test and the colour test. Whichever you choose, be sure to follow the instructions carefully, and to test only the first urine of the day. The time when you can use these tests varies. Some kits recommend waiting until your period is at least four days late; others can be done as early as the day after your period was due, but for a reliable result you need to be certain when your period should have started.

The ring test can give a false result if you allow the tube to get hot, or shake it. Colour tests are not affected by vibration, but may be affected by heat. All results are accurate only for a limited amount of time: some tests are stable for only five minutes; others remain unchanged for hours, even days.

If you get a positive result, or if you get a negative result but your period has not started after five more days, consult your doctor.

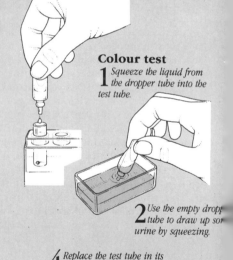

Colour test

1 *Squeeze the liquid from the dropper tube into the test tube.*

2 *Use the empty dropper tube to draw up some urine by squeezing.*

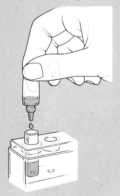

3 *Now put a few drops of urine into the test tube. Replace the stopper and shake the tube well.*

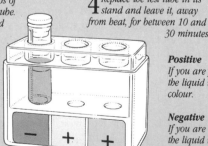

4 *Replace the test tube in its stand and leave it, away from heat, for between 10 and 30 minutes.*

Positive
If you are pregnant, the liquid will change colour.

Negative
If you are not pregnant, the liquid will not change colour.

◆

pregnancy is some 266 days from the date of conception: your doctor will therefore arrive at your expected date of delivery (EDD) by adding 280 days, or 40 weeks, to the first day of your last period (the chart on page 31 is calculated according to this convention). You may find that you pay your first visit to the clinic knowing that it is ten weeks since you conceived, but emerge three months pregnant!

But since not all women ovulate halfway between two periods, the medical convention of adding on an extra two weeks is an artificial one, and an inaccurate method of working out when a baby is due. It is wise to think of the EDD as an approximate date rather than the day when you expect to go into labour.

If you have just stopped taking the contraceptive Pill your dates may be completely wrong. The period which immediately follows your last Pill may not be followed by ovulation or you may have a

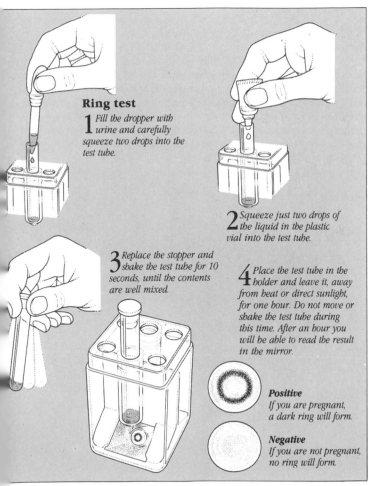

Ring test

1 *Fill the dropper with urine and carefully squeeze two drops into the test tube.*

2 *Squeeze just two drops of the liquid in the plastic vial into the test tube.*

3 *Replace the stopper and shake the test tube for 10 seconds, until the contents are well mixed.*

4 *Place the test tube in the holder and leave it, away from heat or direct sunlight, for one hour. Do not move or shake the test tube during this time. After an hour you will be able to read the result in the mirror.*

Positive
If you are pregnant, a dark ring will form.

Negative
If you are not pregnant, no ring will form.

slight spotting of blood which is not really a period. It may take several months to re-establish your natural cycle, and until then you cannot predict with any certainty when, or whether, you are going to ovulate. You might be a month or more out in your dates. This is obviously very important in estimating when the baby is due, especially since it could mean labour being induced unnecessarily (see page 297). It is advisable to wait for a clear three months after coming off the Pill before trying to conceive; during this time you should use some other method of contraception.

Conceiving while using contraception

If you conceive with an IUD (intra-uterine device, or coil) still inside you, your chances of miscarrying increase. It is important to see your doctor quickly, as the IUD should be removed if possible and this can only be done early in pregnancy. Sometimes doctors advise termination. This is certainly not necessary if you want the baby: even if it is too late to remove the IUD, many women deliver the IUD with the placenta after an uneventful pregnancy and birth.

It is possible to conceive while taking the Pill, if you miss one or more days when you should have been taking it, or if you have a stomach upset with vomiting so that you fail to absorb the hormones, or if you have been on antibiotics. If you do conceive but continue to take the Pill for several months while pregnant, there is a slightly increased risk to the baby of congenital abnormalities. But the vast majority of women who have taken the Pill while pregnant give birth to babies who are healthy and normal.

HAVING A VAGINAL EXAMINATION
You may be examined vaginally early on in your pregnancy. If you are more than 6 weeks pregnant the doctor can detect a slight softening and enlargement of the uterus. The developing embryo is well protected and cannot be dislodged by the examination.

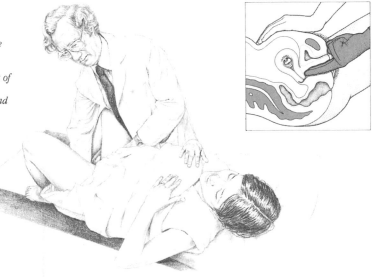

Sometimes a doctor prescribes pills containing the hormones oestrogen and progestogen to discover whether or not a woman is pregnant, the idea being that you take them and if you are not pregnant your period starts. These hormone pills carry the same slight risk to the baby as the Pill does: do not take them.

Pregnancy and AIDS

If you are anxious that you or your partner have been exposed to the virus that causes AIDS (acquired immune deficiency syndrome), you may decide before you get pregnant, or in very early pregnancy, that you should be screened for it. The test does not identify the virus (the human immunodeficiency virus, or HIV) itself, but reveals whether

When is your baby due?

Look down the columns of the chart at the figures set in bold type to find the first day of your last period. The date next to it is 280 days later, and is therefore your estimated date of delivery (EDD).

Jan/Oct	Feb/Nov	Mar/Dec	Apr/Jan	May/Feb	June/Mar	July/Apr	Aug/May	Sept/June	Oct/July	Nov/Aug	Dec/Sept
1 8	1 8	1 6	1 6	1 5	1 8	1 7	1 8	1 8	1 8	1 8	1 7
2 9	2 9	2 7	2 7	2 6	2 9	2 8	2 9	2 9	2 9	2 9	2 8
3 10	3 10	3 8	3 8	3 7	3 10	3 9	3 10	3 10	3 10	3 10	3 9
4 11	4 11	4 9	4 9	4 8	4 11	4 10	4 11	4 11	4 11	4 11	4 10
5 12	5 12	5 10	5 10	5 9	5 12	5 11	5 12	5 12	5 12	5 12	5 11
6 13	6 13	6 11	6 11	6 10	6 13	6 12	6 13	6 13	6 13	6 13	6 12
7 14	7 14	7 12	7 12	7 11	7 14	7 13	7 14	7 14	7 14	7 14	7 13
8 15	8 15	8 13	8 13	8 12	8 15	8 14	8 15	8 15	8 15	8 15	8 14
9 16	9 16	9 14	9 14	9 13	9 16	9 15	9 16	9 16	9 16	9 16	9 15
10 17	10 17	10 15	10 15	10 14	10 17	10 16	10 17	10 17	10 17	10 17	10 16
11 18	11 18	11 16	11 16	11 15	11 18	11 17	11 18	11 18	11 18	11 18	11 17
12 19	12 19	12 17	12 17	12 16	12 19	12 18	12 19	12 19	12 19	12 19	12 18
13 20	13 20	13 18	13 18	13 17	13 20	13 19	13 20	13 20	13 20	13 20	13 19
14 21	14 21	14 19	14 19	14 18	14 21	14 20	14 21	14 21	14 21	14 21	14 20
15 22	15 22	15 20	15 20	15 19	15 22	15 21	15 22	15 22	15 22	15 22	15 21
16 23	16 23	16 21	16 21	16 20	16 23	16 22	16 23	16 23	16 23	16 23	16 22
17 24	17 24	17 22	17 22	17 21	17 24	17 23	17 24	17 24	17 24	17 24	17 23
18 25	18 25	18 23	18 23	18 22	18 25	18 24	18 25	18 25	18 25	18 25	18 24
19 26	19 26	19 24	19 24	19 23	19 26	19 25	19 26	19 26	19 26	19 26	19 25
20 27	20 27	20 25	20 25	20 24	20 27	20 26	20 27	20 27	20 27	20 27	20 26
21 28	21 28	21 26	21 26	21 25	21 28	21 27	21 28	21 28	21 28	21 28	21 27
22 29	22 29	22 27	22 27	22 26	22 29	22 28	22 29	22 29	22 29	22 29	22 28
23 30	23 30	23 28	23 28	23 27	23 30	23 29	23 30	23 30	23 30	23 30	23 29
24 31	24 1	24 29	24 29	24 28	24 31	24 30	24 31	24 1	24 31	24 31	24 30
25 1	25 2	25 30	25 30	25 1	25 1	25 1	25 1	25 2	25 1	25 1	25 1
26 2	26 3	26 31	26 31	26 2	26 2	26 2	26 2	26 3	26 2	26 2	26 2
27 3	27 4	27 1	27 1	27 3	27 3	27 3	27 3	27 4	27 3	27 3	27 3
28 4	28 5	28 2	28 2	28 4	28 4	28 4	28 4	28 5	28 4	28 4	28 4
29 5		29 3	29 3	29 5	29 5	29 5	29 5	29 6	29 5	29 5	29 5
30 6		30 4	30 4	30 6	30 6	30 6	30 6	30 7	30 6	30 6	30 6
31 7		31 5		31 7		31 7	31 7		31 7		31 7
Jan/Nov	Feb/Dec	Mar/Jan	Apr/Feb	May/Mar	June/Apr	July/May	Aug/June	Sept/July	Oct/Aug	Nov/Sept	Dec/Oct

antibodies to it are in the bloodstream. If someone has been infected, antibodies will be present. Even though they themselves may show no symptoms of infection, they can transmit the virus to someone else. A pregnant woman can infect her unborn baby.

Before being tested you will have thought through the implications—social, emotional and physical—of getting a positive result. As one woman carrying the virus said: "The only difference between now and before is this piece of knowledge. And it's such depressing, unhappy knowledge, I find it quite paralyzing."* According to current research, anyone who is antibody-positive has a 10 to 30 per cent chance of developing AIDS within four years. Pregnancy affects the immune system, so it may trigger AIDS in a woman who is antibody-positive but who has had no previous symptoms. It is possible that she may develop the disease during pregnancy or soon after the baby is born.

Babies born to HIV-positive mothers always have antibodies. Some types of antibody, however, can enter the baby's blood without the child becoming infected with the virus, and if an HIV-positive woman is healthy during pregnancy, there is a good chance that her baby will lose its inherited antibodies within 6 to 18 months. It may take a year, with tests every few months, to know for sure whether a baby is carrying the virus. Only about 22 per cent of antibody-positive newborn babies develop AIDS. If a woman has already given birth to an infected baby, there is a 66 per cent chance that her next baby will be infected too. If she herself has AIDS the risk is still greater. A baby infected in the uterus may have birth defects or a characteristic facial appearance with a very small head, box-shaped forehead, flat nose, blue eyeballs, widely spaced eyes and full lips.

Antibody tests may show up negative for three months following infection. It makes sense to have a second test 12 weeks after the first if you or your partner are at high risk of contracting the virus and if you are in very early pregnancy and are sure that you would want a termination if you were antibody-positive. No test is 100 per cent free from error. The "Western blot"—which is the most widely used test in North America and Britain—is 96 per cent accurate.

Early signs of pregnancy

Breast changes Even before your pregnancy is confirmed there may be early indications other than a missed period. Breast changes, in preparation for milk production, occur in the first weeks. The brownish circles round the nipples (the areolae) become darker and the little bumps on them (Montgomery's tubercles) more prominent. If you are pink-skinned you may notice that the lacy network of blood vessels in your breasts has become much more obvious. Blue veins run over the breasts like rivers on a map. Your breasts also feel tender and heavy. Women with small breasts may note an obvious increase in size very early on, and are often delighted. If you have large breasts already you may not notice any size change at this stage.

You may notice changes in your breasts early in pregnancy, including an increase in size, a darkening of the nipples and the areolae, and extra prominence of the little bumps on the areolae known as Montgomery's tubercles.

Tiredness Enormous metabolic changes take place in pregnancy and your whole body has to adjust to the process of growing a baby. It is not surprising that you may feel tired and that you cannot carry on just as before. Many women complain of extreme tiredness in the first eight or ten weeks. But as your body adjusts to the pregnancy the fatigue vanishes and the middle months are often easy. If you are feeling tired it is only sensible to take the message from your body and go to bed early, have a rest at midday if you can, or have an early evening rest when you get in from work.

If it is your second (or third) pregnancy, you may find that you are constantly tired. Women who thoroughly enjoyed their first pregnancy say that the second one is much harder to cope with because they are exhausted by the non-stop pace of their first child's daily life. The only solution is to organize your life as well as you can; try to have at least a short time every day when you are completely free from domestic responsibilities. Even half an hour every evening when your partner attends to the child and the washing-up can be relaxing if you are able to enjoy it to the full. (See page 158 for more about second and later pregnancies.)

Nausea Another common sign of pregnancy is nausea. These waves of sickness often happen early in the morning, when your blood sugar level is low, but they may also occur in the early evening, or even—more rarely—at other times of the day. Some women just feel very sick, others actually vomit. Tiredness contributes to nausea, but so does an empty stomach: small frequent snacks of bland foods like biscuits or a banana may relieve the feeling. If you suffer from morning sickness, a cup of tea and a few biscuits or dry toast immediately on waking may prevent the nausea, or the biscuits alone may be better. A late night snack may help, too. As a general rule cut out all greasy fried foods, tobacco, and alcohol. Some women become really ill with vomiting (see page 123), although most stop feeling sick during the fourth month.

There is some evidence that women who experience pregnancy nausea are less likely than others to have miscarriages. This can be a cheering thought. But nausea does not exist in all cultures; many societies have other illnesses and disabilities or special dreams which they connect with pregnancy. Margaret Mead points out that in some societies of New Guinea boils are considered to be a typical symptom of pregnancy. Some Jamaicans do not acknowledge pregnancy until they have had a special fertility dream of ripe fruit bursting with seed. Dreams of this kind are characteristic of early pregnancy. It is as if all women need definite signs with which to link pregnancy so that they can say, "I feel this, therefore I must be expecting a baby."

You may suffer from nausea for the first time in your second or third pregnancy. This is almost certainly as a result of tiredness, and you may not relieve the nausea within three months unless you can somehow arrange to have more rest.

The first 3 months were wretched because I had continual nausea. I worried about what this might be doing to our baby—but here she is, chubby and beautiful. It doesn't seem to have affected her at all.

Emotional reactions to pregnancy

However much you want a baby, finding out that you really are pregnant can produce a flood of conflicting emotions: triumph ("We've done it!"), a sense of being trapped ("There's no going back—now what?"), fear ("Mother had an awful time having me—shall I be able to stand the pain?"), apprehension ("Will we still love each other in the same way?") and doubt ("Will he still want me once my waist starts getting thicker?"). It is surprising how many women respond to their first pregnancy with shock and feel that it has happened "too soon", even though they very much want a baby and have considered the matter carefully before stopping contraception. Confronted with the reality and the physical changes of pregnancy, they want to say: "Stop! I haven't prepared myself for this. Let's go back and start again."

If you discover that you are pregnant when you did not plan to be, you may also feel unfairly trapped. Yet, perversely, many women (for whom pregnancy is not a disaster) are aware of an odd pleasure that their fertility has triumphed over their conscious wish. Your partner may suspect that you wanted a baby all along and have not been "playing fair". Starting a baby under such circumstances can lead to conflict between you, because he may feel that you have not been open with him. Try not to go off and discuss the matter with other people as if your man were the enemy. Talk about it together: you need to understand each other.

Feelings about motherhood You may have a crisis of self-confidence, feeling that you will be no good as a mother because you have no maternal instincts. But mothering is a learned activity and very little of it purely instinctive. Moreover for the first-time mother in our society, who may never have handled a newborn baby before, most of the learning goes on after the baby is born. The teacher is the baby herself. Even though you may not start off as an expert, your baby soon turns you into one.

Feelings about being on show You may feel suddenly that your most intimate relationship with the man you love is publicly displayed, not just because you are pregnant and everybody knows, but because of the physical examinations and exposure at the antenatal clinic, and the advice that people keep giving you. This sense of becoming public property may be intensified by the obvious pleasure of parents who have long been wanting you to get pregnant.

Yet your body holds life. The wonder of that cannot really be understood by anyone else. You stand naked in front of the mirror and look for changes. You rest your hand on your tummy and wonder if you can feel the tiny seed of a baby beginning to grow inside you. You think back to when you made love, wonder which time it was and if, perhaps, you really knew then that you had conceived.

We're over the moon! I never believed it could happen to me. I feel so pleased with myself. I know it's ridiculous, but it's as if I was the first human being ever to have a baby!

Feelings about your body If you feel on bad terms with your body as it starts out on the work of early pregnancy, arrange to attend some pregnancy exercise or dance classes if these are available in your area. A list of organizations which can help you is on page 383. If these classes are not specially for pregnant women, let your teacher know that you are pregnant. Get out in the fresh air and walk. Buy a maternity swimsuit and swim regularly. Start doing the movements suggested on pages 108–109 a few times each day to pep up your circulation and increase vitality. In some countries massage is an anticipated and very pleasant part of being pregnant, so you could go to a masseuse or your partner could learn how to massage you (see page 172). This can be particularly useful if you are tense and find it difficult to release your muscles at will.

As your pregnancy progresses, you may become fascinated by your body's changing shape.

Your partner's feelings You are not the only person who has to adjust emotionally in pregnancy. Your partner needs to as well. He does not have to cope with physical changes, but the emotional impact of a first pregnancy is no less real, and the passage into fatherhood constitutes a major transition in his life. For a man this process is often delayed until several things have happened: the pregnancy has been officially confirmed; your figure has obviously changed; the baby has moved and he has felt it fluttering.

Emotions of joy, pride and wonder may war with others which are disturbing. There may be financial problems which can cause a man to feel a sense of deep and burdensome responsibility for the woman bearing his child and for the new life that is coming. A man, too, may feel trapped by pregnancy. Perhaps his relationship with the woman was intended to remain free and untrammelled by babies (especially if the couple have not discussed pregnancy and planned for it together). His job may now assume importance not only in its own right, but because he feels an urgent need to be successful before the baby comes, as if it threatens his own powers of achievement. A man, too, may be frightened of birth and even of his partner's pregnant body, which can seem dangerous and not to be touched in case the baby is dislodged. He may feel, quite wrongly, that his own sexual desires are a terrible threat to the baby. For some men the whole pregnancy is a time of stress.

Discussing your emotions together

It does not help to bottle up these emotions. Talk about them together. If you pretend they are not there, they become destructive. What you are feeling is normal and thousands of other couples experience it too. It may be possible to work out together a sensible strategy so that some parts of your lives are left free from responsibility: you could avoid relatives until you feel better able to cope with them. You may be able to arrange to visit the antenatal clinic together, so that your partner can see what happens there, can meet the doctor or midwife and be present during the physical examination. Reading

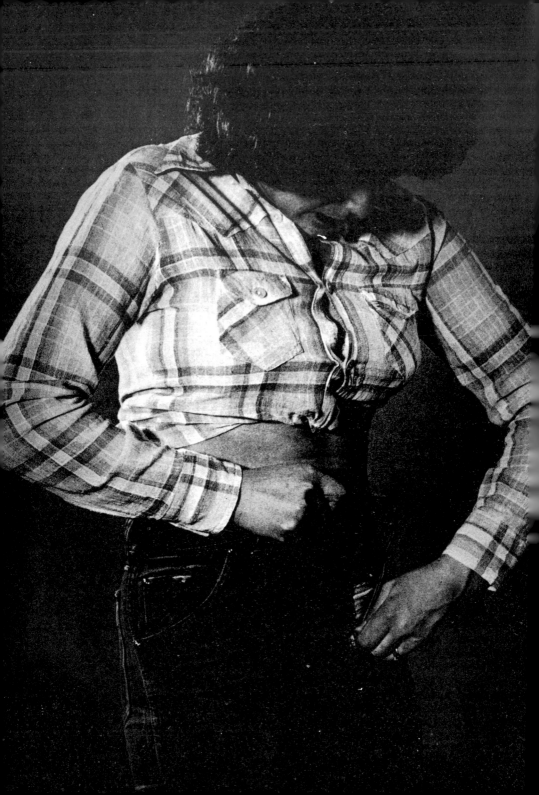

together about pregnancy and birth helps to replace ignorance with knowledge about the role a man can actively play in childbirth.

Lying together in bed, cuddling, and exploring each other's bodies is a way of communicating through loving touch and tenderness. It is a way of nourishing your partnership together, ready for the new person who is entering it. Since words often disguise your real feelings and complicate matters, find opportunities to meet each other through touch.

Pregnancy is not merely a waiting time. It is a time for working out together what you value in your relationship and what kind of world you both want to create for your child. This is not a question of making a nursery and buying things ready for the baby, but of helping each other to change from people who are responsible just for themselves into a mother and a father, with the new responsibility that parenthood brings. A man and a woman need to grow into parents. Then not only a baby, but a new family is born.

The woman alone

Pregnancy and childbirth are not easy when you do not have a partner to give you love and care. It is even more difficult once the baby is born to take complete responsibility for a new life. Yet many women have done this successfully and have reared happy, healthy children.

Talking about the single mother and the challenges she faces is in a way misleading, because women on their own bearing babies do not fall into one category any more than women with partners do. The reasons single women embark on pregnancy, and decide to go on with it, vary widely. Some women continue with a pregnancy only because they are unwilling or unable to face up to it, and drift on hoping that it might go away. Others are bearing a much-wanted child "before it is too late". Others again loved the father of the child and hoped that the relationship would continue, but then found themselves rejected and bearing a child alone. Then there are women whose men die while they are pregnant, leaving them to face the future alone.

Whatever your reasons for having a child on your own, financial problems may loom large. Trying to combine a job with rearing a child, while knowing that there is no-one else to take over in time of need, can be difficult. It is important to anticipate and share the problems, and a good idea to seek counselling from people who understand them and who may be able to put you in touch with other sources of help. Contact the organizations listed on page 383 before you have your baby and see what they have to offer. These organizations are also designed to help you cope with all the practical difficulties that can crop up, such as housing, finding day care for the baby and sorting out to which social benefits you are entitled.

Book into childbirth education classes (see page 164) early. Many women delay until the last minute and then find that the classes are full. The National Childbirth Trust (address on page 383) can tell you

=**66**=
I've always had irregular periods so I didn't notice. The doctor said "Do you realize you're pregnant?" I was stunned! Alan's married you know. It was too late for an abortion.
=**99**=

OPPOSITE
Finding that your clothes don't fit any more may be the first time that you really believe you are pregnant.

about the different kinds of childbirth classes, postnatal support and breast-feeding counselling that are available in your locality.

Sometimes a man who is not your permanent partner is still willing to accept some of the responsibilities of fatherhood. It is quite common in an antenatal class to have couples who do not plan to marry or even to stay together. Be frank with your childbirth educator so that she has a chance to get to know you, and perhaps both of you, as people and not just as pupils. It may be possible for you to arrange to see her privately for a session in which you can discuss the emotional and physical challenges facing you.

Emotional support in labour

Think ahead to the birth and decide whether you would like to have a companion with you. Childbirth can feel very solitary if you do not have someone with you to encourage you and provide continuous emotional support. This person could be a good woman friend, an antenatal teacher, your sister or mother, or a man friend who understands what birth is about and can give the right kind of help. Most hospitals nowadays allow a companion in labour, although they often restrict you to one person, and sometimes they state that it must be the father of the baby. Discuss the matter with your doctor and with your childbirth educator, and if necessary state your request in writing to the secretary of the hospital's Board of Management or to the Director of Midwifery.

If there is no-one who can be with you in labour, discuss the subject in advance with the doctor at the antenatal clinic. Say that you would particularly value someone as a companion to be with you throughout labour, and that you do not know anyone who can come with you; ask whether there is anyone in the hospital—preferably someone you could meet beforehand—who could be with you. The doctor may say that you will have a midwife and will not be left alone. But a labour companion is different and is simply there as a friend, to give you emotional support and to remind you of your relaxation and breathing. If you are in a teaching hospital there will almost certainly be a medical student who can do this. If it is a midwifery training school there is usually a student midwife who can fill the same role.

But suppose that you have to be without a companion in labour. Make your midwife your friend and ask her for help. Unfortunately there is not much continuity of care in hospitals, and you may have to get to know two or three midwives, one after another—a lot to ask of someone in labour. On the other hand, sometimes a midwife will stay on duty so that she can be with you until after the delivery.

Managing alone

If your man has been unwilling to accept responsibility or perhaps even acknowledge your pregnancy, you probably feel angry and resentful. One woman, who had been told she could never have a baby but who found herself pregnant, said, "I hadn't realized just

I was so pleased to see Ann come through the door. I coped with a difficult labour only because of her, and think without her I might have gone under.

how much his marriage was a going concern. Just when I most needed him I had to come to terms with the fact that he didn't want to break up his marriage and was devoted to his kids. In fact, my pregnancy was terribly embarrassing for him! I suddenly felt dreadfully on my own. I didn't hear from him through a large part of the pregnancy because it was the summer holidays and he went abroad with his family."

Another woman's husband left her when she was four months pregnant because he said he could not stand the idea of a third child. He had left her several times before for short periods and the baby was conceived during a reconciliation. Her great fear was that she would find him on the doorstep again, since she had been through so much emotional turmoil that she did not feel she could cope mentally with any more scenes and upheavals. This led to a strained and difficult pregnancy, followed by a prolonged labour and forceps delivery because of incoordinate uterine action.

A university lecturer who had decided in advance that she wanted a baby but not a man said that her colleagues accepted this but that she found it hard to tell her family: "Mother thought I was mad and said how could she ever let her friends know. I thought about them all at their coffee mornings and thought, 'Oh my God, I don't suppose she can'. I thought it would be hardest explaining to my 80-year-old grandmother but she was the one who understood best." This woman could not go home when her pregnancy became obvious because of the effect on her parents' neighbours and friends, although her parents did adjust to the idea after the baby was born and became proud grandparents.

Some women are rejected by parents, although one girl said: "In a way I rejected *them* and their values, by going ahead and having the baby." Even so, however "free" of your parents you feel and however you delight in being independent of them, cutting roots like this can be extremely painful. You may feel guilty, even if you do not accept the social conventions which thrust the feelings of guilt upon you. You may worry about imposing your views on your child, who will learn that in friends' houses there is a Daddy as well as a Mummy.

Being a single parent often brings greater challenges— and rewards.

Yet single mothers all stress that you do need help and must have the grace to accept it, for your child's sake as well as yours. There are the all-important questions of where you are going to live, what you are going to live on, whether you should and can go back to work, and if so when. You must also consider how you are going to retain any sort of mobility with a baby, how you will deal with the relationship between sex, motherhood, the other things you want to do and the needs you want to fulfil, and how you are going to feel when things are difficult or impossible because of the baby. Many of the difficulties confronted by single women are the same as those faced by those with partners, but intensified because the women are alone and unsupported. As one woman said, in order to go through with having a baby on your own, "you need to *really want* that child!"

Planning & preparation

Throughout history most babies were born at home. Maternity hospitals were first started for homeless women and were really extensions of the poor-houses. Many of the babies born in these hospitals were then put in foundling institutions. These first maternity hospitals were convenient centres for medical students to learn and practise obstetrics, but infection was rampant, as doctors conveyed bacteria on their hands from one patient to another, and many babies and mothers died. They were the most dangerous places in which women could possibly give birth.

Today, modern hospitals are no longer dangerous places to have a baby. Yet, despite extremely rapid advances, and the tendency for most doctors to recommend a hospital birth, many women still feel that a home birth would be the most appropriate for them.

Where would you like to have your baby?

Even before you become pregnant, it is worth thinking about whether you would like to have your baby at home or in hospital and discussing it with your doctor. You may have decided, for example, that you would prefer to have your baby at home, yet discover that your doctor is unwilling or unable to attend you. If there are no specific medical reasons for this, you might want to change your doctor before you start a pregnancy. Whether you want to have a home birth or a hospital birth, it is important to inform your doctor as early in your pregnancy as possible, as it is often difficult to change your mind once wheels have been set in motion. It is a good idea to make a list of things that are really important to you about the birth and the time immediately after and to decide which environment best meets your requirements, home or hospital.

HOSPITAL BIRTH

OPPOSITE

Once you know you are pregnant, find out all you can about childbirth so that you know what to ask for and who can help.

Most women who decide to have their babies in hospital do so primarily because they are convinced it is the safest place. They want to be sure that all the skills and equipment of modern obstetrics are at hand for their babies' sake. For some women, especially those having their first child, giving birth is a frightening experience, a step in the dark, and they feel more secure in the knowledge that they are in the hands of people who have been specially trained to cope with any possible emergency. Often a woman who fears that her labour will be painful opts for a hospital delivery, knowing that certain pain-killers are available only in hospital and not wanting to take the chance of finding herself at home without necessary relief from pain when it is too late to do anything about it.

Sometimes a woman may know and trust a particular obstetrician and want to be cared for by this person, while another wants to go to hospital because she feels she would benefit from a period of release from the pressures of home and family. Occasionally a woman's partner wants her to go to hospital because he is very worried about birth at home. He may just be frightened of being involved, but more often he is afraid he might have to deliver the baby himself.

Medical reasons for hospital birth

As well as those women who would prefer the security of a hospital birth, there are those for whom it is advisable to give birth in hospital whatever their personal preferences. It is wise to consider hospital care if you have diabetes, a heart or kidney condition, or if you smoke cigarettes regularly (see page 94). Your doctor will send you to hospital if you get severe pre-eclampsia (see page 126) or if you go into labour three weeks or more before the baby is due; you will probably be advised against home delivery if your baby is breech, since it may need help with breathing immediately after birth (see page 334). There are really no absolutes, but there are certain things which make childbirth a little more risky.

If you are to be a first-time mother over 35 for instance, labour *may* be longer than if you were younger and many doctors would advise you to be in hospital so that you can have labour speeded up or help with the delivery. Some doctors believe that all first-time mothers (primigravidae) should give birth in hospital because, they say, a labour is only normal in retrospect and there is always a small chance that even after a perfectly normal pregnancy you may have complications which will entail you being moved to hospital at the last minute for specialist care.

If you have had a haemorrhage with a previous labour, either before or after the delivery, it is wise to choose a hospital birth because you may need a quick blood transfusion if it happens again. The same goes for a retained placenta or a delayed third stage in a previous labour. If you are very short, under 5 ft 2 in (1·55 m), your pelvis may be a tight fit for the baby to get through, though many short women do give birth easily. Any other indications of disproportion, because of the way the baby is lying, for example, should also make you plan for a hospital birth.

Three or more miscarriages are another reason for having the baby in hospital, because previous problems of this kind *may* mean that labour will present problems (though often everything is straightforward). Obviously, if you have lost a baby because of a difficult birth, you are unlikely to take the small but real additional risk of a home birth and will want to know that, if the baby should need it, intensive care is available at the hospital where you are giving birth. Doctors also advise mothers of twins to give birth in hospital, partly because they are very likely to come early and to be of low birthweight and partly because the second twin can get stuck (see pages 80–85).

Choices in hospital care

If you have decided that a hospital birth is right for you, you will need to think about the alternatives available within the hospital system. There are two main kinds of maternity unit, a consultant unit or a general practitioner unit, as well as the Domino scheme.

Consultant units If you are having your baby under the National Health Service in a consultant unit, you are looked after by a team under the direction of a specialist. If the specialist is attached to a teaching hospital, medical students may also be involved in your care. If you are having the baby privately, the consultant sees you and contracts to attend your birth and deliver you if possible.

It is your GP who refers you to a particular consultant in the hospital. You are not normally asked whether you have any preferences, but you can in fact choose your consultant, provided you make your request early enough in your pregnancy. GPs don't like their patients changing from one consultant to another, mainly because of the administrative difficulties this involves, so it is best to ask around and find out from other mothers about the practices of different consultants and then to discuss this with your GP *before* your case is referred.

Teaching hospitals and general hospitals, in which consultant units are based, tend to have a great deal of technologically advanced machinery and are to be recommended especially for pregnancies where the baby may be "at risk" and where it is vital to keep a careful eye on mother and baby. If there is any indication that the baby may be born before term and be of very low birthweight, birth should be in a unit with a neonatal intensive care unit, equipped with all the sophisticated technology and manned by specially skilled staff to give your baby the best attention possible.

> ==**"**==
> *The hospital's marvellous! They explain everything; I nearly always see the same obstetrician and this morning after examining me he said "Wonderful growth!" and patted my tum. I'm really looking forward to having it there.*
> ==**"**==

GP units In a GP unit, which may be a small cottage hospital or a ward inside a larger consultant unit, you stay under the care of a GP and the midwives who work with that particular practice. The GP may not be your usual family doctor since not all of them are trained in obstetrics. Your doctor may pass you on to another GP for obstetric care or you can find one yourself who, you feel, understands and sympathizes with the style of childbirth you would like to have. These units are for low-risk maternity care where it looks as if everything is going to be straightforward. By the time you are ready to give birth, you usually know the midwife who delivers you and consequently feel more relaxed. GP units far away from consultant units do entail some extra risk, however, and you should only be booked into a hospital of this kind if no complications are expected.

One advantage of having a baby in a GP unit is the chance to get to know your midwife beforehand, when she visits you in the relaxed atmosphere of your own home.

The Domino scheme Some hospitals offer an alternative to the consultant unit in the Domino scheme, in which community midwives bring their own patients into hospital and deliver them themselves. The midwives then go home with the mothers after they have had a rest following childbirth, which may be anything from a few hours to a day and night, depending on the wishes of the mother and the state of her and her baby. Your GP will be able to tell you whether Domino operates in your nearest big hospital.

Looking over the hospital

Some Senior Nursing Officers are happy to arrange for you to look over the hospital before you book in. If it is not the usual practice to do this in a hospital, get in touch with the antenatal out-patients sister and ask if you can talk to whoever runs childbirth classes. There is probably a visit by the antenatal class to the labour and delivery suite and you may be able to go too (see page 169). You can also write to the Senior Nursing Officer asking about the things that matter most to you. (For more about childbirth alternatives, see page 383.)

When you see the hospital, bear in mind that *people* matter more than the architecture and interior decoration. Do you sense a warm, caring atmosphere or do the staff seem brusque? The attitude of the doctors and nurses towards you and your birth is one of the most important factors in making hospital birth a rewarding experience.

I had a traumatic experience in hospital last time, so we've decided to have it at home.

HOME BIRTH

At the same time that hospital birth becomes more and more the standard way to have a baby there is a small but steady increase in the number of women who decide to have their babies at home.

Most women who have a baby at home after a previous hospital birth say that they enjoyed it much more and feel that it must have been pleasanter for the baby. Some opt for home births because they want to give birth in a familiar, comfortable, non-medical environment, surrounded by their own things, in the home they have created with their partner. They want to be able to make their own decisions, to give birth in their own way and behave spontaneously, without being forced into the role of patient and having to conform to hospital rules and regulations. They also want to avoid having to change rooms and move from a bed to a delivery room, and to be able to adopt any position they find comfortable. At home you are in charge and the doctor and midwife are familiar and welcome guests in your home. For some, this continuous relationship and co-operation with just a few helpers is important.

Some women say that since birth is an act of love, personal and intimate, it should take place in one's own environment, without unnecessary observers, among friends in a loving atmosphere. They want to know that the father of the baby or a close friend can be present throughout, can take an active part, and can give emotional support through the labour. Some would like the father to "catch" the baby himself. Most hospitals allow fathers to be present for labour and delivery nowadays, but they are still sent out for a wide range of minor procedures and examinations, often just when the labouring woman feels she needs her partner most. Often a woman would like to ensure that her baby has a "gentle birth" and is welcomed into the world tenderly, without the machinery and bright lights that are almost inevitable in hospitals.

The importance of bonding

Evidence of research on bonding between mother, father and baby points to the importance of the time immediately following birth for the couple to get to know their baby and feel it belongs to them and they to it. In many hospitals separation is still arbitrarily imposed on new parents, time for cuddling is either restricted or denied and routines take precedence over the emotional unfolding which heralds the birth of a family. Many women suspect that medical intervention is often unnecessary and that they will have a better chance of giving birth naturally and without drugs at home. They believe that full awareness of what is happening to them is a valuable experience and that drugs can harm their unborn babies. After a previous difficult hospital birth, one pregnant woman said: "I was determined to have a natural birth this time. Last time I had the whole works, and finished up with an epidural and a forceps delivery. I can't help thinking that if I let things take their own time and keep walking round and can relax and use my breathing and feel comfortable in my own home, with the people I love around me, my body will know what to do."

If you already have other children, you may be concerned that they should see birth as a normal, happy part of life and not, instead, as a surgical operation that entails you going off to a hospital. Birth is a family affair and the baby should belong to the whole family. Some women hope that the other child or children can be involved in the labour and some would like them present at the birth. This is impossible to arrange in most hospitals. Mothers of toddlers often worry that separation from them will lead to emotional and behavioural problems in the older child, and this just at a time when the new baby puts in an appearance. And there are those mothers who just find it impossible to get someone to look after their family while they are away in hospital. It is sometimes stated that women having their fourth or subsequent babies should always give birth in hospital, but if all your previous pregnancies and labours have been straightforward, there is no additional risk with a fourth or fifth birth and some definite advantage in giving birth at home where the other children can also be involved.

Some doctors are reluctant to give their approval to a home birth once you are actually pregnant, even though they have seemed flexible earlier. For example, one woman said that her doctor had agreed to a home birth for her third child "in principle" before the pregnancy but then "did her best to change our minds. She did not

> ═ ❝ ═
> *Of course, I'll go to hospital if it looks as if the baby is at risk, and I'm quite prepared to move there in strong labour if need be, because then I'll know things haven't worked out, and it would be silly to take unnecessary risks. But I want the chance to have a natural birth. And I don't think I'll get it in hospital.*
> ═ ❞ ═

As your toddler helps you to sort out clothes for the new baby, it may be hard to believe that he ever wore them himself...

rcally understand that there was absolutely no-one who could come to look after the other children, and that I would not have my husband with me if the baby was not born at home. .... There were many occasions when I was reduced to tears on my arrival home. Had I been less determined, or without my husband's support, I should have given in."

If you would like to give birth at home and your doctor is unsympathetic, contact the organizations listed on page 383.

ANTENATAL CARE

I like being with all the other pregnant women. I thought "We're all growing babies!" And everyone is so friendly and they explain everything. I revel in it.

One ingredient of a happy birth is good antenatal care, so that you are confident that you are healthy and the baby starts life under the best possible conditions. But the care you give yourself is probably more important than the care you receive from professionals. It also includes learning how to cope with stress in everyday life, and understanding how to work with your body. You do not need to attend classes until you are about six months pregnant, but it is worth thinking about the different classes available and perhaps beginning a few exercises earlier than this.

Antenatal care has developed piecemeal since the nineteenth century and we do not really know which elements in the package are valuable for all women, which are best kept for those at special risk, and which might be discarded altogether. Much of it is not very effective in producing reliable results. It is common for confusion to occur about whether a baby is growing well inside the uterus, for example, and many women are told that there is intra-uterine growth retardation when, in fact, it turns out that everything is fine. In spite of this, good medical care during pregnancy can every now and then make all the difference between life and death for the baby—and even, very occasionally, for you too.*

Unfortunately, because women are crowded into antenatal clinics, often without an appointments system or with block bookings, and because they never know which member of staff they are going to see next, many women say they hate their visits to the antenatal clinic. They often have to wait for long periods before seeing the doctor for a few minutes (just as in most hospital out-patients' departments). This is all the more irritating because pregnant women are not usually ill, and they feel that they are wasting valuable time at the clinic. So take a good book or an amusing friend for a natter while you wait. Or you may be able to make friends with another expectant mother going to the same clinic and you can keep each other company.

Some men brave the clinic along with their partners (a few clinics even encourage fathers to be there) but in many cases this is not expected and fathers may be asked to remain in the waiting room. If, however, it is important to you that you both talk to the doctor and that your partner is involved in the pregnancy, not only the birth, it is worth being quietly but firmly persistent to get what you want.

The clinic cannot give many clues about life on the labour ward, and, even in those hospitals about which women write enthusiastically after their babies are born, the antenatal clinic may have been "grim" and "an ordeal". So do not judge the hospital by its clinic.

If you have any questions or are worried about anything, the best person to speak to is the antenatal clinic sister or, if she is not around, a staff midwife. Since the first clinic visit, which is called the "booking clinic", allows the doctor time for learning a good deal about you while subsequent visits may be comparatively short, take the opportunity to find out all you want to know at the first visit. If there is anything you particularly hope for concerning the way in which you have your baby, tell the obstetrician who examines you and ask if it can be noted down on your record or co-operation card. A record card is retained by the hospital but, if you are having shared care, partly from the hospital and partly from your GP, you will be given a co-operation card to take from one to the other (see pages 48–49).

Frequency of clinic visits

Once your pregnancy has been confirmed, your doctor will make arrangements for your antenatal care. Your first clinic visit will take place when you are about three months pregnant. If your pregnancy proceeds normally, you will then attend the clinic (or see your doctor if you are having shared care) once a month until you are 28 weeks pregnant. At this stage you will be seen every two weeks and in your final month will be given weekly appointments.

Clinic procedures

During the clinic visit you may be weighed before you see the doctor. While the baby is growing, you will probably be putting on weight fairly steadily (see page 87).

Even if a visit to the clinic means queuing up and a long wait you do have the opportunity of meeting other expectant mothers.

Your blood group is determined at your first visit and a test is done to check whether the baby might develop Rhesus disease (see page 103). Your blood sample is automatically tested for syphilis, and you may be offered screening for spina bifida or Down's syndrome (see page 205). Regular blood tests are done for anaemia (see page 128). Your blood pressure will be taken at each visit, and this is especially important towards the end of the pregnancy (see page 125).

At some clinics an ultrasonic scan (see page 202) is performed routinely when you are 16 or 17 weeks pregnant. Other clinics will do this when there is doubt about the expected date of delivery. In late pregnancy a single scan can show the size of the baby's head in

Understanding your co-operation card

Para 0	The mother has had no previous birth.
Para 1 (or 2)	The mother has had one (or two) previous births.
Para 2 + 1	The mother has had two previous births plus a miscarriage (or termination) before 28 weeks.
LMP	Last menstrual period.
EDD/EDC	Expected date of delivery or expected date of confinement.
TCA	To come again.
Alb	Albumin in urine. Your urine is analyzed for the presence of sugar, which is a sign of diabetes, and albumin (protein), which can be a sign of toxaemia. Another name for toxaemia is pre-eclampsia or pre-eclamptic toxaemia (PET for short). When sugar is present, it is noted as a percentage. Two per cent is a large amount. Ideally albumin should not be present at all.
NAD	Nothing abnormal detected.
PET	Pre-eclamptic toxaemia (or pre-eclampsia), another name for toxaemia.
Hb	Haemoglobin, an oxygen-carrying substance present in red blood cells. If your haemoglobin level is lower than 10·5 per cent, you are considered to be anaemic and will be prescribed iron. Because of the greater quantity of circulating blood, most pregnant women have reduced haemoglobin.
Fe	Iron. This means that you have been prescribed iron.
Bp	Blood pressure. This is the pressure inside the arteries as the blood is pumped from the heart. The pressure built up every time the heart beats is called *systolic* pressure. Between beats the heart muscle relaxes and the pressure drops. This lower level is called *diastolic* pressure. The systolic pressure is the upper figure on your card, the diastolic pressure is the lower one. The lower figure is more significant than the upper one. A woman is considered to have high blood pressure, hypertension, if it exceeds 140/90 when measured on more than one occasion (see page 125).
FMF	Fetal movement felt.
FH	Fetal heart.

relation to your pelvic outlet. If you have a series of scans at different sessions, an estimate can be made of the baby's rate of growth.

At the first antenatal clinic visit you will probably have an internal examination (see page 27). At most subsequent visits the uterus and baby will be felt by abdominal palpation. As this is done, you should give a long breath out and release your tummy completely, then go on breathing slowly, releasing more on each breath out. This makes it easier to feel how the baby is lying and is much more comfortable for you than if you are tense.

The examining hands feel first for the distance between your pubic bone and the baby and then the top of the uterus. This is called fundal

H/NH	Heard or not heard, usually referring to the fetal heart. In the last weeks of pregnancy the actual heart rate is often written in.
Oedema	Swelling. Part of your weight gain is due to water retention, causing puffiness in the feet and ankles, face and vulva. A great deal of fluid retention may be a sign of pre-eclampsia, but it can be perfectly normal.
Fundus	The top of the uterus. As the baby grows, the fundus is pushed up to just above your navel at 22 weeks and under your ribs at 36 weeks. But when the baby drops down into the bony pelvis ready for birth the fundus is lower again (see page 69). You can find your own fundus and chart its position week by week through your pregnancy. Lie on your back, tummy bare and, with the sides and palms of your hands, feel round the hard top of your uterus, pressing against what feels like a wall of muscle.
Cervix	The neck of the uterus, which shortens and opens to let the baby out.
PP	The presenting part of the baby. This is the part which is down at the bottom of the uterus and likely to be the first to press through the opening cervix if you are at the end of pregnancy. In the last few weeks the antenatal doctor may note the presentation more precisely, so that you can get an idea of exactly what part of the baby is in the cervix.
Vx	Vertex. This indicates that the baby's position is head down, as it should be.
Ceph	Cephalic. This also indicates that the baby's position is head down.
Brim	The inlet of your pelvis.
Long L	Longitudinal lie. The baby is lying parallel to your spine.
LOA LOP ROA ROP	Left occipito anterior. Left occipito posterior. Right occipito anterior. Right occipito posterior. These terms all refer to the position (anterior or posterior) of the crown of the baby's head (occiput) in relation to your body (right or left). Therefore ROP means that the back of the baby's head is to your right and back.
RSA	Right sacrum anterior. This is the most common breech presentation.
Eng/E	Engaged. This is written on your card when the baby's head has dropped down into your pelvis, which can happen any time from about six weeks before you go into labour until after you have actually started.
T	Term. The doctor writes this on your card when it is estimated that you are right at the end of your pregnancy and the baby is ready to be born.

A visit to the clinic

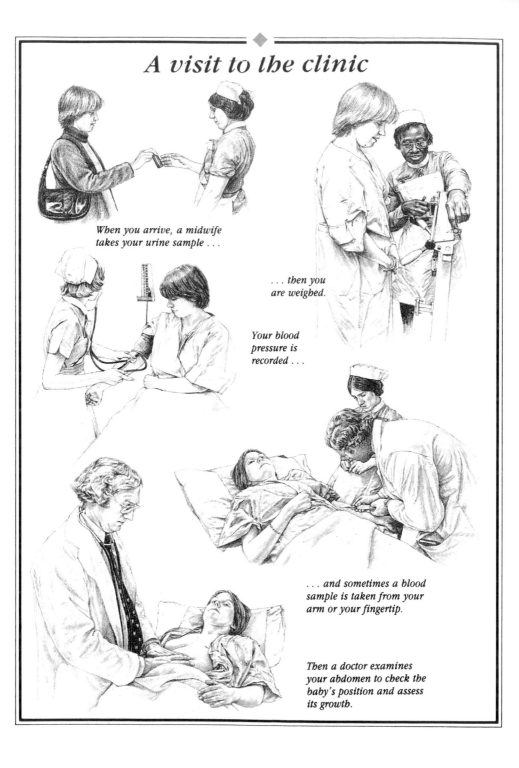

When you arrive, a midwife takes your urine sample . . .

. . . then you are weighed.

Your blood pressure is recorded . . .

. . . and sometimes a blood sample is taken from your arm or your fingertip.

Then a doctor examines your abdomen to check the baby's position and assess its growth.

palpation. The hands move down the sides of the baby so that the back and limbs are discovered. The part of the baby that is over the cervix is said to be "presenting". The doctor or midwife turns to face your feet and presses the hands downwards and from side to side to determine whether the baby's head, buttocks or any other part, is presenting. The next manoeuvre tends to be uncomfortable but is quickly performed. Facing you again, the doctor spreads one hand wide and presses in above your pubic bone to feel the exact position of the presenting part in relation to the pelvis.

In late pregnancy, take the opportunity to find out how your baby is lying and discuss anything that worries you. Notice fetal movements and report any pronounced change in their frequency or type. The best way of monitoring a pregnancy is for the obstetrician, midwife and the expectant mother to work together.

TALKING TO DOCTORS

Some people have doctors with whom they quickly feel at ease, and experience little difficulty in finding out the medical alternatives open to them in pregnancy and discussing their requirements with their doctors. However, the expectant mother and her doctor are likely to meet in a system in which time is at a premium and sometimes one or both of them finds it difficult to break out from a formal doctor-patient relationship with all that this implies of authority and subordination.

Being pregnant is a physiological process. It also involves a kind of emotional journey into being a patient. And as if all this were not enough, it propels you into new kinds of social relationships. Some of these are with the professionals you encounter in the antenatal clinic. So, as well as having to understand the changes taking place in your body and your emotions, you may have to develop new social skills which help you to create a satisfactory dialogue with those who care for you and your baby. This is especially the case where you meet different members of staff at each clinic visit and others again when you are in labour. The lack of continuity in care is one of the main criticisms that women make about childbirth in hospital today.*

The obstetrician was very pleasant. He told me they'd just had a baby 3 months ago. That made a lot of difference.

Some women also feel very vulnerable emotionally when pregnant and cannot help crying under stress, even though (or perhaps because) it is the last thing they *want* to do. You are in no way abnormal if you feel surges of emotion which are difficult or impossible to control, but it means that you may feel at a disadvantage in an interview with a doctor when you want to ask for something or talk about a kind of birth you hope for.

This possibility is a good reason for having your partner or a close friend or relative with you on such occasions. It is important, of course, that you discuss your wishes thoroughly with this person first. You may find it useful for him or her to play "the devil's advocate" and act out an imagined encounter so that you have some practice in discussing the subject and develop a strategy. Do not make the mistake of anticipating opposition from the hospital staff; you will probably be pleasantly surprised. But do be prepared to give carefully thought-out reasons for what you want.

See that you are well briefed about the matters you want to discuss. There is now a good deal of published research on emotional and sociological aspects of maternity care, for example, and many papers on the technology of modern obstetrics and the active management of labour (see page 290) which are published in medical journals. It will help if you have the correct references and a clear idea of some of the most important statements. If you are attending National Childbirth Trust classes, ask your antenatal teacher to help you. The NCT produces booklets and leaflets which may be relevant,* and there are other organizations which may be able to give advice (see page 383).

Preparing your questions

Since questions may go out of your head when you actually have a chance to ask them (pregnancy amnesia is a well-known phenomenon), and because some doctors seem to concentrate exclusively on the lower end of your body to the exclusion of interest in you as a person, it is a good idea to jot down subjects you want to discuss. Different treatments are done routinely in different hospitals. You may not want some or all of these, and it is best to state your preferences as early as possible. On the other hand, you may want a treatment which would not usually be given in your hospital but is probably available if you make a special request. Your list could include questions about the doctor's attitude towards induction of labour, routinely giving enemas or suppositories, the use of intravenous drips, towards continuous electronic fetal monitoring, episiotomy and the use of forceps (see pages 290–307). You could also ask about the availability of epidurals (see page 286) and whether or not you will be able to keep your baby with you through the 24 hours. It may also be important for you to know whether there will be much help with breast-feeding. Be specific in your requests, to avoid misunderstandings later on.

If you have not made an appointment with a discussion in mind, sometimes the antenatal clinic is so crowded that you feel reluctant to take up anybody's time. Even so, it is probably worth saying that you have made a note of things you would like to discuss and ask whether it is convenient that day, or, if not, whether you can arrange to have some time to talk at the next visit. There is no need to be apologetic about wanting further information or asking for the doctor's help to achieve the kind of birth you would like. After all, you are not just a baby-producing machine!

During the interview sit in a relaxed way, check that fingers and toes are unclenched, and breathe out just before speaking for the first time. Make eye contact and address the doctor by name or ask his or her name if you do not know it.

I had to sit in a little cubicle for ages feeling cut off from the world.

OPPOSITE
Regular medical check-ups will help you keep track of your baby's growth and development.

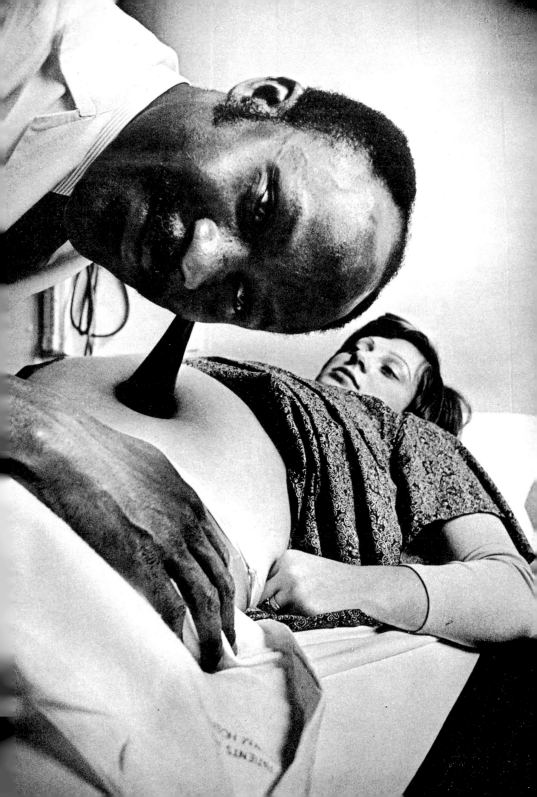

When a woman is nervous, she tends to pitch her voice too high. Modulate it so that it does not sound too demanding. You might smile nervously without realizing it. This can be confusing for the doctor, who may think that you are happy about something when you are not. Or the doctor unconsciously smiles because he or she is concerned to get you to accept another point of view and is sugaring the pill; your spontaneous reaction may then be to smile back, perhaps giving the doctor the idea that you are content when in fact you are not.

Avoid aggression and state your requests clearly and concisely. If you lose your temper, you may be classified as difficult or neurotic. If you encounter opposition or are made to feel that you cannot know what is in your best interests, restate your wishes firmly and give the reasons for them. It is a good idea to include requests that are not top priority, so that there is a possibility of compromise on some matters. Belligerence only provokes further opposition. Tell the doctor instead how unhappy or disappointed you are.

You may want to take notes of the conversation. You can always say: "I'd like to think more about that; may I just make a note of it?" Be careful not to imply that you are cross-examining the doctor and writing down any answers in preparation for a later attack. Listen to the doctor with concentration and make it clear that you are listening by "playing back" the important statements: "Do you mean . . .?" "So you are saying that . . .?" and rephrase whatever has been said as accurately as you can. You can sometimes add to your remark the *implications* that you think such a statement entails. By clarifying a point in this way you may be working towards modifying it. For example, if the doctor says, "I never allow husbands to remain if I have to give the patient a vaginal examination or do a forceps delivery because they only get in the way", you might ask: "Are you saying that it is dangerous for a husband to stay because he might affect your judgment?" Not many experienced obstetricians would say that the presence of a husband could affect their professional judgment, and the doctor might reply by telling you a story about men who have fainted. You might then say: "I take it you feel happier about a man who stays calm and who gives emotional support to his wife?"

If your interview has gone badly, you can consider changing your doctor or, if there is more than one maternity hospital in your area, the hospital where you give birth. But give yourself a few days to simmer down and think it over calmly. You can write a letter to the doctor politely explaining your reasons for seeking other care; it is a good idea to send copies to the Secretary of the Board of Hospital Managers or the Family Practitioner Committee, and also to the local Community Health Council.

But such drastic measures are often unnecessary and you will find that you have opened up the possibility of getting the kind of childbirth you want. Good communication with your doctor means that, if for medical reasons you do not get all you had hoped for, you can at least take an active part in the decision-making.

On one occasion I waited 3 hours before being seen. I felt sorry for mums with toddlers. No provision was made for them except a broken rocking horse.

Physical and emotional changes

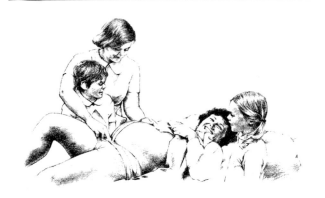

Life in the uterus

In the first days of pregnancy life is budding in cells far smaller than a pin-head. Because everything is happening on such a minute scale, it can be difficult to accept the reality of a baby growing deep inside you. Even when you begin to believe in your pregnancy, other people remain unaware of it. It can seem as if an explosion has taken place without anybody noticing, or as if all the colours have become more brilliant but everyone else is carrying on as usual. The chance meeting of one out of four hundred million sperm with a ripe and waiting egg has resulted in a dramatic series of events, conducted on a scale so miniature that you cannot feel the astonishing life-process unfolding inside you, even though you know it is happening.

Fertilization

At birth the ovaries of every baby girl contain almost 500,000 potential single-cell eggs, but they do not ripen until the menstrual periods begin. Each cell that ripens into an egg is nourished by nearly 5000 others that will never themselves ripen. From your first period until the menopause, when your periods stop, you may carry up to 4000 ripe eggs; each month between 100 and 150 begin to ripen, but usually only one a month reaches full maturity and is capable of being fertilized. The frequency with which eggs are produced and released is determined by hormones, which interact regularly in a system known as the menstrual cycle.

This cycle lasts for about a month, and begins when a hormone released by the pituitary gland stimulates an ovary to start ripening an egg. As the egg matures, the ovary releases oestrogen into the bloodstream. The oestrogen stops the pituitary gland producing its hormone, so no more eggs are stimulated into ripening. It also makes the uterine lining change and thicken in anticipation of the egg, which bursts out of the follicle (a capsule bulging on the surface of the ovary) about midway through each menstrual cycle. It is then drawn by the fingered tentacles of the fallopian tube into its long canal, which is about the thickness of a ballpoint refill.

The egg itself is a minute speck. It is barely visible to the naked eye, yet when it meets with a still more minuscule sperm it has the potential to develop into a human being. The follicle (also known as the corpus luteum) that held the egg begins to produce progesterone, which carries on the work that the oestrogen has been doing. If the egg is not fertilized within a few days, the follicle dries up and the progesterone level falls dramatically. As a result the uterine lining decomposes, and a menstrual period occurs.

Even while bleeding is going on, the menstrual cycle renews itself: the pituitary gland is stimulating the ovary into ripening a new egg.

OPPOSITE

Sperm meets egg and dissolves . . . the two nuclei will then fuse.

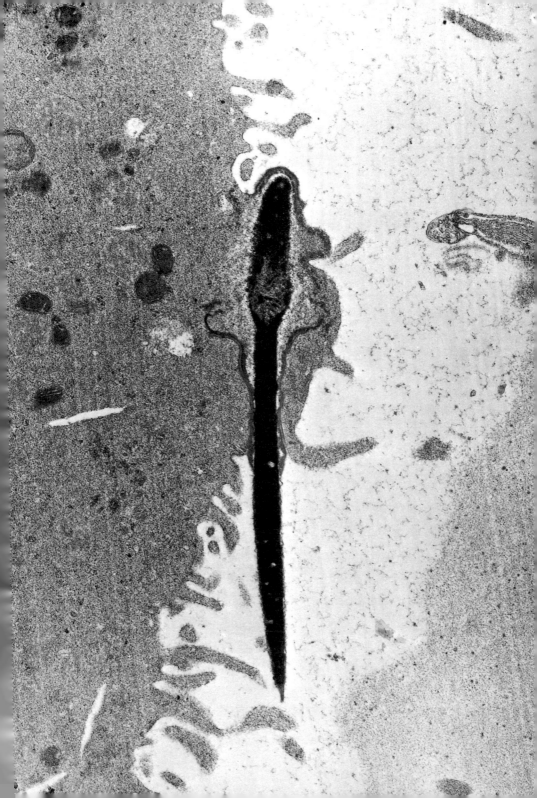

The menstrual cycle

While a follicle is developing in the ovary, the uterus is building up a lining composed mainly of coiled arteries and glands. If the ripe egg released from the ovary is not fertilized, the uterus sheds the top layer of this lining (menstruation) and the process begins again.

This diagram shows an external view of the ovary of a fully grown woman.

This diagram of a section through an ovary shows the stages of development of the follicle during any one menstrual cycle.

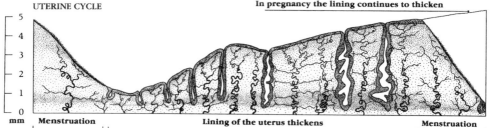

OVULATION CYCLE

| Growth of follicle | Ovulation | Corpus luteum | New follicle |

Days 1 2 3 4 5 6 7 8 9 10 11 12 13 14 15 16 17 18 19 20 21 22 23 24 25 26 27 28 1 2 3 4 5

UTERINE CYCLE

In pregnancy the lining continues to thicken

mm 5 4 3 2 1 0

Menstruation   Lining of the uterus thickens   Menstruation

But if the egg is fertilized, the follicle does not shrivel up, the progesterone level does not drop and the uterine lining continues to thicken, so that you do not have a period.

The usual pattern is that the ovary on one side releases an egg one month, the one on the other side the next. Sometimes one ovary becomes especially active for a few months. Occasionally only one ovary is functioning: if part of a fallopian tube or an ovary has been surgically removed the other one usually takes on the work of both.

Sperm are so tiny that 30,000 of them placed side by side would only just stretch across a beer bottle top. A man ejaculates hundreds of millions of sperm every time he has an orgasm. After intercourse, a mere 2000 of these survive the journey up the vagina, to the fallopian tubes, and only one can fertilize a ripe egg, which immediately puts up a chemical barrier to keep all others out.

Each sperm is shaped like a tadpole with a long, lashing tail which makes it highly mobile. The head is rounded and holds the gene-carrying nucleus. When a sperm meets the egg it burrows deep into it and its nucleus fuses with the nucleus of the egg. It is at this moment that the genes, or units of inheritance, of the parents first meet.

GENETICS

Inside the nucleus of every body cell—with two exceptions—there are 46 chromosomes, making 23 pairs. The two exceptions are the egg cell and the sperm cell, which have 23 chromosomes each instead of 46. Chromosomes are rodlike structures shaped like Egyptian hieroglyphs, each containing thousands of genes.

When the nucleus of the sperm cell fuses with the nucleus of the egg, each chromosome—and each gene inside each chromosome— unites with its opposite number. The newly fertilized cell now contains 46 chromosomes, like every other human cell. The physical characteristics of the future person are determined, and the cell can start to develop into a human being.

Boy or girl?

Out of the 23 pairs of chromosomes in every human cell one pair determines the person's sex. The two sex chromosomes in a female cell are known as XX, and the two in a male cell as Xy. Since the egg and the sperm cell contain half the usual number of chromosomes, every egg cell contains 22 chromosomes plus one sex chromosome, which is an X. Every sperm cell contains 22 chromosomes plus one sex chromosome, which can be either an X or a y.

The sex of the baby depends on these differences between sperm cells. If the egg is fertilized by a sperm with an X chromosome, the union of the two sex chromosomes will result in XX, a girl. If the egg is fertilized by a sperm with a y chromosome, the union of the two sex chromosomes will result in Xy, a boy. There is usually a 50/50 chance that a boy or a girl will be conceived; statistically it appears that as

Your baby's sex

A woman's egg cells and a man's sperm cells each contain 23 single chromosomes, which are not paired until they meet their opposite number. Of the 23 single chromosomes, one is always a sex chromosome. Each egg always has an X (female) sex chromosome but the sex chromosome present in any sperm can be either X or y. Since a y chromosome is dominant, the egg that is fertilized by a sperm carrying a y chromosome will result in a boy, while the egg fertilized by a sperm carrying an X chromosome develops into a girl.

Mother Father

Girl Boy Boy Girl

The female reproductive organs

When a woman ovulates, the released egg from one of the two ovaries is immediately drawn into a fallopian tube where, if intercourse has taken place, it may be fertilized by a sperm. The fertilized egg embeds itself in the lining of the uterus. If the egg is not fertilized, it is shed, along with the lining of the uterus, down through the opening in the cervix and out of the vagina: this is menstruation.

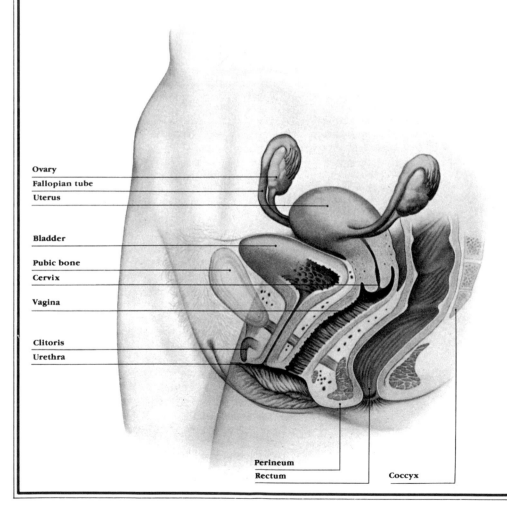

Ovary
Fallopian tube
Uterus

Bladder

Pubic bone
Cervix

Vagina

Clitoris
Urethra

Perineum
Rectum
Coccyx

The male reproductive organs

Sperm mature in both testes, which are enclosed within the scrotum. They travel up through each vas deferens, where they are stored temporarily. When a man is sexually aroused, his penis becomes erect and the outlet from the bladder into the ejaculatory duct is closed, leaving it free for the sperm. The sperm entering the ejaculatory duct are accompanied by secretions from the seminal vesicles, Cowper's glands and the prostate gland. About a teaspoonful of the fluid (semen), containing millions of sperm, is ejaculated from the urethra at orgasm.

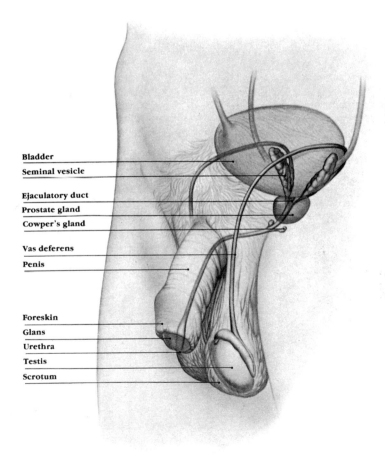

Bladder
Seminal vesicle

Ejaculatory duct
Prostate gland
Cowper's gland

Vas deferens
Penis

Foreskin
Glans
Urethra
Testis
Scrotum

women grow older and also as they bear more children, there is a slightly greater probability that they will give birth to a girl.

Although the baby's sex is determined by the sex chromosome carried by the sperm, it is also partly a consequence of the environment into which that sperm is received. Natural alkalinity or acidity of the secretions in your reproductive tract makes it easier for some sperm to survive their long journey than for others. Traditionally an acid medium has been thought to increase the chances of having a male child, and an alkaline medium a female child; because of this people have douched with acid or alkaline solutions before intercourse, but there is little evidence that this significantly affects your chances of producing one sex or the other.

Dominant and recessive genes

When a y chromosome meets an X chromosome, the y chromosome dominates to produce a boy. Similarly, when a gene encounters its opposite number one always takes precedence. A baby receives half of its genes from each parent. If a gene for brown eyes from one parent meets a gene for blue eyes from the other, the gene for brown eyes will always prevail. This does not mean that a child of one

Dominant and recessive genes

Since the gene for blond hair is recessive, the blond-haired grandparents in this family group must possess two blond-haired genes, one of which has to be passed on to each of their children. This means that the dark-haired mother and father in the group must each have a recessive gene for blond hair, giving them a one-in-four chance of producing a blond child.

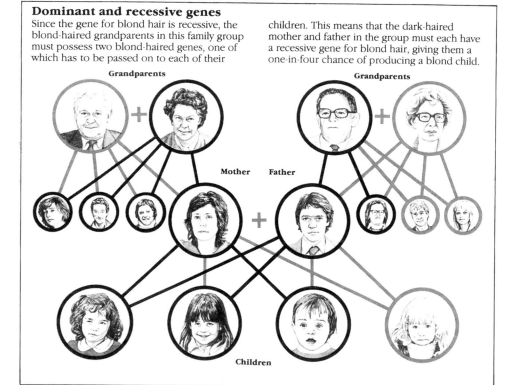

Grandparents
Grandparents
Mother Father
Children

brown-eyed and one blue-eyed parent will always have brown eyes. But the gene for brown eyes is known as *dominant*, the one for blue eyes as *recessive*. So someone with brown eyes who has received a gene for blue eyes from one parent retains the blue-eye gene as a recessive gene. If he or she should have a child by another brown-eyed person also with a recessive gene for blue eyes, there is a one in four chance that both parents will pass on their recessive genes for blue eyes to produce a blue-eyed child. This ability of two brown-eyed parents to have a blue-eyed child is a simple example of the way in which heredity introduces diversification with each generation.

Defective genes

Occasionally genes are defective, but since healthy genes are usually dominant over faulty ones, your baby's normal development is almost always assured. Some defective genes are carried by the sex chromosomes, and then the children of one sex only are affected. Colour-blindness, for instance, is carried by some women in one of their two X chromosomes; since the normal gene in their other X chromosome is dominant over the faulty one they do not suffer from colour-blindness. But if a boy inherits an X chromosome with a faulty gene he has no other X chromosome with a healthy gene to dominate it, so he is colour-blind. Thus colour-blindness is transmitted through alternating generations of affected boys and carrier mothers. Haemophilia is passed on in the same way.

If you are anxious about the possibility of your children inheriting any diseases or handicaps from your family or your partner's, tell your doctor before you become pregnant if possible. Failing that, as soon as your pregnancy is confirmed ask to talk to a genetic counsellor. There is a skilled genetic counsellor in every teaching hospital who can tell you the mathematical chances of your bearing a defective child and about the tests that can be carried out (see page 202). If it is discovered that you are carrying an abnormal child, your pregnancy can be terminated *if you wish*. Nobody has to agree to termination of pregnancy even if bearing a handicapped child.

THE BEGINNINGS OF PREGNANCY

The genetic make-up of the future child is decided at the moment of fertilization. But conception is a process, not a split-second event. Immediately after it has been penetrated, the egg starts to divide. It divides repeatedly as it is swept along the fallopian tube to the uterus, which it reaches seven days after leaving the ovary. By this time it is a clustered ball of cells, called a blastocyst, like a tiny blackberry but hollow in the centre. The blastocyst floats in the cavity of the uterus until about the tenth day, when it succeeds in embedding itself into the uterine lining.

Some blastocysts (estimates range from one in ten to as many as one in three) do not manage to root themselves into the wall of the

◆

uterus, and are swept out with the next menstrual period. Conception is only complete when the blastocyst has successfully nested into the wall of the uterus. You have not yet missed a period.

Implantation

The cells now number several hundred. The blastocyst releases enzymes which penetrate the lining of the uterus, causing the tissues to distintegrate and the blood and cells—on which the blastocyst can feed—to seep out. They make a kind of nourishing soup, whose quality depends on the preparatory state of the uterine lining. Sometimes this is not rich enough to maintain the pregnancy and there is a miscarriage, which just resembles a late and rather heavy period, without you ever realizing that you have been pregnant. An inadequately nourishing uterine lining is one cause of infertility.

Early development

During the second week of the fertilized egg's life, the cells become differentiated. One set becomes the amniotic sac, an envelope of salty water in which the baby will later grow. Another cluster develops into the yolk sac out of which the embryo can make blood corpuscles. Yet another group becomes the placenta (see page 66). In between these structures are other rapidly developing cells which will form the baby. These cells are at first just an embryonic disc, but they grow lengthways in the third week until there is clearly a head and a tail end, with the yolk sac attached by a stalk to the middle of the disc.

At this point you are about one week past the date when you expected your period to come. Although you are not sure, perhaps you suspect that you might be pregnant.

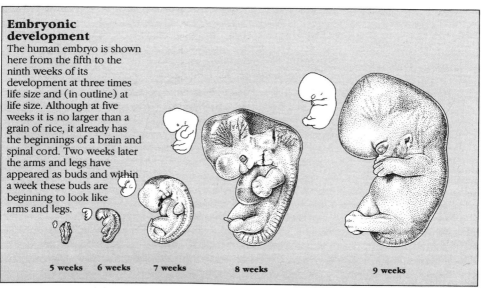

Embryonic development

The human embryo is shown here from the fifth to the ninth weeks of its development at three times life size and (in outline) at life size. Although at five weeks it is no larger than a grain of rice, it already has the beginnings of a brain and spinal cord. Two weeks later the arms and legs have appeared as buds and within a week these buds are beginning to look like arms and legs.

5 weeks   6 weeks   7 weeks   8 weeks   9 weeks

Six weeks pregnant It is three or four weeks after the meeting of sperm and egg, and about two weeks since you missed your period. According to the medical method of dating pregnancy (see page 28), you are about five or six weeks pregnant. The cluster of living cells has now developed into an embryo: there is a head and a neck with rudimentary eyes and ears, a brain, and a heart which is already beating, although it has only two chambers instead of the four which will develop shortly. There is a bloodstream and a digestive system, kidneys and a liver, and tiny buds which will become arms and legs.

A rod of cells develops—the notochord—which later becomes the spine. The embryo develops from the head end down, so that at this stage the lower part of its back is as yet barely formed and looks more like a tail. In fact, while now the size of a coffee bean, the embryo closely resembles a miniature sea horse.

Seven weeks pregnant A week later the embryo is about the size of a broad bean. Its body has plumped out into a baby shape, even though the head is at a strange angle in relation to the body. It has visible nostrils, lips and tongue, and even the buds of its first teeth. Four chambers have developed in the heart. The limb buds have grown into arms and legs, although as yet the hands and feet are no more than ridges.

Eight weeks pregnant The baby is still smaller than your little toe. It floats in the amniotic sac like an astronaut in space, attached to its life-support system. The heart has started the vigorous pumping of blood which will continue for a lifetime. The brain glimmers through skin as thin as greaseproof paper, revealing every tiny branching blood vessel beneath. The jaw is not yet fully formed and the ears are slung low and have not yet been moulded into their correct position. The eyes are covered by an intact skin, which will eventually split to become the eyelids. The head of the embryo is huge in relation to its body. The limbs elongate and elbows and knees appear. Even now the baby is trying out some gentle kicking, though you cannot feel any movement inside you.

All the organs and features of the embryo are completed in the course of the next month. The face grows from the top, and as the lower parts form the neck is elongated and a chin develops. The nose and outer ears are completely formed. Fingers and toes are visible, though webbing stretches between them.

By the time you are 12 weeks pregnant the basic physical equipment of the embryo is in working order. The head is still big for the body and the limbs small; few muscles are working yet. All the internal organs have formed and some of them are functioning. The genitals have developed, but it is not yet easy to tell what sex the baby is. The umbilical cord has started to circulate blood between the embryo and the group of membranes attached to the wall of the uterus. It is at this stage that the embryo begins to rely on these

HANDS AND FEET
These develop at a slightly different rate, the feet being about a week behind the hands until the 13th week.

7 weeks

8 weeks

13 weeks

7 weeks

8 weeks

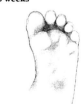

13 weeks

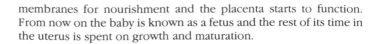
membranes for nourishment and the placenta starts to function. From now on the baby is known as a fetus and the rest of its time in the uterus is spent on growth and maturation.

THE PLACENTA

In the early weeks of pregnancy one cluster of cells begins to develop into the placenta, which is an organ grown especially to nourish the baby and to excrete its waste products. The outside layer of this cell cluster develops into a membrane with hundreds of tiny roots which penetrate the uterine tissues.

Your blood does not flow directly into the baby at any stage of pregnancy. It passes across the tissues on the maternal side of the placenta and the baby's blood passes back across the tissues on the other side. The two bloodstreams are separated by the membrane; chemical substances can be diffused from one bloodstream to the other through the membrane, but the bloodstreams themselves normally never mix. (Some fetal blood cells do cross the placenta, but usually without any significant effect.) The baby can thus have a different blood group from yours, while still taking its nourishment from your blood. In just the same way the baby's waste products are passed back through the placenta into your bloodstream, to be filtered and excreted by your kidneys.

Although the baby makes breathing movements, it does not breathe inside you: it takes its oxygen from your blood and passes back carbon dioxide. The oxygen diffuses through the membrane into its blood in the same way that oxygen from the air passes through the lining of your lungs. The placenta therefore works rather like a coffee filter: the coffee grains never enter the jug, but substances from them filter into it. Changes in your blood as a result of stress, illness, or toxic substances that you imbibe will affect the quality of the substances which flow through the membrane.

Blood takes only half a minute to flow from the baby's heart to the placenta and back again to the baby's heart. The flow of blood through the placenta in the fourth month of pregnancy is already 25 quarts (27·5 litres) a day, and by the end of pregnancy 300 quarts (330 litres) of blood are passing through each day.

As the placenta starts to function, it gradually takes over responsibility for production of a range of hormones, including oestrogen and progesterone, from the glands which normally secrete these hormones. Oestrogen and progesterone control most of the changes in your body during pregnancy. The oestrogen stimulates the growth of the uterus and the development of new uterine blood vessels, and also causes the milk glands in your breasts to develop so that you can feed the baby. The progesterone prevents the uterus from contracting strongly and endangering the baby during pregnancy, and thus holds off the start of labour until term. When the baby is ready to be born, the progesterone level drops. By this time the uterus has become exquisitely sensitive to the level of oestrogen in the blood, so that when the placenta reduces its output of progesterone, the oestrogen takes over: it initiates labour and ensures that the uterus contracts strongly right through to the end of the third stage.

THE GROWING BABY

At 12 weeks The fetus has a large head and small, rounded rump; the sex organs are distinguishable though as yet incomplete; the eyes are closed, the retina showing dark and round through translucent skin. Toes and fingers are formed; the arms are the right length in proportion to the body and the nails are beginning to grow. The ribs and spine are just starting to harden into bone and the baby is moving vigorously. You cannot yet feel these movements, but it is kicking, curling its toes up and down, rotating its feet and wrists, clenching and unclenching its fists, pressing its lips together, frowning and making other facial expressions. The baby is also swallowing the amniotic fluid, gurgling it from its mouth or passing it out through its bladder. There is still plenty of room in the uterus, so the fetus can swoop and undulate in its own enclosed sea.

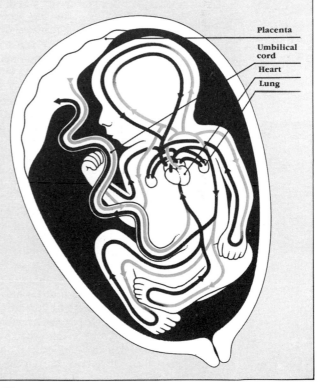

Fetal circulation

This simplified diagram shows how blood circulates around the fetus. The blood that travels along the umbilical cord towards the fetus has received oxygen from its mother through the placenta. Before reaching the fetal heart, it mixes with some of the de-oxygenated blood that has already circulated through the fetus. This mixture travels through the heart and is pumped up into the head and round the body, becoming, as it does so, less oxygenated. To obtain more oxygen, it returns to the placenta via the heart again, most of it bypassing the lungs. At birth the blood vessels around the baby's navel are automatically sealed off and the baby's circulation rapidly adapts to self-survival, with the lungs taking over the function of oxygenating the blood.

Placenta

Umbilical cord

Heart

Lung

KEY

Oxygenated blood

De-oxygenated blood

At 16 weeks Although the baby is growing rapidly, it could still nestle easily into a teacup. Its face is developing specifically human features, though the chin is still small and the mouth wide in comparison. The eyes are huge, closed and spaced far apart. The baby is covered with a fine down, called lanugo. This is the earliest stage at which you may first become aware of its movements. At first these feel like butterflies or little fish zigzagging about in bursts of activity, but soon they are unmistakably the kicking and lunging movements of a live being deep inside your body.

At 20 weeks The baby is half as long as it will be at delivery and about as heavy as a medium-sized Spanish onion (8 oz or 250 g). You could still hold it in the palm of your hand. The closed eyes are bulbous, because the face has not yet plumped out. Hair on the head is starting to grow and there are delicate eyebrows. The baby's movements are becoming more complex and it may be sucking its thumb.

You will probably notice that there are times when your baby seems to be asleep and times when it moves very actively (often when you have just settled down to go to sleep yourself). This seems to be partly because when you lie down it is easier for the baby to move. When moving around you also automatically rock the baby in your pelvis, so when you are busiest the baby is often asleep.

At 24 weeks The baby is about the length of your telephone receiver (13 in or 32 cm). It is covered with vernix, a creamy substance which protects its skin inside the uterus and prevents it from becoming waterlogged. This vernix sticks to hairy parts and many babies are born still coated with it. You may notice that your baby responds to loud noises and to music, especially to the brass section of an orchestra. If you are practising relaxation, you may feel the baby become remarkably active and begin to leap around energetically.

At 28 weeks The fetus is now legally viable; if it is born it must be registered as a birth. If it dies it is considered to be a stillbirth rather than a miscarriage. With modern intensive care a baby at this stage has a 60–70 per cent chance of survival—even higher in some units. The main problem encountered is usually that the baby's lungs have not yet developed bubbles of surfactant, the substance which prevents the complete collapse of the lungs between each breath. There is also still very little fat under the baby's skin, so its temperature control mechanisms cannot yet work efficiently.

The baby has virtually filled all the available space in the uterus. Most babies turn upside down at some point during the seventh month and then seem to fit more comfortably. By now you may be able to distinguish the baby's bottom from a foot or a knee. When you lie in the bath you can enjoy watching the baby swivel from one side of your abdomen to the other. Foot and knee movements are more jerky than whole-body movements and hands produce soft flutters

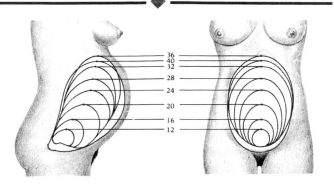

THE CHANGING UTERUS
Although the uterus is expanding throughout pregnancy, this increase in size is not usually visible until the fourth month, when it is too large to stay hidden in the pelvis. From the 12th week the uterus enlarges at a regular rate until the 36th week, when the fundus (the top of the uterus) reaches to just below the breastbone. In women having their first child, the baby sometimes engages in the pelvis at about this date, so that the fundus descends slightly, even though the uterus has not shrunk.

like sea anemones moving. Other people may now be able to feel the baby kicking when they place a hand on your abdomen.

Throughout later pregnancy you can often anticipate the periods of most hectic movement; many babies are at their most energetic between eight and eleven pm.

At 32 weeks By the eighth month the baby lacks only some lung surfactant and a good layer of insulating fat before it is ready to be born. Movements are vigorous: the prods coming from the feet are so energetic that they may make you catch your breath. Every now and again the baby may jerk spasmodically in what can be a rather alarming manner; some women worry that their babies are having epileptic fits. But it is usually an attack of hiccups, brought on perhaps because the baby has been gulping amniotic fluid.

At 36 weeks At some point between 36 weeks and term (which is 40 weeks from the first day of your last menstrual period) the baby will probably descend into the pelvis with its head firmly fixed like an egg in an egg-cup. It is then said to be "engaged"; this is a good sign and one indication that the baby can pass through the pelvic cavity without difficulty. Once your baby has engaged you are slung lower and can often feel the head like a coconut hanging between your legs. It is uncomfortable to sit down fast on a hard chair and you may also experience peculiar sensations in your vagina like mild electric shocks (see page 209).

After the baby has engaged, its larger body movements tend to be limited; you will probably feel only the kicking of legs and feet, the action of the head as it uses the pelvic floor as a trampoline and the fainter movements of the arms. But although the movements change in type no day should pass without some lively indications from the baby of its presence (see page 218).

The last weeks may be tiring and involve tedious inaction. The baby is three times heavier at delivery than it was at 28 weeks, weighs anything from $5\frac{1}{2}$ to 11 lbs (2·5–5 kg) and is between 18 and 22 in long (44–55 cm). It is now ready for its extraordinary journey to life.

Forty weeks of life

The next ten pages show different stages of the development of a baby from the moment of conception to its last week in the uterus. The illustration below shows the journey of the egg along the fallopian tube, where it is fertilized, to the uterus. During this five-day journey, the single-cell egg divides into over a hundred cells.

One of the sperm that have arrived in the fallopian tube penetrates the ripe egg.

The head of the sperm separates from the tail and approaches the egg's nucleus.

The chromosomes of the two nuclei pair off to create a two-cell egg.

The two cells divide as the egg continues its journey along the fallopian tube.

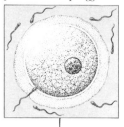
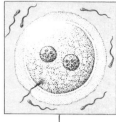
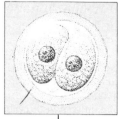
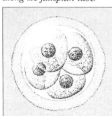

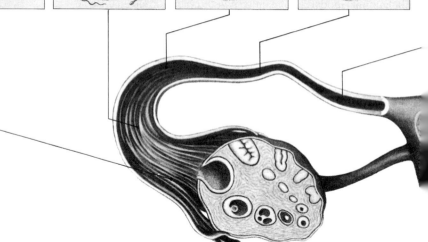

As the cells continue to divide they gradually get smaller and smaller.

On about the fifth day the egg reaches the uterus and loses its jelly-like coating.

Six or seven days after fertilization the egg embeds itself in the uterine lining.

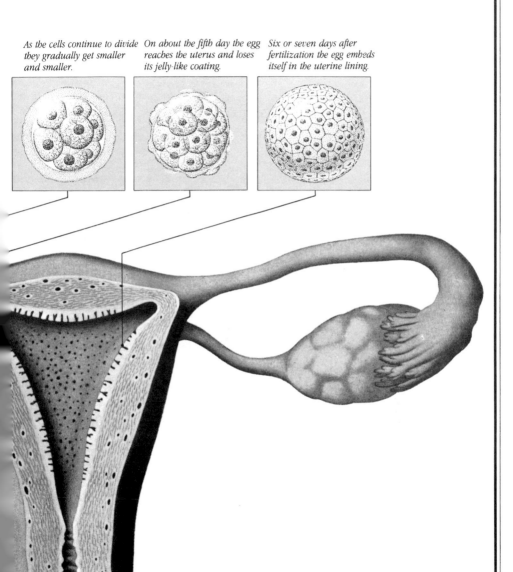

Eight weeks pregnant

The baby is just under 1 in (2·5 cm) long. The bones of its arms and legs start to harden and the baby makes slight movements, still too feather-light for the mother to notice. The baby's face is developing. Some time during this week the baby starts to open its mouth and the upper palate forms. The lower jaw is taking shape, with muscles which will enable the baby to suck and chew. The sound-perceiving mechanism of the ear has now developed.

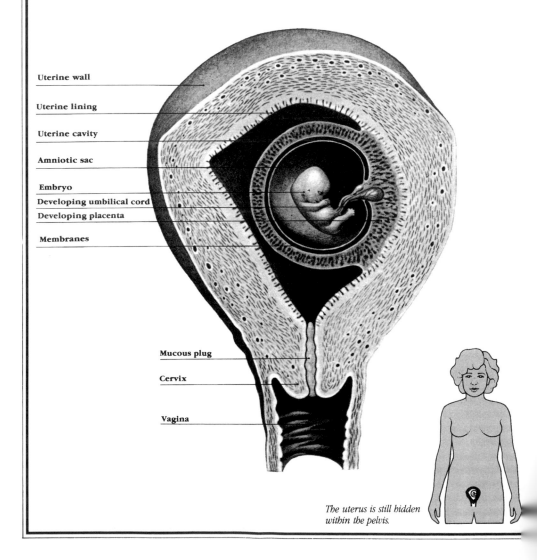

Uterine wall

Uterine lining

Uterine cavity

Amniotic sac

Embryo

Developing umbilical cord

Developing placenta

Membranes

Mucous plug

Cervix

Vagina

The uterus is still hidden within the pelvis.

Twelve weeks pregnant

The baby is now just over 2 in (5 cm) long. Its head is more rounded and is no longer so top-heavy: it is about two-thirds the size of the body. The eyes are widely separated in a broad face. The jaws have 32 permanent tooth buds and the baby is starting to suck. It is already exercising the muscles that will be used in breathing after birth.

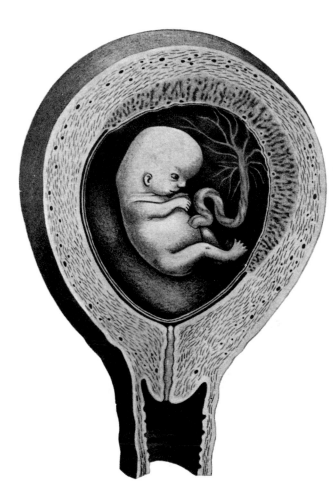

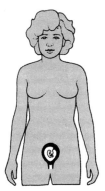

The growing uterus can now be felt through the abdominal wall.

Twenty weeks pregnant

The baby's rate of growth, which has been very rapid, slows down a little at this stage. It is about 10 in (25 cm) long. Legs are now the right length in proportion to the body and there are miniature nails on the toes. The mother feels movement, at first faint then growing stronger. Hair on the baby's head and delicately etched eyebrows have appeared and there is a fine downy hair called lanugo over much of the body.

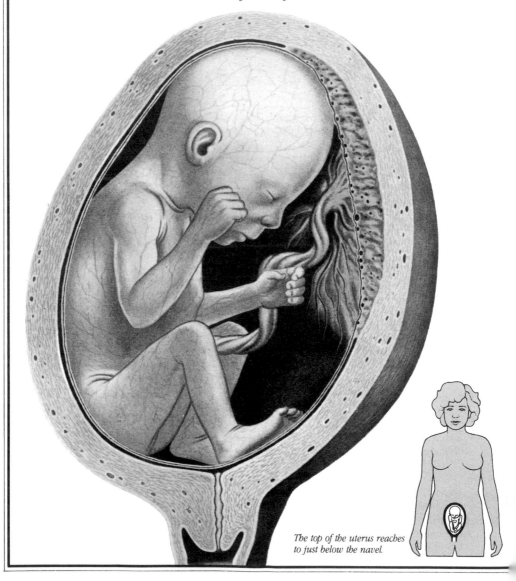

The top of the uterus reaches to just below the navel.

Twenty-four weeks pregnant

The baby is thin and the skin is wrinkled. The face is now fully formed and the eyes are rather prominent because fat pads have not yet built up in the cheeks.

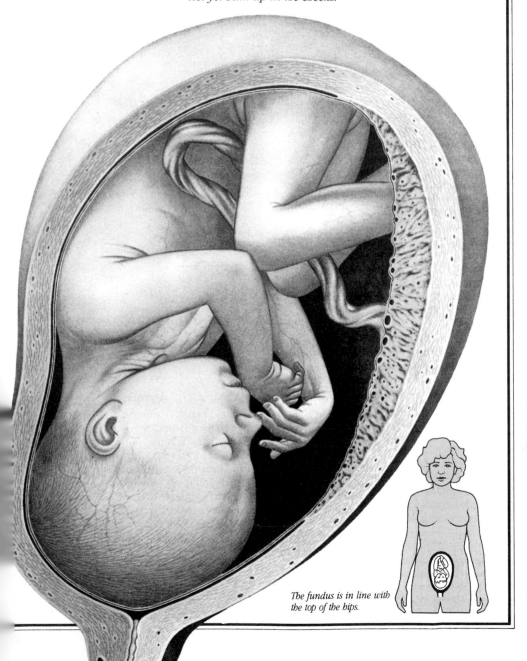

The fundus is in line with the top of the hips.

Thirty-six weeks pregnant

There is no longer enough room in the uterus for the baby to move about freely. It has settled into one position and the main movements the mother feels are jabs from the arms and legs. By now the skin is smooth and peach-like and the body has plumped out. When the baby is awake, the eyes are open and it is aware of strong light flowing through the tissues of its mother's abdominal wall. If it is born at this time, the baby has an excellent chance of survival.

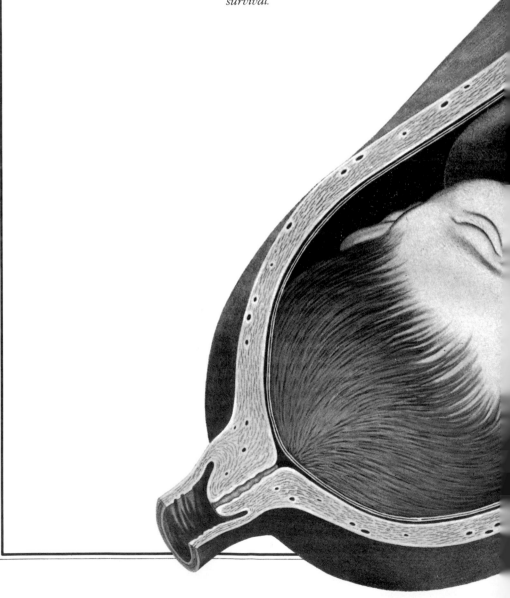

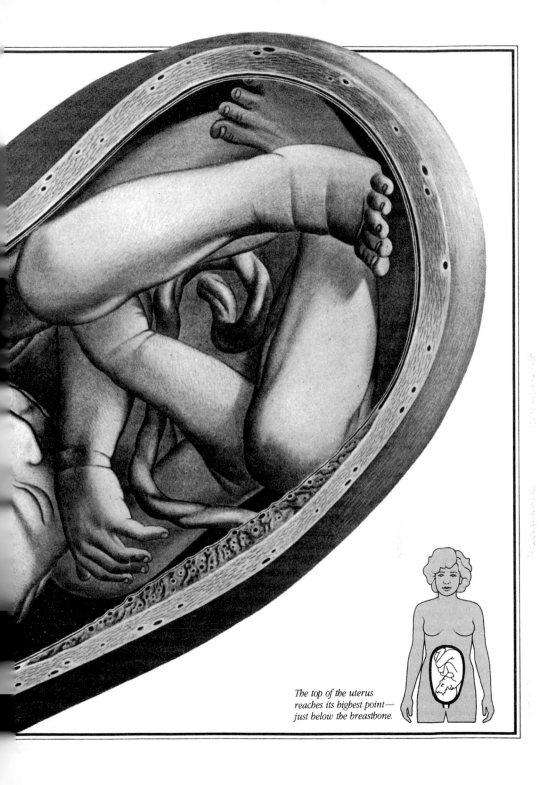

The top of the uterus reaches its highest point—just below the breastbone.

Forty weeks pregnant

The baby is now about eight times bigger than it was at three months, when all its vital organs were formed, and has increased in weight approximately 600 times. Most of the lanugo has dropped off, though there may still be some down the centre of the back, in front of the ears and low on the forehead. The fingernails extend beyond the fingers and may need cutting at birth so that the baby does not scratch its face.

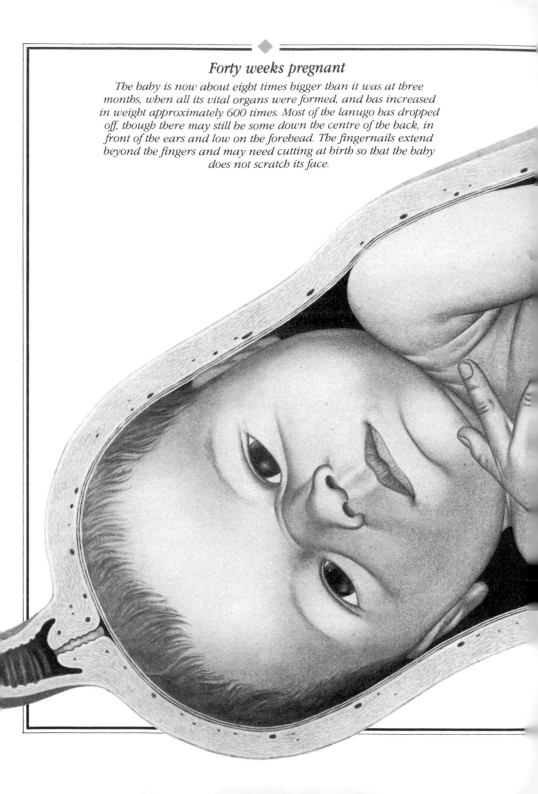

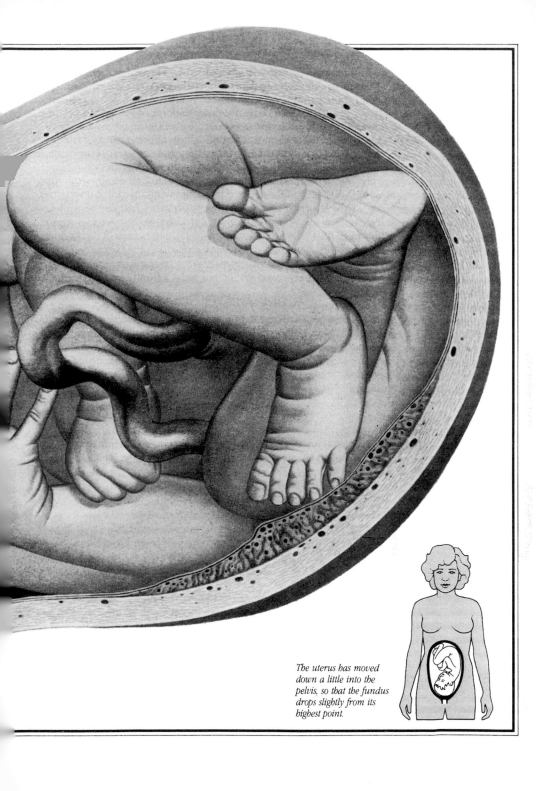

The uterus has moved
down a little into the
pelvis, so that the fundus
drops slightly from its
highest point.

Expecting twins

Finding out that you are going to have twins usually comes as a shock. Some women suspect quite early in their pregnancy that this will be the case, especially if they have already had a singleton pregnancy with which they can compare this one. If you are a fraternal twin (see below), you are about twice as likely to give birth to twins yourself as are other women, so you may be on the lookout for any confirmation of your suspicions. The chances of having fraternal twins depend on heredity, age, race and the number of children you have already had. Although fraternal twins often skip a generation, the chances of them occurring in successive generations are high. The frequency of identical twins seems independent of these variables.

Mixed feelings

However, if nothing has led you to suspect that you are carrying more than one baby, it can be very upsetting to be told, after a scan at the

---

How twins are conceived

Normally conception occurs when one egg released from a woman's ovary is fertilized by one male sperm. Seven out of ten pairs of twins result from the woman releasing two eggs, which are then fertilized independently by two sperm (fraternal twins). Usually the two eggs then implant and develop separately in the uterus. Less commonly, one egg fertilized by one sperm divides, resulting in two developing babies with the same inherited characteristics (identical twins). Often this division occurs after implantation in the uterus.

IDENTICAL TWINS
Identical twinning occurs after, rather than at, fertilization, and often after implantation in the uterus. As a result the twins almost always share a placenta although each has its own cord and bag of water.

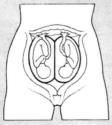

FRATERNAL TWINS
Fraternal twins have separate water bags and cords, and separate placentas. Occasionally the two eggs implant close together in the uterus, so that the placentas become fused and it looks as if there is only one.

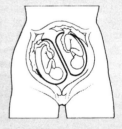

Monozygotic (one-egg) or identical twins

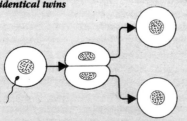

Dizygotic (two-egg) or fraternal twins

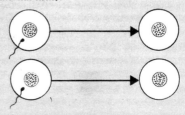

antenatal clinic perhaps (see page 48), that suddenly all your expectations of birth and the time afterwards need re-adjusting.

If you are to be a mother for the first time, the natural apprehension you originally felt about the labour and how you would cope with a new baby is greatly increased. Added to this you wonder how you will manage two babies at the same time in all their noisy reality—two mouths to feed, two nappies to change each time, two babies to bath, two lots of clothes to wash, two budding personalities who will need your love and attention.

One woman, who was dismayed on hearing that she was expecting twins, said that she never really veered from this attitude throughout the rest of her pregnancy. During a stay in hospital in her eighth month of pregnancy, she took the opportunity of watching mothers who had recently given birth to twins, and felt that all her worries were justified, since they seemed to have such trouble in managing two babies. However, shortly after her twins were born, she was able to comment on the "totally unexpected delight of being able to breast-feed both, often simultaneously". She did admit, though, that it was hard work at first and that "the intense joy and delight the babies now give has only come as we have got to know them".

> *I heard that I was expecting twins when I was about 29 weeks pregnant, spent two days weeping intermittently, and didn't really whip up much enthusiasm about the idea right to the end of the pregnancy.*

Positions of twins in the uterus

Twins fill the available space in the uterus more quickly than a single baby, so they may adopt the positions in which they will be born at an earlier stage.

The pictures below show fraternal twins (with two placentas), but the same positions apply to identical twins (with a single placenta).

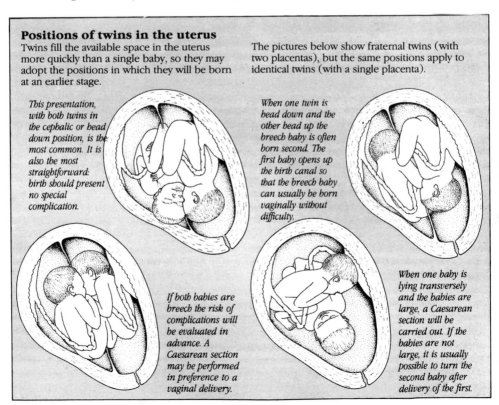

This presentation, with both twins in the cephalic or head down position, is the most common. It is also the most straightforward: birth should present no special complication.

When one twin is head down and the other head up the breech baby is often born second. The first baby opens up the birth canal so that the breech baby can usually be born vaginally without difficulty.

If both babies are breech the risk of complications will be evaluated in advance. A Caesarean section may be performed in preference to a vaginal delivery.

When one baby is lying transversely and the babies are large, a Caesarean section will be carried out. If the babies are not large, it is usually possible to turn the second baby after delivery of the first.

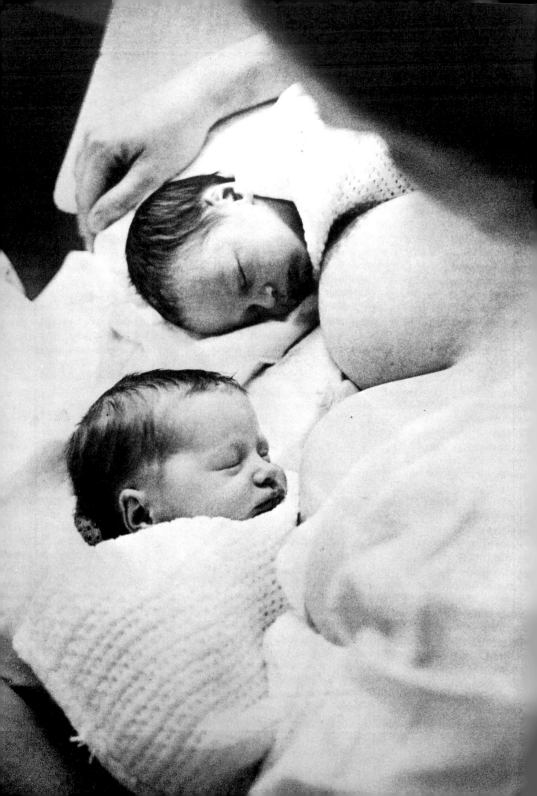

Sometimes a woman is unhappy to discover that she is expecting twins because she has been planning for a home birth and this may no longer be possible. Doctors usually advise hospital birth for twins, since the chances of a complicated delivery, especially for the second twin, are increased and it is possible that the babies will be premature and underweight.

Alternatively a woman may be overjoyed to find that she is going to have twins. Perhaps she had wanted more than one child, but was not particularly enjoying her pregnancy and certainly not looking forward to another. Suddenly she discovers that she can have two children for the price of one pregnancy and labour!

Rest

The first thing to accept is that a pregnancy with two babies tumbling about inside can be more of a strain than an ordinary pregnancy. The risk of developing pre-eclampsia (see page 126) is higher; since the babies are more likely to be born prematurely, they may not be so strong. Because they have to share the space in the uterus and the nutrition available through the placenta, twins are often of low birthweight. To help avoid extra strain, you need regular rest times and frequent early nights. If you already have other children, it is worth making an effort to find some motherly (or fatherly) person who can look after them for an hour or so each day so that you can relax without feeling that you will be needed in a minute.

In late pregnancy a baby who has not been growing well in the uterus invariably grows better if the mother has more rest and actually stays in bed (lying down in a darkened room for three hours every afternoon is ideal). This is why many obstetricians move you into hospital for a compulsory rest. But if you are able to plan ahead and make other arrangements, you may avoid any anxiety about the babies' growth and be able to convince your doctor that you can re-organize your life well enough to take adequate rest at home.

There is no need to be an invalid. But if you think about the extra demands made on your body by a multiple pregnancy you will realize that your whole system has to adjust to the babies' needs. Such an adjustment involves widespread metabolic changes; there is also extra pressure put on your digestive organs and on your diaphragm and lungs, as well as stress on bones (on your lower ribs, which tend to splay out, and on your spine, for example). Your muscles, too, cope with much of the stress of a twin pregnancy, especially your tummy muscles, your pelvic floor, and the muscles of legs, feet, arms, shoulders and back, which have to support the extra weight and do the work of lifting and coping with your body mechanics. Above all this a general crowding out may make you feel very full up.

So rest is good for you and will help your body adjust to the increased demands made on it by a multiple pregnancy. And the rest that helps most is rest taken *before* you become exhausted and irritable and *before* you feel that you cannot carry on a minute longer.

═ ❝ ═

We didn't find out until the 8th month that we were expecting twins, and then we were delighted. The initial shock of the news left me feeling physically a bit weak at the knees, but there was never any question about our joy at the prospect.

═ ❞ ═

OPPOSITE

The prospect of twins may come as a shock, but the reality may more than compensate.

Comfort

You may find it very uncomfortable to lie flat. The heavy uterus is pressing on major blood vessels in that position too, so, both for your own comfort and for the blood supply to the babies, lie either well propped up or in a three-quarters-over position (see page 118). Prop your breasts with one pillow and put two under your upper knee if this feels good. Even more so than with a singleton pregnancy, special back supports may be needed in the last few weeks. A large bean bag may be comfortable; so might a boomerang pillow with other pillows. You may be able to borrow two firm foam wedges from the National Childbirth Trust or your hospital if it has them. Whatever you choose, try to get something solid which will support the exaggerated curve of your lower spine.

BACK SUPPORT
If you are carrying twins you are most likely to feel the strain caused by the extra weight in the small of your back. A large bean bag or firm floor cushion or a special boomerang pillow (far right) will give the support you need.

Exercise

Sensible body mechanics are also more important when you are expecting more than one baby (see pages 115–119). Learn how to counteract the effect of the enlarged and heavy uterus by standing straight and tall, with tail tucked in. Aim to balance on the balls of your feet rather than being flat-footed and waddling like a duck, which is only too easy to do when you are overtired. Above all learn how to get up from a lying-down position by rolling over, if necessary kicking off with your foot and hand against solid objects, and then rising on to all fours (see page 113).

Pelvic-floor exercises (see page 107) are important throughout, whether you are carrying one baby or two; with twins they will be especially vital after the birth, as the muscles around the vagina have been stretched by the extra weight of two babies. It is a good idea in any case to do these exercises from early pregnancy, before there is any appreciable change in weight, as muscle tone is really best built up before there is any particular stress on the muscles. If your pelvic-floor muscles are under a great deal of strain, you should do these exercises while lying on the floor with your lower legs raised on a chair. In this position weight is not pressing on the pelvic muscles, and it is easier to feel what is happening there, even in advanced pregnancy when the babies may be very low down.

You will probably be aware of the babies moving a great deal inside you. Your abdomen feels like a basket full of puppies. It can be difficult to sleep, and you are often woken by all the internal activity. Practising release from tension and deliberately letting muscles relax all over your body can help enormously (see page 172).

Some mothers worry in case the babies are harming each other. They can certainly shuffle each other up a bit, but each one is sealed off in its own bag of waters, and this also means that each baby bobs around like a cork in a tumbler of water. The water cushions them from shock and allows free movement until the very last weeks of pregnancy when the pelvic girdle cradles the babies so neatly that you may feel only small movements.

Diet

For a detailed discussion of diet in pregnancy see page 86. The demands made on your body by a twin pregnancy require an even more careful attention to diet than is necessary in a singleton pregnancy. Aim for a nutritious diet with plenty of salads and fruit and only those foods which are of positive value to yourself and the babies. Cut out the ice creams, flabby slices of bread, sickly doughnuts and biscuits. The easiest way to do this is to convince yourself how nasty they are and to think instead of rich golden hunks of cheese, glowing fruit salad, a peach that melts in the mouth, jade-green watercress, tawny apples and a luscious, long glass of milk.

To save labouring over a hot stove have at least one raw-food meal a day, which will give you a good supply of vitamins. You may like to buy some new cookery books that concentrate on salads and fruit and stimulate your imagination. If you normally eat white bread and cereals, now is the time to switch to granary bread and flour, brown rice and whole grains. Eating like this will help you after the babies come, too, as you cannot feel full of vitality if you are poorly nourished and weighed down with "junk" foods.

The more tired you become the more you may feel that you cannot be bothered about arranging meals and shopping for food. But your health depends on your having a good diet and not skimping on protein, vitamins and minerals. Is there any chance of getting help with shopping? Could someone else shop for you? Or could you and your partner or a friend do it together in bulk, loading up a car? (But do not lift boxes and bags into the boot yourself or attempt to unload them!) If you have to shop unaided, use a wheeled shopping basket and avoid carrying bags. There may still be a shop in your area which will deliver goods provided that you order enough at one time. If you live in the country, a village shop may do this when they know you are expecting twins. Or could your partner take a neighbour who has no car to the supermarket, so that she can help him shop for you?

Your baby's wellbeing

Looking after yourself in pregnancy, from the very first weeks, is probably more important for the welfare of your baby than anything else you can do. It ensures that you provide the best possible environment for the developing baby—and, equally important, it gives you the best chance of being healthy and full of vitality, ready for the birthday and the first stages of motherhood.

NUTRITION

Your baby depends on what you eat and drink for adequate nourishment in the uterus. In the sixties it was thought that provided the expectant mother had a "sensible" diet there was no need to give her any advice about what she should eat, because the fetus would always take what it needed. There were certain "do nots", the most important of which was "do not eat for two". But such a vague instruction led to large numbers of women going through pregnancy on inadequate diets.

Then, in the seventies, research revealed that when pregnant women have an inadequate diet, their babies may die or be born in poor health, and women may have difficult pregnancies and labours, as well as subsequent illness*. If a woman is nutritionally deprived, her baby is deprived too; she is more likely to have a miscarriage and, if the pregnancy is maintained, her baby is more likely either to be born prematurely or to be of low birthweight because it has not received sufficient nourishment in the uterus. The research also revealed that poor nutrition in the later part of pregnancy can affect the development of the child's brain*.

Weighing yourself gives an indication of the progress of your pregnancy, but it should not become an obsession.

Weight gain in pregnancy

Your total weight gain in pregnancy is made up as follows:		However much weight you gain during your pregnancy, you will gain it at approximately the following rate:	
Weight of baby	38%	0–12 weeks	0%
Weight of placenta	9%	12–20 weeks	25%
Weight of amniotic fluid	11%	20–30 weeks	50%
Increase in weight of		30–36 weeks	25%
uterus and breasts	20%	36–40 weeks	0%
Increase in weight of blood	22%		
Total weight gain	100%		

So, as a rough guide, you can assume that if—for instance—you are 30 weeks pregnant, the weight you have gained since the beginning of your pregnancy will be about 75% of your total weight gain.

However, recent research has shown that sometimes too much emphasis has been placed on having huge quantities of food and a great deal of animal protein. Metabolic changes in pregnancy mean that most women can make better use of the food they eat, and this increased efficiency extends into the period of breast-feeding, too*. So there is no need to worry too much about whether you are having the right diet, routinely taking vitamin pills and mineral supplements, or to feel you ought to be eating foods you dislike just because you are told they are good for the baby.

Weight gain

It is normal to put on between 20 and 30 lbs in pregnancy (9–13·5 kg). Some women put on more, with no ill effects. It is wrong to assume that because your baby will only weigh $6\frac{1}{4}$ to $8\frac{1}{2}$ lbs (3–4 kg) at birth, all the rest of the weight that you put on is fat. You must consider the weight of the placenta, the membranes and the amniotic fluid, as well as the increase in size of the uterus and breasts, and the increase in volume of your blood. Fluid retention also accounts for a substantial weight gain in some women (see page 92). All these things return to normal after the birth.

Since different women gain weight at different rates it is impossible to be dogmatic about how much weight you should put on. Responsible medical opinion now is that "arbitrary weight restriction is potentially harmful to both mother and baby"*. If you start off your pregnancy underweight you and your baby may benefit from a bigger weight gain than the woman who begins pregnancy already overweight. It is certainly most unwise for any woman to try to remain slim during pregnancy, and an attempt to keep your figure might result in the eventual loss of your baby. On the other hand, if you start pregnancy overweight, you are likely to put on more weight than a woman who is not fat at the onset of pregnancy, and you are more likely to suffer from high blood pressure and urinary tract infection*.

One way of checking to see whether you are putting on superfluous fat, which you will be left with after the birth, is to measure your upper thighs each week, keeping a record of the measurement. This is a way of recording the increase in your own body fat as distinct from the weight you gain as a result of the pregnancy. The measurement should stay about the same, although fluid retention may increase it slightly in the last weeks of pregnancy.

Your upper thighs should stay about the same size throughout pregnancy.

Protein

Women who are not pregnant are recommended to have $1\frac{1}{2}$ oz (46 g) of protein a day for optimum health. When you are pregnant you may need about twice as much. The foods rich in protein are lean meat, fish, beans, nuts, brewer's yeast, milk, yoghurt, all the various cheeses and the other dairy products.

All proteins are made up of chemical substances—called amino acids—in different combinations. Animal or "first-class" proteins contain all the amino acids necessary for the protein to do its body-building work; vegetable proteins, which used to be called "second-class", only contain some of these amino acids, and therefore they should be eaten either with a small quantity of animal protein or in different combinations. If you are a vegetarian who eats no animal products, combine beans with a wheat product at the same meal—say, beans with whole grain flour pastry, chickpeas with pasta, or lentils with wholewheat bread*.

You will obtain adequate protein if every day you have one dish from each of the following categories: a) one helping of meat or fish, two eggs, or a cup of peanuts or cashew nuts; b) 4 oz (100 g) of hard cheese, 8 oz (200 g) cottage cheese or 1 pint (0·5 litre) of milk (substitute soya, nut milk or tofu); c) four slices of whole grain bread, a helping of brown rice or whole grain pasta, or one large potato baked in its jacket. If you are a vegan and do not eat any animal products, you obviously will not want cheese and milk, and should have a good helping of pulses instead.

Protein becomes particularly important if you are ill or fighting an infection, or if you feel overtaxed and exhausted. If you cannot face proper meals, protein and other essential foods can be obtained in the form of a drink. Try the following high-energy cocktail:

High-protein shake

1 cup of low fat milk

⅓ cup of instant nonfat dry milk powder

4 tablespoons of soy powder (available from health food stores)

1 cup of chopped fruit (strawberries, banana, pears, apricots, etc.)

1 tablespoon of honey

4 ice cubes

Blend all the ingredients on high speed until smooth. You can either drink the shake (try chilling it for an hour or so first), or freeze the mixture until slushy before eating it with a spoon.

A high-protein, low-fat refresher can give you an instant lift when you are feeling weary.

Carbohydrates

You need carbohydrates for energy. They are found in sugar, and in the foods you eat in bulk, such as bread, flour, cereals and root vegetables. Most foods containing carbohydrates have other valuable nutrients too; potatoes—especially if you eat them in their jackets—can contribute protein and vitamin C as well as carbohydrate, and wholewheat bread provides B vitamins, iron and the fibre which helps to prevent constipation. If you eat small quantities of these foods daily, you should need no other carbohydrates. But if foods rich in carbohydrates are the foods you enjoy most, you may put on unnecessary weight.

If you are overweight before starting pregnancy, or if you are putting on a lot of superfluous fat (see page 87 for a method of checking this), it is a good idea to cut out all white flour and sugar, and all products containing them. Cakes, puddings and biscuits do not do much to help your unborn baby's health. If you like sugar in tea and coffee, train yourself to enjoy both of these without it.

Fats

Your body's need for fat is minimal. You can deliberately reduce your intake by trimming fat off meat, by using less butter, by boiling or steaming foods rather than frying or sautéing them, and by cutting out rich sauces. You will find that cottage or curd cheese and yoghurt are both useful ingredients of low fat sauces, and that you can make fat-free sauces with puréed vegetables.

Milk and dairy products

Milk is usually recommended for the pregnant woman, but unless your diet is grossly inadequate in protein you do not need more than 1 pint (0·5 litre) a day. Consumed in large quantities milk is fattening, and if you fill yourself up with milky drinks you are likely to dampen your appetite for other foods you and your baby need. Some women do not like milk or are allergic to it. You can have fat-free milk or take cheese or yoghurt instead; if it is simply a matter of taste, disguise the milk in sauces or dishes where you are not aware of it.

Vitamins

It is important that most of your vitamin intake should come from food. Trying to get the right dosage of vitamins, and the right balance between different vitamins, from supplements is unwise. The chart on page 90 tells you which vitamins are in which foods, what they are for and whether it is ever advisable to take a supplement.

Minerals

Minerals and trace elements are a vital part of your diet, but if you are eating plenty of food rich in protein and vitamins you are unlikely to suffer from a mineral deficiency. Iron, calcium and zinc are probably the only minerals about which you need to be especially concerned.

Iron is necessary for the formation of red blood cells. Red blood cells contain a substance known as haemoglobin; if your blood contains insufficient haemoglobin not enough oxygen is carried to your baby and you become very tired. Vitamin C helps your body to absorb iron, whereas antacid medicines stop you from benefiting fully from it. Liver is a good source of iron, as are dark molasses, egg yolk, whole grains, pulses, all dark green leafy vegetables such as watercress, raisins, prunes, brewer's yeast and nuts.

Extra iron is often prescribed in pregnancy. If you eat plenty of foods rich in iron, you should have good reserves stored in your liver,

Vitamins in pregnancy

Vitamin	What it does	Foods it is in	Increase needed in pregnancy	Supplement needed
Vitamin A	Maintains skin, body tissues, vision; helps your body to resist infection.	Mainly green and orange vegetables, liver. Also dairy foods.	None.	None.
B VITAMINS B₁ Thiamine	Maintains brains, heart and nerves. Enables your body to make use of carbohydrate.	Most foods, but especially whole grains and yeast products. Lost in over-cooking.	None.	None.
B₂ Riboflavin	Helps tissue growth and regeneration, especially skin and eyes. Allows your body to use carbohydrate, fat and protein.	Mainly yeast, pulses and green vegetables. Also milk, eggs, brains, kidneys and liver. Often lost if exposed to light.	None.	None.
B₆ Pyridoxine	Allows your body to make use of protein. Ensures cell division.	Most foods, but especially meat, fish, dried vegetables, whole grains, potatoes, bananas.	None.	None. In fact it is wise to avoid a supplement as large amounts can suppress lactation and some cases of "rebound" deficiency have been reported in babies whose mothers took enormous doses during pregnancy.
B₁₂ Cyano-cobalamin	Helps to form haemo-globin and the baby's central nervous system. Allows your body to make use of protein, folic acid and fatty acids.	Meat and fish, especially liver.	None.	A capsule might be advisable for vegetarians.
PP Niacin	Helps to keep tissues healthy and allows your body to use protein.	Meat, fish, peanuts, pulses, eggs, milk.	None.	None.
Pantothenic acid	Maintains nerves and red blood cells. Essential for breakdown of fat and carbohydrate.	Most foods, especially meat, eggs, cheese, whole grains, peanuts and some green vegetables.	90%—nearly double the normal intake.	None.
Folic acid	Aids cell division and the development of the baby's central nervous system.	Liver, green leafy vegetables.	100%—double the normal intake.	Often prescribed at the same time as iron.
Vitamin C	Helps form connective tissue and assists absorption of iron. Maintains blood vessel walls, helping to prevent haemorrhage; assists healing and the formation of bones.	Fresh vegetables and fresh fruit, especially citrus fruit.	None.	Occasionally prescribed to help the absorption of iron.
Vitamin D	Helps form and maintain bones.	Liver and fish liver oils. Butter, egg yolk, milk.	None.	None.
Vitamin E	Helps to protect cells from damage and degeneration.	Most foods, especially wheatgerm.	None.	None.
Vitamin K	Plays vital part in process leading to blood coagulation.	Manufactured in human colon. Also in green leafy vegetables.	None.	None.

and not need to take extra. The fetus draws on these reserves, so that it can store enough in its own liver to last for several months after birth—a vital need, since milk contains almost no iron. But if you are iron-deficient (slightly anaemic) before embarking on pregnancy (and many women are, without realizing it), a supplement is probably advisable.

You probably need about twice as much iron when you are pregnant as you do before conception.

Calcium is necessary for the formation of strong bones and teeth. It enables blood to clot and your muscles to work smoothly. The oxalic acid in spinach and cocoa reduces the absorption of calcium: do not depend on a milky chocolate drink for your calcium intake.

Your baby's teeth start to bud very early on in pregnancy, so your calcium intake in the first four months matters a great deal. Milk is a useful source, as are other dairy foods. Calcium is also present in leafy vegetables, whole grains, pulses and nuts. You need almost twice as much when you are pregnant.

Zinc deficiency may result in miscarriage, growth retardation in the uterus, stillbirth or congenital handicap*. There is also some evidence that zinc is necessary for muscles to contract well and, though it is difficult to measure accurately the concentration of zinc in human tissues, that shortage of zinc is one cause of long labour*. Taking an iron supplement can interfere with the absorption of zinc. High fibre foods—especially bran—contain zinc, as do brazil nuts, cheddar and other hard cheeses, seeds, herrings and meat.

Women at risk

Certain women are at "nutritional risk" and need to pay special attention to diet; for them vitamin and mineral supplements may be useful. The ones who may be at risk are those pregnant during adolescence (while they are still growing themselves), women who are underweight when they become pregnant, women who are overweight because of excess consumption of carbohydrates and fats, those living on a very restricted range of foods like a macrobiotic diet, women who have lost a baby from miscarriage or stillbirth before, and women who have had three pregnancies within two years. Also included in this category are women suffering from some chronic diseases involving the regular use of drugs, women who smoke, heavy drinkers and those with multiple pregnancies*.

Research* suggests that if a woman who has previously given birth to a baby with a neural tube defect (spina bifida or anencephaly) takes a multi-vitamin preparation for at least one month *before conception* and up to the second missed period, the chance of having another handicapped baby is much reduced. The woman is well nourished both at the time of conception and during the crucial early stages, when the baby's spinal cord is being formed and a neural tube

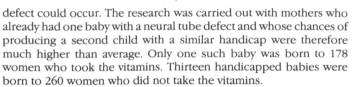

defect could occur. The research was carried out with mothers who already had one baby with a neural tube defect and whose chances of producing a second child with a similar handicap were therefore much higher than average. Only one such baby was born to 178 women who took the vitamins. Thirteen handicapped babies were born to 260 women who did not take the vitamins.

What we cannot conclude from this research is that because women at high risk benefit from multi-vitamins then *all* women should have them. Some researchers suspect that, in some cases, high doses of vitamin supplements may prove to have a mild teratogenic effect and lead to babies being born with handicaps.

Salt and fluid retention

It used to be thought that salt was dangerous in pregnancy and was one cause of pre-eclampsia (see page 126). It has now been established that salt is necessary for a normal pregnancy. When a group of expectant mothers had no-salt diets they had *more* pre-eclampsia than a control group of women who had as much salt as they wished*. Cutting out salt can also cause cramp in hot weather. Since you tend to retain more fluid when you are pregnant, you will only maintain the usual level of saltiness in all your body fluids by having as much salt as your appetite dictates*.

Occasionally special diets are prescribed for pregnant women in order to reduce fluid retention, which used to be thought dangerous in itself. But these special diets can harm the unborn baby. Women with mild fluid retention (oedema) usually produce babies in just as good a condition as those who have no signs of it at all. Ankle, foot and leg swelling on very hot days, when you have been on a plane trip or after you have been standing for a long time, is therefore nothing to worry about. If your skin is looking very puffy, take more rest and look at your diet to see if you should increase your protein intake (see page 87); if your fingers and face become swollen you should mention it to the doctor, as it is a sign that your kidneys are not coping well with the excretion of waste products from your body. This in turn may mean that your placenta is not working efficiently.

You cannot prevent oedema by cutting down on fluids, so drink as much as you want. Four or five glasses of water a day will help your kidneys to function well throughout pregnancy.

Eating a balanced diet

I'm taking the opportunity of reforming Chris's eating habits. It's all salads and wholemeal bread and food that's good for you.

Bear in mind that you are providing nutrition for three distinct but interdependent biological entities: your own body, the developing baby and the placenta*. This triple nutritional task demands a good, high-protein diet rich in vitamins and minerals.

A salad a day is a must, but remember that you can use finely chopped cabbage when lettuce and other greens are out of season, and that it is usually tastier than hothouse lettuce. Experiment with salads and try mixing fruit and vegetables. Apples go with most savoury things. A baked potato with cheese and a cabbage-based salad are a good source of protein, vitamin C and calcium. If you can spare time to bake your own whole grain bread, add extra wheat germ or soy flour and you have added to your diet another valuable source of protein, iron, B vitamins and fibre.

Eating well does not always mean eating expensively. Some women save money by avoiding unnecessary foods such as carbonized drinks, coffee, packet desserts and soups, confectionery, shop cakes and starchy sugary puddings. Milk and cheese are relatively cheap, and a delicious main course can be made from a selection of vegetables in season covered with a white sauce and topped with a layer of grated cheese browned under the grill.

DRUGS

The full range of substances to which the embryo and fetus may be vulnerable is not yet known. It is wise to take the fewest possible medicines of any kind during pregnancy, especially in the first few weeks when the embryo is forming and when the placenta is only just starting to be active. (You should therefore take care during the second half of the menstrual cycle if there is any chance that you might be pregnant.) It used to be thought that the placenta acted as an effective barrier to all poisons in the maternal bloodstream. But it is now known that many drugs—including nicotine and alcohol—can cross the placenta and may affect the baby*.

Everything you read in the papers about drugs in early pregnancy, it's so terrifying! I can't remember what I took in those 8 weeks and it's haunting me.

If you think of how the fertilized egg has to segment, travel along the fallopian tube, embed itself into the lining of the uterus and develop into a baby, you can imagine how such delicate and complex processes can be interfered with by chemicals which have been introduced into your bloodstream.

The liver and the kidneys are the organs of your body which deal with drugs and turn them into material which can be excreted in the urine. In an unborn—and even a newborn—baby these organs are still immature. The fetus is therefore not able to excrete many of the drugs which may reach it through the placenta. Instead, such drugs can accumulate in its body in toxic quantities. It is vital to remember, when taking any drug, that a dosage which may be right for you is far in excess of that which is suitable for your tiny baby.

Everyone remembers the thalidomide disaster*, when a sedative which was thought to be mild and safe was prescribed for women in early pregnancy. As a result of this sedative more than five thousand babies were born with badly deformed limbs, or none at all. Thalidomide is an extreme example of the effect that a drug can have on the development of an unborn baby. But all drugs are potentially harmful if misused. You should think carefully before taking any drug when pregnant, especially in the early weeks. The word *drug* here includes not only prescribed drugs, but also nicotine, alcohol, and medicines bought over the counter such as laxatives or aspirin.

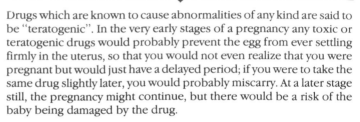

Drugs which are known to cause abnormalities of any kind are said to be "teratogenic". In the very early stages of a pregnancy any toxic or teratogenic drugs would probably prevent the egg from ever settling firmly in the uterus, so that you would not even realize that you were pregnant but would just have a delayed period; if you were to take the same drug slightly later, you would probably miscarry. At a later stage still, the pregnancy might continue, but there would be a risk of the baby being damaged by the drug.

Weighing up different risks

Clearly some pregnant women need drugs, and may be very ill without them. Illness in the mother can also affect the developing baby. For instance running a very high temperature (see page 102) seems to be teratogenic at certain phases of pregnancy, so it may be safer to take aspirin to get your temperature down than to try and cope without any medicines. It is always a question of balancing the risks to the baby against your need and the stress which may be caused to you by not having drug treatment.

Since the thalidomide disaster there has been acute awareness of the need to screen all new drugs before they are prescribed to pregnant women, and doctors are being increasingly careful. But drugs which have been in use a long time remain on the market without being tested. And it is difficult to be certain about any drugs, because animal experiments may produce damage in one species, yet not in another. This can work either way: rats may be affected, but not human babies, or babies may be affected when rats are not.

People are often ignorant about the chemical substances they introduce into their bodies. Antacids for the relief of indigestion, cough medicines, sleeping pills (barbiturates), antihistamines used in the treatment of hay fever and antibiotics are just some commonly used drugs which alter the body's chemical balance. A great many pregnant women take over-the-counter as well as prescribed drugs of one kind or another in the first weeks of pregnancy, and no-one has much idea of the possible risks. There are other substances which you may not think of as being drugs, including cigarettes and alcohol. Even tea and coffee have been researched for harmful effects, though normal use (half a dozen cups a day) seems to be fine*.

Smoking

There are positive steps you can take to give your baby the best start in life and other things which you should avoid since they are known to be detrimental. First and foremost among the dangers is smoking. Whether or not you inhale, nicotine passes into your bloodstream and from there into the baby's. It makes the fetal heart speed up and interrupts the baby's respiratory movements which are a rehearsal for breathing. In effect, the baby coughs and splutters.

Smoking interferes with the efficiency of the placenta and is the most widespread and efficient way of pumping a powerful poison into an unborn baby's bloodstream. Nicotine makes the blood vessels in the placenta constrict so that less oxygen and fewer nutritional substances reach the baby.

Mothers who smoke bear babies who weigh less than babies of mothers who do not smoke and the baby's weight drops in direct relation to the number of cigarettes consumed*. This does not mean that some smokers do not have good-sized babies but that statistically babies of smokers can be shown to be deprived of the best possible nutrition in the uterus. The reason for this is not just that a woman who smokes tends to eat less. Cigarettes have a direct effect on the growth of the baby*. It could be that some women make the mistake of thinking that labour will be easier if their babies are lighter in weight. Labour with a tiny, underweight baby is no easier or shorter than labour with a good-sized baby, and your baby is much more likely to be healthy and easy to care for if you have not smoked.

Smoking after the fourth month of pregnancy is a major cause of prematurity and the birth of underweight babies who, although they have had the full time in the uterus, are stunted in development and may have to be cared for in a special care baby unit. Smoking also increases the chances of bleeding during pregnancy, miscarriage (women who smoke are twice as likely to miscarry as those who do not), premature rupture of the membranes, premature separation of the placenta, haemorrhage before or early in labour, haemorrhage after delivery, congenital abnormality, stillbirth, and death of the baby in the week following delivery*. The more a woman smokes, the more likely these things are to happen.

I really get scared when someone lights up. I think, "Why should my baby have that poison in its bloodstream?" I can get quite rude about it!

How to give up If you are a heavy smoker and dependent on cigarettes to get through the day it may be very difficult to give them up, even for the sake of your baby. Fortunately, the nausea of early pregnancy or just a sudden dislike of cigarettes prompts many women to cut them out. Even if this does not happen spontaneously you can use the techniques of aversion therapy to condition yourself to break the habit. Every time you feel queasy or vomit make yourself think "cigarette" and use the association between vividly picturing the act of smoking and the overwhelming sensations of nausea to train yourself to develop a dislike of cigarettes.

How to cut down If you are past the nauseous stage of pregnancy or feel perfectly fit throughout, as many women do, you should still try to reduce your cigarettes to at least half of the usual number. Ask your partner to help by cutting down his consumption in the same way; if the two of you are making the same effort, your determination is strengthened. Also, recent studies suggest that even being in a smoky room for a long time—being a "passive" smoker—should be avoided. The more you can both cut down the better.

You may be feeling terribly guilty about smoking while still unable to give it up. You might feel like a murderer, but the guiltier you become the more you want a cigarette to help you calm down. It is certain that guilt and emotional stress can also affect your metabolism adversely, including your heart rate, blood pressure, breathing, muscle tone and the adrenalin in your bloodstream. The question then arises as to how much stress you should tolerate in trying to give up smoking. If you know how to release tension you may be able to cope by smoking each cigarette only halfway down and still find that it helps you enough to "unwind".

This is where your own judgment of the relative importance to you of smoking or not smoking in pregnancy is essential. Every pregnant woman has the right to be fully informed of the risks of smoking and also to make her own decision on the subject. No-one can *make* you stop smoking, however many dire warnings they give: you decide.

On the other hand, your baby cannot choose whether or not to smoke. A mother chooses for her child.

Alcohol

Alcohol is as much a drug as anything you may take in the form of a pill. The safe minimal dose in pregnancy is not yet known, but because alcohol is socially accepted it is easy to forget that its use should be restricted. Fortunately, many women develop an aversion to it in any form.

Some women's metabolisms are unable to break alcohol down into harmless substances and it passes straight through the placenta to the fetus in its poisonous form. If you are one of these women, you should not drink at all. You can have a blood test after drinking to discover how well you are able to metabolize alcohol, but this is not done routinely. There is no reason why you should not ask your GP to do this simple test before you even start a pregnancy.

The less well you metabolize alcohol the more careful you should be. Even if you metabolize it normally, there is evidence that a single "binge" during pregnancy may affect some babies, depending on the stage of development they have reached. So although common sense would indicate that you can drink in moderation and still have a perfect baby, unfortunately you cannot assume that this is the case. Limit your intake of alcohol to an occasional glass of wine.

Being careful about drugs

Think about any drugs you may be taking when you intend to conceive, and ask your doctor's advice. Do not wait until your first antenatal visit or even—if possible—until you are sure you are pregnant. If there is any chance that you might be pregnant, avoid taking any drugs which are not absolutely essential to your health.

If a doctor other than your obstetrician is treating you, especially in the early months of pregnancy before it is obvious that you are having a baby, make sure that he or she realizes that you are pregnant before prescribing. This may be particularly relevant if you are taken ill when away from home and have to consult a different doctor.

Go through your medicine cupboard when you stop using contraception. Make a list of the contents and ask your doctor whether there are any which are likely to be unsafe during pregnancy. Throw away, by flushing down the lavatory, or return to the chemist, any drugs which were not prescribed for you, which are out of date, or which your doctor advises you to get rid of.

Mood-changing drugs

Because so little is known about the effect of mood-changing drugs it is wise to limit their use or cut them out altogether. Cannabis or Valium may help you to relax on an occasion when you cannot easily "switch off". But explore other ways of releasing tension. The effects of disciplined relaxation (see page 172) are likely to help your unborn baby more than anything you can take in through your mouth. They are positive things you can do for yourself and your baby, ways of tuning in to your body rather than making an attempt to escape from it or deaden its sensations.

Cannabis Little is known of the effects of cannabis on the baby. Its strength varies widely, and its immediate effects on the user vary with expectation, the company in which it is taken, and previous experience of it. Claims have been made that it can be teratogenic, but this is still being investigated.

Cocaine Whether the drug is taken by inhaling a powder (snorting), smoking it (crack) or injecting it (free-basing), a woman using cocaine is very likely to have a baby who is small for dates or premature, and who is addicted to the drug. These babies tend to be irritable and jumpy, and it is difficult to calm them down so that they take a satisfying feed*.

Read the labels on all medicines, including over-the-counter ones, and keep a list of anything you take right from the beginning of pregnancy.

Mild tranquillizers are often prescribed during pregnancy and do not seem to be harmful. Diazepam (Valium) is sometimes used in treating pre eclampsia (see page 126) to bring blood pressure down. But it is best to stop taking even a mild tranquillizer as you approach the time when you expect to go into labour. Valium taken just before labour starts or during the course of labour can result in the baby having a low Apgar score (see page 328) at birth and breathing difficulties. The baby may also take a long time to start feeding properly, as well as become chilled more easily than usual*.

Powerful tranquillizers such as chlorpromazine (Largactil) and haloperidol (Serenace) should not be used in pregnancy. If you think you might have conceived, change to a milder tranquillizer and see if it is sufficient to control your anxiety and reduce tension. The strong tranquillizers can affect the development of the baby's nervous system. In particular, Largactil taken over a prolonged period of pregnancy can damage the baby's eyes*.

Sleeping pills

These include tranquillizers, antihistamines (see opposite) and hypnotics. Hypnotics are of two different kinds. Some are barbiturates, which are highly addictive even over a short period and are now almost never prescribed: phenobarbitone, Luminal, Veronal, Amytal and Sodium Amytal, Soneryl, Nembutal, Phenoderm, Rapidel, Medomin and Seconal. Others are non-barbiturate: Chloral, Welldorm, Doriden and Mandrax (which also contains an antihistamine). Welldorm is often prescribed in pregnancy. Non-barbiturates also seem to be addictive if taken over a long period. Not enough is known about the effect of hypnotics on the unborn baby, but they are cumulative. The drug concentrates in the mother's fatty tissues. Certainly large doses of barbiturates can cause respiratory depression at birth and feeding difficulties. The baby is doped along with the mother. Over-the-counter sleeping tablets have not been tested for safety in pregnancy. The best solution is to try to do without sleeping pills if you can; try to overcome insomnia by altering the pattern of your daily life so as to allow for more conscious relaxation and daily exercise in the open air.

Pain-killers

Aspirin The most widely used pain-killer is aspirin (salicylate) and its derivatives. If you have a headache or other pain, try to get rid of it by resting in a quiet, darkened room before resorting to aspirin. If rest is not an effective remedy, a few aspirin are unlikely to be harmful. But never dose yourself repeatedly: a recurring headache should be discussed with your doctor. If taken regularly (say every four to six hours) during the few days before you go into labour, aspirin can produce difficulties in blood clotting in the newborn baby and neonatal jaundice; sometimes it can damage the baby's central nervous system.

It is possible, however, that aspirin assists the circulation of blood through the placenta, and trials are currently taking place to see whether a low daily dose of aspirin can help in those pregnancies where there is inadequate flow of blood to the baby.

Codeine is addictive: the baby whose mother has been taking several pills daily throughout pregnancy may be born dependent, have severe withdrawal symptoms, and even die. Use it sparingly.

Paracetamol can cause liver and kidney damage in the person taking large doses. It should be used with caution in pregnancy, since the baby's liver and kidneys can suffer from relatively small doses.

Drugs to treat migraine can cause the uterus to contract during pregnancy, thus endangering the fetus. Discuss alternative ways of treating migraine with your doctor.

Anti-sickness drugs

Medicines against nausea and vomiting are of three different kinds: anti-cholinergenic drugs, antihistamines and phenothiazines*. They can all have side-effects.

The first category treats nausea by acting on your nervous system; it reduces secretions, including stomach acid, and relieves muscle spasm. No-one can be sure whether these drugs are completely safe for the fetus. Antihistamines, which include Cyclizine, Ancoloxine and Avomine, block the action of histamine (a substance to which some people are allergic) and may cause drowsiness. Cyclizine and Ancoloxine are best not used in pregnancy as high dosage may cause fetal abnormalities. The last category, the phenothiazines, are major tranquillizers, and are therefore inadvisable in pregnancy: the fetus may suffer the same adverse effects as from Largactil (see page 97).

It seems then that drugs to control pregnancy sickness should not be used unless specifically prescribed by a doctor who knows you are pregnant, and then only when you have weighed up together the advantages and disadvantages of taking the drug. Do not take any pills for travel sickness if you think you may be pregnant.

When I decided to get pregnant, I cleared the medicine cabinet and threw out all the half-used drugs and old bottles.

Antibiotics

Antibiotics may be prescribed in pregnancy; obviously their use is sometimes necessary and any disadvantages to the baby are outweighed. Never use antibiotics left in a bottle which were prescribed for a previous infection, even if you have exactly the same kind of infection. Tell your doctor that you may be pregnant, or remind him or her that you are pregnant, when you ask for a prescription.

Penicillin appears to be a safe antibiotic to take at any time during the period of pregnancy.

Sulphonamides (which are not really antibiotics but effective antibacterials) are used to treat urinary infections. If you need to have sulphonamide treatment you should stop a week or so before the baby is due, to let it out of your system before you go into labour. Otherwise the newborn baby's kidneys may not be able to cope with excreting the drug and the baby may develop jaundice which can damage its central nervous system.

Tetracycline, a wide spectrum antibiotic, is deposited in the unborn baby's teeth and may cause yellow mottling and staining. It can also stop the growth of the baby's bones during the period when it is taken, so should not be used during pregnancy.

Streptomycin, another wide spectrum antibiotic, should never be taken in pregnancy. One of the drugs used to treat tuberculosis, it can cause deafness in the baby.

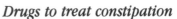

Drugs to treat constipation

Stool bulk producers, such as Normacol, do no harm provided that they are used in moderation.

Stimulant laxatives, which include senna-based aperients such as Senokot, cascara, Dorbanex and Dulcolax, seem to be safe for the fetus, but they may cause you to lose excessive amounts of fluid. Make sure that you drink plenty of liquids if you are taking any of these preparations.

Saline laxatives, including Milk of Magnesia, Epsom salts and Andrews salts, can also cause dehydration if you do not drink plenty of fluids, but otherwise they do not appear to be harmful to the fetus.
Various types of oil lubricate the bowels. But avoid liquid paraffin which reduces the absorption of vitamins A, D and K. A lack of vitamin K may lead to disorders of blood clotting in the baby. Extra fluids alone may cure your constipation, especially if you adjust your diet to include bran. (See page 121 for more about constipation.)

Drugs to reduce fluid retention

Diuretics increase the excretion of salt and water from the body, and in so doing make your kidneys work very hard. They are used in the prevention and treatment of pre-eclampsia (see page 126). Ammonium chloride, a drug which is sometimes used, can affect the baby's blood. Since there is no proof that reducing fluid retention avoids pre-eclampsia, it is best to avoid diuretics altogether*. Discuss the matter with your doctor.

Steroids

Steroids are used for the treatment of asthma or hay fever, for eczema and other skin disorders, and for rheumatism and arthritis. They affect the salt and water balance of the body, as well as sugar, carbohydrate, protein, fat and calcium metabolism. Steroids may cause fetal abnormalities with prolonged use through pregnancy (although this is by no means always the case). But some women cannot avoid using them—women, for example, with severe asthma. If you are on steroids and plan to become pregnant, let your doctor know. It may be possible for you to change to a milder drug before starting the pregnancy.
Since steroids are often used in the form of skin ointments, do not use any cream or preparation prescribed for skin irritation when you are pregnant unless there is real need for it.

Drugs to treat thyroid conditions

You may need to take drugs for an under- or over-active thyroid, but be aware that such drugs can have an effect on the baby's thyroid. One drug, Carbimazole, should be used only in low doses during

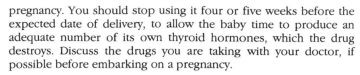

pregnancy. You should stop using it four or five weeks before the expected date of delivery, to allow the baby time to produce an adequate number of its own thyroid hormones, which the drug destroys. Discuss the drugs you are taking with your doctor, if possible before embarking on a pregnancy.

Anticoagulants

These drugs are prescribed for deep vein thrombosis or for a pulmonary embolism—both serious conditions caused by blood clots. Anticoagulants can cause haemorrhage in the baby and some, such as Warfarin, should not be taken in the last three months of pregnancy. If an anticoagulant needs to be given towards the end of the pregnancy, Heparin by injection is the safest. Any adverse effects on the fetus can be reversed in some cases by small doses of vitamin K given to the baby after delivery*.

Drugs to treat diabetes

Drugs which are taken by mouth to reduce blood sugar should not be used during pregnancy*. They can cause miscarriage or fetal abnormalities. Injections of insulin, however, are safe. If you are diabetic and want to get pregnant, let your doctor know and discuss in advance how the pregnancy will be managed (see page 127).

Anticonvulsants

If you normally take anticonvulsants or anti-epileptic drugs, discuss the possibility with your doctor of modifying your treatment before you conceive. These drugs may cause cleft palate in the baby.

General anaesthetics

There are times when a general anaesthetic may be necessary during pregnancy; but if possible such anaesthetics should be avoided because the baby becomes anaesthetized too. Make sure that if your doctor or dentist recommends general anaesthesia for anything he or she knows you are pregnant.

OTHER HARMFUL INFLUENCES
X-rays

In pregnancy it is wise to cut down the use of X-rays to the minimum, because there is no safe threshold for radiation, and hence no minimum level at which you can be assured that X-rays are safe for your unborn child. So avoid X-rays during pregnancy if possible, or in the second half of the menstrual cycle if there is a chance that you might be pregnant.

Radiation can partially destroy the genetic material which acts as the blueprint for the normal development of each cell of the body. A damaged cell is called a mutation. Radiation can have the greatest effects on an embryo which is in the initial stages of development, and a badly affected embryo is likely to be aborted spontaneously. But X-rays taken in pregnancy can also have an effect after birth*: there is evidence that X-rays are associated with a higher than usual chance of developing diseases of the respiratory system, blood disorders and infectious illnesses in childhood.

There are some cases in which diagnostic X-rays are important and the only means of discovering certain disorders. If a doctor or a dentist advises X-rays, take professional advice, but always check first to ensure that they really are essential.

High temperature

I had some sort of virus, with a high temperature, sore throat and everything. And it scared me stiff. In fact, it haunted me right through the pregnancy, wondering if the baby was normal. And she's gorgeous.

If you find you are running a temperature, go to bed, drink plenty of fluids and sponge yourself down with cold water, or have cool baths or showers to lower your body temperature. Do not just let your temperature rise. There is a slight chance that a very high temperature—say, over 39°C (102°F)—in the first four months of pregnancy can damage a baby*. The most crucial time is during the third and fourth weeks after conception. This is a horrifying thing to learn in late pregnancy if you know you had flu earlier on, but most babies are born whole and healthy even when the mother has run a high temperature. Nevertheless, it is sensible to avoid becoming run down, and so more susceptible to infection, if you think you may be pregnant. Keep up a high intake of protein and vitamin C in your diet so that you reduce the risk of contracting an infection.

As far as we know, there does not seem to be any risk of serious damage to the fetus from a high temperature at any time after the 16th week of pregnancy.

Hot saunas and hot baths lasting for a long time can also produce a temperature high enough to harm a developing baby, so it makes sense to keep the temperatures down in pregnancy. Your own comfort is probably the best guide.

Vaccination

Vaccinations are not recommended during the first four months of pregnancy, during which time there is a small risk of damage to the fetus. In the later months, most vaccinations (apart from rubella; see below) are considered harmless, although you should avoid small-pox vaccination throughout pregnancy, especially if you have never been vaccinated against smallpox before. If you are travelling to a country which still insists on smallpox vaccination, you can obtain exemption with a certificate of pregnancy from your doctor.

Rubella (German measles) is such a mild disease that many people have it in childhood without knowing it. Unfortunately, if you contract rubella when you are pregnant, the virus may cross the placenta and in the first 20 weeks of pregnancy it can have a serious effect on the baby. It is therefore sensible to have a blood test before you even become pregnant: if the test shows that you have never had rubella you can be vaccinated against it. Alternatively, if you are already pregnant when you discover that you are not immune, you can be vaccinated immediately after the birth of your baby.

The protection afforded by rubella vaccination lasts at least seven years, and probably much longer. After you have been vaccinated, be very careful about contraception for the next three months, since you should not conceive until you have had time to build up immunity to the virus in your system. Never have a rubella vaccination if you think you might be pregnant.

If you did not have a rubella vaccination before you started your pregnancy and have never had the disease, avoid all contact with children who might possibly have it. If you think you have been in contact with rubella, get in touch with your doctor immediately. He or she will offer you an injection of gamma globulin, but the chances of the baby being damaged by rubella in the first three months of pregnancy are high, especially in the first eight weeks; if you contract the disease you may want to consider termination.

The Rhesus negative woman

All blood is either Rhesus positive or Rhesus negative. Some 86 per cent of people are Rhesus positive, which means that their blood contains something known as the Rhesus factor. This factor is tested for early on in your pregnancy as part of your routine blood test. Its presence or absence is noted, but is only important in one comb-ination of circumstances: if you are Rhesus negative and the baby's father is Rhesus positive. There is no problem if the baby is Rhesus negative, but 40 per cent of all Rhesus positive babies of Rhesus negative mothers become anaemic, and if this is untreated the baby may die before or after birth.

If you are a Rhesus negative mother bearing a Rhesus positive baby, the danger arises when some of the baby's red blood cells leak into your circulation. This is particularly likely after an accidental haemor-rhage in late pregnancy and at delivery, or if you have miscarried or had an abortion. Your body then responds to the Rhesus factor present in the baby's cells as if to an invader, and begins to manufacture antibodies against it. If some of these antibodies leak back from your circulation into the baby's, they proceed to destroy large numbers of the baby's own red blood cells.

The flow of red blood cells each way across the placenta is not usually substantial enough during a first pregnancy to cause your body to develop such antibodies. But when your first baby is born, some of its blood may flow from the placenta into your circulation. This triggers the creation of antibodies to the Rhesus factor in your blood. From then on you produce antibodies to the Rhesus factor, and the next time you are pregnant with a Rhesus positive baby your antibodies may attack the baby's blood vigorously. It may get jaundice, its brain can be damaged, severe anaemia may develop and, in the worst cases, it may not even survive.

There are several things that can be done about this. The first and simplest is an injection, given to the Rhesus negative mother immediately after the birth of her first baby. It consists of a serum which stops her biological defence mechanisms acting against foreign Rhesus substances. A fresh injection of this serum is given after each subsequent delivery. The same routine is followed after a miscarriage or a termination of pregnancy too, since it is possible that the fetus was Rhesus positive and that some of its blood entered the mother's bloodstream.

It is no good giving this serum *after* a woman's body has already produced antibodies. If a high proportion of antibodies is detected in your blood during a second or subsequent pregnancy, and your baby is known to be at risk, amniocentesis may be performed (see page

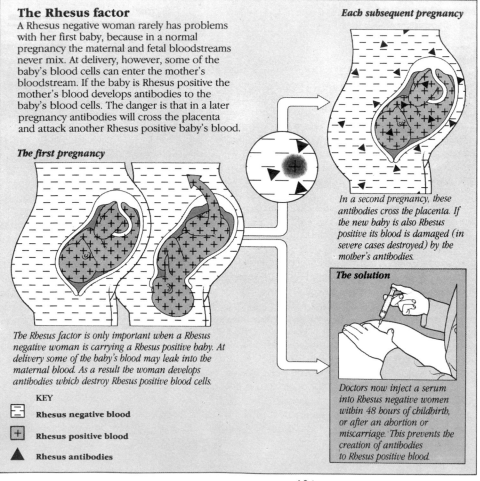

The Rhesus factor

A Rhesus negative woman rarely has problems with her first baby, because in a normal pregnancy the maternal and fetal bloodstreams never mix. At delivery, however, some of the baby's blood cells can enter the mother's bloodstream. If the baby is Rhesus positive the mother's blood develops antibodies to the baby's blood cells. The danger is that in a later pregnancy antibodies will cross the placenta and attack another Rhesus positive baby's blood.

The first pregnancy

The Rhesus factor is only important when a Rhesus negative woman is carrying a Rhesus positive baby. At delivery some of the baby's blood may leak into the maternal blood. As a result the woman develops antibodies which destroy Rhesus positive blood cells.

Each subsequent pregnancy

In a second pregnancy, these antibodies cross the placenta. If the new baby is also Rhesus positive its blood is damaged (in severe cases destroyed) by the mother's antibodies.

The solution

Doctors now inject a serum into Rhesus negative women within 48 hours of childbirth, or after an abortion or miscarriage. This prevents the creation of antibodies to Rhesus positive blood.

KEY

Rhesus negative blood

Rhesus positive blood

Rhesus antibodies

206) and the amniotic fluid analyzed for the presence of bilirubin (bile pigment). An anaemic fetus excretes into the fluid large amounts of bilirubin from destroyed red blood cells.

A woman who is Rhesus negative and whose partner is Rhesus positive is tested for Rhesus antibodies every two to three weeks. If there are antibodies, a blood test is done on the baby in the uterus, using ultrasound to guide the needle into the umbilical cord. If necessary, the baby can be given one or more transfusions before birth, again using ultrasound to guide the needle. If the baby is sufficiently mature to face life outside, labour may be induced early. If necessary, the baby can be treated immediately after delivery and given a complete blood transfusion to eradicate all the antibodies from its bloodstream.

Fortunately, as more and more Rhesus negative women are routinely immunized after delivery, this situation is increasingly rare.

An "incompetent" cervix

Occasionally a woman's cervix may be torn from a previous difficult labour or mid-pregnancy termination, or is damaged by a cone biopsy. She would not find this out until her next pregnancy, when she might lose her baby after the fourth month as a result of "cervical incompetence" (see page 340). The term "incompetent" is an unfortunate one and makes women feel as if they have failed to reach some standard of reproductive ability.

An obstetrician may recommend cervical cerclage—sewing the cervix closed for the duration of any subsequent pregnancy. This is a relatively simple procedure: once the pregnancy is established, a suture is inserted under anaesthesia and is threaded through and around the cervix like the drawstring of a sponge-bag. The suture is removed at about the 36th week of pregnancy or later. Some obstetricians like to induce labour at this point because they say it is simpler, since contractions often start shortly after the removal of the suture anyway. You are not compelled to have labour induced, however, and should decide whether this is what you want in such circumstances.

There is wide variation in the degree to which obstetricians in different countries use cervical cerclage. It is fashionable in France, for example, whereas in Britain it is used more by private obstetricians than those working in the National Health Service. A randomized trial of this procedure, conducted on women at high risk of giving birth prematurely, produced no evidence of its benefit*.

Your physical wellbeing

To get the most out of the experience of being pregnant, you should ensure that your body is in good condition. Remember that healthy activity can be pleasurable in itself as well as being an excellent preparation for labour. Sometimes books on pregnancy and even antenatal teachers give the impression that childbirth is an athletic event for which you have to train like a marathon runner, a kind of examination for which you must study assiduously, or even an ordeal with which you are unlikely to cope but which will be quickly forgotten afterwards. No wonder expectant mothers become anxious! No mention is made of the excitement, joy and sheer pleasure that many women experience in childbirth.

Most women look forward to childbirth with excited anticipation. They know that there is a slight chance of something going wrong but that the better they have prepared themselves by doing body-toning movements and exercises, the more likely they are to be able to handle any emergencies.

=66=
I've never been fitter. The doctor says I'm not a very interesting case. I don't really know I'm pregnant!
=99=

GETTING TO KNOW YOUR BODY

Before beginning exercises, it is useful to gain an awareness early in pregnancy of how your body works and what is taking place in your reproductive organs. One way of doing this is to have a closer look at your genitals. For a clear view, you can kneel or squat over a mirror. A torch might help you to see the area better.

The perineum

The perineum is the tissue around your vagina and between your vagina and anus. Just before delivery it begins to bulge and its tissues fan out and open up as the ball of the baby's head presses through it.

The vagina

Your vagina is the soft, cushioned canal which holds the penis during sexual intercourse; it is also the passage through which the baby is delivered. The outer part of the vagina is the vulva, consisting of layers of outer and inner lips (labia) constructed like the overlapping petals of a rose. During pregnancy they change in colour from red to violet, the effect of the pregnancy hormones which have also darkened your nipples, maybe your face, and other parts of your skin.

Insert one or two fingers into your vagina and feel around the stretchy folds inside. Though the sides of the vagina are normally touching each other and there is no hollow space, notice how readily they spread apart. They open like an accordion when the baby is pressing down through them to be born, and the action of hormones that are released into your bloodstream will make them become even softer and more flexible during the last few weeks of pregnancy.

The clitoris

Your clitoris is like a bud rising from the inner lips at the upper (front) end of your vagina. Its base and the inner lips around it are very sensitive, and pressure on or stroking of these parts produces sexual excitement. As you touch its root, you may notice that it swells up. You will feel that there is a hood or fold of skin surrounding the clitoris and that this connects up with the inner lips. So anything in your vagina which stretches the inner lips apart will also pull on this hood and the clitoris will be stimulated in this way, too.

A woman's genitals vary as much as a man's. Just as penises are different sizes, for example, the clitoris may be the size and shape of a small pea or more like the curved centre of an orchid. Women's labia vary too. Some are firm, some soft, some large and fleshy, others smaller. A woman may worry that masturbation might have changed the shape of her labia or clitoris, but these organs are so flexible that pulling, pressing or rubbing them does not produce permanent structural changes. Doctors and midwives cannot tell anything about your sexual habits by examining your vulva, though many women harbour a secret fear that they can.

At delivery the baby presses against this whole area that you are examining, easing forward the tissues so that they open up like elastic, and then slides out with a rush of liquid. After the baby is born these flexible tissues spring back again; at first they will not be as firm as they were before, but they will gradually gain in tone.

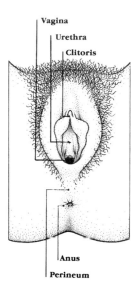

Vagina

Urethra

Clitoris

Anus

Perineum

The cervix

Now introduce your longest finger deep inside your vagina and you meet the rounded, firm cervix (the neck of the womb), the part of the uterus that will open (dilate) when you are in labour. Early in pregnancy it will feel like the tip of your nose. You may notice a little dip in the middle, like the dimple in the centre of a buttoned cushion. This is where the mucous plug is situated, and this plug, like the cork in a bottle, seals off the uterus from the outside. At the end of pregnancy the cervix will have softened and, when you touch it with your finger, it will feel more like your mouth when it is soft and relaxed than like your nose. This is one of the signs that you are ready to go into labour. The cervix is "ripe".

The pelvic floor

The muscles which support everything inside the pelvic cavity (including the uterus, the bladder and the rectum) form the pelvic floor. They have special significance for your health, whatever age you are and whether or not you are pregnant. The upright position that humans have adopted in preference to the all-fours stance puts an extra stress on these muscle layers in pregnancy.

Keeping fit during pregnancy

While you are pregnant it is easy to allow muscles that were previously firm and elastic to sag. You are putting on weight, your figure is changing and you may assume that sagging muscles are an inevitable accompaniment to these changes. However, gentle toning exercises, aimed at firming up your abdominal muscles and avoiding back strain, can do you and your baby nothing but good.

Pelvic rocking

Lie on a flat surface, your head and shoulders supported by pillows and your knees bent with the feet flat. Experiment with pressing the small of your back against the floor or bed and then releasing it so that you produce a gentle, rhythmic, rocking movement. Then roll your hips round in a slow, circular, hula-hoop movement.

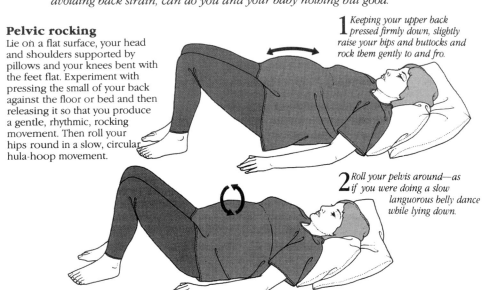

1 *Keeping your upper back pressed firmly down, slightly raise your hips and buttocks and rock them gently to and fro.*

2 *Roll your pelvis around—as if you were doing a slow languorous belly dance while lying down.*

Wrong

Although double-leg raising and sit-ups are exercises often recommended for pregnant women, they do not in fact strengthen the abdominal muscles. These muscles do not work to lift the legs but to stabilize the lower back. If they are not strong to start with, they cannot cope with the effort involved when the legs or trunk are raised, and the result is back strain or torn abdominal muscles.

Double-leg raising is rarely effective in toning abdominal muscles and should never be done in pregnancy or in the 4 weeks following birth.

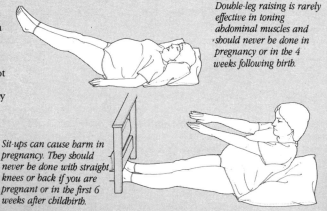

Sit-ups can cause harm in pregnancy. They should never be done with straight knees or back if you are pregnant or in the first 6 weeks after childbirth.

Leg sliding

Leg sliding is a gentle exercise that allows you to tone up your tummy muscles efficiently without straining them. Do it five or six times at first and gradually build up until you can do it comfortably 10 or 15 times. If at any point you feel your back aching, stop. Leg sliding is best done lying on your back on a firm surface with a pillow under your head and shoulders.

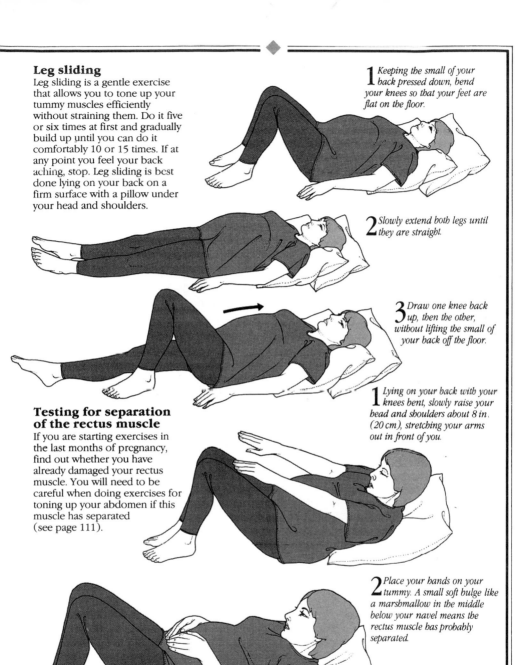

1 *Keeping the small of your back pressed down, bend your knees so that your feet are flat on the floor.*

2 *Slowly extend both legs until they are straight.*

3 *Draw one knee back up, then the other, without lifting the small of your back off the floor.*

Testing for separation of the rectus muscle

If you are starting exercises in the last months of pregnancy, find out whether you have already damaged your rectus muscle. You will need to be careful when doing exercises for toning up your abdomen if this muscle has separated (see page 111).

1 *Lying on your back with your knees bent, slowly raise your head and shoulders about 8 in. (20 cm), stretching your arms out in front of you.*

2 *Place your hands on your tummy. A small soft bulge like a marshmallow in the middle below your navel means the rectus muscle has probably separated.*

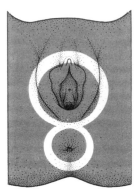

The pelvic-floor muscles form a figure-8 around the front and back passages. Learning to contract and release these muscles efficiently during pregnancy will help you both during labour and after your baby is born.

Though these muscles form a co-ordinated working structure, they are not really a "floor" at all. They are slanted at different angles and levels and can be held with varying degrees of firmness. The easiest way to find these muscles, of which some women are not aware, is to interrupt a stream of urine, since you bring all of the pelvic-floor muscles into play when you do this. Or you can think of them as forming a figure of eight round the front and back passages. In the middle of the eight is a horizontal bar, the transverse perineal muscle. When the muscles of the pelvic floor are contracted, the circular shapes of the eight change to almond shapes and the transverse perineal muscle is pulled up and over towards the pubic bone (the firm ridge of bone just above the clitoris) like the opening lid of a roll-top desk. You can feel this happening from both inside and outside if you put one finger inside the vagina and a thumb over the pubis.

Your pelvic-floor muscles contract spontaneously during love-making, increasing your sensations of pleasure and those of your partner. Awareness and control of these muscles are important in labour too, when you will need to be able to release them as you press the baby down the birth canal.

Some people can hold their pelvic muscles contracted much longer than others, and you may notice, when you first try to contract these muscles, that they tire and tremble. To exercise your pelvic-floor muscles gradually, you can pretend that this area is a lift which you are taking up to the first floor. You hold it there, then move on to the second floor, and so on until the muscles are fully contracted. Then release them gradually to the ground floor. Finally end with a toning movement by drawing the muscles up to the first floor again. If you do this between 20 and 30 times a day you will be able to hold them firm for longer periods, building up to a count of eight or nine without holding your breath or tightening up your shoulders. But always alternate tightening movements with resting spaces to allow the muscles to be re-oxygenated in the intervals between activity.

TONING YOUR ABDOMINAL MUSCLES

The human backbone is curved, not straight as in many four-legged animals. In some people it is almost S-shaped. Because of the forward load produced by pregnancy, strain is put on the spine, especially in the small of the back, and the upper spine may be pushed into the wrong position to compensate.

The abdominal muscles

Four-legged mammals take the extra weight of pregnancy on their abdominal muscles slung evenly between the front and back limbs. Despite their upright stance, human beings also need well-toned abdominal muscles for comfortable pregnancy because, if these are flabby, the back muscles are forced to take on too much work to support the spine. When this happens, the vertebrae of the lower spine are forced into an unnatural position and the discs between them are subjected to great pressure. They may slide and become displaced. This leads to exhausting backache. Girdles cannot help much; they just take over some of the work that healthy muscles should be doing. The best girdle is composed of your own tummy and buttock muscles, and both sets need to be toned to provide mutual support.

To understand what will benefit your abdominal muscles and what might be harmful to them, it is useful to know how this girdle of muscles is constructed and how it works.

The muscle running from top to bottom down the front is called the rectus muscle and it bears much of the load of late pregnancy. It is separated into two halves by a line down the centre which is like a seam. When you are about halfway through your pregnancy, this may show as a dark line in your skin from your navel down to your pubic-hair line, although it does not occur in all women. You can see the same line as an indentation about the width of a pencil in photographs of Mr Universe flexing his muscles and caving in his abdomen. The two sides of the rectus muscle can be pulled apart if the muscle is subjected to too great a stress and then the muscle "unzips". Constipation and straining on the lavatory can sometimes cause this muscle to separate.

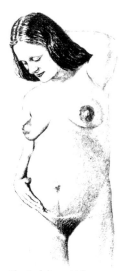

The dark line which may appear on your skin from your navel down to your pubis is a sign that the rectus muscle is being stretched.

You can test yourself to find out if there is any separation of the rectus muscle. Lying on your back with a pillow under your head, knees bent, rest your hands on your tummy and *very slowly* lift your head and shoulders with your chin tucked in. If you can feel a soft bulging area the width of a matchbox or more the muscle has separated. If this is the case, you can rehabilitate the muscle after the baby is born (see page 353). Meanwhile concentrate on leg sliding (see page 109).

Some exercises that are intended to strengthen the abdominal muscles can also cause the rectus muscle to separate. You should never try double-leg raising exercises while you are pregnant, or even single-leg raising unless the muscles are already in very good condition. Nor should you do exercises that entail putting your feet under heavy furniture and then raising the upper body or any kind of sit-ups without using your hands. Not only can these exercises damage the abdominal muscles, they can also strain the back.

Exploring pelvic movement

The bones that form the pelvis are like a cradle for the baby growing inside you, a cradle that can rock in all directions. Feel your pelvic bone with your fingers. Start with your hip bones. Press in over their upper ridges and then walk your fingers round and down into the small of your back where your hip girdle joins your spine. The point at which it does so is the sacrum, the bone which forms the back of the pelvis and the outlet through which the baby descends.

Posture and balance

Good posture is essential to your physical wellbeing during pregnancy. This means not only learning to stand and walk in the best way, so that your baby is cradled in the pelvis in a position that is comfortable for both of you, but also performing other everyday movements, such as getting out of bed, in a way calculated to avoid unnecessary strain. To achieve good posture you need to improve the tone of your muscles and to learn how to use only those muscles necessary for whatever you are doing. If you are looking good and walking with a spring in your step, you will probably also feel much better.

Maintaining good posture

Make a point of tucking in your buttock muscles, and feel your tummy muscles working to straighten out your spine. Keep your shoulders dropped. Now imagine a string is pulling your head straight up, and notice the back of your neck lengthening.

Wrong
If the weight of your uterus makes you stand back on your heels, with your bottom stuck out and your shoulders back, your spine hollows and you get low backache.

Tailor sitting

Tailor sitting is an ideal way of rounding out the lower back. As long as you take care not to slouch over, it can be one of the most comfortable positions for sitting during pregnancy.

Bridging

In late pregnancy your tummy muscles can feel so stretched that it might be difficult to exercise them consciously. If this is the case, it helps to tighten your buttock muscles, since this means that you pull in your tummy muscles too. Bridging improves the tone of your buttock muscles and helps the circulation in your legs.

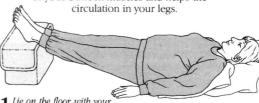

1 *Lie on the floor with your heels raised on a low table or stool.*

2 *Tighten your buttock and abdominal muscles and lift your bottom up off the floor, keeping your back straight.*

3 *Hold this position for several seconds, then slowly lower your hips.*

The rocking-chair exercise

This exercise encourages good posture by allowing you to press out the small of your back while keeping the rest of your body aligned. You become like a rocking chair that rocks to and fro, and you need a partner to set you in motion and provide the firm surface against which you press your lower back. Avoid hollowing your back at any time.

1 *Your partner stands in front of you with his hands on your hips.*

2 *You rock your pelvis gently backwards and forwards between his hands several times.*

3 *Now he stands at your side and puts one hand on the small of your back and the other over your lower tummy.*

4 *You continue rocking, pushing against his hand with the small of your back then moving away from it.*

Getting up from lying down

If you sit up suddenly after you have been lying on your back, you put great pressure on your tummy muscles, especially in advanced pregnancy. The method below is a way of avoiding strain on these muscles, and since it involves changing from a horizontal to an upright position in gentle stages, it is also good for the circulation.

1 *Roll over on to one side, swinging your shoulders round and drawing up your knees.*

2 *Push yourself up with your upper arm while swivelling your legs from the hips over to the edge of the bed.*

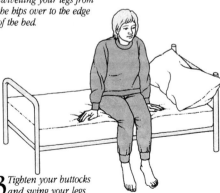

3 *Tighten your buttocks and swing your legs over the side of the bed in a smooth, co-ordinated movement.*

Now walk the fingers round again to the big bones at the side, then down into the groin and around the front till they meet at your pubic bone. This forms the front of the pelvis and the baby dips down under this bridge of bone just before delivery. Notice that your pubis is much lower than your sacrum. The human pelvis is tilted. Once you have found exactly where these bones are and have a clear picture of them, get your partner to feel them too. Guide his hands so that he is able to track your pelvis accurately.

Pelvic rocking

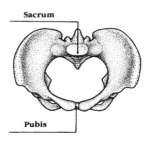

Sacrum

Pubis

Lie on any flat surface (it can be a firm bed), with your head and shoulders supported by two pillows and your knees bent with the feet flat. Explore the capacity for movement in your pelvis. Experiment with gentle, rhythmic rocking. Then try rolling the cradle round as if you were doing a very slow hula-hoop movement. This is a kind of belly dancing while lying down, in which you tighten your tummy muscles while pressing your buttocks together. As you do so, notice how the different sets of muscles are alternately tightened and released and the way in which tummy and buttock muscles work together in a co-ordinated fashion.

Now combine this movement with controlled breathing. Each time you pull your tummy muscles *in* and press your buttocks together, give a strong breath *out* through your mouth. Then, as you release the muscles and rock your pelvis gently forward (it is a very slight movement), allow your lungs to fill up with air, breathing in through your nose. Do it at your own pace, emphasizing the breath out and letting the breath in take care of itself. This movement done in early pregnancy is a good way of toning abdominal muscles for the work they must do later.

Now rest your fingers on the big bones at the front of the pelvis on either side. Continue the movement with the breathing and notice the swing up and down of these bones. This is the distance the bony cradle rocks as you walk and move around in pregnancy. The baby is accustomed to these movements during its intra-uterine existence, and it is not surprising that rocking a newborn baby quietens and soothes it. Research shows that a baby being rocked is most likely to be comforted by a swing of 3 in (7·5 cm) to either side*. This corresponds exactly with the arc of the pelvic rock.

A position with firm support for your spine is best for practising this pelvic rocking. Other positions allow you to hollow your back in an exaggerated way, which can be harmful, especially in advanced pregnancy, because it puts stress on the sacro-iliac joint, which is situated at the top of your buttocks. Such strain is particularly bad for you when you are pregnant because your ligaments are already softened by hormones released into the blood during pregnancy to make the vagina and cervix more flexible in preparation for the birth. Once these ligaments have softened, any form of pelvic rocking which involves back *hollowing* can cause more backache.

EXERCISES IN PREGNANCY

Exercises to help you cope with the stresses of pregnancy should be matched by others designed to help your adjustment after childbirth, since this is the time when the speediest and most dramatic physical changes are happening to you. Post-natal exercises are simply a modification of the ones you learn in pregnancy, so there is no need for you to learn completely new ones after the birth. In this book post-natal exercises are described on pages 352–353.

Posture and balance

Good posture maintained every day is more important than pregnancy gymnastics. As the weight load changes you should give conscious thought to balance and body mechanics, something that is usually taken for granted. It is not just a matter of "standing straight, head up" like the girl who won the school deportment medal, but of understanding how to economize on muscle work and use only those muscles that are needed for any task. This always results in more graceful and comfortable movement without straining and effort.

Standing To achieve good posture, you should stand with your back to a wall, heels far enough away from it for your seat and shoulders just to touch it. Press the small of your back towards the wall and you will feel your seat tucking under and your tummy muscles working to straighten out your spine. Make sure that you do not tighten your shoulders. Keep them dropped. Now imagine that a string is pulling your head up from the centre at the top and notice the back of your neck lengthening. Relax your jaw. (Your jaw muscles cannot force your head up!) Walk a few paces away from the wall. You will find that you are in a stiff, exaggerated stance like a soldier on duty. Let the muscles settle into a more comfortable state. The rocking-chair exercise (see page 113) encourages good posture, and can be done with the help of your partner.

Walking Whenever possible, walk rather than stand. The healthiest, most rhythmic and natural all-round exercise is walking. If you have to stand around, exercise your feet while you do so, even if only by screwing up and extending your toes, going up onto the ball of the foot and down again and shifting weight from one foot to the other. Muscles in the feet and legs pump blood back to the heart, so movement is important to maintain good circulation in the legs.

You can also increase the tone of your buttock muscles and help the circulation in your legs by bridging (see page 112)*.

Sitting Sit back on your chair and see that your spine is well supported. If necessary, put a small cushion in the small of the back. In the last few weeks of your pregnancy you may need more support than this; try sitting well back against a large bean bag or a firm floor

Aches and pains

In late pregnancy you are carrying more weight which, instead of being evenly distributed, is centred in one area and so affects your balance. This extra weight alone can cause aches and pains by straining muscles and causing you to adopt an unnatural stance, leading to further strain. The way the baby is lying can also cause discomfort and occasionally sharp shooting pain when the baby is pressing against a nerve.

Foot exercises

Foot exercises discourage varicose veins in the legs by stimulating the blood flow back to the heart. When you are sitting down or having a rest, practise drawing the alphabet with your feet, one foot at a time, keeping your legs still. You will find that you can easily read or do some work at the same time.

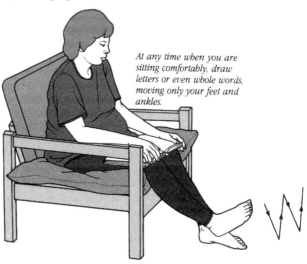

At any time when you are sitting comfortably, draw letters or even whole words, moving only your feet and ankles.

The angry cat

However many exercises you do with your back supported, it feels good to get the weight of the baby off your spine occasionally. You can do this by going on to all fours and rocking your pelvis, an exercise sometimes known as "the angry cat". This is a kind of pelvic rocking reversed.

1 *Get on to all fours, keeping the small of your back flat, not hollowed.*

2 *Without moving your elbows or knees, tighten your tummy muscles and hump up your lower back. Relax back to the flat position after a few seconds.*

Wrong

Never under any circumstances allow the lower back to cave in.

The wheelbarrow

Towards the end of pregnancy many women have pain in the groin. This usually occurs as a result of pressure from the baby on the joints of the pelvis. To relieve the discomfort, try this exercise, your partner kneeling very close to you.

1 Lie on your back with your knees bent. Your partner holds your hips at either side.

2 Your partner slowly lifts your hips. He holds them up for a moment, then gently lowers them.

Wall stretching

A good way to lift your ribs off your expanding uterus is simply to stretch high with first one arm then the other, until you are comfortable. A similar exercise may be done by sitting with your back pressed against a wall to help alignment.

2 Swing your arms out to shoulder height and, with your hands pressed against the wall, walk your fingers up it.

1 Sit with your back pressed against a wall and your legs stretched out in front of you.

3 Turn your palms outwards when your hands have reached as high as they can go.

The shoulder roll

Upper backache, which is caused by poor posture or heavy breasts, can be relieved by doing the shoulder-roll exercise.

Rest your fingertips on your shoulders and rotate your elbows back.

cushion. If you have to write or type at a desk or table for any length of time, remember to rest your head down on it occasionally and gently stretch the back of your neck.

Bending and lifting Use your legs, not your back, when you reach down for anything. This means that, whenever possible, you should bend your knees and get right down to the load. Kneel or squat when you are working low down, cleaning the bath or making a divan bed, for example. Avoid misusing your spine as if it were a crane. For some jobs, such as wiping or polishing a floor, it is most comfortable to get onto all fours. This takes the weight of the baby off your spine and is surprisingly comfortable, especially if you do have backache.

Lying down and getting up The front-lateral or "three-quarters-over" position is often the most comfortable when you are lying in bed. It may help to put a pillow under your upper knee. Allow good space between your legs. Avoid hollowing your back when you are lying down, too. This is likely to happen if you have a soft mattress and like to lie on your front. If necessary, put a small pillow under your hips so that your back does not cave in.

Squat or kneel down to pick up a toddler, rather than using your back like a crane.

Whenever you get up from lying on your back, roll over onto one side first, swinging your shoulders round, and push with your upper arm, drawing up your knees at the same time till you are in a kneeling position; tighten your buttocks and then rise from that position (see page 113). This movement will avoid unnecessary strain on your abdominal muscles. It may sound complicated but it can come to be a beautifully smooth, co-ordinated movement, making you feel like Cleopatra rising from her barge.

Aches and pains

Although bad posture is often responsible for aches and pains during pregnancy, you may have other aches and pains that are just the result of being pregnant. If this is the case all you can do to relieve them is concentrate on relaxation and experiment with different positions in which you feel more comfortable.

The front lateral or three-quarters-over position is often comfortable for resting.

Low backache In late pregnancy, if the baby is facing towards your front and engages as a posterior (see page 257) with the back of its head pressing against your sacrum, you may develop backache. Rest in positions in which the weight of the baby is tilted off the spine, and take every opportunity to get onto all fours. Scrubbing a kitchen floor can provide extraordinary relief from backache. The angry cat (see page 116) is an exercise that combines this position with pelvic rocking to relieve your spine of the baby's weight.

Upper backache This occurs when you try to compensate for the weight of your pregnancy dragging you forward, by flinging your shoulders back and tightening the muscles in the upper back. To relieve it, roll your shoulders backwards whenever you have the opportunity and do the shoulder-roll exercise (see page 117).

Tingling and numbness You may sometimes feel a tingling and numbness in your hand. This is known as the carpal tunnel syndrome. It results from pressure on the nerves and tendons caused by swelling of the hand and wrist. You will be most aware of it in the morning after your wrists have accumulated fluid during the night. To relieve the sensations of discomfort, try the shoulder-roll exercise or hold your hand above your head for a few minutes and flex and gradually extend the fingers upwards.

Pain under the ribs You may experience pain below the ribs at either side when the top of the uterus (the fundus) is high after 30 weeks (see page 69). This pain tends to come on whichever side the baby is lying.

You will discover that you are only comfortable when sitting straight on a rather high chair and will not want to slump down onto your uterus. In spite of folklore about the dangers of an expectant mother lifting her arms above her head, you will find that it helps to stretch upwards so that your whole rib cage is lifted off the uterus. You can also do stretching exercises while sitting with your back against a wall for support (see page 117).

Lifting your arms above your head may help if you have a tingling sensation in your hands.

Pain in the groin In late pregnancy it is common to have pain around the pubic area, where the pelvic joints have softened in readiness for labour. Avoid standing for long periods, and even when sitting change position often. Symptoms can be relieved by doing the wheelbarrow exercise (see page 117). Some women get a stitch in the side because the round ligament at either side of the uterus is stretched. If you are lying down, you may find it easier to get up if you roll over slowly and sit up gently while supporting your sides with your hands (see page 113).

Cramp in the leg A few pregnant women get cramp because they are trying to go on a salt-free diet. Eating something salty before you go to bed may make the cramp disappear. However, most cramps are probably caused by a calcium deficiency and, if you are plagued by recurring cramps, you will be prescribed calcium tablets. Avoid curling your toes under. Use a duvet or make up the bed loosely so that your toes are not pressed down by the bedlinen overnight.

Lifting your feet above the level of your heart will also help circulation and hence relieve cramp. However, in advanced pregnancy this may give you indigestion, so you are left with a choice between two discomforts. While you are lying with your feet up, roll them round in circles from the ankles to help stretch the calf muscles, or practise drawing the letters of the alphabet, one foot at a time, keeping your legs still. If you do get cramp, ask your partner to grip

your heel and push your foot up while pressing down on your knee with the other hand. It is a useful precaution to do this regularly about ten times before you settle down for the night.

COMMON PROBLEMS DURING PREGNANCY

Although your baby can grow inside you without your having to think consciously or do anything about it, this growth affects your whole body and every system in it. You may worry about these disconcerting changes taking place in your system if you do not understand what they are and why they have occurred.

Varicose veins

The valves which help direct the blood through the veins back to the heart may soften in pregnancy and become unable to propel the increased amount of blood through the legs.

Avoid all positions which allow pooling of blood in the legs: sitting with your legs crossed or with your thighs pressing against the edge of your chair, for example. Foot exercises will help keep the blood moving. If you are advised to wear elastic stockings, choose semi- or full-support tights and put them on *before* you get up in the morning. Bend a knee, put one leg of the tights on and wriggle it up; then do the same with the other.

Vaginal varicose veins Sometimes a woman develops varicose veins in her vagina. The discomfort may be relieved by wrapping some ice chips in a clean handkerchief, knotting it and packing it against the sore and tender areas. Obviously you cannot walk around like this, but it is a good excuse to lie down for a while, so offering a position in which the whole weight of your uterus is not pressing down on the swollen veins. Sometimes vitamin B6 (pyridoxine) can help (see page 90), and you should take three tablets a day.

Haemorrhoids (also known as piles) are varicose veins of the rectum and can be caused by constipation. If you have piles avoid any straining on the lavatory. This condition should be treated as quickly as possible because the haemorrhoids can become prolapsed (protrude through the anus) causing extreme pain. Your doctor may give you a prescription for a pain-relieving cream. Alternatively a lint pad soaked in witchhazel can also bring relief.

Constipation

You are more likely to be constipated during pregnancy because some of the extra hormones produced while you are pregnant cause the intestine to relax and become less efficient. First of all ensure that you are eating the right kinds of food (see page 86). Eat plenty of fruit, vegetables, fibre and whole grains and drink as much water as

=**"**=
I feel enormous and old and exhausted. I used to be a ballet dancer—and this is the end! I never imagined I could be so gross.
=**"**=

OPPOSITE
Swimming when you are pregnant is a good way of maintaining a state of physical wellbeing.

you can. When you are on the lavatory, allow your pelvic floor to be fully released and bulging down. Take your time over emptying the bowels, and take a brisk walk every day if possible.

Bladder control and infections

In the first three months or so of your pregnancy the developing baby and enlarging uterus are pressing against your bladder, while the extra progesterone flowing through your bloodstream softens the tissues. So it is quite normal for a pregnant woman to have to pass water very often. This may be even more noticeable at the very end of pregnancy when the baby has gone down into your pelvis.

Cystitis Pressure and engorgement of blood vessels in the pelvic area mean that a pregnant woman is more exposed to the risk of urinary infection. If you notice a stinging, burning feeling when you pass urine, this usually indicates that you have developed cystitis. If left untreated, cystitis rapidly becomes very uncomfortable.

If you suspect that you have cystitis, go to your doctor, who will probably prescribe a course of antibiotics to be taken for 10 to 14 days. It is sensible to seek help when you first notice the symptoms as delay can mean that the infection takes hold more firmly. As a general treatment, drink plenty of liquid. Drink a glass of water every time you have used the lavatory. Drinking lemon and barley can help, or try an alkaline-based drink such as a mixture of sodium bicarbonate and sodium citrate. One nature-cure remedy is marshmallow tea.

Wear cotton pants and avoid any clothing that is tight on the crutch. If you wear tights, get some that have a cotton panel or air holes between the legs. Spend time on the lavatory to empty your bladder as completely as possible. When the baby is pressing against your bladder in late pregnancy, you will be able to shift position so that the baby moves a little, allowing you to void some more.

Pyelitis If you have a temperature and low back pain, and if it hurts when you apply pressure over your kidneys, on one or both sides, you may have pyelitis (a kidney infection). Sometimes the infection causes nausea and vomiting too. Seek treatment immediately, since this is not only painful for you, but can affect the functioning of the placenta. Antibiotics are effective, but all the measures suggested for coping with cystitis are also helpful and you will probably appreciate a hot water bottle against the painful area. Women with pyelitis are often admitted to the antenatal ward to allow a proper diagnosis. The right drugs usually clear up the problem within two weeks.

Yeast growths

It is normal to have an increased vaginal discharge in pregnancy, but if your vulva becomes itchy and your vagina is red, sore and burning, you probably have thrush ("candida" or "monilia"). Nystatin or Canesten pessaries are usually prescribed. Cut out sugar and white flour and try a diet based on whole grains, fruit, vegetables and protein. Painting gentian violet (which you can get from the chemist without a prescription) over the affected area works well but is messy. If you try this method, wear a sanitary pad to stop staining.

Breast tenderness

The normal breast tenderness of the early weeks of pregnancy can be acutely painful for some women, and they walk about with stiff arms to protect themselves in case anyone brushes against them. A good supporting bra (see page 130) is important even if you do not normally wear one, since if the breasts are increasing in size, as they usually are at this stage, their own weight can be uncomfortable. If your breasts become extra-sensitive like this, you will not enjoy your partner's most gentle touch until about the middle of pregnancy.

Inverted nipples

Some women have one or both nipples shaped like dimples. These are called "inverted" nipples. If you have a nipple like this but can press it out, or if it projects when you are sexually excited, the baby will be able to get hold of the nipple well and draw it out further. Otherwise you may find it more difficult to fix the baby on to the breast with a good mouthful. However, if you do manage to start the

WEARING A NIPPLE SHELL
Using a dome-shaped plastic nipple shell under your bra in the last 2 months of pregnancy may help an inverted nipple into an easier shape for the baby. The pressure of the shell on the breast coaxes the nipple through the hole in the middle.

Usual nipple shape

Shape of inverted nipple

Plastic nipple shell

baby off, he or she will suck the nipple into a good projecting shape. It is a fallacy to think that you have to have prominent nipples in order to breast feed successfully.

Vomiting

For some women the nausea and vomiting that is very common in the first three months of pregnancy (see page 33) goes on much longer, and this prolonged sickness is known by the medical term of hyperemesis. A woman with hyperemesis is really ill because she cannot take any food by mouth. Surprisingly, the cure may simply be admission to hospital and often no further treatment is necessary. This is why some psychiatrists and obstetricians have suggested that hyperemesis is a symptom of disturbed relationships and that, if the woman has a chance to get away from the relentless day-to-day contact with a partner, mother, mother-in-law, or anyone who is part of the stress to which she is reacting, the vomiting will ease.

If you find that you are vomiting at all hours of the day, cannot be sure of keeping any meal down and are feeling really wretched, it is worth trying to get away, preferably among people you know only slightly or not at all, and who will not fuss over you. If this gives you the opportunity to do something you have never done before (not hang-gliding!) or see something you have never had the chance of seeing before, so much the better. There is a phrase that is sometimes used about a person who is "run down": "she needs taking out of herself". A woman who is vomiting almost without interruption may need to be taken "out" of herself and her usual relationships until she can cope emotionally, and then, when her pregnancy has settled down, she can come back "into" herself with new strength.

Nasal congestion

Sinusitis The mucous membrane inside the nostrils and sinuses often swells up during pregnancy because of the action of hormones liberated in the bloodstream which are also, fortunately, softening up your vagina and cervix. Some women seem to have a permanent cold in late pregnancy for this reason. It does not interfere with your breathing during labour, so there is no need to worry about this, though you may be more comfortable breathing through your mouth than through your nose. This means that you will need to take frequent sips of water or have a small plant spray filled with ice water to spray into your mouth between contractions and lip-salve to smooth on your lips. The symptoms will go after delivery.

In three pregnancies I had slight bleeding in the first 10 weeks each time. After that it was plain sailing. The births went fine and the babies were perfect.

Nosebleeds are very common in pregnancy. These, too, are associated with higher hormone levels and congestion. A tiny blob of vaseline in the nostril will usually stop a nosebleed, and you should avoid blowing your nose hard.

Vaginal bleeding in early pregnancy

Bleeding from the vagina at any stage of pregnancy is always worrying. In early pregnancy it may be that the level of your pregnancy hormones is not sufficiently high to avoid breakthrough spotting. There is no way you can stop this without possibly affecting the developing baby, but it is sensible to take it as a message from the body that you need rest. Go to bed and stay there till the bleeding stops. Cut out unnecessary exertion and, if the bleeding started at a time when your period would normally have been due, take life especially gently then and see if you can manage a few days in bed. Practise deep relaxation every day. There is further information about how to deal with a threatened miscarriage on page 339.

Vaginal bleeding in late pregnancy

If you notice bleeding in late pregnancy it may be a sign that labour is about to start. It is usually blood from around the cervix and, except in those cases where there is a polyp in the cervix that has started to bleed, shows that thinning out and some dilatation is taking place. If your baby is due within a month and the bleeding looks like the beginning of a period, a blood-stained mucous discharge (a "show", see page 228), accept it as a normal sign that your body is in working order for labour and that you may start within a week or two.

Bright red bleeding, which flows as if you were at the height of a period, is another matter. It is called antepartum haemorrhage (APH) and, although quite rare, is serious. If you start to haemorrhage, you should ring your doctor or the hospital immediately.

Placenta praevia Sometimes blood flows from the placental site when it is too low-lying and partly in front of the baby's head. Intermittent APH from 27 weeks onwards is a typical symptom of this condition, known as placenta praevia. Placenta praevia occurs in about one in every 200 births and it almost certainly means that delivery will be by Caesarean section. During a vaginal birth, as the lower segment of the uterus thinned out, the placenta would be torn away from its roots, depriving the baby of nourishment and oxygen. If you start to bleed when you are as much as 37 weeks pregnant, or thereabouts, you will be admitted to hospital and, if bleeding continues, will be advised to stay there until the baby is mature enough to be born.

In fact, ultrasound at 16 weeks often reveals that the placenta is lying in the lower part of the uterus. Although this tends to be taken by some obstetricians as an indication of the need for Caesarean section, it is normal in early pregnancy and, by the end of pregnancy, when the wall of the uterus has stretched and enlarged, the placenta is usually in the right place in the upper part.

Abruptio placentae APH can also mean that a tiny part of the placenta, situated in the upper part of the uterus as it should be, has peeled away. This is called accidental haemorrhage (accidental in that the haemorrhage has occurred by chance) or abruptio placentae. The severity of accidental haemorrhage depends entirely on how large a portion of the placenta has separated from the lining of the uterus, but it is always a potentially serious problem, and the doctor should be informed at once. You will be advised to go to hospital for bed-rest and, if the bleeding stops and all is well with the baby, will be discharged after four to five days. It is probably wise to avoid intercourse and orgasm until after the baby is born.

Blood pressure

Every time you go to the antenatal clinic your blood pressure is checked (see page 48). This is because, although slight fluctuations are normal during pregnancy, any significant rise may be an indication of pre-eclampsia (see page 126). If the diastolic figure in your blood-pressure reading rises by as much as 15, you are considered to have hypertension—high blood pressure. Hypertension can be a signal of pre-eclampsia, which reduces the efficiency of the placenta. Bed-rest will be prescribed, since the placenta will begin to work more efficiently if you stay in bed.

Pre-eclampsia

The full name of this condition is *pre-eclamptic toxaemia*, but it is usually known as pre-eclampsia, and sometimes just as *PET* or *toxaemia*. The Australian name for it is *hypertensive disease of pregnancy* or *HDP*, and it is also called *pregnancy induced hypertension* or *PIH*, even *gestosis*. All these names reflect the uncertainty as to the cause of the illness. One doctor in the nineteenth century called it "the disease of theories" and this remains true today.

Pre-eclampsia affects between 5 and 10 per cent of all pregnant women, but rarely occurs in the early part of pregnancy, unless a woman has been malnourished for years.

Symptoms Your blood pressure rises, the level of uric acid in your blood goes up, and you retain a lot of fluid. A rise in blood pressure alone does not mean that you have pre-eclampsia, and neither does an increase in fluid retention. The two symptoms in combination, however, indicate the need for some form of treatment. If mild pre-eclampsia goes untreated, eventually protein appears in the urine. Babies of mothers with a high proportion of protein in their urine may be born prematurely; once a woman is excreting a lot of protein pregnancy is unlikely to continue longer than two more weeks*.

The danger of pre-eclampsia is not so much to you as to the unborn baby. If the condition is allowed to progress, clots and fatty acids build up in the placenta, blocking the arteries and causing the placenta to fail. This means that labour occurs prematurely, before the baby is necessarily mature enough to survive. In its severest form pre-eclampsia becomes eclampsia, and then it can seriously affect you as well as the baby, causing fits and possibly a state of coma. The following symptoms can be signs of eclampsia: headache, flashing lights, nausea, vomiting and pain in the abdomen. Don't make the mistake of thinking that you have gastric flu if this happens to you in late pregnancy. Get in touch with your doctor immediately and ask if he or she would take your blood pressure and test your urine.

Causes No-one is absolutely certain what causes the disorder, but research at Oxford indicates that it may be because the blood vessels in the placenta are thinner than usual. The problem starts between the 6th and 18th week of pregnancy, when placental cells do not infiltrate arteries in the uterus deeply enough to make the blood vessels expand so that they can nourish the baby (see page 66).

There is another element in pre-eclampsia, too; it seems to be a process similar to graft rejection. It is as if the baby is a transplant in the mother's body, and her immune system recognizes it and produces cells in order to expel the intruder.

The risk of pre-eclampsia is highest in the first pregnancy. But it also has something to do with the man; if the woman has a new partner for a subsequent pregnancy, the chances of her developing pre-eclampsia are about the same as if it were her first baby.

Poor nutrition may play an important part in pre-eclampsia. You may be able to avoid the disorder by eating well, ensuring you have adequate protein throughout pregnancy (see page 87). If you have had pre-eclampsia in a previous pregnancy, start out on a programme of good nutrition *before* you conceive again.

You are more likely to develop pre-eclampsia if any of the following apply: you have diabetes or kidney disease; you have high blood pressure anyway (140/90 or higher); you are having twins or more; members of your family have high blood pressure or have had pre-eclampsia; you are still in your teens or are over 40; you are under 5 ft 3 in (1·6 m); you have had pre-eclampsia with a previous pregnancy (in which case there is a one in ten chance of it recurring); you suffer from migraine.

Treatment Many doctors think that staying in bed at the first signs may avoid further developments. Certainly bed-rest coupled with relaxation of body and mind will reduce your blood pressure and improve the blood flow to the baby. Don't lie flat on your back in bed, but on your side or well propped up.

If you have high blood pressure with protein in your urine, or high blood pressure alone above 170/110, your doctor will probably admit you to hospital the same day. You will be kept in bed and your blood pressure and urine will be checked every four hours. Sedatives are sometimes prescribed. After a couple of days you will be allowed up for short periods: if your blood pressure falls below 90 and stays there, and if there is no longer any protein in your urine, you will be probably allowed home after three or four days.

Many women feel trapped in hospital when they have pre-eclampsia, because they may not feel at all ill. In these circumstances, knowing what is happening to you and why means that you can help to care for yourself rather than just put up with having things done *to* you. Ask questions: find out about your condition and its progress, and understand the reasons for the treatment you are receiving.

Eclampsia If your pre-eclampsia has developed into eclampsia an intravenous drip will be set up through which a drug is introduced into your blood to prevent convulsions; injections will lower your blood pressure. Your baby may be delivered by Caesarean section.

Sugar in the urine

Your urine is tested whenever you attend the antenatal clinic (see page 48). If more sugar than usual is detected in your urine, you may have a tendency to be diabetic which has remained hidden until pregnancy. Nearly all women at some time during pregnancy produce sugar in their urine. They are not diabetics. The diagnosis of diabetes is more likely to be correct if you have not previously had a highly sugared meal or snack, if you have a parent who is diabetic, or if you have already had a baby weighing 9 lb (4 kg) or more at birth.

When you are pregnant, the amount of blood in your system rises and so does the amount of blood sugar to be dealt with by your kidneys. You may be able to reduce the sugar level by modifying your diet and cutting out all sugar, cakes, puddings, sweets and chocolate. The accumulation of glucose in a diabetic woman who is pregnant is absorbed by the fetus, which then grows very fast. The obstetrician may recommend induction of labour before the baby grows too big to pass easily through your pelvic outlet. Although large, the baby will not be mature and may need special care after birth (see page 334). Some babies of diabetic mothers are delivered by Caesarean section because the mother's cervix is not soft and ready to open.

If you become diabetic during pregnancy, the diabetes may be controlled by insulin and will probably disappear after delivery. It is now possible for a woman to monitor her blood sugar levels at home using a glucose meter; when linked to a computer at the hospital, the meter provides details of the levels of blood sugar in the average day, so that the woman can adjust her sugar intake as necessary.

There is no reason why a diabetic woman should not breast-feed, and many diabetics do so successfully.

Anaemia

When you are anaemic (see page 89), you tend to feel very tired, easily become exhausted when you do anything vigorous and may also have dizzy spells and be short of breath. If you have vomited a great deal during early pregnancy, are having a baby within two years of the previous birth, have had a number of babies in quick succession and are on an inadequate diet, or are pregnant with more than one baby, you are most at risk of being anaemic. Women who suffer from anaemia in pregnancy are less able to cope with any heavy bleeding at the time of the birth and are more likely to have an infection. The baby suffers because less oxygen is carried by the mother's blood to the placenta and premature labour often results. Adjust your diet so that you get more iron-rich foods, protein, vitamin B, especially B12, vitamin C and a folic-acid supplement which your doctor will prescribe (see page 90). All are necessary to ensure that your blood can carry enough oxygen to all the tissues. Your doctor will also prescribe iron tablets. If they make you constipated, ask for another kind. If you have a low haemoglobin level (see page 48) after 30 weeks, injections of iron may be prescribed.*

Headache

There is no reason why you should have more headaches when you are pregnant than when you are not pregnant. In fact, some women who usually suffer from migraine find that it disappears throughout pregnancy. You can have tension headaches while you are carrying a baby just as at any other time. If your pregnancy is fraught with anxiety, or you are taking on more than you can handle, you will probably be prone to headaches. Decode the messages from your body, modify your life style and, if you are worried about labour, find out how you can help yourself (see page 135).

A sharp, blinding headache that affects your eyesight in late pregnancy should be reported to your doctor as it could be associated with pre-eclampsia.

Digestive disturbances

Indigestion and heartburn are problems of the last three or four months of pregnancy. There seems to be so little room in your abdomen and it feels as if all your organs are being crushed.

It is better to have many small snacks than several larger meals a day, and it is sensible to avoid fried or rich, spicy foods. Some people find that they cannot digest bread or products containing yeast and that, by cutting out these foods, they can eliminate heartburn. Many women discover they cannot drink during a meal and that meals have to be taken dry. You need to experiment with different combinations of food and liquid to find the kind of diet that suits you personally. There is no perfect diet that is right for everyone.

Since heartburn results from acid normally present in your stomach flowing back into the oesophagus, try to find positions for sitting and sleeping in which the upper part of your uterus is not pressing against your stomach. You will probably prefer upright chairs and at night will feel better if you sleep well propped up with pillows. Make sure jeans, trousers and skirts are comfortably loose at the waist if you want to avoid indigestion.

Shortness of breath

When the baby is high, after about 34 weeks and before it drops into your pelvis, you will probably find that you are short of breath whenever you exert yourself or even just climb the stairs. Your uterus is putting pressure on your lungs, and your diaphragm may be shifted out of place by as much as 1 in (2·5 cm). Again, sitting straight and sleeping propped up can help and you will probably discover that you have to take life rather more slowly in order not to get breathless. There is a rhythm to everything in nature, and this is a phase of pregnancy when your body is telling you to slow down.

Towards the end of pregnancy you may find you are short of breath when climbing stairs or doing anything energetic.

DAILY CARE AND COMFORT

When you are pregnant you find that you carry round your own very efficient central-heating system. You do not need to dress as warmly as usual and in hot weather you will probably feel more comfortable in cotton dresses, skirts and so on and should avoid synthetic materials. Many pregnant women suffer from varicose veins in the

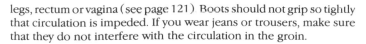

legs, rectum or vagina (see page 121) Boots should not grip so tightly that circulation is impeded. If you wear jeans or trousers, make sure that they do not interfere with the circulation in the groin.

Shoes

Shoes should allow the feet to keep their normal shape and should not be so high that your weight is thrown forward onto the balls of your feet. In late pregnancy you may find that your feet are wider than usual and so need a wider-fitting shoe or a half size larger. Although lace-ups give good support to the arches, you may not be able to tie them easily in late pregnancy. For the same reason slip-on sandals are better than shoes that have elaborate buckles.

Brassieres

Since breast changes and enlargement occur from the first days of pregnancy, you will need a bra which gives good support and, if you are heavy-breasted, choose one with straps sufficiently wide not to dig into your shoulders.

Heavy breasts, allowed to hang without support, may develop stretch marks (see opposite), which will leave you with silvery streaks after the pregnancy. A woman with large breasts may prefer to wear a lightweight bra at night too during pregnancy.

WHAT SORT OF BRA?
Bras you wear in pregnancy should have a band around their lower margin and wide straps over the shoulders, adjusted to provide firm support for your breasts. The cotton bra (right) can be adjusted at the back for girth, but opens at the front: it is suitable for nursing as well as pregnancy.

Teeth

Although the baby needs calcium to grow strong teeth, your own teeth are no more likely to fall out in pregnancy than at any other time. However, as your gums soften and become spongier along with other tissues in the body as the result of the action of pregnancy hormones in your bloodstream, you may be liable to a gum infection. Good nutrition (see page 86) is the first line of defence against this. Mouth hygiene is also important, with regular tooth brushing, especially after breakfast and before you go to bed at night. Arrange a dental check-up when you know you are pregnant and again for mid-pregnancy. Since it may be difficult to fit in appointments immediately after the baby is born, arrange another shortly before the baby is due. The dentist's waiting-room is an excellent place to practise your relaxation for labour, and slow, full abdominal breathing in the dentist's chair works wonders.

Skin pigmentation

For many women pregnancy is better than a beauty treatment: skin improves, eyes shine and hair is in better condition. But some women develop patches of darkened (pigmented) skin on the face, and this can be distressing. The technical term is "chloasma", but it is also called "the mask of pregnancy". It is a result of the high level of pregnancy hormones and also occurs in some women taking the Pill. It is made worse by exposure to sunlight. The kind of cosmetic cream sold as "undereye" cream for minimizing birth marks often disguises it effectively. The mask usually disappears once the baby is born.

You will notice that other parts of the body that are already pigmented become darker, for example the circles around your nipples and the skin of your labia. You may also develop a dark line down the middle of your tummy from your navel, and this is where the rectus muscle is being stretched (see page 111). It is particularly obvious in dark-haired women. All these colorations should disappear once the baby is born.

Stretch marks

Stretch marks (striae) may appear over your tummy, buttocks and breasts. They are dark streaks and are a sign that the skin has been stretched from underneath. They never disappear completely but, after the birth, they change from being brown or deep violet to a silvery shade, rather like the marks on some fine, gauze-like fabric that has not been properly ironed. Many women use a rich cream or oil to "feed" the skin, and there are even some on the market especially for stretch marks. However, these are expensive and any cream that is readily absorbed, or even vegetable oil, will do. If your skin is very stretched, and especially if you are having twins, it is marked like this because of pressure on the layers underneath which cannot be reached by anything applied from outside. Still, it can feel good and be relaxing for you to stroke your tummy; even though you may still have stretch marks, there is nothing to be lost and some pleasure to be gained from regular gentle massage with a rich, slippery cream applied by you or your partner.

Sport

Any sport you do well is probably fine during pregnancy: if you are really good at something, you do not waste muscular energy and your movements are smoothly co-ordinated. As pregnancy advances, you will notice your balance changing as the centre of gravity is concentrated in your tummy. This will almost certainly limit your activities, although I heard of a tightrope walker who practised daily on the high wire until she went into labour—an exceptional woman! Swimming is splendid exercise during pregnancy, and dancing too, provided you are not in a stuffy room. Cycling is also beneficial although, if you can avoid heavy traffic, it is kinder on both you and your baby.

=**"**=
I've always been very active physically and was determined I wasn't going to give up because I was pregnant. So I've cycled everywhere and gone on with my yoga and swum every day.
=**"**=

Travel

Travel in pregnancy is usually quite safe, but the exhaustion which may result from it is not. It is important to divide up long journeys into short, manageable sections if you can; rest in between. Do not sit immobilized in a car, train or plane for longer than two hours at most without getting up and walking around for five minutes. Sitting for long periods reduces the circulation of blood in the pelvic area. Also remember to empty your bladder regularly as you are more likely to get a bladder infection during pregnancy (see page 122).

Travel in loose, comfortable clothing, and in shoes that allow for a little expansion. Soft slipper-socks are usually the most comfortable. Take any opportunity of dropping off to sleep. Pack an eye shade made of soft material to block out lights.

Flying On an aeroplane drink water or fruit juice; avoid alcoholic drinks, as air travel is dehydrating, and alcohol will dehydrate you further. If you are over 25 weeks pregnant, most airlines will require a letter from your doctor saying that it is all right for you to travel. Your doctor will probably agree to write such a letter as long as the risk of your going into labour on board a plane is slight. It would be reasonable of your doctor to refuse consent if, for instance, your blood pressure was high, or if you had suffered a threatened miscarriage in early pregnancy. In such cases a change in altitude could bring on premature labour. Similarly, it is unwise to fly in a small unpressurized plane, as the supply of oxygen to the fetus can sometimes be drastically diminished.

You might also bear in mind, if you are thinking of flying a long distance, the strain caused to you by jet lag.

Driving is perfectly safe if you do not find it exhausting and obviously if you are not subject to dizzy spells. Bear in mind that if you drive in city traffic you are almost certainly breathing in other cars' exhaust fumes. This does not do your baby any good, so try to avoid the rush hour if you can. If you have a heavy gear lever, the sheer hard work of changing gear can cause discomfort in the later months. An automatic car makes lighter work of driving in pregnancy. Make sure your seat belt is strapped under your tummy and that it is not too tight or it will cause indigestion and interfere with your breathing.

Rest and sleep

During the first and last three months of pregnancy you will probably feel much more tired than usual, and it is advisable to rest as much as possible, rather than trying to fight off the tiredness. Towards the end of your pregnancy there may be several reasons why you cannot sleep as much as you would like.

Nearly every pregnant woman goes through a period when she either cannot drop off to sleep or wakes in the night because the baby

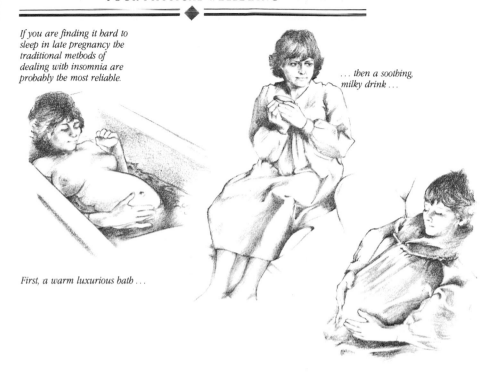

If you are finding it hard to sleep in late pregnancy the traditional methods of dealing with insomnia are probably the most reliable.

... then a soothing, milky drink ...

First, a warm luxurious bath ...

... and finally deep, relaxing breathing, all the while concentrating on the new life within you.

is kicking her, she needs to empty her bladder, or she has been woken by a violent and disturbing dream and cannot get back to sleep. Sometimes the insomnia occurs because she is lying worrying and in the darkness her fears gain the upper hand.

If you have recently given up work, you may feel that your pregnancy has become a time of passive waiting and is stretching out longer and longer, so that you cannot see an end to it. You probably cannot sleep because you need action, and sometimes vigorous exercise during the day can be a remedy for this problem. You could also try the traditional remedies for sleeplessness, such as a hot milky drink after a luxurious warm bath at bedtime.

The stillness of the middle of the night actually provides a marvellous opportunity for practising your relaxation and breathing. Use the time to centre down into your body and become more aware of the developing life inside you. Allow your breathing to flow right down to where the baby nestles deep inside you. Cup your hands over the lower curve of your abdomen and breathe so that the wave of the inhaled breath presses your hands up and, as you give a long breath out, you sink on the receding wave.

Relax and enjoy lying there with your baby. Once you have begun to lose yourself in these feelings, you will probably find that your deep breathing has relaxed you back into sleep.

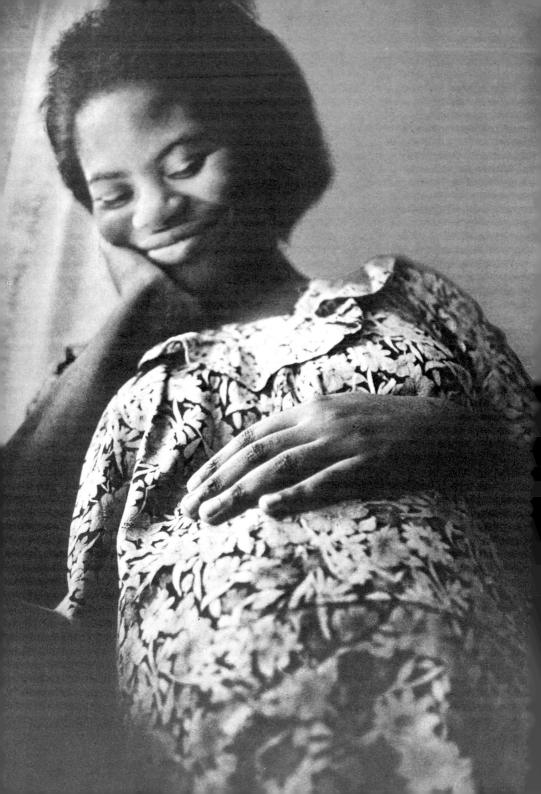

Emotional challenges in pregnancy

Many expectant mothers look and feel radiant. A healthy woman who is looking forward to a much-wanted baby, who has a loving and secure relationship with a considerate partner, and some knowledge about childbirth and what she can do to help herself, often revels in her pregnancy. Many women say "I feel fitter than I ever have before" or "I'm really enjoying being pregnant" and are surprised at the vitality and sense of inner fulfilment which they experience.

Yet probably all of us are assailed by darker thoughts at times when we are overtired or under some special stress. Some of the more negative feelings that women experience in early pregnancy have been discussed on page 34. But as your pregnancy advances, more specific anxieties may preoccupy you at times. Anxiety may grip you in the middle of the night when the baby has kicked you awake or when you have had to get up to empty your bladder and cannot get to sleep again. Every fear is magnified in the darkness as you lie trying to sleep and unable to relax.

66
Everyone's thrilled to bits, except it's me that's got to have it!
99

Worries about the birth

Labour can be an intensely pleasurable, all-absorbing and deeply satisfying activity which it is really possible to enjoy. But just as some people do not like climbing a mountain, even though the view at the summit is magnificent and the climb exciting, and just as some feel that sex is over-rated and not worth the effort, whereas others think it is one of the best experiences life offers, different women have very different attitudes towards childbirth. This is not just a matter of what happens physiologically or how you are treated in hospital, but also depends on what kind of person you are. Anxiety can cast a shadow over childbirth and produces the speeded-up heart rate, high blood pressure, muscle tension and other physical results of stress which actually make birth more difficult. It is important to think through it and to understand why you are anxious.

Anxiety about labour is probably best dealt with first of all by finding out more about it, not just its mechanics, but the physical and emotional sensations of each phase, and the relaxation, breathing and focused concentration which can help you to work with your body instead of against it. The simple process of sharing fears also often results in women feeling much more lighthearted, so that they begin to enjoy their pregnancies. A good antenatal class where discussion is encouraged and women can talk freely about their apprehensions as well as about their hopes is often effective in

OPPOSITE
There are bound to be doubts and anxieties, but for many women there is also a new-found serenity and a sense of inner fulfilment.

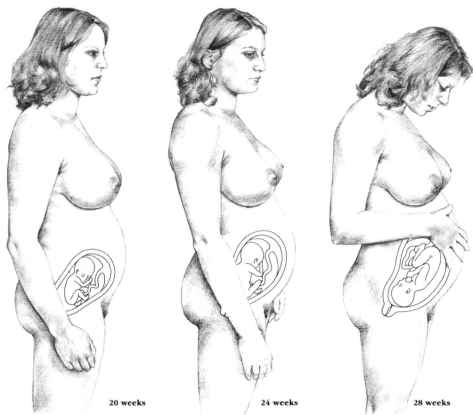

20 weeks   24 weeks   28 weeks

YOUR CHANGING SHAPE
Some women delight in the physical changes brought about by pregnancy. Others feel threatened by the inevitability of the process. Taking pleasure in your expanding form is good preparation for working with and expressing yourself through your body in labour.

developing self-confidence and helping you to look forward to labour as a peak experience which brings delight and fulfilment, not just an ordeal to be endured.

Pain A woman having her first baby often thinks "I have never had anything really painful. How shall I stand up to the pain of labour?" and since she has no idea what that pain is like or what contractions feel like, the thought can bring terror. Learning about labour, about how contractions work and how they may feel at different stages of labour, is the most effective way of coming face to face with this anxiety and doing something about it. There is a whole chapter in this book about pain and pain relief (pages 278–288), but the important thing to understand is that for most women the pain of labour is quite different from the pain of injury. Some women describe it as "positive pain" or "pain with a purpose".

Loss of control For many women anxieties about labour are linked with a dread of losing control. For your whole life you have been

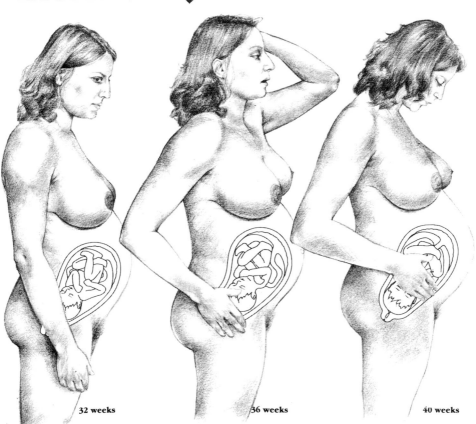

32 weeks   36 weeks   40 weeks

taught to control physical processes and your own behaviour, and suddenly something is about to happen which clearly cannot be controlled and which is about to take over your body. You are told that you may cry out or groan, for example, that you may lose inhibitions, be impatient or irritable with your partner or whoever is helping you in labour, and swear and say things you never meant to, and are horrified to hear that during labour you may involuntarily empty your bowels or your bladder.

You also learn that the waters may go suddenly. In any group of women discussing the events of labour, first-time mothers nearly always ask those who have already had babies when the waters went, whether it was sudden, and if so where it was; they express keen anxiety that the bag of waters may break in the supermarket or on a bus. What these women are saying is that they are fearful of letting their bodies function freely because of the embarrassment and social stigma attached. It is as if degrading physical processes, above all dirty ones which involve getting rid of waste products from the body, are taking place in public.

Think through why you find the thought of the waters breaking in public so upsetting. You are having a baby and it is perfectly obvious that you are going to give birth soon. If the waters do break in public, is it really so very terrible? You will attract interest and sympathy, but not disgust. You may see it as a kind of sexual act in front of other people. You are quite right, and understanding this can help you in labour. Birth, just like lovemaking, is a sexual process. If you can go *with* your labour instead of fighting it the experience can be fulfilling in a strangely pleasurable way. Prepare the way to this through body awareness and relaxation. Touch relaxation (see page 173) is a special kind of release which teaches you to flow towards sensations of pressure and heat. It will help a lot in labour.

Loss of dignity and failure An anxiety closely connected with loss of control is the fear of making a fool of yourself. Some women think doctors and nurses will laugh at them if they find themselves making uncontrollable noises, for instance. You may feel that you are on public display in labour and approach it as a test of endurance. You may also be anxious about "letting down" a partner who puts great faith in your ability to cope, or even of "failing" a keen antenatal teacher. Some men who participate in classes and the other preparations for the birth become so enthusiastic and obsessional that they are in effect "trainers", rather like athletic coaches. The woman then feels that she is expected to put on a performance and must excel in it. Antenatal classes which are geared exclusively to techniques used in labour rather than focusing on wider aspects of the total experience can reinforce this feeling.

Just as the elaborate techniques performed to "ensure" satisfaction in lovemaking can sometimes disturb the spontaneous rhythm of sex and interfere with the intense feeling and play of emotion between the couple, so breathing exercises and "distraction" techniques can sometimes intrude on the experience of labour. Exercises need to become "second nature" and be made a part of yourself. It is like learning to play the piano: there is a vast difference between laborious scales and playing a sonata. The exercises are important because they prepare you for playing music. But the eventual aim is to let the music flow through you, rather than to superimpose tricks and techniques onto it. Such a physical and emotional surrender is simple in labour because of its intensity. Birth involves mind and body working together in a completely absorbing, exciting and passionate way. There is no success or failure in labour. You cannot make a fool of yourself, let anyone down or flunk an examination in birth.

Fear of managing alone Some women approach labour as a medical incident like having an appendectomy, an unwelcome interruption of normal life rather than an experience which can be satisfying in itself. They feel totally dependent on the technology provided by the hospital and worry about whether they will get there on time, or whether the right people will be present to deliver the baby. Such women's dependence is reinforced by contemporary obstetrics and by every programme on television which illustrates the latest marvel of science applied to childbearing. The impression is readily given that women must depend on life-saving machines, and that without them it is not safe to have a baby.

The fact is that although these machines can be extremely useful in diagnosing difficulties when a baby is at risk or when special problems are met in pregnancy or labour, the majority of women can give birth perfectly well without them.

It is not advances in medicine but improved conditions, better food and general health which have made childbirth much safer for mothers and babies today than it was 100 years ago. The rate of stillbirths and deaths in the first week of life is directly related to a country's gross national product and to the position of the mother in the social class structure.

It is a disturbing thought that it is twice as safe for a woman in the professional classes to bear a child than it is for an unsupported mother at the bottom of the social scale. The challenge is to find out which mothers and babies are at risk, to offer them everything possible which can make birth safer, but to let those who are at no special risk give birth naturally if they can.

Loss of autonomy Another frequent anxiety is that of being denied the right to function as an adult and fear of being under the control of doctors, nurses and even machines. Many pregnant women resent the feeling that they cannot make their own decisions. Increasing numbers feel that they do not want to hand their bodies over to professional care-givers in pregnancy and childbirth, and are seeking maternity care in which they can take an active part, sharing the decision-making with their advisers.

If you are not sure whether your doctor is being quite open with you, or whether the hospital will really let you do the things in labour which you have asked to do, the uncertainty can produce a sick fear in the pit of the stomach. Too often pregnant women are treated like children or as patients in categories of "high risk", "low risk", "primigravida", "multigravida", "PET" and so on, who have to be processed through the hospital system, passive receivers of care rather than active birth-givers.

Fear of hospitals For many women hospitals are threatening places. People usually go to hospital when they are ill. This may be the first time that you have been a patient in a hospital and the sights, sounds and even smells of hospitals may alarm you. Society has given little thought so far to designing and decorating maternity units so that they look more like home, or at least a good hotel. Hospitals are still places with long porridge-coloured corridors and white tiles and instrument trolleys. Delivery rooms in otherwise splendid modern

I can still remember when I had my tonsils out when I was 7. I can't bear hospitals.

hospitals can be windowless boxes, and antenatal clinics, your first introduction to the hospital, are often forbidding places without pictures and with backache-inducing chairs set in rows. Even more important than the physical surroundings are the attitudes of members of hospital staff and the way in which they interact with patients. If you meet cool indifference, rigid authoritarianism or obvious hostility, you may dread going to the antenatal clinic, and this anxiety can colour your whole approach to labour.

There is a certain kind of emotional climate in which anxieties flourish and unfortunately it is one which our society provides for many pregnant women. If there is no-one readily available of whom you can ask questions and be answered in terms you can understand, the seeds of anxiety are often sown. They are nourished by the insecurity of seeing different members of staff in the antenatal clinic at each visit.

Women often feel apologetic about anxiety, about not being "sensible", as if they were revealing some shameful lack of emotional stamina. They are sometimes regarded as having something psychologically wrong with them if they show anxiety. But many of the fears you have during your pregnancy are not the result of inadequacy but a response to stresses caused by an environment which is alien and unfriendly and by care which is impersonal. In such a situation anxiety is *realistic*.

Although you may not be able to eradicate anxiety about the birth itself, it is sensible to tackle it directly. Ask to see round the labour and delivery rooms, including the machinery which may be used; attend antenatal classes at the hospital so that you can get to know at least some of the staff, and talk with your doctor about the style of childbirth which you would like if possible; ask him or her to note down any particular request on your record card. Read the section in this book on talking to doctors (pages 51–54) before you go.

Loss of attractiveness Some pregnant women are deeply concerned that their sexual attractiveness may be completely destroyed by childbearing. They are frightened of losing their figures; they may also be anxious that the vagina will be slack and changed in shape, and that as a result they will not be able to make love with their partners in a mutually satisfying way.

The fear of a tear or a cut (see page 294) often discussed in childbirth education classes is not so much about pain resulting from stitches, although it is often dealt with by the antenatal teacher in terms of coping with discomfort after the birth. It is really anxiety about genital mutilation.

Episiotomy Until recently, in many hospitals episiotomy was routinely used for all women having their first babies and for a large percentage of those having second and subsequent babies. Now this is changing fast. Women are questioning the need for what amounts

All the coming and going and the noise makes me feel really het up. I can practically feel my blood pressure rising.

OPPOSITE
Finding time to concentrate on yourself when an older child is constantly present creates its own particular challenge.

to surgical intervention in normal birth and the creation of an artificial wound. Doctors are asking how it was that this intervention became so widely used without any proper evaluation.

Women are often more anxious about episiotomy than any other invasive procedure. The thought of being surgically cut, or injured, in such a sensitive place is horrifying, and some women feel as if they are being punished for enjoying sex. Many worry that childbirth will so damage them that they will never be the same again.

There are various ways in which you can prepare your body and the tissues of your perineum—the area between your vagina and your anus—to become soft and supple, so that you enter labour fully confident that you can give birth without injury.

Pelvic-floor exercises (see page 107) can help create the sensitive awareness, co-ordination and control which help you in the second stage of labour, preparing you to open your body for the baby to be born, and reducing stress on the pelvic muscles and perineal tissues. Many women find that massage with vegetable oil also helps. Certainly getting in touch, literally, with this part of your body and feeling how flexible the tissues are, will give you confidence that your vagina and perineum are able to fan out and open wide. Since in late pregnancy it can be quite difficult to reach your perineum and exert firm pressure, you may want to ask a loving partner to help with this massage. It feels especially good if the oil is warmed first.

=**"**=
I'm not sleeping very well. Things keep running through my mind . . . what if it's got no arms or legs?

=**"**=

If you are concerned to avoid an episiotomy, discuss the subject with your midwife or doctor in advance. Say that you would like help at the delivery so that you can breathe the baby out rather than push it out, and ask for this to be noted on your card. It is wrong to think that a woman who is anxious about episiotomy is in any way "neurotic", though doctors sometimes assume this.

Sometimes episiotomy must be performed for the baby's safety, so that he or she can be born quickly, or to avoid a large tear. It can help you to understand the healing process afterwards if you know what has happened, and exactly where. Exploring the vagina with your fingers during pregnancy (see page 106) and after the birth, and looking at it in a mirror, helps you to feel that it belongs to you; you can then rehabilitate the area through gentle pelvic-floor movements.

Worries about the baby

Almost every woman wonders at some stage of her pregnancy whether her baby is normal. Fear of producing a handicapped child is often connected with anxiety about not being able to live up to standards set by somebody else, usually either or both of the woman's own parents. You may feel it almost impossible that you could produce from the dark interior of your body anything which is perfect. This is probably the most persistent, gnawing fear of all, and the only way of coming to terms with it is to develop self-confidence, a process which, not surprisingly, takes time. This is where regular attendance at childbirth education classes which encourage you to

If you are pregnant for the first time and maybe living in a different area, make the effort to meet other people with young families. You will build a new set of social relationships which will stand you in good stead after your own baby is born ...

have trust in your body and in your ability to give birth, rather than depend on others to get the baby born for you, can help enormously.

One woman who had disappointed her parents academically became pregnant outside marriage, in a desperate effort to show them that at least there was *something* she could do. She now lay awake wondering if her baby was deformed. Talking about this fear in an antenatal discussion group led her to reveal that she was having awful dreams. It then emerged that five out of the twelve women in the group were having very vivid dreams, and that even some of those who had not admitted to any worry about whether the baby would be "all right" were having dreams in which the baby was disposed of because it was not "good enough", or was taken away and looked after by other people because *they*, the mothers, were not themselves good enough. Dreams can often reveal emotional tangles which cause great distress in pregnancy until they are brought out into the open.

Most women who fear bearing an abnormal baby have little reason to expect that the baby will not be perfect. The minority of women who are aware of the possibility of inherited diseases or handicaps in their or their partners' families, or who are pregnant after the age of 40, will realize that they can seek genetic counselling and can have alpha-feto-protein (AFP) screening (see page 205) and, if necessary, amniocentesis performed (see page 206).

Worries about the future

Loneliness Many women having their first babies move away from their own homes during pregnancy, often to a larger flat or house, so that they find themselves in an area where they know nobody at all. They stop work in late pregnancy and no longer even have the daily contacts with friends and colleagues at work. At home and alone for the first time, they are initially delighted, but often quickly become bored and depressed.

If you are in this position plan to take up some activity which brings social contacts; learn something new; join a club of some kind; attend childbirth education classes; track down interesting places in the locality to which you have moved, and invite people to your home. If you do not know anyone with young children and would like to discover more about what babies are like, seek out your nearest playgroup or nursery school and go when parents are meeting their children, or go to the welfare clinic and say that you want to get to know somebody who has a baby. Your doctor or health visitor may be able to tell you about other pregnant women or mothers with new babies who live near you. It is worth investigating the possibilities while you are still pregnant. When you are busy with a baby it may be more difficult to make new friends, especially during the winter months, so take the opportunity of making them now.

Change When a woman expresses anxiety about "things never being the same again", it helps to think through what exactly this means for her. If things are irrevocably altered, what might happen? One couple who had a deeply satisfying relationship saw the pregnancy and the upset connected with the birth as an "interruption". "We don't want to change our lives for a child," the woman said, "to be swamped by it. How long will it take before we get back to normal again? Sometimes I'm frightened we'll *never* get back to normal." When I asked what she found frightening about this, after some thought she explained that she did not want to become the same kind of woman as her mother and did not see herself as bound to babies and a home. Most of all she was afraid that because of the pregnancy her partner would not love her any more and that she would be de-sexed by maternity.

Social expectations Another woman said that her pregnancy made her feel that at last she was fulfilling a socially acceptable role and that her own mother was proud of her for the first time in her life. In a way, she resented this. Other women acted as if they knew how she felt and what she thought and wanted. The doctors at the hospital expected her to be a "good patient" and be processed through the busy antenatal clinic like all the others with their swelling bumps. She suddenly felt miles away from her former colleagues and the others with whom she had worked, separated from them by the inescapable fact of her pregnancy. But by the end she felt guilty that she had resented the baby at the beginning of her pregnancy. At night as it moved inside her she lay thinking whether she would ever be a good mother. She said, "I sometimes feel so sorry for the little thing in there that I end up crying."

In an antenatal discussion group both of these women had the chance to talk about their disturbing feelings. It emerged that several of the others were also lying awake at night thinking and worrying about much the same things. What had seemed personal handicaps proved to be an experience shared by a number of women.

If you realize that you are not all alone with your fears, and are not being "odd" or neurotic, the anxieties usually become much less disturbing. Thinking about inevitable change may worry you in different ways: you may be afraid that the relationship with your partner will deteriorate; that you have no maternal instincts and will be no good as a mother; that the loss of a job and the money and sense of freedom associated with getting out of the house and earning your own living may bring a real deprivation. You may wonder if you will be able to tolerate being at home all day with a "screaming brat", and whether you will miss all the interesting people at work.

Although such anxiety is realistic in the sense that these changes are dramatic and demanding for many women, most expectant mothers are more aware of anxieties about labour and the baby than they are of how they will cope after the birth. Many take the unknown "afterwards" more or less for granted. It is as if they can only see as far as the birth, which dominates the horizon. The post-partum experience may then come as a shock for which they are not prepared. So some anxiety about life after the baby arrives is a healthy sign, and indicates that the emotional work is taking place which prepares a couple not only for the birth but for parenthood.

Many anxieties during pregnancy, both for the woman and the man, offer clues to the challenges confronting the couple. It is a waste of emotional energy to try to "forget" them or put them to the back of your mind. They are there to be worked with. It is often the man and woman who are determined to take it all in their stride and carry on as usual, and who do not acknowledge feelings of apprehension on the threshold of the unknown, who are likely to face the most shattering crises, both in the experience of birth and also when they have a baby in the house.

The discomfort anxiety produces can force you to think through the meaning for you of the coming of a child into your lives. Without stress and challenge of this kind emotional preparation for birth and parenthood may be overlooked. Fears and anxieties are an important element in the emotional changes necessary if you are to face up to the reality of birth and then to the astonishing reality of the new baby.

Becoming a father

Becoming a father is a major step in a man's life. It can also be a daunting one. Yet it is an experience usually treated as insignificant in comparison with that of becoming a mother. As a result the emotional upheavals and stresses of the future father are little understood and men are not prepared for the impact of pregnancy. If people do notice that a man is finding the going difficult they tend to laugh rather than sympathize. In fact the nervousness and anxiety of the father-to-be are favourite subjects of jokes and anecdotes, ranging from the picture postcard variety—showing a man wide-eyed and desperate in the hospital corridor as his wife produces triplets— to those amused tales about male ignorance and incompetence shared between women over coffee.

I reckon that babies have been born for thousands of years and I don't know what all the fuss is about.

In childbirth classes and hospital lectures for parents-to-be a man is often discussed only in terms of how he can help his partner, and his own profound emotional needs are neglected. One result of this is to make him feel isolated and resentful, finding it difficult to reach out and give his partner the support she needs. She is the fairy princess going to the ball and he feels a bit like the back legs of a pantomime horse.

An expectant father may feel jealous of all the attention given to the future mother, absurdly envious of her reproductive powers and sometimes even jealous of the coming baby. Then he feels guilty about succumbing to these emotions and decides to concentrate on his work—because that at least is one thing he can do properly. And the more he immerses himself in his own preoccupations, the more isolated and left out of the pregnancy he feels.

Some men become really depressed during pregnancy or experience violent mood swings similar to those that a pregnant woman may go through. A few even walk out of the relationship because the stress is too great for them to handle. So it is important to remember that usually there are *two* people having a baby and that the man also goes through a transitional period of stress when very deep emotions may be stirred and his behaviour may be difficult to understand.

Reacting to fatherhood

The sheer responsibility of having a baby can be frightening. The woman may be going to give up work outside the home for a time, or even for good, and the man is expected to support the family. The financial burden alone may be too great for some men to shoulder without anxiety. But for many men money problems constitute a rationalization, a socially acceptable explanation for anxiety, without getting to the root of what they find disturbing. In fact, some men find that the prospect of becoming a father brings with it a crisis of identity. Although it is a common occurrence and one which in due course brings about creative change, it is nevertheless still a crisis.

The changing relationship One element in this crisis involves grieving over a relationship that is bound to change. The easy ways, the lack of routine, the spontaneity of the early stage of the relationship, all have to give way to an existence centred round a baby. Some men see their partners as their mothers. When the woman becomes pregnant it is as if the man is losing a mother and is being replaced in her love by a new baby. As she becomes more involved in the pregnancy and the coming baby he feels increasingly rejected and finds this inevitable shift of focus very threatening.

The changing woman Some men acquire a woman as a show-piece, proof of their success in hunting down and possessing a desirable sexual object, or evidence of their social success, a demonstration and symbol of a life style which embodies achievement. Delighted as such a man may be to be fathering a child, he may find it difficult to cope with his partner's new concentration on the pregnancy rather than on him. He feels that the physical changes in his partner's body are upsetting as conventional attractiveness is replaced by a very different body—no longer the outline of a neat figure but a melon-shaped abdomen and heavy, swelling breasts covered with a network of tiny blue veins. A man who has valued a woman as a status or sex symbol may feel that he is being cheated.

The developing baby It is sometimes difficult initially for a man, who does not have the baby growing inside his body, to feel its reality. He often begins to become more aware of the child at about the time when he feels it bump and kick at night. Some men find this sensation not only astonishing and exciting but rather eerie, and they take a while to adjust to the idea of another being living and growing inside the body of the woman they know so well.

I'm deeply moved by this baby growing inside her. I feel we're very close in a new way.

The future grandparents When a couple have a first baby they may have to work through a painful transitional period in which they forge a new adult relationship with their own parents, which allows for the responsibility and commitment they have to the child they are bearing. This may produce stresses with the future grandparents, and a man may get caught up in a difficult relationship with his own mother just as a woman may with hers. When a man's mother is fearful that she is losing her son she becomes demanding. He may feel the pull of her possessive love drawing attention away from the needs of his wife and baby. Sometimes a woman sees this, whereas the man is completely unaware of it. It is important to understand that the older women, the ex-mothers, are being replaced, and they may feel hurt and unwanted. If there is a problem of this kind, the couple should talk about it together and be honest about their feelings.

The father's new role

Having a baby used to be solely the concern of the woman, with her mother standing in the background giving advice. Nowadays it is much more something for woman and man to share.

There are still some men who say they do not want to get involved in "women's things" and who feel that their manliness is being threatened. They have the uneasy suspicion that learning about childbirth means that they will no longer be potent, virile males. Some imagine that it is only "good form" to hand the woman over to the care of the experts and retire from the scene. They believe that the professional must know so much more than they do that they are bound to be in the way and have no function in the delivery room.

Thirty years ago some midwives and obstetricians looked askance at men who became involved in the process of childbirth, as if they were slightly odd. Go back fifty years or so and men kept well away from anything to do with birth; pregnancy was a "certain condition" which a man pretended he knew nothing about. My mother told me that my father felt embarrassed to go out with her in advanced pregnancy, so that walks they took had to be after dark, with her enveloped in a wrap-around coat. And as for a father wheeling a pram, or changing a nappy—it was unheard of; even a man who might have liked to try his hand at such things rarely got the chance. This was partly because there used to be what one perceptive psychoanalyst called a male "taboo on tenderness". Men were frightened that to become involved with women's activities would humiliate them in the eyes of other men. And childbirth was the epitome of all feminine mysteries. Both women and men were prevented by these rules from discovering their full potential.

Many modern men are determined to share as much as they can in pregnancy and birth. They enjoy the woman's changing shape and the reality of the baby kicking against their hand. But a man often still feels a novice at fatherhood. He wonders just how much he can do, since the baby is growing in her body, not his. In a way, the partnership between the mother and her unborn child is complete. And pregnancy often seems to be so carefully managed by the obstetric team that a man can feel an intruder.

But a woman depends on her partner's support and needs the special relationship with him, which is quite different from any others that she has. She may not realize just how much her partner is sharing in the pregnancy emotionally and the heights and depths of his own feelings about it. There is no longer any need for a man to square his shoulders and pretend he is not stirred by what is happening. Take the opportunity to talk together about your feelings.

Feelings about being present at the birth

Most expectant fathers today approach childbirth with curiosity and interest and in a very different spirit from that thought suitable by their fathers and grandfathers. Though they may wonder whether they are going to make fools of themselves while playing an unfamiliar part, and may be nervous of unpleasant procedures involved in labour, they want to understand what is going on and to help and support their partners. They realize that hospital staff are usually extremely busy and working with more than one patient at a time. It is therefore impossible for other people to give the constant companionship and loving care which a woman craves as she is swept through the powerful physical and emotional experiences of labour; and the very unfamiliarity of the surroundings can make the most courageous woman apprehensive. She needs her partner or someone else who loves her. She needs someone who is there not simply as an onlooker but as a companion, who has studied what happens in childbirth, who knows what the antenatal preparation has been like, and who is able to help her in labour. (For more about the father's part in the birth, see pages 267–277.)

The man who fully involves himself in the birth shares in an experience which is exciting, challenging, intensely moving and deeply satisfying. It is not only a question of helping his partner have their baby but of an often surprising encounter with his own emotions and a discovery that he is swept into a peak experience which is bigger than anything he anticipated. There may be an astonishing, an incredible joy and wonder at having been close to the beating centre of life. In a very direct way, love is made flesh.

BEING SUPPORTIVE ABOUT ANTENATAL CARE
The antenatal clinic

Pregnancy can be a time of great emotional upheaval as a woman adapts psychologically to the extraordinary things happening inside her body. She has to go through all sorts of manipulations and physical examinations that are not always conducted in a warm, sympathetic way. It is clear that many women are made anxious by the kind of antenatal care they receive.

Some men find this difficult to understand. They say that they find the sophisticated technology which is used today reassuring and fascinating. But if the man imagines something happening inside his own testicles or penis, he may find it easier to comprehend. How would he feel if his testicles started to swell up and change shape dramatically, forcing him to visit hospital regularly and be prodded, poked and examined by strangers who seemed only concerned with the lower end of his body? He might find it impossible to get information about what was happening to him, knowing only that he faced an ordeal at the end of nine months when whatever was occurring must be terminated and the thing inside him somehow got out. How would he like lying flat on a high table, sometimes with his legs up high and wide apart in metal stirrups, while various women in white coats peered at him with little lights and probed his body with special machines? Out of the corner of his eye he could see them writing up case notes full of technical terms and abbreviations apparently suggesting a disease.

A man only has to go to the antenatal clinic once to get an idea of how intimidating it can be. In the rushed atmosphere of a busy clinic women often feel that they have become part of a factory process for producing babies. Questions about treatment or requests for advice go out of their heads, or else seem to interrupt the smooth running of the clinic and mean that other women waiting in the queue have still longer to wait. All too often a woman returns from a clinic session depressed and anxious. If her partner can get away from work to attend occasionally and to meet the doctor, he can give her moral support and, through good relations with the staff, help to pave the way for being there with her throughout labour.

Even if this is not possible, he can still help his partner by providing comfort and security if this is what she needs, and by talking to her about the things that ought to be discussed with the doctor. It is helpful to write questions down and keep a notebook for this purpose, as well as for any instructions given during pregnancy.

Childbirth education classes

When a woman starts attending classes in preparation for the birth there is usually an opportunity for her partner to share in some or all of the meetings. He can then learn a good deal about the physiological process and emotional changes of labour, can understand his own part in it, and often has the chance to see films of birth where women are using techniques similar to those learned in classes.

Everyday help

In the last three months a man can help his partner by seeing that she takes more rest and lies down for a nap every afternoon or evening. Sometimes extra labour-saving equipment, additional help in the house, or the use of services like a laundry, can ensure that she does not get worn out. She should not be carrying heavy shopping so he may take over supermarket duty, or come as well to load the boxes into the car. If there are jobs in the house which entail moving furniture, these are his now. And if the woman cannot get down to bath the toddler or strip the bed and make it afresh the man can take over these chores too while she does some of the easier tasks. On the other hand the woman does not need to be treated like an invalid, and the couple can enjoy going out together, especially at the end of pregnancy when time may seem to pass very slowly and she feels she has been pregnant for ever.

A man can also protect his partner from all the well-meaning advice, often very contradictory and confusing, that comes from other people both before and after the birth. He can support her in doing things the way they have both decided.

Practical help is important, especially in the last few months.

OPPOSITE

With a new baby on the way, a father helps by becoming more involved in the older child's daily routine.

150

Your changing relationship

Pregnant women are not only antenatal patients or even just future "mums". They are also usually in a loving relationship with a man. Pregnancy can be a time of great opportunity for both partners in the relationship to discover things about themselves and each other. However two people feel about each other, the emotional changes of pregnancy are bound to affect them. If they do not communicate easily it can be a time when small irritants turn into major crises.

The couple under stress

There are some couples who find the transition period of pregnancy an especially stressful time. It can put stress on the couple who have an informal, even casual, relationship and who have not attached particular importance to getting married, but who perhaps marry when a baby is on the way. It can put equal stress on a couple who both enjoyed their careers and never saw themselves as parents, but who nonetheless decide to continue with the pregnancy when the woman conceives by mistake. It can bristle with challenges, too, when a woman has been on the Pill, stops taking it because the couple think it might be a good idea to have a baby, and then immediately becomes pregnant before she has had time to switch her mind to the possibility of motherhood. In these situations rapid adjustment is necessary, and either or both parents may feel trapped, at the same time that they are feeling delighted.

As soon as they tell other people about the pregnancy they may feel that a social machine has swung into action. Some couples say that they felt strong disapproval from relatives, especially their parents, when they put off having a baby; then when the woman eventually did become pregnant they were overwhelmed by the relief and pleasure these people expressed, as if at last they were doing the socially acceptable thing. In some ways the reactions feel like a public intrusion on their intimate and personal relationship with each other.

Sharing the problems

When a pregnancy starts, a man and a woman often begin inhabiting different worlds. He may think that she becomes psychologically unpredictable and vulnerable. In her turn she may see him as unsympathetic, unloving and crude. He may feel he can no longer talk to her about "rational" matters, and that she has lost interest in everything except the coming baby. He may even feel pushed out into the cold, as if he were living with a different woman. Because they are often isolated from other couples facing similar difficulties, they may be under the impression that such problems are unique to them. Talking to other couples expecting babies can help them to see the social pressures on prospective parents and the cultural style of childbirth in modern Western societies which often creates emotional stress. Attending classes together can provide a bridge between the different socially assigned gender roles of a man and woman, and can help draw them closer.

Talking in a group

At one antenatal group couples discussed together the effect of pregnancy on their relationship. One woman, who was feeling that she had lost her individuality in the universal category of expectant motherhood, remarked that she was frightened of what this was doing to her relationship with her husband. Would they, she worried, become just "Mum and Dad" and cease being lovers? Her concern about this was even making her resent the baby at times.

In discussion the members of the group found that other couples too were experiencing these pressures and the same kinds of anxiety. Some of them felt strongly that they wanted to be different kinds of parents from their own parents and to have a happier marriage than their parents had. It was agreed that it was important for a couple to share these thoughts with each other and to discuss not just the practical arrangements for preparing for the baby, but their ideas about the kind of parents they hoped to be, and what they thought about their partners as prospective parents too.

Becoming a mother involves emotional "growing pains" which can be no less disturbing than those of adolescence. A similar psychological process often occurs in a man too, but he usually feels he has even less justification to talk about it because *he* is not pregnant. Yet to be able to nurture their young, both the man and the woman have to change and become different kinds of people.

Another couple, who had been through this process with an earlier pregnancy, said that talking about it had helped them understand each other better and that they came to like their changed roles. At first the parts of "Mummy" and "Daddy" were merely play-acting, but then they found they were good at them. The new roles made each see qualities they had never imagined the other possessed.

One of the things to emerge from that discussion was that becoming parents is not just a matter of physical changes but also of learning. The adjustment and adaptation take time, and pregnancy is the ideal time to start this process of growing up.

Developing confidence

Many couples have a funny name for the unborn child, and talk about it as if it were a friend whom they know well but have never met. When doctors prod and poke and the hospital takes the woman over at the antenatal clinic or when she goes into labour, the couple can feel as if a very personal and intimate relationship between the three of them has been invaded. "Our" baby has become "the" baby, or even "the hospital's" baby. A woman needs to feel that the baby really belongs to her. This may be important in pregnancy, and is vital after the birth, if she is to have a chance to fall in love with her baby.

Other couples have problems in family relationships (especially with their in-laws), which they imagine to be peculiarly their own and which they do not realize are shared by many others. Each partner may be resenting the other for his or her insensitivity and ineptitude at handling these situations, or for being over-dependent on parents. In a childbirth education class there is a chance to talk through these problems, to discuss the future grandparents' feelings and any other situations which are causing stress. The very fact of finding that they are not alone with such difficulties may help a couple.

Parents can start to get to know their baby even before it is born, and this knowledge may give added depth to their own relationship.

Growing through the experience

Many couples have their babies before they are really emotionally ready for them. As a result, some babies come into the world in spite of, rather than because of, what their parents feel about each other. When a woman decides to continue with an unplanned pregnancy, the accidental product of an impermanent relationship, she needs special emotional support. Even if a man has nothing else to offer a woman he can give her this. It is bound to be painful for them both if they decide to part with the baby, but the experience can be important for both of them and can help them to grow in understanding. In fact, when a couple are unhappy together, there is an even more compelling reason to use the time of pregnancy for joint preparation for the birth of their child, if only because the task can in itself bring a new perceptiveness and sensitivity to the other's needs.

So, in all circumstances, preparation for birth is not merely the acquisition by the woman of a set of instructions and exercises, but a process in which two people start out together on a shared enterprise. It provides opportunities for increased understanding of each other's needs and enrichment of their whole relationship. For both parents pregnancy can be a time of growing up. If a man and woman can understand what the pregnancy means to the other partner they are well on the way to growing up *together*.

The emotional changes of pregnancy exist for *all* couples expecting a baby, and it helps to realize that others share these experiences and find them challenging. Sharing brings relief from anxiety and a new understanding of the emotions involved.

SEX IN PREGNANCY

It is important for your sense of wellbeing that you are physically loved in pregnancy, whether or not this involves sexual intercourse. Stroking, massage, loving touch and sexual pleasuring are all part of this physical expression of the relationship.

Attitudes to sex

Many couples make love right through pregnancy. At the beginning nausea and vomiting can mean that the last thing you want to do is to make love, but usually by the middle months lovemaking is enjoyable and satisfying, sometimes for the first time. Pregnancy is a good time for you to learn more about how your body works. A woman who begins to learn about her uterus, vagina and pelvic-floor muscles may become sensitively responsive to this part of her body when she was not before. Some women have their first experience of orgasm during pregnancy. Many do not realize the function of the pelvic-floor muscles (see page 107) in active lovemaking and some have never looked at or explored the way in which the vagina, labia and clitoris are constructed.

But this is not just a matter of intellectual information and diagrams of the female genitals. Some women dislike and have a general and profound distrust of their bodies. For the first time in pregnancy they can learn to know and be comfortable with themselves. If you have never before allowed feelings to sweep through you, you may find that preparation for the intensely emotional experience of labour, with its storms and currents, and the extraordinarily powerful drama of delivery, unlocks a capacity for "letting go" which can apply to lovemaking also.

But some couples (especially in the later months) feel that they do not have the doctor's approval about lovemaking. You may have guilty feelings and be anxious that you are somehow harming your unborn baby. This is one of the subjects that expectant parents often talk about in childbirth education classes. Couples say that they often find sex a very difficult subject to discuss with their doctor.

=**❝**=
Sex? I can barely remember what that is!
=**❞**=

Positions for lovemaking

The conventional "missionary" position (with the man lying on top of the woman) is rarely comfortable, unless the man gets on all fours and puts no weight on the woman. It is worth experimenting with some other positions in which she is uppermost or in which entry is from the side or from behind (see page 156). No harm will come to the baby: the bag of waters cushions it and a seal is provided by the mucous plug, which is rather like a stopper in a bottle. Even when your abdomen is bumped hard the only effect on the baby is that it bobs like a cork in a tumbler of water.

Can orgasm start labour?

Although the female orgasm involves contractions of the uterus, it will not trigger off labour unless everything is ready to start anyway. But it is quite natural after intercourse to feel uterine contractions, which usually die down after a few minutes. The uterus is an active organ and contracts regularly from the time of a girl's first period right through to the menopause. It is especially active in pregnancy and the contractions (known as Braxton Hicks contractions) which you feel in the last months are rehearsals for the labour. If you have had a premature labour before, notice spotting of blood or if the mucous plug has already gone (the show—see page 228), it is wise not to have intercourse. Once the cervical mucus has been disturbed by contractions (and this *can* happen in the last four to five weeks), ascending infection is a possibility.

I love her luscious, pregnant curves!

Using sex to induce labour

If you are "due", especially if induction of labour has been suggested by your doctor, lovemaking is one of the ways in which you might be able to start things off naturally. Some women are thought to be especially sensitive to prostaglandins in the semen. (Prostaglandins cause the uterus to contract, and semen has a higher proportion of them than any other body substance.) It is best to choose a position—such as the woman lying on her back with her legs raised on the man's hips—in which semen is deposited right up against the cervix. But since such a position may be very uncomfortable at this late stage of pregnancy, it should be done gently.

Breast stimulation in late pregnancy also sometimes produces a strongly contracting uterus. This worries some people, but unless

Lovemaking in pregnancy

Whatever position you choose . . .

. . . your partner on top, but with his weight off your abdomen . . .

. . . you on top . . .

you have reason to think that the baby may come too early it is equally harmless, and may actually be a good thing, because the Braxton Hicks contractions which result (see page 229) help to prepare the way for labour, softening and drawing up the cervix, and—just before the baby is due—dilating it a little even before labour begins.

Nipple stimulation during labour

It has been discovered that stimulation of the nipples can reactivate a labour that has come to a halt. Some doctors have tried using it in place of the oxytocin drip (see page 298) to augment a slow labour. Unfortunately they have discovered that it does not always work. It may be that its success depends on how the stimulation is provided: perhaps someone you love may be more effective than simply using a breast pump. The midwife and doctor may agree to go out for a while and leave you to it. Though there may be a few raised eyebrows, it makes sense to try the natural way of stimulating the uterus first.

The emotions you have as lovers are not in conflict with the feelings of compassion and tenderness everyone agrees it is right to have about a baby. The sexual excitement felt by two people bound in love and caring for *each other* is a good basis for becoming parents able to give love to their baby and growing child.

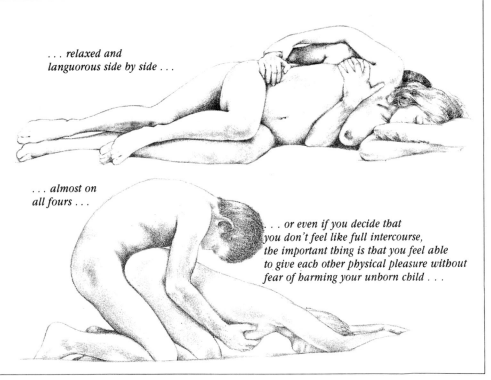

. . . relaxed and languorous side by side . . .

. . . almost on all fours . . .

. . . or even if you decide that you don't feel like full intercourse, the important thing is that you feel able to give each other physical pleasure without fear of harming your unborn child . . .

Pregnant again

Pregnancy the second or third time round is a new experience. It will not be exactly like the first time. It holds different challenges. Coping with them involves flexibility and resourcefulness on the part of both parents. In some ways things are much easier because you know what to expect and have probably developed self-confidence in your role as a childbearer. You may sail through the pregnancy with style and thoroughly enjoy it. But there may be difficulties which come as a surprise because you thought it would be simple this time.

Reactions to another pregnancy

Other people's reactions The first problem you may encounter is the reaction of other people to a new pregnancy. Whereas your first was greeted with delight, friends and relatives are usually far less interested in the next pregnancy and may even raise their eyebrows and criticize you if you already have three children or if you are pregnant again after a very short interval. They can make you feel that what you are doing is not very public-spirited and even socially harmful. Some women say they were asked "Do you want it?" or "Don't you think you've had enough?", others that sympathy was offered by well-meaning friends, "How ever will you manage?" Being prepared for this reaction will help you cope with it.

Your partner's reaction You may find that your partner is not so excited about the next pregnancy. He may be busy and preoccupied and even seem totally uninvolved. Many men feel an extra burden of responsibility and financial anxiety when a second or subsequent baby is on the way. One baby was fun but now he feels "trapped" into having to provide for a growing family for years to come. Some women are desperately disappointed at their partners' reactions to later pregnancies and feel that they are missing out on all the joy of the first baby and the companionship that drew them close together the first time round. Talk about your feelings together so that you can come to appreciate what the experience means to each of you.

Finding time to relax

When you already have a lively two- or three-year-old or a group of energetic youngsters to look after, pregnancy can be very tiring. The first time round you were able to look after yourself and luxuriate in afternoon rests, with time for thinking, planning and dreaming. Caught up in the hustle and bustle of family life, ferrying children to and from school, coping with the enormous meals they can consume and facing the everyday battle with egg on the stairs, tricycles in the hall, crumbs on the carpet and dishes in the sink, you may have to

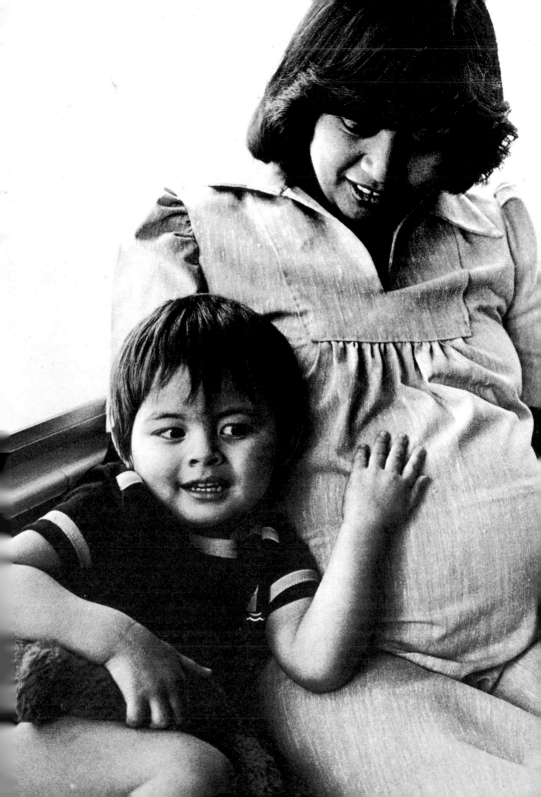

relegate pregnancy to the back of your mind. You simply do not have time for it. This may result in your neglecting yourself, your nutrition, your relaxation, and also missing out on times when you can just "centre down" and focus your thoughts on the baby and yourself.

When you realize this, in the short intervals between your commitments as wife, mother, nurse, psychotherapist, teacher, hostess, house cleaner, chief cook and bottle washer, the chances are that you will feel guilty. You begin to feel apologetic to the little baby growing inside you, and perhaps also fearful that you cannot give him or her the time or even the love that you have devoted to the others. This feeling may be intensified after the birth, when to some extent the new baby has to be fitted into family life rather than your own activities being modified to the baby's needs. If you are sitting a two-year-old on the lavatory, or calming down three children in the bath having a very splashy game which threatens to submerge the toddler, it is difficult at the same moment to fix the new baby comfortably on the breast and to enjoy the release of milk.

Talk about these feelings of inadequacy with other women who are facing the same problems. If you do feel guilty, the only solution is to try to organize your life so that every day you have at least some time to think about and plan for the coming baby, or, once the new baby has been born, to give him or her your whole concentration. It is certainly difficult to find even a short space of time for such attention; but you may be able to find someone who is willing to take your other children for a walk some afternoons or your partner might bathe them and put them to bed every evening, giving you a time when you will be able to concentrate on yourself and your new baby.

I feel I'm cheating this baby. There's not enough time to think about this pregnancy.

Taking care of yourself

A new pregnancy may produce aches and discomforts which you have not experienced before. Lifting bigger children and the inevit-able clearing and cleaning may contribute to backache associated with bad posture. This is accentuated by fatigue and doing things in a rush. If your child still wakes in the night, doesn't like the idea of an afternoon nap, *ever*, or wakes very early in the morning and, because he or she is still too young to read quietly, comes jumping into your bed and remains during the hours after dawn, a restless bundle, you may be running short of sleep and long for a solid uninterrupted 10 or 12 hours. Perhaps it is possible to arrange this when your partner is at home at the weekend.

The chances are that you look and feel more pregnant with this baby too, partly as a result of poor posture and tiredness, but also as a consequence of the stretching your uterus has had during previous pregnancies. This may mean that you don't feel at all happy about your body; such a lack of pleasure in yourself is then expressed automatically in the way you stand, walk and sit. It is a vicious circle.

Ask your childbirth educator to help you firm up your abdominal muscles. Use buttock and leg muscles to help support your spine and

Try to set aside a small part of every day when you can relax completely and focus your thoughts on yourself and the coming baby.

Preparing your first child

Borrow a friend's baby for a few hours so that your child can discover what babies are really like . . .

. . . let your child feel the baby moving inside you . . .

. . . make a book showing pictures of your first child when she was a baby so that she can see how babies change and grow . . .

. . . and let father take responsibility for some of your child's daily routine before the new baby arrives.

tummy and do a few rhythmic exercises each day (see pages 108–109). Your older child may enjoy doing them with you. Then make an opportunity to cherish yourself a bit. Ask your partner to give you a massage session. Think about what would cheer you up.

Preparing the older child

Some parents worry a great deal about how to prepare the older child for the new baby. This problem can seem almost insurmountable if the older one is clinging and still very dependent. Some American childbirth educators* have come up with the idea of making a book for the child, illustrated with photographs of himself and starting with a simple description of how a baby grows inside its mother, illustrated with line drawings and a photograph of the mother when she was pregnant. You could show preparations for the birth, and then your child as a newborn baby, being suckled or bathed. These pictures could be followed by a series of photographs of the older child showing him eating, drinking, playing, helping in the house and garden. Perhaps the last page of the book can be left blank for a photograph of the new baby. All this helps the older child to prepare for the new baby and to realize that he was once just as small and incapable as it will be.

If possible borrow a baby for a few hours or have a mother and her small baby in the house for half a day or so. This will help your child to understand the reality of a baby and also how a mother holds and cares for it. Many older children expect a new baby to be either a passive bundle that can be handled like a doll or a playmate who can join in their games immediately.

If you are moving the older child from a cot to a bed, do so several months before the birth, so that it does not seem a consequence of the baby's arrival. And, if you are going to have extra help after the birth, encourage the helper to become friends with the older child well before the advent of the new baby.

When another baby is on the way, the relationship between the father and the older child is of great importance. It is a time when the two can draw closer together and enjoy each other's company for longer periods, something that will help you a great deal after the birth when you are busy with the new baby.

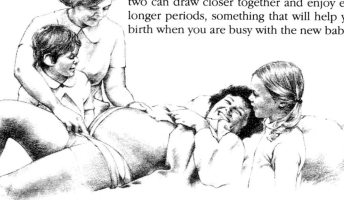

Towards the end of pregnancy take your older children with you to the antenatal clinic. Ask if they can listen with a stethoscope to the fetal heart, or help measure your tummy.

Anticipating the birth

In tune with your body for labour

Windows into the uterus

The last few weeks

In tune with your body for labour

Part of preparation for birth is doing exercises, but it is even more important to *think* about labour in a constructive way. Give yourself time to imagine what is going to happen in your body and what you may feel, and so build up a picture that has meaning for you. This picture will be quite different from illustrations in obstetric textbooks: it is vital that it relates to *feelings* and is not just built up of intellectual information. Only then can the subjective sensations you experience in labour fit into a pattern that makes sense to you and that can help you adjust to each challenge as it comes.

So during pregnancy take time to imagine the birth of your baby. Think of different kinds of labour (see page 257) and how you might cope with them. Avoid restricting your fantasies to only one kind of labour when it may turn out that the labour you have is very different.

Childbirth education

If you are having a baby without having had instruction in childbirth, your body will probably respond naturally. However, education for birth helps you to know more about your body and so feel happy with it during pregnancy. You learn how to prepare yourself so that when you are in labour you can work *with* your body instead of fighting it, so that you can understand the activity of the uterus, and so that, through relaxation, breathing and focused concentration, you can gradually come to achieve harmony with the birth process.

CHOOSING AN ANTENATAL CLASS

The discussions in class helped me to face all the possibilities in labour with a minimum of fear.

Once you have booked into an antenatal clinic (see page 46), it is time to think about arranging antenatal classes, so that you and your partner can learn about the physiological changes of pregnancy and labour and the possible emotional impact of the stresses likely to be involved. It pays to shop around for classes and discover the different ones available in your area. You would not dream of walking into any hairdresser's and asking them to cut and style your hair without first finding out what sort of work they did. Learning your task in childbirth is even more important, and so you should approach childbirth education classes with the same discrimination. For teaching to improve, more critical, informed consumers are needed. Any antenatal teacher worth her salt learns from her students, and continues to modify her teaching on the basis of the feedback she receives from them and the ideas they share with her.

Finding out about classes

When you enquire about classes, do not assume that they are successful only if those who have attended them have had easy labours and births. If you have to have a forceps delivery or a Caesarean section it does not mean that you have "failed" in applying what you have learned. Having a baby is not like passing an exam or winning a race. You are not expected to come out "top" with a two-hour labour, or no pain-relieving drugs or whatever. It is much more a question of learning how to adapt your responses—mainly those of breathing and relaxation—to the particular challenges of your own labour. So it can be useful to talk also to women who have had labours that were not straightforward, and to find out from them if attending classes helped them at all.

Even though women all the world over have babies in much the same way, birth can be a vastly different experience for different women; just as, even though sexual intercourse involves certain mechanical and physiological processes which are the same everywhere, what people feel about it, exactly what they do and the meaning the total experience has for them, varies with the individual and the occasion. Childbirth is not primarily a medical process, but a psychosexual experience. It is not surprising that adapting your responses to the stimuli it presents should involve a subtle and delicate working together of mind and body.

I didn't realize how scared I was till I went to classes and then it hit me. I'd been kidding myself. But after a few classes I started to feel a new confidence.

When asking about classes, ask a woman whether she found the techniques that she learned in class helpful when she was actually in labour, and whether she felt confident and as if she understood exactly what was going on. If she says "Nothing helped", implies that the classes did not relate in any way to the reality of labour, or says that she was absolutely terrified from beginning to end, it sounds as if the classes did not help her, even though she may have enjoyed getting to know the other expectant mothers.

Your local hospital may have classes, though frequently hospital and clinic classes concentrate on baby care rather than on education for birth. Find out how many of the classes deal with labour: you will need at least five or six sessions on what to do then. Your doctor may know of classes, and possibly your midwife or health visitor. If you write to the National Childbirth Trust (address on page 383), it will let you know where classes are held by its teachers. The NCT has a training and study scheme for its teachers, and in this way aims to continue improving the standards of childbirth education and keeping its teachers up to date.

What makes a good antenatal class?

Good classes are progressive in the sense that you learn a little more each time; you should not feel at the third or fourth lesson that you have sat through it all before. There should be opportunities for you to ask questions, discuss freely and practise the exercises rather than

simply listen to a formal lecture. Breathing and relaxation exercises which can be of practical use in labour should be included. Their relevance to labour should be specifically described, and why and how they are used. Relaxation is not as simple as it might sound. It is not just a question of flopping in front of the TV screen or of lying down with a bar of chocolate and a good book, but of learning complete awareness and control of muscle groups all over the body so that they can be contracted or relaxed at will, including muscles you may not even know you possess. Relaxation also means learning how to relax *under stress*, not just lying in a deck chair on a sunny day or in a classroom while a cool voice tells you that a contraction is beginning, continuing and then fading away.

It helps to learn different patterns and rhythms of breathing for the different phases of labour (see page 187). So when you are asking about classes enquire of any woman who has been to them whether she learned breathing in detail.

An effective teacher helps her students realize something of what labour feels like, and the reality and power of its challenge. She also explains things fully, without fear that she is burdening her students' minds, and does so honestly and clearly. In some classes there is far too much talking down to pregnant women. You have a right to understand what is happening to your own body and what people are proposing to do to you. A good teacher does not answer a query with "Oh you don't have to bother about that", or imply that everyone will do what is best for you and your baby, and that all you need to do is trust your birth attendants. Discussion should be a real exchange of ideas, not simply a few questions to which answers are given without recognition of the apprehension and the sometimes nightmarish fears that can lie behind them.

You can see from this that a good deal depends on the personality of the teacher. It is not so much "the method" that is good or inadequate as the quality of the teaching itself, and perhaps most of all the relationship that the teacher has with her students. I have seen teaching in different countries—including Western Europe, the USA and beyond the Iron Curtain—which seemed woefully inadequate or mechanized, or which involved learning a number of rather irrelevant physical exercises, and yet, because of the personality and attitude of the teacher, the women participated joyfully in their labours.

> ==66==
> *Now I've had the baby I do miss the classes! It was such fun meeting every week.*
> ==99==

The Dick-Read method

There are different approaches to childbirth education and the names associated with them can be confusing for expectant mothers. The Dick-Read method is named after Dr Grantly Dick-Read;* it is the oldest method and is usually associated with "relaxation classes". The philosophy behind this approach is that ignorance produces fear, which leads to tension, which in turn quickly produces pain. So teachers concentrate on overcoming fear by teaching deep relaxation and the breathing that accompanies it, along with providing full

OPPOSITE
Learning to relax for labour can benefit both of you and be enjoyable too.

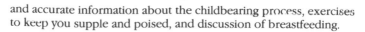

and accurate information about the childbearing process, exercises to keep you supple and poised, and discussion of breastfeeding.

Psychoprophylaxis

Psychoprophylaxis is a highly systematized training centered on techniques of breathing rather than relaxation. This method originated in the USSR, was developed in Paris, and then adapted in the United States by Elisabeth Bing. Psychoprophylaxis classes start by deconditioning the women from their fear and doubts about childbirth, and then recondition them to respond to labor contractions as helpful stimuli and not as pains. Exercises are taught both for limbering up and for use in labor. Full information is given about the anatomy and physiology of pregnancy and labor. This system is taught by the American Society for Psychoprophylaxis in Obstetrics teachers and is one of a range of approaches taught by International Childbirth Education Association teachers.

Here, women know psychoprophylaxis as "prepared childbirth" or by the name of its French originator, Lamaze, whereas in France itself it is often called *accouchement sans douleur* (labor without pain). This name is misleading and might make any woman having pain in labor feel that something is going wrong. For most women who have been to classes the pain of labor is not the most important thing about the experience and is a side effect with which many, helped by techniques of adjustment and by emotional support and guidance at the time, can cope well without pharmacological aids. Others want some additional pain relief, and should have it.

In North America and Britain, psychoprophylaxis methods have changed radically since they were first introduced. Dogma has disappeared, breathing is no longer regimented, and the whole approach has become more relaxed. Many teachers have learned skills in group dynamics and psychological counseling, and, from psychoprophylaxis, several people have evolved their own approaches to childbirth education.

The Bradley method

An American obstetrician, Robert Bradley, has created "husband-coached" childbirth, in which the man acts as the woman's teacher and supporter in pregnancy and labor, breathing is slow and full, obstetric intervention is kept to the minimum, and painrelieving drugs are not used. Many Bradley enthusiasts opt for home birth. The American Academy of Husband-Coached Childbirth can refer you to a Bradley instructor nearby (see page 383).

The autogenic method

On the European continent, a system of training based on Schulz's methods of relaxation and breathing is taught in many hospital classes. A woman learns to relax by conceptualizing warmth and weight in different parts of the body; breathing is slow and relaxed.

A typical delivery room

It is a good idea to have a look at a delivery room in the hospital where you are going to have your baby. Many hospitals arrange tours of labour wards and delivery rooms so that expectant mothers can see them well in advance of labour. Some of the equipment can seem rather daunting until it has been explained to you.

The clock is useful for recording the length of each stage of labour and for noting the time of the baby's birth. The second hand can be helpful for timing contractions.

The drip stand will hold the fluid if a doctor decides to set up an intravenous drip for the mother.

The delivery table is high and hard, with a firm rubber mattress. The lower end can be pushed in level with the mother's buttocks so that the doctor or midwife can easily receive the baby.

The lamp can swivel at different angles and is directed onto the mother's legs in the second stage of labour. The ceiling lights can be dimmed if the mother wishes.

Near the bed is a gas and oxygen machine for the mother to use is she needs to relieve any pain.

Behind the bed is the apparatus for measuring blood pressure. There is also oxygen should the mother need it.

The resuscitation trolley for the baby is equipped with oxygen and with suction apparatus to extract any mucus from the lungs.

Beside the bed is an electronic fetal monitor, which can be used to record the baby's heartbeat throughout labour.

The crib trolley is waiting for the baby. There is often an electric blanket in it.

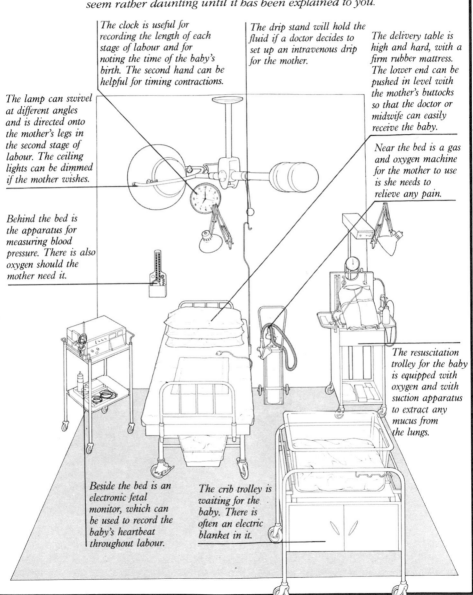

Active birth

Janet Balaskas has developed a method of preparing for birth based on hatha yoga, with the focus on moving around and changing position throughout labour, and giving birth squatting, kneeling or on all fours. To be able to do this freely and with comfort, "stretching" exercises are important beforehand, and a woman learns how to adopt "open" positions with help from her partner.*

Methods of preparation for active birth are now often incorporated into other classes, and Janet Balaskas's great achievement is that in many hospitals all over the world she has succeeded in getting women down from the labour bed and delivery table onto the floor.

The Odent approach

Although a surgeon, Dr Michel Odent perceives that childbirth is very different from surgery. For him, the most important thing is to provide an environment that facilitates a spontaneous psychophysiological process in which the woman who is left undisturbed will feel as if "on another planet".

Instead of childbirth classes, Odent organized singing get-togethers in which new parents, pregnant women and their partners, midwives, doctors and little children all joined. He has rediscovered the use of water in birth, offering the woman a deep bath of warm water in which she can float in a peaceful, darkened room. For delivery, he favours the standing squat, with the woman supported from behind by her partner or a female helper.

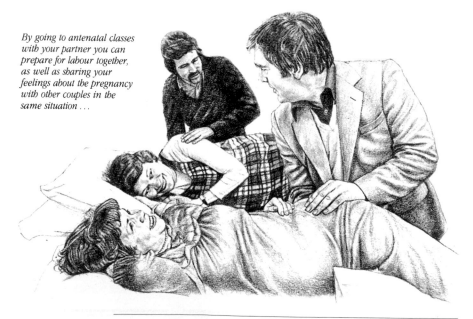

By going to antenatal classes with your partner you can prepare for labour together, as well as sharing your feelings about the pregnancy with other couples in the same situation ...

Michel Odent's ideas have been incorporated into many classes run by birth centres, by midwives amd by other childbirth educators.

The Kitzinger psychosexual approach

My own *psychosexual approach* originally grew out of both the Dick-Read and psychoprophylaxis systems and now incorporates many active birth positions and movements. It is based on the idea that the woman is an active birth-giver rather than a passive patient. It focuses on birth as experience rather than as a series of exercises in breathing and relaxation.

Psychology and social anthropology have contributed much to my own approach, and especially my observations of how women behave in and feel about labour in many different cultures. I have learned most from women themselves. Labour involves often barely glimpsed feelings about ourselves which have developed through the formative years of childhood: attitudes to and fantasies about our bodies, feelings about the relative size and positions of organs and orifices, and concepts of cleanliness and pollution, beauty and ugliness. All of these are partly social in origin, products of our upbringing and family relationships.

Labour is a social situation, not just a physiological or even a private emotional experience. Because it involves human relationships at a sometimes tense and demanding time, it helps to know how to talk with the different people assisting at the birth and how to understand what may be in the doctors' and midwives' minds. All antenatal teachers agree that students require plenty of information about how their bodies work and what goes on in hospitals. Most classes include a visit to the hospital and a tour of the delivery room (see page 169). But it is not just a question of knowing what will happen to you when you are giving birth, but of learning how to negotiate to get the kind of birth you want.

The aims of antenatal classes

So you will see that there is wide variation in exactly what is taught and how, although there is general agreement that six sessions of one and a half to two hours each are the minimum required. The aim is not to retreat from contractions but to adjust to them and respond actively. There is more and more emphasis on a woman being in the kind of setting and having the loving emotional support which enables her to be confident in her own powers and to behave spontaneously, without having to do "exercises" or wondering whether her performance is good enough. Classes for fathers should also be offered, so that they can learn how to help in pregnancy and labour and understand something about the feelings involved in becoming a father. Many teachers offer couples classes where the whole of preparation for birth is shared. If you are offered less than this in the classes you attend, you will probably feel the need to supplement them with other classes, reading, or extra private tuition.

When to start antenatal classes

Whatever method you finally opt for, do not leave booking for classes or reading up on the subject till the last moment. Start finding out what is available and begin your course of reading four or five months before the baby is due, even though classes may not be offered till the last nine weeks or so. Where teachers run classes only for those in the last two or three months of pregnancy there is often an opportunity to meet the teacher earlier. This is an excellent idea, although some teachers of psychoprophylaxis believe that students get bored if they start too soon. Even if you do not start to practise any breathing techniques till the last weeks, it can only be beneficial to learn good posture in early pregnancy, something about how the baby develops inside you and how to cope with any minor discomforts of pregnancy. It is also an advantage at any time, whether or not you are pregnant (and for men as well as women), to know how deep relaxation can help you get to sleep.

Whatever approach you select, provided you are happy with your teacher and develop confidence in yourself through the instruction, the teaching will be right for you, and you will find that you have a variety of suitable tools with which to adapt to contractions in labour. Labour need not be an ordeal to be feared, but a positive, rewarding experience, and a really *happy birthday.*

RELAXATION AND MASSAGE

Relaxation is the art of letting go and allowing peace to flow through you. The skill is in being able to release your muscles at will and not only when you are in a special mood to relax. It is not just an exercise, but as necessary a partner to—and interlude in—strenuous activity as the breath out to the breath in.

The importance of relaxation

I hadn't realized that I clenched my jaw when I tensed up around my eyes or how often I curled my toes when I concentrated. I am much more aware now of how I react when under stress.

Relaxation is vital for labour. If you cannot relax you are likely to become exhausted as a result of tightening up muscles all over your body in reaction to the challenging stress of contractions. By tensing muscles unnecessarily you are wasting energy, and if you are exhausted any pain experienced will be felt more keenly and your ability to control it is bound to be diminished.

Generalized tension and anxiety can sometimes affect the way the uterus contracts, producing incoordinate uterine action, which means that the contractions are painful but are not very effective in pulling open the cervix. Because it alters your whole body chemistry, marked tension lasting a long time can also reduce the oxygen supply to the baby. Just as the smooth co-ordination of the digestive system, the beating of your heart and your breathing are all affected by acute tension, so stress and anxiety can slow down the unfolding process of childbirth and make it more difficult.

When you know how to relax you can adjust to your labour with special ways of breathing, positions and other techniques. Relaxation helps keep your mind clear so that you are able to understand what is happening and can respond to it purposefully and creatively.

Centring down

To explore the skills of relaxation, you need to be able to "centre down", to use an old Quaker term, and be still and enjoy peace of body and mind.

Lie on your back, well propped up with plenty of pillows, or sit in a comfortable chair with cushions supporting all of your back, including the back of your neck. You may also like a cushion under each arm or under your thighs. If you prefer, lie on your side, back rounded, head and shoulders forward, legs and arms bent. Before starting any exercises spend time thinking of the journey the baby makes to be born. Read page 246 and then focus your thoughts on that part of your body. Feel muscles and flesh heavy and released.

Touch relaxation

With touch relaxation, a partner gives you a message of touch to say, in effect, "release here". You respond to the pressure and warmth of the hands with immediate relaxation. If you learn to respond to your partner's touch in this way during pregnancy, it will be a spontaneous reaction when you are in labour. In effect, your partner will be able to draw the tension out of you.

To practise the technique, you contract different sets of muscles one set at a time. Your partner then rests his or her hands over the area that feels tight, and as soon as you feel the touch, you release, as if you are flowing towards it. Sometimes it helps if the touch develops into a gentle massage over the part of the body that is tense. This massage should be very slow; a partner who is worried or excited may massage in fast, jerky movements and this has the effect of communicating tension rather than relieving it. Whenever massage is done against bare skin, it is a good idea to use a little talcum powder or warm oil, so that the hands glide smoothly and you do not feel itchy.

Between each exercise it is important to discuss whether it feels right for you—whether you want the touch firmer, lighter, or in a slightly different place. During labour, too, you can talk together

=**66**=

We are enjoying it a lot. We do it each night when we go to bed and to tell you the truth we like the massage and everything so much that we don't always get round to finishing the exercises!

=**99**=

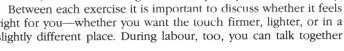

Settle into a truly comfortable position for a while each day; make sure that there are no distractions to prevent you concentrating on your baby's presence inside you ...

between contractions so that your helper understands exactly what you want. Some examples of touch relaxation for different parts of the body are given on pages 178–186.

In childbirth, touch can be enormously comforting. It helps you release all the muscles you do not need to use in order to have the baby. It relieves psychological stress, too, because you are able to feel secure and nurtured.

On the other hand, some women find that the experience of giving birth is so total, so overwhelming, that touch would be superfluous. While touch relaxation can be an important part of preparing for the birth, when you are in actual labour you may come to a phase when you do not want to be touched at all. If so, simply tell your partner this. It is vital that you have the kind of support *you* want and that your partner is willing to stand back and let you do things your way.

Release of tension By practising relaxation with you like this, your partner becomes aware of any tensions in your body, and when you are in labour will be able to notice if there is a build-up of tension long before anyone who does not know you well realizes what is happening. All that is needed is to reach out a hand with the message: relax! If your shoulders are getting tense, for example, a firm hand is rested on your shoulder. If your legs are tense, loving hands stroke your legs firmly.

One great advantage of this is that it does not involve giving directions and "coaching" in labour. There may be times—especially at the very end of the first stage—when positive guidance is invaluable, but there is no place at all for bullying a woman in childbirth. Through learning touch relaxation, your partner will have the self-assurance to give you just the kind of help you need.

Responding to the doctor or midwife Experiencing touch relaxation together also means that you are preparing yourself to respond to the touch you receive when the doctor or midwife examines you. Instead of feeling threatened, tensing up and pulling away from their touch like a snail drawing in its horns, you will be able to relax. This makes having your tummy palpated and pelvic examination much easier and more comfortable.

Pressure from the uterus During childbirth the stimulus coming from the uterus is remarkably like a strong, intense kind of touch radiating from inside. As the uterus contracts it squeezes tightly. A powerful pressure builds up and there is a sensation of heat. When the cervix is being opened and pulled wider, still more pressure is exerted. Then, as the baby moves down through the cervix, pressure is produced by the ball of its head. It feels as if a grapefruit were being pressed down first against the anus and then through the vagina. To all these stimuli a woman may respond either by tightening up, or by releasing her muscles.

Learning to flow with a contraction Now imagine that you are in labour and that the pressure of the uterus is building up with each contraction. Visualize the pressure of the baby's head, too, then release and flow towards these sensations. Some women feel each contraction as warmth building up to heat and then dying down again. One woman told me that every contraction was like an oven door swinging wide open; at its peak she received the full blast of the heat and then the oven door closed again.

When the baby's head is on your perineum and coming through the vagina, all the tissues are fanned out like the petals of a flower. As they open you may feel a warm, tingling sensation, as if the whole area is flooded with heat. If you have learned always to relax in response to the pressure and warmth from your partner's hands, you will be able to respond to these messages from *inside* your body too, not by pulling back, but by releasing and *flowing towards* them. In this way the sensations you get from within your body can guide you in labour.

Puppet-strings relaxation

Of course you do not always have someone to help you with relaxation. You can practise relaxation by yourself, using a method that I call the puppet-on-a-string method.

Lie in whatever position you usually sleep. Make yourself really comfortable, well supported by pillows, and give a long, sighing breath out and relax. Imagine that strings are attached to all your joints. Think of one fixed to your elbow, being tightened gradually so that your elbow is pulled up with the string. Depending on the position in which you are lying, your elbow may be moved a lot or a little. Then let it go. Notice the different feelings. Now the angle of the string is different, so feel the pull in a different direction. It lifts your elbow higher and higher. Now the string is released. It may take a little practice, but try not to allow any parts other than those operated by the string to move. The hand hangs limp at the wrist. The shoulder is not lifted. Only the elbow is activated.

Now do the same thing with an imaginary string attached to the other elbow. Let it be pulled in various directions. Continue as if a string were fixed to one big toe, then the other one, the back of one ankle, then the other, the left knee, the right knee, the left wrist, the right wrist, the index finger, the middle joint of a finger, one shoulder, the other shoulder, your left hip, your right hip.

Then imagine two strings, attached to your right elbow and right wrist, for example, tightening one after the other till both are drawn taut; first the wrist string is released, then the elbow string. Experiment with the strings working in a different order. Keep your mind focused on the tightening string rather than on the muscle you are contracting. Only when the invisible string is taut should you turn your mind to analyzing which muscles are tightened.

Imagine one string fixed to the top of your head, another to the base of your skull. First one is pulled, then the other. One goes slack, then the other. You will find that you can make the strings pull in different directions and at varying angles. This saves it from becoming a repetitive exercise that you do just from habit, without focusing on what your body is doing. It is important that any body movements you do bring awareness, an increased sense of working *with* your body. Mechanical exercises have no place in learning to relax.

Stanislavsky relaxation

There are acting techniques for increasing body awareness and learning which muscles contract and work together. The precise combination of muscles working together varies with each individual and the nature of the task, the angle at which you tackle it, the weight, dimensions and even the texture of the tools used. You will find that tasks you perform, even ordinary, everyday tasks, often cause you to change your breathing, and sometimes you hold your breath altogether. You may discover too that you tense up muscles that you do not need to use because you tackle a job in the wrong way or over-work at it, or because you are emotionally keyed up about what you are doing. All this is a valuable process of self-discovery and you can gradually learn more and more about yourself.

The method of relaxation based on Stanislavsky acting techniques explores different sets of muscles in the body that naturally function together and the way they work in response to different imagined activities and tasks and even thoughts and feelings. You think of certain situations—things you might be doing with your body—and mentally involve yourself in these situations as if you were actually performing them. Notice which muscles have become tense. Once the observation is made, switch off the picture in your mind and deliberately release those muscles.

Start by sitting or lying against a firm support and let the pillows take your whole weight. Listen to the sound of your own breathing. Breathe so that you can just hear yourself—in through your nose, and out through your mouth. Allow the breathing to flow through your mouth, letting the breath out be long and slow. The sound is like a little sigh as you breathe out. You may notice that there is a slight pause after you breathe in as if you have reached the crest of a wave. Enjoy that slight pause. Then give a long breath out. And with each breath out, relax a little more.

Suggested exercises for Stanislavsky relaxation

The jaw Imagine that you have some very sticky toffee in your mouth, and chew it well. It is sticking to your teeth. Work this great hunk of toffee out of your teeth. Notice what is happening. Then rest and drop your jaw. Let it relax, quite soft and loose. Notice the different feeling of complete release of the jaw muscles.

The eyes We do not usually notice when our eye muscles become tense. Imagine that there is a fireman climbing a ladder to rescue a little dog stranded at the top of a house. Focus on the fireman as he climbs all the way up. Observe the feeling in the muscles behind and around your eyes. Follow him with your eyes—up and up—until he is at the top. He has the little dog under his arm and is bringing it down and down. Now he is at the bottom. Relax your eyes, and if you want to, let them close. Notice how different they feel.

The feet Imagine that you are at the seaside standing on a very pebbly beach with no shoes on. Making very slight movements, imagine that you are walking on the beach with the sharp pebbles underfoot, and really feel them under your bare feet. Pick your way carefully over them. Oh! That was a sharp one! Observe the tension in your feet. Now go on to the soft sand. Really feel the difference. Then imagine that you lie down and let your feet relax completely.

The hands Can you recollect the feeling of making a snowball? Imagine that you are picking up snow and are patting the hard cold mass into a firm snowball. You are hurrying so that you can throw it at someone. As you quickly make your snowball, notice the tension in your hands. Then drop them and let them relax beside your body on the bed or floor again and notice how warm, soft and loose they feel.

Taste Imagine that you are sipping some water. Place the glass to your lips. It is sharp, neat lemon juice! Really taste it. Notice what is happening in your mouth and the tension that is spontaneously produced. Now it is gone. Let the muscles of the mouth soften.

Now you have a large, ripe peach. Take a good bite of it. It is very juicy and the juice is dribbling down. You need to suck it and draw in the juice. Smell it, too. Chew it, swallow it. Now it has gone. Notice the very different feeling in your mouth. Relax completely and think through what happened to the muscle inside your mouth and nose and the other facial muscles as you imagined you ate the peach.

Smell Muscles around the nostrils, in the cheeks and the mouth work together as we smell and taste things. Imagine that you have in your hand a bottle of liquid. Take out the stopper and take a good sniff—it is ammonia! Notice how you have become stiff down the back of your neck. Then relax. Breathe fresh, pure, clean air. Let yourself breathe easily.

Here is another bottle. Do the same with this one. It is scent this time: lily of the valley. You will find yourself drawing in the perfume of lily of the valley in long, slow breaths, holding the fragrance as if it were suffused behind the surface of your face. Now the fragrance has gone and you are just breathing air. Relax.

Go on from this to re-create in your imagination actions that you usually perform without thinking, simple things like writing a shopping list, tying shoe laces or unlocking a door, and discover exactly how you use your body.

Stanislavsky relaxation gives you a greater awareness of how your body works.

Touch relaxation

Tension makes childbirth unnecessarily painful. Learn how to relax to your partner's touch, so that this will be a spontaneous reaction in labour. To practise touch relaxation, first sit on the floor, well propped with cushions, and with legs and arms bent and spread a little. Give a long breath out through a soft, relaxed mouth. Now you are going to contract different sets of muscles— especially those you tend to tighten under stress—noticing how you feel when they are tight. Your partner will watch carefully, and then will rest one or both hands over the area you have tightened. As soon as you feel the touch you should relax and allow yourself to feel as if you were flowing out towards the touch.

The abdomen

Pull the muscles of your abdomen towards your spine. You will find that you have also tightened muscles at the bottom of your back and that your breathing is affected, too. Now your partner rests both hands gently over the lower curve of your tummy. Relax as soon as you feel the warmth and pressure of the hands. Then they can be slowly lifted away.

This touch can be comforting during contractions in the first stage of labour.

Light massage just above your pubic bone, where the pull of the dilating cervix often feels painful, usually helps too. The massage should be very light, as if stroking the baby's head. And it must be slow.

Sitting or kneeling at your side, your partner can massage with both hands in a continuous, flowing movement, one hand following on the other, and stroking slowly and evenly from the groin in a half circle down and over the other groin.

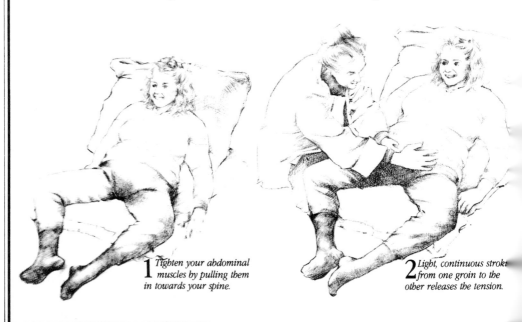

1 *Tighten your abdominal muscles by pulling them in towards your spine.*

2 *Light, continuous stroke from one groin to the other releases the tension.*

The shoulders

Most people tighten their shoulders when under stress. Tight shoulders result in strained breathing and, because the tension usually involves the back of the neck too, can cause a headache. In labour, tension in the shoulders very soon results in heavy, panicky breathing which, in turn, leads you to hyperventilate. A side-effect of this is a reduction in the amount of oxygen reaching the baby. If you know how to release your shoulders, you will not hyperventilate.

1 Tense your shoulders and throw them back against the cushions.

To feel exactly what happens with shoulder tension, press your shoulder blades back towards each other as if they were angel's wings and you could make them meet at the back. This is what a woman may do when she is finding it difficult to cope with big contractions in the first stage of labour. She tenses her shoulders and presses them and her head back into the pillows. Notice how you feel when you do this. Is it affecting your breathing?

Now your partner rests one hand firmly over each shoulder, applying pressure with the heels of the palms at the front of your shoulders. You release immediately, flowing out towards the touch. Then the hands are slowly removed.

It is astonishing how often, when tension is building up in labour, that firm pressure on a woman's shoulders, or only the shoulder on the side nearest her helper, enables her to release.

2 Firm pressure applied over one or both shoulders helps you release.

The face

If a woman in labour is concentrating hard, or feels anxious about what her body is doing, the muscles around her eyes become tense and her brow furrows. Her jaw stiffens, her mouth gets tight, and it becomes difficult to release the vagina and perineum.

Frown as if you had a headache and were in a very bright light. Notice how you feel when you screw up your eyes and forehead. Using two fingers on each side of your head, your partner presses on the bone of the temples. Release as soon as you feel this touch. Then *very gradually* your partner reduces the pressure, as you visualize any residual tension flowing out and away.

The head

This exercise helps you to release the muscles of the scalp, which we often forget because they are under our hair. Shoot your eyebrows up towards the top of your head until your whole scalp feels tight. Your partner forms his or her hands into a cap, which is then rested against the top of your head. As soon as you feel the pressure, release. Let your eyes close slowly.

As your partner becomes aware of your tension easing, he or she slowly reduces the pressure. As this happens you can visualize any residual tension flowing up and out of your head. It is as if the hands are drawing out the tension from deep inside your head.

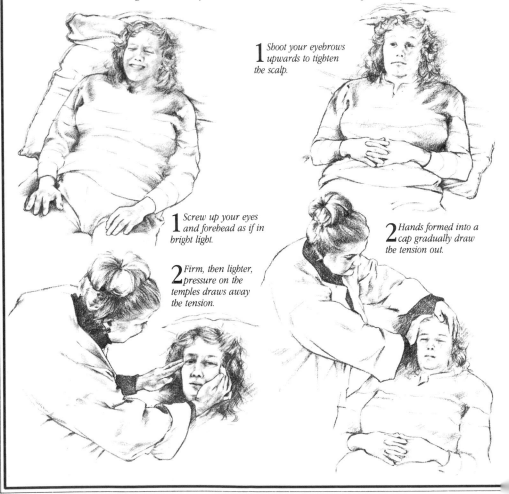

1 *Shoot your eyebrows upwards to tighten the scalp.*

1 *Screw up your eyes and forehead as if in bright light.*

2 *Hands formed into a cap gradually draw the tension out.*

2 *Firm, then lighter, pressure on the temples draws away the tension.*

The arms

Tighten the arm nearest your partner. Notice how it feels. Your partner watches carefully, then places one hand firmly on the front of your shoulder, with the other over the inside of your upper arm, cradled around the big muscle there, the biceps. The hands are as if moulded to your body. As soon as you feel the warmth and pressure of the touch, relax.

Then the hand on the inside arm moves slowly and firmly, stroking right down to your wrist. The other hand stays firm and sure on your shoulder. As the hand moves, focus on the feeling of any residual tension flowing down your arm, out and away.

Movements like this, from the centre of the body towards the periphery, are helpful because tension always flows from the centre, out and away. This slow, firm stroking down the inside arm can feel very good in labour. Try it at the start of each contraction.

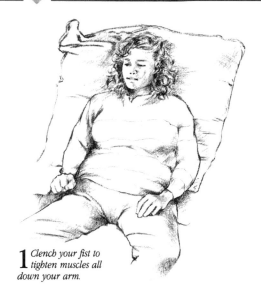

1 *Clench your fist to tighten muscles all down your arm.*

2 *The touch of hands on your shoulder and biceps eases the stiffness.*

3 *Slow, firm strokes down the length of the arm help you relax completely.*

The legs

Press your knees very firmly together. Notice how it feels. Your partner rests one hand on the outside of each leg, and you relax, letting your knees roll outwards. The muscles released are those of your inside thighs—the adductors. When a woman feels her baby pressing down to be born she often tightens these muscles unknowingly. A vital part of opening up to let the baby be born is complete release of the adductors.

Easing cramp Sometimes in labour the inner thigh muscles get so tight that the woman's leg becomes stiff and her foot drawn up, with the result that she gets painful cramp.

Stretch one leg out straight, so it feels stiff and taut, then flex your foot. To release the muscles, your partner places one hand on the *inside* of your thigh, moulding the hand to the leg, then strokes slowly and firmly down to your ankle. You release to the warmth of the touch.

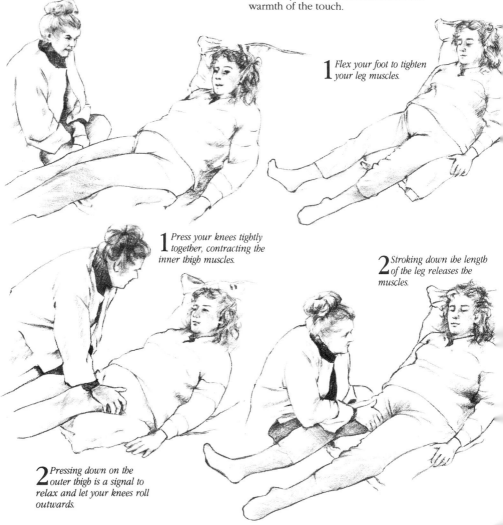

1 *Flex your foot to tighten your leg muscles.*

1 *Press your knees tightly together, contracting the inner thigh muscles.*

2 *Stroking down the length of the leg releases the muscles.*

2 *Pressing down on the outer thigh is a signal to relax and let your knees roll outwards.*

Releasing tension Now see what happens when you press your knees out. Feel the tension as you do so. Then your partner rests both hands on the inside of your upper thighs, and you relax to the touch. With hands shaped to your inside thighs, your partner strokes slowly from the top of your legs down to your knees.

This massage is particularly useful as you reach the end of the first stage of labour, when contractions are coming about two minutes apart, and last a minute or more. At this time a woman often feels that her legs are cold. She may begin to shiver and shake, until her whole body is trembling.

1 *Press your knees out and feel the tension in the outer thighs and the stretch in the inner thigh.*

2 *Hands resting on the inner thighs, with fingers down, ease the tension.*

3 *The hands slide firmly down the inside leg to the knees.*

If this is your experience, you will find that massage of the inner thigh muscles warms your legs so that you feel they belong to you again and you can consciously release them. Your partner should use a very firm stroke as the hands slide down the inside of your thighs, and a gentle stroke coming up over the outside of the legs in a continuous flowing movement, helping tension flow out from the centre of the body, down and away. It is as if the hands are giving the message: "Open up, open up, the baby's coming out."

Releasing the pelvic-floor muscles This type of massage also reminds you to release your pelvic-floor muscles so that you can help the baby's head bulge forward in your vagina. Each downward movement of the hands has the effect of releasing the muscles through which the baby is coming to birth. To focus on this feeling, first contract your pelvic-floor muscles as if they were a lift going up to the first, second and then the third floor of a building. Pull them up and hold them. Then your partner rests both hands on your inside thighs, and you release the pelvic-floor muscles down towards them, as if the lift were going down to the basement. As the hands slide towards your knees, release still more, bulging your perineum forward.

The shoulders

For the next set of exercises, lie on your side, making yourself comfortable with pillows. Your back should be rounded, your head and shoulders well forward, and your underneath arm behind your back.

If a woman is lying on her side during childbirth and she becomes tense, she often adopts a fetal position. She curls up into a ball as if she were hugging pain to herself. Notice how you feel when you do this. Your shoulders will have tightened up so that they are near your ears. Your breathing will probably be affected too. Now your partner rests his or her fingers on your shoulders and applies firm pressure with the palms. You release, flowing out towards the touch.

Having your shoulders held in this way can be helpful if you tend to over-breathe during contractions. A thumb massage over your upper back and shoulders, or at either side of the spine, may also help.

The small of the back

Many women experience backache in labour, usually around the sacrum—the bone in the small of your back where the pelvis joins the spine. To find out exactly where this is, ask your partner to place his or her fingers over the large bones at the side of the pelvic cradle and then trace them round until the pelvis dips down at the back to meet your spine.

Imagine that you have a bad pain just there. Pull in the small of your back. You will find that you are sticking your bottom out and throwing your shoulders back. This is the typical picture of a woman with back pain in labour.

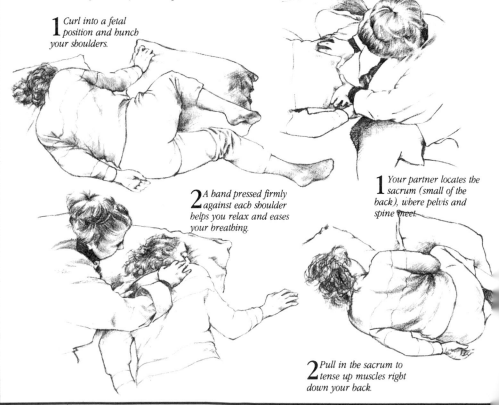

1 *Curl into a fetal position and hunch your shoulders.*

2 *A hand pressed firmly against each shoulder helps you relax and eases your breathing.*

1 *Your partner locates the sacrum (small of the back), where pelvis and spine meet.*

2 *Pull in the sacrum to tense up muscles right down your back.*

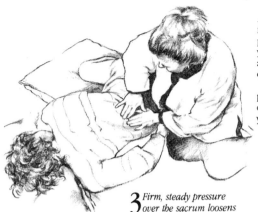

Applying pressure The tension that results from backache means that you suffer *more* pain from your own stiff muscles. To help you release, your partner now presses firmly and steadily over the sacrum, using the heel of the palm (not the fingers).

As soon as you feel the warmth and pressure, you relax, letting go and flowing out towards the hands. Muscles right down your back immediately soften and loosen.

3 *Firm, steady pressure over the sacrum loosens the muscles.*

4 *Deep massage around the sacrum may bring relief.*

Deep massage In childbirth, firm counter-pressure like this may feel good, or you may prefer to be massaged. Massage is usually best done by moving the flesh—both skin and muscle—on the bone, rather than by merely creating friction. Your partner can use either a firm, circular motion with hands more or less stationary, or slide the hands across the top of one buttock to the top of the other and back again.

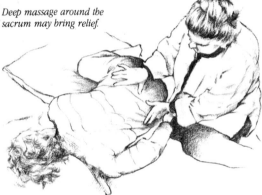

5 *Sliding one or both hands firmly across the top of the buttocks helps you to relax.*

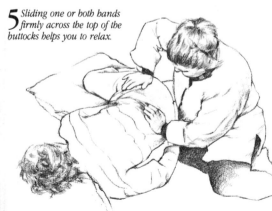

Helpers and backache When a woman has backache in labour she may experience it for hours on end. The baby's head is pressing back against the sacrum and has to slide past it down into the birth canal. Helpers using counter-pressure or doing back massage often develop backache too, because they are relying on muscle strength in the arms rather than allowing their own body weight to flow down *through* the arms. Your helper may want to rest one hand on your hip, but should be careful not to exert pressure there, or lean on you, since that will cause you discomfort.

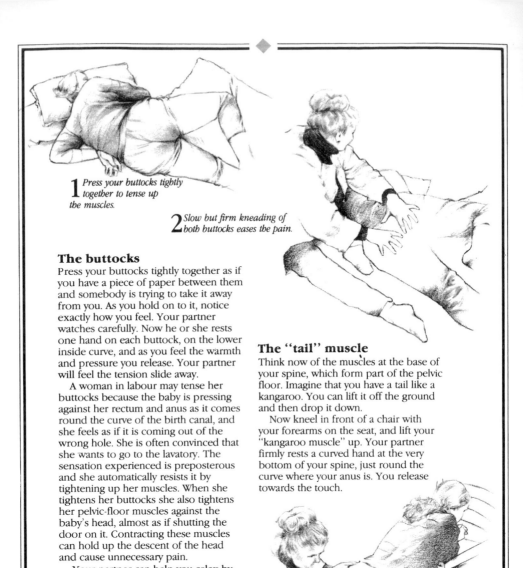

1 *Press your buttocks tightly together to tense up the muscles.*

2 *Slow but firm kneading of both buttocks eases the pain.*

The buttocks

Press your buttocks tightly together as if you have a piece of paper between them and somebody is trying to take it away from you. As you hold on to it, notice exactly how you feel. Your partner watches carefully. Now he or she rests one hand on each buttock, on the lower inside curve, and as you feel the warmth and pressure you release. Your partner will feel the tension slide away.

A woman in labour may tense her buttocks because the baby is pressing against her rectum and anus as it comes round the curve of the birth canal, and she feels as if it is coming out of the wrong hole. She is often convinced that she wants to go to the lavatory. The sensation experienced is preposterous and she automatically resists it by tightening up her muscles. When she tightens her buttocks she also tightens her pelvic-floor muscles against the baby's head, almost as if shutting the door on it. Contracting these muscles can hold up the descent of the head and cause unnecessary pain.

Your partner can help you relax by firmly massaging your buttocks as if working bread dough. It is important to get down into the fat and muscle, very slowly kneading both buttocks at once. As soon as you feel the firm, reassuring touch, you relax.

The "tail" muscle

Think now of the muscles at the base of your spine, which form part of the pelvic floor. Imagine that you have a tail like a kangaroo. You can lift it off the ground and then drop it down.

Now kneel in front of a chair with your forearms on the seat, and lift your "kangaroo muscle" up. Your partner firmly rests a curved hand at the very bottom of your spine, just round the curve where your anus is. You release towards the touch.

1 *Firm pressure, or rhythmic "rocking" massage, at the very base of the spine relaxes the "tail" muscle.*

BREATHING FOR LABOUR

Relaxation and breathing are so closely associated that it is important to explore them as part of a unity. You cannot really breathe correctly for labour unless your body is relaxed. As labour progresses you will spontaneously breathe more rapidly. If you breathe more quickly and at the same time heavily, you are bound to hyperventilate and flush carbon dioxide out of your bloodstream. This can make you feel very uncomfortable and, if severe enough, you will even pass out. The more you hyperventilate, the more you are likely to under-breathe— or even not breathe at all—*between* contractions. This is especially so if you have also had pethidine to relieve the pain. Though your body can cope with this, your baby needs you to go on breathing. Over-breathing, "forgetting" to breathe, and holding your breath are all harmful to your baby during childbirth.

In many cultures breathing in labour is deliberately regulated to help a woman work with the forces bringing her baby to birth. Among the Zulu, for example, breathing exercises are taught in pregnancy. A woman is supposed to go to the door of her hut each morning as the sun rises and take careful, controlled, full breaths through each nostril alternately.* She uses the same breathing in labour. In other cultures breathing is regulated by background sounds, including prayers, music, the beating of hands or repeated phrases of encouragement, or by the swaying movement of attendants holding the mother.

Breathing for relaxation

Smooth, easy breathing rhythms can also help release tension and create a state of pleasurable relaxation. In labour this is particularly important because, since contractions come like the waves of the sea, there is a strong natural rhythm built in to the physiological activity. A woman can either resist this, trying to "switch off", escape from or dominate it, or she can go with it and adjust her breathing to the compelling sweep of uterine power. She can only go with the rhythm if she can accept what is happening in her body and assent to it.

So the breathing taught for labour is nothing to do with "distraction techniques" and is certainly no magic method of eradicating sensation or guaranteeing that you do not feel pain. It is another way of getting in tune with your body and especially with your uterus.

Rest your hands over the lower curve of your abdomen. In late pregnancy you have a lovely melon shape there. Breathe as slowly as you comfortably can. As the breath enters your nostrils, allow them to dilate, notice the slight pause between the breath in and the breath out, and then breathe out through a soft, relaxed mouth as if you had on a new, glossy and rather expensive lipstick. Enjoy that breath out. Notice what is happening to your abdomen. Feel it rising under your hands as you breathe in—a gentle swelling, like a wave building up. Then as you breathe out, the abdomen sinks back again and the wave

Practising smooth, easy breathing helps you to relax and get in tune with your body for labour.

recedes. Be aware of the slight pressure under your hands as you breathe in, and feel the pressure withdrawing as you breathe out and the abdomen goes back to its former position.

Breathing down your back

You need someone to help you rehearse this. Try kneeling in front of a chair with your forearms and head resting on the seat and your knees well apart. Ask your helper to rest one hand firmly on each side of the base of your spine. Then breathe slowly right down your back, noticing the pressure against the hands as you inhale and how it gradually falls away as you exhale.

The greeting breath

When you are in labour, meet each contraction with your breathing, giving first of all a complete greeting breath. This is a deliberate, slow breath *out.* Imagine an early first-stage contraction lasting 45 to 60 seconds. Breathe slowly through the contraction, with the lower back spreading out and pressing slightly against the bed or floor as you breathe in, and the pressure being lifted as you breathe out.

The resting breath

As a contraction fades away, you give a long, slow, complete breath out through your mouth—a resting breath. This is important partly because it offers you complete relaxation at the end of a contraction so that you can rest and get refreshed before the next one, and partly because it signals to everyone in the room that a contraction is over. If the midwife or obstetrician wants to talk to you, or ask you to turn over, now is the time, between contractions—never during them.

In strong labour you may want to give several of these complete resting breaths once a contraction finishes. Do whatever feels good. If you always respond to the end of a powerful contraction by one or more resting breaths you can be sure that, however difficult contractions are, you are giving your baby oxygen by breathing fully.

Full-chest breathing

You need a partner to help you practise this. Lie on your side with your back rounded, head and shoulders curved foward, legs well apart and the upper leg drawn up and bent at the knee. Now lift your head as if stretching your spine all the way up the back so that you feel taller. Stretch your neck at the back, stretch all the way up your spine and then simply let it drop back into place; let your head settle comfortably on your shoulders. See that there is a good space between your legs. Then give a long breath out and relax completely. Allow your eyes to close if they feel heavy.

Think of your back. Your spine is not stiff like a lamp post. It is constructed with small vertebrae in a curving shape like a string of sausages. We often act as if our spinal columns were very stiff. Yet think of the way a cat moves and how movement ripples up and down

OPPOSITE

Preparing for labour need not be a solemn drill: you can make it a natural part of your daily life and involve your other child too.

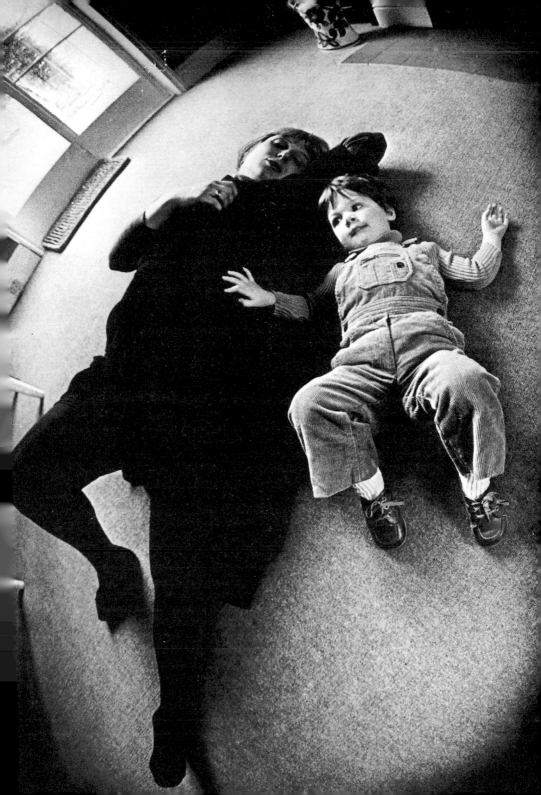

the back. Now your partner rests one hand on each shoulder and massages with the flat of both hands from the top of your back right down to the bottom. The hands should be relaxed. Say if you would like the massage to be heavier or lighter, slower or quicker. Is it in exactly the right place? It should feel good. Relax towards the hands.

Then your partner rests the palms of both hands firmly above your waist on either side of the spine over the ribcage. They should be in a position that is comfortable for you and should not be pressing in on your waist (or where it once was!). Notice their warmth and strength. Breathe in through the nose and out through the mouth again so that the main level of breathing awareness is just where you feel the pressure and warmth of the hands, and listen to your breathing. Breathe down to where you feel the hands, expanding your ribcage, so that it is swelling out under the hands as you breathe in, and then it falls away from the pressure of the hands as you breathe out. Listen to it for a moment. Can your partner feel the pressure, building up as you breathe in and falling away as you breathe out? This is full-chest breathing. It can be very useful, once labour starts, to meet the earliest contractions of the first stage of labour. You may be able to breathe like this all the way through your early contractions, concentrating on breathing into the area against which your partner is pressing the hands. When you are actually in labour you will not need the hands there because you will do it automatically and the contracting uterus itself will provide sufficient stimulus.

Upper-chest breathing

As contractions strengthen, you may want to lift your breathing above them, as if over the crest of a wave. Contractions come like waves and you will find that you can cope with them more easily if you breathe more lightly and more quickly. At this phase of labour they may be coming every four or five minutes and lasting about a minute.

To practise breathing with these contractions, your partner should rest the palms of both hands on your upper back just below your shoulder blades. You breathe so that your main level of breathing activity and awareness is where you feel the pressure of the hands. You may find that you want to breathe more rapidly, perhaps through parted lips. You should be able to hear a crisp little sigh or "huff" with each breath out. Now if you rest your hand over your upper chest you will feel it rising and falling at the same time, rather like a seagull floating on a wave. In labour the wave of a contraction will be underneath and you will be breathing over the top of it. Remember to relax your shoulders; they are not doing any of the work.

If you can still breathe all down your back, do so. Only "lift" your breathing if you need to.

Butterfly breathing

As you go over the tumultuous waves of contractions at the end of the first stage of labour, just before the cervix is fully dilated and the

BREATHING OVER THE WAVE
Experiment with the different sorts of breathing you may need in the first stage of labour ...

... full-chest breathing if you no longer find it easy to breathe all down your back ...

... upper-chest breathing to lift you over the top of stronger contractions still ...

uterus and vagina become one birth canal, you may need to move up to the quickest, shallowest breathing of all—butterfly breathing.

When the going is hard, women tend to raise their chins in the air, tense the muscles of the neck and jaw, and start to gasp and over-breathe. Instead, let your head drop forward onto your chest like a heavy flower on its stalk. Remembering to keep your shoulders loose, the back of your neck long, and your jaw released will help you to keep a steady rhythm and let your breathing "dance".

Butterfly breathing is the lightest, most rapid breathing you will want to use in labour. With all breathing you are bound to be using your diaphragm and lungs, but butterfly breathing is easier if you think of it as being centred in your mouth behind your cheeks and not in the throat. If you centre your breathing in the throat, you will probably tense up your neck. Think of the space in your mouth, the space behind your warm, plumped-up cheeks. Either sit up in a chair or lie well propped up on the bed for this exercise. If you are lying flat, you can easily find yourself gasping and panting heavily when you are doing this type of breathing. So pile three or four pillows behind you, or try squatting, kneeling, all-fours or standing positions.

Resting the plump pads of the tips of your fingers against your cheeks will help you to concentrate on this area. Part your lips in a slight smile like the Mona Lisa. Relax your mouth and you will probably find that you are salivating a little. Breathe lightly in and out through your parted lips. Start gently, then gradually double the rate of your breathing till it is like the ticking of a wristwatch.

Butterfly breathing may be quite difficult at first. You may feel that you are taking in or letting out too much air. Most people do to begin with, and find this the most contrived kind of breathing to learn. They think that they will never be able to manage it in labour, but then it

... butterfly breathing if you need it, to take you through to the end of the first stage.

comes quite naturally and they do not know how they could have coped without it. You may find that it helps to think in terms of a definite rhythm in which one beat is slightly accentuated: *one*, two, three, four; *one*, two, three, four; or *one*, two, three, four, five, six. If you do this, be careful not to expel a great deal of air on the accentuated breath or you will gasp in the following breath and start to hyperventilate. If you find it difficult to keep the rhythm, or find your throat getting tight, give a quick blow out through pursed lips and carry on with the light breathing immediately after.

After you have experimented with this breathing, try it once again, and this time notice especially if your shoulders or the back of your neck become tense. Drop your shoulders and relax. Under stress, it is tempting to breathe too heavily and sound as if you are a chugging piece of machinery. Try to keep your breathing as light as a whisper. When you rehearse, think of the sound of leaves in the forest floating to the ground, but bear in mind that in actual childbirth you will naturally make more noise than that.

You will only want to use this sort of breathing when you are coping with the biggest contractions, at the end of the first stage. When you reach this point, you may feel like a little ship in a storm at sea in the middle of huge waves and confusing cross-currents. For most women this is the most difficult time of labour. Grantly Dick-Read used to call it "the pain period of labour". This does not mean that you may not feel pain at other times, but it is the time when you will need all your concentration and control.

Sheep's breathing

If we watch any mammal giving birth, a cat, for example, or a sheep, we notice that she does not take great breaths in and then "block" the birth canal by holding her breath. A sheep gives birth with rather light, quick breathing. Her breath is involuntarily held as she bears down and then she continues the light, accelerated breathing again.

During the second stage of labour, when the baby is travelling down the birth canal (see page 245), most women feel the urge to push during contractions. As a contraction builds up you move from full to lighter, quicker breathing, your cheeks plumped up. Then the surge of desire to bear down comes and you hold your breath. As soon as you can breathe again you do so, then feel you have to bear down again—and so on until the desire fades, your breathing slows down and then the contraction ends. You can practise this with only the slightest, most gentle push.

DIFFERENT POSITIONS FOR LABOUR

Once you are fairly confident about your ability to relax and breathe rhythmically, explore some different positions which you may want to use in labour. There is no reason why you should have to be tucked up in bed all the time. There are definite disadvantages with the supine position (lying flat on your back) for your baby, since the blood-flow in the large veins in the lower part of your body may be obstructed by the heavy weight of your uterus and this can reduce the blood-flow through the placenta to and from the baby.

During the first stage of labour you will almost certainly feel happiest walking about or standing up. During contractions you will probably want to lean against a wall or your partner. If you have low backache, you can lean forward onto a heavy piece of furniture. Once labour is advanced, it will be easier if you already know the positions in which you are likely to feel most comfortable. Avoid getting stuck in one position; the essence of labour is *movement*. You can try sitting well up, firmly supported right up your spine; kneeling, leaning back over your heels or forward onto a pillow placed on a chair or bed or over the top of the bed-head; a knee-chest position with your knees placed either side of your body, rather like a frog; on all fours or squatting, with your back firmly supported. Some of these positions are illustrated on pages 198–199.

Your aim in all these positions is to give the baby as much room as possible in your pelvis by having your knees well apart and to allow the uterus to tilt forward onto your abdominal wall and away from your spine. In this position it assumes an egg shape, whereas when you are lying flat on your back it tends to be distorted from this natural shape. When you are upright you are also allowing gravity to help the baby down. In all these positions contract only those muscles you need to use to support yourself, and whenever possible use pillows, furniture or another person to help you.

You can relieve low backache in labour, especially common when the baby is in an occipito-posterior position (see page 258), by getting into a position in which your abdomen can hang forward, tilting the baby away from your sacrum. It will also be convenient for back massage and counter-pressure, and because the longitudinal axis of the uterus is then in line with the birth canal it may help the baby to rotate into the correct anterior position. If the baby is posterior, you will probably have bearing-down sensations before you are fully dilated, and are more likely to be able to control the urge if you take pressure off your rectum.

Pressure on the umbilical cord interrupts the baby's blood flow through it. Resulting decelerations of the fetal heart which last after the end of the contractions may be noted if you are having continuous electronic monitoring (see page 303). This will lead your doctor to consider a forceps delivery for fetal distress. If you adopt a position in which your tummy is hanging forward, however, such as on all fours, both the baby and its cord will be tipped away from your spine and the pressure on the cord may be relieved.

Incidentally, it is a good idea to adopt an all-fours position for delivery if the baby has large shoulders that get stuck (shoulder distocia). It gives the assistant more room for manoeuvre, as the baby's head can be extended and drawn out and up towards your anus, so delivering the shoulder nearer your front, and the rest will then follow easily.

Sometimes contractions are inefficient from the start of labour and do not seem to pick up or, having been effective, become weak. In either case it is worth trying a position in which the uterus can most easily form a sphere. It may help to stand facing a wall, legs well apart and leaning forward with your hands resting against the wall.

PRACTISING FOR CONTRACTIONS AND PUSHING

The experience of labour is difficult to imagine before you have had a baby. Will contractions be unbearably painful or hardly noticeable? Some women think of the contractions as bigger and bigger hills they have to climb, each hill having its own peak, until they reach the mountain range at the end of the first stage.

The action of the uterus

When the uterus contracts, it is tightening up, just like any working muscle in the body. Make a very tight fist with one hand and raise your arm so that the big muscle on the inside of your upper arm, the biceps, tightens; then feel it with your other hand. You will notice that the biceps has gone hard and is sticking out. If a man does the same thing, his biceps may stick out a good deal more than yours does, because his is probably a bigger muscle. The biceps goes hard as it

PRACTISING FOR CONTRACTIONS
By simulating contractions you learn to respond to painful stimuli with the use of breathing. It is best to practise this technique with your partner, who acts as your "uterus" by pinching a little flesh on your inside thigh between his fingers. You adjust your breathing rhythms according to the degree of pressure you feel. . . .

. . . and after a while it may be a good idea to change places. "Contractions"—like the real ones—can vary: some short, some long, some easy, some harder; some may even have double peaks. . . . For your partner it may be the first real inkling of what labour can be like.

contracts and it also protrudes. This is because the muscle fibres are shortened and thickened. The same thing happens, on a much larger scale, when the uterus contracts. Like your bulging biceps, the uterus bulges forward in your abdomen when you have a really strong and effective contraction. The strong contractions are the best of all for helping the baby to be born.

Place your hand just above your pubic-hair line at the very bottom of the abdomen. The cervix lies under this area and it is here that you are likely to feel the strong, rhythmic pull as it opens, a pull that will feel tightest at the height of each contraction (see page 229).

You cannot do anything actively to help the baby down the birth canal until the cervix is wide open. A relaxed body and a mind at peace are the most important contributions you can make to the birth process at this stage. It is possible to train yourself to respond with neuro-muscular release whenever you want to. Your breathing techniques can help your relaxation and your relaxation can help keep your breathing smooth and rhythmic.

Simulating contractions

Contractions are felt mainly as powerful pressure which comes whether or not you want it to, so when you are practising for them work with a partner and allow him or her to simulate the contractions, deciding when they start, how strong they become and how long they last. Meet each contraction with a welcoming breath *out* and use the rhythmic breathing you have learned right through each one, with a long resting breath out at the end. Your partner sits beside you so that you have eye contact with each other. He (or she) pretends to be your uterus by taking hold of a piece of your flesh, the inner thigh, say, and squeezing it. He will find that grasping a small piece of flesh rather than a big area is more effective. He should be particularly careful if you have a varicose vein, lifting the flesh up off the leg instead of pressing down into the leg, and avoiding the area around the varicose vein. First he squeezes gently, and then tightens his grip to a strong pinch that lasts for about 15 seconds, after which he gradually releases his hold. The contraction should last about 45 seconds in all. This will help him to be aware of what you are feeling and how you react to stress of this kind, so that he can give you emotional support and encouragement.

In between these mock contractions, you can discuss with him how each one felt, and perhaps how he can improve his performance and you can improve yours. In labour this rest space between contractions should be used to prepare you for the next one: do not waste time discussing the contraction that has just ended.

It is a good idea to change places so that you become your partner's "uterus" and he can experience this firm gripping sensation and learn how to respond to it. This is important if he is going to be with you during labour and wants to be able to help you by breathing with you when and if contractions become difficult.

Practising for stronger contractions

Switch roles again and imagine that labour is progressing, with longer and stronger contractions, each reaching its peak about halfway through. Remember, however, that contractions vary and that it is no good wishing for a "textbook labour" if your own labour proves to be different. Some contractions have their peaks about a third of the way through; some may even have two peaks. The important thing is that if you go with your uterus, you tune in with it rather like an orchestra responding to a conductor. The conductor in this case is the uterus. You have to be able, as it were, to "listen" to your uterus in order to react to it, and be in harmony with it. For these stronger contractions your partner grips the flesh of your thigh for a minute or a little longer.

When necessary during these longer contractions you respond by lifting your breathing above the contraction—breathing more shallowly and more quickly (see page 190). Relax your shoulders and toes; then, as the contraction becomes slightly less intense, allow your breathing to become slower and fuller.

Pushing

Pushing or bearing down is often described as an extraordinarily athletic activity, as if you could learn to do it the way you learn to do a gymnastic exercise. It should not be like this. It is, rather, a spontaneous welling up of energy which culminates in a triumphant push and an opening of the vagina.

However you are sitting now, rest your hands beneath the lower curve of your abdomen. Take a breath and hold it. Drop your chin forward on your chest and at the same time allow the bulge underneath your hands to press downwards and forward, so that *from inside* your abdomen you are pressing your hands out and moving them forward. You probably feel your perineum moving forward too. Allow the movement to carry right down through you until you feel the tissues of the vagina spreading out, and then rest. Did you get that feeling of something moving forward? When the baby is ready to be born, this movement helps its head to bulge farther down the birth canal. Though it is useful to learn how to do this beforehand, especially if you practise it without straining and useless effort, most women feel a spontaneous urge to do it anyway during labour (see page 245).

Before going on to practise this pushing movement, make sure that your bladder is empty. You can sit on a bed, or on the floor, with four or five firm pillows behind your back, knees flopped apart and your heels drawn up near your buttocks. Or you can adopt any of the positions suggested on pages 198–199.

One of the best ways of rehearsing pushing is on the lavatory since we also release pelvic-floor muscles for defecation and so they are not put under strain. If you happen to be constipated, as many women are in late pregnancy (see page 121), this movement will help relieve the constipation and is an excellent exercise for encouraging spontaneous, easy bowel movements.

You will probably feel more comfortable in an upright position. This will be an advantage during labour as you will be more in control of what is happening, can open up easily for the baby to be born, and can see over the bulge to watch the birth if you want to. Gravity can help you. If you are lying flat, or almost flat, you are pushing the baby uphill because the uterus is almost at right angles to the vagina (see pages 246–247). In an almost upright position you can lean on your uterus and press the baby down.

After you have done this gentle pushing a few times, begin to work with your partner. To start with you might like to try sitting. Your partner sits near your head with a pillow over the forearm and supports your head and shoulders with it. This gives you a very wide base of support. With your helper's hands over your lower abdomen, you can both feel what is happening inside. Drop your head forward onto your chest, so that you do not strain with your throat muscles and produce a grunting sound. Take a breath. Lean forward and press from inside steadily out, slowly, gently; a little bit more; let it go; let the breath out and rest. While you are practising, your partner's hand pressed firmly against your lower abdomen gives you something to press against and guide you. It is easier to bear down when your baby is actually in the birth canal waiting to be born because you have something to press against. Allow your pelvic-floor muscles to bulge foward like a heavy sack of apples. When you have felt and noted the sensation this produces, lift your pelvic floor up again so that it is well toned and not sagging (see page 107). Think of it smiling.

Trying other positions

When you are confident that you have the feeling of pushing with complete release of your pelvic-floor muscles in this position, go on to explore other positions which may feel right when you are in labour. Experiment with every open position—on a mattress on the floor, on the bed, leaning over or against furniture, using cushions and other kinds of support, cradled by another human body—in which you can feel in touch with what is happening and free to let the energy of the uterus sweep through you to birth. An almost impossible posture in which to do this is, as you can imagine, lying flat on your back with your legs in the air in the standard lithotomy position, or with your knees scrunched up to your chest while you try to roll yourself into a ball—both standard positions for the second stage and delivery in contemporary hospitals.

During the eighties, however, there have been widespread changes in practice. Now in many hospitals in Britain, for example, women are encouraged by their midwives to find any position, and make any movement, which is comfortable for them, and, if they wish, to give birth on a sheet or mattress on the floor.

With your partner's hand over your lower abdomen, you can both feel what is happening inside.

Practising positions for labour

There is no reason to spend labour in bed. In fact, lying flat on your back diminishes the oxygen supply to your baby and prevents your uterus contracting efficiently. While you are pregnant, try out different positions to find those which are most comfortable for you.

STANDING LUNGE
A standing lunge position, feet wide apart, is often comfortable. You can lean your forearms against the wall and rest your head on them.

ON ALL FOURS
Getting down on all fours is one of the best positions for relieving low backache.

SQUATTING
When you are squatting, your pelvis is wide open and the baby's head is pressed down. You may want to rest your hands on the floor to give yourself firm support. If a full squat is uncomfortable, use a low stool or a pile of large books.

KNEELING UP
Kneeling up, legs apart with your ankles turned out and toes towards each other, opens your pelvis and releases tension in the back.

SUPPORTED SQUAT
You may find it easier to squat with the help of a partner. Grasp each other's wrists and squat down together. Start with the weight on the balls of your feet and your heels raised; with practice, you may be able to get your feet flat on the floor.

KNEELING FORWARD
Kneeling with your legs spread wide, ankles out and toes turned in, gradually lean forward until your forearms are on the floor. This extends and relaxes back muscles and buttocks, and takes the baby's weight off your back.

HANGING ABDOMEN
Try kneeling on all fours, with your forearms on the floor, your knees spread wide and your abdomen hanging between them. In this position, you may like to rock backwards and forwards.

LYING DOWN
You can relax almost on all fours, but flopped forwards onto a big floor cushion or bean bag.

Practising positions for delivery

Try to explore different positions for delivery with the people who will be helping you at the birth, so that everyone has some idea of what to expect. Using a doll, a ball, even a grapefruit, as a substitute for the baby may be helpful.

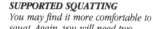

SUPPORTED SQUATTING
You may find it more comfortable to squat. Again, you will need two helpers, who can support your knees when you are bearing down.

SUPPORTED KNEELING
Kneeling opens up the pelvis fully and aids the descent of the baby. You will feel most secure if you have the support of two helpers, one on each side of the bed or delivery table.

HALF KNEELING, HALF SQUATTING
This is the easiest position if you are delivering your own baby. It should give you greater stability than kneeling or squatting and allows you to guide the baby out.

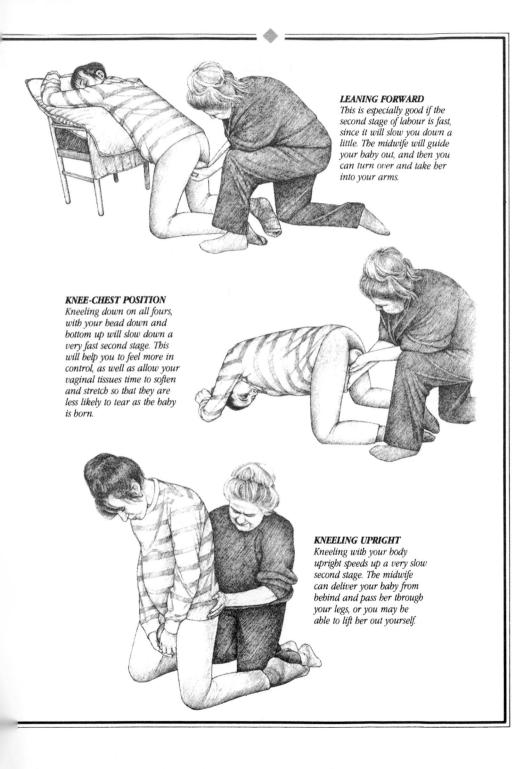

LEANING FORWARD
This is especially good if the second stage of labour is fast, since it will slow you down a little. The midwife will guide your baby out, and then you can turn over and take her into your arms.

KNEE-CHEST POSITION
Kneeling down on all fours, with your head down and bottom up will slow down a very fast second stage. This will help you to feel more in control, as well as allow your vaginal tissues time to soften and stretch so that they are less likely to tear as the baby is born.

KNEELING UPRIGHT
Kneeling with your body upright speeds up a very slow second stage. The midwife can deliver your baby from behind and pass her through your legs, or you may be able to lift her out yourself.

Windows into the uterus

Apart from the routine urine and blood pressure tests you will have every time you go to the clinic (see page 48), there are certain other investigations that may be done during pregnancy. Whether they are done at all, or how often they are done, will depend not only on there being some specific reason for them, but on the part of the country you are in and therefore on the sort of hospital or clinic you attend. Teaching hospitals have far more sophisticated equipment and are also engaged in research, so—for example—if you are in a large city you may have ultrasound two or three times during your pregnancy, whereas if you live in a small country town you may never have it at all.

ULTRASOUND

I found the scans at 16 and 30 weeks exciting because the images on the screen were explained to me.

Ultrasound (also referred to as a scan, or an ultrasound scan) works on the principle of bouncing very high frequency sound waves (far higher than the human ear can detect) off solid objects. It is a method which has been used for many years by fishermen to locate shoals of deep-sea fish, and by navies to locate submarines in wartime. Echo-sounders in yachts work in a similar way.

Uses of ultrasound

In pregnancy ultrasound is used to obtain a picture of the baby in the uterus. It is possible to see the tiny fetus kicking from the end of the second month, and after 28 weeks breathing movements can be observed. There are a number of reasons why scans are done:

To confirm pregnancy A scan can be used to confirm pregnancy very early on, before clinical tests are effective: it is capable of detecting changes in the uterus that cannot yet be revealed by physical examination. You can find out if you are having twins, for instance, when you are only eight weeks pregnant.

To establish the estimated date of delivery Scans are often routinely used in large hospitals, where you may expect to have them done at least two or three times during pregnancy. Your first scan will probably be done at about 16 weeks in order to establish the estimated delivery date. At this stage the age of the baby can be established to within 10 days (later in pregnancy it is more difficult to be precise because babies of the same age may grow at very different rates). You may then be scanned again in the middle and at the end of pregnancy, or even more frequently, at intervals of a few weeks. This is called serial assessment and does not mean that anything is wrong. Only when the scan is used in this way can the clues that it gives about the rate of fetal growth be taken seriously. In smaller hospitals you may never have a scan at all, unless there is a specific reason for it.

To detect certain handicaps Between 18 and 20 weeks, ultrasound can be used to detect certain abnormalities in the fetus, including spina bifida (see page 206), congenital heart defects, and gastro-intestinal and kidney malformations.

To assess maturity in late pregnancy Late in pregnancy a scan is often used to indicate whether or not a baby is ready to be born. It cannot show whether the lungs are mature enough for breathing, but by measuring the size of the baby's head it can establish the approximate age of the baby and its stage of development.

To detect how the baby is lying If it is important to find out how your baby is lying in the uterus and a doctor cannot know for certain from manual examination, ultrasound can tell with accuracy. This knowledge may make all the difference to you if you want to have your baby at home, for instance.

If the baby is shown to be in a good position, you can proceed with confidence in your plans for a home birth. If the baby is seen to be lying awkwardly, you will accept that it might be more sensible to come into hospital for the birth. Either way, you and your doctor can be guided by the information provided by the scan.

To assess the condition and position of the placenta When there is bleeding in late pregnancy ultrasound can be used to locate the position of the placenta. The danger is that the placenta might be

HAVING A SCAN
Because it involves such sophisticated equipment, an ultrasound scan may seem intimidating; if the picture on the screen is blurred and meaningless it may be disappointing; but if it is explained to you so that you can actually recognize your baby, it may be the most exciting moment of your pregnancy so far ...

blocking the baby's way out of the uterus (a condition known as placenta praevia, described on page 125). In fact a scan done in the first few months of pregnancy often gives the impression that the placenta is lying low on the wall of the uterus, but as the pregnancy progresses and the uterus enlarges the placenta usually proves to be in the right place after all. Occasionally bleeding in late pregnancy means that the roots of the placenta are becoming dislodged with pre-labour contractions, indicating that the baby's lifeline would be cut if labour were allowed to proceed. A scan can show this clearly, and a Caesarean section can be performed to save the baby. Used in this way, or as a preliminary to amniocentesis (see page 206), ultrasound has undoubted advantages.

AN ULTRASOUND PICTURE
Here is a photograph of a scan of a 14-week-old fetus. Unlike many other scan photographs, the image of this baby is easily distinguished. Often scans are meaningless to the untrained eye, partly because the baby is hidden behind other organs.

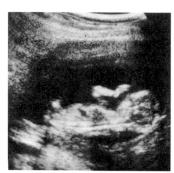

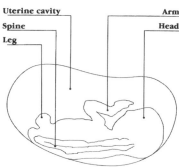

Uterine cavity   Arm
Spine   Head
Leg

How ultrasound works

You undress, put on a hospital gown and lie on your back beside the scanner. Your abdomen is oiled and then a transducer is slowly passed over it in different directions. The transducer is a machine which picks up echoes from the different planes of your own organs and the developing baby's tissues, and which then translates the information into the form of a map on a screen like a television screen. A scan done in the first few months of pregnancy gains in clarity if your bladder is full and therefore clearly visible, so you will probably be asked to drink a pint of water first and not pass water for an hour or so before the scan. Do not expect to see an immediately recognizable picture of your baby, even in late pregnancy; if a doctor is present, ask to have the picture interpreted, because it may look more like a map of the moon than a baby, and you may find it difficult to make out the different parts of the baby.

The safety of ultrasound

So far as we know ultrasound is safe, certainly much safer than X-rays (see page 101), which provided the only method of finding out about the baby in the uterus before the scan was developed. On the other hand, high frequency sounds continued for a long time can cause damage to hearing in an adult. Questions have therefore been raised about possible effects on the baby's hearing since although the sound waves are only bounced off the baby for a short time, the baby may be vulnerable at certain stages of its development. Babies are not born deaf after having ultrasound, but no-one yet knows if any of them will suffer delayed effects in later life.

Ultrasound does have other effects that are not yet fully understood. It causes heat to be generated in body tissues and tiny bubbles inside tissue may dance in reaction to the sound waves. Studies in animals show that powerful or prolonged doses of ultrasound can cause cell changes, and Doreen Liebeskind, a radiologist at Albert Einstein College of Medicine in New York City, has been able to produce permanent genetic changes in human white blood cells on the laboratory bench. This does not necessarily mean that diagnostic ultrasound at the level at which it is normally used in pregnancy is dangerous. But it does imply that we should be asking searching questions about possible long-term effects. It could be that ultrasound has some subtle deleterious effects on especially vulnerable babies in the first 12 weeks of pregnancy, during the time that the major organs of the body are being formed.

I feel I could have been given more information about the ultrasound scan beforehand. My husband waited for me outside and if I had known what a moving experience the scan would be I would have brought him in with me.

Some safety measures

It makes sense to expose pregnant women and the babies inside them to ultrasound only when a diagnosis is needed which cannot be made without ultrasound, and when that diagnosis would result in some change in the kind of care that is given. This rules out routine scanning at 16 weeks—now the accepted practice in many countries. It also rules out using ultrasound simply because parents would like to see a picture of the baby or to enable a woman to "bond" with the fetus. Many obstetricians are rather keen on this and believe that they can make a contribution towards ensuring that babies are well mothered by doing routine ultrasound scans. They do not realize that there are other—better and more intimate—ways of becoming aware of the baby (see pages 218–219).

When ultrasound is used, the length of time you are exposed to it should be limited, and when you are discussing what you can see on the screen, ask for the image to be frozen. Understandably, a woman is fascinated by seeing her baby's movements on the screen; in Denmark the scanner is linked to a video-recorder so that the examination can be replayed later, the woman can see her baby moving, and there can be full discussion about it without exposing the baby unnecessarily to ultrasound.

AFP SCREENING

Alpha-feto-protein (AFP) is a substance produced in the early phases of pregnancy by the embryo's yolk sac and later on by the fetal liver. It is known that when the levels of AFP are abnormally high a large proportion of babies are found to be suffering from neural tube defects such as spina bifida (when part of the spinal cord is outside the baby's body) and anencephaly (the absence of a brain). The baby without a brain cannot live, but babies with spina bifida do sometimes live, although they are usually paralyzed below the waist and often develop hydrocephalus (water on the brain) as well.

Levels of AFP in a pregnant woman's blood double about every five weeks in the fourth, fifth and sixth months of pregnancy, but earlier than this they are usually low. The best time to screen your blood for AFP is therefore in early pregnancy, before the 18th week. Results come through in two to three days.

If your dates are wrong and pregnancy is more advanced than you think, you may find that the AFP level seems suspiciously high. The proportion will also be high if you are expecting twins. In both these cases ultrasound will be used to tell you the real age of the baby and whether you are expecting more than one.

If the rate appears to be high for no obvious reason another blood test may be done to double-check; if the level of AFP is then found to be two or three times higher than the median level of a sample group, you will be offered amniocentesis (see below). But this means two or three out of every hundred women having amniocentesis, with the risk attached to it (one or two babies out of every hundred are miscarried). Some people say that the risk of amniocentesis is greater than the risk of bearing an affected baby if your AFP level is high. Because of these differences of opinion within the medical profession, AFP screening is done as routine in some parts of Britain, but not in others; the point at which you are offered amniocentesis will also vary depending on the centre where your blood is tested.

As with all medical intervention, solving the problem is a matter of a delicate balance between risks and there is no easy answer. If AFP testing shows that your level is high, discuss the matter with your doctor, taking your partner or a family member with you so that you can talk it over together afterwards and make a shared decision about whether or not to have amniocentesis.

AMNIOCENTESIS

Amniocentesis is a procedure which has been developed to detect abnormalities of the central nervous system (spina bifida and anencephaly) and some other forms of mental handicap such as Down's syndrome (mongolism). The sex of the baby can also be determined, so you can discover if any sex-linked disorders might have been inherited.

How amniocentesis works

Under a local anaesthetic a hollow needle is inserted through your abdominal wall into the uterus, where about half an ounce (14 g) of the water in which the fetus is lying is sucked out. This fluid has been swallowed by the fetus and passed out of its body again either through its mouth or bladder; it is full of cells from the skin and other organs which can provide clues to the baby's condition. The fluid is then spun in a centrifuge to separate the cells from the liquid.

In the 1950s, when amniocentesis was first invented, mistakes were sometimes made and the needle penetrated placental tissues, causing occasional miscarriage. But now that ultrasound techniques have been developed, the position of the placenta can be accurately located beforehand and the risks of damage to the placenta have been very much reduced. There still remains a one or two per cent chance, however, that amniocentesis may cause miscarriage.

Because of this small but definite risk, there is no point in having amniocentesis unless there is a well above average chance of your baby being born abnormal. You must also have thought carefully about the implications of discovering that something is wrong with your baby and have decided that you would opt for termination. In some parts of Britain, amniocentesis is offered to all women over 35, since the incidence of some of the disorders it is designed to detect rises sharply with age.

If an abnormality is revealed, counselling should be made immediately available to both parents. Since amniocentesis cannot be done until some time between the 14th and 16th weeks of pregnancy, when many women have already felt the first fluttering of fetal movement, the decision is often a distressing one to have to make and the termination is riskier than one performed earlier in pregnancy. The woman who is going through this experience needs generous emotional support from her partner and family.

CHORIONIC VILLUS SAMPLING

Chorionic villus sampling—CVS for short—entails taking a sample of tissue from the part of the outer membrane around the embryo that will later become the placenta, in order to diagnose whether or not a fetus will have a genetic handicap. One of the handicaps it cannot detect, however, is spina bifida. The great advantages of CVS over amniocentesis are that it can be done before 12 weeks—even as early as six weeks after conception—so that an abnormal fetus can be terminated much earlier; and that the test is done through the vagina rather than through the abdominal wall.

CVS is, however, still on trial and there are many questions to be answered before it becomes common practice. The trials are designed to discover whether CVS is sufficiently accurate for routine use, and whether there are risks which outweigh the benefits—such as a high incidence of infection and bleeding or spontaneous abortion (miscarriage) following CVS. If you are asked to take part in a controlled trial of CVS—in which this technique is compared with amniocentesis—it makes sense to do so. We do not as yet know enough about either test to be able to say which is better.

Ultrasound device

Placenta

Umbilical cord

Uterus

UMBILICAL VEIN SAMPLING
A technique, performed after the 18th week of pregnancy, that enables a sample of fetal blood to be taken for testing. Guided by ultrasound, a very fine needle is passed through the mother's abdominal wall and into the blood vessels in the umbilical cord. The technique can also be used to give blood transfusions and administer drugs.

UMBILICAL VEIN SAMPLING

At the end of the seventies fetoscopy—photographing the baby with a telescope introduced into the uterus—was the latest technique for finding out what was happening to babies known to be at risk. Unfortunately, the risk of miscarriage proved to be as high as 5–10 per cent. Fetoscopy has now been superseded by umbilical vein sampling, hailed by Dr Stuart Weiner of the University of Pennsylvania as opening up "a whole new area of fetal medicine"*.

In umbilical vein sampling, a very fine needle is passed through the mother's abdomen and uterus into the fetal vein in the umbilical cord and blood is withdrawn so that it can be tested. Intra-uterine blood transfusions can also be given in this way, and drugs can be injected directly into the baby. Because the fetal vein is frail in early pregnancy, the technique cannot be performed until after 18 weeks.

Although still experimental, umbilical vein sampling is being used in addition to amniocentesis and ultrasound; it is also used when there is Rhesus disease (see page 103), in order to diagnose haemophilia in a baby, and to check for metabolic disorders.

Dr Kytros Nicolaides, of King's College Hospital, London, estimates that when the method is used by experienced doctors, the risk of losing a baby is only 1 per cent—the same as that for amniocentesis and chorionic villus sampling in that hospital. He emphasized to me that "the greatest risk of any operative technique in pregnancy is always the skill and experience of the operator."

The last few weeks

Your baby is almost ready to be born. The firm body is nestled in the cup of your pelvis, and the little arms and legs are plumper as the last layers of fat form to help the baby's temperature-control system function efficiently after birth. Sometimes the baby gains as much as 8 oz (226 g) in a week at this stage of pregnancy.

Physical sensations

You may feel fewer big body movements but an insistent kicking underneath your ribs on one side or the other. If your abdominal wall is thin you may even be able to hold your baby's foot. There may be other strange movements, perhaps a sudden urgent knocking which continues intermittently for half an hour or more. This can be so pronounced that you may worry in case your baby is having something like an epileptic fit. But it is definitely not that. The baby may have hiccups, perhaps because it was gulping amniotic fluid; or it may have lost its thumb which it was contentedly sucking, and is "rooting" to find it again, with quick, darting movements of the head from side to side, just as after birth it will search for the nipple. The baby's head feels like a melon or coconut pressing through your bulging perineal tissues, making you sit down with care.

There may also be odd sensations in your vagina. Sometimes there is a sharp buzz like a mild electric shock or a tickle. The baby may be lifting and lowering its head against your pelvic-floor muscles in another movement which it will do naturally after birth too, when put down on its front in an alert state. There are times when your baby is sleeping or drowsy and other very active times, often in the evenings.

Mixed emotions

Conflicting emotions are characteristic of these last weeks. You may be tired of being pregnant but on the other hand the state you are in now is a condition you know and understand, whereas in front of you there is an unknown challenge. So sometimes you want the baby out and long to get on with the labour. But at other times you feel safer as you are, and anxious about the future. Some women say that as the birthday draws nearer they feel irritated with the pregnancy and even with the baby. This produces an emotional state which makes them welcome the start of labour. Other women relish these last weeks.

Antenatal depression

It is very common for a woman to feel low and become depressed some time in the last six weeks of pregnancy. If you have been practising carefully and preparing yourself for a natural birth you may experience a kind of stage-fright and be convinced that you are going

I'm really enjoying this time and am looking forward to the birth.

You know how workmen whistle at you? Well, they always have at me, and I don't say I like it, but I'm used to them doing it. And now, of course, they don't.

to forget everything when you are actually in labour. You may also be feeling physically tired and heavy with the weight of your burden.

Antenatal depression, though usually short-lived and spasmodic, is a fact of life for some women. It is made more severe by anaemia (see page 128), so ask at the clinic what your haemoglobin level is at present and if necessary have extra iron. It is also partly a result of a need for more rest. You may feel very different if you lie down to rest in a darkened room in the middle of the day, have some early nights and adjust your activity to slower, gentler rhythms if possible.

If you find yourself becoming depressed at this stage of pregnancy have a talk with your childbirth educator who, probably a mother herself, will understand what you are feeling.

> *It feels as if the pregnancy is just going to carry on for ever and ever, and it is never going to come out.*

Diet in the last three weeks

As you come to within three weeks of the estimated delivery date you will probably find that you need small, frequent meals rather than several large ones each day. There seems to be no room for anything else. This is a time when you can build up reserves of energy for labour by adopting a diet similar to that used by marathon runners.

One California doctor works with long-distance runners, in particular with cardiac patients who adopt running as part of their cure. He describes the typical nutrition of marathon runners as "a fresh, raw, high-fiber diet rich in linoleic acid and silicon."* Apparently they experience cravings for certain foods and also share a kind of folklore about what makes for vitality and endurance. Their diet is rich in high-fibre foods (roughage), and the active ingredient in all such foods is called silicon. It is also high in polyunsaturated fats, the most important of which is called linoleic acid, found in seeds, nuts and whole grains. Linoleic acid, incidentally, is easily destroyed by exposure to oxygen, heat and light. Marathon runners are mostly vegetarians, avoid greasy fried foods, believe that plenty of onions and garlic is good for them and take large quantities of vitamin C.

As part of your build-up to labour in the last two or three weeks you might like to plan a high-energy diet on the same principles as these Californian runners. Start the day with some muesli mixture, including bran. You can eat this mixed with some raw fruit and yoghurt—two other foods which the runners enjoy—and add some freshly chopped or ground nuts, seeds and grains.

Buy a new book on the preparation of salads at this late stage of pregnancy to stimulate your imagination. A handful of peanuts on a fresh vegetable salad will provide you with extra linoleic acid without giving you a high-fat diet. A little finely chopped raw onion and garlic with seasoning added to cottage cheese adds something solid and particularly tasty to any salad. Have an occasional baked potato in its jacket, or sometimes whole grain or granary bread. Otherwise plan to eat mainly unprocessed foods with plenty of raw vegetables, citrus and other fruits of every kind, nuts and lots of yoghurt. You will then be at peak form for the hard work of labour.

OPPOSITE

The last weeks of pregnancy are a time of conflicting feelings—uncertainty, impatience and excitement.

210

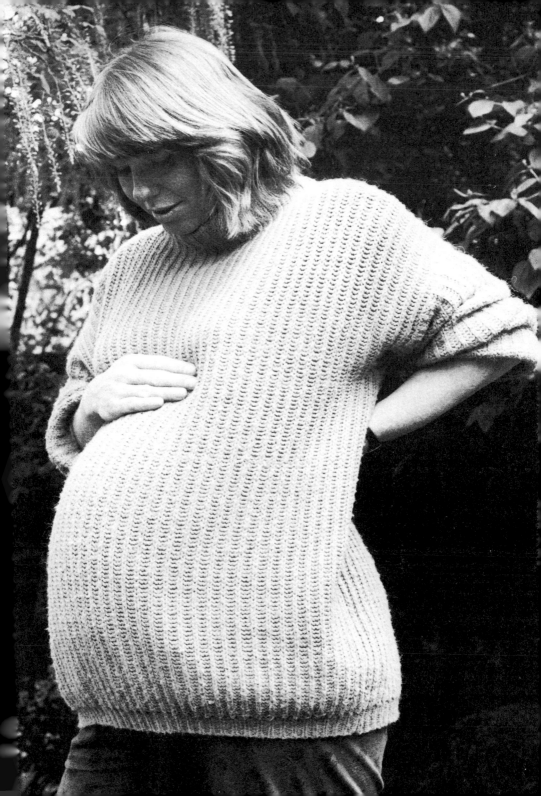

THINKING AHEAD TO LABOUR

You will probably be thinking a great deal about labour at this time, wondering what it will be like. One of the things you can find out is the position your baby is in; remember to ask when you are being examined at the clinic. The ideal position for a straightforward labour (and by far the most common) is head down and anterior. But some babies present in different positions, as posterior or breech for example. Delivery may be less straightforward with the baby in these positions (see pages 257–264).

The baby who is presenting as a posterior

If your baby is lying head down with its back against your spine, limbs towards your front, it may be because you have a roomy pelvis so that it can still move around a lot. Women who think they are due but who really have another two weeks or so to go before delivery can have a baby who is still moving freely like this—sometimes posterior, sometimes anterior, sometimes lateral (ear forward). In this case

---

What do you need to pack?

Now is the time to be thinking about the things you want to have available during labour and afterwards. Gather them together in a lightweight, easily carried container.

Comfort aids for labour

Thermos flask for ice cubes, which are sometimes available in hospital.

Two small sponges to be dipped in iced water and used for sponging your face, wetting your lips and sucking between contractions.

Chap-stick or vaseline for dry lips.

Plant spray for moistening face with cold water, or Evian spray.

Baby's hot water bottle or a picnic thermal pack to be heated up in water for use as a hot compress in the small of your back, between your legs etc.

Talc, cornflour or massage lotion to avoid skin friction when massaged.

Rolling pin to iron away backache (see page 261).

Hairbrush and ribbons or bands if your hair is long.

Books, cards, chess, Scrabble, crosswords etc.

Honey to keep your strength up in early labour.

Fruit juice, herb teas.

Eau de cologne or toilet water.

Paper bag to breathe into in case you hyperventilate.

Beautiful object on which you can focus when necessary.

Nourishing snacks for your labour companion.

Camera.

Exercise book to serve as labour log book.

Writing materials.

Phone numbers of relatives and friends.

Money for pay phones if in hospital.

Comfort aids for after the birth

Calendula and hypericum cream from a homeopathic pharmacy, for a sore perineum.

Bottle of witchhazel lotion with which you can soak the sanitary pad next to stitches.

Sanitary belt.

Soft lavatory paper.

Cotton nightdresses, dressing gown or housecoat.

Nursing bras.

Deodorant (you will perspire heavily in the few days after delivery).

Toilet bag.

Writing paper and envelopes.

Earplugs if in hospital ward.

◆

pre-labour and early-labour contractions usually turn the baby into the anterior position without any intervention by the doctor.

If your baby seems to have settled in a posterior position, you may find that you can coax it to change during one of its waking periods by very firm hand pressure. The posterior baby is usually lying with its head on your right side. You want to shift it round and over towards the left. Treat the baby as if it were a sleeping cat which you were trying to scoop off the middle of a sofa and move over to the left side. Curve the side of your hand round the most solid section of its bulk and firmly, little by little, edge it over. Keep the fingers of your other hand over your navel. If you are successful the saucer-shaped dip there (the space between the arms and legs of a posterior baby) will become—at least temporarily—a hard convex curve (the back of a baby in an anterior position). You will be able to detect the change as your navel will probably stick out. Talk to your baby as you move it. This is not simply a clinical exercise, but a bit of maternal persuasion.

Once the baby is stretching the uterus to its utmost it is a tight fit and you will probably not be able to move it. You will have to wait and see whether the first-stage contractions will do the work for you.

The baby who is presenting as a breech

Most babies tip head down—in the vertex or cephalic position—between the seventh and the eighth month. If your baby is still presenting buttocks first (breech) at around 36 weeks the doctor may decide to try and turn the baby—a procedure known as external version. This is a skilled manoeuvre and should always be done by a doctor—do not attempt it yourself.

> **“**
> *I can't help thinking, what if the baby drops out? I might have it anywhere! I'm in a state of constant expectation, thinking, is this it, and then deciding, no it isn't.*
> **”**

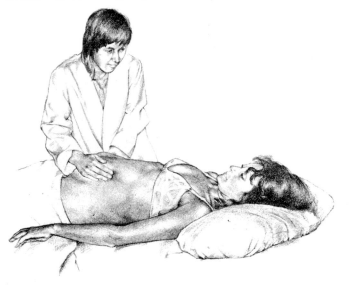

EXTERNAL VERSION
Your doctor may attempt this skilled manoeuvre if your baby has settled in a breech position. Sometimes the version is successful and a normal delivery can follow, but frequently the baby turns straight back into a breech position after the procedure is over. External version must always be done by a doctor; if done by an unskilled person there is a risk of the placenta separating from the uterine wall.

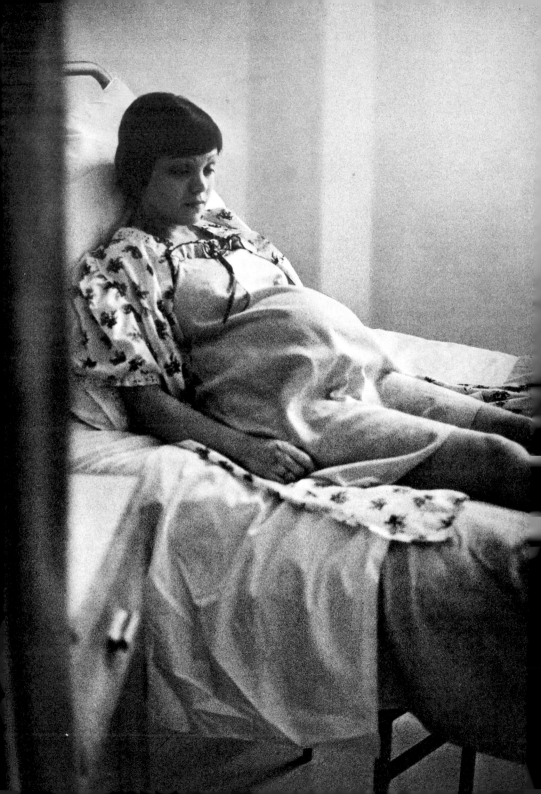

How external version is done You empty your bladder and then lie down on you back with your knees drawn up. The doctor will probably do an ultrasound scan to find exactly how the baby is lying and will listen to the baby's heartbeats before and after turning the baby. You may be asked to lie on a sloping examining table with your legs up and head down for about a quarter of an hour before the manoeuvre, so that the baby is encouraged to move clear of the pelvis. Spend this time relaxing deeply; use abdominal massage to help you release your tummy muscles and use your breathing to help you as well. Because the uterus often contracts when hands are pressing on it, and this makes it more difficult to turn the baby, the doctor may also use a muscle relaxant to lower the tone of the uterus.

When you feel the doctor's hands on your tummy, release and flow towards the touch. Give a long, slow breath *out* and let your lower tummy bulge out in a great wave as you do so.

Helping a breech to turn You can try to tip the baby up out of your pelvis yourself by adopting a position with your head down and your bottom in the air for 15 minutes three times a day. Some babies turn a somersault once clear of the pelvis—even after 37 weeks*.

A knee-chest position, leaning over a firm bean bag on your front with your head on the floor and your hips as high as possible, or lying in the same position on a steeply sloping, cushion-padded ironing board propped between the bed and the wall or a solid piece of furniture, offer a range of options—none of them, it must be admitted, very comfortable in advanced pregnancy! But if you are able to turn your baby, it may make the difference between a vaginal delivery and a Caesarean section.

If the version is successful and the baby turns, walk about for an hour or two so that there is the best chance of fixing the baby head-down. Some babies turn straight back into the breech position. Seven times out of ten, however, external version at 37 to 39 weeks is successful*. But if the baby tips back again into a breech position you will have to accept that she prefers it; discuss with your doctor the sort of delivery you will have (see page 261).

BEING "OVERDUE"

Concern about the best things to eat, the position of the baby, and whether labour will be straightforward can be preoccupying in the last few weeks. If you actually go *past* the estimated date of delivery you may really begin to worry; you are now consigned to the category of the woman who is "overdue".

The estimated delivery date

The date that you are given at the beginning of pregnancy for your baby's birth (EDD or EDC) is only a statistical mean. Studies show that only 5 per cent of babies arrive on that day. If you look at the 95

OPPOSITE
It is natural to feel despondent if the hospital is concerned because you are "overdue", but the majority of babies arrive after the predicted date.

◆

babies out of 100 who do not put in an appearance on the "correct" date you find that three out of ten babies come before the EDD and seven out of ten come *after* it. This is partly because women's menstrual cycles are of different lengths, and ovulation—and hence conception—may occur at different times within it. But by the time you reach the end of your pregnancy you may not be able to prevent yourself from fixing on the expected delivery date as your goal. If it comes and goes and nothing happens, you may become very depressed. Each day that passes seems like a week, and each week more like a month. Unless you plan for activity and recreation during this time your morale will drop to rock bottom.

The doctor says he wants to induce me on my due date because my blood pressure is up. I do want to have a natural birth but the time is coming nearer and nearer. It's hanging over me like a date set for execution.

If you find that you are getting despondent, remind yourself that, though very few babies are born on the day predicted for their birth, nine out of ten do put in an appearance within ten days of the expected date. There is nothing abnormal about a baby who is nine days "late". Many women, however, are made to feel "under sentence of induction" if they go as much as a week past their expected date. In some hospitals it is routine policy to induce labour when you reach the tenth day following the estimated date, and this is done without further investigation. If your pregnancy is normal and you are in good health, being ten days "late" is a very poor reason for induction.

Whether induction (which is described on page 297) is really necessary or not depends entirely on the baby's wellbeing at the end of pregnancy. The baby's wellbeing, in turn, depends on the condition of the placenta.

The aging placenta

At the end of pregnancy the placenta looks like a piece of raw liver about the size of a dinner plate and the thickness of your little finger. Like every other human organ, it has a youth and an old age. An elderly placenta works less well. If labour does not start at the right time (which may be anywhere between two weeks before and two weeks after the estimated date of delivery—and very occasionally later still) the placenta may fail to support the baby in the uterus. The baby is then deprived of nourishment. This is why obstetricians are concerned if a pregnancy is prolonged much past the date worked out for the birth. Even so, a baby who is thought to be overdue may prove at birth not to be postmature at all. There are various ways in which the condition of the placenta can be assessed. Some are tests which doctors do to you; probably the most reliable method is one which you can do for yourself (see page 218).

Urinary oestriol tests

One way of finding out whether your placenta is functioning well is to measure the output of oestriol in your urine or blood. (Oestriol is a form of the hormone oestrogen, important for the baby's growth.) The level of oestriol produced by the placenta rises throughout pregnancy; just before labour starts, it drops. The level also drops if you have high blood pressure or pre-eclampsia (see page 126), as it will if you have bleeding in late pregnancy, kidney disease or diabetes. A lower level than normal suggests that the placenta may not be doing a good job of nourishing the baby and excreting its waste products. If doctors are considering whether to induce labour, they may therefore perform this test.

But the proportion of oestriol in urine can vary by as much as 30 per cent with different readings; there are day-to-day variations, even when everything is normal. You therefore cannot rely on one or two tests alone. There should be a series of readings of all the urine passed over a period of 24 hours, or weekly blood tests. If you are admitted to hospital with pre-eclampsia, regular tests may be performed. If they indicate that the placenta is not functioning well your obstetrician will suggest induction of labour. But the oestriol level is only a clue to the condition of the placenta, and it should not be acted on alone. When levels of oestriol output are compared with the information provided by ultrasound to assess the baby's growth, there is often a discrepancy, so obstetricians tend to use the two types of test together to try to find out what is happening.

If there is no urgent need for induction (and your doctor will certainly make it clear if there is), you may first want to monitor fetal activity as an additional check on how the baby is faring (see page 218). There is some evidence that observations you can make yourself are more likely to give an accurate picture of the baby's condition than medical tests.

Non-stress test

This test uses an electronic fetal monitor (see page 303) to see if the baby's heartbeat shows the usual variations. If the heart rate is satisfactory, there is no need to induce labour or to do the more complicated oxytocin challenge test (below).

Oxytocin challenge test

This test is sometimes called a "stress test" to distinguish it from fetal movement recording (see below), which is a "non-stress test". It is occasionally used when a baby is thought to be overdue to see if it would be better off born.

How the test is done The uterus is made to contract with oxytocin dripped straight into your vein; the reactions of the fetal heart are then observed. The heart rate will probably react to each contraction by slowing down. As long as it returns to normal as soon as the contraction ends, the baby is not considered to be under any particular stress and induction is therefore unnecessary.

On the other hand, if contractions affect the baby's heart rate so much that it slows down and remains slow for a time between contractions as well, then this is considered to be evidence of fetal distress. In these circumstances labour may be induced immediately:

larger amounts of oxytocin will be introduced into your veins to stimulate contractions, and the delivery will be very carefully monitored throughout; alternatively the doctors may decide that the safest option is to perform a Caesarean section.

Fetal movement recording

Just when I think there's never going to be a movement there's a terrific leap and then the baby's wriggling all over the shop. Keeping a kick chart has made me much more aware of the baby's waking and sleeping times.

One of the most accurate ways of knowing if a baby is doing well while still inside the uterus in late pregnancy is something you can do for yourself. This is to note the baby's movements. In the last weeks of pregnancy, until it engages, the baby usually wriggles, dips and turns, bangs and kicks, and moves like a porpoise from side to side in great sweeps of activity which you can actually see through your clothing. Once it has engaged it often moves less because it is a rather tight fit. Even so, a vigorous baby moves even after it has gone down into the pelvis, though the movements then tend to be just the knocks from knees and feet. You feel as if you have a rolling coconut in your groin or just behind your pubis (the head turning), and later the strange buzzing sensation of the engaged head bouncing against the pelvic-floor muscles (see page 209).

You may not normally be aware of most of these movements while you are busy but as soon as you sit down to rest, or lie down hoping to sleep, you cannot help noticing them. They are a good sign that your baby is healthy. Studies of fetal activity show that every baby has its own individual pattern of waking and sleeping inside the uterus, and by late pregnancy you will have probably noticed what your baby's pattern is. But sometimes you may be awake and expect a kick; if nothing happens it can be disconcerting. In fact, the baby is probably fast asleep; if you have had an alcoholic drink or taken sleeping tablets, your baby will probably be affected by them too.

Often it is when you go to bed that you both notice your child's vigorous movements ... regular movements are a sign that all is well ...

Mothers do vary a great deal in the extent that they observe fetal movements. Sometimes this awareness is related to the amount of amniotic fluid, since the water cushions movements. If you are preoccupied and concentrating hard on something else you may also be less aware of fetal activity. If you are still working outside the home, or busy inside it, there may be too much going on to notice fetal movements. But each woman's experience of the movements is fairly consistent if her baby is thriving in the uterus, bearing in mind that the nature of movements changes after the baby has engaged, as described above.

If for any reason it is thought that your baby may be "at risk" (usually because you have not put on weight for two or more weeks, your tummy has not got bigger during this time, or because you are "overdue" in relation to your EDD), you can use your own knowledge about your baby's movements to keep a check on its wellbeing inside you. It is a satisfying feeling to know that monitoring your baby's activity is more likely to be an accurate gauge of how the baby is than a series of complicated tests done by other people. Researchers compared what they called a "daily fetal movement" chart, drawn up by women, with a placental function test designed to measure the total excretion of oestriol in the urine over a period of 24 hours (see page 216).* When the amounts of oestriol in the urine were low but the mother said that she was aware of a normal number of fetal movements, every single baby was born alive. Unfortunately when the oestriol levels were normal but the mother noticed that her baby was hardly making any movements in the uterus at all, three out of ten babies died.

Suppose that you have gone past your dates, and the obstetrician is beginning to suggest taking you into hospital for observation and to talk about possible induction; you can then start to keep a systematic fetal movement chart. If your baby is not being adequately nourished in the uterus and your placenta is failing in its function, fetal movements will diminish over a period of three or four days and some time after that they will stop altogether. If you leave it this late, birth will probably be by Caesarean section in order to ensure a speedy delivery and to care for the baby. But if you monitor the gradual decrease in movements, and tell the doctor as soon as you observe this happening, you will probably be induced, but be able to deliver the baby normally and a Caesarean won't be necessary.

When to take action

If you have observed no movement at all over a period of 12 hours and your baby does not wake up at night, go to the hospital or to your own doctor and ask if you can have the fetal heart checked. If you are in hospital fetal activity can be checked immediately with ultrasound. A transducer is placed on your tummy near the baby's heart. You tell the doctor or midwife as soon as you feel movement.

It has been discovered that there is an effective minimum number of movements which can tell you that the baby is all right; ten movements, of any kind, in a 12-hour period indicate that all is well. If you notice fewer than ten movements in that time your baby may *still* be fine, since 2·5 per cent of daily counts made by women who have healthy babies fall below that, but the indications are that the baby would be better off born in the majority of cases.

The "Count to Ten" chart

The "Count to Ten" chart* is a way in which the mother records fetal activity in half-hour blocks of time on squared paper. It is very boring to have to observe your baby's movements all day and much easier simply to note down the first ten movements in a 12-hour period and stop when you have recorded them. The way in which the chart is often used in hospital is to tell the mother to start recording fetal movements at 9 am and go on until ten are recorded. She is told to black in the square corresponding to the time at which she has felt the tenth movement.

If you are going to do this as a record for yourself use squared paper and indicate the days of the week along the top. Put the hours of the day down the left-hand side, beginning with the time at which you have decided to start recording. It is probably better to start at teatime or thereabouts (but it should be at the same time each day), and record during the evening. This seems the sensible half of the day because you are more likely to have a stretch of time when you are sitting down, reading, listening to music, chatting or watching television, and from experience this is known to be a time when fetal movements are often felt. If you start at 4 pm and go to bed at 10 pm or later you then have a clear six-hour period for noting movements.

On your chart you fill in the block in which the fifth movement occurs. A baby who is not very active will take a longer time to get to the fifth movement. If you do not feel any movements by the time you lie down to sleep at night ring the hospital first thing in the morning, say that your baby is hardly moving at all and ask if they will check the fetal heart and activity. (You will probably find that as soon as you settle down to sleep the baby starts moving. If this happens, record the time; but if it is not yet the fifth movement of the day do not shade in the square.)

The point about this method of assessing the baby's welfare is that it is something active you can do for yourself. From both your and the baby's point of view it is completely non-invasive, as well as being incredibly simple.

FETAL MOVEMENT
RECORDING
This way of assessing your baby's wellbeing is especially useful if you are apparently "overdue". Starting at the same point each day, mark the square against the time when you feel your baby's 5th movement. If you do not feel any movements by the end of a 6-hour period contact the hospital without delay. And if you feel fewer than 5 movements it is also advisable to ring the hospital.

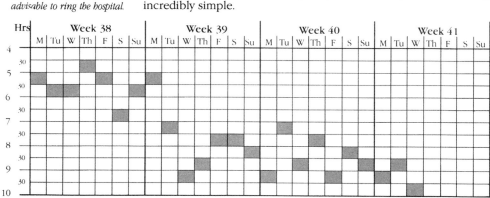

Number of movements if fewer than 5 have been felt by 10pm

The experience of birth

Moments of birth

The cervix is fully dilated to 10 cm and the midwife feels the position of the baby's head as it moves down the birth canal. The mother is now free to go with the great sweeps of energy that accompany the overpowering urge to bear down and is caught up in an act that requires intense concentration. Her partner gives himself fully to helping her cope with each contraction.

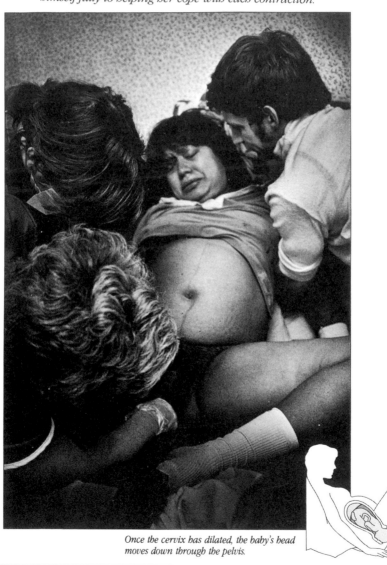

Once the cervix has dilated, the baby's head moves down through the pelvis.

The appearance of the head

The baby's head has slipped under the mother's pubic bone and emerges. Because it has rotated in the birth canal, it is now facing downwards. The midwife feels to make sure that the cord is not round the baby's neck.

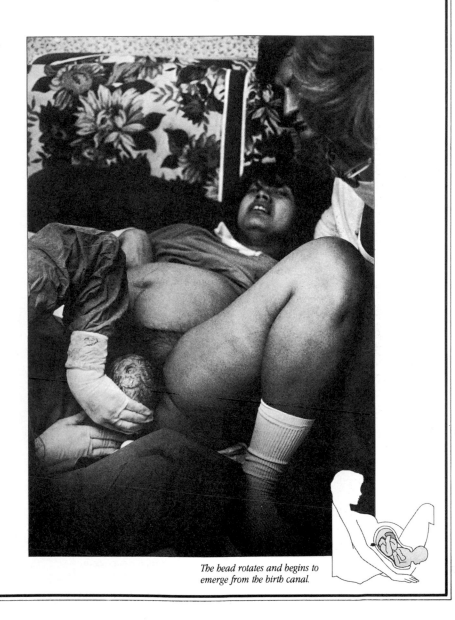

The head rotates and begins to emerge from the birth canal.

Rotation of the head

The baby's head starts to rotate again, so that it is once more in line
with the shoulders. Now that she has pushed the head out, the
mother is relaxed and happy, and sits up to catch the first glimpse of
her child.

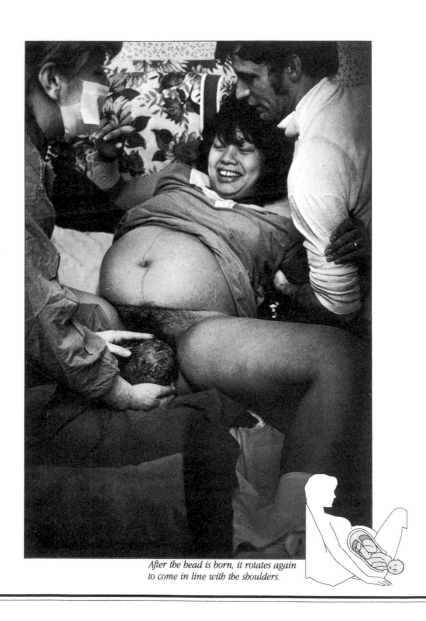

After the head is born, it rotates again
to come in line with the shoulders.

Birth of the body

The baby's body follows, helped out by the midwife. He is already breathing. The hair is damp and the skin still crinkled up like a rose petal before it has opened. The parents look on in wonder.

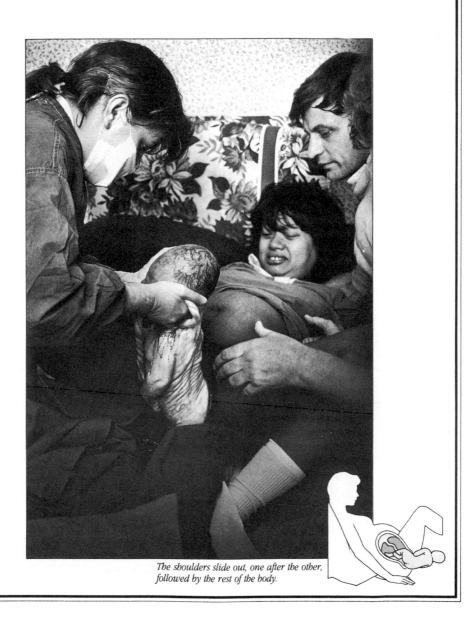

The shoulders slide out, one after the other, followed by the rest of the body.

Becoming a family

The long-awaited moment. Joy and a celebration as the mother holds her child in her arms for the first time. Still attached to the placenta by the umbilical cord, he lies safe and warm against her tummy after his journey to life.

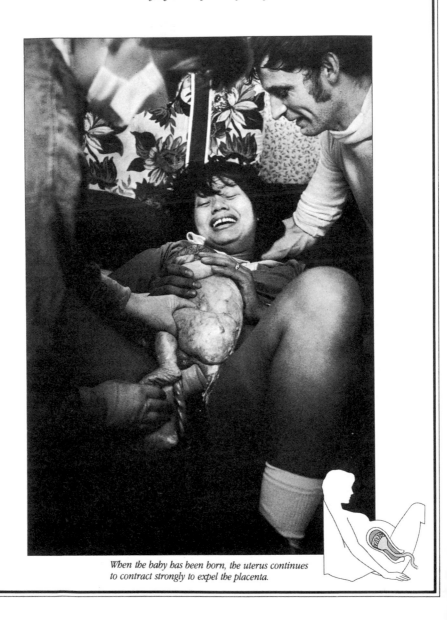

When the baby has been born, the uterus continues to contract strongly to expel the placenta.

What happens in labour

There are three stages of labour. During the first the cervix is being drawn up into the main body of the uterus and dilating; in the second the baby is pressed down through the birth canal and this stage culminates in delivery; during the third the placenta and membranes are sloughed off the lining of the uterus and expelled.

Having said this, it is important to add that for many women labour is an overwhelming and dramatic experience and you certainly are not sitting around thinking in terms of neat stages. There is no fanfare of trumpets to tell you when the first stage is really under way or when the second stage has started. Some women have a clear physiological message, such as the breaking of the waters or sudden strong, regular contractions, leaving them in no doubt that labour has started and that this is unmistakably *it*, and when they reach the end of the first stage they know with equal certainty that they are now in the second stage and *have* to push. For a great many women, however, the different stages of labour shade over into each other. The experience is rarely as tidy and compartmentalized as books on labour seem to suggest, and the third stage may even pass completely unnoticed as you hold your newborn baby in your arms and marvel at it.

Build-up to labour

Labour starts with the gradual softening and ripening of the cervix at the base of the uterus. This can take days and days or can happen overnight, especially if you have had a baby before. Once the cervix is soft and stretchy the uterine contractions—which are occurring anyway in late pregnancy—tend to draw it up bit by bit, so that it gradually changes from being a long canal hanging down in your vagina to being a dip in the bottom of the uterus, the tissues having been pulled up into the lower segment of the uterus.

You are not considered to be in labour when all this is happening. Your labour has not started in medical terms until you are having regular contractions which are effectively dilating (widening) the cervix; it is work that has to be done before it is possible for the cervix to open up. Usually this means you are at least 3 cm dilated (see page 244) before you are considered to be in labour. In fact many women already have a partially dilated cervix by the time they realize that they are having contractions.

It is obviously more pleasant for you if your body is working for you while you are carrying on with your work and shopping and eating and sleeping and seeing your friends. You cannot possibly be tensing up and fighting your body when you are busy doing all these things and leaving your uterus to work undisturbed and unremarked on. So carry on normal living for as long as is comfortable.

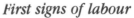

First signs of labour

Three things can indicate that labour has started or is about to start: a show appears, the waters break or contractions begin.

A show appears This is the blood-stained mucous discharge that you have when the cervix is beginning to stretch. Until the start of labour this mucus has acted as a gelatinous plug in the cervix, sealing off the uterus. Its appearance is a good sign that there is some definite activity round the cervix. But it can come out two or three weeks before you actually go into labour and contractions are established, or it may appear when your labour is so far advanced that you do not notice it. So, although you can take it as an encouraging sign, do not rush off to hospital. Go on with your everyday activities or, if it is night, have a hot milky drink and go back to sleep.

The bag of waters breaks When the membranes surrounding the baby have been pressed down like a wedge in front of its presenting part (usually the head) and pressure has built up, the bag pops. It may do this suddenly with a rush of water or, and this is more likely, with a slow trickle. In fact, you may not be quite sure whether the bag of waters has burst or you are wetting your pants. If you are not sure, forget it (if you can) and carry on as usual, unless you are still several weeks away from your EDD, in which case you should go to the hospital at once. If it is more than three weeks before your baby is due it is important for you to be in a place where special care is ready for the baby at delivery.

You will probably have been told to ring the hospital or your doctor or midwife if the waters break and you lose a lot of water at once. This is because, if labour is slow, taking 24 hours or more from the rupture of the membranes, there is a chance of your baby becoming infected. Also, if the baby's head does not fit properly into the cervix, there is a chance that the waters might sweep the cord down through the cervix, which in turn might mean the blockage of the oxygen supply to the baby. If, therefore, you do not know how your baby is presenting before you go into labour, you should be prepared to go to hospital immediately after the waters break, in case the baby is breech or its head is high. Today obstetricians usually decide to stimulate the uterus into activity once the waters have gone. If you are sure of the presentation, give nature a chance and allow yourself three or four hours of gentle everyday activity before leaving for hospital. Contractions will usually start during this time.

There is no need to worry about having a "dry" labour, with the baby travelling down an unlubricated birth canal, as there is no such thing. Your amniotic fluid is completely reformed every three hours. Actually a "wet" labour is more likely and can be uncomfortable, since a continual leaking throughout labour is cold and unpleasant. If you are leaking, wear a sanitary pad and change it frequently.

Contractions start They usually feel like a tight elastic belt slung under your bump and round into the lower part of the small of your back, being drawn tighter, gripping for 15 to 20 seconds, and then being released. This sensation occurs again after ten minutes, or even sooner. These might be the Braxton Hicks "rehearsal" contractions, which some women experience as quite painful at times in the last three weeks or so of pregnancy. These then tend to be called "false" labour. All this means is that you thought you were in labour, with good reason, but were not.

If you want to be fairly sure about being in labour, time your contractions over a period of 30 minutes or an hour; make a note of the interval between the start of one and the start of the next, and also note down the length of each contraction. The contractions need to come closer and closer together and to last longer (40 seconds or more) before you can be confident that labour is being established.

During contractions the muscle fibres at the top of the uterus tighten, pressing in and down on the centre and producing an upward pull on the cervix. When the baby's head is pressed down by

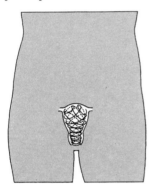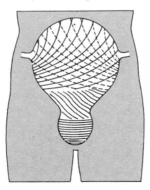

MUSCLE BUNDLES
The uterus is composed of spiral muscle bundles which in early pregnancy start to unfold into an open-latticework formation at the top of the uterus. If you think of the uterus as a clock, the muscle bundles are spaced out most between 9 and 3— that is, over the fundus of the uterus. By the end of the pregnancy these bundles of muscle have unfolded much more and are stretched lengthways.

a contraction, the muscles and fibrous tissues of the cervix are drawn apart. In a straightforward labour most of the physical sensations caused by contractions come from this area in and around the cervix, apart from a hardening and swelling felt at the top of the uterus.

Once the contractions are going well, they have a regular rhythm, a wave-like shape, and last longer and longer, while the interval between them is reduced. One woman said she felt her contractions like heat from an oven. First the oven door opened a little and then more till she was in the full blast of heat. Then it closed again.

The first stage of labour

Although we do not know for certain what starts labour off, one theory is that when the tissue in the baby's adrenal gland is mature it produces cortisone. This triggers off a remarkable process. It changes the balance between the amount of oestrogen and pro-gesterone produced by the placenta, the oestrogen level dropping

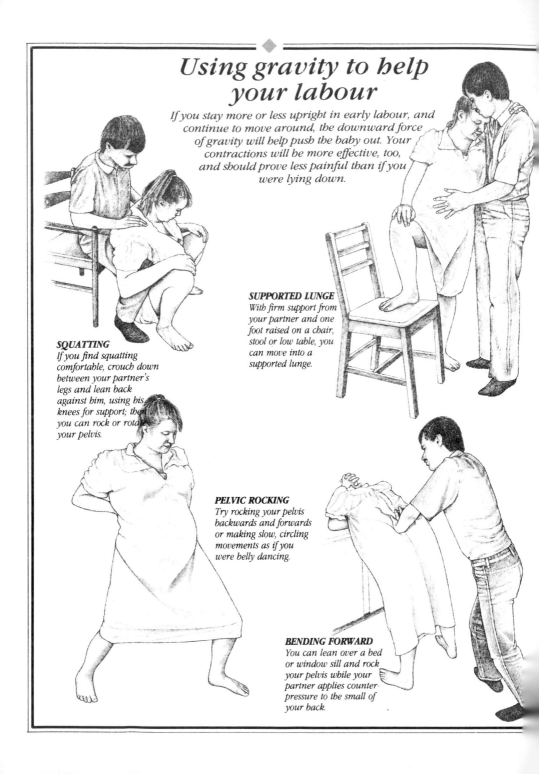

Using gravity to help your labour

If you stay more or less upright in early labour, and continue to move around, the downward force of gravity will help push the baby out. Your contractions will be more effective, too, and should prove less painful than if you were lying down.

SUPPORTED LUNGE
With firm support from your partner and one foot raised on a chair, stool or low table, you can move into a supported lunge.

SQUATTING
If you find squatting comfortable, crouch down between your partner's legs and lean back against him, using his knees for support; then you can rock or rotate your pelvis.

PELVIC ROCKING
Try rocking your pelvis backwards and forwards or making slow, circling movements as if you were belly dancing.

BENDING FORWARD
You can lean over a bed or window sill and rock your pelvis while your partner applies counter-pressure to the small of your back.

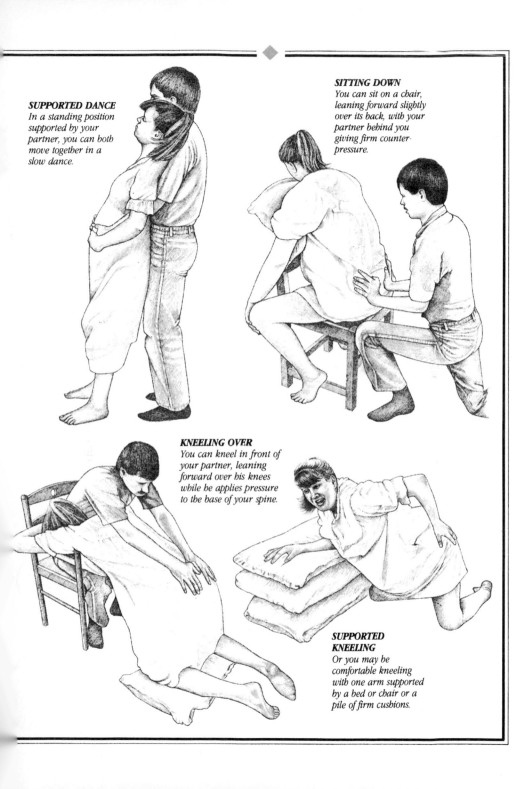

SUPPORTED DANCE
*In a standing position
supported by your
partner, you can both
move together in a
slow dance.*

SITTING DOWN
*You can sit on a chair,
leaning forward slightly
over its back, with your
partner behind you
giving firm counter-
pressure.*

KNEELING OVER
*You can kneel in front of
your partner, leaning
forward over his knees
while he applies pressure
to the base of your spine.*

**SUPPORTED
KNEELING**
*Or you may be
comfortable kneeling
with one arm supported
by a bed or chair or a
pile of firm cushions.*

and the progesterone level going up, and this in turn initiates the production of prostaglandins. The prostaglandins act on the uterus to make the contractions you have been having in late pregnancy bigger and closer together. So the contractions of early labour may feel like Braxton Hicks contractions, but heftier and more regular.

These more efficient contractions press the baby's presenting part down to the base of the lower segment of the uterus and against the cervix. This then becomes progressively more stretched and thinned out as the muscle fibres are pulled up into the upper segment. The effacement and stretching of the cervix next trigger the production of oxytocin from the posterior pituitary gland, and this stimulates the uterus into a steady rhythm of contractions. Labour is under way!

Moving around in labour

Going to bed early in the first stage of labour and becoming more or less immobile can slow down labour or interfere with it starting effectively because the presenting part may not be pressed down against your cervix. When you are upright, moving around, you have gravity to help you; everything is being pressed down.

In this position the uterus is contracting against the force of gravity.

It was not till the end of the eighteenth century in Europe that women began to lie down to give birth. Before that time they had walked around during much of labour and used labour stools or sat up in bed or on a chair. Birth stools were designed like horseshoes, with the open part at the front, were low on the ground so that the woman squatted, and sometimes provided support for her lower back as well as handgrips. As a result she was in a physiologically excellent position.

Mauriceau, then the obstetrician to the French court, introduced the lying-down position and it soon caught on because people sought to imitate the manners of the court. When forceps were introduced (see page 306), obstetricians found that they were easier to use on a woman who was lying flat. Still later, the lithotomy position, in which the patient lies on her back with her legs fixed to raised stirrups and which was first devised for surgery on bladder stones, was introduced. This highly artificial posture is often terribly uncomfortable for the woman, pressing her uterus against the big blood vessels in the lower part of the body. This interferes with her circulation, causing hypotension (low blood pressure), and also with the production of urine; it can cause fetal distress.

Research on the effect of different positions in the first stage of labour* has shown that most women prefer to be up and about, not lying in bed, and that contractions are stronger and labour shorter with the woman in an upright position. The uterus is working nearly twice as efficiently to dilate the cervix.

So, between contractions keep walking about. Try full pelvic rocking and circling movements as if you were belly dancing. If dilatation is taking a long time, also try soaking in a warm bath or squatting on a low stool under the shower.

The first stage of labour

*The first stage of labour is by far the longest,
and it helps to be upright and moving about.
A woman needs a loving partner or someone
else she trusts to hold and encourage her and
to share the experience with her.*

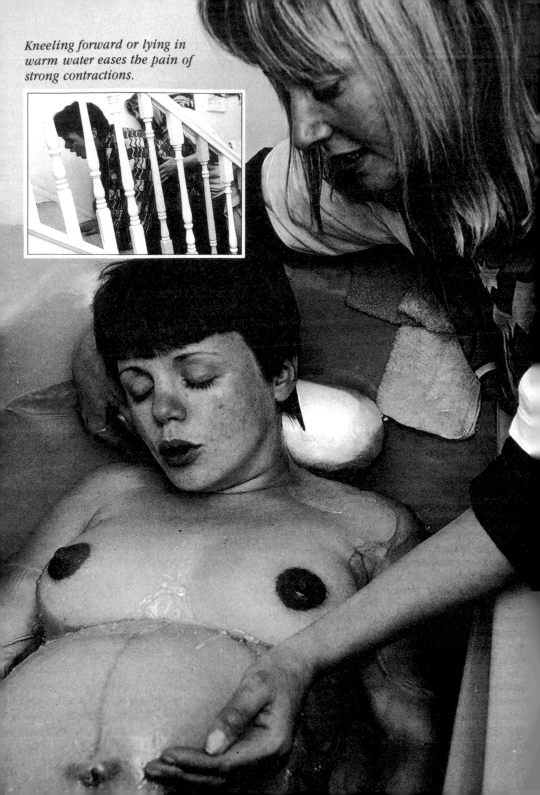

Kneeling forward or lying in warm water eases the pain of strong contractions.

A firm back massage—your partner breathing with you—gives comfort and reassurance.

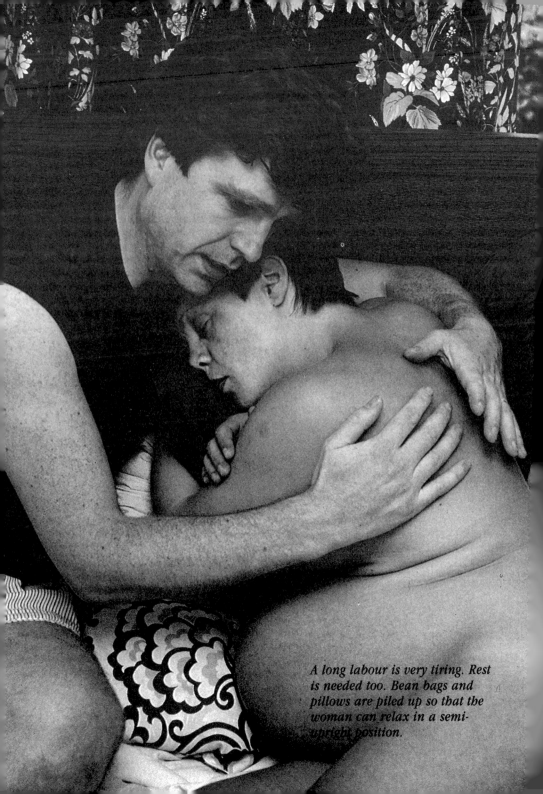

A long labour is very tiring. Rest is needed too. Bean bags and pillows are piled up so that the woman can relax in a semi-upright position.

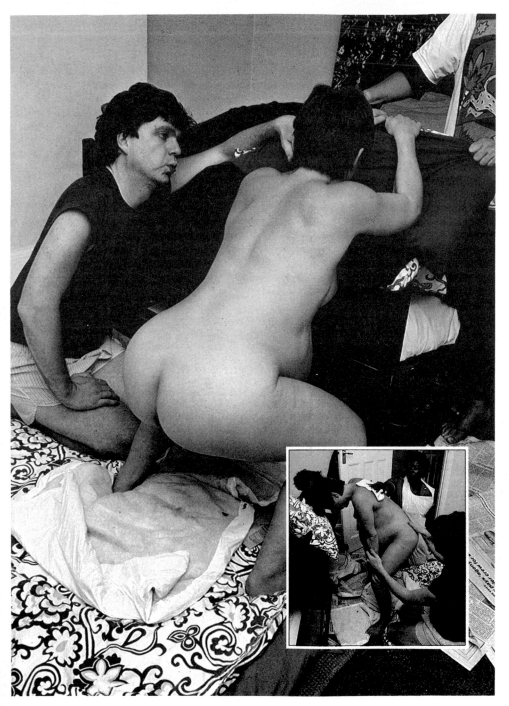

Open positions, legs well apart, help the progress of labour.

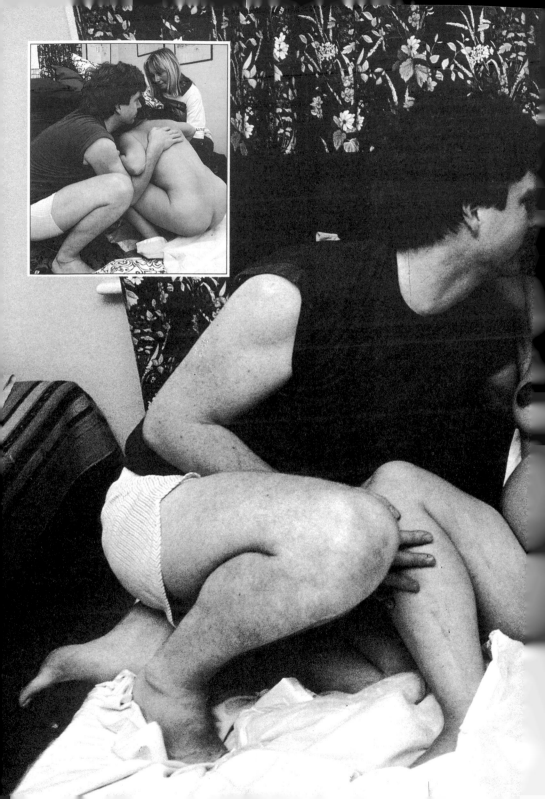

*In the late first stage huge
waves swell and rush
through the woman's body.
Her helpers are like anchors
in a stormy sea.*

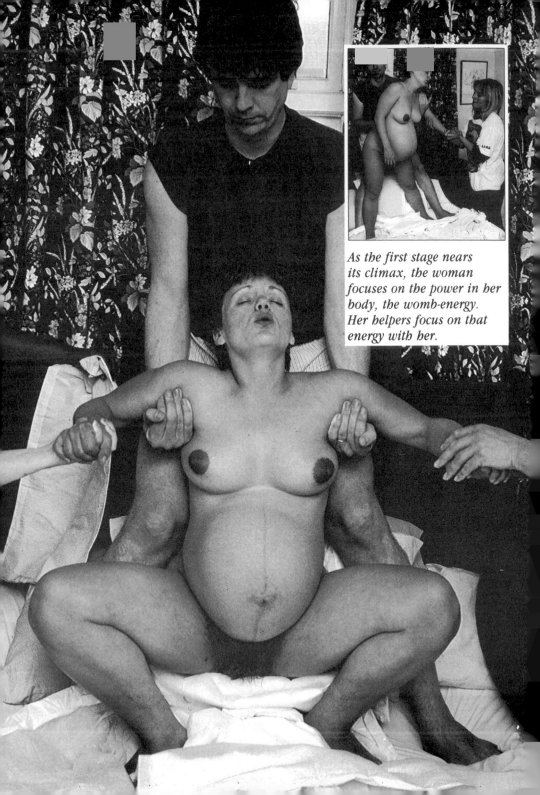

As the first stage nears its climax, the woman focuses on the power in her body, the womb-energy. Her helpers focus on that energy with her.

When to go to hospital

Unless you feel strongly that you need to be in hospital during this time, or your doctor has advised that there is a special reason why you should come in as soon as there are any signs of labour starting, it is best to stay at home and carry on as usual. This is partly because of the psychological effect of going to hospital, being admitted and prepared and getting into bed. If you have only just begun labour, all this can stop it entirely. There are many women who have gone to hospital with regular contractions that are still more than five minutes apart and who have then gone out of labour and have either had to wait around with their morale dropping steadily or have had an intravenous oxytocin drip inserted in an arm vein to stimulate the uterus into action.

Knowing that your contractions will be coming one every two minutes and will last about one minute or longer just before the baby is born may give you some perspective on your labour when it is just starting. Having contractions every five minutes can be tiring and some women experience this for 12 hours or more (usually when the baby is in a slightly awkward position, facing the mother's front instead of her back, see page 257), but the baby cannot possibly be born when contractions are coming this far apart, so if you are happier at home, stay there. Keep a careful record of what is happening, time the contractions now and again, and be ready to go to hospital as soon as the membranes rupture or contractions come more often than every five minutes.

Of course you must bear in mind the distance from your home to the hospital and the difficulty of getting there. If you are going in your own car, it is as well to have done a dummy run beforehand at the rush hour to see how long it can take and to be sure that you know the way, even in deep snow, hail or fog, and also any short cuts that may be convenient. Your partner should drive steadily, but not fast, and certainly not braking suddenly at corners or at lights. Decide early what you will need to make the journey comfortable and whether you would prefer to be in the front or back seat. If you are calling an ambulance, find out well in advance how to do this and, if you are relying on getting to hospital by taxi, have a list of several numbers pinned up by the telephone in case one is not immediately available.

Admission procedures

When you arrive at the hospital, a midwife will take you to a little room where you will be "prepped" (prepared) for labour. She will ask you questions about how labour started, if the waters have gone, and if so when, how often contractions are coming, and so on. She will do some of the things you are already familiar with from the antenatal clinic, such as checking your blood pressure, feeling the position of the baby through your abdominal wall and listening to the fetal heart. Feeling through your vagina and into your cervix, she will be able to tell if you have started dilating. If you are already partially dilated, she may break the waters (see page 291). This is done routinely in many hospitals at 3–4 cm dilatation, and sometimes before this phase has been reached. If you want your membranes to remain intact until they rupture spontaneously, say so before your internal examination.

It used to be hospital practice to shave a woman's perineum, and in some hospitals every perineum was required to be as bald as a hard-boiled egg. Still today some attendants like the hair surrounding the vagina to be clipped short. Women have spoken out strongly against the unnecessary, uncomfortable and degrading practice of perineal shaving; research has shown that it is useless in avoiding infection and, however carefully done, always results in some injury to the skin.

Some midwives still give an enema or suppositories to empty the lower bowel, but there is no point unless a woman is very consti-pated. In the hours before labour starts, most women have loose motions. In this way the lower bowel is cleared naturally.

After you have been examined you will have a shower. In older hospitals and birth centres you may be able to soak in a bath. You will probably be asked to don a hospital gown; it is usually done up at the back, but if you hope to have your baby at the breast immediately following delivery you will find it easier to wear the gown with the opening at the front. In many hospitals now you can choose to wear your own clothes. If you would like to do this, select something made of cotton rather than a synthetic fabric, as giving birth is hot work and hospitals are often over-heated. Whatever you wear should be loose, so that you can move freely.

Make a note of the length of contractions and any other physical signs so that this information is available when you phone the midwife.

In some hospitals your partner may be asked to wait outside while you are prepped, but today many midwives take it for granted that a couple want to stay together. It can seem a very long time to be separated and if your partner has been helping you cope with contractions up till now, it is good to go on having the same kind of support. It also gives the midwife a chance to talk with the father, which means that she is meeting you not as an isolated patient but in your relationship with your man. If you have chosen to have someone other than the father with you, they should be able to stay, too. Labour is not a good time in which to have people coming and going. You will be able to relax knowing that you are with someone who understands you and is giving continuous emotional support.

A doctor may come into the room, too, to assess progress or to discuss your case. If you have any questions, take this opportunity to ask them. If you are planning a natural birth, want to walk around in labour, or have any other wishes, remind the doctor and midwife of these and ask if they have been or can be noted on your chart.

Countdown for birth at home

If you are having your baby at home, plan ahead and make sure that any major chores do not pile up. When you think you are in labour, start to prepare for the birth. Put a plastic sheet (the kind of sheeting you can get from builders' merchants is the cheapest) on the bed and if the bed is not already at right angles to the wall move it to this position. Put out the things that the midwife has asked you to have ready on a small table or better still a trolley, arranged on a freshly laundered towel, teatowel or pillow slip and cover them with another piece of cloth. Arrange the lighting so that the midwife can direct some light onto your perineum for delivery and so that the other lights can be dimmed or turned out. Put the baby's clothes to air and a hot water bottle in the cot. Boil some water: this will be used mostly for tea, but is also useful for washing your perineum after delivery.

Then turn your mind to what you are going to eat and drink for the next three days and also what you may want to offer visitors. You will have been wise to have stocked up your store-cupboard and freezer well in advance. If you put anything in the oven at this stage, take a timer with you when you go to the bedroom and write a reminder, pinning it in a prominent place, or your labour may be accompanied by the smell of burning.

Call the midwife, if possible before she goes out on her rounds, to let her know that you may be needing her later, and pin all important phone numbers by the phone. The midwife will probably call to check how you are doing and will leave you telephone numbers of where she can be contacted throughout the day.

Transition

Towards the end of the first stage, when you are between 8 and 10 cm dilated, you are in transition.

For most women the very end of the first stage is stormy and challenging. Contractions follow each other relentlessly with hardly a pause between, and they tend to become arhythmic, with sharp peaks and sometimes with more than one to each contraction. The build-up of energy with each may be so sudden and tumultuous that there is no time for slow breathing and you must adapt straight away and breathe much more lightly and quickly if you are to soar over the top of the peaks with your breathing. The very length of the contractions may demand every bit of concentration and determination you are able to summon, and you will need strong emotional support and unfailing encouragement. Your partner's attention must not waver for a minute and he should repeatedly communicate to you his confidence in you and his love.

Every time a big contraction came part of me said "No no" and I answered mentally "Yes yes".

At the same time other physiological signs may occur which can be unsettling, until you remember that they are indications of progress and that if you are aware of three or more of them, then you are likely to be 8 cm dilated and hence in transition. Feeling hot then cold, then hot again, your cheeks flushed and your eyes shining bright, suggests that you are in transition. So does a fit of hiccups or belching, or you may even feel nauseous and actually vomit. Perhaps your legs feel icy cold and begin to shake uncontrollably. One of the surest signs is feeling that you have a large grapefruit pressing against your anus or that you want to empty your bowels. You might have a catch in your throat that stops your easy rhythmic breathing or you involuntarily hold your breath or start to grunt. You may suddenly feel that it is all too much hard work and that you cannot go on and would like to go home and forget about having a baby. Or you may become irritable with everyone and hypercritical of the help your partner is giving.

Not all women experience these signs, but a sufficient proportion do to make it a good idea for your partner to memorize them, so that at the right moment he can say: "I think you are in transition". You may have forgotten you are having a baby by this time and are simply concentrating on the work of handling each contraction. You are also very likely to feel that you are not making any progress at all and have lost all sense of time. Since in transition you may get an urge to push before you are fully dilated, you may be told to continue breathing and not to hold your breath until you absolutely must.

Pushing powerfully and for a long time against an incompletely dilated cervix can make it puffy and swollen so that the opening actually closes rather than opens wider. This is why you may be asked not to push until you cannot avoid pushing. This is wise advice, because then you can be quite certain that your body is really ready to push and you will also enjoy the surrender to the great sweeps of energy that come with the contractions in a way you cannot if you are just pushing because someone has told you to do so.

I liked to feel a warm hand on my arm through the contractions.

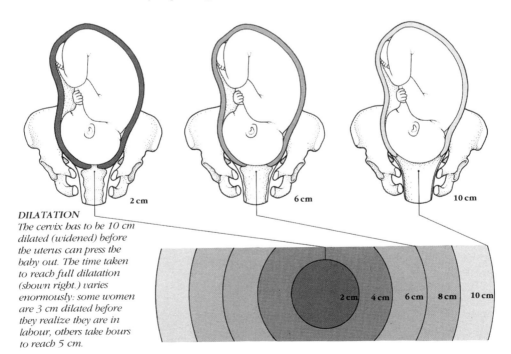

DILATATION
The cervix has to be 10 cm dilated (widened) before the uterus can press the baby out. The time taken to reach full dilatation (shown right.) varies enormously: some women are 3 cm dilated before they realize they are in labour, others take hours to reach 5 cm.

2 cm   6 cm   10 cm

2 cm 4 cm 6 cm 8 cm 10 cm

Transition may be very brief—just a few contractions—or it may last an hour or more. It is likely to last longer if the baby is in an occipito-posterior position (see page 257). The cervix has to dilate to 10 cm before the baby can be pressed down through the opening. At full dilatation (10 cm or the width of the palm of a large man's hand including the thumb joint) the cervix is open enough for the baby's head, its largest part, to ease through. There are spaces between the baby's skullbones, the fontanelles, which can close up as the baby slides down the birth canal, so shaping its head to make the journey much less arduous, even for a 9 lb (4 kg) baby. This is why, especially in first labours, the baby's head is moulded, sometimes into a rather peculiar shape; this gradually disappears in the first week or so after the birth (see page 331). As soon as the cervix has dilated to 10 cm, the second stage of labour starts.

The second stage of labour

The second stage of labour is the most exciting. During the first stage the cervix has thinned out and opened. At the end of the first stage the cervix is open to 10 cm, making the uterus and vagina one birth canal. Then follows a wonderful time when you can begin to push. The second stage of labour is often described as if it were sheer, grinding, hard work, but you will *want* to do it. You will probably have an overpowering urge to bear down and press the baby through the birth canal. This is passionate, intense, thrilling and often completely irresistible, and for some women it is the nearest thing to overwhelming sexual excitement. Pushing is not something you decide to do with a rational part of your mind, but a force that sweeps through your body and culminates in the delivery of your baby.

There are a few women who do not feel much of an urge to bear down. Sometimes women who have had other babies do not experience a strong pushing urge. The whole process may be gentler; the mother seems not to need to do much bearing down because that baby is going to be born very easily anyway.

There are three to five urges to bear down with each second-stage contraction, though sometimes we talk about these contractions as if they were all push. Frantic pushing results in your becoming desperate, straining to press the baby just that little bit farther. This is not necessary, because surges of desire to bear down come with each contraction, and it is important to go with each as it comes; allow yourself to hold your breath, bear down and open up with the surge, which usually lasts five or six seconds, no longer. Only you can know when these surges are there. Some people think it is a good idea for a woman to hold her breath for as long as she possibly can in the second stage and only then is she really working hard. However, research suggests that prolonged breath-holding is not only exhausting for the mother, but can also be dangerous for the baby because it reduces the oxygen content of the blood. So trust your spontaneous feelings and do what comes naturally.

I felt wonderful sensations of involuntary pushing. The midwife examined me and I heard the blessed words, "There's no cervix left."

Your baby's head appears

When the top of your baby's head can be seen for the first time, it looks like a wrinkled walnut in the vagina, not like a baby at all. Your partner will probably see this before you can, and will be able to tell you the colour of the baby's hair. With the first baby the second stage make take one or two hours. With the second or subsequent baby it may take only ten minutes.

Then there comes a time when the widest part of the baby's head is just at the birth opening and does not go back in between contractions. You feel stretched to your utmost. At this moment of "crowning" it is important not to go on pushing, even though you feel very much like it, otherwise you might tear the surrounding perineal tissue. The doctor or midwife may perform an episiotomy if they think you might tear (see page 294). If you want to avoid having one, just before the head crowns start to *breathe* the baby out instead of pushing it out (see page 192), and in this way it may slip forward without being forced. The midwife or obstetrician checks to see that the cord is free of the neck and may insert a mucus catheter in the baby's mouth and suck any mucus out.

The baby's head slips under your pubic bone and extends, the chin being automatically lifted off its chest. As the head emerges, damp and sticky with mucus, it is often a violet or purple colour. This is nothing to worry about: the child has not yet taken that first great gasp of air that will oxygenate the blood.

The journey through the pelvis

About 80 per cent of women have good, well-rounded pelvises for childbirth. Problems may be encountered if your pelvis is narrow: an android pelvis, for instance, is shaped like a triangle at the brim, which is hard for the baby to negotiate. Even when the pelvic shape is not ideal, the uterus works to press the baby into a neat package which, given time, can often make the journey without difficulty. Basically the baby consists of two balls which move against each other. The ball with the largest diameter is the baby's head. The other ball is the baby's trunk with the limbs well tucked in. The action of a uterus that is contracting well results in the baby being moulded into the right shape for the journey down the birth canal.

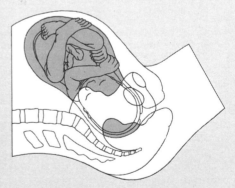

1 *The vagina is almost at right angles to the uterus. So the baby has to negotiate an angle similar to that of the foot putting on a wellington boot. But there are several bones that may stick out and hold up the baby's progress. The sacrum is the big bone in the spine which forms, together with the pubic bone at the front and the hip girdle at the sides, the pelvic brim. Once the baby's head has travelled below the pelvic brim, it is in the pelvic cavity.*

Normal female pelvis

Android pelvis

The baby may be covered in vernix, a cold-cream-like substance which coats the baby's skin in the uterus and makes it look as if it has been spread with cottage cheese. The head has been moulded by its journey down the birth canal, so it may be an odd, pointed or bumpy asymmetrical shape, and the forehead may recede and the baby be almost chinless. The nose is often flattened like a prize-fighter's and there are little red marks between the eyes and on the eyelids.

At delivery, the baby's head is facing downwards but the shoulders are still turned sideways inside you. Once the head is free, it turns to come in line with the shoulders. You may need another push for the shoulders. The doctor or midwife may press the baby's head down so that the shoulder nearer your front slides out first, then the head is lifted up so that the lower shoulder slides out next. Then the whole body slithers out and your baby is born!

There is often a great gush of water, and the baby may be already breathing and crying, its limbs lashing and its face puckered up with what looks like rage. The lower end of the body seems very small in comparison with the head end, apart from the genitals which often look extraordinarily large. All this is normal. If the baby is not yet breathing, attendants suck out the respiratory tract, and hold the child's head downwards, or they may give oxygen or an injection. If you are well propped up, you will be able to reach your baby, provided he or she is lying over your thigh or has been delivered up on to your tummy, and you may want to reach down straight away and take your daughter or son in your arms.

═ **"** ═

I felt the baby's head pop round and she was born. And she was a girl! All the time I had been desperate for a son but I didn't mind. I held her and she just lay there and liked it.

═ **"** ═

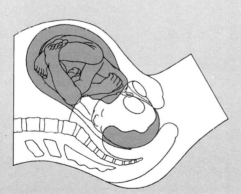

2 *Once the baby has negotiated the pelvic brim, it moves on to the pelvic outlet, bordered by the coccyx (the tiny bone at the base of the spine) at the back, the bottom of the pubic bone at the front, and the ischial spines, which are the two projecting crests on the side walls of the pelvis. The coccyx slips out of the way as the head comes through.*

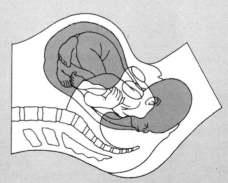

3 *Usually the downward pressure from above that is provided by good contractions will ease the baby's head down so that as it comes through the steepest curve at the beginning of the vagina the muscles at the back of the neck extend. In effect this means that the baby is facing downwards just before and as it is delivered.*

The third stage of labour

Though you may not feel the contractions, your uterus continues to contract after the birth of the baby. This makes the placenta separate from its lining, since the placenta cannot contract. As the uterus squeezes down into a firm, hard ball the placental mass is automatically peeled off. This process has been compared to stretching a piece of rubber on which a postage stamp has been stuck; when the rubber moves, the stamp becomes detached. The sinuses in which the placental blood vessels were rooted are closed by the tight squeezing of the uterus, and these contractions prevent excessive bleeding from the uterine wall.

When the placenta has detached itself, the midwife or doctor may pull on the cord (see page 296). Take a breath, hold it and bear down at the same time to help this process. You can ask that instead of having cord traction, you can push again and do it by yourself.

There is a squelchy, slippery feeling as the placenta slides out. The person who delivered you examines the placenta carefully to see that every part is there. Pieces of placenta left inside could cause unnecessary bleeding, pain and infection in the post-partum period. Though the placenta looks like a large piece of raw liver, it was the tree of life for your baby. You may be interested to examine it yourself and see the difference between the rough side, which was against the wall of the uterus, and the smooth side, which lay towards the baby like a soft, velvety cushion, and to note the network of blood vessels that provided your baby with its life-support system.

The midwife will help you on with a couple of sanitary pads, as there will be some bleeding now and for several days, resembling the height of a heavy period. The length of time during which there is a bloodstained vaginal discharge (lochia) varies greatly between women. Some new mothers bleed for just a few days after the birth, others for as long as five or six weeks.

Being together

In many hospitals the staff tidy up at this point. They wipe and weigh the baby, examine you to see if you need stitches, give you a wash, change your gown, shorten the baby's cord and reclamp it. But practice is changing fast and many now give the parents the opportunity for a quiet time with their baby immediately following the birth, only doing the basic essentials and leaving the couple for an hour or so to get to know their baby. Being together should always come first. Tidying up can be done later. It is far less important. If you need stitching, it is usually possible to have the baby with you throughout this procedure. Suturing (the technical term for stitching) is done under local anaesthetic and usually takes a long time, sometimes as long as an hour, since careful embroidery has to be done and the underlying layers of muscle must be correctly aligned. So keep your baby in your arms or near enough to touch.

Birth under water

*Babies can be born in water—either in a
special pool or in the bath. In warm water,
contractions are less painful, it is easier to
relax, and the tissues of the perineum are
soft and supple.*

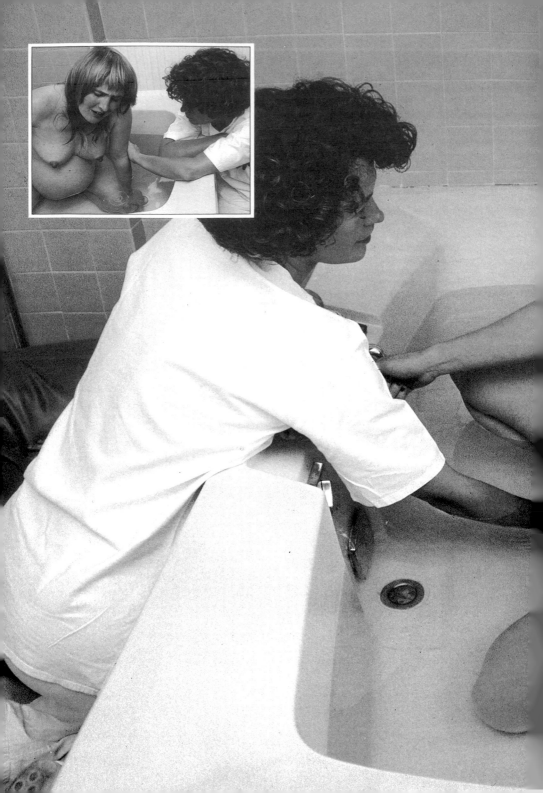

The mother kneels and her midwife can feel the baby's head just inside the vagina. As the midwife monitors the fetal heartbeat, one child watches, eager, quiet and intent.

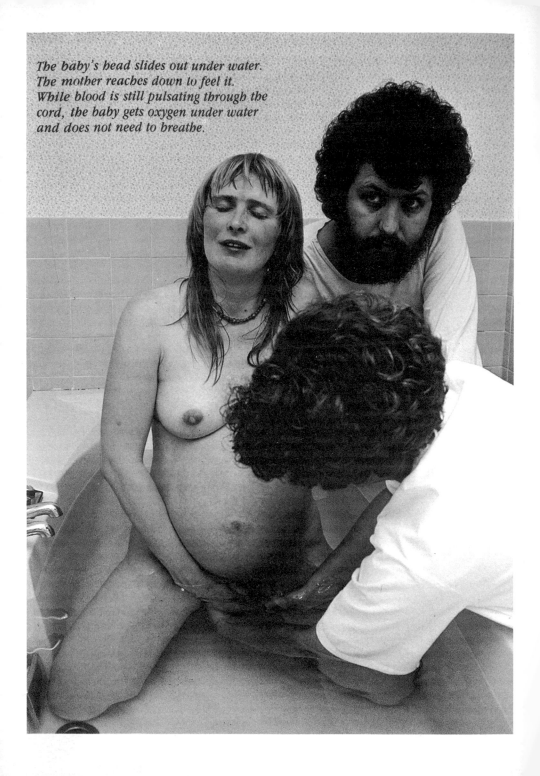

The baby's head slides out under water.
The mother reaches down to feel it.
While blood is still pulsating through the
cord, the baby gets oxygen under water
and does not need to breathe.

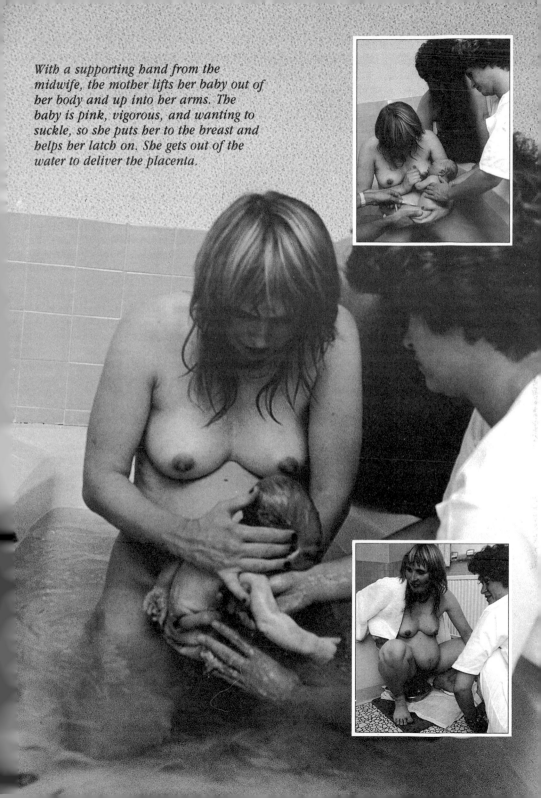

With a supporting hand from the midwife, the mother lifts her baby out of her body and up into her arms. The baby is pink, vigorous, and wanting to suckle, so she puts her to the breast and helps her latch on. She gets out of the water to deliver the placenta.

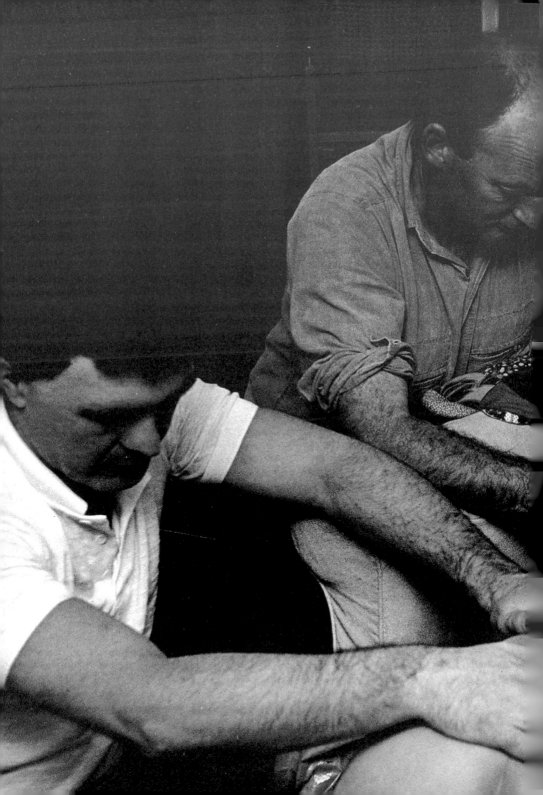

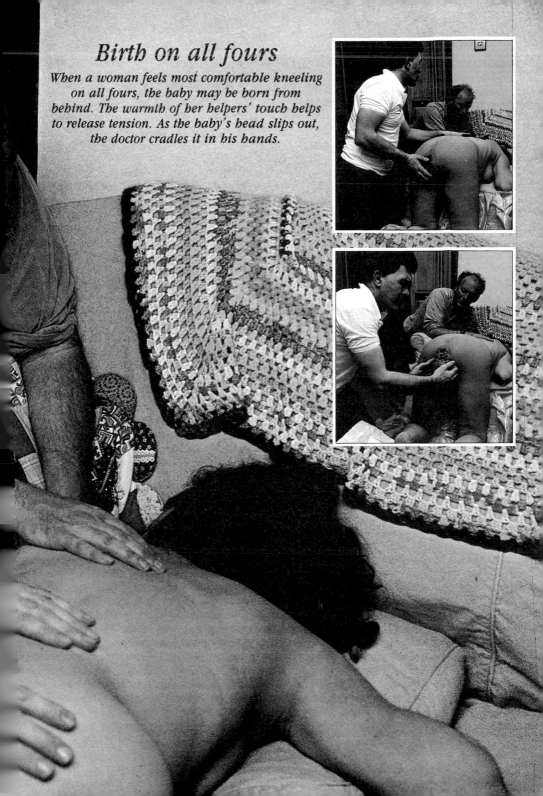

Birth on all fours

When a woman feels most comfortable kneeling on all fours, the baby may be born from behind. The warmth of her helpers' touch helps to release tension. As the baby's head slips out, the doctor cradles it in his hands.

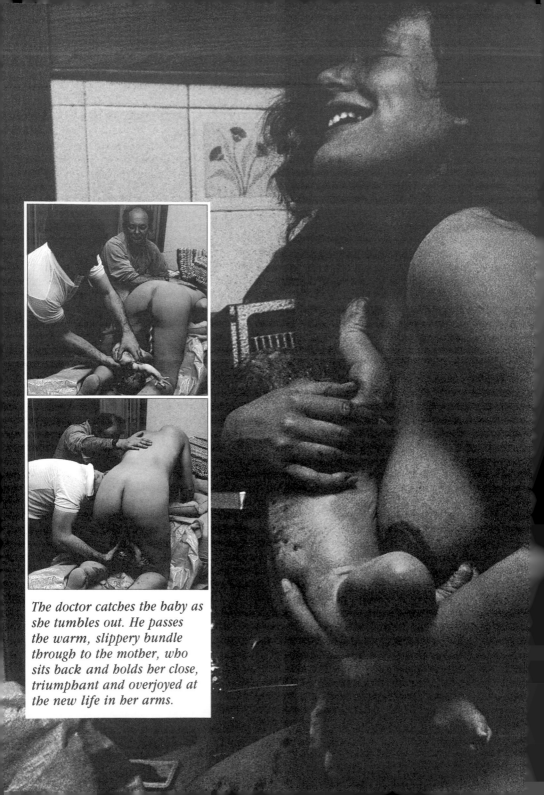

The doctor catches the baby as she tumbles out. He passes the warm, slippery bundle through to the mother, who sits back and holds her close, triumphant and overjoyed at the new life in her arms.

Different kinds
of labour

However much people may advise you not to have any preconceptions about your labour, just to be ready for whatever comes, it is difficult not to have some, because it is almost impossible to prepare yourself to cope with a situation that you have not imagined in advance. So it is useful to think ahead to the major variations on the theme of childbirth which you might confront. However, it is still vital to keep in the forefront of your mind the normal, rhythmic and harmonious pattern of a straightforward labour. Otherwise all the medical technicalities may seem bewildering, and you may interpret each uncomfortable physical sign as an indication that something has gone wrong.

This chapter looks at some different types of labour, all of which can throw you unless you understand what is happening.

Labour with a posterior baby

When the hard back of the baby's head presses against your sacrum or slightly to one side of it, the baby is said to be in an occipito-posterior position. Most women have some backache in labour, but women with posterior babies may have it all the time, so much so that the labour can be described as a "backache labour". Few women with posterior babies do not have backache, which can be the most tiring and stressful thing about a labour—especially if, as is often the case when the baby is posterior, it continues *between* contractions as well as during them.

Another characteristic of labour with a posterior baby is that it starts very slowly, often over a period of several days, and contractions are usually experienced as one big one followed by a feeble one. Plan for morale-boosting activity during a long first stage. Don't go into hospital too soon. A walk in the park or the country is probably better. Eat and keep up your strength in early labour and have plenty of fluids, remembering to empty your bladder regularly. Your partner also needs stamina in a backache labour, to keep you going by giving you his total attention during difficult contractions.

The baby will probably rotate at the very end of the first stage or on the onset of the second and things will be plain sailing from then on. About 5 per cent of posteriors do not rotate and then the hard work has to be continued in the second stage and you may need obstetric help (see page 306) to deliver the baby. But the chances are that the baby will swivel round by herself and then be able to complete her journey down your birth canal with ease.

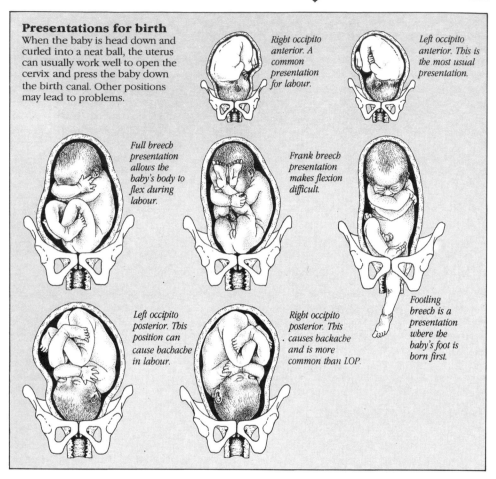

Presentations for birth
When the baby is head down and curled into a neat ball, the uterus can usually work well to open the cervix and press the baby down the birth canal. Other positions may lead to problems.

Right occipito anterior. A common presentation for labour.

Left occipito anterior. This is the most usual presentation.

Full breech presentation allows the baby's body to flex during labour.

Frank breech presentation makes flexion difficult.

Left occipito posterior. This position can cause backache in labour.

Right occipito posterior. This causes backache and is more common than LOP.

Footling breech is a presentation where the baby's foot is born first.

Ways of dealing with a backache labour

You may find that some of the things described on the following pages are helpful in the first stage of backache labour.

Heat A hot water bottle wrapped in a towel, or a hot compress (in the form of a face-cloth or small towel wrung out in really hot water) may bring relief, applied to where you feel most pain. A hot shower with the water pulsing on your back also helps.

Changes of position Keep upright and moving around for as long as possible. In this way you tip the baby down to press through the pelvis and birth canal instead of right into the small of your back. Crouching, leaning forward, kneeling, squatting, getting onto all fours, and lying on your side with your back well rounded, your head and shoulders curved forward and a good space between your legs, may all be positions in which pain is eased. They may also encourage the rotation of the baby's head.

Pressure Ask your partner to provide firm pressure, either right over the place where your pelvis joins your spine or to the left or right of this if the pain is more to the side. He should use the heel of the palm of one hand, with the other resting over it, and press his body weight down through his arm. Or you may prefer the feel of knuckles. It is sometimes comfortable to sit on your own knuckles, one hand under each buttock, so that firm pressure is applied there as your own weight is put on them.

Stimulus on pressure points may help you to handle the pain more effectively. One place where deep pressure of a thumb or finger may feel good is on your bottom, level with the top of the slit between your buttocks and a little more than the width of your palm out towards the leg on each side. Experiment to find the spot: it feels tender, but pressure on it is satisfying. If you are in a position in which you are tilted forward, your partner can apply pressure to the spot on both of your buttocks at once. If you are on your side he will only be able to reach one, but even this may help. These areas are called "pain prevention points" in one system of psychoprophylaxis.

Chinese pressure points Your partner can exert pressure on parts of the body far away from where you are feeling pain, but where a really strong stimulus can offer almost miraculous relief. Known as *shiatzu* or acupressure, this can be particularly effective in childbirth when used on the feet. One pressure point is just below the centre of the ball of the foot. Another is between the fleshy pads under the big toe and next toe. Your partner holds one foot firmly, exerting very strong pressure with a finger or thumb on the chosen spot, and providing light counter-pressure with the rest of the hand over the top of the foot.

There are many acupressure points on the buttocks, too. Kneel forward over the seat of a chair or lie three-quarters over on your side so that your partner can "map" the places on your buttocks where it feels good to have strong, steady pressure. Try, for example, pressing up just under the curve of the buttocks, and beneath the bony pelvis at either side of the buttocks. Another place where pressure can be very effective is on the inside wrist, between the tendons. Care should be taken to press only with the fleshy pad of a finger or thumb—not with the nails.

FOOT WORK
Applying pressure to certain parts of the feet can relieve pain from contractions. One spot is just below the centre of the ball of the foot; another is between the fleshy pads under the big toe and the next one.

It is surprising how strong the pressure from finger and thumb can be on the right spot, and in all these places continuous pressure will produce a tingling, buzzing sensation. Acupressure can provide effective pain relief during powerful contractions, whether they are felt on your front or back, and wherever the pain is centred.

Relieving a backache labour

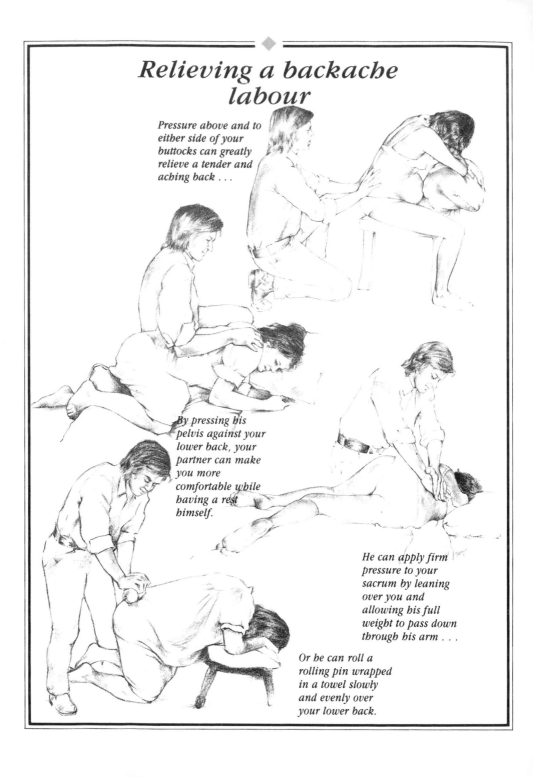

Pressure above and to either side of your buttocks can greatly relieve a tender and aching back . . .

By pressing his pelvis against your lower back, your partner can make you more comfortable while having a rest himself.

He can apply firm pressure to your sacrum by leaning over you and allowing his full weight to pass down through his arm . . .

Or he can roll a rolling pin wrapped in a towel slowly and evenly over your lower back.

Massage Massage may feel better than pressure, or can feel good alternated with pressure. The massage that suits most women best is firm, slow and steady, moving the flesh and muscle on the bone. You can use powder, cornflour or massage oil to avoid skin irritation, and your helper should have some cream to rub into his hands if he has to apply massage for a long time.

Another effective way of giving massage is to use a rolling pin. Knot a face towel or hot compress towel round it to get more grip.

If you are in the kind of environment where you can really do as you please, your partner can sit on the bed with his pelvis against your lower spine and lean back against you. This provides welcome rest for someone who after several hours of working to relieve backache may develop back pain himself!

Labour with a breech baby

Labour with a breech sometimes starts with the waters leaking. This is because the baby's bottom does not fit the opening cervix as well as the oval of the crown of the head, and so part of the bag of waters becomes wedged between the baby's bottom and your cervix. It is important that you call the hospital if this happens to you and the baby is not yet engaged. The risk is that the cord might slide down as well and be caught between the baby and the cervix, so that the oxygen supply to the baby is cut off.

If the waters do not break early in labour, stand up and keep walking around through the first stage, until they break spontaneously. There is a strong case to be made for not doing an amniotomy (see page 291), since if a breech baby is left in its bag of waters there can be no pressure on the cord.

After the waters have gone, the best positions are on all fours or on your side. You may have backache and if so your partner could exert pressure with the knuckles over the small of your back.

The second stage of a breech labour

You may be moved to an operating theatre before the second stage starts, in case you should need an emergency Caesarean section. Sometimes your partner is shown to the waiting room at this time. If you want to stay together make this clear.

Many doctors prefer to deliver breech babies with the woman in the lithotomy position (see page 232), since they feel that they have most control over the birth this way. But you will probably be more comfortable sitting, with your partner giving you a firm base with his shoulders and arm behind you, or sitting on the bed behind you, or you may prefer to squat or be on all fours.

It is usually best to let the second stage proceed with no voluntary exertion on your part until the body is born and the head is about to slip out, so that the baby's body is born on contraction waves only. (It may be easiest to do this if you are on all fours.) Concentrate on total release: breathe, rather than push, the baby out.

Breech birth

Breech babies can be born vaginally as long as the pelvic outlet is wide enough for the head to pass through it.

1 The buttocks are usually delivered first, followed by the legs.

2 The baby turns so that the shoulders can emerge as easily as possible.

3 The baby's own weight draws the head down and its legs are then lifted to deliver the head.

If the baby has both feet up by its head the doctor may slip a gloved hand in to draw down a leg and turn the baby into a footling (see page 258). Relax and breathe as this is done. Once the foot is down the baby can then take the curve of the birth canal more smoothly, as its legs are no longer splinting its spine. If you are not having an epidural (see below), an injection of local anaesthetic is given in your perineum if an episiotomy is to be done (see page 294), before the baby's head is delivered. It takes one or two minutes to be effective.

Most obstetricians do a large episiotomy with a breech so that the head can be delivered unimpeded, and some do two cuts, one each side of the perineum (a bilateral episiotomy). But if you give birth with breathing instead of pushing, your tissues may fan out well and an episiotomy may not be essential. Since there is unlikely to be an opportunity for discussion at the time, when things will be happening fast, talk about this earlier on in your labour (between contractions). Otherwise the doctor will probably do an episiotomy.

Once the episiotomy is done, the doctor can deliver the head, using hands or forceps to cradle it. You will be asked to push for the head and will probably find that you need to bear down only once.

Sometimes women can help to deliver their own breech babies by leaning forward and lifting the baby's legs up, while the doctor or midwife controls the delivery of the head and supports a shoulder. I first saw this done by mistake when a very helpful midwife told a first-time mother to put her hands down and touch her baby while its head was still inside her. The mother was so excited that she held the baby's legs, lifted them, and as she did so the head slipped out without an episiotomy.

Epidural anaesthesia (see page 286) is often used for breech deliveries and indeed has largely replaced general anaesthesia. It means that you only feel a pulling sensation, and that even if delivery is complicated you are awake and aware and can hold your baby as soon as it is breathing well. An increased number of obstetricians routinely do Caesarean sections (see page 308) for all first-baby breeches. Discuss this with your obstetrician. Even if a Caesarean section is the safest option for your baby, there is no need to be unconscious if you do not want to be.

Some doctors prefer to do routine Caesarean sections for all breech babies, and explain their practice by saying that vaginal delivery lowers a baby's IQ. In fact, it is doubtful whether there are any long-term benefits for the baby of Caesarean section over vaginal birth. Carefully controlled follow-up studies of the health and behaviour of $2\frac{1}{2}$- and $8\frac{1}{2}$-year-olds who were born bottom-first have revealed that the mode of delivery makes no difference at all*.

When thinking ahead to the kind of birth you will have for your breech baby, it is important to remember that the pelvis is not a rigid, confined space. During pregnancy the joints relax, bones move more freely on each other, and the pelvis actually expands to make more room for the baby. Moreover, both the width and the size of the

Breech birth in the squatting position

Taking up a squatting position, with your partner supporting you from behind, is a good way to give birth to a breech baby. It allows the pelvis to open up completely and makes the best use of the force of gravity.

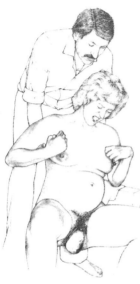

1 *The mother is supported by her helper standing behind her. The baby's buttocks emerge first.*

2 *The baby's body and legs are born.*

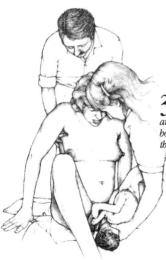

3 *The baby simply uncurls and drops into the attendant's hands. The baby's body is supported as the head is born.*

4 *The mother can then sit back and take her baby into her arms the moment after the birth.*

opening from front to back are increased in 28 per cent of women when they switch from lying down to a squatting position*.

In Dr Michel Odent's practice most women with breech babies have vaginal births. He likes the woman to be upright: "Our only intervention will be to insist on the supported squatting position for delivery, since it is the most mechanically efficient. It . . . is the best way to minimize the delay between the delivery of the baby's umbilicus and the baby's head. . . . We would never risk a breech delivery with the mother in a dorsal or semi-seated position*." If the first stage of labour goes well without any intervention, a woman has every chance of a vaginal birth. But if first stage contractions are inefficient and yet painful, and dilatation does not progress, a Caesarean section is decided on.

Short sharp labour

> She came so quickly there was no time to get to the delivery room. All was calm and peaceful. A mother in the next bed slept right through.

It is wrong to assume, as do some obstetric textbooks, that a short labour is bad for the baby. In many apparently short labours the cervix is dilating gently (see page 227) over a period of days before you realize you are in labour. And some short labours can be delightful. But however easy it might be physically, a violent precipitate labour is emotionally demanding and may leave you feeling drained and shocked.

If, from start to finish, your labour lasts less than an hour or two, you may need a great deal of active help from your partner, as well as his emotional support: in effect it is like starting straight in at the very end of the first stage. Your partner needs to concentrate with you and to maintain eye contact and breathe with you. Remember that breathing has to be light to avoid hyperventilation. Your partner may hyperventilate if everything is happening quickly and he becomes anxious or excited. So remind each other to keep the breathing butterfly-light over contraction peaks.

When you feel the baby pressing like a grapefruit against your anus it may be easiest to avoid pushing if you turn on your side, with your knees drawn up. But whatever position you choose, push only when you have to and then for as short a time as you can. Open your mouth, drop your jaw and relax your lips. Then continue breathing in and out through a relaxed mouth and concentrate on releasing all the tissues around your vagina as they fan out and open wide.

If the baby is coming very fast in the second stage you will probably need to blow as well as breathe quickly to stop yourself from pushing. If you feel as if you really must push, blow as if you were extinguishing a candle flame to reduce the intensity of the push (see page 192). You will not stop the push altogether, because the expulsive power of the uterus is there whatever you do, but you can limit it to a certain extent.

Some women feel after a labour of this kind that they want the baby inside them again; they wish that they could go back to the beginning, because everything happened so fast that they cannot make sense of it. Some even feel "cheated". If this is so with you, talk through each event of labour with your partner, fitting the pieces together, and relive the birth in your thoughts until you can see its shape.

Long-drawn-out labour

A lengthy labour can be psychologically taxing as well as physically exhausting. You need constant confident emotional support from someone who loves you and does not leave you. Yet unfortunately a prolonged labour tends to make a man anxious about what is happening, unsure of his role and often feeling that he ought to leave it all to the professionals.

A long-drawn-out labour can seem prolonged for two reasons: you may be unable to differentiate clearly between the lead-in to labour proper—sometimes called the "latent" phase—and active labour; and active labour itself may then be prolonged because contractions are faint and infrequent, or because they are not achieving dilatation of the cervix. In these cases, psychological support, accurate information and an opportunity to rest are vitally important. Even if contractions seem ineffective and dilatation is slow until you reach 4 cm, everything may seem to co-ordinate suddenly so that from then on labour goes like a bomb. Over 90 per cent of women having a lengthy latent phase go on to have a normal labour and delivery if given the chance*. So don't immediately assume that if labour takes several days to start it is going to be like that right through. Have relaxing hot baths, sleep or rest in different beds if possible so that you have a change of scene and automatically take up different positions. There may be a couch, an easy chair or even a hearthrug to lie on as a change from your usual bed. Do not go into hospital until you think you would feel happier there. Even if you have a long first stage the second may be completely normal.

The progress of your labour is assessed in terms of the rate of dilatation of the cervix (see page 244). Provided the baby is all right and its heart tones are regular, *slow dilatation at the onset of labour does not harm the baby*, however tiring you find it. Slow dilatation in the early phase is not the same as complete lack of progress over several hours once active labour has started (that is after about 3 cm); then the baby may be exposed to special risk and the heart rate may slow down. Do remember that it is difficult for people to be accurate about dilatation: you may be examined by someone who says you are 5 cm dilated, but an hour later someone else says you are only 4 cm or perhaps 5 cm dilated, when by then the first person examining you would have reckoned you to be 5½ cm dilated.

A squatting, crouching or kneeling position during contractions often helps.

Ways of dealing with a long labour

In hospital it is often difficult to walk about and alternate periods of rest with sessions of activity. But if you can do this, it is the best natural way of helping a uterus which is contracting ineffectually to start working far more efficiently.

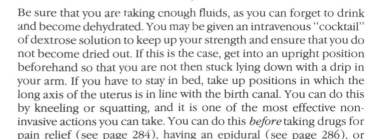

Be sure that you are taking enough fluids, as you can forget to drink and become dehydrated. You may be given an intravenous "cocktail" of dextrose solution to keep up your strength and ensure that you do not become dried out. If this is the case, get into an upright position beforehand so that you are not then stuck lying down with a drip in your arm. If you have to stay in bed, take up positions in which the long axis of the uterus is in line with the birth canal. You can do this by kneeling or squatting, and it is one of the most effective non-invasive actions you can take. You can do this *before* taking drugs for pain relief (see page 284), having an epidural (see page 286), or accepting hormone acceleration of labour (see page 301).

Sometimes fear or anxiety seems to prevent a uterus from functioning well. If physical difficulties have been ruled out, work together with your partner on facing up to any worries that may be on your mind. Together create an atmosphere which is psychologically positive, concentrating on the reality of the baby who is coming to birth and on the visual image of the cervix opening up. In parts of New Guinea when labour is long drawn out the woman is urged to confess any hidden anger she may feel because it is thought that labour will proceed smoothly and easily once she has got rid of the negative feelings she is bottling up.

Throughout labour I was conscious that I could only go with the contractions. It was like a marathon.

Dysfunctional labour

One thing that may hold up labour is incoordinate uterine action. Unfortunately it is possible to have massive contractions and yet for the upper segment of the uterus not to be able to draw up and pull open the lower section. It is as if one part of the uterus is working against another part. The result is dysfunctional labour and failure to progress. With this kind of labour, floating or crouching in a deep bath, with lights dimmed, might help; if there is still no progress, an epidural and augmentation of labour with an oxytocin intravenous drip set up may be the answer. If you choose an epidural, you will have time for a rest and then, if you wish, the anaesthetic can be allowed to wear off so that you can push the baby out yourself.

Giving support
in labour

It is now accepted in most hospitals that there is a place for fathers in the birth room and that many couples want to be together for the birth. There is still some way to go before many hospitals are as welcoming to a woman partner. Any woman should be able to choose exactly whom she wants with her for this important experience in her life. If the baby's father cannot be with his partner, or if the woman feels he is not the right person to help her, she may want to have a woman friend or relation with her instead. In many cultures it is not acceptable for the husband to be present. In the past, women in childbirth have always been supported by other women. And a woman should not be deprived of personal support because she does not want her partner with her, or because religious or cultural tradition prohibits it.

Research has shown that the presence of a birth partner reduces the need for pain-relieving drugs, shortens labour, makes it an easier and happier experience for the woman giving birth, and results in fewer babies needing intensive care*.

Whoever is going to support a woman in childbirth, it is important to learn in advance exactly how to help most effectively. Childbirth education classes can be very useful in teaching how to give emotional and physical support, in exploring emotional aspects of birth, and in understanding the stresses felt by a birth partner. Although this chapter is addressed mainly to fathers, it is also meant to give guidance to anyone helping at the birth.

The father at the birth

The man who knows what he can do to help is in a much better position than the one who is merely invited in to the labour room, but who has no idea of what is going on. He has every opportunity to be an informed and knowledgeable participant. It is not just a question of holding his partner's hand, although this can be a way of giving emotional support, but of being able to judge where and when she needs guidance and encouragement with relaxation.

He has also learned how to breathe "over" the contractions so that he can breathe with his partner at times when she needs extra support. He knows how to rub her back and do gentle, light massage over her lower abdomen when the uterus is opening up, and how to apply firm pressure to her shoulders, arms and legs.

It can, however, be one thing to learn how to give support in the friendly atmosphere of a small antenatal class where couples are

> **"**
> *We didn't plan on him being there for the birth. But the doctor took it for granted that he would come into the room, so he did. And he was pleased as Punch! He was grinning from ear to ear afterwards and he told everyone that he had been at the birth. His family thought it was disgusting.*
>

267

working together, with much discussion interspersed with laughter, and quite another to put that learning to use in a large, impersonal, hospital. Confronted in labour with masked figures in white or green whom he has never met before, whose names he does not know, in a strange clinical environment, he can feel out of place, in spite of consent by the hospital to his presence at the birth.

This is why it is a good idea for him, as well as for his partner, to have seen round the hospital and especially the labour room before the birth. Women sometimes say that it was when they were approached with some unfamiliar piece of equipment in birth that they began to tense up, and that if they had known what it looked like and how it worked they would have found it much easier to stay relaxed. And men who have been giving good support to their partners before apparatus of this kind is used sometimes give up, as they feel that the machinery is controlling the labour.

This is understandable, because when a drip stand or monitoring equipment is brought to the bed it is difficult for the man to get close to his partner, and because a monitoring belt which fits round her abdomen may make it impossible for him to massage that area. In most hospitals, too, once the labour is monitored and speeded up, a midwife stays with the patient all the time, so the intimacy that the couple had in earlier labour is lost. This can lead to them feeling that experts and machinery have taken over.

THE KIND OF SUPPORT YOU CAN GIVE

It is not a question of just being there for her sake, but for your own. You don't know what you're missing if you're not at the birth. It was the most tremendous experience of my life!

The first and most important thing for a companion helping a woman during the long first stage of labour is to be relaxed. This is difficult in an exciting situation, but any tension or anxiety is immediately communicated to the mother. If labour is different from what you expected, awareness of what is happening can worry you more than the woman, who is enveloped in the force sweeping through her body and who may actually shut out all irrelevant stimuli. You, however, may be made anxious by the doctor's tone of voice, the midwife's remark to a colleague, or by the (quite normal) appearance of blood-stained mucus during a contraction. Ask for information, because if you are in doubt about anything, it is better to find out *early* rather than late. In many hospitals you will not be given full information unless you ask. Speak slowly and quietly. Move slowly and deliberately. Touch your partner without haste, resting a relaxed hand on her body and, when you lift your hand away, do so slowly. If you are massaging her, stroke very slowly.

Distractions in the labour room

When helping her to achieve focused concentration on what is happening in her body during contractions, never break that concentration by chatting to anyone else, watching a machine or allowing yourself to be distracted by what is going on around you. As well as causing the woman in labour to tense up, modern equipment often fascinates her companion, who may become so involved with watching the monitor, for example, that the pregnant woman takes second place and feels that emotional support has been withdrawn. You should not forget that, however sophisticated the machinery, it is in fact the woman who is having the baby. Once labour is well under way, your attention should be on her, and encouragement by word, touch or look should be given with every single contraction.

On the hospital's side too an induced or speeded-up and monitored labour becomes an interesting clinical exercise. Midwives, doctors and students may come in to watch. Teaching may go on at the bedside. Discussions about the equipment sometimes take place while the woman is busy with a contraction and would appreciate silence so that she can concentrate better. Although you cannot insist that everyone is quiet during contractions, you can indicate politely by your own silence and attention to the woman in labour that you are not available for conversation, and by doing this can help her to enter a "circle of solitude" with you, and the baby coming to birth.

Occasionally machines break down and engineers arrive. This can be very distracting for the woman in labour, and may even be alarming. Fortunately she is not dependent on the monitor or other pieces of equipment to have her baby. Give her your full and undivided attention. Be on the same level, at the head of the bed, not towering over her. Use eye contact to give her emotional support. If she is coping well, she may like to close her eyes and handle contractions without looking at anybody, but if the going gets hard, suggest that she open her eyes and that you go through it together. This is likely to be of special help at the end of the first stage of labour, when her cervix is anything from 6 cm to fully dilated.

Positive support during contractions

Everything you say should be positive. Avoid saying "You're not relaxed here" or "Your shoulders are tightening". Instead say something such as "Your feet are beautifully relaxed. Do the same with your hands" or give her positive instructions such as "Pull your shoulders down and now let them go". When she is doing well, tell her so: "Good. Good. Beautiful. You're doing really well." This helps most as contractions reach their peak. It can be useful to hold her shoulder firmly during big contractions, and if she has practised relaxation techniques that help her flow out towards your touch (see page 173), these will help her keep her shoulders loose and so avoid hyperventilating. Between contractions talk together about where she likes to be stroked or held.

She may find it helps her to work with her contraction if you describe to her what is happening as the uterus goes into action: "You are opening up wider and wider. Your cervix is being pulled up and open and the baby's head is pressing right down." Ruth Wilf, an

Hold her firmly but gently and give her encouragement with each contraction . . .

experienced American midwife, suggests that if the woman seems out of touch with her body the support person should quietly discuss with her, between contractions, any negative thoughts she may be having. This gives you something to work on during the next contraction. Create an image for the next one—the baby pressing down, the cervix opening up—and use your hands to suggest gradual opening. After the next contraction ask, "How was that compared to the last one?" The woman may be able to suggest other things you can do to help her focus her concentration.

Understanding the labour's progress

As well as needing to be told what progress she is making, she also needs information about what is being done by her birth attendants. Being in labour can be very disorienting. Chloe Fisher, Nursing Officer for Community Midwifery in Oxford, who has the art of helping women get in touch with their bodies in labour, says that fear of the unknown is the main reason why women panic in labour and that a request for pain-relieving drugs is usually one for reassurance about what is happening. A woman may be distressed because she does not realize the progress her labour is making. She loses all sense of time and each contraction may be so enveloping that she cannot see the pattern of her labour. So be clear about progress and, if you can, prepare her also for what is about to happen. For instance, if the waters have not gone by the time contractions are coming every two minutes, you can be fairly sure that they will go soon. If she is about to have an amniotomy (see page 291), prepare her for the renewed strength of contractions after it and discuss with her how she might change her breathing to cope with them. In the second stage remind her that the hot, throbbing, tingling feeling is a sign that the baby is just about to be born and will soon be in her arms.

◆

Know when to be quiet. This depends very much on your empathy with her. Talk when it helps, but keep quiet when you can give other forms of support. Facial expression, gesture, touch and massage are important. One of the best ways of helping is to rest a hand on her shoulder with the other hand at her wrist as she goes through the contraction. If she has backache, she will welcome firm pressure or massage over the sacrum, or slightly to one side of it (see page 260).

How to help with breathing

Breathe with her through difficult contractions. Do not wait until she is tense to start the breathing. Begin with a relaxed breath out together. Keep closely in rhythm with her own breathing at the beginning of the contraction so that there is a partnership. Do not impose a radically different level or rate of breathing on her or it will become a fight between her breathing and yours. If she starts to drag through the contraction with heavy gasping breaths, this is the time to differentiate your breathing from hers.

When appropriate, move your hand in a light butterfly-wing movement to stress the lightness of breathing necessary when the uterus is at its tightest.

Help her enjoy complete relaxation between contractions. This is especially important in stressful labours, as otherwise the woman carries her tension from one contraction to the next and it is cumulative. When she is relaxed, you can talk together about how to meet the next contraction. Avoid complicated anatomical and physiological terms. When you speak about the uterus or cervix, remember it is "your" uterus and "your" cervix, just as it is also "your" or "our" baby. Words used during contractions should be simple, rhythmic and repetitive.

Coping with pain

Labour companions are often unsure whether or not they should mention the word "pain". For some it is taboo. It is imperative to acknowledge pain when it exists and not pretend that it is not there. To do so is to deny a woman the validity of her own experience and to say in effect: "You aren't feeling what you think you are feeling, and if you are, there must be something wrong with you or with your labour." If she tells you it hurts, agree and say, "I understand" or "Yes, I realize that". It might be the moment to add, "Your uterus is working very hard" or "The baby is pressing right down" and also to help her see the pattern of her labour. If she is more than 6 or 7 cm dilated, you will know that she is at the most difficult part of labour. Show her with your hand how far she is dilated. Help her change position, freshen her up with a face wash, brush her hair, use massage. Give her your total, undivided attention. Emotional support of this kind can take the place of drugs for pain relief.

The most undermining thing you can do to a woman in labour is to encourage her to feel sorry for herself. The woman who is told, "Oh,

271

my dear, I can't bear to see you in such pain," or words to that effect, is being deprived of emotional support. Even the expression on a helper's face can give that message, sometimes more clearly than words. We would not think much of someone who leaned over the side of a liner and called to the person in the water, "It looks terrible down there. The waves are so huge and, poor thing, you look as if you are drowning. Do you want an injection?" Yet this is the equivalent of the sympathy and the offer of "something to take away the pain" that some attendants offer to a woman in labour. The woman who has prepared herself for labour often wants help to cope with the mountainous waves rather than the offer of a drunken stupor or sensation-free childbirth. If she wants drugs for pain relief, this should be her own decision. If she does ask for pethidine or an epidural, she should do so freely, not because she has been persuaded or coerced by someone else.

Staying together

If you feel queasy or that you must have a break, just tell your partner you will be back in a moment and stroll out. Although you may be asked to go out when the doctor comes in or when examinations are done, this is not necessary. It seems that fathers are sometimes asked to go out because doctors and nurses are embarrassed to do things to the woman in front of her partner. But women often feel they especially need support when they are being examined or when drugs for pain relief are offered, and for you to go out then can be the worst time. This is one point in labour when the woman, who is at the focus of all the care provided, can herself speak up and state her preferences. She could say, "I'd very much like my husband to stay, please. Don't send him away. I really need him," or "I don't think I'll

Sometimes it can help her just to know that you are there . . .

be relaxed if he goes out." If the doctor and midwife are doubtful, she could add, "He's learned about what happens and understands it pretty well. He's being a wonderful support!" You have no legal right to insist on being present so, if the doctor is adamant, you must go out, but you can ask if you may come back in at the earliest possible moment and can linger outside, making your message clear. Problems of this kind may not arise, and in labour reports couples often say how helpful and friendly everyone was, but it is wise to have a contingency plan in case everything is not straightforward. It should not be forgotten whose labour it is: the hospital staff and any machines should be there to assist, not take over.

Start-stop labour

Some labours seem to come to a full stop for a time and a woman may be stuck at 4 cm dilatation or more for several hours. This is a sign for a change of activity and if possible a change of scene. Lying flat on one's back is not a good position for labour, from either the woman's or the baby's point of view. You can see that she does not slip down in the bed. Remember that when she is lying on her left side or is upright the blood flows more freely through the placenta to the baby than it does when she is lying flat on her back.

It is not a good idea for the woman to lie still for long periods and you can suggest that she may like to roll over onto the other side occasionally or to sit well up. If she is sitting up, supported by four or five pillows, there is not the same problem of decreased blood flow to the baby. It is also fine if she wants to squat, kneel, sit upright, stand, or adopt any of the many positions which women often spontaneously choose in labour (see page 198). But these are obviously limited if drips and machinery are in use.

If no machinery is being used when labour comes to a stop, encourage her to get up and move about. If she is already walking about, suggest a bath or a shower, perhaps a back massage, and then rest in bed with hot water bottles wherever she aches. Jamaican folk midwives give the woman a good douse down and then wrap her in hot towels and offer a drink of hot thyme or mixed-spice tea when labour fails to progress. Perhaps we could learn something from this.

A full bladder can cause unnecessary pain. It used to be thought that it could also hold up labour but there is no evidence that this is the case. For her own comfort, remind the woman to empty her bladder every hour and a half, or more frequently if she seems to need that. If progress is slow, help her to feel that her natural pace is the right pace. Each labour is different and having a baby is not a competition to see who can do it fastest or who can, most nearly conform to a norm. Especially when labour is long drawn out, affirm your confidence in her own body rhythms.

Between 8 and 10 cm dilatation the woman may feel lost and tossed in the sweep and turmoil of contractions following on each other almost without a break. Keep eye contact and breathe with her through each contraction. Letting her know that you trust her own natural rhythms is nowhere more important than at this point, when many women are made to feel that it is a race to the finishing line. Her legs may feel very cold and begin to shake, and you can help her by firmly massaging the inside of her thighs.

The lull

There is often an apparent pause in labour of 20 minutes or more when the woman's cervix is just about fully dilated. She may have no urge to push, and may feel no contractions, yet her attendants are alert for the start of the second stage. They expect action but nothing seems to be happening. They may worry that the uterus is not going to do its job of pushing the baby out, and some may try to get the woman to push even though she does not feel like it, so that she quickly gets exhausted.

If the woman feels rushed and that there are anxious eyes upon her at this point, she becomes tense and anxious herself. Reassure her that there is all the time in the world. This is a normal part of the unfolding birth process—the "rest and be thankful" phase when the baby's head is still not deep in the pelvis. She does not need to do any straining for the head to drop lower. This almost always occurs naturally if she is able to rest and refresh herself.

So help her stand up, perhaps take a shower, offer her a sponge down and put some fresh music on the tape recorder. She may want to walk around, gently rocking and circling her pelvis, perhaps enjoying slow belly dance movements. You can stand cradling her body against yours as she does so, holding her shoulders, elbows or wrists, and move *with* her. After half an hour or so—occasionally an hour or more—contractions pick up, and with renewed energy and excitement the woman enters the expulsive stage of labour. She has had a welcome interval before the drama of the second stage.

Support for the second stage

When the woman begins to push the baby out, she can be in any position which feels comfortable to her: held firmly in your arms, or cradled by your body, or with something solid to grasp or over which she can lean. She needs to be free to round her back, roll her shoulders forward and rest her chin on her chest during contractions. You can help by providing physical support if she wants it and, perhaps, by reminding her to keep her head forward at the height of each pushing urge (without making any attempt to force it forward). From time to time give her a wrung-out sponge or ice cubes to suck.

Do not mention the word "push". Say "open up" instead. Straining only wastes energy and results in unco-ordinated expulsive efforts. If you suggest she does not push at all unless she feels she has to, she will push in the right way at the right time.

Avoid clock-watching, too. It can be as disastrous to have one eye on the clock all the time in the second stage of labour as it would be if

OPPOSITE
Yours to share—the birth not only of a new human being but of a new family.

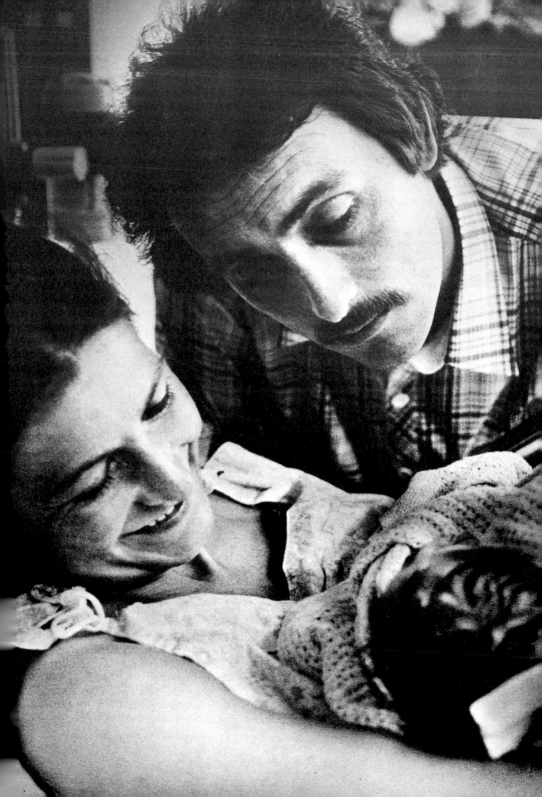

you were watching the clock while trying to make love. The woman needs to feel secure in a world without time or standards of performance, simply able to be herself and experience the intensity of what her body is telling her to do. If the pushing urge is strong and difficult to control, and it looks as if everything is happening too fast, help her lie on her side or get down on all fours, as this may lessen the impulse. Encourage her to put her hands down and feel even before any part of the baby's head is oozing through the vagina, then use a mirror for her to see the top of the head as it crowns. If you see that the crown is moving forward, but she is still holding her breath, say quietly *"Breathe"*. She should immediately breathe out and go on breathing in and out with a dropped jaw.

Sharing in the birth

Many women are anxious that they might be too small. Reassure her that there is room, and her own feelings of openness and flexibility will help to make room. The power of suggestion is so great that each word and phrase used can affect her ability to work with her body.

When you are with a woman in childbirth, you share with her a journey into the unknown. The helper is like the lookout on a yacht sailing at night, watching for the coastline and helping to steer her through. She needs your constant presence and to be left alone is the most frightening thing of all. Giving support in labour needs vigilance, skill, patience, an understanding of that particular woman—her rhythms, her responses to stress—an awareness of what she is thinking and how she is feeling at each moment, and your complete commitment to this task. Sometimes it demands endurance and courage. It can be hard, exhausting work. But yours, too, is the excitement, the deep satisfaction and joy when a child is born.

SURPRISE DELIVERY

If you are with a woman in labour who is giving birth before a midwife arrives or before you can get to the hospital, the most important thing is for you to stay calm and give her quiet, confident support. Drop your shoulders and relax! Tell her she is doing well. Hold her in your arms and help her feel secure.

Wonder, astonishment at the reality of this new person, and overwhelming tenderness are some of the feelings a new father may experience.

Making her comfortable

If the room is cold, heat it. The baby will need a warm environment after birth. If you can, place a pile of newspapers or a plastic sheet or tablecloth under the mother. She may like to sit or kneel on a firm cushion or bean bag. Cover whatever she is on with a sheet if there is one available. Find some big towels, a jumper or something else warm to wrap the baby in. Offer her sips of water if her mouth is dry.

Put pillows or some sort of support behind her back, shoulders and head to allow her to sit up comfortably unless she prefers some other position: her own feelings about this are likely to be right. If traces of faeces appear at her anus, wipe with cotton wool or lavatory paper down and away from the vagina. Boil some water and leave it to cool. It can then be poured between the mother's legs after delivery to clean her up. Wash your hands and scrub your nails thoroughly.

If she is already pushing, remind her to "open up" and not to hold her breath or push at all unless she feels she needs to. Just before the head crowns, tell her to pant, so that from then on she breathes the baby out instead of pushing it out. She can push gently between contractions if delivery is slow.

If there is a loop of cord round the baby's neck as its head slides out, hook a finger round it and lift it over the head. *Do not pull the baby or the cord*, as this may detach the placenta from the wall of the uterus before it has stopped being the baby's life support. If a membrane is over the baby's face, lift it off. When the head is born, allow it to hang by its own weight and this will tend to draw forward the shoulder nearer the mother's front. Either you or she can catch the baby. Lift it up on to the mother's upper thigh or tummy, head slightly down so that any mucus can drain.

After the delivery

Cover the mother and baby with a coat or blanket, or better still a duvet, which is light and warm. Put a bowl between the mother's legs ready to receive the placenta as soon as she feels more contractions. There is no need to cut the cord immediately. Enjoy the peace after delivery as you together admire the baby and wait for the placenta. Make her comfortable. She may be shivery and appreciate a hot water bottle. She might like a cup of tea and may even be ravenously hungry. When the baby is ready to suck put it to the breast and see that the nipple is well back in the mouth. Telephone for a midwife or doctor.

The help a woman needs in childbirth is usually very simple and straightforward. The most important element in it is to stay calm, confident and emotionally supportive.

If this surprise delivery happens in a car, away from any help or home comforts, there is no need to do anything about the placenta or cord. However, if you have a plastic bag or some newspaper, you can wrap the placenta in it and try to keep it above the level of the baby.

If you are at home and are not able to get a midwife, boil up shoe laces or soft string for tying the cord, and scissors for cutting it. If the placenta does not come after about 20 minutes, get the mother to kneel and give some long, slow blows out. It should slip out then. (Do not pull on the cord.) Put a bowl under her buttocks and pour warm boiled water between her legs. She can keep her uterus contracting and reduce bleeding from the placental site by massaging it firmly.

Tie the cord about 4 in (10 cm) from the baby and again about 6 in (15 cm) and cut with sterilized scissors or a new razor blade between the ties. Check that there is no bleeding from the cord stump. If there is, do another tie nearer the baby.

The greatest heat loss from a newborn baby is from its head, so cover the back of the head. Keep mother and baby cuddled together. When birth comes by surprise it is unlikely that anything will go wrong. This is just nature at its most efficient.

Dealing with pain

"I've got a very low pain threshold. I can't stand going to the dentist, so I can't *think* what labour is going to be like!"

"The idea of the pain really worries me. I've never really experienced severe pain, and I can't imagine what it's like to be in pain for hours and hours and hours."

"What is labour pain like? I mean is it like breaking your arm or a bad headache or menstrual cramps or indigestion—or what? If I knew more what it was going to be like I could face it better."

These three statements express what many women who are pregnant for the first time feel, but perhaps do not acknowledge or put into words: fear that pain is going to be overpowering, a sense that they have never experienced pain that tested their inner resources, and ignorance of the kind of pain that is likely to be felt.

Putting pain in its context

People often think that pain is just a matter of a "high" or "low" threshold. There are very few women who think that they have a high threshold and can bear pain as well as other women. In fact, the idea of simple thresholds like walls, with some of us possessing high walls and others low ones, is a myth.

It is now known that in human beings the pain-sensation threshold is exactly the same*. In one study in the United States, members of Italian, Jewish, Irish and Old American ethnic groups were all given electric shocks ranging from mild to fairly strong, and every single person said pain occurred at exactly the same point. Yet obviously people do not *react* to pain in the same way and there are times when a pain which you once bore easily becomes too much to take and you cannot stand it any more. Toothache that you can cope with when you are busy and preoccupied can be absolutely shattering when you go to bed, lie down and try to sleep. So you cannot judge the degree of pain by how an individual reacts.

People may see a pain-producing stimulus as a test of their power to *endure* pain, and so may not be ready to admit to being hurt. In the Sudan, for instance, a young man who cannot bear pain loses social esteem and is unlikely to find a girl to marry him. As in many cultures, the ability to bear pain stoically is part of a code of values.

In every society there are cultural stress points, situations which are seen as threatening and thus predispose people to feel pain. When we know what makes people anxious in a particular society, we can begin to understand these stress points. In many societies some painful stimuli are linked with pleasure. Take lovemaking for example: slightly painful stimulation may be deliberately sought because it is sexually exciting.

The context within which pain occurs is important. As an experiment*, electric shocks were given to test people first when they were feeling relaxed and cheerful, and then when they had been made anxious. The electric shocks were felt as much less painful when the subjects were feeling cheerful. In another study*, as many as 35 per cent of a doctor's patients experienced marked pain relief when given a placebo, an inactive substance which they believed was a pain-killer. It has also been found that the degree of pain tolerated bears a direct relation to the rate of increase in pain, rather than to the level of pain reached*. A person experiencing a pain stimulus that gets worse rapidly feels it more than someone experiencing just as strong a stimulus that takes longer to reach the same point.

This may have particular relevance to very rapid labour, especially an induced labour (see page 297), when the pace is more than a woman can cope with. We sometimes talk about labour as if a long labour were difficult and a short one easy. But speed alone can give no indication at all of how a woman experiences her labour.

Pain perception always involves not only a recording of the stimulus by the brain, but judgment as to its importance, its precise significance, and its place in the scheme of things—the meaning of the total situation in which the stimulus occurs. Labour pain, like all other pain, is a function of the whole person, and we can go even farther than that and say that the experience of pain in labour is profoundly influenced by the values of the society in which the woman grew up.

So labour pain is partly a product of personal and social values about the meaning of childbirth. The way we eat, sleep, empty our bowels, make love, have babies and die makes these experiences more than simple biological acts. They all express ideas, for the most part shared, about good and evil, beauty and ugliness, the pure and the polluting, what is considered to be healthy and what diseased, and what is normal and what abnormal.

Pain relief in other cultures

There are two myths about the ways in which women in the Third World give birth. One maintains that labour is always horrific and dangerous, but that women do not cry out because of strong taboos against showing that they are in pain. The other suggests that the women all have completely painless births, and just squat down in the fields and have their babies before getting back to work again. The truth is probably in between. In many Third World countries healthy women have straightforward labours. Other, malnourished women suffer a great deal.

Most cultures have methods of relieving pain in childbirth, so there is obvious recognition that it exists. But the ways in which pain is relieved and labour made more comfortable are radically different in the technological Western countries. We can give complete relief of pain and remove all sensation from the waist down with regional anaesthesia. This is what an epidural does (see page 286). We have other forms of pain relief which partially remove pain or which eradicate the memory of it. We rely on pharmacological substances to do this for us. Herbal medicines are used in the Third World and some of them have narcotic or mood-changing properties, just like modern drugs, though it is much more difficult to prepare the right dose when you are using plants. There are also other kinds of help which are much favoured in these countries and which used to be employed in the West but tend to be ignored in hospitals today. They include religious and magic rites, different kinds of counter-stimulation, massage, hot and cold compresses, changes in position, and emotional support from others sharing the experience with the woman in labour. These supporters hold her, stroke her, rock her back and forth, and live through the birth *with* her rather than do things *to* her as a patient.

Much of what is done by birth attendants in other cultures is meant to provide simple, practical help based on the handed-down experiences of generations of women. It is also intended to have a psychosomatic effect, helping the baby to be born by influencing the mind of the woman in labour. This practical and psychosomatic help in labour may be forgotten or not understood in our modern hospitals. Yet there are advantages in being able to cope without drugs if possible, because all powerful drugs have side-effects and they all go through the mother's bloodstream to her baby.

Imagining your labour in advance

In preparing for birth it is a good idea to work out how you might like to be helped to be more comfortable and also how you can use your mind to help your body through relaxation, focused concentration and ideas and mental images that produce a pattern and harmony between what is going on inside your uterus and the way you think about it. You may find that this is difficult to conceptualize before you have your first baby.

Trying to master your body or running away from the sensations you are experiencing can actually produce pain, because you are bound to become tense and then chemical messages are sent instantaneously into your bloodstream which affect your whole metabolism. This causes changes in blood pressure and heart rate, breathing, sweating and skin, digestion and defecation, and muscle tone. Psychosomatic factors can even change the action of the uterus itself in ways we do not yet fully understand. A woman who is very anxious may have a long labour because her uterus does not work efficiently or stops contracting altogether.

What labour feels like

In a normal labour any pain experienced is quite different from the pain of breaking a leg, for example, or being injured. The physical feelings produced by a strongly contracting uterus are powerful and challenging. They are likely to involve a combination of sensations, a very tight squeeze, a pulling open of tissues and the firm downwards pressure of the solid ball of the baby's head through a passage which is being slowly stretched wide.

In films you sometimes see a pregnant women suddenly double up, her hands clasped over the top of her abdomen. The director is telling viewers that labour has started. But it *never* happens like this in reality. Instead there is likely to be a sensation of being gripped by tightening muscles low down in your abdomen or in the small of your back. All the sensations are at hip level. Nor is the feeling a sudden one. It has a wave-like shape, building up to a crest and then subsiding and disappearing until the next contraction. There is always a rest period between each. As contractions get stronger, longer and closer together the tightening may extend right round your body, so that it feels more like a circle of thick, wide elastic across your pelvis which is being steadily drawn in, held firm, and then slowly released again. Or you may be conscious of expansion during contractions and be most aware of the top of the uterus spreading and rising, tilting forward in your abdomen, while the great muscle squeezes its lower part open and presses the baby down.

As your contractions reach their peak, you may feel as if a wide band of elastic is being stretched tightly round your body.

"Pain with a purpose"

The feelings that this produces may be painful, but it is pain with a purpose and different from the pain of injury. Contractions are not painful in themselves, and in fact the uterus contracts strongly and rhythmically at intervals in the second half of pregnancy usually without causing any pain. It is the peak of the contraction, when the muscle is working hardest and is making most progress, that is most likely to be perceived as painful, and this may last as long as 30 seconds or as little as 15 seconds.

The idea of a pain that is *qualitatively* different from other kinds of pain is difficult to accept for anyone who has not experienced it. Yet sheer physical effort, like that involved in running a race or climbing a mountain, produces just that kind of "functional" pain, the ache of muscles that are working very hard. If the athlete thought only of pain instead of about winning the race, she would give up. If the mountaineer thought that her aching muscles were the sign of some dreadful physical injury instead of the natural result of working them so hard, she would forget all about her goal and lose the feeling of triumph when she reached the summit.

Pain in labour is the by-product of the body's creative activity. Contractions are *not* pains. They are tightenings which may be painful, especially when they are being most effective. There is an art in approaching each new contraction, thinking "Splendid! Here's another one!" and later, as you approach the end of the first stage, when they are their biggest, "Oh, this is a really good one!"

When you are in the thick of labour, your whole self is involved. It is almost impossible to think about other things or to hold a part of yourself back in any way. The intensity of labour can be frightening, especially for the unprepared woman who does not know what to expect, or for one who wants to keep it all at the level of a learned skill, doing her exercises in much the same way as she might carry out a three-point turn in a driving test. This is why preparation merely for handling contractions is never enough. You also need to prepare yourself mentally and emotionally for the overwhelming nature of the sensations and feelings of labour.

Hypnosis

Some women find that hypnosis is an effective method of relieving pain in labour, and it has the great advantage over chemical anaesthetics in that it does not reduce the baby's oxygen intake. In fact, about a quarter of women who have had hypnosis in childbirth say that they experienced no pain, but results do vary and most women who have hypnosis need chemical pain relief as well.

The common belief that hypnosis involves some kind of magic trickery and that you can be made to do anything the hypnotist wishes is very wide of the mark. Hypnosis is simply a state of increased suggestibility and you can prepare yourself with a good practitioner so that you can, if you wish, use *auto*-hypnosis.

People who are able to go into a deep trance are completely immune to pain while in the trance and can have a forceps delivery or be stitched up after an episiotomy without a local anaesthetic. It has been calculated that two out of every hundred women can go into such a deep trance that they could even have a Caesarean section without feeling any pain*.

If you agree to have hypnosis in childbirth you are usually trained in progressive relaxation to remove anxiety, and taught to think positively about childbirth. If you want to do auto-hypnosis, the hypnotist will suggest that you can put yourself to sleep and wake up when you wish. After the birth the doctor will suggest that you will in future only be hypnotized by a medical person for a therapeutic purpose, so that you need not be afraid of being put into a trance by anyone using hypnosis for their own purposes or for fun.

It may be that all good antenatal classes teach an element of auto-hypnosis. Antenatal teachers do not usually like to admit this. Yet in many ways thinking ahead to labour constructively, when one is deeply relaxed, is using the power of suggestion. Whether or not you decide to try hypnosis, you can use auto-suggestion and fantasies about labour and the baby in a creative way to prepare yourself for childbirth, knowing that this is the safest analgesia of all.

Acupuncture

Acupuncture is another way of reducing pain in childbirth. There are basically three kinds: the traditional Chinese method involving the use of needles in the limbs, and two European methods—one in which needles are inserted in the ear, and another providing transcutaneous electronic nerve stimulation (TENS) with pads attached to the woman's back or sometimes other places. The great benefit of TENS is that the woman can move around as she wishes and herself controls the timing and degree of stimulation. In Peking nowadays acupuncture is used in preference to epidural anaesthesia for 98 per cent of Caesarean sections*. It is sometimes combined with small quantities of drugs.

The advantages of acupuncture are that it is non-invasive, easily administered by someone trained in the method, instantly reversible, and babies are in better condition at birth than after pethidine has been given. Some studies show that acupuncture shortens the first stage of labour for women having their first baby. Women say that they feel more in control of labour and delivery than when they have drugs for pain relief*.

TENS is increasingly available in Britain under the National Health Service. It is being used in some hospitals in the USA. If you want acupuncture you will usually have to make your own arrangements for your acupuncturist to be with you during childbirth.

Using water

You probably already know how soaking in a hot bath can relieve pain, whether you have experienced backache, aching muscles from strenuous exercise or menstrual pain. And many women have discovered that it can be comforting in labour. Lying in warm water increases venous pressure so that veins can return blood to the heart more efficiently. It enhances cardiac action and slows the pulse rate. Total relaxation in the warmth and comfort of a bath may help the uterus contract more effectively. But it does more than this. Water both counteracts the force of gravity and any pressure a woman feels against her back and buttocks, and also reduces pressure felt from inside the body, so there is a further pain-relieving effect*.

Sometimes pain is so much reduced and dilatation proceeds so fast as a woman surrenders herself to the water that a baby slips out while she is still enjoying the bath. This is quite safe, since the baby only takes a breath when lifted clear of the water, and for a few minutes after delivery blood is still pulsating through the cord, thus providing the baby with oxygen. After the baby has slipped out of your body, the midwife will rest a finger on the cord so that she can feel the blood pulsating through it. You may like to do this too.

Dr Igor Charkovsky in the USSR has the woman give birth in a deep transparent tank, and the baby is born under water. He does this, however, not so much for the mother's sake as in order to produce what he has claimed are super-intelligent babies. He believes that since the fetus has been floating in the amniotic fluid for nine months, if the baby is born into an ordinary atmosphere, the brain suddenly becomes much heavier, and this causes brain cells to die.

In a water birth, the baby should never be left in the water, but should be lifted into the mother's arms. You know yourself how cold you can feel after getting out of a bath. The baby quickly becomes chilled too, so she should be dried at once and then wrapped with you in big bath towels so you do not get cold.

Some birth centres are now installing deep pools in which women can float in labour. There are other portable pools on the market which can be used for home births, including plastic pond liners (which can be bought from garden centres and placed inside a timber frame), or you can buy specially constructed water-birth tanks which are thermostatically controlled.

It is probably unwise to decide in advance on giving birth in water. A woman for whom floating in water feels blissful late in the first stage of labour is very likely to want to get out of the water once the second stage starts. She should do whatever feels right at the time.

DRUGS FOR PAIN RELIEF IN LABOUR

There is a variety of pain-relieving drugs available, and different drugs suit different women. It is important to understand what can be used and how each type works so that you can make your own informed decision as to whether you want the help of a drug, and if so which kind. Whether or not you have drugs—and how much you have—is up to you. As one obstetric anaesthetist has stated: "The only arbiter of pain is—or should be—the patient ... a stereotyped prescription cannot cope with individual variations in response to pain"*.

All drugs for pain relief in labour, whether given by injection or inhaled, pass through the mother's bloodstream to the baby. They all affect the baby—some more than others. None of them actually does the baby any good. When you are considering whether or not to accept drugs in labour, bear in mind also that some forms of anaesthesia and analgesia can interfere with your first meeting with the baby and subsequent bonding.

Tranquillizers and analgesics

Tranquillizers are used to relax you if you are anxious and tense and also to lower your blood pressure. Given intramuscularly, tranquillizers take effect in 15 minutes; taken by mouth they are effective in 30 minutes. If taken during labour, tranquillizers tend to make the baby limp and floppy at birth, and probably also slow to suck. They interfere with the newborn's temperature control, too.

They are sometimes used in combination with analgesics, pethidine for example (see opposite), to increase their effectiveness, though some obstetricians are critical of this practice.

Valium The effects of diazepam (Valium) last half an hour to four hours and pass rapidly to the baby. The manufacturers of Valium report that it reduces the woman's recall of labour and delivery and that in 70 per cent of cases complete amnesia occurs. Twelve per cent of women separated from their babies immediately after delivery cannot even remember whether they have had a boy or a girl*.

Valium, when given to the mother in labour, is known to change the pattern of the baby's heart rate.

Pethidine The most widely used drug used for analgesia (taking the edge off pain) in labour is a narcotic, pethidine. It is usually given by intramuscular injection in doses of 50 to 150 mg. It takes effect in 15 minutes and lasts for two to four hours. Some women like it and say it helped them cope with difficult contractions by making them feel relaxed and slightly drunk. Others hate the effects of pethidine and call it "stupefying", and say they were woozy and out of control.

A fairly common side-effect of pethidine is nausea. One or two women out of every ten vomit when they are given pethidine. It is sometimes combined with an antihistamine to prevent sickness, but this tends to make you even sleepier.

Large amounts of pethidine are present in the baby if this is injected within five hours before delivery, and especially in the three-hour period before delivery. When it is given intravenously the concentration of pethidine in the baby's cord blood is only slightly below that in the mother's bloodstream. Pethidine can cause breathing difficulties in the newborn, who may then need to be given oxygen.

To reduce the depressant effects of pethidine, it was combined with a drug called levallorphan. However, pethilorfan, the combined drug, was not satisfactory and is rarely used. Doctors prescribed larger and larger doses of it because the combined injection was not such a good pain reliever as pethidine on its own, and it still affected the baby. If a baby is born with respiratory depression after its mother has had pethidine, it is given an anti-depressant.

Omnopon is a derivative of morphine and is usually more effective than pethidine in providing pain relief. But it too can cause respiratory depression in the baby. Morphine in any form, like pethidine, reduces the transfer of oxygen across the placenta and tends also to lengthen the labour*.

Metrazinol This is sometimes offered in place of pethidine, and it is claimed that it relieves pain more effectively. It is given in doses of 100 mg. Its side-effects are like those of pethidine—drowsiness, nausea, vomiting, dizziness, light-headedness, shivering, sweating and restlessness—and it may also affect the baby.

Gas and oxygen (Entonox) is a mixture of a maximum of 70 per cent nitrous oxygen and 30 per cent oxygen which is available in a machine that you can use yourself. It is not cumulative and is cleared from the baby's system with the first breath it takes at delivery. The mask through which you breathe it in must fit firmly against your face or the gas will leak out.

=**"**=

With the pethidine I felt the pain but was so dizzy that I couldn't do anything about it. But the omnopon deadened the pain . . .

=**"**=

Inhaling gas and oxygen just before the start of each contraction may take the edge off the pain.

The analgesic effects, which are slight and not enough for some women, occur within 15 to 30 seconds and last for up to a minute. Timing is therefore important. In the words of one woman: "As I felt the very start of the contraction I took three full breaths of gas and oxygen in and out through my open mouth. I remembered to make them really slow. . . . Then as the contraction got bigger I dropped the mask and went into the quick breathing. It was fantastic . . ."

Local anaesthetics

I felt very woozy and out of control. I didn't really know what I was doing after I had it. I couldn't concentrate on my breathing or remember what I had learned in classes. And I was just overwhelmed by the pain, but helpless to do anything about it. Never again.

Local anaesthetics can also cross the placenta but they are least likely to affect the baby when they are injected into the area around the vagina and the perineum. This is done before an episiotomy (see page 294) and before a forceps delivery (see page 306) if other anaesthesia has not been given.

When local anaesthetics are used to bathe nerves that cover a large area of the body, they are called *regional* anaesthetics.

Paracervical block is a series of injections of local anaesthetic around the cervix. It affects the baby immediately and in three out of ten babies the heartbeat becomes slower (a condition known as bradycardia)*. Some babies have died as a result. Paracervical block is rarely used in Britain for this reason.

Epidural anaesthesia is injected into the space between part of the spinal cord and the dura, the outer membrane around the spinal cord. Top-up injections can be given through a fine plastic tube which is left in place after the first injection. This is preferable to another injection, as an epidural takes about half an hour to set up. An epidural may be given with you sitting up and curled forward or lying on your left side curled up into a ball—a difficult position for the pregnant woman.

HAVING AN EPIDURAL
It is important to make your back as convex as possible when you are being given an epidural so that the vertebrae are spread out. This makes it easier for the anaesthetist to insert the needle between the bones. You must, of course, stay completely still while this is being done.

An epidural can provide complete relief from pain and can even be used as an anaesthetic for a Caesarean section. It removes sensation from the waist down, or sometimes from your navel down, either completely or partially, while allowing you to remain conscious and to see what is happening if you want to. For a painful labour which is difficult and prolonged it seems the perfect answer. Many women have said how marvellous the epidural was, but it should be your own choice—no-one should be put under pressure to have one. Some hospitals give epidurals to all first-time mothers, unless there is no time to give one.

Epidurals do not always work. It may be difficult to inject into the right place or the anaesthetic may take on one side only, so that you get the odd lop-sided feeling of contractions occurring in half your body, which can be disconcerting.

The anaesthetic used is similar to that used by dentists, and you feel it like liquid ice numbing your tummy, bottom and legs. Even though it only anaesthetizes part of you, it must be given by a skilled anaesthetist and under sterile conditions. If by mistake the needle punctures the dura you get a complete spinal: you are more heavily anaesthetized and may have a bad headache which can last a week or more after the birth.

An epidural lowers blood pressure, sometimes drastically, so that other drugs may have to be given to raise your blood pressure again. Because of this, an epidural is sometimes given to a woman whose blood pressure is high, even though she may not be having a painful labour. In one study 39 per cent of women having epidurals experienced hypotension, though it did not last longer than one hour. The proportion went up to 47 per cent when women were also receiving an oxytocin intravenous drip (see page 298)*. When your blood pressure suddenly drops, you feel sick and faint and may vomit. This sudden lowering of blood pressure and the reduction in the amount of blood coming from your heart affects the baby too, since the oxygen-bearing blood supply is pumping more weakly and slowly through the placenta.

Having an epidural may mean that a whole train of other procedures is started which you did not bargain for. Because you have no feeling in your bladder, it will need to be emptied by catheter. Because you may not feel any urge to push, the obstetrician may rotate the fetal head with forceps or manually*.

Since there is an increased chance of having a forceps delivery once an epidural has been given, you may want to let the anaesthetic wear off as you reach the very end of the first stage and to refuse a top-up. On the other hand, if you have not felt first-stage contractions at all and have to cope with the long hefty ones near full dilatation, the experience can be an overpowering one.

Research into women who have had epidurals reveals that they are sharply divided in their opinions about them. In one study many women were very happy with their epidurals and said things like "It

Nearly every mum in this hospital has an epidural; anyway they wire you up to things and do so many things to you that I thought, well, at least I won't feel all that. I mean, they might have forgotten that I could feel if everyone else couldn't.

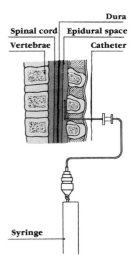

	Dura
Spinal cord	Epidural space
Vertebrae	Catheter

Syringe

If you have an epidural a needle containing a catheter is inserted between the vertebrae into the epidural space and then withdrawn; the catheter is left in place in case a top-up is needed.

was a miracle!" and "It was pure magic." But 18 per cent of women regretted having the epidural and said, in effect, "Never again!"*

Women praise epidurals when: it was their own decision, and theirs alone, to have one; they felt among friends; the epidural provided effective pain relief; there was minimal other intervention; and the mother managed to push the baby out herself. Women are highly critical of epidurals when: they felt that they were not able to make a free choice about having one; they did not feel that they were in an emotionally supportive environment; the epidural was not effective; delivery was by forceps; and there were side-effects—they felt sick and giddy, suffered headache, or had long-term problems such as pain or numbness which they attributed to the epidural.

An epidural anaesthetic passes into the baby within ten minutes and studies are still being carried out on the possible effects of an epidural on the baby*. Some studies suggest that the baby becomes nervous and jittery while others show that it is very drowsy after delivery,* but this may vary according to what drug is used.

If you decide to have an epidural, bear in mind that some of the difficulty you might have in coping with the baby in the week or so after the birth may be connected with the anaesthetic, not because you are incompetent. You will soon be over this period and interaction between you and the baby will rapidly become easier.

I had to look at the machine to see when I was having a contraction . . . I did want to feel him slide out, and not feeling that was terribly disappointing, that and not really knowing that he had been born.

Caudal A caudal is like an epidural, except that it is injected into the epidural space around the sacrum and blocks only that area rather than the larger area blocked by an epidural. A greater dose of anaesthetic is necessary, and a caudal is usually given for short-term pain relief to a woman having a very difficult second stage.

The future of drugs in childbirth

Hospitals should provide an environment and the kind of personal care in which each woman is free to accept or reject pain-relieving drugs as and when she wishes. Whatever drugs are given to you in labour, your consent should always be obtained beforehand and their effects should be explained.

Fear, anxiety, loneliness and feeling you are part of a factory for producing babies all increase the experience of pain. Understanding what is happening inside you and what is being done to help you and your baby, knowing what you can do to help yourself, feeling you are among friends, and having someone you love with you, all make pain much more easily bearable.

Modern obstetric anaesthesia, used only when necessary, is fairly safe for the baby, but one consultant anaesthetist warns that "numerous questions about the effects of drugs given to the mother on mother-baby interaction and future child development require an answer"* and stresses that long-term studies should be carried out to assess exactly what risks are being taken. For the present this still remains a largely unexplored field of research.

Towards the medical control of birth

You have the right to decide what happens to your body before, during and after childbirth. You are not bound, either in law or out of politeness, to agree to procedures and investigations to which you object. If things are done without your consent, it is a form of assault. Your consent is implied when you are forewarned about some kind of obstetric intervention and concur by remaining silent.

You are also entitled to be given full information about anything that is being done to you and your baby, can reasonably expect to be able to ask questions about it and to be given honest answers. If you do not ask questions, professionals may take it for granted that you do not want to know any more, and even that to offer further information might make you uncomfortable.

Your right to choose

In all medical procedures it is a question of carefully balancing the relative risks of a policy of intervention on the one hand and a policy of "wait and see" on the other. To be able to make an informed choice you may value the counsel of skilled professionals, but ultimately *you* make the decision. This applies both to *where* you have your baby and *how* you have your baby. If you want natural childbirth, go all out to get it. Plan for it, prepare yourself for it and do everything you can to create the right setting for it to take place. But also be flexible so that if something in your physical condition or that of your baby indicates that modern technology can be used with advantage you do not miss out on its undoubted benefits even if this means that the birth is less "natural".

A woman having a baby has responsibilities as well as rights. One of the most important of these is the responsibility to give the baby the best possible start in life. Some obstetricians believe that whenever a machine or a procedure is available which permits greater medical control of childbirth it ought to be used. An equally valid view is that one should be selective in the use of technology, employing it where necessary, but bearing in mind that birth is also a psychological experience which affects the relationship between mother, father and baby—perhaps for a long time after.

The best environment for birth

The highest-quality childbirth and the best welcome into life for the baby must include emotional as well as medical aspects of birth. If you accept medical help, it does not automatically follow that you give up concern about the psychological dimensions of the experience. Technology need not, and should not be permitted to, ruin a woman's personal experience of childbirth.

When machines are used *in place of* warm and friendly human relations they seem to take over. But when they take second place to emotional support and encouragement and you feel free to reach your own decisions about how much aid to accept, they can be a useful adjunct to good care, especially when the risk to a baby is considered to be higher than usual.

Many couples can bear witness to ways in which sophisticated modern apparatus made them feel more secure in childbirth and was used to help rather than hinder. But for this to happen the environment provided for birth has to be a very special one and all those coming into contact with the expectant parents need to be able to give of themselves and not only their technical skills. For it is only in such a setting that there can be trust, honesty and self-confidence.

The growing use of technology

Obstetricians are discovering new ways of controlling a process which 30 years ago was left to nature. Many now say "Why stand by watching and intervene only when something goes wrong?" and believe that instead labour should be regulated from start to finish. To do this effectively they need to be able to monitor exactly what is going on in the uterus and what is happening to the fetus at every second and to intervene at any point to ensure that cervical dilatation, the strength of contractions and the biochemical state of mother and fetus conform to a predetermined norm. This is called *active management of labour**.

Many inventions are appearing on the market which obstetricians, quick to seize an opportunity to reduce the perinatal mortality rate, want to buy for their units. Some women hate this intrusion of machinery into what they feel should be a natural process and question its benefits for the labour and the baby. Others find security in knowing that labour is controlled by the obstetrician with all his machinery; they like knowing exactly when the birthday will be and are relieved to know that labour will not last longer than 12 hours at the most. In some hospitals the love affair with technology is gradually giving way to a new concern about the quality of human relations. But there is no standard recipe that will suit all women. The vital element is *personal* care.

COMMON PROCEDURES IN LABOUR

When you arrive in hospital, you may be given an amniotomy, linked to a fetal monitor and hooked up to an intravenous drip. During the second stage, an episiotomy may be performed to hasten delivery. Some women experience many kinds of intervention during the course of their labours and unless you specifically tell the obstetrician or midwife that you do not want your labour controlled in this way there is a chance that you will have at least one of them.

Artificial rupture of the membranes

Artificial rupture of the membranes (ARM for short) or amniotomy has come to be accepted as a normal routine in most hospitals and is often performed as part of the "prepping" done after you are admitted. The membranes surrounding the fetus are punctured with a small tool like a crochet hook through the open cervix. Routine amniotomy is now open to question, however. When the membranes are allowed to rupture spontaneously, they tend to do so towards the end of the first stage of labour*. In 12 per cent of women the membranes remain intact right through to delivery. Some membranes rupture spontaneously when the midwife or doctor touches them during a vaginal examination.

Since there are no nerve endings in the membranes their rupture is not painful. All you feel is a gush of warm liquid. Be prepared for contractions to increase in intensity after this has happened. ARM can speed up labour by 30–45 minutes if the membranes have not ruptured spontaneously by the end of the first stage, since the baby's head is pressing harder against the cervix once the cushion of fluid has gone, and this produces a rush of oxytocin in your system which triggers off strong contractions.

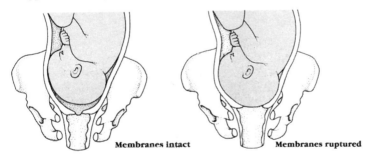

Membranes intact   Membranes ruptured

RUPTURE OF THE MEMBRANES
Spontaneous rupture of the membranes usually indicates that the cervix is starting to open. The baby's head then presses right against the cervix and contractions are intensified. This may also happen after artificial rupture of the membranes.

Reasons for amniotomy

Besides being a part of induction, rupturing the membranes also allows the obstetrician to assess the state of the amniotic fluid. When a fetus is in distress it passes meconium, the first contents of the bowels, into the water, which is easily seen in the fluid released. Many obstetricians believe that amniotomy is important to assess the condition of the baby. Once it has been done, it is possible to insert an electrode in the baby's scalp, so that its heartbeat can be recorded throughout labour (see page 303).

Some obstetricians prefer to use an *amnioscope* to examine the amniotic fluid while keeping the membranes intact. A cone-shaped

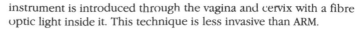

instrument is introduced through the vagina and cervix with a fibre optic light inside it. This technique is less invasive than ARM.

The risks of routine amniotomy

Pressure on the cord Intact membranes protect the baby's head. The amniotic fluid equalizes pressure on the head and amniotomy takes away the cushion of water in which the fetus lies, so exposing its head to the direct effect of contractions. Rupture of the membranes also gives rise to the possibility of pressure on the cord, which may hinder the flow of blood through it. It is not rare for a baby to have the cord round its neck, and without the cushion provided by the amniotic fluid, such babies are particularly vulnerable to pressure on the cord. It has also been suggested that once the amniotic fluid has gone, the fetal surface of the placenta is compressed, which may reduce the flow of blood to and from the baby*.

Pelvic infection Amniotomy introduces the possibility of pelvic infection*. Since infection is more likely if labour continues for more than 24 hours after amniotomy, operative delivery may be necessary if the baby has not been delivered naturally by that time.

Sometimes, when the membranes are ruptured before labour is going strong, contractions later become weak or stop altogether, and it turns out that the woman was in "false" labour. Because of the risk of ascending infection if labour takes a long time following rupture of the membranes, it is often decided to stimulate the uterus with an oxytocin intravenous drip.

Deceleration of the baby's heartbeat Some studies have demonstrated that after amniotomy there are more early decelerations in the baby's heartbeat. These early decelerations come at the start of a contraction and the heart is back to normal by the end of the contraction. The slowing down is slight, by less than 40 beats a minute. Many obstetricians consider this innocuous and quite normal*. Because babies born after amniotomy have been demonstrated to be in good condition, with high Apgar scores (see page 328), some doctors have concluded that the procedure does not subject the fetus to any special stress during labour.

Head moulding Other obstetricians are concerned about head moulding and disalignment of the cranial bones, which may be increased after amniotomy. There is some disagreement about this but, in any case, the moulding of the baby's head gradually disappears during the first week or two of life.

So amniotomy raises many questions which have not yet been adequately answered. It is a subject that you may want to discuss with your obstetrician. You have a right to be fully informed. You can, if you wish, request that amniotomy be done not as a routine but only if the baby is showing signs of distress.

The partogram

The partogram consists of a series of graphs used in hospital to record the main obstetric events of labour against a time scale of 24 hours. It is particularly useful for isolating problem labours, for instance when the baby is posterior and the mother is getting worn out. In the course of a normal labour it is also a clear record of progress made so far for any new staff that may come on duty. But sometimes the routine use of the partogram can lead to a slow labour being accelerated even when the woman is not tired and the baby is not under stress.

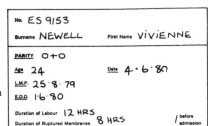

No. ES 9153
Surname NEWELL   First Name VIVIENNE

PARITY 0+0
Age 24   Date 4·6·80
L.M.P. 25·8·79
E.D.D. 1·6·80
Duration of Labour 12 HRS
Duration of Ruptured Membranes 8 HRS   / before admission

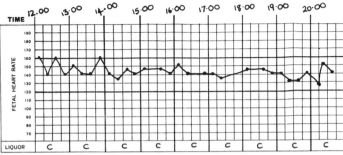

Fetal heart rate *Charted in beats per minute, with 120–160 beats considered normal. (Any deceleration is shown as an arrow down to the lowest level.) The condition of the amniotic fluid (liquor) is also recorded. C means "clear", M "meconium-stained", and B "blood-stained".*

Contractions *Frequency, strength (by shading) and length of contractions in seconds are shown here.*

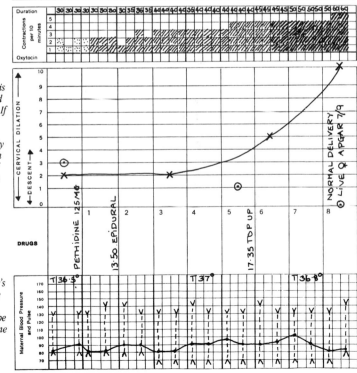

Cervical dilatation *The degree of cervical dilatation is noted every 3 or 4 hours and a dilatation curve is drawn. If there is a 2-hour delay compared with the statistical norm, the obstetrician usually stimulates the labour with an oxytocin drip. The descent of the head through the pelvis is also indicated.*

Drugs *Any drugs given are noted, as well as general remarks. After delivery the Apgar score is recorded (see page 328).*

Blood pressure *The mother's blood pressure and pulse are recorded about every 20 minutes. The upper level is the systolic pressure, the lower one the diastolic pressure (see page 48).*

The intravenous drip

In many American hospitals, and increasingly in British ones, a drip is set up for every woman in labour. A fine catheter (hollow tube) is introduced into a vein in your arm or hand and fixed with sticky tape so that fluids can be infused straight into your bloodstream. The argument for setting up a drip is that once a vein is open, emergency action can be taken rapidly and your strength can be kept up without you needing to eat or, sometimes, even drink anything. This means that if a Caesarean section is necessary (see page 308) and general anaesthetic is used, your stomach is likely to be almost empty already and therefore there is not a great deal of risk that you will regurgitate or inhale its contents.

Dextrose, a glucose solution, may be given through a drip to act as a "pick-me-up" in labour. Since it bypasses the stomach you do not have to digest it. Dextrose is useful if labour is long and tiring and you are becoming dehydrated, or if lactic acid builds up in the course of a difficult labour, causing acetone to appear in the urine—an indication that your body is short of glucose.

If you have a drip set up, it is especially important to remember to empty your bladder regularly: every hour is not too frequent. You will be accumulating fluid and should urinate frequently to stop urine building up in your bladder.

Once a drip is set up, other substances can be introduced by the same route. This may be done without you consenting to or even being aware of the administration of drugs. If you have an intravenous infusion and the bag or bottle is changed, ask what it is. Your partner will be able to get close enough to read the label. Oxytocin is introduced by this means. The label will probably read "syntocinon". You can read more about this in the section on induced labour.

You need not consent to an intravenous drip unless you are confident that there are good reasons for it. It is yet another way in which women are sometimes made needlessly uncomfortable in labour. The drip can be very useful when needed, but used routinely it merely makes it difficult for you to move. In most hospitals where intravenous drips are used as a matter of course it is taken for granted that the woman in labour stays in bed.

Episiotomy

An episiotomy is a surgical cut made to enlarge the birth opening. It is done with scissors, under local anaesthetic, just before the baby is born. In the United States episiotomies are usually midline (down from the bottom of the vagina towards the anus). In Britain they are usually medio-lateral (sloping out to the side, away from the anus, or down and then out again in the shape of a hockey stick). Occasionally, an episiotomy is made on each side of the vagina, for example when a breech baby with a large head is being born. This kind of incision is known as a bilateral episiotomy.

Since the incision is made through both skin and muscles, careful repair of the wound must be done afterwards. The local anaesthetic given before the episiotomy was performed is topped up when necessary. It takes a few minutes to take effect, and the doctor or midwife should wait until the area is fully anaesthetized before stitching the wound. The suturing is done with a curved needle and it may take as long as an hour to sew up a medio-lateral episiotomy or one which has been extended by tearing. Stitching a midline episiotomy is usually simpler and quicker because there is a natural dividing-line between muscles in the midline.

The stitches may be of the kind which dissolve, in which case they should not need to be taken out. But have a look at the area in a mirror every couple of days to check that they have disappeared, since sometimes they do not drop out and become embedded in tissue. You may feel as if you are sitting on thorns. When this happens the stitches should be snipped out by a midwife or doctor on or before the tenth day after the birth.

Reasons for episiotomy

Some obstetricians believe that all first-time mothers should have an episiotomy to relieve strain on their tissues and to get the baby delivered quickly. When there are signs of fetal distress, an episiotomy can speed delivery and make birth easier for the baby. You may be told that it is a good idea to have an episiotomy because "a straight, clean cut is better than a nasty, jagged tear" which is more difficult for the obstetrician to sew up. Sometimes episiotomy is done in an attempt to prevent damage to tissues inside the vagina when there is evidence of "buttonhole" tearing (that is, a series of very tiny lacerations deep inside the perineum).

The practice of routine episiotomy is still favoured by many North American obstetricians and those on the European continent, but is declining in British hospitals. In the seventies, almost 100 per cent of women had episiotomies in some hospitals in Britain. Now the proportion is generally below 40 per cent. As soon as a research project investigating episiotomy was begun in any hospital—that is,

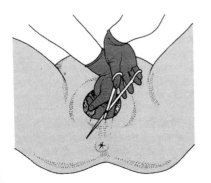

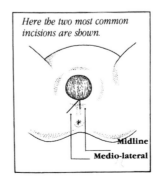

Here the two most common incisions are shown.

Midline

Medio-lateral

HAVING AN EPISIOTOMY
An episiotomy is done as the baby's head crowns and between contractions. The local anaesthetic, combined with the numbing effect of the baby's head pressing against the perineum, means that the cut is rarely felt.

as soon as questions were asked about its necessity—the rate dropped by about a third, even before any results were obtained.

Problems with episiotomy

A trial conducted in Dublin revealed that women with an intact perineum or only a superficial tear experience less pain after childbirth than those who have an episiotomy. The pain after an episiotomy is about the same as that from a second-degree tear (one that affects the underlying muscle). Women are more likely to have severe tears into the anus when they have had an episiotomy than if they have not had one*. Another trial, in England, showed that there is no advantage in episiotomy over a first- or second-degree tear*.

Many women say they feel terribly uncomfortable when making love for several months after having an episiotomy, and they tend to resume intercourse later than women who have had a tear.

There are other problems with episiotomy which should be borne in mind: if done too early—before the perineum has thinned out—it can cause unnecessary bleeding; sometimes the cut is much larger than a tear would have been; and quite often the stitches get infected and antibiotics are necessary*.

With skilled guidance at delivery and a gentle birth (see pages 313–324), more and more women are now having no injury to the perineum—and this makes an enormous difference to how they feel in the days and weeks after the baby is born.

Managing the third stage

A now widely accepted method of controlling the third stage of labour, the expulsion of the placenta, is to give an intramuscular injection of oxytocin after the delivery of the shoulder nearest your front (the anterior shoulder). The placenta then usually separates from the lining of the uterus with the next contraction and is expelled within five minutes of the birth.

However, if the placenta does *not* separate completely after the injection, it can be trapped by the powerfully contracting uterus. So attendants clamp and cut the cord as soon as the baby is born and then press a hand on the top of the uterus, pulling on the cord at the same time in order to get the placenta out.

If the placenta is left to separate naturally, it may take half an hour. Clamping of the cord immediately at delivery may make a retained placenta more likely. If the cord is not clamped until after it has stopped pulsating there is much less chance of a retained placenta and post-partum haemorrhage. This may be because when the cord is clamped blood cannot flow out of it, so encouraging the now defunct placenta to be peeled away from the uterine wall. Instead the placenta stays firm and full.

If the third stage is allowed to proceed naturally, your first physical contact with your baby produces a rush of emotion that is accompanied by the release of oxytocin. This *natural* oxytocin keeps the uterus firm and causes further contractions. Once the placenta has separated the midwife gently places one flat hand over your lower tummy, just above the pubic bone, and you push against the hand, so delivering the placenta and membranes. It is often a help to have a hand to push against like this. The alternative is to squat over a bowl or pail and to deliver the placenta with gravity to help.

CONTROLLED CORD TRACTION
After the birth of your baby, your uterus continues to contract strongly to expel the placenta. You may be asked to push the placenta out, once it has peeled off the wall of the uterus, by pushing against the doctor's or midwife's hand placed against your lower abdomen, while he or she gently pulls on the cord with the other hand.

There is no reason for a cord to be clamped before the placenta has been delivered except for convenience, although occasionally the cord is so short that it is impossible for the mother to hold her baby unless it is cut first, or it is twisted in a succession of loops around the baby's neck at delivery and so is cut to enable the baby to slide out. In fact, if a woman is Rhesus negative and her baby is Rhesus positive (see page 103) there is a strong case for delayed cord clamping. If the cord is clamped before it has stopped pulsating, when there is still blood flowing through it, the chance of a flow of Rhesus positive blood back into the mother's circulation increases.

INDUCED LABOUR

Induction is the medical way of starting off labour, and keeping it going. When labour begins naturally, the uterus becomes sensitive to hormones present in your bloodstream at the end of pregnancy. When labour is induced the doctor tries to obtain a similar result by flooding your system with hormones, until they reach a level much higher than that which occurs naturally. This can be done by introducing synthetic hormones into your bloodstream, through a continuous intravenous drip, or by inserting prostaglandin pessaries into your vagina. Both these methods are usually combined with artificial rupture of the membranes.

Induction procedures

At present a great deal of research into these methods is taking place in hospitals. Remember that you have the right to receive full details of what is going to be done and why, *before* being admitted to hospital for induction, and you can choose to accept or refuse it once you know the facts.

> *I was made to lie flat on my back for hours. I felt like a lump of meat being poked and prodded.*

Stripping the membranes Some doctors strip the membranes to stimulate labour. This is done by pushing the membranes away from the cervix by hand, while leaving them intact. This is a rather uncomfortable procedure, but may start things off.

Artificial rupture of the membranes (see page 291) will be performed as the only means of induction if you are near your dates. Most obstetricians believe that, once the membranes are ruptured, the baby ought to be born within 24 hours, because there is some risk of infection if labour is long drawn out. So you need to be aware that if your labour is started by ARM, but is slow to get going, it may then have to be accelerated with hormones.

Prostaglandin pessaries One way of inducing labour commonly employed in Britain is to use pessaries of prostaglandin gel which are introduced into the cervix. If the gel is inserted during the evening, labour may have started by the following morning. In fact, it may be unnecessary to have amniotomy and an oxytocin drip as well, and prostaglandin gel has the great advantage of allowing you freedom to move about in labour.

Oxytocin drip If induction involves being connected to an oxytocin drip, ask if the syringe can be introduced into the arm or the hand you use least. If the connecting tube is short, you cannot easily move your arm or change position without dislodging it, but there is no need for it to be short, and you can ask for it to be securely fixed so that you can still change position. Many women have discovered that when they are in labour they get backache simply from lying in one position for too long, quite apart from the backache that is often a result of contractions. A glucose solution is often passed through the drip first. The drip can be turned down or even stopped once 5 cm dilatation of the cervix has been reached. It is usually kept in until after the end of the third stage, since it can control bleeding from the uterus by keeping it contracting hard.

Why induction may help

Induction is an invaluable obstetric technique when a baby must be born without delay. Many doctors believe that between 15 and 25 per cent of women and their babies benefit from either induction or acceleration of labour. Some believe that these figures are too high, while others again that 60 per cent or more of labours ought to be induced. If you have symptoms of pre-eclampsia (see page 126), including high blood pressure, albumin in the urine, sudden excessive weight gain, and oedema (puffiness resulting from fluid retention), this is a good reason for induction, since the baby may not continue to be well nourished inside your uterus if the pregnancy is allowed to go on. If you have had a previous forceps delivery because a baby was a tight fit, inducing the next baby before it is at term may allow you to give birth more easily.

Induction after the EDD

Some babies stop growing because the placenta, through which they receive nourishment and oxygen, is not working well at the end of the pregnancy, even before there is any question of being "overdue", and even though the mother may be feeling fit and healthy. Such babies may do better outside the uterus.

Induction before the EDD

Between 10 and 12 per cent of women go two weeks or more "overdue" (known as "post-dates"), but in only 1 per cent of these babies is there any evidence of post-maturity. What has often happened is that the date of the start of pregnancy has been miscalculated. In only 3 per cent of women is pregnancy unusually long.

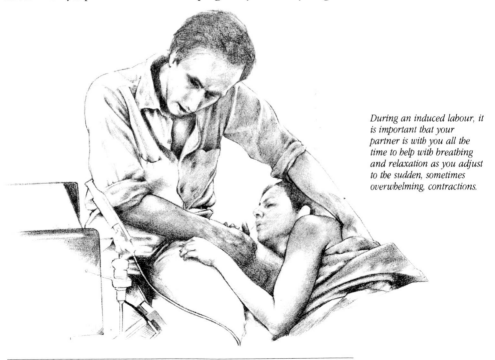

During an induced labour, it is important that your partner is with you all the time to help with breathing and relaxation as you adjust to the sudden, sometimes overwhelming, contractions.

If you are 42 weeks pregnant there is a chance of the placenta not functioning so well because it is aging. However, *premature babies are most at risk,* so the obstetrician needs to be sure that the baby really is overdue before inducing it. Some doctors make it a rule to induce if you are more than a week overdue, others like all their patients to deliver at about term and bring you into hospital if you are a few days past your dates. Tests can be done to find out whether the placenta is working efficiently and therefore whether induction is really necessary (see page 216).

The length of induced labours

Although you may have a rapid labour with induction, this cannot be guaranteed. Some obstetricians prefer labours not to last longer than ten, eight or even five hours and deliver with forceps or by Caesarean section if labour is longer than they believe it should be. When a policy of routine induction is introduced in a hospital, there is a big increase in the number of Caesarean sections performed. Since there is so much variation in obstetric policy, it may be a good idea when discussing the possibility of induction with the doctor to ask what his or her practice is. Depending on whether or not you want a short, sharp labour, this may affect your decision about whether to agree to induction if it is not urgently necessary for your baby's sake.

Possible problems

Induction is a form of intervention which, while extremely useful when really necessary, is not without risks, and in coming to a decision the relative risks of leaving the baby inside your uterus and inducing labour have to be assessed.

Unripe cervix It has been stated that "the major factor governing the success of induction is the state of the cervix."* When the cervix feels soft—like your lips when you hold your mouth slack—then it is ripe and ready for labour. Unfortunately, induction is often done before the cervix is ripe, and in consequence the uterus may not respond to the hormones. If the membranes have been ruptured, then the only way to get the baby born is by Caesarean section.

Powerful contractions If the uterus is triggered to work harder, labour is more violent than it would be if it started naturally. In an induced labour there are often two "peaks" to each contraction, and each may last one minute or longer. Women who have had babies before, and whose previous labours were not induced, say that contractions start more powerfully and that there is not much lead-up to each contraction, but instead a sudden "explosion". There may be only a short interval between them; just time to let out one relaxing breath and then you are into the next one! You may find you need to go straight into the breathing techniques you will have learned for about half dilatation (see page 190).

Interrupted blood flow Extremely powerful contractions are likely to interfere with the blood flow through the uterus and so cause fetal distress. In one study it was discovered that fetal distress was significantly more common in women having oxytocin, that the babies were more likely to have low Apgar scores (see page 328), and that far more babies went to the nursery to have special care*.

So it is important to have expert assistance if you are being induced and essential for the baby's heart to be continuously monitored. If you experience a contraction that lasts longer than 90 seconds, let the obstetrician know immediately. Even with a small dose of oxytocin some women have a prolonged contraction in which the uterus clamps down on itself—and on the baby. There is no test by which the sensitivity of your uterus to oxytocin can be known beforehand, so it is best to start with a small dose and gradually build up till good contractions result. The aim should be to simulate normal labour.

Measuring contractions

During an induced labour a machine called the Cardiff Pump may be used to monitor the pressure of uterine contractions and stop the flow of oxytocin when the uterus is contracting too hard. Another machine, the FM3R, automatically adjusts the flow according to the amount of pressure in the uterus which is measured by a small intra-uterine pressure catheter so that the woman does not have to be strapped into a tight belt to record the contractions. Both these machines solve the problem of the too strong, harsh labour which often results from infiltrating more oxytocin into a woman's blood-stream than her particular uterus needs.

Accelerated labour

Labour is said to have been accelerated (or augmented) when it has already started and then, for some reason, has been speeded up by the use of an oxytocin drip. If a drip is used *before* the cervix has started to dilate progressively, even though you have felt contractions and have had a "false labour" or many Braxton Hicks contractions, you are being induced, not accelerated.

Labour may be accelerated when there is uterine inertia or incoordination, that is, when the uterus is not working effectively (see page 266). Some of the most difficult labours are long ones, and if you are becoming tired out with back pain for example, acceleration may help you cope, because it stimulates uterine action.

If it looks as if labour ought to be induced or accelerated, there are breathing skills you can use to deal with the challenge (see page 190). You need not give up, feeling that the doctors have taken over.

Induction with epidural anaesthesia

In some hospitals you may be offered a "package deal" of induction combined with epidural anaesthesia. (For more about epidurals see page 286.) Women who accept the package deal offered know that labour will take place on a certain day and that complete pain relief will be available. This new style of childbirth is attractive to many obstetricians and to many women too.

As with any intravenous drip, if you are receiving a large quantity of fluid, it is important that you should remember to empty your bladder regularly. If you cannot pass urine (and you usually cannot if you have had an epidural) the midwife will insert a catheter and draw off the urine for you. A full bladder makes contractions painful by acting as a barrier between the baby's head and the base that forms the front of your pelvic arch.

Elective induction

Elective induction, also called induction for convenience, is induction that has no medical benefit.

Some doctors believe that most women should be induced. Some think it is the only way in which *all* labours can be efficiently managed. They say it is important for women to be in labour when staff are on duty, that hospital organization is easier when it is known how many women will be in labour each day, and that it is better if women are not in labour at night.

There will always be those women who go into labour spontaneously at inconvenient times, but the earlier they are induced the less this is likely to happen. So some obstetricians believe that induction any time after 38 or 39 weeks is right for most women. The logical development of this approach to obstetrics is that spontaneous labours will be considered "emergencies" and the "normal" labours will all be induced.

The US Food and Drugs Administration has, after considering the research, withdrawn approval for the use of oxytocin for the elective induction of labour, asserting that it can expose both mother and baby to unnecessary danger.

Coping with induction

While there are basic questions that women need to ask about induction and acceleration of labour in terms of our whole style of childbirth in the West, these may not seem very relevant if your doctor advises you that your labour should be induced. It may come as a shock. You may even feel that all your careful preparation for the birth of your baby is pointless now.

Many women have enjoyed induced labours and coped with them well. But unfortunately many whose labours were induced say that they did not have any choice and that they were given inadequate information. Yet the British Department of Health and Social Security has stated: "A mother should have learned about induction at antenatal classes and if later it appears that induction would be the safer course of action for her, she should have every opportunity of discussing it with professional advisers. Knowing what is likely to be involved, she can make a fully informed decision about it."*

The important thing is to ask questions. Do not wait and hope that the obstetrician will explain things to you. Discuss it all fully, learn about what happens and share in the decision-making rather than feeling it is all being decided for you. When you have the facts and your obstetrician's advice, take time to weigh it up and choose what seems to be the best way, always leaving your mind open to new evidence which may later point to a different course of action. It is your baby and your body and the experts are there to help you.

ELECTRONIC FETAL MONITORING

The electronic fetal monitor is used to track the fetal heartbeat and to record the pressure of the uterus during contractions. Either a transducer is placed over your abdomen near the baby's heart (external monitoring), or an electrode is inserted through the open cervix and clipped to the baby's scalp (internal monitoring). A printout, which is usually in the form of a continuous graph on a long spool of tape rather like ticker tape, shows the baby's heart rate in relation to the work done by the uterus. The monitor is a compact box which can amplify the baby's heartbeat so that it becomes clearly audible. It incorporates a flashing light which also registers the baby's heart, but this can be turned off. If anything goes wrong the monitor sounds an alarm, though this often indicates something wrong with the machine rather than with the baby.

The external monitor

An external monitor has two straps which are attached to your abdomen. One strap holds the tochodynamometer (a pressure gauge to record contractions), the other holds an ultrasound transducer which registers the baby's heartbeats.

The internal monitor

The internal monitor, which is more accurate, is inserted through your vagina and cervix and fixed to the skin of the baby's head. It is

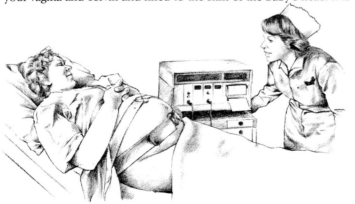

ELECTRONIC FETAL MONITOR
The monitor is usually near the bed and you can see when the next contraction is starting even before you feel it, and can get ready to meet it with your breathing. On the right of the monitor is a printout which shows the fetal heartbeat on the left and contractions on the right.

connected to a catheter leading to the machine and another catheter is inserted into the uterus to record electronically the pressure of contractions, or you may wear a single strap around your abdomen to hold the tochodynamometer. An internal monitor cannot be used until the membranes have ruptured spontaneously or have been ruptured artificially, and until the cervix is dilated at least 2 cm.

Advantages of monitoring

The monitor is particularly useful in high-risk pregnancies and when labour is induced or augmented with an oxytocin drip, since the length, power and frequency of the contractions produced by the drip must be carefully watched and their effect on the baby observed lest they prove too stressful for it. Until recently induction was often done "blind", and enormous, turbulent contractions were produced which sometimes cut off the fetal blood supply. This is much less likely nowadays since, by monitoring all these artificially aided births, it has been discovered that small amounts of oxytocin are effective.

Another undoubted advantage of monitoring is that the monitor indicates when the next contraction is beginning, so that, however drowsy you are feeling during labour, you can breathe out and relax, and get ready to breathe over it.

Problems of monitoring

Many women say that the abdominal strapping for the external monitor is very uncomfortable. Some even say that the pressure of the transducer on their tummies was the most painful thing about labour. Sometimes the internal electrode slips off the baby's head or, if an external monitor is being used, the baby moves and its heartbeat is lost. Some new external monitors have transducers which track the position of the baby's heart so that they do not lose it in this way.

As with an intravenous drip, having an external monitor means that you must remain more or less in one position lest the transducer slips off. As we have seen, this immobility means discomfort for you (page 294) and possibly problems for the baby. So monitoring may actually sometimes produce the failing fetal heart rate which it then records. If you are being monitored, turn on your side before the monitor is put on, although you may find that even this position becomes uncomfortable after a while.

Some women in labour are wired up to the monitor only to find that nothing is being recorded at all because the machine is not operating. It is very irritating to be immobilized and connected to a machine when it cannot possibly be doing anything to help. Yet staff sometimes appear shocked at a woman's request for the transducer to be detached so that she can move about and get on with her labour unhindered. If this happens to you, you are entirely justified in being insistent that the monitor is disconnected. But when the monitor is working well some women find it reassuring to know that every heartbeat of the baby is being recorded.

Telemetry

Monitoring by telemetry (radio waves) is an advance on the older method and allows you to be up and about in labour unattached to wires but continuously monitored at the same time. The equipment is less cumbersome and the machinery can be placed at some distance from you. Most women prefer it, labours seem to go faster and babies do better. Because you are able to be upright, you may feel less pain, and the uterus can work more efficiently, producing stronger and more powerful contractions.

But even monitoring by telemetry is usually invasive, since an electrode is clipped onto the baby's scalp, though a method of sticking the monitor on with epoxy resin is now available. Any invasive technique (one which entails entering your body) introduces added risk of infection. This is a risk worth taking when there is reason to suspect the baby is encountering difficulties, but *not*, many people would think, when everything seems to be straightforward.

A scalp electrode probably causes the baby some pain. (It is uncomfortable to prick your finger on one.) It remains on the baby's head till after delivery, when it should be removed gently and deftly, not merely pulled. In 85 per cent of newborn babies a rash appears at the site of the electrode and in 20 per cent a small abscess develops*. Sometimes the child is left with a permanent bald patch.

Interpreting the data

Although it is estimated that the fetal monitor enables an obstetrician to save one life for every 1000 babies monitored, the interpretation of data is of first importance. The machine by itself can do nothing to make childbirth safer. It is only too easy to interpret normal variations in the fetal heart as pathological, sometimes because of the design of the machine, or to miss out on clinical signs that something is wrong because the monitor indicates that everything is normal. Obstetricians and midwives experienced in auscultating the fetal heart and assessing clinical conditions have a skill which is being neglected today as more and more confidence is put in electronic machines.

Half of all babies show some irregularities of heartbeat during labour. Usually this is of no significance. We don't know how they manage it, but babies actually sleep during labour. They change from rapid eye movement (REM) or dreaming sleep to deep, quiet sleep for a period of up to 40 minutes, and then back again. As the sleep state varies, so the heart rate changes; in deep sleep, the heartbeat stays steady, and the printout of the heart rate tends to be flat. Until the deep sleep was understood, this kind of trace made doctors anxious; but it has now been discovered that the baby only has to be roused a little for the heartbeat to pick up. One way of doing this is to touch the top of the baby's head. Mothers have their own ways of achieving the same result—changing position, for example, or even talking to the baby—and this may reassure the doctors.

The baby's heart rate is usually between 120 and 160 beats per minute. A quicker rate than this is termed tachycardia, and a slower rate, bradycardia. Incomplete understanding of the normal range of variation in the fetal heart rate during and between contractions leads to a great deal of intervention. In Spain and West Germany, for example, when abnormal fetal heart patterns are recorded, obstetricians stop the uterus contracting by introducing drugs into the mother's bloodstream. In all countries, electronic fetal monitoring has led to more forceps deliveries and Caesarean sections being performed, and the introduction of a monitor in any hospital is associated with a sharp increase in the rate of operative deliveries— though this often drops after a while.

Testing the baby's blood

Some obstetricians believe that the baby's blood should be tested to check the findings when the monitor suggests fetal distress since, if the baby is in difficulties, this always shows up in the blood chemistry. This extra test might cut down the number of unnecessary Caesarean deliveries. One kind of electrode both records the baby's heart rate and tests its blood.

It has usually been accepted that if a blood test reveals high levels of lactic acid, which builds up if the baby is short of oxygen in the second stage of labour, the baby's brain will be damaged. But it is now known that, if it does become short of oxygen, a healthy baby can switch to another kind of metabolism which allows it to draw on energy reserves built up over the previous weeks; in this way the baby can survive on less oxygen with no ill effects. Indeed, babies whose blood is acid at birth often have high Apgar scores (see page 328). And neurological studies on four-year-olds whose blood was acid at birth due to oxygen shortage show that this had no harmful effects.*

HELPING THE BABY OUT

In British hospitals nowadays about one woman in every ten is delivered by forceps, though the rate is higher in some hospitals.

Forceps delivery

Forceps look like metal salad servers and dovetail into each other so that they cannot press too far in on the baby's head. If the woman has not already had an epidural an injection to numb the birth outlet is given first. The curved blades are inserted one at a time and cradled round the baby's head, one at each temple. Forceps are of different shapes for different situations: most bring the baby down the birth canal, though some are simply used to lift the baby out. If the baby's head is occipito transverse or occipito posterior (see page 257), the obstetrician may first turn the head manually or may use curved Kiellands forceps for the delivery to rotate the head from the transverse or posterior to the anterior.

Vacuum extraction

Sometimes a vacuum extractor, or ventouse, is used instead of forceps. This works like a miniature vacuum cleaner to suck the baby out. A vacuum cup is attached to the baby's head. It may take between 10 and 20 minutes to be applied. During this time if you want to push, push. Once the cup is on, it helps if you can bear down, so that the baby is pressed down from above as well as being pulled by the suction applied from below.

Reasons for forceps or ventouse delivery

Forceps or vacuum extraction is used when delivery needs to be hastened because your blood pressure has risen dramatically, for example, or because there are signs of fetal distress, or when the baby is in an unusual position, making its journey through the pelvic outlet more difficult. The obstetrician has to use clinical judgment to decide whether your baby will pop out like a cork from a bottle given a firm, long pull or whether it is so firmly wedged that it might harm both the baby and you to deliver vaginally. Sometimes after forceps have failed a Caesarean section is performed (see page 308).

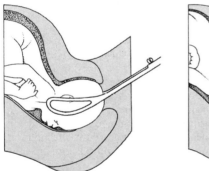 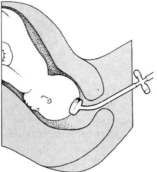

HELP WITH DELIVERY
These forceps (far left) are the kind used simply for lifting the baby's head out of the birth canal. Vacuum extraction (left) can sometimes avoid a difficult forceps delivery, and the suction cup may be attached to the baby before it has started to descend the birth canal.

Forceps may also be used if you have had an epidural (see page 286), as you may feel too numb to work with contractions.

A forceps delivery is frequently advised if you are having a prolonged second stage. Different obstetricians have different ideas of what a prolonged second stage is. Some would say that it is any second stage of longer than half an hour in which there are no signs of progress. Many set a definite time limit on the second stage and instruct midwives to call them when it looks as if this stage is extending. Some believe that this is rather doctrinaire and that the important thing is to observe whether or not the baby is coming down the birth canal progressively, while checking its condition carefully and regularly.

Some women seem to be able to cope with long second stages without tiring, whereas others quickly become exhausted. If you have already had a long labour and then a slow second stage it is difficult to retain enthusiasm and, unless given a great deal of encouragement, you might hope that someone would just come and take the baby out of your body one way or another.

Sometimes a woman may be given encouragement to push or is persuaded to hold her breath too long, when she does not feel any spontaneous urge to bear down. This is because the midwife knows that the delivery will be by forceps unless the baby is born within the time decreed by the obstetrician, so she tries to avoid the intervention by getting the mother to push more strenuously in the hope that this will help the baby to be born before the deadline comes.

Avoiding a forceps delivery

If you have been struggling to push the baby out and it is suggested that forceps may be necessary either because the second stage is taking too long, you are becoming too tired, or the fetal heart rate is slow, explore the effect of *not pushing*. You may find that you do not need to push at all for several contractions—a welcome rest for both you and the baby—and then there is an unmistakable and irresistible pushing sensation which is much more effective than pushing just because you are following instructions. It is a good idea to stand, squat or kneel so that gravity can help the baby out.

CAESAREAN SECTION

The doctor gave me an internal exam and said, "It's not dilating any more—I'll have to do a C-section on you." And I remember saying, "Oh no, I don't want to have a C-section!" I was so emotionally involved in this whole process that it was like robbery.

If the obstetrician tells you that you need to give birth by Caesarean section, this means that you will be anaesthetized and your baby will then be delivered abdominally rather than vaginally.

The most common reason for Caesarean section is cephalo-pelvic disproportion, when the baby's head is too large to pass through the pelvis. Some obstetricians prefer to deliver abdominally all breech babies, or all breech babies of first-time mothers, because they believe it is safer for the baby. But size of the baby in relation to the maternal pelvis and the way the baby is lying are factors which should also be taken into account. If fetal distress is picked up by an electronic monitor and the obstetrician becomes anxious about the state of the baby, he or she may decide to do an emergency Caesarean section. Abdominal delivery may also be performed for twins, or when amniocentesis has revealed that a baby is damaged, for very low-birthweight babies and on women suffering from diseases such as diabetes, renal disease and chronic hypertension.

The rise in Caesarean births

Caesarean rates vary but, in Britain, they make up between 10 and 15 per cent of all births. In some cities in Latin America, 85 per cent of babies are delivered abdominally, whereas in the Netherlands the overall rate is less than 10 per cent. The rate is much higher in the United States and is increasing rapidly—in some hospitals it is 50 per cent or more. But there has not been a corresponding rise in the fetal survival rate. And Caesarean section imposes on women extra risk, unnecessary pain and, often, post-operative infection.

Where in the past the obstetrician would have corrected a baby's bad position by external version through the mother's abdominal wall (see page 215), the tendency now is to deliver by section rather than attempting to turn the baby first. As a result many doctors nowadays no longer know *how* to perform external version.

More and more women are now included in the category of "high risk". The age at which a woman is considered obstetrically high risk went down from 40 to 35, then to 30, and now in some hospitals anyone over 27 is included in this category. If you are over 27 and it seems likely that there may be problems with your labour, you may find that you are advised to deliver by Caesarean section.

Throughout North America it is also the practice to do *repeat* Caesarean sections even when the conditions which resulted in the first section are not present in a subsequent pregnancy: "Once a Caesarean, always a Caesarean". American doctors argue that the uterine scar might break open during a subsequent labour, but British obstetricians differ. They normally use a "trial" of labour, allowing the labour to proceed naturally but being ready to do a Caesarean if necessary. One experienced professor of obstetrics says that problems of scar separation are "much less than the one per cent that is often quoted" and that even if the scar is pulled open by strong contractions "careful monitoring of the fetus and mother usually means that any harm to either is rare"*.

> ══ 66 ══
> *I felt no pain. I looked at trees through the theatre window. I could feel the skin incision like a finger being run over my abdomen. When the uterus was cut open it felt rather as if somebody was rummaging in a chest of drawers.*
> ══ 99 ══

Planned Caesarean section

The decision to perform a Caesarean section is often made days or weeks in advance. A section will usually be planned if it is known that the baby is in a difficult position to be delivered vaginally, or if there is evidence of cephalo-pelvic disproportion—although you can only be certain that there is genuine CPD when you are actually in labour. The baby must be delivered abdominally if the placenta is lying at the bottom of the uterus in front of the baby's presenting part (placenta praevia). Surgery is either arranged for the 39th week or in some cases you are allowed to go into labour naturally, knowing that a Caesarean section will be performed.

Unplanned (just-in-case) Caesarean section

During a long labour in which there is little progress, the obstetrician may make the decision to perform a Caesarean section for no other reason than that dilatation is slow.

Emergency Caesarean section

Some reasons for a planned Caesarean section (such as cephalo-pelvic disproportion) may also apply to an emergency section, when they have not been obvious until labour. An emergency section may

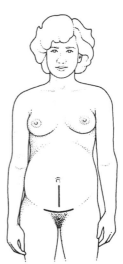

The classic Caesarean incision is vertical. Though it is still used in emergencies, the horizontal incision is now more common, mainly for cosmetic reasons.

also be decided on during a long labour in which the baby is in obvious difficulties and is short of oxygen; if the placenta is failing to service the baby sufficiently or is becoming detached from the lining of the uterus—causing the mother to haemorrhage; or if there is a prolapsed umbilical cord.

Anaesthesia for Caesarean section

Caesarean section has traditionally been performed with the patient under general anaesthetic, but epidural anaesthesia (see page 286) is becoming more common for this operation. Though general anaesthesia has to be used when a very quick decision is made to do a section, those women who have had epidural anaesthesia usually like being awake and aware of what is going on and being ready to welcome the baby as soon as it is lifted out.

General anaesthesia If general anaesthesia is used, you are given as small a dose as possible for the baby's sake, and you may be unconscious for only a few minutes. All the preparation for the operation is done while you are awake and you are often given pure oxygen to breathe in during this time. It should be possible to arrange for the baby who is in good condition to be held by the father while you are unconscious.

Epidural anaesthesia You are given the epidural after being taken to the operating theatre—the dosage is larger for this surgery than it would be if an epidural were being given just for pain relief. An anaesthetist checks carefully to see that the anaesthesia is sufficient for the operation and is ready with general anaesthesia should the epidural not take effectively. There is no post-operative nausea and vomiting as there often is with general anaesthesia. An epidural is also safer for you because you cannot inhale your stomach contents, and safer for the baby, who does not receive a knock-out dose of anaesthesia. Another advantage is that you can hold your baby and put her to the breast immediately after the operation.

Horizontal or vertical incision

Incisions for Caesarean section are either horizontal or vertical. The classical incision is vertical but is rarely done now unless there is no time to spare. The main advantages of the horizontal incision are that it is done low down near the line of the pubic hair, in the area which would be covered by a bikini, and that a horizontal scar is less likely to break down than a vertical scar.

What happens during a Caesarean section

Before you have a Caesarean section a midwife will shave off your pubic hair and slip a catheter into your bladder so that it is kept empty. In the operating theatre sterile drapes are put around your tummy and if you are going to be awake a screen is erected at about

=66=
They told us it was a girl so I thought she'd been born and asked if she was all right. "Have a look" they said and pushed the screen down to show us her spindly little legs sticking out from my body. A few seconds later out came her head and I felt wonderful. I don't think I've ever enjoyed anything so much in my life.
=99=

waist level so that you do not see the surgery. Your tummy is washed in antiseptic solution. If there is anything you want to know, ask.

You will be given an epidural or general anaesthetic. When your whole tummy is numb or you have become unconscious, a small cut is made through the lower abdominal wall below your navel to reveal the lower uterine segment. Packs of surgical swabs are pressed in to keep other organs out of the way. A horizontal slit is made through the muscle and the bag of waters bulges through it. The obstetrician pops the bag and sucks out the amniotic fluid—if you have had an epidural, you may hear the glug-glug-swoosh sound—and uses one blade of the forceps or a hand under the baby's presenting part to ease it out of the small opening, at the same time pressing with one hand on the upper part of the uterus so that the baby is pressed down through the incision.

If you have had an epidural, it may be possible for you to watch the birth at this stage. Ask the doctor to put the screen down for a few moments. You will see your baby emerging and, from your horizontal position, will not see anything gruesome. In fact you will only have eyes for your baby and will not think about the surgery that has been done. The baby is lifted out, suctioned with a mucus catheter, and once it is breathing well can be handed to you or your partner. The whole birth process from the beginning of surgery need take only about four minutes.

As the baby is being delivered you may be given an injection of oxytocin to make the placenta peel away from the wall of the uterus. It will then be lifted out through the abdominal opening that has been made. The obstetrician stitches the cut in the uterus, layer by layer, with absorbable sutures. Suction instruments are used to draw out blood and amniotic fluid, and then the obstetrician repairs the abdominal wall. This takes much longer than the birth—up to an hour—and entails repairing the skin with non-absorbable sutures, staples or metal clips which have to be removed later.

Having your partner with you

Not all couples want to be together during surgery. You may worry that perhaps it will be too much for your partner to cope with, or he may expect to find the experience so distressing that he feels he will be unable to give you any support. Those couples who do want to be together do so because they feel that the birth of a baby, by whatever route, is something they want to share, that it should be family-centred, and that, if the mother is not able to cuddle the newborn baby, the father should be there to do so.

If you do want to be together and your Caesarean is planned try getting to know your obstetrician well in advance. Once you have built up a relationship, ask if your partner can be with you at the birth. If the answer is no, ask politely for the doctor's reasons. If it is not normal practice at that hospital, you may convince the doctor that you are both concerned enough to want to be the first couple to

It was Joanna, our antenatal teacher, who convinced us not just to accept the word of a doctor who said "No, husbands cannot be present at a Caesarean birth."

experience a Caesarean birth together there. There is always a first time. If your partner is present, he sits up by your head supporting you emotionally; there is no necessity for him to watch the operation, since the screen restricts his view.

After the delivery

After the operation, say you want to hold your baby if he or she is not already beside you. An intravenous drip is left in for some hours so that you can be given plenty of fluids straight into your bloodstream if necessary. If you had general anaesthesia, you may feel sick and weak for the first day or so. As soon as you feel you can move about in bed a little, do so. Even wiggling your toes and rotating your ankles is good and prevents pooling of blood in your legs.

Whatever anaesthesia you have had, the chances are that the nurses will help you get up later the same day. Though it hurts, moving around is important to avoid thrombosis. To move off the bed, work your way to the side of it, pressing your buttocks together and taking some of the weight of your body on your hands. As you get up you may have a lot of bleeding from the vagina. This also happens after a vaginal delivery and is simply the blood that has pooled in your pelvic region while you were lying still. Stroll around the room to encourage good circulation and use the slow, complete breathing you learned in antenatal classes.

If you feel you need drugs for pain relief, ask for them. Though you probably want to be awake to enjoy your baby you cannot do this if you are in severe discomfort. The more your partner can be with you, even while you doze, the more you can relax, feeling that the baby is being looked after by someone who loves her.

Dressings will probably be removed three or four days later. Because the obstetrician has had to cut through muscle, your tummy will look very big and soggy. Once the dressings are off you will be able to have a bath. The stitches inside your body dissolve naturally, but the external stitches will be removed towards the end of the first week. Do not worry about them bursting open—with every layer stitched separately there is little chance of any such damage.

After general anaesthesia fluid collects in the lungs and has to be coughed up. A physiotherapist will teach you how to do this so that it causes least discomfort. The breathing techniques you learned in pregnancy can help you too.

It is natural to feel a flood of conflicting emotions after Caesarean birth. Some women say that they are grateful to have the baby, but at the same time they feel "cheated".

A Caesarean birth is a surgical operation and you need time to recover from it as from any abdominal surgery. For the first six weeks after the birth you should avoid any heavy lifting. If it is possible to arrange for extra help at home, especially if you already have a toddler who expects to be lifted, it is an enormous benefit to have someone else to do the more strenuous work.

After a Caesarean birth it helps your circulation if you can get moving soon.

Gentle birth

At birth eyes open for the first time on a new world. Your baby's life outside your body begins. Yet your baby already has nine months' experience of life inside the uterus. The ancient Chinese dated life from conception rather than from delivery and perhaps this corresponds more nearly to reality. The baby started off as the chance collision of a ripe egg and a sperm. Forces which have their origin far back in creation poured energy into the cells, nourishing and multiplying them to make an embryo budding on a stalk and drawing sustenance from your uterus. Gradually as the days passed a fully formed being developed, albeit in miniature, and there was already at the third month a fetus whose main task was one of growth and maturation. As week followed week its senses became sharper so that it was increasingly aware of its surroundings, responding to your movements, and to bright light, loud sounds and music. This long-drawn-out period of preparation culminates in the dramatic journey into the brilliance and bustle of our own world.

WHAT IS IT LIKE TO BE BORN?

Birth is an intense experience not only for you: for the baby, too, it is the climax of a time of growing and waiting. The new human being is caught up in a rush of powerful uterine activity, which squeezes it out from the confines of the tight muscle enveloping it and the cradle of bone in which it has been rocked, into a separate existence.

Travelling from the depths of the uterus, under the arch of bone and out through the soft, opening folds of the vagina, the baby passes through a barrage of different kinds of sensory stimulation. It is the original magical mystery tour and must be more astonishing and full of surprises than any mystery tunnel travelled through in search of excitement in a fairground.

The baby's experience of labour

Pressure builds up over the crown of the baby's head where it is directed through the dilating cervix, which is pulled up over its head like a polo-neck sweater. Pressure is also directed over the baby's buttocks as the uterus contracts down on them and propels the baby forward. So the baby is fixed between the uterus gripping its bottom and the cervix being progressively drawn over its head. This pressure causes the baby to roll into a ball, head tucked in and knees bent up, arms folded over its chest. The upper part of the head, not yet hard bone all over, is moulded so that the brow is pressed backward.

As the baby is forced downwards the crown of the head also confronts resistance from the pelvic-floor muscles, which are springy

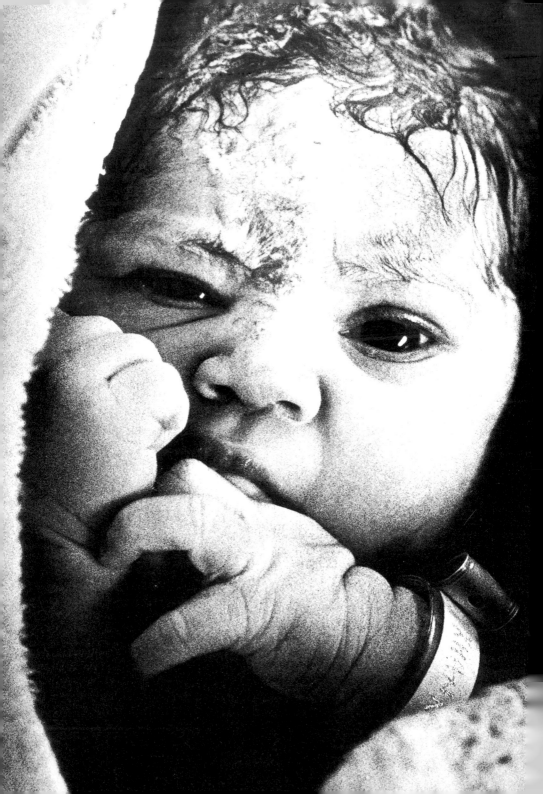

and firm and which are also little by little eased over its head. The passage is narrow but yielding and the baby's whole body is massaged vigorously with each contraction as it gradually descends.

Beneath the stretched abdominal skin and the thinned translucent wall of the uterus itself the baby in the last weeks of pregnancy has been aware of glowing light whenever bright sun or artificial light shone on your body. It must be rather like firelight or the light cast by a red-shaded lamp. When the journey to birth begins the baby is pressed deeper into the cavity of the pelvis, under arches of bone and a canopy of thick supportive ligaments and muscles. Perhaps it is a sensation rather like travelling through a long, dark avenue of overhanging trees.

The baby is not just a hunk of flesh or a life-sized doll. It is a human being fully equipped to feel pain and pleasure, a *person* coming to birth. The baby cannot remember or anticipate in the same way that we can, but it nevertheless feels keenly and is a fully sentient being. The uterus holds and presses tightly in on the child not yet born, with steadily escalating power. By the end of the first stage of labour it is embracing the baby tightly for one or two minutes at a time. Each hug begins gently and grows tighter and tighter till at the height of the contractions the baby is being gripped fast for 20 to 30 seconds. Then the wave of pressure recedes again and the baby floats once more in its inner sea: it is in labour along with you.

Newborn reflexes in labour

In some obstetric textbooks the baby is described simply as "a passenger", and purely in mechanical terms, as two ovoids, the head and the trunk, the long axes of which are at right angles to each other and which can take the curve of the pelvic axis independently. While this is accurate as a description of the mechanics of fetal descent, it leaves out any mention of what the baby might be doing during this process and how the reflexes with which it is born are probably also functioning during labour.

The baby changes its position in response to the power unleashed in your body, and does this not only because of mechanical forces which act on it but probably also because it is making active movements. It is working *with* you towards birth, your partner in the struggle, not just a passenger, and can do this because of inbuilt reflexes (see page 329). A newborn baby turns his head in the direction of a touch, moves his head up and down against a firm surface, curls his toes down when pressure is applied to the ball of the foot, lifts his foot up and puts it down at a higher level when pressure is applied over the top of the foot, and makes forward stepping movements when tilted forward with his feet against a firm surface. Two of these actions probably operate to help the baby onward in its journey. One is the reflex to move its head up and down against firm resistance, which means that it actually wriggles its way forward through the cervix and the fanned-out tissues of the vagina

OPPOSITE
Still damp from birth, the gently delivered baby is alert to learn about the world . . .

with much the same action that we make when putting on a new jersey with a rather tight neck. The other is the stepping movement when the resistance is offered to the feet, so that in effect the baby pushes away from the solid wall of the uterus as it tightens around it.

The impact of the outside world

In the second stage the head has to take nearly a right-angled bend. The pressure builds up until it swivels the neck round so that the baby is facing downward ready to slide out. You can imagine that this provides a very sharp stimulus to the baby, a message which says unmistakably "Things are changing. Wake up! It's all systems go!" At last the crown of the head oozes through the vagina and remains there. Perhaps you reach down with eager hands to stroke the damp, warm top of your baby's head. This is the first greeting.

The head slips out and suddenly the baby encounters space and air. The shoulders and chest slide forward, followed by the whole body. There is a gasp and air rushes into the lungs, inflating them for the first time. The damp inner surfaces of the lungs, previously clinging together like wet polythene bags, open up with the first cry with which the baby meets life.

Air, space, the baby's own limbs moving in an unfamiliar medium, weight, strange sounds, glaring lights, cold hands picking the baby up, turning it over—all at once a myriad of new sensations assail the newborn. Not only must lungs fill with air and start to function rhythmically, but the circulation must find new pathways.

Labour as a stimulus

In his book *Birth without Violence**, Dr Frederick Leboyer calls the mother "a monster" because of the pain he believes she cannot help but inflict on the baby as it passes through the throes of birth. But the process of being born can also be seen to involve stimulation and awakening for which the baby is ready and which prepares it for life. Looked at from this point of view, muscles hold and embrace the baby, triggering powerful sensations, then soften again in a rhythmic pattern. The space between contractions is like the trough between two waves. Inevitably the next wave comes and again the muscles tighten firmly around the child.

Though labour is undoubtedly traumatic for some babies, others look extraordinarily peaceful and contented after delivery. It may feel to you as if you are swimming in a stormy sea when you reach the end of the first stage of labour. You may be anxious that these massive squeezings of the great muscle of the uterus are causing your baby suffering. Yet in spite of the relentless onslaught of contractions as full dilatation approaches, the baby who is pressed through the cervix and down the birth canal in this way responds more vigorously to life than most babies do who are merely lifted out through an abdominal incision. The 9 in (23 cm) journey squeezes out fluid and mucus from its nose and mouth so that the baby born vaginally has less mucus in its respiratory tract than one delivered by Caesarean section and is better prepared for the great new activity of breathing.

Welcoming your baby

Have you thought about how you want to welcome your baby into the world? Frederick Leboyer believes that just as our attention has now been drawn to the mother's experience of birth, so we must focus on the baby's needs and learn how to reduce its suffering. For him this is not just a matter of safe or speedy delivery, a question of making sure that the baby has enough oxygen or is not traumatized by delivery, but one of greeting the baby with consideration and gentleness.

Most babies cry at the shock of birth and this first cry ensures that a rush of air enters the lungs. But if they *go on* crying Leboyer asserts that there is something wrong. The crying of abandonment and distress is quite different from the healthy crying of the newborn. Yet people often take persistent crying for granted and even smile indulgently and say, "She's got a fine pair of lungs!" The newborn baby continues to scream because of insensitivity to her needs and the lack of a sufficiently caring environment. If the setting for birth is changed and, above all, if the attitudes of those assisting are different, so that the baby is treated with respect, Leboyer says, the child will become quiet, will open her eyes, will reach out with her hands and start to discover herself. But if this is to happen the birth room must be calm and hushed, the lights dimmed and those handling the baby must do so slowly, carefully and lovingly. This is *gentle birth*.

CREATING A CARING ENVIRONMENT

Gentle birth need not start only as the baby is born. In the way that labour is conducted and in the whole atmosphere of the birth room an environment of peace and serenity can be created. Though Dr Leboyer is concerned with what is done to the baby *after delivery*, a mother and baby are so close and in such a subtle and yet intense relationship that everything done to you during labour must affect the way in which you are able to respond to your newborn baby. If you are treated as if your body is merely the container from which a baby is removed, or as an irresponsible child who has to be given orders, you will find it very difficult to be in harmony with the forces which are bringing the baby to birth, with your own body in its work of creation and also with the baby. The caring environment for the newborn starts with a caring environment for you, a respect for your rhythms, patience to wait and watch and loving support.

I lifted her out and up on to my tummy and held and stroked her. It suddenly burst on me that this incredible little creature had come out of my body—and I was bathed in love for her.

Dimming the lights

It is irritating for you to labour under bright lights, just as it is for the baby to confront brilliant fluorescent light at delivery. For a gentle birth all unnecessary lighting is switched off so that the room is softly

◆

illuminated, with a clear light only on the perineum. Instead of lying flat on your back or with your legs suspended in lithotomy stirrups you need to be in a position you find comfortable and in which you can be an active birth-giver. Many women like to be sitting up, crouching or kneeling so that they can catch the first glimpse of the baby's head and can put their fingers down to touch it even before it has started to emerge through the vagina. We have already seen (on page 232) that an upright position has many advantages for the mother in terms of mechanical function. If you are well raised you are also in a splendid position for greeting your baby.

When the head crowns some women put their hands down to caress the top of the baby's head. It feels warm and firm and as it eases forward you touch more and more warm, damp, silk hair. This first contact between mother and child is beyond excitement; it is a moment of awe and for some women it approaches spiritual ecstasy.

Then the head slides out and turns to align with the shoulders still inside and you can see your baby's profile; with a rush the shoulders and whole body are born. As the baby slips out and starts to breathe the lights can be dimmed further so that the baby can take its time to open its eyes in the half-light. Many years ago Maria Montessori, the educationalist, stressed that babies are assaulted by bright light. She said that they should be able to begin the gradual exploration of the world with their senses in a soft glow and shadows, similar to the uterine environment they have just left. Yet in the past we have subjected newborns to harsh hospital lights and have acted as if they were unable to see or hear.

Reducing the noise level

In non-violent birth there is no unnecessary conversation and those attendants who speak do so in hushed voices. Leboyer believes that the mother should be quiet too and that excited voices can startle the baby. He thinks that there is too much emphasis nowadays on the father's presence in childbirth and that fathers sometimes get too emotional. Couples who value sharing birth together would not agree with him. I feel myself and know many women who also feel that it would not have been possible to go through labour and birth without the child's father there.

In fact couples often do cry out with astonishment and wonder when they see their baby leap into life and this is a spontaneous outpouring of emotion, an integral part of childbirth with joy, which *in itself* is a life-enhancing experience for both parents. We don't work out carefully exactly what we are going to do when we are caught up in other sorts of peak experience; we don't weigh up the different factors and come up with a calculation. To do so would be to diminish the experience. Life is exultant and we are borne along with it. Birth is that kind of climactic process. It is an act of love, the continuation and culmination of the passion which started the development of that baby.

OPPOSITE
Hold your baby close, against the warmth of your skin, and share with her the first moments of life.

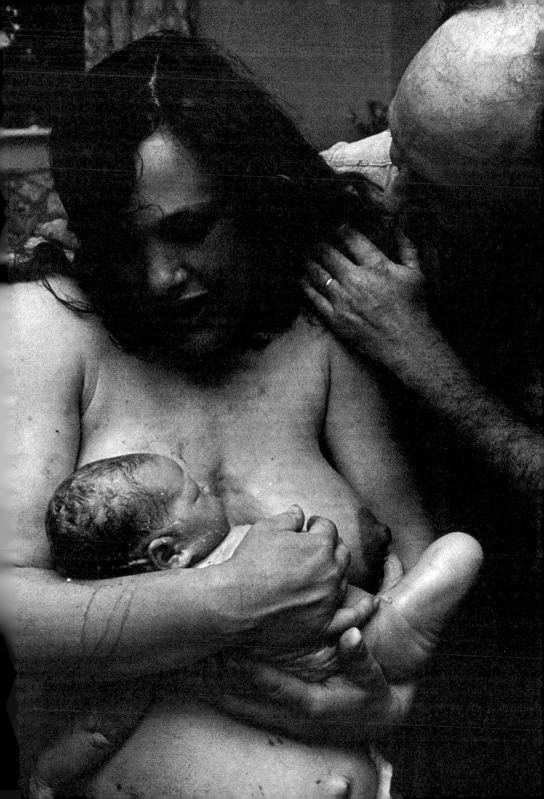

Physical contact

It is because birth is a peak experience that arms reach out to take and hold the baby and draw it close. It is not just that this small, wrinkled, vulnerable baby is yours and that therefore you decide to take it in your arms (though unfortunately this is just how it is for some women in a loveless, uncaring environment); if the right atmosphere exists you are totally enveloped in a rush of intense feeling. This does not mean that the baby is neglected in an orgy of self-indulgent emotion, as Dr Leboyer believes. The baby is drawn into the warm circle of love between the parents and becomes part of it. This is what it is for not only a baby to be born but also a *family*.

In non-violent birth the baby is handled gently and slowly without haste. There are no rough, quick movements. He or she is delivered up onto your tummy or over your thigh. If you ask beforehand it is often possible to do this yourself and the midwife and doctor will remind you to reach out and draw the baby onto your body.

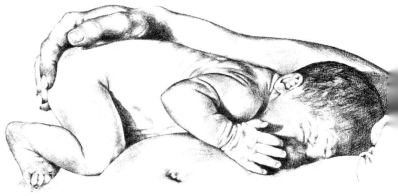

The baby can be delivered straight onto your tummy for its first moments of life; there it is in direct contact with your warm skin and can also still hear the familiar, reassuring sound of your heart beating.

Frederick Leboyer believes that the baby should be lovingly and gently massaged until he or she stops crying and becomes calm. Only then does he think the baby is ready to go to the mother's arms. In his own obstetric practice he used to do this massaging. But many women think that this is yet one more way in which professionals, however caring, attempt to take over childbirth and to intrude on the mother's natural role. Wherever gentle birth is done today it is usually the mother who holds and caresses her baby. You do not have to learn how to massage your newborn. The way you explore and stroke it is spontaneous and right. But this is only possible if the baby is naked and in skin contact with you. Babies are often bundled up in wrappings in case they lose heat. It is true that new babies quickly become chilled unless they are in a warm atmosphere and are held close. Research now taking place shows that the baby, even the low-birthweight baby, keeps warmer when in flesh to flesh contact with his mother and nestling against her breast than the baby who is wrapped up and put in a cot. So ask a helper to slip your gown down over your shoulders or to take it right off before delivery.

A blanket can easily be thrown over you and your baby or a heater can be placed over both. Mothers often feel chilled and shaky after delivery and appreciate the warmth themselves.

If your baby is handed to you bundled up in a cloth, unwrap the covers and cuddle it close. Do not be afraid to talk to your baby. He or she will respond to the sound of your voice and will be especially sensitive to the higher-pitched tone of a woman's voice*. The baby is also getting to know your unique scent and by the time she is a few days old will already prefer a cloth which has been against your body to one which has been close to another new mother's body.

Delaying the clamping of the cord

Frederick Leboyer believes it is important to wait to clamp the cord until it has stopped pulsating. Midwives always used to wait, but nowadays the whole birth is so often rushed that the cord is sometimes clamped and cut immediately while blood is still flowing. Even though this blood is not particularly well oxygenated—because the placenta begins to peel off the wall of the uterus as soon as delivery takes place—it is blood which really belongs to the baby. Unless there are reasons for clamping (such as a Rhesus negative mother who has already produced antibodies against her Rhesus positive baby—see page 103) it seems a good idea to wait a few minutes for the cord to become flaccid, when the baby has no further use for it. There is no reason why the cord has to be cut at all until after the placenta is delivered; it is separated only for convenience.

You can rest your fingers on the cord and feel the blood throbbing through it and wait for the moment when it stops completely. Cutting the cord between two clamps is a very simple procedure and something which a father may enjoy doing. If you would like to do this, ask in advance.

Some obstetricians are concerned that blood could drain back into the placenta and the baby even become short of blood if it is placed above the placenta with the cord still unclamped. This is not a good reason for early clamping or for refusing to place the baby against your body. The baby can be rested over your thigh, where it will be below the placenta and you can easily see and touch it if you are well propped up. Mucus usually drains out naturally and there is no need to use a mucus extractor, though the baby should be carefully observed and an extractor used if the airways are blocked.

Waiting for the rooting reflex

Your baby may emerge from your body already wanting to suck. But many babies are not quite ready and need time to feel secure before they reach out to find the nipple. The rooting reflex (see page 329) is a sure sign that the baby is ready to be put to the breast. Wait until the baby shows interest rather than stuff your breast into her mouth.

It was a forceps delivery. But the doctor took the forceps off after the head was born and said "Come on, deliver the rest of your baby yourself!" I reached down and lifted him up. And they dimmed the lights and he lay making sucking noises on my tummy.

Leboyer believes that mothers often try to feed before the baby is ready and that then even breast-feeding can be another assault on the newborn. Many women today are anxious to feed immediately after delivery and perhaps their anxiety to do this in an alien environment, and one which they may even feel is hostile, makes them rush things. Be patient if you can. Let the baby rest against your bare breast and in his own time he will start to explore with mouth, hands and eyes. This time is precious for you and your baby. It cannot be speeded up without interfering with spontaneous, natural rhythms. After a while the baby will probably begin to lick your nipple and then will seek it and, with a little help as you lift your breast into its searching mouth, will latch on and begin to suck.

The Leboyer bath

An important part of the Leboyer style of birth is the warm bath in which the baby is supported shortly after delivery and in Leboyer's film illustrating gentle birth, the bath is given even before the mother holds her baby. Leboyer believes that the baby needs time to feel safe again in the medium which it has just left in the uterus—water—and that suspended in a bath the baby becomes peaceful and sometimes positively beatific, discovers itself and starts to open its eyes and explore the world around. It is true that some babies seem to enjoy the bath very much, but only if it is done slowly and calmly and if the water is deep enough for the baby to float. The ideal way of giving a bath is to use a deep container with a thermal lining (such as a picnic coldbox) and to have an air heater over the bath.

You may find that the hospital where you are having your baby does not allow a bath because of the risk of hypothermia (chilling). Unfortunately cold air ventilation ducts have been incorporated into the design of many modern maternity units and the baby in water or exposed to this air is likely to get chilled. Many hospital paediatricians are concerned that the baby can lose a great deal of body heat while wet or in a bath, through evaporation, and say that if it is done at all it should be done speedily, which defeats its purpose. You obviously cannot top up a bath with hot water when the baby is in it and you know yourself how shivery you feel when you get out of a hot bath into a relatively cold atmosphere. It is much harder for a baby, who cannot shiver yet and whose largest area of heat loss is her big head, to keep warm.

The baby can maintain heat by using brown fat to create warmth, just like a hedgehog or any cold-adapted hibernating animal, though a low-birthweight baby does not have enough brown fat to do this. Muscular activity and crying also help the baby keep warm, and a baby in a cool room will hyperventilate, though one with respiratory depression cannot do this. Another way in which heat loss is reduced is that blood vessels near the surface of the skin tighten up, so increasing tissue insulation, rather like double-glazing over the surface. But babies who have received some drugs from their

A bath in warm water can be very comforting for the newborn baby.

OPPOSITE

Slowly, carefully, lovingly . . . sensitive handling is what your newborn needs most after the turbulent journey from womb to world . . .

322

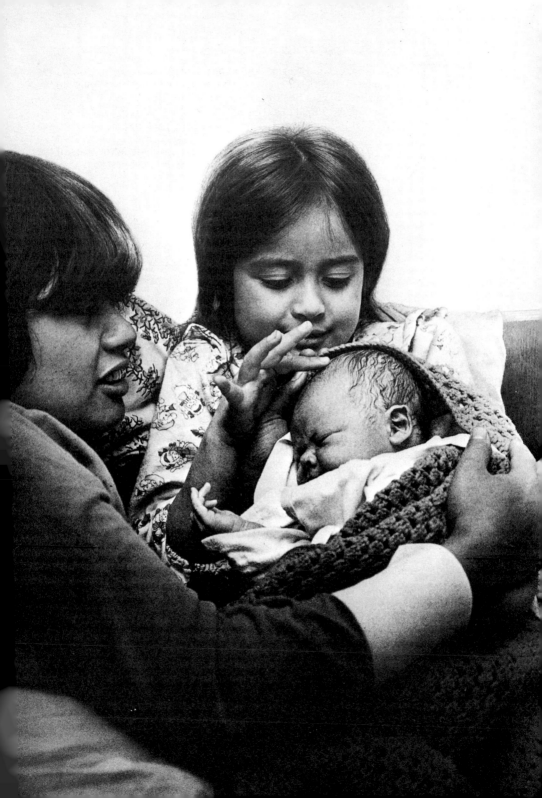

mothers' bloodstreams, including pethidine and Valium, are not only sedated but unable to prevent heat loss efficiently. So if you want the Leboyer bath to be given, bear in mind that you should not have had pethidine or Valium in the last five hours, that your baby should be full term, weigh more than $5\frac{1}{2}$ lb (2500 g) and should not have had breathing difficulties at delivery.

Parents are sometimes very doubtful about the advantages of the bath, preferring to be in skin contact with their baby and to let him or her suck at the breast indefinitely instead. If a baby is happy lying against his mother and ready to go to the breast after a little while it seems purely ritualistic to insist on putting him in a bath because of preconceived ideas about how babies *ought* to behave.

Dr Michel Odent* uses the bath in a different way. The baby goes first to the mother's arms and sucks if he is rooting; only then is he immersed in a bath, and instead of the doctor bathing the baby the father takes over this responsibility, but close enough to the mother so that she can see and touch too. It can be moving to watch a father doing this first service to his newborn child and to see them both looking for the first time into each other's eyes.

A midwife described what happened in one case when a father bathed his baby in this way: "The baby, who had been resting quietly with its mother, gradually opening its eyes, now seemed to wake to its surroundings and gaze serenely around. It is this serenity which is so remarkable and such a joy to watch. The baby's body was totally immersed in the water, which kept it warm, and gave it total relaxation. After five to ten minutes a midwife took over and gently lifted the baby on to the warmed towel below the overhead heater. Not one cry while all this was going on, and all handling was done with an awareness that the baby had never been handled before and that its skin was acutely sensitive. There were no sudden jerks, movements, or pulling while the baby was being dressed. I now realize that the crying which so often accompanies these tasks is the result of sheer fright."*

Sometimes both parents give the bath together and in some home births the mother baths with her baby in a well heated bathroom.

After the delivery

Gentle birth does not finish with the minutes after delivery. It is part of a continuum, a flow of interaction between you and your baby beginning in pregnancy and going on into the weeks following childbirth. It is not just a question of how the delivery is conducted or even whether you are able to hold your baby right away. It is a matter of creating an environment in which throughout the 24 hours you have free access to your baby, feel it is yours and can act spontaneously. You need to know that everyone round you understands what you are feeling, and to be confident of emotional support as you learn to be parents and start to discover more about this unique being who has come into the world.

You and your newborn

The first hours of life

The hours immediately following birth are for many women some of the most intense they experience in their lives. A peak experience like that of giving birth does not suddenly end after you have had half an hour holding the baby or terminate conveniently when the lights are turned out. After such a dramatic and exciting time it is not surprising that some women are unable to sleep for a while, and that many remain in a party spirit for hours or even days after.

Unfortunately many hospitals treat the time after birth as a time when, once clean and tidy, you should be quietly resting; if you are too excited to sleep you may be offered sleeping pills or tranquillizers. Most hospitals do not make provision for the continuity of passionate feeling which ensures that motherhood becomes part of you as a person and is not just something which you are trying to learn. These overpowering emotions impel you through the interim period between the time when you feel you know nothing about your baby and are meeting her as a stranger, and the moment when you realize you know *everything* about her and have become centred in this tiny new existence as much as you are in yourself.

══ 66 ══
I felt I could have got up and danced the rest of the night.

══ 99 ══

Your first meeting with your newborn

You look down at this new little person, feel the weight of the body as he or she begins to relax after the struggle to birth. The head is the biggest part, the hair silken and perhaps still wet and curled in damp fronds or streaked back as if after a swim. Ears are tiny and carved like convoluted shells and the fingernails too are like the little pink shells you picked up from the sand when you were a child. If the baby is still crying the mouth looks huge, a most efficient organ capable of reaching out and grasping on to the breast for its essential nourishment. And the cry itself, a high-pitched, almost animal wail (though when the baby is sleepier it is more of a lamblike bleat), is well adapted to summon immediate attention, to drive you to find out what is wrong and how you can answer the baby's needs, and to be intensely anxious until you have stilled the crying. It is a biological mechanism of vital importance for survival.

As you hold the baby, the hands start to scan the air, encountering space, meeting the face, perhaps brushing against your body or hand. The fingers move and undulate like sea anemones, starting on the important task of finding out about this new world.

If lights have been dimmed the baby will open wide eyes and look straight at you some time during this process of unfolding. It has been discovered that newborn babies find the human face the most attractive thing to look at, far more so than woolly bunnies or painted ducks, and the moving, speaking human face is best of all.

E

Testing the newborn

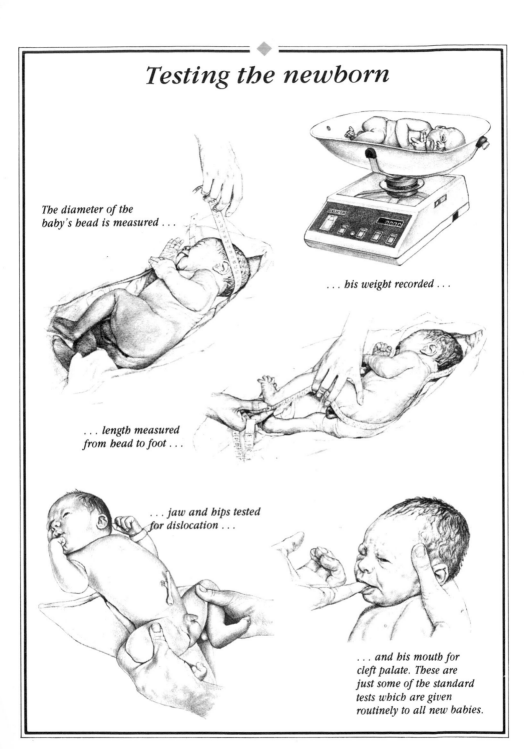

The diameter of the baby's head is measured . . .

. . . his weight recorded . . .

. . . length measured from head to foot . . .

. . . jaw and hips tested for dislocation . . .

. . . and his mouth for cleft palate. These are just some of the standard tests which are given routinely to all new babies.

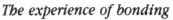

The experience of bonding

The environment into which the baby is born and the attitude of all those handling the baby are important not only for the baby's sake but for yours too, and for the relationship between you. It is far more difficult for a mother to feel her baby belongs to her and she to it—to *bond*—if she does not have time immediately following birth to begin to get to know her baby*. An important element in this is naked skin contact. The baby should not be wrapped up and turned into a solid little package which you are allowed to hold but not to explore. It should be delivered onto your body and you should be able to put the baby to the breast as soon as it is ready to suck.

Marshall Klaus and John Kennel*, working at a hospital in Cleveland, recommend that mothers should be able to hold their babies naked on the delivery bed and have undisturbed time to get to know them, and should then be encouraged to look after them themselves, with help available if they need it. They should have their babies with them and be responsible for them for at least five hours a day and be given ample emotional support from hospital staff.

Still in many hospitals the hours after birth are considered to be time in which you and your baby are medically processed, during which you must pass tests of fitness before being pronounced not "at risk" and discharged into society.

What tests are carried out?

As soon as the baby is born the midwife or doctor assesses the baby's condition and rates it according to something known as the Apgar scale. This is done by simple observation of the baby's breathing, skin colour, muscle tone and general vitality. The highest number of marks is ten and most babies get seven or over. Once you have had a cuddle a further check is made on the baby. Many women say they like this check-up being done close beside them so that they can see what is happening and can discuss anything that they find worrying with the paediatrician. If the baby stays by your side and never leaves you this will happen as a matter of course.

The Apgar scale	What is tested	Points given		
Immediately after birth your baby is tested on five basic points; it is tested again when it is about five minutes old. Even babies who get low marks the first time usually score nine or ten when they are tested the second time.		**0**	**1**	**2**
	Heart rate	Absent	Below 100 beats per minute	100 beats per minute or more
	Breathing	Absent	Slow or irregular	Regular
	Skin colour	Blue	Body pink, extremities blue	Pink all over
	Muscle tone	Limp	Some movements	Active movements
	Reflex response	Absent	Grimace only	Cry

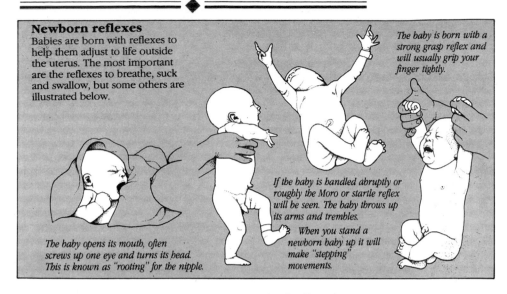

Newborn reflexes

Babies are born with reflexes to help them adjust to life outside the uterus. The most important are the reflexes to breathe, suck and swallow, but some others are illustrated below.

The baby is born with a strong grasp reflex and will usually grip your finger tightly.

If the baby is handled abruptly or roughly the Moro or startle reflex will be seen. The baby throws up its arms and trembles.

The baby opens its mouth, often screws up one eye and turns its head. This is known as "rooting" for the nipple.

When you stand a newborn baby up it will make "stepping" movements.

The baby's weight and length are recorded. The depth of breathing is noted, whether or not his or her extremities are still blue, whether he or she responds vigorously to stimuli and seems strong and healthy. Certain specific things are looked for, too. These include the head size, a check that the genitals are normal and —in a boy—whether both testes are descending. If the baby has not already passed meconium the anus is checked to ensure that it is formed normally. And the baby's heart is listened to (auscultated). The upper part of the mouth is examined to ensure that the palate is complete, and the legs are gently bent up and circled outwards to make sure that there is no dislocation of the hips. Gentle feeling of the baby's tummy will disclose whether the liver and spleen are the right size and feeling around the top of the baby's head reveals the state of the skull bones.

Relating to your baby

Such tests are reassuring. But unfortunately sometimes the adjustment of mother and baby to each other is treated as of secondary importance to this process of medical screening. As a result many new mothers lack confidence in handling and relating to their babies. In our society it is almost as if women are *expected* to be unsure of themselves, awkward and readily depressed. Much of what is called "post-natal depression" probably results from a mother's inability to relate to her baby and feel comfortable as a mother; it feels to her as if the baby belongs not to her, but to the hospital. If other people are making all the decisions, it can be terribly difficult to take over responsibility for this new life you have brought into the world.

It can be even more difficult for a man to feel that his baby belongs to him than it is for a woman. In one Stockholm maternity hospital men were shown how to handle, change, bath and weigh their babies and were helped to understand the emotional and physical stresses of pregnancy and birth on their partners. This was done on two separate occasions while the women were on the post-partum ward. It was discovered that these fathers became more involved in baby care later on and it seemed that they were more understanding than another group of fathers who had not been given the chance to become involved with their babies in this way.

Research shows that *both* parents need an unhurried and peaceful time with their baby in the hour following delivery.

HOW YOUR BABY MAY LOOK

Your new baby may have a low, sloping forehead, a receding chin, hair in sideburns (low on the brow, in the nape of the neck and sometimes down the back as well), an odd, bumpy-shaped head which has been moulded like a ripe grapefruit in its passage down the birth canal, a squashed boxer's nose and blotchy skin. Yet to most new parents their baby looks beautiful! You respond in a protective, caring way to the wonder of this new human being who has come out of the inner depths of your body, having been pressed and kneaded and squeezed out of the uterus and down the vagina to the outside world and into your waiting arms.

Even if you are unaware of feeling anything remarkable at the time, you will probably look back at those moments as being special, as you piece together the fragments of the birth experience and place it in its setting of life lived. This kind of reflection and thinking back is especially important after a difficult labour and probably comes spontaneously to most women if they allow themselves time and do not try to forget about what happened to them.

How the baby has had to adjust

Enormous changes occur as the baby adjusts to the challenges of an extra-uterine existence. One of the most dramatic things that happens, though unseen, is the change from fetal to newborn circulation, with the blood flowing along different pathways. When the baby is inside you all the blood flows in and out through the umbilical cord and bypasses the lungs which do not need to function (see page 66). And since the placenta is doing much of the work that will later be performed by the baby's liver and kidneys, little blood needs to be carried to these organs in the intra-uterine state.

At birth the first great gasp of air causes pressure changes in the whole circulatory system so that blood enters the lungs, liver and kidneys. The increased pressure in these organs brings about the collapse of the umbilical blood vessels and of the bypasses round lungs, liver and kidneys. Once these pressure changes have taken place the system goes on working for a lifetime and the blood vessels which are no longer used waste away.

Why your baby may look strange

Many things you notice about your baby may worry you. It helps to understand the wide range of the normal and to realize that the baby may look very different once it has uncrumpled after a few days.

Lanugo The dark hair which may be over large parts of the newborn's body, especially if it is premature, is called lanugo and drops out over the next week or so. The hair on the head is often a different shade from that which will grow in a few weeks' time as the original hair gradually disappears. One of my babies was born with almost black hair and in a few months was a flaxen blond.

Vernix The creamy substance which may be on the baby's skin, sometimes covering it thickly, is vernix. It is produced by skin cells as they drop off into the amniotic fluid and forms a protective coating. Vernix is gradually absorbed, so it is not necessary to wipe it off, except on the head, where it tends to stick to the hair, and in the folds and creases under the arms, in the neck and the groin.

Caput Some babies are born with a peculiar bump like a large blister on their heads, often just off centre. This is where the head was pressing down through the inadequately dilated cervix before the second stage of labour; the swelling does not affect the baby's brain, and will gradually go. The bump is known as a caput.

Sugar-loaf moulding Usually the brow is sloped back and rather low in the newborn baby, but some babies have high, domed heads like figures in an Egyptian hieroglyph. This is the result of moulding of the head of a baby who was posterior.

A baby who was presenting by the face is usually very swollen, bruised and puffy but, again, this gradually goes.

Some babies are born without any covering of vernix; others are still quite thickly coated with it.

Mongolian spots Some babies have patches of slate-blue skin on their tummies or backs. These are called "Mongolian spots", are nothing to do with mental handicap or Down's syndrome, and are completely harmless. They occur most often in families of Asian and Mediterranean origin.

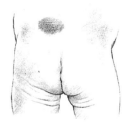

Sexual characteristics A newborn baby's genitals can look very large, especially if the baby is premature. Sometimes there is milk in the breasts of both girl and boy babies (called "witches' milk"). It is harmless and disappears without treatment. It is a result of withdrawal of oestrogen received from the mother's bloodstream and the action of prolactin released by the baby's pituitary. Some baby girls even have a kind of period—pseudo-menstruation—as the result of the withdrawal of maternal oestrogen. Again, it is nothing to worry about, and stops within a few days.

Mongolian blue spots look like bruises and gradually fade with time.

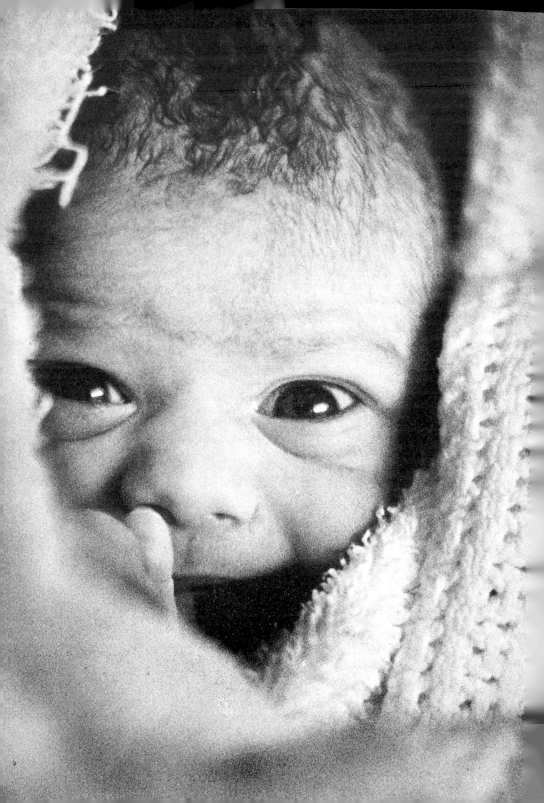

Bonding as a gradual process

Some of the reactions that you have to your newborn baby are instinctive. You respond to the sight of the baby's plumpness, the rounded head, the large forehead, the smell of the skin, the bright gaze of her eyes which look as if they say "So that is who you are!", to the baby's cry, her exploring hands and mouth, and to her vigorous movement and the extraordinary compactness of her neat little body. But even instinctive behaviour needs the right setting if it is to be released and unfold into appropriate nurturing. Then you can go on to learn from the baby how to respond to her signals.

Bonding is often talked about as if it were instant glue which sticks a mother and baby together the minute after delivery, and some women who do not spend the time after the birth with their babies worry that they have failed a test in motherhood and are anxious that this will have lasting effects. In fact bonding is a gradually unfolding process which only *starts* then and develops during each hour you and your baby are together. During all this time you are learning about each other and further physical changes in you are triggered off by stimuli provided by the baby. The most obvious of these is the milk ejection reflex (let-down response), which is stimulated by the baby's crying and searching for the nipple, the touch of his mouth against the breast and his sucking.

One aspect of hospital care which Klaus and Kennel stress is the way in which doctors and nurses can support the family—not just the mother, father and baby, but also other children. Older brothers and sisters should be able to have close contact with the baby too and be made welcome in the hospital. In practice, some hospitals are restrictive about sibling visiting.*

The importance of the time after birth

Wherever you are having a baby, and even if you are "high risk" and need obstetric help, provision should be made for a quiet, intimate time together after birth during which you can begin to feel that you belong to each other. It can be done in a big teaching hospital just as it can in a small GP unit and *it is part of the job of the hospital to create that environment for each mother, each father and each baby.* Discuss it with your doctor. It is only when doctors, nurses and midwives know what women want that they will be sufficiently tuned in to offer the loving environment which is every baby's birthright.

The minutes, hours and days after birth are a time for emotional "work" which may be no less significant in the lives of the newborn baby and of both parents than the sheer physical work of labour. The hospital should provide an environment which supports these unfolding emotional processes. New mothers and fathers do not need to be shown how to develop a relationship with their babies. They do need, however, to feel that they are among friends, to be handed the baby at birth and to be left in peace and privacy together.

OPPOSITE
Cocooned in the cradle of your arms . . . the most comforting security in the first hours of life . . .

The baby who needs special care

About 6 per cent of all babies weigh 5½ lb (2500 g) or less (the internationally agreed definition of a low-birthweight baby). Such babies can be divided into two categories—pre-term and small for dates—and they will probably require special care.

Half or more of low-birthweight babies are born too soon—pre-term or premature babies. There seems to be no obvious reason why such babies should be expelled from the uterus so early, and research is still being carried out into the causes of pre-term delivery.

Small-for-dates babies are born at the right time but have not flourished in the uterus in the last months of pregnancy for a variety of reasons. Sometimes this happens because of malnutrition in the mother, her smoking, high blood pressure or pre-eclampsia, because the placenta has not been working well (placental insufficiency), or because she was carrying twins or more. These undernourished babies often have difficulty during labour, are short of oxygen and have problems with breathing after delivery. They may suffer from hypoglycaemia (low blood sugar, see opposite) and have fits. A few small-for-dates babies, however, are small right through pregnancy for genetic, chromosomal or other reasons.

The baby with poor temperature control

Low-birthweight babies may have problems during labour too and are also more likely to have poor temperature control, because there is very little fat under the skin. They may be jaundiced, difficult to feed and susceptible to infection. Their skin is usually red because the blood vessels are visible through the thin layer of fat. Such babies are kept warm in a nursery which is warmer than the wards and are cared for in incubators. A thermostat may be strapped to a baby's tummy so that the temperature can be regulated according to his or her needs. Sometimes a baby is placed under a plastic heat shield and wears a hat. Tiny babies who are kept warm grow faster*.

The baby with breathing difficulties

Premature and low-birthweight babies may have interrupted breathing (apnoea) in the early days. This is why a very tiny baby is nursed on a special mattress which sets off an alarm if breathing stops. All that is usually needed to start the baby's breathing is a little stimulation of the baby by touch.

One in every ten premature babies has insufficient surfactant in its lungs. Surfactant reduces the surface tension in the lungs, allowing them to expand and stopping them deflating entirely with each breath out; it normally develops before the baby is ready to be born.

A baby usually inflates its lungs with the first breath after delivery and they pop open like parachutes. With the first breath out, half the air is retained, so that breathing after this is much easier. The baby who has not enough surfactant has to work hard to breathe and may become exhausted in the struggle to get enough air. It breathes very quickly, its chest collapses with each breath out, and it looks blue and grunts as it breathes. This condition is called respiratory distress or hyaline membrane disease. It is obviously important in these cases to give the baby oxygen and to help its breathing.

Other babies who may suffer from respiratory distress are those born to diabetic mothers (even though they are large babies), those who have not had sufficient oxygen during labour, those delivered by Caesarean section (see page 308), and babies who develop pneumonia as a result of infection.

If the paediatrician decides to give the baby oxygen, a small catheter is inserted through the cord stump into an artery so that blood samples can be taken about every three hours to test the amount of oxygen in the baby's blood.

Oxygen can be given with continuous positive pressure so that the baby's lungs are kept open. A tiny catheter is inserted through the baby's nostrils, or a face mask or headbox is used. Another method is to apply negative pressure around the baby's chest so that he or she does not have to work hard to breathe. The baby is put into a machine that looks like a miniature iron lung with a neck seal, so that all you can see is the head. Sometimes a mechanical ventilator is used, which takes over all the work of breathing for the baby.

It was difficult to believe he was mine, fighting for life in the incubator, red like a boiled lobster, and pathetic little arms and legs and bulging eyes like a frog. I didn't feel anything except pity.

The baby with low blood sugar

A baby may have low blood sugar (hypoglycaemia) if it has a low birthweight or is premature and also if its mother is diabetic or if the delivery was difficult. The hypoglycaemic baby may have breathing difficulties and be jittery or lie limp and apathetic.

Treatment involves making sure that the baby is getting ample nourishment, so the paediatrician may decide to set up an intravenous glucose drip. It is because of the risk of hypoglycaemia that a very tiny baby may be given additional feeds, even though there are no obvious symptoms of low blood sugar.

Neonatal jaundice

If your baby looks beautifully suntanned as if just back from a Greek island cruise, he or she has jaundice. A newborn baby has a surplus of red blood cells which are broken down after birth. During this process a yellowish substance called bilirubin is produced, which has to be excreted by the baby's liver. Sometimes the liver is unable to cope rapidly enough with the large amount of bilirubin and it builds up in the blood, giving the skin a yellowish tinge.

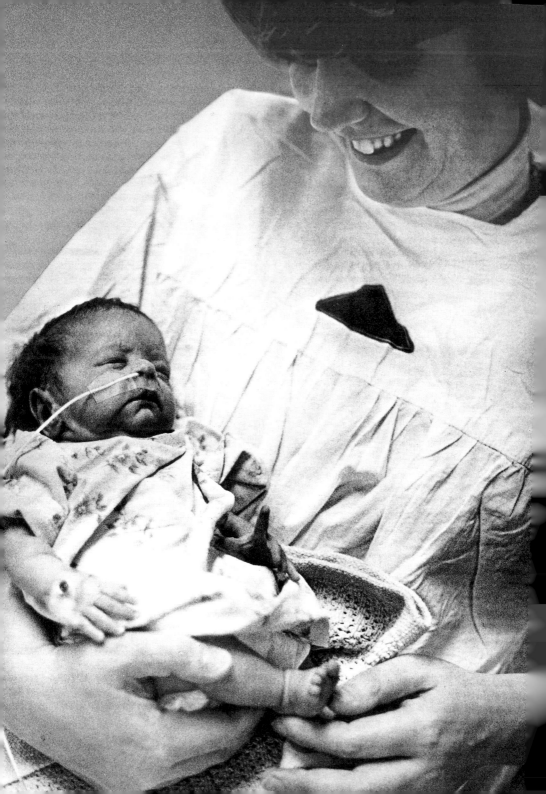

Physiological jaundice About half of all babies develop jaundice. It is usually harmless and is then called physiological jaundice. Jaundice is most likely to develop after the second day of life and to disappear after a week. In premature babies jaundice tends to be most marked on about the fifth or sixth day of life and to go on longer—often for ten days or more.

A jaundiced baby needs sunlight and frequent feeding. If you have the chance, put your baby beside a window and, if it is warm enough, uncover the baby so that light can reach its limbs and trunk.

Jaundiced babies tend to get very sleepy and do not readily wake for feeds. Yet they should have plenty of fluids to cope with the bilirubin, so need to be roused for feeds—perhaps every two hours.

If the bilirubin level is high, the paediatrician may decide to use phototherapy on a baby to bring the level down. This light treatment produces a photochemical breakdown of bilirubin into substances which are then passed out in the baby's urine. The baby is blindfolded so that the light cannot possibly harm its eyesight. This can be especially distressing for a mother who feels out of touch with her baby when she cannot make eye contact with it. When you lift your baby away from the light for its feed, take off the eye covering.

Haemolytic jaundice Paediatricians always watch the jaundiced baby carefully because, although neonatal jaundice is a common and not very serious complaint, the baby may be jaundiced as a result of a blood-group incompatibility between the mother and baby. This is called haemolytic jaundice and can damage the baby's nervous system and brain cells. Sometimes too the jaundice is associated with infection, with a metabolic condition such as low blood sugar, or even with the administration of drugs to the mother in pregnancy.

Feeding the baby in special care

It has been shown that very small babies do best if they are fed soon after delivery,* so a low-birthweight baby may be given a milk feed within two hours of birth. The best food is its own mother's breast milk, but this will take a few days to be produced in quantity. The baby can, however, be put to the breast if strong enough to suck, to derive benefit from the protein and antibodies in the colostrum that is already there (see page 350). Supplements of vitamins D and K are often given, and if phosphate in the baby's bloodstream falls, supplementary phosphates, too.

A baby who cannot suck is usually fed through a small, soft catheter, a nasogastric tube, which is passed through a nostril down into the stomach. Feeds should be small and frequent—about every half hour—or a slow continuous drip is often best for a sick baby. If your baby is being fed in this way it is usually possible for you to help with the feeds once you can express your own breast milk. If you have any difficulties, contact one of the breast-feeding organizations, which are listed on page 383.

OPPOSITE
Even if your baby has to spend some time after birth in special care, she still needs your loving presence.

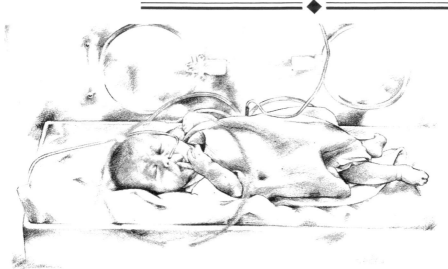

Your baby may look lost and lonely if she has to be cared for in an incubator. You will feel she belongs to you if you talk to her and touch her reassuringly through the portholes.

Relating to the baby in special care

It is distressing for parents to see their baby in intensive care, attached to tubes and wires, isolated in an incubator. They may feel as if the baby is just another interesting specimen. Very low-birthweight babies look so fragile and weird that it can be difficult to see them as real people: your baby may look to you like an odd, misshapen doll or a little animal and not your child at all. On the other hand you may feel passionately that the baby belongs to you and want to grab it away from all the machines and other contraptions so as to hold it close. The obvious skills of those working with sophisticated technology can make parents feel hamfisted and awkward so that they lack confidence to handle their baby. Yet it is important to do this. *All* babies need touching and talking to and, if they are well enough to be taken in your arms, they like being cuddled. If your baby is in an incubator, you can stroke her through the portholes. Tender, loving care may be just as important for the health of your baby as modern medical technology.

Many hospitals now have rooms where mothers of babies in special care can stay to be close to them, help look after them and breast-feed them. It is better for both mother and baby and makes it easier to build close links between them if the mother stays in the special-care unit rather than merely visiting. When a woman can start to look after her baby herself, she begins to feel that her baby belongs to her. One intensive-care unit has rooms where babies are cared for by their mothers, with a glass wall at the side of the baby's cubicle so that nurses can keep a constant eye on the babies. A Sister in this unit said: "One thing the nurses must not do is to take away responsibility for the baby. We always try to make a mother feel it is her baby, even when it is very small and sick."

I looked at her lying there with tubes and sticking plaster everywhere and I felt a wave of longing to grab her and pull out all the equipment and take her away with me.

338

Losing a baby

Many women know what it is like to have an interrupted pregnancy, although the distress caused by even an early miscarriage is often underestimated. Stillbirth, on the other hand, is now rare. But still today, for a small number of women, the birth is also a death.

Women who make the painful decision to have an abortion, because of fetal handicap, or for any other reason, may grieve deeply, too. This is so even though they know they have made the best possible choice in the circumstances and have behaved sensibly. Abortion should never be dismissed as simply getting rid of an unwanted pregnancy. Yet it is still largely a taboo subject, and women often have to go through the experience alone, without help, deprived of the emotional support they need, and socially isolated.

It might seem easier for people to sympathize with a woman whose baby dies at birth. Yet often they do not know how to help and they withdraw from her grief in embarrassment. After all the happy expectations and preparations the woman has made, she goes through a labour which culminates in the delivery of a stillborn baby, or a frail or handicapped baby who dies a week or so after birth. Her arms are empty and she is left alone. The more we reduce perinatal mortality, the more isolated is the woman whose baby dies.

MISCARRIAGE

A miscarriage usually comes as a shock, yet one in every five pregnancies probably ends in miscarriage or "spontaneous abortion". In three out of four cases this occurs before the tenth week and sometimes even before the woman realizes she is pregnant.

Threatened miscarriage

In the first three months of pregnancy, you may notice a heavy feeling around your pelvis and in the pit of your tummy and have period-like twinges and aches.

Sometimes you may have bleeding that is really a suppressed period. This happens when there is insufficient pregnancy hormone to stop your period, even though it will be scanty. Such bleeding is not a miscarriage and the blood comes from the endometrium, not from the placenta or the baby. Sometimes this too occurs at the time when each period would have been due, and right through the early months of pregnancy each would-be period is marked by slight bleeding. Your doctor may advise you to have injections of progesterone to stop this bleeding.

If you have any bleeding or pinkish staining of mucus from your vagina, probably the best treatment is rest in bed. The blood that you see is not the baby's blood but yours, and comes from the maternal side of the placenta where it is not adhering to the uterus, or from around the cervix. Lying down increases the blood flow to your uterus and, if the placenta is not firmly rooted, gives it a chance to attach itself more firmly to the lining of the uterus.

Inevitable abortion

An "inevitable abortion" is a miscarriage which occurs because the baby is no longer alive and, whatever you do, the bleeding is bound to continue. If the fetal heart cannot be detected by ultrasound (see page 202), the abortion is inevitable and you might just as well be up and about and let it run its course. If ultrasound picks up the baby's heartbeat, there is only a 10 per cent chance that you will miscarry, even though you may go on bleeding for a while.

Possible causes of early miscarriage

The cause of early miscarriage is often not known. Fortunately defective embryos with abnormalities that would not allow them to survive after birth are usually miscarried, and a large proportion of miscarriages are probably the natural way of getting rid of imperfect babies. Sometimes there has been no development beyond the very early stages of segmentation and what is termed a blighted ovum is passed. It is estimated that one in six miscarriages results from fertilized eggs that do not develop properly.

After it had been noted that more women than usual miscarry in early pregnancy during flu epidemics it was discovered that a high fever can result in miscarriage. There is more about this on page 102. Sometimes the presence of uterine fibroids (common in older mothers) or an oddly formed uterus means that there is not enough space for the pregnancy to develop.

Late miscarriage

Miscarriage after the 12th week of pregnancy is about three times as rare as early miscarriage. Miscarriages are more likely to occur as you grow older (over 35), if you have had difficulty in conceiving (if it has taken more than six months), and if you have had two or more previous miscarriages. If you have had only one miscarriage before, there is no obvious reason why the next pregnancy should not be straightforward. After three miscarriages there is a 50/50 chance of miscarrying again, so talk to your doctor *before* you become pregnant and plan extra rest from the first days after possible conception.

"Incompetent" cervix Late miscarriage is often the result of a weak or "incompetent" cervix which starts to dilate long before it should. The bag of waters is wedged between the baby and the cervix and ruptures as the cervix starts to dilate, so the first sign may be the breaking of the waters. This type of miscarriage is particularly likely if a woman has already repeatedly miscarried in mid-pregnancy. An

Don't believe it when they say it doesn't matter if you lose a baby early in pregnancy. This was my baby and I wanted her, not just any baby, but that special baby.

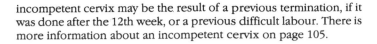
incompetent cervix may be the result of a previous termination, if it was done after the 12th week, or a previous difficult labour. There is more information about an incompetent cervix on page 105.

Placental insufficiency Miscarriage after the 20th week may mean that the placenta has failed to function in servicing the baby. (After 28 weeks the loss of the baby is termed a stillbirth.) If there is evidence of poor placental function and inadequate growth of the baby in the uterus, bed-rest will allow a better flow of blood through the placenta to the baby. One of the ways in which you can affect the efficiency of the placenta is by making sure that you have a good diet during pregnancy. If you have had a miscarriage, it is a good idea to start a high-standard diet before you become pregnant again (see page 86). If you have had a series of miscarriages, keep any large blood clots from the latest one (a vacuum-sealed jar is suitable) for the doctor to have tested in a laboratory.

Guilt about a miscarriage

Every woman who has had a miscarriage wonders if anything she did or failed to do caused it. A miscarriage can happen at any time so that most women will be able to think of some event that might have triggered it off. You had a row with someone in the office, your mother-in-law came to stay, you slipped in the street, had just had intercourse, or were overtired from a party the night before. But, whatever your guilty suspicions, none of these things has been shown to cause miscarriage. However, it can be difficult to convince yourself that you are in no way responsible.

Grieving for the lost baby

Talk with your partner about your feelings. Even if you have not yet felt fetal movements, the loss of your baby is sometimes emotionally shattering. If you have had miscarriage after miscarriage or are slow to conceive, you may experience every single period as the loss of a baby and grieve as a result. This grieving is necessary for you to be able to look forward to the future with confidence in yourself as a "real woman". Suppressed grief always causes trouble later.

Your partner, however, may not have accepted the reality of the pregnancy by the time you miscarry and so it can be difficult for him to understand why you need to mourn, but it will help you if he can give time to listen. Or you may find you can talk more easily with another woman who has been through a miscarriage herself.

After it is all over, the longing to start another pregnancy can interfere with relaxed and spontaneous sex. And the more anxious you are to conceive the more tense you become and the less likely to get pregnant. If you feel that you are getting anxious and that this is spoiling your sexual relationship, try having a holiday from each other and coming together again at the time when you expect to be ovulating (see pages 56 and 367).

STILLBIRTH

"I'm so sorry. Your baby has died." Almost every expectant mother has thought at some time that someone might say these words to her. For some women it is a nagging fear which haunts them and threatens to punish them for negative feelings they have about the baby and becoming a mother or for daring to expect too much of the birth and the baby. Sometimes, not as often as in the past, but nevertheless in about 10 out of every 1000 births, it really happens and the baby dies before, during or shortly after birth.

The experience of loss

In spite of everything that anyone can do you are suddenly confronted with the experience of loss. This is a loss not only of the baby, but of all the hopes and expectations of yourselves as parents and the new images of the self that have been built up through pregnancy.

Nothing can take away the suffering that comes as a result of stillbirth. This is so even when the care given to you is loving and sympathetic, though such emotional support can help you gradually deal with the experience and eventually come to terms with it. Unfortunately some members of hospital staff cannot cope with their own feelings of guilt and distress when a baby dies, and you may be left alone in a side-ward, avoided as much as possible by nurses and doctors who do not want to "upset" you by referring to what has happened. When they do talk to you, they may urge you to put it behind you, say that you will forget what happened when you have another baby, or tell you to think of your partner. The more such advice is given the longer the experience may take to live through.

The task of grieving is a personal and intimate one. It consists of slowly and painfully—and sometimes you may feel that you will never succeed—integrating the experience into the total pattern of your life and finding a place for it in which it has meaning. Once you have done this you will be able to stand back from it a little and will no longer be overwhelmed by it. This process cannot be hurried and, if an attempt is made to force the pace, grieving will be delayed and you may be overpowered by grief at a later stage of your life.

Stillbirth in Third World societies

A hundred years ago everyone expected a certain proportion of babies to die. You bore ten and reared six if you were lucky. In many Third World countries even today babies are not named or publicly spoken of for the first few weeks because the chances are that they will not survive. It has been suggested that the mothers themselves are able to remain slightly emotionally detached from a new baby whose life may be transitory*.

In these societies death is incorporated into the web of life and there are supportive rituals to deal with it, whereas we are ill-prepared in Western society for facing death. We each struggle to find

We were left alone together and we sat and held her. She was perfectly formed. We wept together. It was a very important time for us.

our own way and often feel that we are the only people who have ever faced such emotional upheavals. Death is a shocking intrusion into the normality of existence.

Facing up to the loss

If professional helpers know that something is going wrong with your birth, you have a right to expect them to give you information, discuss the difficulties openly and honestly and stand by you as you try to cope emotionally with what is happening. Women who have been through this ordeal say that it helped to realize that they were being told the truth and to be fully involved rather than shielded from the event by the mystique of medical practice.

If your baby dies while still inside the uterus, you know that you are carrying a dead baby. It is as if your uterus, a place of life, has become a grave. The obstetrician may advise that it is safer to wait to go into labour naturally, which often happens within a couple of weeks, but may offer you induction if you wish. Many women feel an urgent need to "get it over with"; others that they want to spend the last remaining days possible with the baby inside them.

When something so distressing happens, there is no easy "solution", no one course of action that can wipe out the anguish. Sometimes a man asks what he can say or do to help his partner and to make the suffering less, or other family members or friends want to help but do not know what to do. People are so different in their responses to loss that the most helpers can do is to make themselves available, to reach out and be ready to receive whatever the bereaved person wants to tell them, without holding back for fear of intruding or feeling embarrassment at her grief. The most valuable thing they can offer is a *waiting silence*, without tension or unnecessary words, so that the sufferer's pain can flow into them.

I wish I'd asked to see him. It all happened so fast. Now I long to have seen him and held him. But it's too late.

Mourning for the baby

This may sound simple, but in fact it can be very difficult, because grieving is not just a matter of tears and sadness, but also numb shock and guilt and anger, all of which are felt at different phases of the experience. It is not easy to acknowledge destructive guilt, and perhaps even harder to cope with anger which may involve hostility against people, including doctors and nurses, who tried to help.

For you the time immediately following the death of a baby may be one of frozen half-awareness of what has happened and it is often not till three weeks or so afterwards that you begin to live through these other phases of grieving.

It is sometimes difficult for a mother to mourn her stillborn baby because she never really knew this person over whom she is grieving. It can be still more difficult if you have not *seen* the dead baby and realized that your bulging tummy held a living creature that has since died. This is why some paediatricians think it is a good idea for a mother to touch her stillborn child and encourage her to do so.

The baby's burial

You and your partner may wish to discuss together arrangements for the baby's burial. Some women do not wish to know where the baby is buried, but others do. It is up to you to learn as much or as little as you wish to know. Some women feel afterwards that perhaps the baby was a figment of their imagination and never existed at all. It was removed from them like a tooth which was causing trouble and extracted. You may think of your baby's body being handled with indifference and lie wondering what "they" did with it.

The effect on your relationships

Being depressed affects all our relationships with other people, including those we love and need most. Though the death of a baby may draw you and your partner closer together, it introduces stresses into the relationship which may be too severe for you to cope with. You may both need help from other people. Your partner has to grieve too and yet may feel that it is "unmanly" for him to show weakness and that he must be strong to support you. The result may be that he simulates a matter-of-fact acceptance of the inevitable and leaves you feeling isolated because he does not understand.

If the baby lived for a time and went to the special-care nursery, your partner probably had a chance to go there and see and touch the baby while you may have stayed in the ward. So you rely on his descriptions and the details he can give you to be able to build up a complete picture. Yet a man who is himself depressed and grieving may find it difficult to talk about such things without showing his own distress and may resist it, so giving you the impression that he is holding back on vital information.

Losing a baby almost invariably causes a deterioration in the couple's sexual relationship too. It is difficult to feel sexually excited when you are depressed. And even as time goes on, when you are beginning to "function" again, feelings of pleasure can be followed by a rush of grief. When you start to enjoy life again, even when you start to feel sexually aroused, you may both feel at times that you are betraying your dead child*. So both of you need to give understanding to each other.

If you have lost your baby and want to be in touch with others who have gone through this experience, contact the Compassionate Friends and the Stillbirth Association at the addresses on page 383.

THE NEXT PREGNANCY

If you are pregnant following an abortion or if you have lost a previous baby as a result of miscarriage or stillbirth, or if your baby died after birth, the previous experience tends to cast its shadow forward. Strangely, this tends to happen even if you really did not want that particular pregnancy to continue.

A woman who has lost a baby through accident, who has had miscarriages, for example, or a cot death, may feel angry that the emotions of one who has had an abortion should be discussed in the same context as her own ordeal and even that the woman who got rid of a baby deserves whatever happens to her. Yet the experience of loss may be equally haunting and the sense of guilt even greater.

We tend to compare and contrast the progress of the present pregnancy with past pregnancies. If a previous pregnancy had an unhappy outcome, it colours our view of the whole experience and it is natural to become acutely conscious of risks and dangers. We do not always realize that this is what we are doing, since a common way of trying to deal with fear and anxiety about repeating a distressing experience is to attempt to shut out thoughts of it, to protect ourselves from the painful experience of yet another failure.

A woman who feels guilty about aborting a previous baby or who feels somehow responsible for a miscarriage may transfer this guilt to the present pregnancy and be anxious that she is going to have a terrible labour, bear an abnormal baby or lose the baby as a kind of retribution or punishment. It is not a rational or even necessarily a conscious thinking through of the risks, but a kind of primitive expectation that automatic punishment comes from the gods.

If you try to forget what happened or to put it to the back of your mind, you will be unprepared for the emotions that may assail you in situations of stress, when you have a vaginal examination or when you go into hospital. And when labour starts you may find that you cannot help thinking back to the loss of the other baby.

You may tell yourself to be sensible and not to dwell on negative thoughts. Though understandable, this is rarely successful. You are right to acknowledge your feelings and also justified in getting those who care for you to take them seriously. But do not leave this till the end of pregnancy and certainly not until you go into labour. Try to find the kind of preparation for birth and parenthood that includes frank and open acceptance of any previous unhappy experience.

In a pregnancy following the loss of the baby women often experience painful, disturbing dreams about bearing a damaged child or losing the baby and feel that in some awful way this is their own fault. The dreams may be clearly about birth and babies or may be heavily disguised. The baby is often represented in such dreams as a doll or small animal or one's own tooth or limb, and death as the irretrievable loss of anything that is treasured.

The joy of another pregnancy may be suffused with grief at the loss of your previous baby.

You may feel that you are carrying a baby of the same sex as the previous one or even that you are pregnant with the child you lost before. That is one way of trying to cope with the painful experience. In fact, some people even say, "Have another baby and you'll forget about it". But of course you cannot really substitute one baby for another or replace a lost baby by getting pregnant again. It is vital for both you and the baby you are bearing that you work through to an acknowledgment that this baby is its own unique self.

The first ten days

It is recognized that a woman who bears a child who is handicapped or ill, or who has a baby who dies, needs to pass through a period of grieving. It is less well understood that for *any* woman the time immediately after birth is experienced as a loss which she needs to grieve over, however perfect the baby. As a new mother you are on the threshold of a new beginning which entails the death of some aspects of your self and, with the birth of a first baby, the relinquishing of the self as child and as adolescent.

EMOTIONS AFTER DELIVERY
Unexpected emotions

Many women need time to part with the fantasy baby which they carried inside them before they can come to terms with the real baby who has been born. The real baby is often astonishingly different from the one they imagined they were bearing. The death of a fantasy which has been cherished can be a painful process. It is especially threatening if the baby is premature and needs to have special care, or if it suffers from any form of handicap. But even a healthy, mature baby may be so unlike what you expected that you cannot come to terms with its reality or with the fact that it turns you into a mother with different responsibilities from those you had before, who is emotionally committed to that baby for every minute of every day.

Changes in mood

All the intense feelings you have during the hours and days after giving birth have a biological survival value for the baby. Without them you would be just a caretaker. Sometimes your emotions are mind-moving and if you had not just had a baby would rightly be thought pathological. But during the first week after birth they are perfectly normal and experienced by many more women than ever openly admit to them.

It is not just a matter of depression. In fact you may feel you are on a permanent high. But it is likely that at some time during the first five days after the birth you will experience an abrupt drop in mood and a sudden feeling of depression. Your stitches are uncomfortable, the hospital routine is intolerable, you start to worry about the baby or whether you will be a good mother, or you simply feel flat because the party is over and it is now "the morning after the night before". Then again you may experience violent mood swings and feel you are on an emotional roller-coaster in the days immediately after the birth. You are probably more likely to feel like this if you usually have pronounced mood swings anyway. Our society often has a very

OPPOSITE

A mother "teases" her newborn with the nipple . . . soon her baby will be enjoying one of the great pleasures of the early months of life . . .

346

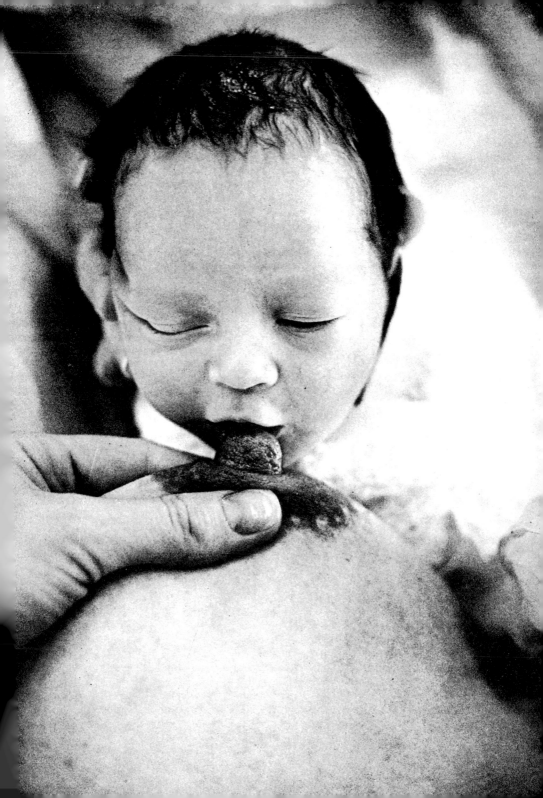

romanticized stereotype of the new mother in a frothy pink negligée, a cherubic baby in her arms. The violent mood swings of the post-partum period can come as a shock because they are so different from the way you think you *ought* to feel.

Needing to behave spontaneously

Some women who have their babies in hospital are emotionally unstable until they get home. For them an institutional setting for the post-partum experience is unsettling and confusing. They seem to have a great need to be *in their own place*. There is nothing abnormal about you if you feel like this. The important thing is to acknowledge the kind of person you are and for your partner to accept it too and make arrangements decisively and as speedily as possible.

If all seems to be well with you and the baby, the best thing is to arrange to leave hospital as soon as possible. Ask to see the paediatrician and let him or her know how you feel. The community midwife will then visit you at home for ten days following delivery. This is one reason why there is a strong case to be made for being in contact with your community midwife before you go into hospital to have your baby, even if you are not having shared care and are in a consultant unit; your partner should have her name, address and phone number in advance. You will then avoid the occasional breakdowns in liaison between hospitals and community health services, or the times when the whole machinery suddenly grinds to a halt, such as public holidays or even weekends.

=**"**=
Hospital was so busy and there was so little opportunity to sleep that I came out exhausted.
=**"**=

The complexity of your emotions

Your partner may be experiencing violent emotions himself at this time; he too may be torn between laughter and tears after the delivery. Our society tends to stress that men ought to be strong and

Being in a hospital ward where the atmosphere is friendly means that you can discuss your baby and any worries that you might have with other mothers.

348

offer wide shoulders for the new mother to lean on, but in fact some men are so deeply touched by the experience of birth that they undergo much the same emotional turmoil as the new mother. A new father may suffer acutely on leaving the hospital, because he is surrendering you and his baby to the care of strangers. In spite of the rejoicing and excitement, there may be a strange undercurrent of grief. The intimate bond linking him to the woman who has borne his child is cut by an enforced separation. When he returns to the hospital it is to come as a visitor.

> *The awful thing was having to go away and leave them both in hospital 1½ hours after the birth. The separation then was very hard to bear and I felt quite sick.*

YOUR CHANGED BODY

After you have had a baby you encounter your body in a dramatically changed state. Whereas before you enjoyed your smooth body heavy with fruit, the curve of your abdomen like an enormous melon still awaiting the harvest of birth, you may feel after delivery astonishingly alone, bereft and empty. If you are in hospital without people you love near you, in the care of people who treat you as just another "mum" or worse still as an involuting uterus, a sutured perineum and a couple of lactating breasts, you need time to come to terms with your changed body and to rediscover yourself as a person.

For many women the euphoria of having given birth and of having produced a real baby, which comes as a delightful surprise at first, gives way to this confrontation with the body. Changes in the breasts associated with breast-feeding can be an ordeal for some women. Many set their sights at the birth, seeing labour and delivery as the challenge, and are ill prepared for the new challenges that follow immediately after. One mother who felt a revulsion at her much changed body exclaimed: "But it was all supposed to be *over!*" Once the baby had arrived she wanted her self back again.

Weight loss

Immediately following delivery you probably feel beautifully slim and light-weight. You have lost the combined weight of the baby, the placenta, the amniotic fluid and membranes. It is only when you first put your hand down on your tummy that you become aware of the folds of skin, like a soft and soggy cream puff. When you first catch sight of yourself naked in a full-length mirror you may be horrified at the amount of weight you have put on: the thickened waist, the heavy thighs and (if you are breast-feeding) the ballooning breasts—which you and your partner may enjoy if you were small and flat before, but which can be too much of a good thing if you were top-heavy anyway.

Water loss During the week after childbirth most women sweat out the excess fluid they no longer need, and any puffiness you may have noticed in your legs and ankles will disappear; so will the plumped-out facial features and the fluid which might have been retained in your fingers, making them fatter than usual.

◆

Restoring muscle tone If you use your abdominal muscles your tummy will flatten after a few weeks, but you cannot achieve this if you go without exercise. Some exercises suitable for the early post-partum period are illustrated on pages 352–353. Brisk walking is good for abdominal muscles: if the weather is suitable fix the baby in a carrier against your body and walk, in the country if possible.

At first your pelvic-floor muscles may feel as if they are sagging like a heavy hammock, but their tone will be gradually restored over the next three months and if you use them regularly, without straining them, rehabilitation will be complete.

BREASTS AND BREAST-FEEDING

The sooner you put your baby to the breast the sooner its gut will be lined with colostrum, a substance which forms a protective "paint" and a barrier to invading bacteria. Colostrum also provides the baby with antibodies to diseases to which you yourself are resistant. Ready in your breasts at the end of pregnancy, it is the earliest form of milk, rich in protein and an ideal first concentrated food for your baby.

The milk ejection reflex

When your baby sucks the action stimulates an area in your brain (the hypothalamus), which in turn stimulates the pituitary gland at the base of your brain to release oxytocin into your bloodstream. Oxytocin flows into the blood vessels in your breasts and causes specific cells around the milk glands deep inside your breasts to contract. This has the effect of squeezing the milk out through the tiny holes in your nipples.

You will probably feel the warm, tingling glow of the milk ejection reflex immediately preceding the flow of milk. This occurs as the oxytocin-carrying blood rushes into the breasts and you feel them getting warmer. Infra-red photographs of lactating breasts show that they really do grow hotter in response to the baby's cry.

The first few feeds Notice what happens when you put the baby to the breast. Fix her well on, with the nipple deep in her mouth and as much of the areola as will make a good mouthful. Cuddle the baby close and wait. Drop your shoulders: if they feel really stiff *pull* them down and then let them go. It may take a few minutes for the sensation to come and then suddenly it is there: deep inside both breasts, not just the one the baby is sucking, there is a prickling, buzzing feeling as if champagne is flowing through your veins and at the same time a wave of heat flowing towards your nipples. And then you see the baby's jaws beginning to work, and the strong steady movement of the bone at the top of the baby's jawbone, just by her ear, as she begins to swallow as well as suck. The milk ejection reflex can happen when you just think about feeding the baby or if you hear her cry. If she is not in your arms you can press the palm of a hand

A baby needs to suck at the breast, not just the nipple.

firmly against your breast and the milk flow—which will be a slow but steady dripping from the nipple—will come to a stop.

The difference between sucking and feeding

Having milk in your breasts is just the beginning. Obviously the important thing is to *release* it so that it flows into your baby. For nutritional purposes it is not enough to have a baby sucking at your breasts, though he will enjoy this anyway. He needs to *swallow* and until this happens is not feeding. Hospitals are more relaxed than they used to be about the time babies spend at the breast, but if you are on a ward where feeding time is still restricted, you should count this time from the moment the baby is actually feeding, not from when he is just sucking.

Even before the reflex occurs the baby gets some milk, because it collects in the ducts just behind the nipple. This is called "foremilk" and is rich in protein. It usually keeps the baby happy until the rush of milk comes with the reflex. But if you give a baby foremilk only, because he is not sucking for long enough to stimulate the reflex, your milk supply will dwindle or never build up.

If you feel embarrassed or self-conscious or experience strong emotions of anxiety, fear or anger, the milk ejection reflex will probably be slower in coming and sometimes does not occur at all. This is why the setting for breast-feeding in the first days after birth is so important and why emotional support from someone who understands how you feel is helpful. Even though you may think you have emptied a breast, a fresh reflex can occur when you put the baby back to it again. A breast is not like a jug of milk, but has a constant supply provided that the baby gives the right stimulus.

I had an image of glowing with motherly calm, but breast-feeding isn't a bit like that: it's so sexy, I can't believe it!

Little and often

If you are concerned about the amount of milk the baby is taking, bear in mind that the frequency of feeds is more important than the length of feeds. Though some babies, especially in the first four to six weeks of life, enjoy sucking more or less continuously at certain times of the day, the main nutritional content of the milk has been obtained during the first five to seven minutes. This is why many short feeds, the baby dropping off to sleep in between, is for many mothers and babies the perfect style of feeding in these first weeks. You may be able to unplug the baby's mouth gently from your nipple by depressing the breast with a finger or by slipping a finger just inside the baby's mouth to break the vacuum—but don't, whatever you do, just pull the nipple out.

Babies who like sucking for comfort

Some babies always wake up and fuss when you do take them off the breast. These are usually babies who have such a strong need to suck in the first six weeks or so that they never drop off the nipple for long. Then it makes sense to consider providing the baby with a dummy for

Post-natal exercises

Many of the exercises recommended during pregnancy are also good for getting your figure back after delivery. It is important to remember, though, that post-natal exercises should be progressive. Do only the gentlest exercises for the first day or two then move on to the more strenuous ones shown here. Never do an exercise that hurts you.

Toning the abdomen

To restore the muscle tone of your tummy after childbirth, try gentle leg sliding (see page 109) for the first few days then practise these abdominal exercises five times each. Always raise your head on a breath *out*.

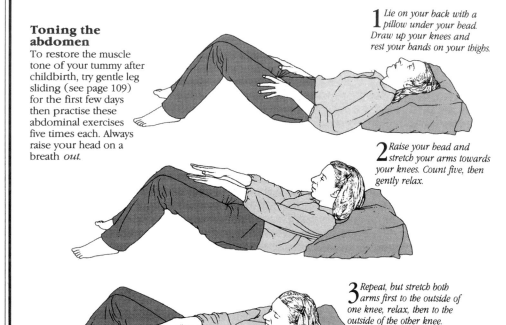

1 *Lie on your back with a pillow under your head. Draw up your knees and rest your hands on your thighs.*

2 *Raise your head and stretch your arms towards your knees. Count five, then gently relax.*

3 *Repeat, but stretch both arms first to the outside of one knee, relax, then to the outside of the other knee.*

Abdominal exercise

A gentle exercise for toning up abdominal muscles is done lying on your back with the small of your back pressed against the floor or bed.

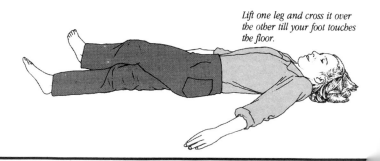

Lift one leg and cross it over the other till your foot touches the floor.

Lying comfortably

If you have had stitches, lying on your front may be the most comfortable position for you. Pillows placed under your hips help your pelvic organs to return to their usual position and allow you to practise pelvic-floor exercises and pelvic tilting. A pillow under your head and shoulders will take pressure off your breasts.

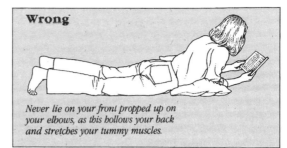

Wrong

Never lie on your front propped up on your elbows, as this hollows your back and stretches your tummy muscles.

Put two pillows under your hips not your abdomen, so that your back is not hollowed and the abdominal wall is relaxed.

Repairing the rectus muscle

If your rectus muscle has separated, this exercise, done from about three days after delivery, can help.

Lie on your back, knees bent and hands crossed over your tummy. As you breathe out, raise your head slowly, pulling in your tummy and holding the rectus muscle together. Do this exercise a few times twice a day.

Encouraging the milk flow

Many women find that their milk flow slows down when they are resting. The first sign is usually a red patch of inflammation, often in the outer part of the breast where your arm has been pressing against it. If your breasts are not too tender, the answer is vigorous arm movement.

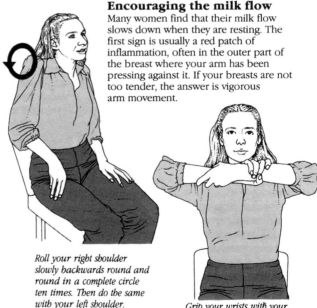

Roll your right shoulder slowly backwards round and round in a complete circle ten times. Then do the same with your left shoulder.

Grip your wrists with your hands and hold your arms in a square in front of you with your elbows well up. Push the skin of your wrists towards your elbows, gripping firmly. Do this ten times.

alternative sucking satisfaction, and with some additional help in dropping off to sleep, such as rocking, regular rhythmic sound or the old-fashioned lullaby.

You may feel very "drained" when feeding is long-drawn-out: if you are tired and the baby is constantly demanding to be fed, it is easy to think that you cannot be providing enough milk. Though this is sometimes the case, many babies want to go on feeding non-stop because they like it so much, not because they are starving. So after about ten minutes' sucking it is sensible to put the baby down or hand him or her over to a friend or your partner for a cuddle. Relax a bit; top up with some more breast milk at whichever side feels most generously supplied; then have another break, and so on.

Each baby's feeding pattern is different

The first 6 weeks I felt I was doing nothing but feeding her. I was partly proud, partly outraged at not being able to get on with my ordinary life.

Breast-fed babies do not suck continuously through a feed. They enjoy bursts of sucking, stop for a while, then start again. This is normal. If you think about meals you enjoy you will realize that you do not chomp away non-stop either. Nor do you want the same quantity of food at each meal. Babies are the same.

Think of each feed as divided into different courses. Some will be seven- or eight-course banquets, but others will be only two courses. You will gradually be able to work out when the baby likes the banquets, and then you may be able to cater for them by arranging your day to fit in with this pattern. Somehow anticipating and preparing for feeding sessions of this kind makes them much easier to cope with and you are less likely to feel exhausted by them.

Is breast milk enough?

You may wonder if and when your baby needs any food other than your breast milk, especially if you secretly feel that your baby is not having enough milk from you.

Water Many hospitals still give water to babies. If the room temperature in the hospital is high this may be a good idea, but it is usually not necessary when you go home. The baby needs milk, not water. If your baby is producing six or more wet nappies in the course of 24 hours and is having no other fluid, and if the urine is pale amber or colourless, this is an indication that she is having enough milk from you. You will probably find that *you* are thirstier than usual. Drink as much as you like, though there is no point in having more than you want, since it will not produce more milk.

Top-up bottles If you are concerned that your baby is not having enough milk and you start to give top-up bottle feeds, the amount of milk you are producing will diminish, since it is demand that stimulates supply.

Using a bottle for top-ups (complementary bottle-feeding) or to replace breast-feeds (supplementary bottle-feeding) in the first two months of life can mean that the baby grows accustomed to the type of sucking action which is used at the bottle. The large bottle teat can provide a sort of super-stimulus to which the baby responds more readily than to your nipple. And if the teat has a large hole in it so that the milk comes quickly she may soon come to prefer bottle to breast.

Solid foods When you introduce solid foods be prepared for your milk supply to be automatically reduced. This is one reason why the early introduction of solid foods is counter-productive. It replaces food the baby needs, human milk, with food which she does not need until she is about six months old. A baby's appetite cannot possibly cope with human milk *plus* all the other foods which are on the market. Manufacturers of so-called "baby foods" are often responsible for breast-feeding difficulties which start at three to four months, a common time for mothers to discover that they are failing to produce enough milk.

Test weighing Weighing the baby before and after a feed (test weighing) is a method of finding exactly how much breast milk he or she has taken. It is pointless unless done over 24 hours, since the baby takes different quantities at different times; even then it tends to increase your anxiety and make you feel inadequate. A much better guide to a baby's wellbeing is feeling good muscle tone and noticing if she is alert and responsive.

More frequent breast-feeding When you want to increase the quantity of milk you are making, put the baby to the breast more often. If the baby has not gained weight, or has lost weight, feed him every time he stirs over a 24 hour period. If the baby is very sleepy rouse him after every two and a half hours if you can, except at night. Unwrap him, talk to him and "woo" him with the breast. I call this my *Twenty-Four Hour Peak Production Plan*. It works in the first weeks after birth and is also useful at about six weeks.

Breast-feeding difficulties

Engorged breasts Many new mothers find that they are engorged on the third or fourth day after delivery, when the milk really floods in. The longer you go between feeds the more likely you are to be painfully engorged. A cold compress, such as a nappy with some ice inside, resting against your breast, will ease the pain of engorgement, and with the baby's frequent sucking will help you through this difficult transitional phase. The hospital will have a breast pump that you can use if it is important to draw off some milk and if you find it difficult to express by hand, but only draw off enough for comfort.

Sore nipples Nipple soreness, especially when the baby is a vigorous sucker, is common in the first few weeks and does not mean that you will fail at breast-feeding. Studies show that those mothers

◆

who go on to enjoy breast-feeding include many women who have had initial trouble with sores and cracks, and that the only difference between these and others who give up is that they persevere. Go topless whenever you can; avoid using soap on your nipples or using cotton wool against them, and let them dry off after a feed, exposed to warm air (it is best not to use a towel).

Cracked nipples Sometimes a crack appears at the point where the nipple joins the areola. This is almost invariably because the baby has not fixed well on the surrounding tissue and obtained a really good mouthful. If a baby drags on the nipple stem and does not draw the nipple into the back of the mouth, not only will you have problems with sores and cracks but also the baby will not be able to take enough milk after the first spurts at the beginning of a feed.

A soft, flexible nipple shield made of rubber with a wide brim like a Mexican sombrero can sometimes help to relieve soreness caused by cracks and make feeds tolerable until the nipple has time to heal. Avoid using plastic-lined breast pads, since if there is any leaking your nipples will be sitting in the damp.

Breast tenderness If you develop a red patch on a breast, feeding more often can help. Ensure that the baby is well latched on. Exercise your arms to increase the circulation to your breasts (see page 353). If an infection develops and you run a temperature at the same time as having a red patch, cold compresses and oral antibiotics prescribed by the doctor will quickly treat it. Continue feeding the baby, as this makes it far less likely that you will develop an abscess.

Excitable babies Some babies feed with great bluster and excitement, spluttering and coughing and really making a meal out of it. In the first weeks they suddenly draw back as they start to choke, pulling on the nipple at the same time. Or they may let go for a second and then grab on again, but because they have jerked their heads back they now have only the nipple stem in their mouths so that they are dragging on the place where the stem joins the areola. These babies need a calm environment in which to feed. Talk to yours soothingly

EXPRESSING YOUR MILK
If you need to use a breast pump because your breasts are engorged or because your baby cannot take milk from the breast, it is a good idea to use one that converts into a bottle.

and reassuringly, and reposition her firmly and securely. If your milk comes with a sudden rush after the ejection reflex has occurred, see if a little boiled water or mint tea, which can be given by spoon or in a mini-feeder dummy, encourages her to be more relaxed at the breast. If your milk streams out fast you may need to express a little at each feed before putting the baby to the breast.

Sore abdomen After a Caesarean section breast-feeding may be difficult because you find it almost impossible to settle with the baby in a position where she is not pressing on the wound. Try placing a pillow on the wound and lie on your side, or sit up and pop the baby's legs under the arm on the same side as the breast you are using.

Giving breast milk in a bottle

When you desperately need sleep and your partner wants to give some feeds, it can be a good idea to express some breast milk after each feed, and store it in the refrigerator (perfectly safe up to 24 hours). Use a sterile plastic container. If you want to keep your milk longer than 24 hours, freeze it. Express after each feed, either immediately or about 30 minutes later. If you find that milk shoots out of one breast when you put the baby to the other you can collect this milk too. If you are not good at expressing by hand buy a small breast pump. There are different varieties on the market.

BOTTLE-FEEDING

If you decide to bottle-feed or want to give occasional bottles for convenience, the artificial milk you choose for your baby should be as much like your own milk as possible. No manufacturer has yet been able to invent anything but a product which *approximates* to human milk, because your milk adapts to your baby's individual needs. Substitute milks are a great improvement on unmodified cow's milk, however, and those which "humanized" have the proportions of fats, sugars and trace elements changed so that they are more like the real thing. Discuss with your doctor, midwife or health visitor the choices available. Most babies thrive on artificial milk. But you do need to be scrupulously hygienic in preparing it.

Hold your baby close, cradled in your arm, when giving a bottle.

Making up bottle feeds

If you are using bottles it is vital that your kitchen and all utensils are clean and that you sterilize both bottles and teats carefully, following the instructions that come with the sterilizer or that are on the can of artificial milk. You can make up enough feeds for 24 hours straight into the bottles, put caps on them and store them in the refrigerator. It is then easy to feed your baby whenever he or she shows signs of hunger, just as you would if you were breast-feeding.

Never leave warm milk about for more than a few minutes as bacteria will multiply. After the feed, always throw away any leftover milk, clean out the bottle immediately and leave it soaking in sterilant. Keep teats in sterilized covered containers. When you go out do not take warm milk with you. Take it cold, straight from the refrigerator, and reheat it in a pan of hot water or an electric bottle warmer. It is tempting to tuck the bottle under the carry-cot covers to keep it snug and ready immediately the baby wants it. But if you do this you are running the risk of feeding your baby milk which is harbouring bacteria capable of causing gastro-intestinal illness.

Though it seems pleasanter for a baby to have warm milk, this is not strictly necessary; if the baby is impatient for a feed and you are in a hurry it is quite all right to give her a cold bottle.

Powdered milk must be thoroughly mixed. Some brands dissolve more easily than others. Even the tiniest lumps can block the hole in the teat and, if your baby splutters or vomits, can be inhaled and cause trouble with breathing. When you are making up dried milk, measure it very carefully and never put in an extra scoop to make it richer, as this overloads the baby with minerals which his system can only absorb with difficulty.

The baby who is fed on artificial milk may go longer between feeds since the milk takes longer to digest. If you were worried about whether your baby was having enough breast milk it can be very reassuring to know how much he or she has had from the bottle. But avoid trying to make the baby finish the bottle just because it is there. In hot weather give drinks of water too and introduce sips of fruit juice, since the bottle-fed baby will need extra vitamin C. But artificial baby milks do contain some extra vitamins, so do not give vitamin supplements unless advised to do so by your doctor, and then take care that you do not exceed the prescribed dose.

Feeding for pleasure

When bottle-feeding, remember to hold the baby close, cheek against your breast, just as if you were breast-feeding. Though it may produce a less comfortable cushion for the baby's head, a man can do this too. The baby may sometimes like to lie nestled against your partner's bare skin, and fathers who give a feed in the middle of the night like this say how much they enjoy it.

Never prop a baby up to feed on its own in a cot, however rushed you are. It can be dangerous, and it means that the baby misses out on one of the most important experiences of early life.

My baby's doing very well on the bottle! My husband shares looking after him, enjoys giving the feeds. All the gushing about breast-feeding from women who were willing to go on for years really put me off!

SLEEP AND CRYING

After being awake and alert, eyes wide open, for an hour or so after birth, the baby often sinks into a deep sleep for about 24 hours, waking only to suck and then dropping off to sleep again while still at the breast. It is a period often followed by another lasting about 24 hours, in which the baby may be sucking almost continuously. This is a normal pattern. It is the frequent sucking which stimulates your milk supply. Some babies suck in short bursts, get drowsy, then suck again. Others will sleep for two to three hours between more prolonged sucking sessions. Some babies start a pattern of evening fussing when they are one or two weeks old which may continue for as long as three months. Though tiring and perhaps worrying for you, this is also completely normal.

Sleep patterns of newborn babies

When your baby is asleep you will sometimes notice that the eyelids flicker and the eyeballs are moving behind them. This is rapid eye movement (REM) sleep similar to that which adults have—the dreaming time. It has been discovered that REM sleep is essential for mental wellbeing and if people are not to become exhausted*. These little eye movements also stimulate the flow of blood to the brain. Even if the baby seems to be stirring and is making little jerking movements or fussing noises, this is not a time to wake her. This kind of sleep is probably just as important for babies as it is for adults.

The meaning of your baby's cry

Another innate biological mechanism is your baby's cry on waking, which alerts you to care for her. The baby may also cry whenever you undress her and seem to hate being without clothes. This is nerve-racking for the new mother and father, especially if you are about to bath her. But remember that the baby was held firmly inside your uterus, hugged by its tightly enclosing walls. If your baby startles and cries when you change a nappy or when you start taking off her clothes, keep your movements slow and firm. With one hand hold the baby's arms over its chest, as they would have been folded inside the uterus at the end of pregnancy, and speak soothingly.

You will soon discover that the baby has different cries to express different needs. But in the first weeks the cry nearly always means *hunger* and the right thing to do is to let the baby suck. A wet or dirty nappy does not really matter to the baby.

PRACTICAL CARE

There is a great gap between studying something in a book and doing it in practice. Experiment and see what works for you.

Bathing your baby

It does not matter how you bath your baby, for example, so long as he is head-above-water, keeps warm and has a chance to enjoy it. Many babies hate being undressed and abhor being bathed in the first weeks of life, and make you feel you must be a tyrant for ever doing either of these things to them. And because they cry you are convinced that you must be utterly incompetent and hopeless as a mother. The single most important thing to remember is to talk to your baby while dressing, undressing and bathing him.

OPPOSITE
Content, asleep and oblivious of the world, your baby may well be dreaming . . .

If you do not want a very hot bath yourself, you can take the baby with you into your own bath. This provides the baby with a personal swimming pool. Start by placing him facing you on your knee and have a conversation. Then you will discover that you can work out little games together and the baby will find out what fun it is to splash. Have ready the biggest bath towel you can find and make the patting dry fun too, so that the whole process is enjoyable.

Changing nappies

Nappy-changing can be done any way you like. At first take it gently and give yourself time and privacy so that you can work out your own style of doing it. A firm surface helps. Have everything you need close at hand before you start, including a bucket into which you drop the soiled nappy. If this is a terry nappy you can then carry it to the lavatory, tipping any lumps straight in, before putting it to soak in whatever antiseptic solution you are using. It is a good idea to stick the safety-pin in your clothing or you will not be able to find it when you start to do the baby up again.

How you decide to fold your nappies will depend on whether you have a boy or a girl, and will also vary according to how big your baby is. It helps to fold a whole pile ready in the shape you like them. You may decide that it is simplest to buy nappies which are already shaped so that they do not need folding at all, but if you enjoy making geometric patterns it is not difficult to work out what suits you in practice: the only thing you need to remember is that the baby should not be placed into a permanently bow-legged attitude because of all the material stuffed between the legs.

You don't need a layette!

Though it can be fun to collect together tiny clothes for your baby, it is not really necessary, and since he or she will quickly grow out of these first- and even second-size garments there is little point in spending much money on them.

Your older child will not feel left out if you involve her in looking after the new baby...

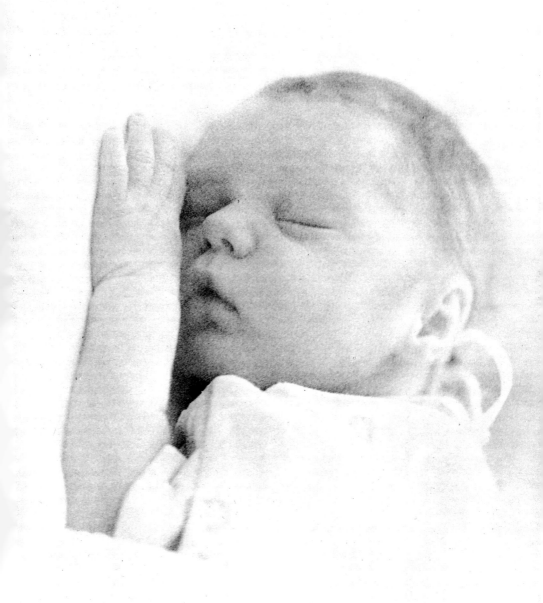

Nappies You will not be able to manage without nappies. The choice is between disposable and washable nappies. Disposables either come with a plastic backing or fit into plastic pants. Their obvious advantage is that they eliminate washing, but they are rarely absorbent enough to last a baby through the night. Washable terry nappies are cheaper than disposable ones, as well as being highly absorbent. Bear in mind that babies often dirty their nappies before, during and after a feed, and that many like to suck every two or three hours at first. You will have to decide how often you are prepared to change your baby! You may find you need as many as 24 terry nappies to see you through the 24 hours, and possibly more if you do not have an efficient tumble drier. You can save some washing by buying disposable nappy liners and tie-on plastic pants. Alternatively, there may be a nappy laundering service available in your area.

Clothing New babies lose heat rapidly, so need to be kept warm and cosy. You can do this in any way you like, but several fine layers are usually warmer than one thick one. When you can, choose things which do not have to be pulled over the baby's head, as most babies hate narrow neck holes. In very cold weather the baby's head ought to be covered outdoors.

Avoid strings and ribbons near the baby's mouth and hands, and large-holed lacy knitted jackets and shawls in which the baby will catch little fingers and toes. You are bound to be given bootees and mittens; these are wriggled off, lost, and get dirty and probably germ-ridden. Stretchy one-piece suits are better for keeping feet covered, and babies should be able to get at their hands and explore with them when they are awake.

A baby carrier is not strictly clothing but is important for your mobility. The most useful item of clothing is something for you, not the baby. It is a big wrap-around overcoat, cape or other voluminous top garment. Then you can tuck the baby in a baby carrier against your body underneath your cloak with just her face peeping out, and you know that your own body heat is providing warmth and that the outer garment is holding the warmth in around the baby.

The challenge of new parenthood

Though most women look forward to the time when they will have their baby at home, taking an important part in family life, the first days at home alone with a new baby can be ones of worry and even panic. You may suddenly feel like a stranger in your own home as you try to understand and cope with the needs of this demanding new person. You will soon learn to interpret the different cries of your baby, however, and will be visited regularly by a health visitor with whom you will have a chance to discuss any problems.

Midwives and health visitors

In Britain the community midwife visits you daily at home, and more often if necessary, until the tenth day after delivery and longer if she thinks it desirable. Then the health visitor calls and comes whenever you need her. She may start by visiting every week, but if you seem to be coping well will make her visits less frequent. She is concerned with the physical and emotional wellbeing of every member of the family, not only with the baby.

Post-natal check-up

Your post-natal check-up will be arranged for between five and seven weeks after the birth, and is an important way of ensuring that you have complete physical rehabilitation after childbirth. The obstetrician will give you an internal examination to see if your pelvic-floor muscles are well toned and the uterus and bladder correctly positioned, and will check on the state of any scar tissue. If sexual intercourse is difficult and uncomfortable or if you are feeling depressed and unhappy, tell the doctor at this visit. If you are dissatisfied with any aspect of care you have received or seek further explanation of things that have happened to you in labour, take the opportunity to discuss these things with the doctor.

SEX AFTER CHILDBIRTH

For many women the full flood of passion is slow to return after childbirth. So much has happened in your body that you may need time to find yourself again and get in touch with your feelings. If labour was unpleasant or delivery traumatic you need time, too, to *like* yourself again and to trust your body.

If you have had stitches you may feel at first as if you will never want to make love again. If you are one of the minority of women who do not have stitches you may not be able to wait to make love. So there is a great difference in attitude, depending very much on the state of your perineum. The initial healing of the episiotomy wound (and it is a wound) often takes two weeks or longer and even then you may be very conscious of scar tissue at the lower end of your vagina.

Rediscovering each other's body

Make sure first of all that your partner knows which areas are likely to feel sore and help him discover what feels good and where. Do not attempt to have intercourse at first and certainly do not try to *prove* anything to yourselves. Choose a quiet time when you need not be rushed, perhaps after a feed when you know the baby is most likely to settle and sleep soundly. Use a lubricant jelly, squeeze a little on your partner's fingers and, taking his hands in yours, guide him, showing him where you like to be touched. Many couples need two or three exploratory sessions like this before they feel sufficiently confident and passionate to have complete intercourse. If you rush it, you may have unexpected discomfort and will then tense up in anticipation of pain next time, and because your pelvic-floor muscles have contracted will experience more pain.

When you feel you are ready for intercourse, adopt a position in which your partner's weight is not going to drag on the lower part of your vagina or, if you are breast-feeding, is not on your breasts. For example, if you lie or sit with your legs over the side of a divan bed, feet on the floor, your partner is able to penetrate you gently without pressing against or pulling on any tender areas. You will probably feel extraordinarily full up. Release your *throat* and this will help the release of muscles around your vagina. Do not aim for simultaneous orgasm. It is usually much more comfortable and pleasurable for you in the weeks immediately after having a baby if your partner comes to orgasm first and then stays still inside until you have an orgasm too.

Adjusting to your changed body

You will learn a lot about each other and sometimes sex will be funny, sometimes tender, occasionally passionate. Even if you do not feel that you are making a wild success of your sex life in the first few months, lovemaking helps you and your baby by releasing oxytocin into your bloodstream which helps the uterus contract so that it returns to its previous size and shape and encourages the flow of breast milk. When you do have orgasm, milk may actually shoot out from your nipples.

You will probably find that your shape has changed after a first baby. The labia, like the outside petals of a flower, are softer and fleshier, and away from the site of the episiotomy you may find the entrance to the vagina also more yielding. If your uterus is still involuting, you will feel after-contractions following lovemaking. This is a good sign. If they are uncomfortable, use a hot water bottle against your lower tummy or back.

OPPOSITE
As you gain confidence, caring for your baby becomes an exciting opportunity for you to learn more about each other.

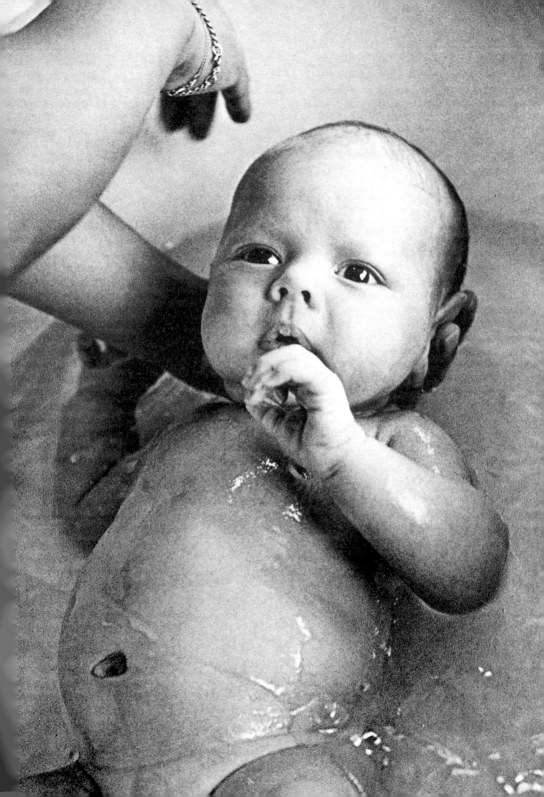

Even if you thoroughly enjoyed lovemaking, you may feel slightly sore afterwards, once the sexual intensity has faded. Again, this is normal. A cold witchhazel compress may feel soothing.

Painful intercourse

For some women intercourse after childbirth is acutely painful and no amount of trying to relax does away with the pain. This is called "dyspareunia". It can occur when stitches have been inserted too tightly and the surrounding flesh has become puffy and swollen (oedematous) and perhaps is infected. Go to your GP or ask your community midwife to look at the sore area as soon as possible. Sometimes it is just a question of nicking a few stitches, sometimes a matter of taking antibiotics. If you have pain up near your cervix, it may be that the transverse cervical ligaments have been torn and it takes time for them to repair themselves. Make sure that your doctor knows that you are having this sort of pain.

Many women worry that they have become "frigid" after childbirth. Often a lack of interest in sex is caused by tiredness. Try to rest with your feet up and if possible sleep at some time during the day when your baby sleeps. Even the most active baby sleeps sometimes, and it is a question of discovering your baby's pattern and taking advantage of it. This is more difficult if you have a toddler too, but many toddlers enjoy a cuddle in bed or on the sofa.

Although you may not feel like making love for some time after childbirth, it is sensible to have explored sensations and had intercourse *before* your post-natal check-up. Most women with new babies are so busy that it is not easy to fit in another appointment to discuss sexual difficulties and they hope that if they take no notice the problems will disappear. Make a note of where and when you feel pain and let the doctor know that you are experiencing dyspareunia and that you want help.

Sex after childbirth takes you on a new journey with your partner. It involves discovery, change, in some ways for many women a fresh awareness of the depth and drama of their sexual feelings, and for both of you a new closeness and tenderness as parents of the baby who has been born of your love.

CONTRACEPTION AFTER CHILDBIRTH

There is no easy answer to contraception and what pleases one couple is completely unsuitable for another. Many couples now consider the matter in advance so that they can have intercourse safely whenever they feel ready. You may find that a combination of methods works best for you but, whatever kind you select, study carefully the correct method of use and never deviate from the routine. It is not worth being worried about another pregnancy when you are only just beginning to enjoy the results of the last!*

Breast-feeding

If you are breast-feeding, your periods may not come back till you wean the baby or start introducing her to some form of solid food. Ovulation, and hence the possibility of conception, can occur a couple of weeks or so *before* you have this first period. Breast-feeding tends to reduce fertility but is not an effective contraceptive unless you are suckling the baby intermittently right through the 24 hours and are giving her no other food or fluid at all.

Coitus interruptus

Hoping that your partner will withdraw before ejaculation, and deposit semen outside your vagina, is not a reliable method either, though it is very common throughout the world. In spite of working well for some couples, it demands great control on the man's part and may lead to dissatisfaction for you both. Sperm can flow from the penis *before* ejaculation and if you have intercourse again within a short time, live sperm may already be present in your partner's urethra and be introduced into your vagina before ejaculation. Sperm do not have to be deposited right inside your vagina for you to become pregnant, and even a drop or two of semen leaking against the labia may contain a million sperm or more.

Natural birth control

Natural methods of birth control entail identifying the period of ovulation, the phase of the menstrual cycle at which you are most fertile, and then abstaining from intercourse during that time. It is impossible to calculate the time of ovulation accurately using a calendar alone. The traditional rhythm method, the only method of birth control officially approved by the Roman Catholic Church, relies on keeping a record of the menstrual cycle and daily monitoring of basal body temperature, using a special thermometer. More effective is the symptothermal method which combines charting your temperature with observing changes in the cervical mucus. There are drawbacks, however: in the first year or so after childbirth a woman may not have a regular menstrual cycle, and it can be difficult to work out the significance of the changes she observes; natural methods require instruction from someone who is really skilled in using them, and a commitment from both partners.

Ovulation prediction There are DIY kits on the market that can tell you if and when you are ovulating, though they are expensive. They work in a way similar to chemical pregnancy tests (see page 27), and signal, by a colour change, the presence of luteinizing hormone in your urine, which increases a couple of days before ovulation. You start testing the urine several days after the beginning of a period and go on testing, at the same time each day, noting exactly when the equipment records a surge in luteinizing hormone. You should not

◆

empty your bladder for four hours beforehand. Two to three days after you have observed a colour change you are at your most fertile.

The condom

The condom (sheath) is the most widely used of the barrier methods and, employed carefully, is effective and safe. The one big disadvantage after childbirth is that your vagina may not be well lubricated and may be tender following episiotomy. Unless you use a lubricant cream the latex rubber sticks and drags, interfering with pleasure and reducing confidence. So have some artificial lubrication ready, but avoid vaseline, as this rots rubber. Do not use old condoms; their shelf life is about two years.

The diaphragm

If you used a diaphragm before you became pregnant you will probably need a larger size after you have had a baby, and it must be fitted by a doctor, who cannot do it accurately until about six weeks after childbirth. The diaphragm should be left in place for at least six hours after intercourse; do not, however, leave it for longer than eight hours if you have had any kind of bladder infection during pregnancy or following the birth, since pressure of the rubber rim on your bladder can sometimes cause irritation and exacerbate an infection. Use one teaspoonful of spermicidal cream on the diaphragm; never use vaseline. It is probably best not to dust with talcum powder as some manufacturers advise, since some kinds of powder contain carcinogenic substances. The diaphragm is completely safe to use when breast-feeding and the spermicidal cream or jelly cannot harm the unborn baby if you should conceive accidentally. The success rate ranges from four pregnancies for every 100 years of use to as high as 29, but the efficiency of the diaphragm depends very much on the motivation and care of the user.

Sometimes ligaments running across the cervix are slack after childbirth and the diaphragm cannot be wedged snugly up under the pubic bone but slips out of position, especially when you bear down. In this case you may want to consider a cap.

The diaphragm is more effective when used with a spermicide.

The cervical cap

This is a rigid, thimble-shaped rubber dome which fits by suction right over the cervix itself and has to be placed in position very carefully by you. It can remain in place the whole month, from period to period. It is about as safe as the diaphragm.

The sponge

This is a soft round sponge of polyurethane foam, looking rather like a doughnut, which is impregnated with spermicide. It is inserted deep into the vagina and over the cervix. Each sponge is used only once. It must be left in position for at least six hours after intercourse. Its reliability is still in question.

Spermicides

Foaming spermicides are more effective than creams or gels because they effervesce into every crevice. However, you may find that this characteristic in itself interferes with your pleasure in intercourse. Spermicides in the form of foaming tablets or pessaries are not so reliable, because women often do not place them sufficiently high up in the vagina.

If you notice any vaginal irritation with a particular brand, try changing to another. Some spermicides come in pre-filled applicators; others have to be measured out into an applicator. One problem is that you are supposed to lie on your back so that the spermicide does not drip out before intercourse, and this may not be your position of choice.

Spermicides are safest used in combination with a diaphragm, cap or condom. The pregnancy rate is anything between five and 30 pregnancies for each 100 years of use.

The intra-uterine device

It is usually easier for an intra-uterine device (IUD) to be inserted into your uterus and retained without excessive cramping once you have had a baby. So it may be that the IUD will suit you. The failure rate is between one and five pregnancies for every 100 years of use, depending on the skill of the doctor who inserts it. Copper IUDs need to be replaced every few years and after each insertion you may feel faint and sick. You should not have intercourse for the first few days, and may notice some bleeding after intercourse during the first month or so. Plastic IUDs can be left in longer; some need to be changed only every seven years.

Many problems associated with IUDs are related to the way in which they are inserted, so the longer you can go without changing an IUD, the safer it will be.

Pelvic infection is common with an IUD and is more likely when there is a string attached to it, since infection ascends from the vagina up through the cervix. Infection should be treated with antibiotics, all of which pass through into your milk, though the only obvious effect on the baby may be that his or her motions become loose. In some ways the thread is reassuring: occasionally an IUD is expelled or buries itself in the uterine lining and many women like to have some means of knowing whether their IUD is still there.

The copper 7 is the type of IUD most commonly prescribed.

Rarely an IUD actually perforates the uterus, and this is more likely to happen if it is inserted within a short time after delivery when the uterine wall is thin and soft. An IUD with a rounded rather than a spiky edge is less apt to do this.

In Scandinavia there is an IUD which releases 20 micrograms of levenorgestrel, the hormone used in the progestogen pill. It is an effective contraceptive and has fewer side-effects than many other kinds of IUD that are commonly available.

The Pill

Though the Pill is the most reliable method of contraception so far invented, there are certain conditions, some of which are not evident until pregnancy, that indicate that you should not choose the Pill as your post-natal contraceptive. If you have high blood pressure which continues after the birth or if it has been discovered during pregnancy that you have diabetes, you should *probably* not go on the Pill. If you are suffering from severe post-natal depression, it may be wiser to avoid the Pill. If you developed varicose veins during pregnancy, you should watch for any pain in your legs which could be a sign of a blood clot. If you have had a blood clot in a vein (thrombophlebitis), you should *not* take the Pill

Progestogen changes the bacterial flora of the vagina and some women develop thrush for the first time when taking the mini-pill (see below). If you have already had thrush this may not be the contraceptive you should choose.

The Pill also needs reassessment as you get older. If you are over 35, the risk of a cardio-vascular disorder is increased significantly. If you smoke heavily as well, you should not be taking the Pill, as you are running grave risks with your health.

The combined oestrogen-progestogen Pill, almost 100 per cent effective in preventing pregnancy, is definitely *out* if you are breast-feeding. It affects your metabolism and therefore indirectly the baby. It may alter both the quantity and the quality of milk and there may possibly be long-term effects on the child.

The progestogen-only Pill Many women who breast-feed are prescribed the progestogen-only Pill, the "mini-pill". Since it contains no oestrogen, it probably does not prevent ovulation but works by thickening the cervical mucus, making it difficult for sperm to travel beyond the cervix, and by preventing the normal cyclical changes in the endometrium (the lining of the uterus) which allow a fertilized egg to implant. It is a less effective contraceptive than the combined Pill, but has fewer side-effects. The failure rate ranges from one to four pregnancies for every 100 years of use. It has to be taken every day without a break and must be taken at about the same time each day to be effective.

Many women say that though their milk supply was diminished for a few days after they started taking the mini-pill, feeding on demand, more or less continuously, for a day or two brought the supply back to normal. On the other hand, we do not really know what effects these powerful synthetic hormones may have on the baby.

The morning-after Pill A series of high-strength contraceptive pills is taken within three days of unprotected intercourse. Two pills should be taken as soon as possible after intercourse, and another two 12 hours later. This morning-after Pill is useful in an emergency but, because of the strength of the hormones taken, it is not a wise form of contraception and often makes a woman feel nauseous.

GAINING CONFIDENCE AS PARENTS

Many women in our society have no experience of babies and some have never had a newborn baby in their arms before. They are anxious that they will not know when the baby is hungry, that they will drop or drown it in the bath, that they will never be able to stop it crying or that the baby who is not crying has stopped breathing. New mothers are often too ashamed to talk about such feelings and may even repress recognition of them. Talk with other mothers and you will find that you are not alone with such anxieties. Talk about good feelings too—when the baby falls asleep and lies in your arms in perfect contentment, the soft, downy head resting against your skin, when he opens his eyes wide and gazes at you with excited attention, or when you watch her satisfied sucking at your breast.

You are not just a caretaker of the baby but a partner in a unique and evolving relationship. You learn more about each other every day, synchronizing with each other as dancers do. You respond to facial expression, eye movement, muscle tension—even breathing— quite spontaneously. When you act like this *you are invariably doing the right thing*. When you are self-conscious, you miss steps in the dance and confidence drains away.

The developing relationship between a mother and her baby is a process that needs time to unfold and blossom, patterned, just as a hyacinth bulb or a crocus is patterned, by the laws of its own inner energy. Yet this is only part of the dance. The baby's father too has his own special kind of interaction with his child as well as with you. When a man is fully involved with his baby, enjoying her, responding to her needs and getting to know her as intimately as you do, the pattern becomes even more intricate and exciting.

Twins can give you twice the pleasure if you take time to enjoy them...

Sharing in parenthood

Parenthood is a shared task. In the past fathers missed out on the baby's early months and were supposed to be interested in their children only when they started to play games and talk. Babies have astonishingly strong personalities and are different from each other even in the early weeks. It is worth getting to know the person who is your child from the outset. The man who turns his back on this opportunity to share in the relationship with the newborn baby may be denying a whole aspect of himself.

Being a parent is not just an endless series of repetitive tasks or a heavy responsibility, though all parents see it like that at times. It is a journey of discovery—discovery of the baby's personality, of who you are, who your partner is and who you are *becoming* together.

Pregnancy week by week

This is a week-by-week guide to what may be happening to you and your baby throughout pregnancy. As different women's pregnancies develop at different rates, do not expect to be at exactly the same stage for the week described. Read the information for the two weeks either side, too.
Since pregnancy is dated medically from the first day of your last period, the record begins with what is termed the third week of a 40-week pregnancy, the week of conception.

WEEK 3

You have ovulated and an egg is travelling along one of the two fallopian tubes towards your uterus. During intercourse one of the millions of sperm your partner has ejaculated has fertilized the egg while still in the fallopian tube.

Your baby is a cluster of cells which multiply rapidly as they continue the journey along the fallopian tube.

WEEK 4

You have probably not noticed anything different, though some women have a strange, metallic taste in their mouths.

The fertilized egg has arrived in your uterus and, after floating in the uterine cavity for about three days, has embedded itself in the uterine lining. It is nourished from blood vessels in the lining of the uterus, and the placenta begins to form around it.

WEEK 5

You are beginning to think that you may be pregnant. Your period is late, but you can't be sure, because you may feel as though it is about to start at any time. Your breasts are slightly enlarged and tender and you may find you need to pass urine more often than usual.

The embryo is about $\frac{1}{10}$ in (2 mm) long and would be visible to the naked eye by now. Its spine is beginning to form and the brain has two lobes.

WEEK 6

You may be feeling sick first thing in the morning or when you are cooking a meal. Your vagina will have become a bluish or violet colour. From the 6th day after your period was due it should be possible to find out by a urine test whether or not you are pregnant. Your uterus is now the size of a satsuma.

The baby has developed a head and trunk, and a rudimentary brain has formed. Tiny limb buds are beginning to appear. By the end of this week its circulation is beginning to function. The jaw and mouth are developing and 10 dental buds are growing in each jaw.

WEEK 7

You may sometimes feel dizzy or faint when you stand for a long time. Your breasts are noticeably larger; small nodules (Montgomery's tubercles) may appear on the areolae at about this time, while your nipples may become more prominent. By this date the doctor should be able to confirm your pregnancy by a vaginal examination.

The limb buds have developed rapidly and now look like tiny arms and legs. At the end of these limbs are small indentations which will later become fingers and toes. The spinal cord and brain are now almost complete and the head is assuming a human shape. The baby is now about $\frac{1}{2}$ in (1·3 cm) long.

WEEK 8

You may find that you have "gone off" certain foods. Many pregnant women can no longer drink alcohol, even if they previously enjoyed it, and a dislike of cigarettes or tobacco smoke is common. Your hair may seem less manageable than usual. You may also have a slight vaginal discharge. This is quite normal as long as it is not irritating or painful.

The baby now has all its main internal organs though they are not yet fully developed. The eyes and ears are growing, and the face is beginning to take on a human shape. The baby is just under an inch (2·5 cm) long.

WEEK 9

You may notice changes in your skin because of the pregnancy hormones in your system. Any wrinkles you have may be less obvious. Your gums may be softening, again because of these hormones, and you need to be especially careful about dental hygiene now and through the rest of the pregnancy. The thyroid gland in your neck may be more prominent.

The baby's limbs are developing very rapidly, and fingers and toes are beginning to be defined on the hands and feet. The baby is moving about gently to exercise its muscles, although you cannot feel these movements. At this point the baby weighs only about as much as a grape.

WEEK 10

Your uterus has expanded to the size of an orange, but is still hidden away within your pelvis. You should be wearing a bra with good support by now. If you buy a bra that fits your breasts but is adjustable to allow for later chest expansion, you may not need to get another size during the rest of your pregnancy.

The placenta, to which the baby is attached, begins to produce progesterone in a process which is completed by the end of the 14th week, when the progesterone produced is sufficient for the placenta to take over the function of the corpus luteum. The baby's ankles and wrists are formed, and fingers and toes are clearly visible. The baby has grown to about $1\frac{3}{4}$ in (4·5 cm) long.

WEEK 11

If you have been nauseous during the last weeks, the sickness should gradually lessen from now onwards. The amount of blood circulating through your body has started to increase, and will go on increasing until about the 30th week. You should be thinking about arranging antenatal classes, as they often tend to get booked up early.

Your baby's testicles or ovaries have formed, as have all of its major organs. Since these organs will not develop much further, but will merely continue to grow during its time in the uterus, the baby is relatively safe from the risk of developing congenital abnormalities after the end of this week.

WEEK 12

You will probably attend your first antenatal clinic this week. You will have a complete medical examination and the doctor will be able to feel the uterus by external examination, as it has risen above your pelvis. Arrangements are made for you to attend the clinic once a month until you are 32 weeks pregnant. The first visit is the time to ask about anything bothering you.

The baby's head is becoming more rounded and it has eyelids. Its muscles are developing and it is moving about inside the uterus much more. It is now about $2\frac{1}{2}$ in (6·5 cm) long but still weighs only $\frac{1}{2}$ oz (18 g).

WEEK 13

If you have had early-morning sickness this will probably have gone completely by the end of this week. From now on your uterus will be enlarging at a regular and noticeable rate.

The baby is now completely formed. From now on its time in the uterus will be spent growing and maturing until it is able to survive independently of its mother.

WEEK *14*

You will be feeling less tired than you were at the beginning of your pregnancy and will probably feel quite fit and active. You may notice a dark line (the linea nigra) down the centre of your abdomen. This will probably start to fade after the baby is born. Your nipples and the area around them are also starting to darken. Your uterus is the size of a large grapefruit.

The baby now has eyebrows and a small amount of hair has appeared on its head. Its heart can be heard by ultrasonic scan. The baby drinks some of the amniotic fluid and can pass urine. It is now receiving all of its nourishment from the placenta and measures about 3¾ in (8–9 cm).

WEEK *15*

Your clothes will be getting too tight for you. It is best not to try to cram yourself into tight jeans. To cope with the increased amount of blood circulating in your body and the baby's need for oxygen, your enlarged heart has increased its output by 20 per cent.

The hair on your baby's head and brows is becoming coarser. If it has a gene for dark hair, the pigment cells of the hair follicles are beginning to produce black pigment.

WEEK *16*

Your second antenatal clinic is now due. Some clinics do a scan at this visit. You will be able to see the outline of the baby's head and body. You feel butterflies in your stomach that just *might* be the baby moving. Your waistline will be starting to disappear. If you have not already done so, book childbirth education classes. Sometimes an "early-bird" class is available to discuss diet, exercise, posture, emotions and health.

Lanugo (fine down) is starting to form all over the baby, following the whorled pattern of the skin, and the baby has grown fingernails and toenails. It is 6¼ in (16 cm) long and weighs nearly 5 oz (135 g).

WEEK *17*

You may find that you are sweating more than usual (due to the extra blood in your system) and also that your nose feels congested. This is a common result of pregnancy and will end after delivery. Vaginal secretions may increase now.

The growing baby has pushed the top of the uterus to halfway between your pubic bone and your navel. From now on the baby weighs more than its placenta. It is probably aware of—and may be startled by—sounds outside your body.

WEEK *18*

If this is your first baby, this is the time when you may feel the first prod which is definitely nothing to do with indigestion! At last you know that there really is a baby in there! Trouble in sleeping at night will be helped by increasing the number of pillows supporting you.

Measuring about 8 in (20 cm) long, your baby is now testing out its reflexes. As well as kicking, it is grasping and sucking. Some babies find their thumbs and are confirmed thumb-suckers before they are born.

WEEK *19*

Now is not too early to start practising deep relaxation and steady, rhythmic breathing. Keep aside some time each day for this. You may notice that you are putting on weight on your buttocks as well as your abdomen.

Buds for permanent teeth are forming behind those that have developed for the milk teeth.

WEEK *20*

You will notice your baby being more and more active, and may even be able to see some of its movements. The growing uterus is pushing up against your lungs and pushing your tummy outwards. Your navel may suddenly pop out and stay that way until after delivery. Your chest (rather than breasts) has expanded and, if you do not already have an adjustable bra, now is the time to buy one.

Sebum from the sebaceous glands mixes with skin cells and begins to form the protective vernix which clings to the lanugo all over the skin, especially on the hairier parts and in the creases. The baby is now about 10 in (25 cm) long.

WEEK 21

You may start having heartburn—a burning sensation in the lower part of the chest—and may also bring up small amounts of acid fluid. Get your doctor to give you some antacid tablets.

The baby weighs just under 1 lb (450 g). It is still moving about freely in the amniotic fluid and can be felt kicking, sometimes high in your tummy, at other times down near your pubis.

WEEK 22

Your gums may be swelling because of the pregnancy hormones in your system. Do not forget that dental hygiene is important throughout pregnancy.

The baby is settling into a pattern of activity and sleep. It is probably at its most active while you are resting.

WEEK 23

The different parts of the baby can be felt (palpated) through your abdominal wall. You may feel a stitch-like pain at times down the side of your tummy; this is the uterine muscle stretching and the pain should go after you have had a rest.

At about this time the Braxton Hicks "rehearsal" contractions may become more pronounced, gripping and massaging the baby regularly.

WEEK 24

Your next visit to the clinic—by now the doctor will be able to hear the baby's heart through a stethoscope or a special fetal trumpet. The top of your uterus (the fundus) now reaches to just above your navel.

The baby is growing rapidly—it is now about 13 in (32 cm) long and weighs over $1\frac{1}{4}$ lb (0·5 kg). Although its vital organs are quite mature by now, its lungs are not yet sufficiently developed for survival outside the uterus.

WEEK 25

You may get cramp now and later. Avoid pointing your toes down. The baby may also be pressing against your bladder, causing you to go to the lavatory little and often.

The baby's bone centres are beginning to harden.

WEEK 26

If you think you may qualify for a maternity allowance from the DHSS (see page 377) now is the time to apply for it. If you leave applying for maternity allowance till after the birth, you may be entitled to less money.

The baby's skin is beginning to change: instead of being paper-thin and transparent, it is gradually becoming opaque.

WEEK 27

You will be putting on weight fairly regularly now until about the 36th week. It may be a good idea to start thinking about what to get for the baby before you become so big that shopping becomes an unpleasant chore.

The baby's skin is very wrinkled, but is protected and nourished by the covering of vernix.

WEEK 28

Colostrum may leak from your breasts. From now on you will probably be visiting the clinic every two weeks. If you are Rhesus negative, an antibody check is done.

At this stage of development, the baby is considered legally viable, which means that if delivered it must be registered. It is about 14 in (38 cm) long and weighs around 2 lb (0·9 kg).

WEEK 29

You probably feel as if all your internal organs are being crowded out by the baby. There is pressure on your diaphragm, liver, stomach and intestine.

By now the baby's head is more or less in proportion with the rest of its body.

WEEK 30

It is important to remember to maintain good posture when you are standing or sitting, even though the weight of the baby seems to be dragging you off balance.

The baby is probably very aware of the Braxton Hicks contractions, coming at regular intervals, even when you do not notice them.

WEEK *31*

You may be getting very breathless when you climb stairs or exert yourself.

However breathless you feel, the baby is getting enough oxygen. It now weighs 4 lb (1·8 kg).

WEEK *32*

At each clinic visit the baby's position is felt, its rate of growth assessed and its heart checked.

The baby is 16 in (42 cm) long. It is perfectly formed but the fat reserves beneath its skin are only gradually laid down. Born at this time it would still need to be cared for in an incubator.

WEEK *33*

You may be able to distinguish the baby's bottom from a foot or knee. You feel its movements more as prods and kicks—it may be too big now to swoop around in the amniotic fluid.

Your baby has probably adopted the most usual head down ("vertex" or "cephalic") position, in which it will now stay until delivery.

WEEK *34*

You will be attending antenatal classes by now.

The baby can differentiate between dark and light, and is bathed in a red glow when sunlight is on your tummy. Its skin is becoming pinker.

WEEK *35*

You may have some backache at about this time. This is because the ligaments and muscles supporting the joints in the small of your back relax.

The fetus measures approximately 18 in (44 cm) in length and weighs around 5½ lb (2·5 kg).

WEEK *36*

Clinic visits will be every week from now on. If this is your first baby, it will probably engage some time this week or soon after, and may have done so already. Your lump will settle lower down and you should find that your breathing becomes easier, though you may also need to pass urine more often.

The baby is almost fully mature and any time now the presenting part may drop into your pelvis ready for birth. It is about 18 in (49 cm) long.

WEEK *37*

You may have a chance to tour the maternity ward and labour room of the hospital in which you are planning to give birth.

The baby may be rehearsing slight breathing movements, though there is no air in its lungs. In this way amniotic fluid passes into the baby's trachea, giving it hiccups!

WEEK *38*

You may notice that the baby moves less now and that, instead of whole body movements, there are only jabs from the feet and knees, and the strange buzzing sensation inside your vagina of the baby's head moving against your pelvic-floor muscles.

The baby may be putting on as much as 1 oz (28 g) in weight a day at this stage.

WEEK *39*

Your cervix is ripening in preparation for labour. You may feel heavy and weary and be having quite strong Braxton Hicks contractions.

The amniotic fluid is renewed every 3 hours. The baby's bowel is filled with greenish-black meconium, excretions from the baby's alimentary glands mixed with bile pigment, lanugo and cells from the bowel wall—its first motion after birth.

WEEK *40*

The long-awaited day is near, and perhaps after the long wait you are now wishing that it had not come so quickly! You will soon hold your child in your arms.

The baby is about 20 in (55 cm) long. The presenting part is in the lower segment of your uterus and pressing through the softened, partially opened, cervix. It is about to leave the security it has always known and then it will need all your love and care.

Appendix 1

The Department of Health and Social Security publishes leaflets on general maternity benefits, and these are available from your local DHSS office or Citizens' Advice Bureau. If you are in any doubt about whether you qualify for any benefits, it is probably best to apply for them anyway.

There are two main types of maternity benefit: statutory maternity pay, which is paid by employers, and maternity allowance, paid by the DHSS.

Statutory maternity pay

If you have worked for your employer for at least six months up to the 26th week of your pregnancy, you may be entitled to statutory maternity pay (SMP). To qualify, you must earn enough to pay Class 1 National Insurance contributions (although you *may* still qualify if you pay reduced rate contributions).

SMP can be paid for up to 18 weeks after you stop work, beginning between the 30th and 35th weeks of pregnancy. Within these limits, you can normally choose when to stop work and start getting SMP. You are entitled to SMP even if you do not intend to return to work after the baby is born.

If you have been with the same employer without a break for at least two years (five years if you work part-time for at least 8 hours a week), you can get SMP at the rate of 90 per cent of your earnings for the first six weeks, followed by payments at a lower rate for 12 weeks. If you have worked for your employer for at least six months but less than two years (or less than five years part-time), you can get SMP at a lower rate for the full 18 weeks.

You do not have to claim SMP (it will normally be paid in the same way as your earnings), but you need to tell your employer at least three weeks before you stop work.

Your contract of employment may entitle you to paid maternity leave from your employer at a rate more or less than SMP, but all employers must pay at least SMP to all those who qualify for it.

For more information, see leaflets FB 8 (*Babies and Benefits*) and NI 17A (*Maternity Benefits*).

Maternity allowance

If you are not entitled to SMP (for example because you are self-employed or have recently changed jobs), you may be able to get a weekly maternity allowance from the DHSS. It is paid by order book cashable at your local post office.

To qualify, you must have been working and paid your own National Insurance contributions for 26 weeks of the 52 weeks ending with the 26th week of your pregnancy.

Maternity allowance can be paid for 18 weeks, starting from the 30th week of pregnancy—or later if you want to work longer. You can work up to the 34th week and still receive payments for the full 18 weeks, but if you work longer than this the allowance will be reduced.

You can claim after you are 26 weeks pregnant, even if still working. Use form MA 1 from your antenatal clinic or DHSS office, together with your Maternity Certificate (from your doctor or midwife). Don't delay sending in your application or you may lose some of your allowance.

Social Fund maternity payment

If you are on a low income you may be able to get a maternity payment from the Social Fund to help you pay for things for your new baby. The payment may be made if either you or your partner get Income Support or Family Credit, and you can apply for it (using form SF 100 from an antenatal clinic or DHSS office) up until your child is three months old.

Employment protection

If you have been working full time for two years with the same employer, you have two basic rights under the present law. First, you are protected from dismissal because of your pregnancy. If you cannot carry out your usual job, your employer has to try to find an alternative job for you.

Second, you have the right to return to the job you held before your pregnancy for up to seven months after the baby's birth, but you must let your employer know well in advance and in writing that you plan to return.

For more information, get a copy of *Employment Rights for the Expectant Mother*, a booklet available from your local DHSS office or Jobcentre.

Health benefits

You are entitled to free NHS dental treatment and prescriptions during pregnancy and until your baby is a year old. Family planning services are also free.

If you are receiving Income Support, you may also be entitled to free milk and vitamins while pregnant and until your child is five.

Appendix 2

These research references relate to the asterisks in the main text. Where there is more than one asterisk on a page the references appear in order, with each entry on a new line relating to a different asterisk.

p. 32 Quoted by Pamela Nowicka, *Independent*, November 23, 1987.

p. 46 M. Enkin and I. Chalmers (eds), *Effectiveness and Satisfaction in Antenatal Care*, Spastics International Medical Publications, 1982. Ann Oakley, *The Captured Womb*, Blackwell Ltd, 1984.

p. 51 Sheila Kitzinger, *The Good Birth Guide*, Penguin 1983.

p. 52 Sheila Kitzinger, *Birth at Home*, Oxford University Press, 1979. Sheila Kitzinger, *Some Women's Experience of Induced Labour*, NCT, 1978.

p. 86 Sir Dugald Baird, *Journal of Biosocial Science*, I, 113, 1974.
☐ R. W. Smithells *et al.* "Maternal nutrition in early pregnancy", *British Journal of Nutrition*, 38, 3, 497–506, 1977. *Nutrition and Fetal Development* (ed. M. Winick), John Wiley & Sons, 1974. H. A. Kaminetzky and H. Baker, "Micronutrients in Pregnancy", *Clinical Obstetrics and Gynecology*, 20, 2, 363–380, 1977. R. M. Pitkin, "Nutritional support in obstetrics and Gynecology", *Clinical Obstetrics and Gynecology*, 19, 3, 489–513, 1976.

p. 87 P.J. Illingworth, R. T. Jung, P. W. Howie, T. E. Isles, "Reduction in postprandial energy expenditure during pregnancy", *British Medical Journal*, 294, 1573–1576, June 1987.
☐ Gary K. Oakes and Ronald A. Chez, "Nutrition in Pregnancy", *Contemporary Obstetrics and Gynecology*, 4, 147–150, 1974.
☐ M. D. G. Gillmer, "Obesity in pregnancy—physical and metabolic effects", in *Nutrition in Pregnancy: Proceedings of the Tenth Study Group of the Royal College of Obstetricians and Gynaecologists* 213–230, RCOG, London, 1983.

p. 88 Ellen Buchman Ewald, *Recipes for a Small Planet*, Ballantine, 1977.

p. 91 A. Malhotri and R. S. Sawers, *British Medical Journal*, 293, 465–466, 1986.
☐ M. Puig-Abuli *et al.*, "Zinc and uterine muscle contractivity", paper given at European Congress of Perinatal Medicine, Dublin, 1984.
☐ Jacqueline Gibson Gazella, *Nutrition for the Childbearing Year*, Woodland Publishing Co., Wayzata, Minn., 1979.
☐ R. W. Smithells *et al.*, *Lancet*, I, 8164, 339–340, 1980.

p. 92 M. Robinson, "Salt in Pregnancy", *Lancet*, I, 178–181, 1958.
☐ B. S. Worthington, J. Vermeersch and S. R. Williams, *Nutrition in Pregnancy and Lactation*, Mosby, 1977.
☐ B. S. Worthington *et al.*, *op. cit.*

p. 93 Jonathan Scher and Carol Dix, *Pregnancy*, Penguin, 1983.
☐ G. M. Stirrat, *Obstetrics*, Grant McIntyre Ltd, 1981.

p. 94 Federal Register, 43, 114, US Department of Health, Education and Welfare, 1978.

p. 95 *Perinatal Problems* (eds N. R. Butler and E. D. Alberman), Livingstone, 1969.
☐ M. B. Meyer, "How does maternal smoking affect birth weight and maternal weight gain?" *American Journal of Obstetrics and Gynecology*, 131, 888–893, 1978.
☐ J. Kline *et al.*, "Smoking: a risk factor for spontaneous abortion", *New England Journal of Medicine*, 297, 793–795, 1977. R. L. Naeye, "Relationship of cigarette smoking to congenital anomalies and perinatal death", *American Journal of Pathology*, 90, 289–297, 1978. M. B. Meyer and J. A. Tonascia, "Maternal smoking, pregnancy complications and perinatal mortality", *American Journal of Obstetrics and Gynecology*, 128, 494–502, 1977.

p. 97 I. J. Chasnoff *et al.*, "Cocaine Use in Pregnancy", *New England Journal of Medicine*, 313, 666–669, 1985.
☐ Cree *et al.*, *British Medical Journal*, 4, 251, 1973.
☐ J. V. Kelly, "Drugs used in the management of pregnancy", *Clinical Obstetrics and Gynecology*, 20, 395–410, 1977. See also G. M. Stirrat, *op. cit.*

p. 99 Peter Parish, *Medicines: a Guide for Everybody*, Allen Lane, 1976; Penguin, 1976.

p. 100 Federal Register, 41, 115, 1976.

p. 101 Roger Hoag, "Perinatal psychology", *Birth and the Family Journal*, 113, 1974.
☐ Parish, *op. cit.*

378

p. 102 Studies of babies born in England and Wales between 1943 and 1965 revealed that the children of mothers who had had pelvic X-rays in pregnancy were almost twice as likely to develop leukaemia before they were 10 years old as those whose mothers had had no X-rays. The greatest risk is in the earliest weeks, when the mother may not even know she is pregnant. The risk of cancer was increased 15 times when X-rays were done in the first three months of pregnancy. See A. Stewart and G. W. Kneale, "Radiation dose effects in relation to obstetric X-rays and childhood cancers", *Lancet*, I, 1495, 1970.
□ David W. Smith, Sterling K. Clarren and Mary Ann Sedgwick Harvey, "Hyperthermia as a possible teratogenic agent", *Journal of Pediatrics*, 92, 6, 878–883, June, 1978. Peter Miller, David W. Smith and Thomas H. Shepard, "Maternal hyperthermia as a possible cause of anencephaly", *Lancet*, I, 8063, 519–521, 1978.

p. 105 *British Journal of Obstetrics and Gynaecology*, 91, 724–730, 1984.

p. 114 Aidan MacFarlane, *The Psychology of Childbirth*, Fontana, 1977.

p. 115 E. Noble, *Essential Exercises for the Childbearing Year*, John Murray, 1978.

p. 126 Christopher Redman, "Old-fashioned alertness is the key", *General Practitioner*, 1979.

p. 128 Pregnant women often have "physiological" anaemia. There is a greater volume of blood circulating in their bodies; hence the red blood cells are dilated. This is normal and does not mean that they are suffering from anaemia.
Having iron supplements when you do not need them may do more harm than good; excess iron enlarges the red blood cells (macrocytosis) until they are too big to pass through some of the capillaries in the mother's and the baby's circulatory systems. This deprives the baby of essential nutrients and can lead to its growth being retarded. See T. Lind, *British Journal of Obstetrics and Gynaecology*, 83, 760, 1976.

p. 162 Sherry L. Jimenez, Linda C. Jones and Ruth G. Jungman, "Prenatal classes for repeat parents", *MCN*, 4, 305–308, Sept./Oct., 1979.

p. 167 Grantly Dick-Read, *Childbirth Without Fear*, Pan, 1969.

p. 168 Erna Wright, *The New Childbirth*, Tandem, 1969.

p. 170 Janet Balaskas, *Active Birth*, Unwin, London, 1983.

p. 187 Sheila Kitzinger, *Women as Mothers*, Fontana, 1978.

p. 208 G. Kolata, "Fetuses Treated Through Umbilical Cords", *The New York Times*, March 29, 1988.

p. 210 T. J. Bassler, "Dietary practices of marathon runners", in *Health Aspects of Endurance Training, Medicine and Sport*, 12, Karger, 1978.

p. 215 F. Chenia and Ch. B. and C. A. Crowther, "Does advice to assume knee-chest position reduce the incidence of breech presentation at delivery? A randomized clinical trial", *Birth*, 14, 2, 75–78, June 1987.
□ J. P. VanDorsten, B. S. Schifrin and R. L. Wallace, "Randomized controlled trial of external cephalic version with tocolysis in late pregnancy", *American Journal of Obstetrics and Gynecology*, 141, 417, 1981.

p. 219 J. F. Pearson and J. B. Weaver, *British Medical Journal*, I, 1305, 1976.
□ J. F. Pearson, *op. cit.*

p. 232 Professor Mendez-Bauer discovered that dilatation of the cervix and the efficiency of contractions is much greater when a woman is standing up than when she is lying on her back. The uterus works nearly twice as well.[1]
Professor Caldeyro-Barcia, looking at the difference between contractions when a woman is lying on her left side and on her back, found that contractions were as frequent when a woman was standing as when lying flat on her back but that they were stronger. He concluded that for the uterus to work really effectively the woman should be standing.[2, 3]
Eleven hospitals in seven Latin-American countries joined in a study of the effects of the mother's position in labour. At each hospital half the mothers were told to lie in bed during the first stage and the other half were encouraged to get up or sit or lie in bed as they liked. Some 95 per cent of the women did not want to lie down. The membranes were not ruptured artificially, and the waters went at the end of the first stage or the beginning of the second in 85 per cent of the women. First-time mothers who stayed upright had shorter first stages than those who were lying down. The majority of the women said they were more comfortable when they stayed upright.
To find out whether an upright position could produce traumatic pressure on the

baby's head the researchers looked at the incidence of caput and also at the effect on the baby's heart and discovered that, when the membranes had not ruptured, there was no increased rate of caput if the mother was standing, nor was there an increase in deceleration of the fetal heart as recorded by an electronic monitor. They concluded that in normal labour an upright position is fine for the baby, shortens labour and reduces pain.[4]

Further research at the Queen Elizabeth Hospital, Birmingham, came up with the same results.[5]

See 1 Peter M. Dunn, "Obstetric delivery today", *Lancet*, I, 7963, 790–793, 1976
2 R. Caldeyro-Barcia *et al.*, "Effects of position changes on the intensity and frequency of uterine contractions during labour", *American Journal of Obstetric Gynecology*, 80, 284, 1960.
3 Yuen Chou-liu, "Effects of an upright position during labour", *American Journal of Nursing*, December 1974.
4 R. L. Schwarcz *et al.*, "Fetal heart rate patterns in labors with intact and with ruptured membranes", *Journal of Perinatal Medicine*, 1, 153, 1973.
5 A. M. Flynn, J. Kelly, G. Hollins and P. F. Lynch, "Ambulation in labour", *British Medical Journal*, II, 591–593, 26 August, 1978.

p. 262 S. A. Huchcroft, M. P. Wearing and C. W. Buck, "Late results of cesarean and vaginal deliveries in cases of breech presentation", *Canadian Medical Association Journal*, 125, 726, 1982.

p. 264 J. G. B. Russel, "Moulding of the pelvic outlet", *Journal of Obstetrics and Gynaecology, British Commonwealth*, 76, 817, 1967.
☐ Michel Odent, *Birth Reborn*, Fontana, 1986.

p. 265 Emanuel A. Friedman, MD, *Labor. Clinical Evaluation and Management*, Meredith Publishing Co., 1967.

p. 267 Marshall H. Klaus, John H. Kennell, Steven S. Robertson and Roberto Sosa, "Effects of social support during parturition and infant morbidity", *British Medical Journal*, 293, 585–587, 1986.

p. 278 Ronald Melzack, *The Puzzle of Pain*, Penguin 1973.

p. 279 Melzack, *op. cit.*
☐ *ibid.*
☐ *ibid.*

p. 282 Josephine A. Williamson, "Hypnosis in Obstetrics", *Nursing Mirror*, 27 November, 1975.

p. 283 Song Meiyu, "Acupuncture anaesthesia for caesarian section", *Midwives' Chronicle*, April 1985.
☐ I. F. Skelton, "Acupuncture in labour", Society of Bio-physical Medicine, June 1985.
☐ Christine Brown, "Therapeutic effects of bathing during labour", *Journal of Nurse-Midwifery*, 27, 1, 1982.

p. 284 M. Rosen, "Patient controlled analgesia", *British Medical Journal*, 289, 640–641, 1984.

p. 285 *Obstetrics*, a drug-information publication produced by Roche.
☐ Dianne Houslow *et al.*, "Intrapartum drugs and fetal blood pH and gas status", *Journal of Obstetrics and Gynaecology, British Commonwealth*, 80, 1007–1012, 1973.

p. 286 Michael Rosen, "Pain and its Relief", *Benefits and Hazards of the New Obstetrics*, (ed. T. Chard and M. Richards), William Heinemann, 1977.

p. 287 M. B. Wingate, "Effects of epidural analgesia on fetal and neonatal status", in *American Journal of Obstetrics and Gynecology*, 119, 1101–1106, 1974 and B. S. Schiffrin, "Fetal heart rate patterns following epidural anaesthesia and oxytocin infusion during labour", *Journal of Obstetrics and Gynaecology, British Commonwealth*, 79, 332, 1972.
☐ Andrew Doughty, *Journal of Royal Society of Medicine*, December, 1978.

p. 288 Sheila Kitzinger, *Some Women's Experiences of Epidurals*, NCT, 1987.
☐ A. D. Noble *et al.*, "Continuous lumbar epidural using bupivicaine", *Journal of Obstetrics and Gynaecology, British Commonwealth*, 78, 559, 1971.
☐ Kay Standley *et al.*, "Local-regional anaesthesia during childbirth; effect on newborn behaviors", *Science*, 186, November 15, 1974.
☐ Michael Rosen, *op. cit.*

p. 290 Kieran O'Driscoll and Declan Meagher, *Active Management of Labour*, W. B. Saunders, London, 1980.

p. 291 R. Caldeyro-Barcia *et al.*, "Adverse perinatal effects of early amniotomy during labour", *Modern Perinatal Medicine* (ed. L. Gluck), 431–439, Year Book Medical Publishers, Chicago, 1974.

p. 292 A. Huch *et al.*, "Continuous transcutaneous monitoring of fetal oxygen tension during labour", *British Journal of Obstetrics and Gynaecology*, 84, Suppl. 1, 1977.

□ G. C. Gunn *et al.*, "Premature rupture of the fetal membranes", *American Journal of Obstetrics and Gynecology*, 106, 469–477, 1970.
□ P. J. Steer *et al.*, "The effect of membrane rupture on fetal heart in induced labour", *British Journal of Obstetrics and Gynaecology*, 83, 454–459, June 1976.

p. 296 R. F. Harrison *et al.*, "Is routine episiotomy necessary?", *British Medical Journal*, 288, 1971–1975, 1984.
□ J. Sleep *et al.*, "West Berkshire perineal management trial", *British Medical Journal*, 289, 587–590, 1984.
□ S. Kitzinger and R. Walters, *Some Women's Experiences of Episiotomy*, National Childbirth Trust, 1981; S. Kitzinger and P. Simkin (eds), *Episiotomy and the Second Stage of Labor*, Pennypress, Seattle, 1984.

p. 300 "Caesarean Childbirth", Summary of a National Institute of Health statement, *British Medical Journal*, 1981.

p. 301 A. W. Linston and A. J. Campbell, "Danger of oxytocin-induced labour to fetuses", *British Medical Journal*, 3, 606–607, 1974.

p. 302 *Reducing the Risk*, Department of Health and Social Security, 1977.

p. 305 D. M. Okada and A. W. Chow "Neonatal scalp abscess following intrapartum fetal monitoring", *American Journal of Obstetrics and Gynecology*, 127, 875, 1977.

p. 306 G. S. Sykes *et al.*, "Fetal distress and the condition of newborn infants", *British Medical Journal* 287, 943–945, October 1983. P. W. Howe, "Fetal monitoring in labour",
British Medical Journal, 292, 6518, 427–428, February 1986.

p. 309 Stuart Campbell, *Sharing*, Maternal Health Committee of Social Planning and Review Council of British Columbia, Summer 1979.

p. 316 Frederick Leboyer, *Birth Without Violence*, Fontana, 1977.

p. 321 Aidan MacFarlane, *Getting to Know Each Other*, Farley Products, 1979.

p. 324 Michel Odent, *Birth Reborn*, Fontana, 1986, and *Entering the World: the Demedicalization of Childbirth*, Penguin, 1985.
□ Johnson's Baby *Newsline*, Autumn 1978.

p. 328 Much of the original research was done with monkeys: Robert Hinde discovered that rhesus monkey babies separated from their mothers shortly after birth became very distressed and stayed hunched up in a corner of the cage. He suggested that separation from the mother might be bad for a newborn human baby too.[1] Other research has even gone so far as to indicate that mothers who had greater contact with their babies, and continued this contact through early childhood, produced children whose IQ, when tested at the age of five, was significantly higher than average.[2] Those who advocate bonding between mother and baby at birth also suggest that skin-to-skin contact between mother and child is important. Criticisms have been voiced that the child could become chilled, but a study of heat loss in warmed cots as compared with that in the mother's arms showed that there was no significant difference between
the temperature of babies lying in heated cribs and others left with their mothers.[3]
See 1 Robert Hinde in *Proceedings of the Royal Society*, 196, 29, 1977.
2 F. S. W. Brimblecombe, *Separation and Special care Baby Units*, Heinemann, 1978.
3 C. N. Phillips, "Neonatal heat loss in heated cribs vs mother's arms", *Journal of Obstetrical, Gynecological and Neonatal Nursing*, 6, 11–15, 1974.
□ Marshall Klaus and John Kennel, *Maternal-Infant Bonding*, Mosby, 1977.

p. 333 Klaus and Kennel, *op. cit.*

p. 334 L. Silverman, W. A. Silverman and J. C. Sinclair, *Pediatrics*, 41, 1033, 1969.

p. 337 P. A. and J. P. Davies, *Lancet*, 2, 1216, 1970.

p. 342 Cicely Williams and Derrick B. Jelliffe, *Mother and Child Health*, OUP, 1972.

p. 344 Harriet Sarnoff Schiff, *The Bereaved Parent*, G. K. Hall, 1977.

p. 359 Rudolph Schaffer, *Mothering*, Fontana, 1977.

p. 366 If a woman has never had German measles (rubella), the obstetrician may advise her to have a rubella vaccination after delivery. Since this vaccine could affect any baby conceived within the next three months, it is vitally important for her not to conceive during this time. If the woman is unsure about what kind of contraceptive to use, she may be offered an injection of a long-acting contraceptive called Depo Provera. Some women who intend to breast-feed are reluctant to have this injection which introduces hormones into the bloodstream.

Useful reading

J. Balaskas, *The Active Birth Partners' Handbook*, Sidgwick & Jackson 1984.

J. Balaskas and Y. Gordon, *The Encyclopedia of Pregnancy and Birth*, Macdonald Orbis 1987.

J. Balaskas, *The New Active Birth Handbook*, Unwin Hyman 1989.

B. Dale and J. Roeber, *Exercises for Childbirth*, Century 1982.

D. Elbourne, *Is the Baby All Right?*, Junction Books 1981.

C. Flint, *Sensitive Midwifery*, Heinemann 1986.

Ina M. Gaskin, *Spiritual Midwifery*, The Farm, Tennessee 1978.

S. Inch, *Birth Rights*, Hutchinson 1982.

S. Kitzinger, *The Experience of Childbirth*, Gollancz 1982; Penguin 1987.

S. Kitzinger and P. Simkin (eds), *Episiotomy and the Second Stage of Labor*, Pennypress, Seattle 1986.

S. Kitzinger, *Birth over Thirty*, Sheldon Press 1982.

S. Kitzinger, *Woman's Experience of Sex*, Dorling Kindersley 1983; Penguin 1986.

S. Kitzinger and L. Nilsson, *Being Born*, Dorling Kindersley 1986.

S. Kitzinger, *A Celebration of Birth*, Pennypress, Seattle 1986.

S. Kitzinger, *The Experience of Breastfeeding*, Penguin 1987.

S. Kitzinger, *Giving Birth: How it Really Feels*, Gollancz 1987.

S. Kitzinger, *Freedom and Choice in Childbirth: Making Pregnancy Decisions and Birth Plans*, Penguin 1987.

S. Kitzinger, *Some Women's Experiences of Epidurals*, National Childbirth Trust 1987.

S. Kitzinger (ed.), *The Midwife Challenge*, Pandora 1988.

P. Leach, *Baby and Child*, Michael Joseph 1988.

A. Loader (ed.), *Pregnancy and Parenthood* (the official National Childbirth Trust handbook), OUP 1985.

F. Leboyer, *Birth Without Violence*, Fontana 1977.

F. Leboyer, *The Art of Breathing*, Element Books 1985.

C. Lewis, *Becoming a Father*, Open University Press 1986.

M. Odent, *Birth Reborn*, Fontana 1986.

A. Oakley, *The Captured Womb*, Martin Robertson 1980.

A. Oakley, *From Here to Maternity*, Penguin 1986.

J. Roeber, *Shared Parenthood, A Handbook for Fathers*, Century 1987.

W. Savage, *A Savage Enquiry: Who Controls Childbirth?*, Virago 1987.

Useful addresses

AIDS and Pregnancy
Healthline: 01 980 4848
(6–10 p.m.)
*Confidential telephone
information service.*

Association for Improvement in
Maternity Services,
163 Liverpool Road,
London N1 ORF
01 278 5628
*A consumer pressure group
that campaigns for the rights of
childbearing couples to be
respected as normal reasonable adults and to make their
own informed decisions regarding all matters having to do
with the maternity services.*

Association of Radical Midwives,
62 Greetby Hill,
Ormskirk,
Lancs L39 2DG
0695 72776
*Aims to restore the role of the
midwife for the benefit of the
childbearing woman and her
baby. May be able to help you if
you want a home birth.*

British Acupuncture Association
and Register,
34 Alderney Street,
London SW1V 4EU
01 834 1012

Caesarean Support Group,
81 Elizabeth Way,
Cambridge CB4 1BQ
0223 314211

The Compassionate Friends,
6 Denmark Street,
Bristol BS1 5DQ
0272 292778
*If you have suffered a bereave-
ment, Compassionate Friends
will try to help by putting you
in touch with others who have
gone through a similar
experience.*

The Family Planning Association,
St Andrew's House,
27–35 Mortimer Street,
London W1A 7RJ
01 636 7866
*Advice on all aspects of
contraception and sterilization.*

Independent Midwives'
Association,
54 Mount Nod Road,
London SW16 2LP
*Midwives working outside the
NHS who can be booked for
home birth, mainly in London.*

International Centre for Active
Birth,
55 Dartmouth Park Road,
London NW5 1SL
01 267 3006

International Home Birth,
22 Anson Road,
London N7 0RD

La Leche League (Great Britain),
Box 3424,
London WC1 6XX
01 404 5011
*Information about breast-
feeding and practical
help with any difficulties.*

The Meet-a-Mum Association,
3 Woodside Avenue,
London SE25 5DW
01 654 3137
*Nationwide network which
encourages new mothers to
meet and share activities.*

National Childbirth Trust,
Alexandra House,
Oldham Terrace,
Acton,
London W3 6NH
01 992 8637
*Nationwide education for
childbirth and parenthood.
Gives help with breast-feeding
and postnatal support.*

National Information for
Parents of Prematures:
Education, Resources and
Support,
The Sam Segal Perinatal
Research Unit,
St Mary's Hospital,
Praed Street,
London W2 19Y
01 725 1487

The Society to Support
Home Confinements,
Lydgate,
Wolsingham,
County Durham DL13 3HA
0388 528044 (after 6 p.m.)

Stillbirth and Neonatal Death
Society,
28 Portland Place
London W1N 3DE
01 436 5881

TAMBA (Twins and Multiple
Birth Association),
1 Victoria Place,
King's Park,
Stirling KF8 3QX
0986 72080

In many cities there are now
Well Women Centres or Clinics
and Women's Health
Information Services. You may
find them in the telephone
book, or your local Citizens'
Advice Bureau will be able to
give you their addresses.
Information concerning
women's health resources
generally can be obtained
from:

Women's Health Information
Centre,
52–54 Featherstone Street,
London EC1
01 251 6580

Glossary

Abdomen The part of the body containing the intestines, stomach, bowels and uterus.

Abortion (Miscarriage) Either spontaneous or induced delivery of the fetus before the 28th week of development.

Abruptio placentae (Accidental haemorrhage) The peeling away of part of the placenta from the wall of the uterus in late pregnancy, which may result in bleeding.

Accelerated labour The artificial augmentation of contractions, after the cervix has started to dilate, by the injection of oxytocin through an intravenous drip. Often used to speed up a long labour or to get a "tired" or incoordinate uterus working more effectively.

Active birth An approach to childbirth which entails practising stretching positions and movements and being in "open" and upright positions in labour.

Active management of labour The constant monitoring and technical control or induction of labour.

AFP See *Alpha-feto-protein.*

AIDS Acquired immune deficiency syndrome – the collection of illnesses resulting from infection with the human immunodeficiency virus (HIV).

ALB See *Albumin.*

Albumin A protein present in all animal tissues. Albumin in the urine of a pregnant woman can be a sign of pre-eclampsia.

Alpha-feto-protein (AFP) A substance produced by the embryonic yolk sac, and later by the fetal liver, which enters the mother's bloodstream during pregnancy. A very high level can indicate neural tube defects of the fetus—such as spina bifida or Down's syndrome—but can also mean that the woman is carrying more than one child.

Alveoli Milk glands in the breasts which, when they are stimulated by prolactin, produce a flow of milk.

Amenorrhoea The absence of menstrual periods.

Amino acids The main organic chemical constituents of proteins found in all foods produced from animals, but only in limited and varying combinations in vegetables.

Ammonium chloride See *Diuretics.*

Amnesia Loss of memory, usually short term, which can be a side-effect of certain drugs, especially Valium.

Amniocentesis The surgical extraction of a small amount of amniotic fluid through the pregnant woman's abdomen. Usually done as a test for fetal defects or maturity.

Amnion The layer of membrane immediately enveloping the fetus and the amniotic fluid inside the uterus; it is also referred to as the amniotic sac, or bag of waters.

Amniotic fluid The fluid surrounding the fetus in the uterus.

Amniotic sac See *Amnion.*

Amniotomy The surgical rupture of the amniotic sac, sometimes done to speed up labour. Referred to as ARM (artificial rupture of the membranes).

Anaemia A condition in which there is an abnormally low proportion of red corpuscles in the blood, treated by iron (Fe) supplements.

Anaesthetic Medication that produces partial or complete insensibility to pain.

Anaesthetic, general Anaesthetic that affects the whole body, usually with loss of consciousness.

Anaesthetic, local Anaesthetic that affects limited part of the body. See also *Caudal; Epidural; Paracervical.*

Analgesics Pain-killing agents not inducing unconsciousness.

Anencephaly The congenital absence of the brain.

Antenatal Before delivery.

Antepartum haemorrhage (APH) Bleeding from the vagina occurring after the 28th week of pregnancy. See also *Abruptio placentae; Placenta praevia.*

Anterior position See *Occipito anterior.*

Antibacterials Chemical agents that limit the growth of, or destroy, bacteria. See also *Sulphonamides.*

Antibiotics Substances capable of destroying or limiting the growth of micro-organisms, especially bacteria.

Antibodies Protein produced naturally by the body to combat any foreign bodies, germs or bacteria.

Anti-cholinergic drugs Used in the treatment of nausea and vomiting, partly by limiting the impulses through the nervous system and partly by restricting the secretion of stomach acids.

Anticoagulants   Drugs that prevent the blood clotting.

Anticonvulsants   Drugs that combat convulsions, especially epilepsy.

Antihistamines   Tranquillizers used in the treatment of nausea, vomiting and certain allergies.

Aperients   Laxative or purgative drugs.

Apgar scale   A general test of the baby's wellbeing given immediately after birth to ascertain the heart rate and tone, respiration, blood circulation and nerve responses.

APH   See *Antepartum haemorrhage.*

Apnoea   Interrupted breathing which may occur in pre-term and low-birthweight babies.

Areola   The pigmented circle of skin surrounding the nipple.

Arhythmic contractions   Irregular contractions.

ARM   See *Amniotomy.*

Aspirin (Salicylate)   A mild analgesic. Taken in pregnancy, it may interfere with the clotting of blood in the fetus and can cause neonatal jaundice.

Bag of waters   See *Amnion.*

Barbiturates   Powerful and highly addictive tranquillizers.

Bearing down   The pushing movement made by the uterus in the second stage of labour.

Bile pigment   See *Bilirubin.*

Bilirubin   Broken-down red blood cells, normally converted to non-toxic substances by the liver. Some newborn babies have levels of bilirubin too high for their livers to cope with. See also *Jaundice, neonatal.*

Birth canal   See *Vagina.*

Blastocyst   An early stage of the developing egg when it has segmented into a group of cells.

Blighted ovum   An abnormal development of the egg in which the cells do not develop in the usual way to form a baby. It results in miscarriage.

Bradycardia   A slow heart rate. In the fetus and newborn baby, this is a rate of less than 120 beats a minute.

Braxton Hicks contractions (Rehearsal contractions) Contractions of the uterus which occur throughout pregnancy, but which may not be noticed until the ninth month.

Breast pump   Apparatus for drawing milk from the breasts.

Breech presentation   The position of a baby who is bottom down rather than head down in the uterus.

Brow presentation   The position of a baby who is head down in the uterus, but with chin up, so that the brow comes through the cervix first.

Caesarean section   Delivery of the baby through a cut in the abdominal and uterine walls.

Candida   See *Thrush.*

Caput   A small, temporary swelling on the crown of the baby's head caused by the head being pressed against an incompletely dilated cervix.

Carpal tunnel syndrome   A numbness and tingling of the hands arising from pressure on the nerves of the wrist. In pregnancy it is caused by the body's accumulation of fluids.

Catheter   A thin plastic tube inserted into the body, through a natural channel to draw off urine from the bladder, or into a vein to maintain a constant input of fluids, or into the epidural space to introduce anaesthetic.

Caudal (Caudal epidural block)   An anaesthetic injected into the base of the spine. See also *Epidural.*

Cephalhaematoma   A temporary swelling on the side of the baby's head caused by pressure during labour.

Cephalic presentation   The position of a baby who is head down in the uterus. This is the most common presentation.

Cephalo-pelvic disproportion A state in which the head of the fetus is larger than the cavity of the mother's pelvis. Delivery must be by Caesarean section.

Cervical dilatation   See *Dilatation.*

Cervical erosion   Superficial inflammation of the cervix which sometimes occurs during early pregnancy, and may if infected produce irritation and yellow vaginal discharge.

Cervical incompetence   A disorder of the cervix, usually arising after a previous mid-pregnancy termination or damage to the cervix during a previous labour, in which the cervix opens up too soon, resulting in repeated mid-pregnancy miscarriages. It is sometimes treated by suturing to hold the cervix closed.

Cervicograph   See *Partogram.*

Cervix The lower entrance to the uterus, or neck of the womb.

Chloasma Skin discoloration during pregnancy, often facial.

Chloral drugs Non-barbiturate hypnotic tranquillizers.

Chlorpromazine (Largactil) A powerful sedative often used in conjunction with hypnotics, analgesics and anaesthetics.

Chorion The outer membranous tissue enveloping the developing fetus and placenta.

Chorionic gonadotrophin See *Human chorionic gonadotrophin (HCG)*.

Chorionic villi The layer of tiny fronds which forms around the fertile ovum, allowing it to become embedded in the uterine wall.

Chorionic villus sampling A method of screening for genetic handicap by analysis of tissue from the small protrusions on the outer membrane enveloping the embryo, which later form the placenta. The sample is taken by inserting a needle through the vagina.

Chromosomes Rod-like structures containing genes occurring in pairs within the nucleus of every cell. Human cells each contain 23 pairs. See also *Gene*.

Circumcision An operation to cut the foreskin from the penis, usually performed soon after delivery if desired.

Cleft palate A congenital abnormality of the roof of the mouth.

Clitoris Sensitive small organ at the upper end of a woman's genitals, just under the pubic bone and between the folded external labia.

Club foot A congenital abnormality when the foot is twisted out of shape.

Codeine An addictive pain-killing agent derived from opium.

Colostrum A kind of milk, rich in proteins, formed and secreted by the breasts in late pregnancy and gradually changing to mature milk some days after delivery.

Complementary feed A top-up of the baby's breast feed with a bottle feed.

Conception The fertilization of the egg by the sperm and its implantation in the uterine wall.

Congenital abnormality An abnormality or deformity existing from birth usually arising from a damaged gene, the adverse effect of certain drugs, or the effect of some diseases during pregnancy.

Consultant unit Department of general or teaching hospital under the direction of a specialist (the consultant).

Contractions The regular tightening of the uterine muscles as they work to dilate the cervix in labour and to press the baby down the birth canal.

Co-operation card A progress record of the pregnancy of a woman having shared care.

Cordocentesis See *Umbilical vein sampling*.

Corpuscles Constituents of blood, divided into red and white varieties.

Corpus luteum A glandular mass which forms in the ovary after fertilization. It produces progesterone which helps to form the placenta, and is active for the first 14 weeks of pregnancy.

Cortisone A steroid produced by the adrenal gland which appears in the amniotic fluid immediately before labour.

Count to ten chart A log of the first 10 fetal movements felt by the mother over 12 hours some time at the end of pregnancy. Sometimes called "fetal movement" or "kick" chart.

Crowning The moment when the largest part of the baby's head appears in the vagina and does not slip back again.

CVS See *Chorionic villus sampling*.

Cystitis An inflammation of the bladder and urinary tract, producing a stinging sensation when water is passed.

D and C The surgical *dilatation* (opening) of the cervix, and *curettage* (removal of the contents) of the uterus.

Dehydration An excessive loss of body water.

Demerol The American name for pethidine. See also *Analgesics*.

Depression, respiratory Breathing difficulties in the newborn baby.

Dextrose A solution of glucose used to supplement the level of blood sugar, usually introduced by intravenous drip.

Dextrostix A test to assess the level of sugar in the urine.

Diabetes Failure of the system to metabolize glucose, traced by excess sugar in the blood and urine.

Diastolic pressure The blood pressure between heart beats. See also *Systolic pressure*.

Diazepam (Valium) See *Tranquillizers.*

Dilatation The progressive opening of the cervix, caused by uterine contractions during labour.

Distocia, shoulder A state in which the baby's shoulders get stuck during delivery.

Distress See *Fetal distress.*

Diuretics Drugs which increase the amount of urine excreted.

Dizygotic See *Twins.*

Domino scheme A system by which a woman gives birth in hospital and returns home shortly after delivery while remaining under the constant care of one midwife.

Doppler A method of using ultrasound vibrations to listen to the fetal heart.

Down's syndrome (Mongolism) A severe congenital abnormality producing subnormal mentality.

Drip See *Intravenous drip.*

Dura The outer membrane protecting the spinal cord.

Eclampsia The severe form of pre-eclampsia, characterized by extremely high blood pressure, headaches, visual distortion and flashes, convulsions and, in the worst cases, coma and death. The condition is now rare since the symptoms of pre-eclampsia are treated immediately.

Ectopic pregnancy A pregnancy which develops outside the uterus, usually in the fallopian tube. The mother has severe pain low down at one side of the abdomen at any time from the 6th to 12th weeks of pregnancy. The pregnancy must be surgically terminated.

EDD The estimated date of delivery.

Elective induction Induction done for convenience rather than for medical reasons. See also *Induction.*

Electrode A small electrical conductor used obstetrically for monitoring the fetal heartbeat.

Electronic fetal monitoring The continuous monitoring of the fetal heart by a transducer placed on the mother's abdomen over the area of the fetal heart or by an electrode inserted through the cervix and clipped to the baby's scalp.

Embryo The developing organism in pregnancy, from about the 10th day after fertilization until about the 12th week of pregnancy, when it is termed a fetus.

Endocrinological changes Changes in the secretion of the endocrine glands which occur in pregnancy or the four weeks after delivery (the puerperium).

Endometrium The inner lining of the uterus.

Enema The injection of fluids through the rectum to expel its contents.

Engaged (Eng/E) The baby is engaged when it has settled with its presenting part deep in the pelvic cavity. This often happens in the last month of pregnancy.

Engorgement The over-congestion of the breasts with milk. If long periods are left between feeds, painful engorgement can occur, and can be relieved by putting the baby to the breast or expressing the excess milk.

Entonox (Gas and oxygen) A short-term analgesic inhaled, when desired, by the woman in labour. See also *Anaesthetic.*

Epidural (Lumbar epidural block) Regional anaesthesia, used during labour and for Caesarean sections, in which an anaesthetic is injected through a catheter into the epidural space in the lower spine.

Episiotomy A surgical cut in the perineum to enlarge the vagina.

External version (External cephalic version, or ECV) The manipulation by gentle pressure of the fetus into the cephalic position. This may be done by an obstetrician some time between the 32nd and 34th week of pregnancy if the baby is breech.

Face presentation The position of a baby whose face is coming through the cervix first.

Fallopian tube (Oviduct) The tube into which a ripe egg is wafted after its expulsion from the ovary, along which it travels on its way to the uterus.

False labour Braxton Hicks (rehearsal) contractions that come so strongly and regularly that they are mistaken for the contractions of the first stage of labour.

Fertilization The meeting of the sperm with the ovum to form a new life.

Fetal distress A shortage in the flow of oxygen to the fetus which can arise from numerous causes.

Fetoscope A fine tube inserted surgically into the uterus for photographing the fetus to check for abnormalities.

Fetus The developing child in the uterus, from the end of the embryonic stage, at about the 12th week of pregnancy, until the date of delivery.

FH Fetal heart.

Fibre optics The transmission of light along flexible bundles of glass. Sometimes inserted into the uterus to give a view of the fetus inside.

Fluid retention See *Oedema*.

FMF Fetal movement felt.

Folic acid A form of vitamin B essential to the constant production of blood cells and haemoglobin, the shortage of which can produce anaemia in the fetus. It is sometimes supplemented during pregnancy.

Fontanelles The soft spots between the unjoined sections of the skull of the fetus.

Foremilk Milk which accumulates naturally in the ducts behind the nipple and precedes the main release of milk.

Fraternal twins See *Twins*.

Fundal palpation Feeling through the abdominal wall for the top of the uterus to assess its height.

Fundus The upper part of the uterus.

Gamma globulin A protein-based antibody.

Gas and oxygen See *Entonox*.

Gene The part of every cell which stores genetic characteristics.

Genetic counselling Advice on the probability of recurrent hereditary abnormalities or diseases.

Gentle birth One term used for a method of delivery proposed by Frederick Leboyer in which the shock of birth upon the baby is minimized and the baby is welcomed by loving hands, skin contact and soft lights and is able to discover itself in a warm bath.

German measles See *Rubella*.

Gestation The length of time between conception and delivery.

Glucose A natural sugar found in certain organic materials and in the blood: the main source of energy.

Glycogen The natural source of glucose; glycogen stores carbohydrate materials and is formed by the liver and muscles.

GP unit A small cottage hospital or ward inside a larger consultant unit where the pregnant woman is under the care of an obstetric GP and community midwives instead of a consultant.

Gynaecologist A doctor who specializes in female medicine.

Haemoglobin (Hb) A constituent of the red blood cells which contains iron (Fe) and stores oxygen.

Haemorrhage Excessive bleeding.

Haemorrhoids (Piles) Swelling of the veins around the rectum.

Hb See *Haemoglobin*.

HCG See *Human chorionic gonadotrophin*.

Hegar's sign The softening of the lower part of the uterus that gradually occurs during the first 6 weeks of pregnancy.

Hormone A chemical messenger in the blood which stimulates various organs to action.

Hormone accelerated labour See *Induction*.

Human chorionic gonadotrophin A hormone released into the woman's bloodstream by the developing placenta from about 6 days after the last period was due. Its prescence in the urine means that a woman is pregnant.

Hyaline membrane disease Respiratory distress affecting some pre-term babies resulting from a lack of surfactant which holds the lungs open.

Hydatidiform mole A rare abnormality in which the egg fails to develop after becoming implanted in the uterine wall, so there is no baby, although the placenta and chorionic villi go on developing. If the woman does not miscarry, the growth must be removed.

Hydrocephalus A congenital abnormality in which the baby's head is swollen with fluid.

Hyperemesis gravidarum Almost continuous vomiting during pregnancy.

Hypertension High blood pressure. In pregnancy this can reduce the fetal blood supply.

Hyperventilation Abnormally heavy breathing which flushes carbon dioxide out of the bloodstream, so that the normal chemical balance of the blood is lost.

Hypnosis A state of mental passivity with a special susceptibility to suggestion. This can be used as an anaesthetic, and can be self-induced.

Hypnotics See *Tranquillizers*.

Hypoglycaemia Low blood sugar sometimes apparent in babies who have suffered a difficult delivery, pre-term babies, or those of diabetic mothers. It can be artificially produced by giving the mother intravenous glucose in labour, since this increases the release of insulin, which breaks the sugar down. The baby may have to be given extra sugar.

Hypotension Low blood pressure.

Hypothermia A very low body temperature.

Identical twins See *Twins*.

Implantation The embedding of the fertilized ovum within the wall of the uterus.

Incoordinate uterine action See *Uterine action, incoordinate*.

Induction The process of artificially starting off labour and keeping it going.

Insulin A hormone produced by the pancreas which regulates the level of carbohydrates and amino acids in the system. It may be used as a means of controlling the effects of diabetes. See also *Diabetes*.

Internal monitoring See *Electronic fetal monitoring*.

Intra-muscular injection An injection into a muscle.

Intravenous drip The infusion of fluids directly into the bloodstream by means of a fine catheter introduced into a vein.

Intravenous injection An injection into a vein.

Invasive techniques Any medical technique which intrudes into the body.

Involution of the uterus The process by which the uterus returns to its normal state after pregnancy.

Jaundice, neonatal A common complaint in newborn babies, caused by inability of the liver to break down successfully an excess of red blood cells. See also *Bilirubin*.

Ketosis The accumulation of lactic acid in various body tissues and fluids, often indicated by acetone in the urine.

Labia The folds (or lips) of skin at the mouth of the vagina.

Lanugo The fine soft body hair of the fetus.

Lateral position Transverse lie or horizontal position of a fetus in the uterus (sometimes occurring if the mother has a large pelvis), where the presenting part is either a shoulder or the side of the head.

Leboyer approach See *Gentle birth*.

Let-down reflex See *Milk ejection reflex*.

Lie The position of the fetus in the uterus.

Ligament A fibrous tissue binding and connecting bones.

Lightening The engagement of the fetus in the pelvis, with its presenting part fitting securely in the pelvic inlet like an egg in an egg cup.

Linea nigra A line of dark skin which appears down the centre of the abdomen over the rectus muscle in some women during pregnancy.

Lithotomy position The standard position for delivery in USA, the mother lying flat on her back, with her legs wide apart and raised, fixed in stirrups.

Lochia Post-natal vaginal discharge.

Longitudinal lie The position of the fetus in the uterus, in which the spines of the fetus and the mother are parallel.

Long L See *Longitudinal lie*.

Low-birthweight baby A baby who at birth is below the weight of $5\frac{1}{2}$ lb (2.5 kg).

Meconium The first contents of the bowel, present in the fetus before birth and passed during the first days after birth. The presence of meconium in the fluid before delivery is usually taken as a sign of fetal distress.

Milk ejection reflex The flow of milk into the nipple.

Miscarriage See *Abortion*.

Mongolism See *Down's syndrome*.

Monilia See *Thrush*.

Monitoring See *Electronic fetal monitoring*.

Monozygotic See *Twins*.

Montgomery's tubercles Small bumps on the areola surrounding the nipple.

Morphine A narcotic opium derivative used as an analgesic.

Morula A stage in the growth of the fertilized egg when it has developed into 32 cells.

Moulding The shaping of the bones of the baby's skull as it passes through the birth canal.

Mucus A sticky secretion.

Multigravida A woman in her second or subsequent pregnancy.

Multiple pregnancy The development of two or more babies. See also *Twins*.

Mutation A damaged genetic cell. This can occur naturally or, more commonly, as an effect of outside agents, such as radiation.

NAD A medical term, meaning nothing abnormal detected.

Narcotic A drug which induces a state of stupor.

Nasogastric tube A pliable catheter passed into the stomach through the nose.

NCT The National Childbirth Trust.

Nembutal See *Barbiturates*.

Neural tube defects Abnormalities of the central nervous system. See also *Anencephaly; Hydrocephalus; Spina bifida*.

Nicotine A highly poisonous substance present in tobacco. During pregnancy it enters the bloodstream of a woman who smokes, and affects the efficiency of the placenta, usually producing a low-birthweight baby.

Non-stress tests Tests during pregnancy that do not produce fetal stress. See also *Invasive techniques*.

Notochord The cells which form the primitive nervous system.

Nucleus The central part or core of a cell which contains genetic information.

Occipito anterior The position of the baby in the uterus when the back of its head (the crown or occiput) is towards the front (anterior).

Occipito posterior The position of the baby in the uterus when the back of its head (the crown or occiput) is towards the mother's back (posterior).

Oedema Fluid retention, which causes the body tissues to be puffed out.

Oestriol A form of oestrogen. Its level in the urine or blood may be tested in late pregnancy to find out if the placenta is working well.

Oestrogen A hormone produced by the ovary.

Ovary One of the two female glands, set at the entrance of the fallopian tubes, which regularly produce eggs.

Oviduct See *Fallopian tube*.

Ovulation The production of the ripe egg by the ovary.

Oxygenate To saturate with oxygen.

Oxytocin A hormone secreted by the pituitary gland which stimulates uterine contractions and the milk glands in the breasts to produce milk.

Oxytocin challenge test A way of assessing the condition of the fetus and of the placenta, by which oxytocin is introduced into the mother's bloodstream and the reactions of the fetal heart to uterine contractions are recorded.

Palpation Feeling the parts of the baby through the mother's abdominal wall.

Paracervical Regional anaesthesia sometimes used during labour, involving a series of local anaesthetic injections around the cervix.

Partogram A chart recording the development of labour and condition of the fetus.

Pelvic floor The muscular structure set within the pelvis which supports the bladder and the uterus.

Pelvis The bones forming a girdle about the hips.

Penthrane A general anaesthetic. See also *Anaesthetic*.

Perinatal The period from the 28th week of gestation to one week following delivery.

Perineum The area surrounding the vagina and between the vagina and the rectum.

Pessary A vaginal suppository.

PET See *Pre-eclampsia*.

Pethidine (Demerol) A narcotic analgesic. See also *Analgesics*.

Pethilorfan A mixture of the analgesic pethidine and the controlling agent levallorphan. See also *Analgesics*.

Phenobarbitone See *Barbiturates*.

Phenothiazine Strong tranquillizers used in the treatment of nausea and vomiting. See also *Tranquillizers*.

Phototherapy Treatment by exposure to light, used in the treatment of jaundice.

Pituitary gland A gland set just below the brain which, among other functions, secretes various hormones controlling the menstrual cycle. In late pregnancy it releases a hormone, oxytocin, into the bloodstream, which stimulates the milk glands.

Placenta The organ which develops on the inner wall of the uterus and supplies the fetus with all its life-supporting requirements and carries waste products to the mother's system.

Placental function tests Tests to assess the condition and efficiency of the placenta. See also *Oestriol; Oxytocin challenge test.*

Placental insufficiency A condition in which the placenta provides inadequate life support for the fetus, resulting in a baby at special risk.

Placenta praevia A condition in which the placenta lies over the cervix. This part of the uterus stretches in the last few weeks of pregnancy, but the placenta cannot stretch, so it may separate; the result is antepartum haemorrhage. A woman with a complete placenta praevia is delivered by Caesarean section.

Polyhydramnios An excess of amniotic fluid in the uterus.

Posterior See *Occipito posterior.*

Post-maturity The state of the fetus in an overdue pregnancy. The skin may be dry and peeling, and the fingernails may need cutting immediately after birth.

Post-natal After the birth.

Post-partum After delivery.

PP See *Presenting part.*

Pre-eclampsia (Pre-eclamptic toxaemia) An illness in which a woman has high blood pressure, oedema, albumin in the urine and often excessive weight gain. See also *Eclampsia.*

Premature See *Pre-term.*

"Prepping" Procedures carried out to prepare the woman for delivery.

Presentation The position of the fetus in the uterus before and during labour.

Presenting part That part of the fetus which is lying directly over the cervix.

Pre-term A baby born before the 37th week of pregnancy and weighing less than 5½ lb (2.5 kg).

Primigravida A woman having her first pregnancy.

Progesterone A hormone produced by the corpus luteum and then by the placenta.

Prostaglandins Natural substances, which stimulate the onset of labour contractions. Prostaglandin gel is used to soften the cervix and induce labour.

Psychoprophylaxis A method of preparation for childbirth which is centred on techniques for breathing.

Pubis The bones forming the front of the lower pelvis.

Puerperium The four weeks following delivery.

Purse-string (Shirodkar) suture Stitches passed through and around the cervix, and then drawn tight to support the uterus when the cervix is "incompetent".

Pyelitis An infection of the kidneys. It is treated by a course of antibiotics.

Pyridoxine Vitamin B6.

Quickening The first noticeable movements of the fetus.

Rectus muscle The muscles running up the centre of the abdomen.

REM Rapid eye movement in sleep, indicating mental activity.

Respiratory depression See *Depression, respiratory.*

Rhesus factor A distinguishing characteristic of the red blood corpuscles. All human beings have either Rhesus positive or Rhesus negative blood. If the mother is Rhesus negative and the fetus Rhesus positive severe complications and Rhesus disease (the destruction of the red corpuscles by antibodies) may occur unless prevented by anti-D gamma globulin.

Rooting The baby's instinctive searching for the nipple.

Rubella (German measles) A mild virus which may cause congenital abnormalities in the fetus if contracted by a woman during the first 12 weeks of pregnancy.

Sacrum The big bone at the base of the spine, forming the back of the pelvis.

Salicylate See *Aspirin.*

Scan (Screen) A way of building up a picture of an object by bouncing high-frequency sound-waves off it. The sonar or ultrasound scan is used during pregnancy to show the development of the fetus in the uterus. See also *Transducer.*

Senna Derivatives of the cassia plant, components of many aperients.

Shared care Antenatal care shared between a GP and a hospital consultant.

Shirodkar See *Purse-string suture.*

Shoulder distocia See *Distocia, shoulder.*

Show A vaginal discharge of blood-stained mucus occurring before labour, resulting from the onset of cervical dilatation. Sign of labour.

Small-for-dates Babies who are born at the right time but for some reason have not flourished in the uterus. See also *Placental insufficiency.*

Sodium amytal See *Barbiturates.*

Sonicaid See *Doppler.*

Sperm (Spermatozoon) The male reproductive cell which fertilizes the egg.

Spina bifida A congenital neural tube defect, in which the fetal spinal cord forms incorrectly, outside the spinal column.

Spinal anaesthetic An injection of local anaesthetic into the spinal cord. Not used for childbirth in Britain, except by mistake when an epidural is given.

Spontaneous abortion See *Abortion.*

Stanislavsky technique Acting exercises for increasing body awareness and muscle control.

Stasis of milk A reduction in the flow of breast milk.

Steroids Drugs used in the treatment of skin disorders, asthma, hay fever, rheumatism and arthritis. Because they alter the chemical balance of the metabolism they may cause fetal abnormalities if used extensively during pregnancy.

Stethoscope, fetal A trumpet-shaped instrument placed against the pregnant woman's abdomen for the fetal heart to be heard.

Stillbirth The delivery of a dead baby after the 28th week of pregnancy.

Stool bulk producers Drugs to treat constipation.

Streptomycin A wide spectrum antibiotic which should not be taken in pregnancy. See also *Antibiotics.*

Stress tests Tests during pregnancy that cause stress to the fetus.

Stretch marks See *Striae.*

Striae Silvery lines that sometimes appear on the skin after it has been stretched during pregnancy.

Sulpha drugs See *Sulphonamides.*

Sulphonamides Chemicals sometimes used to combat infections. See also *Antibacterials.*

Supplementary feed Bottle feed given with breast feed.

Surfactant A creamy fluid which reduces the surface tension of the lungs so that they do not stick together when deflated. Pre-term babies may have breathing difficulties because the surfactant has not developed sufficiently.

Suture The surgical stitching together of a wound or tear.

Syntocinon The synthetic form of oxytocin, used to induce or accelerate labour.

Systolic pressure The blood pressure built up in the arteries when the heart is beating. It is the upper figure on any record. See also *Diastolic pressure.*

Tachycardia An abnormally fast heart rate in the fetus and newborn baby. This is a rate of above 160 beats per minute.

Telemetry A method of monitoring, using radio waves. See also *Electronic fetal monitoring.*

Teratogenic A general term for drugs which cause physical defects in the embryo.

Term The end of pregnancy: 40 weeks from the last menstrual period.

Termination An artificially induced abortion before the end of the 28th week of pregnancy. Sometimes used as a synonym for induction.

Test weighing A method of assessing how much breast milk the baby is taking by weighing the baby immediately before and after a feed.

Tetracycline A wide spectrum antibiotic which should be avoided during pregnancy, as it can affect the fetal teeth and bones. See also *Antibiotics.*

Thrombosis A blood clot in the heart or blood vessels.

Thrush A yeast infection which can form in the mucous membranes of the mouth or genitals.

Thyroid gland A gland in the throat which produces hormones that control the metabolic rate.

Tochodynamometer A pressure gauge attached by a belt to the mother's abdomen to record contractions.

Touch relaxation A means of releasing muscular tension by resting the hand on tense areas and drawing out the tension.

Toxaemia See *Pre-eclampsia* and *Eclampsia.*

Toxoplasmosis, congenital Toxoplasmosis is a parasitic disease spread by cat faeces. If it crosses the placenta during the first 12 weeks of pregnancy, it can cause blindness in the baby.

Tranquillizers Drugs used to calm a state of anxiety or

tension without inducing unconsciousness. Mild tranquillizers, such as Valium, may be prescribed during pregnancy, but should be avoided during labour as they can cause fetal respiratory depression. Powerful tranquillizers (along with antihistamines and hypnotics, which are sometimes used for their tranquillizing properties) should be avoided during pregnancy. See also *Barbiturates*.

Transducer   An instrument which is sensitive to the echoes of very high-frequency sound-waves bounced off the developing fetus, and which translates the information to build up an image on a television screen. This form of scan is known as ultrasound.

Transition   A point between the first and second stages of labour when the cervix has dilated to between 7 and 8 cm.

Trial of labour   A situation in which, although a Caesarean section seems necessary, the mother is allowed to go into labour in order to see if a natural delivery is possible.

Trilene   See *Anaesthetic*.

Twins   The simultaneous development of two babies in the uterus, either as a result of the production of two eggs which are fertilized independently by two sperm—dizygotic or fraternal twins—or, more rarely, as a result of one fertilized egg dividing to produce monozygotic or identical twins.

Ultrasound   See *Scan*; *Transducer*.

Umbilical cord   The cord connecting the fetus to the placenta.

Umbilical vein sampling (Cordocentesis) A fine needle is passed through the mother's abdomen into the fetal vein in the umbilical cord. The technique allows fetal blood to be tested, facilitates intra-uterine blood transfusions, and enables drugs to be injected directly into the baby.

Undescended testicle   A testicle which has failed to drop naturally from the lower abdomen into the scrotum.

Uterine action, incoordinate Irregular uterine contractions.

Uterine inertia   Weak and ineffective uterine contractions.

Uterus (Womb)   The hollow muscular organ in which the fertile egg becomes embedded, where it develops into the embryo and then the fetus.

Vacuum extractor (Ventouse)   An instrument, used as an alternative to forceps, which adheres to the baby's scalp by suction and, with the help of the mother's bearing-down efforts, can be used to pull the baby out of the vagina.

Vagina   The canal between the uterus and the external genitals. It receives the penis during intercourse and is the passage through which the baby is delivered.

VE   Vaginal examination.

Ventouse   See *Vacuum extractor*.

Vernix   A creamy substance which often covers the fetus whilst in the uterus.

Vertex presentation (VX) *See Cephalic presentation*.

Vulva   The external part of the female reproductive organs, including the labia and clitoris.

Water birth   Birth while the woman is lying or floating in water.

XX/Xy chromosomes   The chromosomes which genetically distinguish the female and male respectively.

Yolk sac   The sac which stores the nutrients for the developing fertile egg.

Index

Placenta (cont.)
at the end of pregnancy
216–220
dealing with in emergency birth
277
detachment from uterine wall
after birth 248, 296–297
effects of amniotomy on 292
expulsion after Caesarean
section 311
insufficiency of 341
praevia 125, 309
testing by urinary oestriol test
216–217
Positions for delivery 200–201
Positions for labour 193–194,
198–199, 230–231, 232–240
Posterior position 212–213
forceps delivery with 307
labour with 193–194, 257–261
turning baby in 213
Post-natal check-up see Check-up,
post-natal
Post-natal depression see
Depression, post-natal
Post-partum period 346–350
Posture 112, 115
Practising for labour contractions
see Contractions, practising
for
Practising for pushing see Pushing,
practising for
Pre-eclampsia 126–127, 298–299
Pregnancy testing 26–29
by ultrasound 202
"do-it-yourself" 27, 28–29
urine 27–28
Premature babies see Pre-term
babies
Preparation for labour see Labour,
preparing for
Presentations for birth 258
Pre-term babies 334–338
Procedures in labour 290–312
Progesterone 56–58, 66–67
Prostaglandin pessaries 298
Protein 87–88
Psychoprophylaxis 168
"Puppet on a string" relaxation
174–175
Pushing in labour 245
practising for 196–197
Pyelitis 122

R

Rapid eye movement in sleep 359
Rectus muscle 109, 111
rehabilitating 353
Reflexes, baby's
used in labour 315–316
newborn 328–329
Relationship with baby 319–329
in special care 338
Relationship with partner 35–39,
147, 152–157, 345
after losing baby 345
Relaxation 165–201
autogenic method 168
Balaskas method 170
Bradley method 168
centring down 173
Dick-Read method 167–168
Kitzinger psychosexual
approach 171
Lamaze method 168
psychoprophylaxis 168
"puppet on a string" method
174–175
Stanislavsky method 175–177
"touch" 173–174, 178–186
REM see Rapid eye movement
Reproductive organs
female 56–58, 60
female, changes after childbirth
363–365
male 56–58, 61
Respiratory distress 334–335
Responsibilities in childbearing
289
Rest 132–133
importance of in multiple
pregnancy 83
Resting breath 188
Rhesus factor 103–105
Rhythm method of contraception
367
Rooting reflex 321–322
Rubella 102–103

S

Salt intake in pregnancy 92
Scan see Ultrasound
Seconal 98
Second and subsequent
pregnancies 158–162
Senokot 100
Serenace 97
Sex, baby's 59–62
Sexual intercourse
after childbirth 363–366

Sexual intercourse (cont.)
during pregnancy 155–157
Sexual organs see Reproductive
organs
Sheath see Condom
Shoes 130
Shortness of breath 129
"Show" 228
Single mothers 37–39
Sinusitis 124
Skin, darkening 131
Sleep 132–133
Sleep patterns of newborns 359
Sleeping pills see Drugs, sleeping
pills
Smallpox vaccination see
Vaccination
Smoking 94–96
Sodium amytal 98
Soft spots on baby's head see
Fontanelles
Solid foods 355
Soneryl 98
Special care for newborn babies
334–338
Sperm 56–62
Spermicides 369
Spina bifida 91
Sponge, contraceptive 368
Spontaneous abortion see
Miscarriage
Sport 131
Stanislavsky relaxation 175–177
Start-stop labour 273–274
Steroids see Drugs, steroids
Stillbirth 342–345
conceiving after a 344–345
Stitches 248, 295–296, 363, 366
Streptomycin 100
Stretch marks 131
Sugar-loaf moulding 331
Sulphonamides 99
Support in labour 38, 267–276
Surprise delivery 276–277
Syntocinon 294

T

Technology used in labour
289–312
Teeth of pregnant woman 130
Telemetry 305
Temperature during pregnancy
102
Tests on baby in uterus 202–208
AFP screening 205–206
amniocentesis 206–207
chorionic villus sampling 207

Acknowledgments

Dorling Kindersley would like to thank the following for their help: David Ashby, Susan Berry, Sue Burt, Giovanni Caselli, Mary Chesshyre, Penny Church, Kate Duffield, Helen Dziemidko, Eleanor Enkin, Dr Murray Enkin, Jean Flynn, Jeanette Graham, Daisy Hayes, Andrew Heritage, Ken Hone, Dr Meeks Joankins, Elaine and Jerry Kingett, Tess and Jon McKenney, Chris Meehan, Kevin Molloy, MS Filmsetting Limited, Helen Sampey, Spectrum Reproductions, W Photo, Steven Wooster.

Special thanks go to the team who prepared the first edition for publication: Sybil del Strother, Ginger Weatherley, Lindy Newton, Bob Gordon and Julia Harris.

Artists
David Ashby, Giovanni Caselli, Andrew Farmer, Nicholas Hall, Shian Hartshorn, Terri Lawlor, Miriam Mills, Kevin Molloy, Howard Pemberton, Andrew Popkiewicz, Les Smith.

Photographs
The photographs on page 211, between pages 232 and 257 and on page 319 were taken by Nancy Durrell McKenna. All other photographs of mothers, fathers and their children were taken by Camilla Jessel.

The photograph on page 57 is reproduced courtesy of Cornell Medical Center, New York.

The drawings on page 263 were based on photographs in *Birth Reborn* by Michel Odent (Pantheon 1984).

The photographers and the publishers would like to thank all the parents and parents-to-be who allowed themselves and their children to be photographed for this book – especially those who so generously agreed to share the experience of the birth of their babies. They are also deeply grateful to the nurses, doctors and midwives concerned for their warm co-operation and advice. Special thanks go to all the staff of the Delivery Suite, the Special Care Unit, and the Antenatal Department of the West Middlesex Hospital, Isleworth, and to the Hounslow Community Midwife Service.

THE HOLY GRAIL OF
INVESTING

PRAISE FOR *MONEY: MASTER THE GAME*

"Tony Robbins is a human locksmith—he knows how to open your mind to larger possibilities. Using his unique insights into human nature, he's found a way to simplify the strategies of the world's greatest investors and create a simple 7-step system that anyone can use on the path to the financial freedom they deserve."

—Paul Tudor Jones II, *founder, Tudor Investment Corporation, and legendary trader with 28 consecutive years of positive returns for his investors*

"Tony Robbins has influenced millions of people's lives, including my own. In this book he offers you insights and strategies from the world's greatest investors. Don't miss the opportunity to experience the life-changing value of this book."

—Kyle Bass, *founder of Hayman Capital Management and investor who turned $30 million into $2 billion in the middle of the subprime crisis*

"In this book, Tony Robbins brings his unique talent for making the complex simple as he distills the concepts of the best investors in the world into practical lessons that will benefit both naïve investors and skilled professionals."

—Ray Dalio, *founder and co–chief investment officer, Bridgewater Associates, #1 largest hedge fund in the world*

"*Money: Master the Game* will be a huge help to investors . . . Tony Robbins dropped by my office for a 40-minute appointment that lasted for four hours. It was the most provocative, probing interview of my long career, a reaction shared, I'm sure, by the other souls with strong investment values and sharp financial minds who populate this fine book. This book will enlighten you and reinforce your understanding of how to master the money game and, in the long run, earn your financial freedom."

—*John C. Bogle, founder, the Vanguard Group and the Vanguard index funds, #1 largest mutual funds in the world*

"This book is not the typical financial book in any way. It is packed with wisdom and vital philosophies to enrich your life. A lot of books out there have more sizzle than steak to offer. Tony's is different. This book will change your life."

—Dr. David Babbel, *professor of finance, Wharton School of the University of Pennsylvania*

"In this book, Tony masterfully weaves anecdote and expertise to simplify the process of investing for readers—priming their financial education and helping them effectively plan for their future."

—Mary Callahan Erdoes, *CEO, J.P. Morgan Asset Management, $2.5 trillion in assets under management*

"Tony Robbins needs no introduction. He is committed to helping make life better for every investor. Every investor will find this book extremely interesting and illuminating."

—Carl Icahn, *billionaire activist and investor*

"A gold mine of moneymaking information!"

—Steve Forbes, *publisher of* Forbes *magazine and CEO of Forbes, Inc.*

"You can't meet Tony Robbins, and listen to his words, without being inspired to act. This book will give you the strategies to create financial freedom for yourself and your family."

—T. Boone Pickens, *founder, chairman, and CEO at BP Capital and TBP; predicted oil prices accurately 18 out of 21 times on CNBC*

"Robbins's unrelenting commitment to finding the real answers to financial security and independence, and his passion for bringing the insights of the ultrawealthy to the average man, is truly inspiring. This book could truly change your life."

—David Pottruck, *former CEO of Charles Schwab and bestselling author of* Stacking the Deck

"If you're looking for answers and you're committed to creating financial freedom for yourself and your family, then Tony Robbins is your man. Get this book, change your life."

—Farnoosh Torabi, *award-winning author of* When She Makes More: 10 Rules for Breadwinning Women

"Sitting in the back of Financial Destiny nearly twenty years ago, I was a student of Tony Robbins's who had a dream to help teach and empower one million women to be smarter with money. Thanks to Tony, a year later I would be speaking on stage at his events, writing *Smart Women Finish Rich*, and ultimately creating a program that would reach millions of women worldwide. Today there are more than seven million copies of my *Finish Rich* books in print, translated into 19 languages. Tony changes lives, and he will change yours. I, like you, will be reading *MONEY* cover to cover, and sharing it with my friends."

—David Bach, New York Times *bestselling author; titles include* The Automatic Millionaire; Start Late, Finish Rich; Smart Women Finish Rich; *and* Smart Couples Finish Rich; *founder of FinishRich.com*

"We've been selected by *Forbes* as the most innovative company in the world for four consecutive years. Our revenues are now over $30 billion annually. Without access to Tony and his teachings, Salesforce.com wouldn't exist today."

—Marc Benioff, *founder, chairman, and CEO of Salesforce.com*

"Tony's power is superhuman . . . He is a catalyst for getting people to change.· I came away with: It's not about motivation as much as it is allowing people to tap into what's already there."

—Oprah Winfrey, *Emmy Award–winning media magnate*

"Tony Robbins's coaching has made a remarkable difference in my life both on and off the court. He's helped me discover what I'm really made of, and I've taken my tennis game—and my life—to a whole new level!"

—Serena Williams, *18-time Grand Slam tennis champion and Olympic gold medalist*

"I was afraid that my success would take something away from my family. Tony was able to turn it around and show me that I've helped millions of people. Probably the most intense feelings I've ever had."

—Melissa Etheridge, *two-time Grammy Award–winning singer and songwriter*

"No matter who you are, no matter how successful, no matter how happy, Tony has something to offer you."

—Hugh Jackman, *Emmy and Tony Award–winning actor, producer*

"If you want to change your state, if you want to change your results, this is where you do it; Tony is the man."

—Usher, *Grammy Award–winning singer, songwriter, entrepreneur*

"Working with Tony Robbins, I felt unstoppable. From that moment on, there was zero doubt in my mind about what I wanted and how I was going to achieve it. I was so clear about what I wanted that I made it happen: I became world champion."

—Derek Hough, *dancer, choreographer, and five-time winner of ABC's* Dancing with the Stars

"Before Tony, I had allowed myself to be put in a position of fear. After meeting Tony, I made a decision not to be afraid anymore. It was an absolutely game-changing, life-altering experience. I'm so excited and thankful for Tony Robbins and the incredible gift that he gave me."

—Maria Menounos, *actress, journalist, and TV personality*

"What Tony really gave me, a kid sitting on Venice Beach selling T-shirts, was to take risks, take action, and really become something. I'm telling you as someone who has lived with these strategies for 25 years: I'll come back for more again, and again, and again."

—Mark Burnett, *five-time Emmy Award–winning television producer*

"What does this man have that everyone wants? He is a 6'7" phenomenon!"

—Diane Sawyer, *former* ABC World News *and* Good Morning America *anchor*

"Tony Robbins helps you take that first step to making real change in your life. I have a pretty good life, but all of us have aspects of our lives that we want to make greater. It's life-changing. It really is."

—Justin Tuck, *defensive end, Oakland Raiders,*
and two-time Super Bowl champion

"Tony Robbins knows the rhythm of success. He is an incredible source of inspiration, and his methods have improved the quality of my life. I only work with the best, and Tony is the best."

—Quincy Jones, *Grammy Award–winning musician, producer*

"Tony Robbins provides an amazing vehicle for looking at your life, mapping out a mission, and determining what's holding you back and what you need to move forward."

—Donna Karan, *legendary fashion designer, founder DKNY*

PRAISE FOR *UNSHAKEABLE*

"Remarkably, Robbins has produced a book that will appeal to both the beginner and the most sophisticated money jockey overseeing multibillions of dollars in assets. If there were a Pulitzer Prize for investment books, this one would win, hands down."

—Steve Forbes, *publisher of* Forbes *magazine and CEO of Forbes Inc.*

"Robbins is the best economic moderator that I've ever worked with. His mission to bring insights from the world's greatest financial minds to the average investor is truly inspiring."

—Alan Greenspan, *former Federal Reserve*
chairman under four sitting presidents

ALSO BY TONY ROBBINS

Life Force

Unshakeable

Money: Master the Game

Unlimited Power

Awaken the Giant Within

Notes From a Friend

THE HOLY GRAIL OF
INVESTING

THE WORLD'S GREATEST INVESTORS REVEAL THEIR
ULTIMATE STRATEGIES FOR FINANCIAL FREEDOM

TONY ROBBINS

WITH CHRISTOPHER ZOOK

SIMON &
SCHUSTER

London · New York · Sydney · Toronto · New Delhi

First published in the United States by Simon & Schuster, Inc., 2024
First published in Great Britain by Simon & Schuster UK Ltd, 2024

Copyright © Tony Robbins, 2024

The right of Tony Robbins to be identified as the author
of this work has been asserted in accordance with the
Copyright, Designs and Patents Act, 1988.

1 3 5 7 9 10 8 6 4 2

Simon & Schuster UK Ltd
1st Floor
222 Gray's Inn Road
London WC1X 8HB

Simon & Schuster: Celebrating 100 Years of Publishing in 2024

www.simonandschuster.co.uk
www.simonandschuster.com.au
www.simonandschuster.co.in

Simon & Schuster Australia, Sydney
Simon & Schuster India, New Delhi

The author and publishers have made all reasonable efforts to contact
copyright-holders for permission, and apologise for any omissions or errors
in the form of credits given. Corrections may be made to future printings.

A CIP catalogue record for this book
is available from the British Library

Hardback ISBN: 978-1-3985-3315-8
Trade Paperback ISBN: 978-1-3985-3316-5
eBook ISBN: 978-1-3985-3317-2

Interior design by Ruth Lee-Mui

Printed and Bound in the UK using 100% Renewable
Electricity at CPI Group (UK) Ltd

MIX
Paper | Supporting
responsible forestry
FSC® C171272

DISCLOSURE

This book is designed to provide information that the author(s) and the interviewee(s) believe to be accurate on the subject matter it covers, but it is sold with the understanding that neither the author(s) nor interviewee(s) nor the publisher are offering individualized advice tailored to any specific portfolio or to any individual's particular needs or rendering investment advice or other professional services such as legal or accounting advice. A competent professional's services should be sought if one needs expert assistance in areas that include investment, legal, and accounting advice. This publication references performance data collected over many time periods. Past results do not guarantee future performance. Additionally, performance data, in addition to laws and regulations, change over time, which could change the status of the information in this book. This book solely provides historical data to discuss and illustrate the underlying principles. Additionally, this book is not intended to serve as the basis for any financial decision; as a recommendation of a specific investment advisor; or as an offer to sell or purchase any security. Only a prospectus and/or a private placement memorandum and/or a limited partnership agreement may be used to offer to sell or purchase securities, and the legal documents must be read and considered carefully before investing or spending money. No warranty is made with respect to the accuracy or completeness of the information contained herein, and both the author(s), the interviewee(s), and the publisher specifically disclaim any responsibility for any liability, loss, or risk, personal or otherwise, which is incurred as a consequence, directly or indirectly, of the use and application of any of the contents of this book.

Legal disclosure: Tony Robbins is a minority passive shareholder of CAZ Investments, an SEC registered investment advisor (RIA). Mr. Robbins does not have an active role in the company. However, as shareholders, Mr. Robbins and Mr. Zook have a financial incentive to promote and direct business to CAZ Investments.

CONTENTS

PART 1

CHAPTER 1

THE SEARCH FOR THE HOLY GRAIL

Over the past ten years, I have had the privilege of authoring two #1 *New York Times* bestsellers on the topic of personal finance (*Money: Master the Game* and *Unshakeable*). They succeeded not because I am an expert in the field, but because I have one important thing . . . **access!**

Over four decades of work as a life and business strategist have earned me personal access to many of the world's most brilliant financial minds, many of whom happen to also be fans of my work. From Alan Greenspan to Ray Dalio to the late Jack Bogle to Paul Tudor Jones and countless others, I've had the pleasure of sitting down with titans of investing to extract the tools, tactics, and mindset that anyone, at any stage of life, can—and should—apply in the quest for financial freedom. Their generosity of time and principles helped me form a trio of "playbooks," and I encourage you to read the others if you have not already.

I began my deep dive into money mastery after the 2008 financial crisis when the world's economy was on the brink of collapse due to the reckless behavior and greed of a relative few. Nobody escaped the economic pain, myself included. My phone rang off the hook as I tried to coach friends and family through job loss, home loss, and obliterated retirement plans. From the barber to the billionaire, the storm tore through everyone's life with varying degrees of devastation.

Never one to be a victim of circumstance, I decided to take immediate action to become part of the solution. With a healthy dose of cynicism, I set out to answer the most important question facing a financially illiterate society. . . . **Is the game *still* winnable?** In the post–financial crisis world, could the typical investor win the game of investing? Could the average person become financially free even if they never sell a business, inherit a nest egg, or scratch a winning lottery ticket? **After interviewing over fifty of the world's most brilliant financial minds and boiling down hundreds of hours of interview recordings, the answer to the question was a resounding YES!** Although the titans I interviewed shared very different approaches, they all agreed on certain immutable laws and steps the investor needs to take (and avoid) to win the game.

Although there are many, the four of the most common principles among these greats were as follows:

1. **First, don't lose.** As Warren Buffett succinctly says, "Rule #1, don't lose money. Rule #2, see rule #1." If you lose 50 percent in a bad investment, you will need 100 percent return just to get back to even. One thing that all the most successful investors have in common is they know that they will indeed lose at times (yes, even Buffett). To mitigate this, they never get too far over their skis and risk too much on any one investment, which leads to the second principle . . .

2. **Second is the core principle of asset allocation—**i.e., spreading your assets among different types of investments with varying risk-reward ratios. When I sat down with the late David Swensen, the man who took over Yale's hundred-year-old endowment and grew it from $1 billion to $31 billion, he explained that your asset allocation accounts for 90 percent of your investment returns! **As you will learn, the ultra-high-net-worth and biggest institutional investors have a drastically different approach to asset allocation than the typical investor.**

3. **Third, wherever possible, look for opportunities with "asymmetric" risk reward.** Simply put, these investors look for investments where the potential reward far exceeds the downside risk. My good friend, and legendary trader, Paul Tudor Jones will only place trades where he believes the risk/reward ratio is 5 to 1.

He will risk $1 to make $5. This way he can be wrong more times than right and still succeed.

4. **Fourth and final is the principle of diversification.** You want to own a wide variety of investment *types* (stocks, bonds, real estate, private equity, private credit, etc.) across various asset classes, geographies, time frames, etc. . . .

My guess is, if you are reading this book, you are NOT the average investor. You (or your clients) have likely accumulated enough of a financial foundation to move beyond these core tenets and add some additional fuel to your investing fire. **As you will see in the pages ahead, alternative investments have generated outsized returns for the world's most astute investors. For example, between 1986 and 2022, private equity as a whole has outperformed the S&P 500 by over five percentage points annually (9.2% compared to 14.28%). That's a 50 percent plus greater return. Private credit, an alternative to bonds, has generated two to three times the income/yield.***

It is undeniable that the smart money uses high-quality alternative investments as the engine for greater diversification and accelerated growth. This is what the titans of finance do with their own personal capital. I know because they've told me. Over decades, I have fostered ongoing relationships with these "masters of the financial universe." For this book, we have interviewed a baker's dozen, thirteen of the most successful alternative investment managers that have generated extraordinary, compounded returns rarely seen by the general public. Folks like . . .

- **Robert F. Smith**—Founder of Vista Equity Partners, Smith is considered the most successful enterprise software investor of all time, managing over $100 billion and generating outstanding returns relative to the company's peers (over the past twenty-plus years). Vista's portfolio spans more than eighty companies, with ninety thousand employees. As of March 2023, the portfolio companies that Vista owns generate over $25 billion in annual revenue!

*https:/moneymade.io/learn/article/private-credit-vs-bonds

- **Bill Ford**—A pioneer in the world of private equity, Ford has grown General Atlantic's assets under management from $12 billion to more than $80 billion and expanded the firm's global presence. Over its history, General Atlantic has invested more than $55 billion in over five hundred companies within technology, financial services, healthcare, and life sciences.
- **Vinod Khosla**—Founder of Khosla Ventures, Vinod Khosla is a legend in venture capital. His early stage investments in disruptive technology companies propelled him from an immigrant with little means to a self-made multibillionaire. He is famous for turning a $4 million investment in Juniper Networks into a $7 billion windfall for his investors.
- **Michael B. Kim**—The "Godfather of Asian Private Equity," Kim has created the largest independent private equity firm in Asia, with a focus on China, Japan, and Korea. His astounding success for investors has also made him South Korea's wealthiest man.
- **David Sacks**—Founder of Craft Ventures, cohost of the *All In* podcast and original member of the PayPal "mafia" with Elon Musk and Peter Thiel. Sacks has invested in over twenty unicorns, including Affirm, Airbnb, Eventbrite, Facebook, Houzz, Lyft, Palantir, Postmates, Slack, SpaceX, Twitter, and Uber.

And many more!

These individuals play the money game at the highest possible level. Yet they play the game with an edge. **The edge of access!** Their status and professional networks **provide them with extraordinary access to unique investments that, frankly, 99.9 percent of people won't typically have access to.** Perhaps even more compelling, they tend to perform well in good times and in bad. **These investors have shown over and over that while they're not immune to the ups and downs of the economy, they know how to thrive, not just survive, during the economic winters.** Instead of being content to ride out the storm, they go shopping when prices are down. To them, a storm is an opportunity. It's one thing to make money when the markets rise; a rising tide lifts all boats. But to generate returns when markets are choppy? That's what separates the good from the great.

One of the "hall of fame" players in the smart money game is my friend **Ray Dalio.** Ray is the Tom Brady of "macro" hedge fund managers. The G.O.A.T. For those who aren't familiar, Ray is the founder of Bridgewater, the world's largest hedge fund ($196 billion*), with an astounding track record in both good times and bad. He was one of the first who predicted the Great Recession and took advantage. **In 2008, while the market melted down 37 percent, Bridgewater bucked the trend and gave investors a gain of 9.4 percent.** Their "Pure Alpha" fund has averaged over 11 percent annually since its inception in 1991 (compared to approximately 7 percent for the S&P 500).[†] Needless to say, when you consistently beat the market by wide margins for more than thirty years, you become one of the most sought-after hedge funds for the world's wealthiest. From the sovereign wealth funds of the richest countries on earth to the most influential billionaires, Ray is on speed dial to many of the world's most powerful.

In some of our earliest conversations, nearly a decade ago, he taught me what he considers the most important principle of successful investing. A principle of diversification to maximize reward and minimize risk. A principle that has guided my own personal investment strategy and, more important, provided the inspiration for the title and content of this third and final book in my financial trilogy: what Ray calls the **"Holy Grail" of investing.** A simple yet profound strategy that is rarely put into practice. I'm going to tell you how it works.

First, it's important to understand that most traditional portfolios hope to **reduce risk and maximize upside through the core principle of diversification: Don't keep all your eggs in one basket.** But unfortunately, this doesn't always work out as expected. This is because many of today's traditional investments are "correlated," which simply means they move up or down in unison.

Correlation measures how much investments move together in the same direction (positively correlated means they move in unison, while negatively

*https:/whalewisdom.com/filer/bridgewater-associates-inc
†https://www.reuters.com/business/finance/bridgewaters-flagship-fund-posts -gains-32-through-june-2022-07-05/#:~:text=In%20the%20first%20half%20 of%202022%2C%20the%20S%26P%20500%20was,an%20average%20of%20 11.4%25%20annually.

correlated means the opposite). Then you have varying degrees of correlation, meaning they move together but not in complete lockstep. **For example, stocks and bonds are generally uncorrelated. When stocks go down, it is helpful if bonds go up to give you some protection. However, correlations are always changing and can often throw some unexpected curveballs.**

In 2022, stocks and bonds both dropped simultaneously. While this is somewhat rare, it may not be an anomaly going forward. AQR, one of the world's most successful algorithmically driven hedge funds, believes that *"macroeconomic changes—such as higher inflation uncertainty—could lead to a reappearance of the positive stock–bond correlation of the 1970s,'80s, and '90s."* In August of 2023, a Bloomberg headline came across my screen that read *"Bonds are a useless hedge for stock losses as correlation jumps."** The article noted that the positive correlation between treasury bonds and stocks is at its highest reading since 1996!

And it's not just stocks and bonds that have been shown to positively correlate lately. Publicly traded REITs (companies that own and manage real estate portfolios) tend to have a strong degree of correlation with stocks, despite being a different asset class. Between 2010 and 2020, REITs had an 80 percent positive correlation with the S&P 500.† Adding real estate to your portfolio might seem like a smart way to diversify, but in fact, your REITs and stocks are more likely to dance in unison. To be fair, REITs performed quite well over the period from 2010 to 2020. But here's the key point: when stocks came crashing down in 2022, REITs also took a tumble. So much for keeping a portion of your eggs safe and sound.

Likewise, cryptocurrency, often touted by its supporters as "digital gold" and a hedge against market volatility, has been moving in lockstep with stocks in recent years. In 2022, Bitcoin took a 65 percent plummet, from

---

*https:/www.bloomberg.com/news/articles/2023-08-02/bonds-are-useless-hedge
-for-stock-losses-as-correlation-jumps
†https:/www.investopedia.com/articles/financial-advisors/030116/reits-still
-viable-investment.asp#:~:text=REITs%20Offer%20Diversification%20
Pluses,through%20the%20end%20of%202020.

approximately $47,000 to nearly $16,000. The same year, stocks entered a bear market and inflation took root. A Georgetown University study found that "crypto assets followed the market's lead even more closely during periods of high market volatility, such as the Covid pandemic and Russia's invasion of Ukraine."* Who knows how it will perform in the future, but it certainly failed as a hedge of protection most recently.

The problem is that today most traditional diversification strategies tend to involve adding more and more positively *correlated* investments! Some investors, knowingly or not, seem to have given up on finding uncorrelated investments to help manage big swings. **One frightening headline recently came across my newsfeed: Older Americans, those in retirement or near to it, are forgoing bonds for protection and betting most or all of their future solely on stocks.** This is quite the gamble. The *Wall Street Journal* reported of clients at Vanguard, "one-fifth of investors 85 or older have nearly all their money in stocks, up from 16% in 2012. The same is true for almost a quarter (25%) of those ages 75 to 84."† **This abandonment of diversification is a high-stakes roll of the dice, but unfortunately, many American's feel they have no choice when their "diversified" portfolios don't act the part.**

So what is the "Holy Grail" of investing?

According to Dalio, the Holy Grail is a portfolio of eight to twelve *uncorrelated (or non-correlated)* investments which, together, will dramatically reduce risk without sacrificing returns. **Dalio demonstrates that a portfolio structured this way can reduce risk by as much as 80 percent while maintaining the same, or similar, upside potential.** He puts it this way:

> *"From my earlier failures, I knew that no matter how confident I was in making any one bet I could still be wrong—and that proper*

---

*https://www.institutionalinvestor.com/article/b8xcj9wtd1gjb5/Crypto-Is-Becoming-More-Correlated-to-Stocks-And-It-s-Your-Fault#:~:text=They%20found%20that%20the%20correlation,January%202016%20and%20January%202021
†https://www.wsj.com/articles/it-isnt-just-boomers-lots-of-older-americans-are-stock-obsessed-ca069e1a

diversification was the key to reducing risks without reducing returns. If I could build [a portfolio filled with high-quality return streams that were] properly diversified (they zigged and zagged in ways that balanced each other out), I could offer clients an overall portfolio return much more consistent and reliable than what they could get elsewhere."

This sounds simple enough, right? But there's one big challenge: Where do we gain access to so many high-quality noncorrelated investments? **Turns out, access is the tricky part—and that's precisely why I wrote this book.**

THE BILLIONAIRE'S PLAYBOOK

Since embracing the Holy Grail philosophy, I've developed a portfolio of publicly traded stocks combined with a large dose of unique alternative investments. For example, I am a fan of **private real estate** that affords steady income and tax benefits (e.g., depreciation). I am a fan of **private equity,** as nearly every great private company needs capital to grow, and private equity returns have consistently outperformed stocks quite handily. **Private credit,** when managed correctly, has proven to be a great alternative to bonds, especially at a time when rates are surging. I also sprinkle in some venture capital; it's higher risk but is always pushing the edge of innovation and disruption, which resonates with my inner entrepreneur.

As you may already know, once you reach a certain net worth, the SEC invites you into a special club. **They deem you an accredited investor when you achieve $200k in annual income or $1 million net worth (not including your home).** This affords you access to some, but not many, alternative investments. **The good news: At the time of this writing, there is legislation pending that will allow anyone to take a test to become "accredited" regardless of their net worth (more on this later in the chapter).**

The SEC bumps you up to **qualified purchaser** status when you have $5 million in total investments. This opens up the entire universe of alternative investments. But here's the rub . . . Just because you qualify, doesn't mean you can get in the door. **In fact, many of the best alternative investments are closed to new investors or, like a new, limited-edition exotic car, they sell out before they even hit the market.**

Earlier in my investing career, I experienced this frustration numerous times. The truth is, there seems to be simply too much demand—too much cash looking for a home in alternative investments. And who seems to be first in line? The biggest check-writing institutions in the world. Sovereign wealth funds, college endowments, and mega family offices throw their weight around and elbow out the individual investor.

My co-author, Christopher Zook, shared a funny anecdote from early in his career . . .

> *I had been waiting for the fax all morning. Yes, this was more than twenty-five years ago, in the days of the ancient facsimile machines. I had received a call the day before notifying me of the good news that my clients and I would be able to invest in a certain flagship private equity fund. We had been trying for years (to no avail) to get access to this specific manager as every fund was "over-subscribed."*
>
> *Now the time had come to find out just how much of an allotment we would be given. We were finally going to get into the cool kid's club. My clients and I had pooled together approximately $5 million of our own money to invest. The fax machine began to make that unmistakable racket and spit a thin paper scroll onto the floor. My heart sank as I read that our total allotment (aka our allocation) was a whopping $250k. It was like getting a reservation at the best pizza place in New York only to be served a single slice to share with a crowded table of friends.*

AN INSATIABLE APPETITE

The appetite for alternative investments in the areas of private equity, private real estate, and private credit seems insatiable. According to research firm Preqin, in 2006 approximately $1 trillion was being managed by private equity managers. **Today there is more than $6 trillion allocated to**

**private equity, with projections that the market will grow to more than
$14 trillion by 2025.** This "Great Migration" to alternatives seems unstoppable as the smart money is clearly re-allocating. Fewer public equities, more private equity. Less public credit (bonds), more private credit. Fewer public REITs, more private real estate.

My suspicions were confirmed by my dear friend and advisor Ajay Gupta. Ajay has represented my family for over fifteen years. By way of background, Ajay is the former (now retired) chief investment strategist for one of the largest independent investment advisors in the U.S., with approximately $200 billion in assets under management. He sold to one of the larger private equity firms, and he now runs Robbins Gupta Holdings, our joint family office.

One day, Ajay handed me a report from KKR, one the world's largest private equity firms. They had recently conducted a survey in which the world's wealthiest family offices, endowments, and pension plans all gave a peek under the hood. I was surprised by the survey participants' willingness to share their current asset allocation. It bears repeating that our asset allocation, how much we choose to invest and in which asset class, is the greatest driver to our investing success. This is a universal truth among every single investor I have interviewed over the past two decades.

As I scoured the KKR report, this was the most shocking statistic I saw . . .

Ultra-high-net-worth families (those with over $30 million) have nearly 46 percent of their assets in alternative investments, with only 29 percent in publicly traded stocks (see figure on page 13).* Alternative investments used to be a side dish in a portfolio; now they are more like the meat and potatoes. **And get this . . . of the money these groups had in alternatives, more than half (52 percent) was invested in private equity, with the balance nearly equally divided between real estate (25 percent) and hedge funds (23 percent).**

*https:/www.kkr.com/global-perspectives/publications/ultra-high-net-worth-investor-coming-age

ALTERNATIVES AS A % OF TOTAL ASSET ALLOCATION

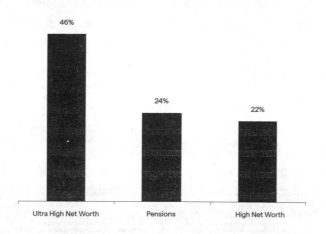

Data as of March 2017. Source: Willis Towers Watson Global Pension Assets Study 2017, publicly available private wealth manager data. KKR 2017 HNW Survey

Why this profound shift toward alternatives? Well, these tea leaves don't take much reading . . .

On a global level, private equity outperformed public markets in thirty-five of the last thirty-five years (between 1986 and 2020)!*

As you can see in the figure below, as an entire asset class, private equity[†] produced average annual returns of 14.28 percent over the thirty-six-year period ending in 2022. The S&P 500 produced 9.24 percent. That's more than five percentage points greater in annualized returns, which translates into runaway compound growth. To put that into perspective, between 1986 and 2022, a hypothetical $1 million investment in the S&P 500 would have grown to **$26,310,105.** Not too shabby. But the same $1 million would have grown to a whopping **$139,604,229** with private equity! Keep in mind, these returns are the average for the private equity industry as a whole, but many firms have achieved far greater returns.

*Global PE vs MPME MSCI All Country World Index—Cambridge and Associates
[†]As measured by the Cambridge Private Equity Index. https:/www.cambridgeassoci ates.com/insight/us-pe-vc-benchmark-commentary-first-half-2021/

SIMULATED PERFORMANCE OF PRIVATE VS. PUBLIC EQUITY

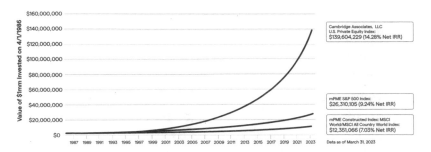

The index is a horizon calculation based on data compiled from 1,505 funds, including fully liquidated partnerships, formed between 1986 and 2022.

Private indexes are pooled horizon Internal rate of return (IRR) calculations, net of fees, expenses, and carried interest. CA Modified Public Market Equivalent (mPME) replicates private investment performance under public market conditions. The public index's shares are purchased and sold according to the private fund cash flow schedule, with distributions calculated in the same proportion as the private fund, and mPME NAV is a function of mPME cash flows and public index returns. "Value-Add" shows (in basis points) the difference between the actual private investment return and the mPME calculated return. Constructed Index: MSCI World/MSCI All Country World Index: Data from 1/1/1986 to 12/31/1987 represented by MSCI index gross total return. Data from 1/1/1988 to present represented by MSCI ACWI gross total return. The timing and magnitude of fund cash flows are integral to the IRR performance calculation. Public indexes are average annual compounded return (AACR) calculations which are time weighted measures over the specified time horizon and are shown for reference and directional purposes only. Due to the fundamental differences between the two calculations, direct comparison of IRRs to AACRs is not recommended.

Sources: Cambridge Associates LLC, MSCI, Standard & Poor's.

PAST PERFORMANCE IS NOT A GUARANTEE OF CURRENT OR FUTURE RESULTS. Historical examples shown do not, nor are they intended to, constitute a promise of similar future results. The information and statistical data contained herein are taken from sources believed to be accurate and have not been independently verified by CAZ Investments. Historical examples are provided for information purposes only and are not intended to represent any particular investment.

As you can see, private equity performs well in good times, but it has also weathered many a storm. When we look at recent history, there have been three major market downturns (and subsequent recoveries). **The Internet Bubble Bursting of 2001, the Great Recession of 2008, and the COVID Pandemic of 2020. In all three cases, the "peak to trough" declines of the S&P 500 were far steeper when compared to private equity.** A study by Wall Street behemoth Neuberger Berman summed it up nicely: *"Private Equity historically experienced a less significant drawdown, and a quicker recovery, than public equities in all three [downturns]."* **Case in point, in 2021, on the heels of the pandemic and a global supply chain crisis, private equity had one of its best years, producing pooled returns of 27 percent.† This is just slightly below the stellar performance of 33 percent in year 2020.‡** Private equity heavyweight Bain Capital wrote,

*As tracked by the US Private Equity Buyout Index of Cambridge and Associates
†https://www.mckinsey.com/industries/private-equity-and-principal-investors/our-insights/mckinseys-private-markets-annual-review
‡McKinsey Private Markets Annual Review 2021

"Private Equity blew the doors off in 2021 as trillions in pandemic-related stimulus produced a historic surge in dealmaking and exits."*

This explains the massive shift to private investments. They simply offer a greater opportunity set. You have to fish where the fish are. Increasingly, companies don't need to go public like they used to. They can get access to capital without dealing with the barrage of legalities and procedures that come with becoming publicly traded. In fact, according to the *Financial Times*,† **the number of publicly traded U.S. companies has fallen by nearly half, to around forty-four hundred, since the peak in 1996. That's just forty-four hundred companies for investors to consider,** and we all know many of them are mediocre at best when it comes to profitability, growth, and future prospects. **In fact, back in 2009, 81 percent of public companies were profitable (post IPO); by 2021, only 28 percent were profitable (post IPO).‡**

By contrast, there are tens of thousands of private companies growing, innovating, and disrupting. Approximately 80% of all companies with more than $100 million in annual revenue are privately held. **When you look at the total value of all publicly traded companies globally, you may be shocked to learn that the value of all companies held by private equity funds dwarfs public stocks by nearly 4 to 1!§**

Now, this is not to say that public stocks don't have a role in our portfolios. They absolutely do, and they are an important ingredient in many Holy Grail portfolios (mine included). Stocks allow anyone and everyone to become owners of our economy, not just consumers. You can own Apple, not just an iPhone. **And stocks allow us to access thousands of global companies, doing business in numerous geographies, with the ability to buy/sell their shares at the click of a button.** There is *not* a competition between public equity vs. private equity. **They are complementary!**

Numerous studies have shown that adding private equity to a typical stock-and-bond portfolio has the tendency to not only reduce volatility,

*https://www.bain.com/insights/private-equity-market-in-2021-global-private-equity-report-2022/
†https://www.ft.com/content/73aa5bce-e433-11e9-9743-db5a370481bc
‡https://www.statista.com/statistics/914724/profitable-companies-after-ipo-usa/
§Prequin: World Federation of Exchanges

but also increase returns.* This is what it's all about: reducing risk (volatility) while increasing returns.

DEMOCRATIZATION

In addition to the many trillions already flowing into private markets, regulations are now being loosened.† Soon, hopefully, average investors will be able to invest in private markets through their 401k plans. This could add more rocket fuel to an already soaring industry. **And here is the best news of all. . . .**

As I mentioned earlier, it has always struck me as unjust that only those with enough net worth can participate in high-quality alternative investments. Heck, many wealthy individuals have become wealthy by selling a business—that doesn't necessarily mean they're sophisticated investors. On the other hand, there are plenty of folks with smaller checkbooks out there who have the desire and intelligence to play ball in private markets. It's my humble opinion that if someone is smart enough and understands the risks, they too should be able to join in. Luckily, Congress agrees. **At the time of this writing, the House of Representatives has passed a bipartisan bill that will allow anyone, even if they fall short of the wealth requirements, to become an accredited investor if they pass a test.** My hope is that by the time you are reading this, the legislation will have become law, and everyone will be able to access great opportunities.

As the bright future of alternatives began to take shape in my mind, my instinctual question was, **How can we participate in this broader trend of the trillions of dollars seeking out alternative investments? How can we ride this wave, this tsunami, beyond just being content with getting access to a handful of opportunities?**

Turns out, many of the best and brightest financial wizards have already figured out a way, and I assure you, most people have never heard of it.

---

*https://www.nb.com/en/global/insights/investment-quarterly-asset-matters-private-equity-and-your-portfolio
†https://news.bloomberglaw.com/daily-labor-report/private-equity-firms-are-winning-the-fight-for-your-401k

MY BIG BREAKTHROUGH

As many of you know, I have been coaching my dear friend Paul Tudor Jones for over two decades. Paul is considered by many to be one of the top ten hedge fund managers in history as well as an incredible philanthropist—his Robin Hood Foundation has donated more than $3 billion toward fighting poverty in New York City.

Nearly a decade ago, one of Paul's former partners (who has since launched his own successful fund) and I were having a conversation about alternative investments. I was commiserating over the common challenge of not being able to get into some of these great investment opportunities. **Getting an "allocation" in a highly sought-after private equity fund is the wealthy person's version of getting past the velvet rope at a hot new nightclub.** More often than not, people are left out in the cold, cash in hand.

Buddy to buddy, he decided to divulge what he does with a good chunk of his personal money. My ears immediately perked up. Here was a top-pedigree fund manager about to tell me what he does with his treasure. Like Tiger Woods telling you where he gets fitted for golf clubs. Better take note! He explained he personally uses a firm out of Houston, Texas, that was taking a slightly different approach. Texas? I thought a guy from Greenwich, Connecticut, would be using an elite firm from Wall Street, London, or Singapore. But like most brilliant financial folks that breathe rarified air, he would be found on the road less traveled.

He spent the next hour educating me on one particular approach that sounded like an exact answer to my question.

How can one participate in this seismic shift toward alternative investments?

As I scribbled notes as quickly as I could, he explained that instead of fighting to get into a fund as an LP investor (a limited partner), there was sometimes a way in which one could join up and become an owner of the entity known as the GP (general partner). The general partner is the actual operating company, also known as the asset manager, who manages the underlying investment funds. The GP is typically owned by the founders and the C-suite employees. *"One can actually buy a piece of the GP!?"* I asked, somewhat baffled. He nodded with the grin of a tenured veteran. This was a paradigm-shifting moment for me. After all, many of the financial titans I have interviewed became billionaires by owning their own asset management firms (and thus being the general partner).

It's no secret that the highest concentration of billionaires on the Forbes 400 are not from big tech or oil and gas. They are the moguls of private equity, private real estate, and private credit. These are the financial masterminds that often generate massive wealth for their clients (the LPs) and for themselves (the GP). These are the people that have mastered the game of money and manage tens or even hundreds of billions. These are the people that, given the opportunity, I want to sit shoulder-to-shoulder with as partners. Could it *really* be possible that I could own a sliver of their business of managing money, especially as trillions are flowing into alternatives? The answer, it turns out, is yes. This world, known as "GP stakes," has become increasingly popular among big institutional investors over the past decade but is only beginning to see mainstream coverage. A story in the *Wall Street Journal** summed it up with a headline: **"Buying Stakes in Private Equity Firms, Not Just Their Funds, Pays Big."**

Why does it pay big? . . .

The client of these firms, the investors/limited partners, pays the GP at least two different fees. First, they pay a management fee that is typically around 2 percent per year on the investment amount. Second, if the investment fund performs well, the firm typically gets 20 percent of the profits. So for the top-tier firms that make investors happy, the firm itself is a wealth-building machine for its founders and owners.

As my brain worked to process what I had just learned, I launched into a game of twenty questions. He boiled it down for me, explaining that becoming a minority/passive owner in an asset management firm (the GP) has three distinct benefits . . .

1. Cash Flow—Predictable income is a wonderful thing. If you run a business, you know how rare, and wonderful, it would be to know in advance that you'll have stable, predictable revenue for years.

---

*https:/www.wsj.com/articles/buying-stakes-in-private-equity-firms-not-just-their-funds-pays-big-1542542401#

Welcome to private asset management. A typical asset management company (GP) manages numerous funds on behalf of investors (LPs). The investors often agree to "lock up" their investments for longer periods of time in exchange for the potential of outsized returns. This creates a long-term horizon for the manager, giving them plenty of time to make the best possible decisions. While putting the investors' money to work, the manager is entitled to a management fee (typically 2 percent per year of all dollars invested). **When investors agree to specific "lock-up" provisions (typically between five and ten years), the asset manager knows they will generate predictable and contractually secured management fee revenue throughout that period. That translates to reliable cash flows for the owners of the firm—in this case, that would include us!** Even better, this steady stream of income will also rise as the firm increases the amount of the money it manages!

2. A Piece of the Profits—As mentioned, in exchange for making their investors money, **the GP receives a handsome percentage of the profits, typically 20 percent, on all the capital they manage.** This is known as carried interest or performance fees. Making money on other people's money, while still giving them great benefits, is a win-win situation that can create outsized returns for the GP (us again!).

3. Diversification—In the wise words of Nobel Prize laureate Harry Markowitz, **"diversification is the only free lunch."** Owning part of the asset management company gets you tremendous diversification. **Why? Because a typical firm manages numerous funds.** Each of those funds has a unique start date or "vintage," which means they are spread across various market/economic cycles. Beyond that, each of those funds contains its own portfolio of companies/investments spread across various industries, sectors, geographies, and stages of growth. This is diversification at the highest level.

There is a fourth and final overarching benefit. Sometimes, a private asset manager will go public or be sold to a larger firm. In this case, the owners, with whom you and I sit shoulder-to-shoulder, may receive a multiple on the equity they own upon the sale. There are a lot of additional benefits that you will learn as you read on, but needless to say, at this point in my conversation I was leaning forward in my chair. It all sounded very appealing (and a little too good to be true). I couldn't help but wonder . . .

Why in the world would a private asset manager sell a stake in their business?

His answer? You need to meet Christopher Zook.

HOUSTON, WE HAVE AN OPPORTUNITY

I was taken aback when I first met Christopher because the first thing he told me was that he was inspired to start CAZ Investments more than thirty years ago after listening to my original *Personal Power* cassette series. (Yes, those ancient cassettes!) It was 1991, and he was working for a major Wall Street bank at the time. He drew a line in the sand and told his wife that within ten years he would launch his own firm. In 2001, true to his word, he launched CAZ Investments—only to be greeted by the post-9/11 bear market. But as you will learn, Christopher is not easily discouraged, and he is an incredibly effective hunter of opportunity, regardless of the market conditions. In addition, he is extremely well respected in the world of alternative investments. **In 2019, the Texas governor appointed him to the state's Pension Review Board, where he serves as the chair of the Investment Committee.**

CAZ Investments is not your typical investment firm. A refreshing candor and a get-your-hands-dirty work ethic are reflective of its deep Houston roots. Under Christopher's more than two decades of leadership, they have forged their own unique path. They had to, because Christopher knew that in order to compete with the big institutions, he'd need to rethink the old, stale model.

Over more than two decades, Christopher and his team have built a network of high-net-worth families that bind together as an "insti-vidual" and use their collective purchasing power to negotiate access to unique investment opportunities. Once again: Access is the name of the game when it comes to alternative investments. As Christopher explained it to me, *"Our role is to wake up each and every day and curate exclusive opportunities for our network of investors to consider (they can always choose to invest or pass). In return, our investors have agreed to lock arms as a unified front. We pool our money for each new opportunity and write a single check that will move the needle as much as any major institution."*

Today, the firm has more than three thousand high-net-worth clients across the globe as well as numerous investment advisory firms who participate in its curated opportunities. The firm has grown to be one of the top 200 allocators to private equity investments worldwide, ahead of major institutional investors like the endowments of Columbia, Duke, and MIT.*

Over dinner, Christopher briefed me on the numerous investment opportunities that have been funded by his network over two decades. I was thoroughly impressed at the scope of timely and thematic opportunities the firm brought to its network. From shorting subprime mortgages during the housing crisis to energy opportunities during an oil crash to buying fractional interests in NBA, NHL, and MLB teams. This list goes on. But it's in the world of "GP stakes" where **CAZ has grown to become one of the biggest players, with ownership in more than sixty prominent private equity, private credit, and private real estate firms that span the globe.**

After extensive due diligence, I became a client, and my family office partner, Ajay Gupta, joined the CAZ board. Over the years, the more we spent time with Christopher and his team, the more we fully appreciated his firm's method of reviewing more than fifteen hundred opportunities each year only to invest in a handful of the best and most timely investments. The team at CAZ was instrumental in helping me assemble my own personal Holy Grail portfolio. I decided I wanted to amplify Christopher's voice and wisdom within my network, and Christopher afforded us the opportunity to join a few dozen others in becoming minority shareholders in CAZ itself. I am not actively involved in the business, but I am passionate about being armed with knowledge about these investment trends, how and where the smart money is moving, and how to capitalize on timely opportunities.

*Source: PitchBook Data as of April 2022

LET'S SPREAD THE WORD

In the middle of 2022, the world was undergoing a major sea change as the era of zero interest rates came to an abrupt end. Persistent inflation, a supply chain crisis, the Ukraine-Russia war, and numerous other factors were sending ripples through the markets. I reached out to my Rolodex of financial titans (many of whom we interviewed for this book), and none were fearful. In fact, they were excited. They sensed opportunity. **For example, while bonds were crashing, rising rates were actually *helping* private credit firms (some of which I own a GP stake in) make substantially higher returns because the rates they charged adjusted upward. Prior to rate hikes, many businesses were accustomed to paying 5–6 percent to private credit lenders; once rates took off, those same businesses were required to pay north of 11 percent as the loans adjusted to the current market rate. Same borrower, same loan—but with a surge in profitability for the lender.**

I recall sitting on my back patio, staring at the ocean, feeling grateful for the principles that Dalio and numerous others had taught me along my journey. Grateful for the strategies I was deploying in my own Holy Grail portfolio. Grateful for the platform I have to share all the insights I have learned through my access. In that moment I knew that Christopher and I needed to write this book. There was simply too much important and empowering material for us to share. Too many interesting strategies to be revealed and explored. Too many voices of seasoned and successful veterans that needed to be heard. I picked up the phone and told Christopher that we needed to write this book for two reasons . . .

1. Between the two of us, we have unique access to many of the most brilliant and successful minds in the alternative investment space. **Folks like Barry Sternlicht, founder of Starwood Capital. Sternlicht has built a global real estate investing empire that spans thirty countries, with more than $115 billion in real estate assets under management. Folks like Wil VanLoh, founder of Quantum Energy, one of the largest private energy investors, with an astounding track record (despite investing**

in an asset class that has major volatility). **Speaking with him was incredibly interesting, especially considering the world's focus on renewables and the opportunities they present.** These incredibly engaging conversations embody the timeless truth that **knowledge is power when it is not only learned but applied.**

2. **Even in the circles of high-net-worth families and the advisors that represent them, there is a general lack of awareness regarding the breadth of the possibilities alternative investments represent.** This was once true for me, and I know it's true for many successful people in my inner circle. Far too often, individuals working with well-intentioned advisors only see a limited set of opportunities, which are often preselected by the advisor's parent company. **We want everyone, investors and advisors alike, to be equipped with the tools, awareness, and opportunities that many of the world's greatest investors are using for their own Holy Grail approach.**

SEVEN UNIQUE STRATEGIES

So let's dive in! This book is divided into two parts. **In Part 1, each chapter is dedicated to a specific alternative investment strategy (or category).** We selected *seven unique strategies* that have created extraordinary returns over long periods of time. **Each of the seven strategies is an entirely uncorrelated investment opportunity, which is why we selected them from the universe of potential options.** We will launch this rocket by first covering GP stakes in more depth. Then we'll reveal how investors can now take part in one of the only legal monopolies in North America: professional sports ownership. Relatively recent rule changes have opened the door for investors to own a portfolio of numerous teams across Major League Baseball, Major League Soccer, the National Basketball Association, and the National Hockey League. These teams have incredibly durable revenue models that have the advantage of powerful tailwinds. **They've evolved from making money off beer and butts in seats to being multifaceted global empires that command billions in streaming rights, sponsorships from those involved in legalized gambling, hotel and restaurant**

revenue, and much more. This is just a taste of what's to come. Every one of the other strategies we present is equally exciting!

In Part 2, we sit down with an all-star lineup of expert asset managers. Collectively, they manage more than half a trillion dollars! They generously took the time to share their origin stories and the instincts, techniques, principles, and strategies that guided them to unimaginable success. We ask each of them to share what *they* think of as the Holy Grail of Investing. Their answers are diverse, surprising, and profoundly wise. So let's turn the page and begin with GP stakes to discover why tens of billions in smart money are chasing this strategy. . . .

A Note from the Authors: We, Christopher and Tony, wrote this book in tandem, conducted the interviews together, and collaborated to bring you the absolute best information. Thus, instead of passing the baton between chapters or paragraphs in the remainder of the book, we decided to write with one clear and unified voice.

CHAPTER 2

GP STAKES

A PIECE OF THE ACTION

"The best route to riches? Finance and investments. More than a quarter of the wealthiest people in America made their money in this industry, which includes hedge funds, private equity and money management."
—*Forbes**

"Do you want to bet on a horse or own a piece of the entire racetrack?"

Since CAZ Investments began investing in GP stakes nearly ten years ago, we have acquired a minority stake in more than sixty different household names in private equity, private credit, and private real estate. All told, we have billions of investor capital allocated to GP stakes, making our firm one of the world's biggest investors in the space. I tell you this not to brag, but because I have an intimate understanding of the many good reasons why a firm would be willing to sell a minority passive interest to investors—particularly if those investors are strategic. We will dive into those reasons in the pages ahead, but first, let's explore what makes these asset management businesses so attractive.

*https://www.forbes.com/sites/rachelsandler/2021/10/26/nearly-half-of-americas
-richest-billionaires-have-fortunes-in-these-two-industries/?sh=79ec65d7445b

THE REVENUE ENGINE

When buying a stake in any type of business, we have to understand its revenue engine. How will the business make money? Let's take a minute to understand the business behind the business.

Most private asset management firms are set up in the same way. The fund(s) they manage is (are) pooled capital from numerous investors. When setting up an investment fund, the firm will often use a legal entity called a limited partnership, and thus, the investors are considered limited partners in the fund. Then there is the asset manager, which is responsible for managing the money. This is the general partner (GP). The GP is the asset management firm/entity that is responsible for creating, marketing, and managing multiple fund vehicles.

To recap, the GP is normally paid at least two distinct sources of revenue for their management services:

1. **Management Fee**—An annual management fee that can range between 1 percent and 3 percent of the total capital being managed (2 percent is the standard at the time of this writing). This is paid regardless of how the fund performs.
2. **Performance Fee**—Sometimes called a carried interest or incentive fee, a performance fee is paid out as a percentage of the fund's investment gains. The standard incentive fee is 20 percent of the profits.

Let us take a simple example of just how attractive these asset management businesses are from a revenue standpoint. Imagine ABC Private Equity, a hypothetical firm that manages a $1 billion fund. The firm will receive 2 percent a year (or $20 million) in management fees, typically for a minimum of five years. That is a total of $100 million in revenue that is as close to guaranteed as one can contractually get. This management fee revenue creates consistent cash flow payments for the general partners (which includes you if you own a stake in the GP). A GP stake will typically produce annual cash distributions in the range of 5 percent to 10 percent annually, beginning on day one of the investment. So, for instance, if you were to make a $1 million investment in a GP stake, it would generate between $50,000 and $100,000 annually in management fee income payments. (For the investment nerds like us, this means it effectively eliminates the J-Curve.*)

Next, let's assume the fund does a reasonably good job and doubles the value of its portfolio over those same five years—$1 billion becomes $2 billion. The investors (LPs) are happy, and the firm is entitled 20 percent of the $1 billion profit. That's $200 million. Not too shabby.

So let's summarize the total revenue potential for the GP. . . .

$100 million in management fees

+

$200 million in performance fees

=

$300 million in gross revenues (per billion in asset managed)

These are incredible economics that are rarely seen in any business on the planet—and that's why we love being partners in these asset management firms. Keep in mind, the example above is relatively conservative. Many top-tier managers have generated much higher returns, resulting in extraordinary revenue for the general partner.

On top of extremely attractive revenue models, these businesses are also highly efficient and extremely profitable when it comes to economies of scale. **A firm of twenty people managing $1 billion can double the size of the funds it manages without coming close to doubling its head count.** I am personally aware of a firm with a mere seventy-five employees that has $47 billion under management. Remember the example above with $300 million of potential revenue per billion? You can quickly do the math and see why these firms that manage multiple billions can be wealth-generation machines for the general partner (and those of us who own GP Stakes).

*In typical private equity investing, the J-Curve means investors in a fund initially show "losses" while their capital is being put to work to buy assets in the fund. This is followed by a reversal once the gains start to materialize, creating a J-like curve on a graph.

To capitalize on economies of scale, most successful firms will launch a new fund every one to three years, adding an additional revenue stream to the firm with each new fund. Firms that have been around for decades, and have multiple business lines, may have twenty or more funds under management. **This is where the math becomes exponential, and we start to understand how the Forbes 400 is dominated by the founders of these types of firms.**

SMOOTHING OUT THE RIDE

In the southwest of France, near the Garonne River, exists one of the most renowned winemakers in the world . . . *Château Lafite Rothschild*. They produce some of the most expensive Bordeaux wines ever made. As a Bordeaux lover myself, I can tell you that certain years, or vintages, are much better than others. The same is true with private investment funds.

Firms will typically raise a new fund every few years, a new "vintage." Each new fund will purchase a diverse set of investments. For example, each private equity fund may acquire somewhere between five and fifteen companies. Without knowing how each of those companies/assets will perform or the economic times/market cycle in which the fund was launched, the performance of each vintage can vary drastically.

But unlike wine, as an investor, you do not know which vintage will be great until *after* you have already spent the money. You have to invest first—and then wait—before seeing the results of the "harvest." **This is precisely why most institutional investors will be invested across numerous vintages managed by numerous managers. This strategy offers greater diversification and ensures exposure to as many vintages as possible.** Needless to say, this is a tall order for an individual investor. Even very wealthy individual investors do not have pockets deep enough to participate in numerous vintages across multiple managers, so they naturally end up with more concentrated risk by investing in a small number of funds.

By contrast, by owning a GP and moving up the ladder to the position of the general partner, one inherits what we call "Vintage Diversification." Why buy one vintage year from Lafite Rothschild when you

can buy a piece of the whole vineyard? Since a typical firm has numerous funds and vintages, the GP stake in said firm will earn its proportional share of profits generated from their entire lineup of funds (past, present, and future). If one specific vintage or fund does not perform as well as expected, it is less damaging to the GP stake, as the firm will typically have numerous funds with different vintages.

To take it one step further, different asset management firms focus on different industries and geographies. From consumer tech to real estate to healthcare to aerospace to enterprise software to hospitality and beyond. While many of these firms are located in the U.S., some are located, or have offices, across the globe. They hunt far and wide for opportunities. While some economies are suffering, others are thriving, so being unconstrained by geography is a huge advantage.

Now imagine a portfolio of dozens of GP stakes with some of the world's most effective and proven asset managers across various market segments. This is the approach our firm takes, and it provides numerous benefits, including . . .

- Diversification by the types of firms you own (private equity, private credit, private real estate, etc.)
- Diversification in the unique expertise (e.g., aerospace, healthcare, software, retail, fintech . . .) of the funds in which you own a GP stake.
- Diversification by the geographic focus (U.S., Europe, Asia, etc.) of the firms in which you own a GP stake.
- Diversification across the vintages/funds (past, present, and future vehicles) managed by the firms in which you own a GP stake.
- Diversification among the portfolio of companies (or assets) within each individual fund/vintage managed by the firms in which you own a GP stake.

Thus, a portfolio of numerous, high-quality GP stakes can offer investors consistent cash flow along with "asymmetric" risk/reward. That's fancy for limited downside with greater upside. This level of uncorrelated diversification is financial heaven for those looking to align with Dalio's Holy Grail philosophy. In fact, many of the nation's top investment advisors are beginning to utilize GP stakes in their clients' portfolios. Creative Planning (managing more than $200 billion in assets), repeatedly ranked #1 investment advisor in the country by *Barron's* and CNBC, is a big believer in alternative investments and GP stakes. "GP stakes are a very unique way for our clients to get access to top-tier private equity from an entirely different angle and experience the benefits of ownership" said Peter Mallouk, president of Creative Planning.

ENTERPRISE VALUE

One final benefit of buying a GP stake derives from the growth in the enterprise value of the firm itself. As the firm grows its "assets under management," and corresponding revenue, the value of the GP stake can be expected to increase. Consulting giant McKinsey reported that *"total assets under management across private markets reached an all-time high of $9.8 trillion as of June 30, 2021, up from $7.4 trillion 12 months prior."* Most industry experts agree this trend is likely to continue.

When private equity, private credit, or private real estate firms raise new capital to manage, this corresponds to increased cash flows from management fees (typically 2 percent annually) as well as increased potential for profit distributions for performance fees. Some of the firms we have purchased stakes in over the years have grown reasonably well, while many more have grown exponentially. One of the private equity firms in which we own a stake had $13 billion under management when we bought it; today they are managing more than $100 billion! The exponential revenue from the management fees and performance fees has made this an extraordinary business to own.

So how does one realize the growing value of the GP stake? Well, this naturally leads to the question *"What happens if I need to get out? How can I get liquidity in the future?"* Outside of the income stream paid to investors, it is true that GP stakes are generally considered illiquid. That said, there are a couple of ways to generate liquidity should you want to sell your position . . .

1. Certain vehicles will periodically provide a "tender offer" for your ownership position. This simply means they will buy you out at the current "net asset value," or NAV, of your position.
2. You will likely be able to sell your positions in a "secondary" transaction depending on the quality of the asset. This means you could sell your position to a third party for a mutually agreed upon price. This is a common occurrence in the alternative investment space (and a topic we cover in more depth later in Chapter 9).
3. Many firms are eventually acquired by other industry players, which creates a harvest event for all the owners of the business. This is often at a significant multiple on the business's profits.
4. Some firms choose to go public, which provides owners of GP stakes with publicly traded stock.

LEAD WITH ALIGNMENT

This all sounds good so far, right? But if you're like me, you might be wondering about the elephant in the room . . .

> *Why in the world would a successful private equity*
> *firm, private credit firm, or any private asset*
> *manager sell a piece of their business?*

We have to rewind a clock a bit to find the answer. The year was 2013. Bain Capital, one the largest private equity firms in the world, had just announced that it was raising more than $4 billion for their first new fund since the 2008 financial crisis. But what could have been just another typical announcement sent shock waves into the private asset management industry. **Bain boldly declared that it would put $800 million of its own capital into the fund.** This was capital that belonged to Bain's general partners, a group made up of Bain executives and partners that ride the elevator every day. **They were signaling to the world that they were willing to put their money where their mouths were. If they win, then you win; if they lose, then you lose too.** Remember, the backdrop to this bold announcement was a financial industry that had nearly imploded thanks to the reckless behavior of many Wall Street firms who brought our economy to the edge of collapse. **In an age of unaccountability, Bain had stepped up and declared that serious personal capital commitments were the way of the future for investors that were understandably trigger-shy.** They were willing to lead with alignment.

To many, Bain Capital launched a new era. Today, following their example, it's customary for firms (the GP) to invest a significant amount of their own personal capital in every fund they manage. This can be tens or even hundreds of millions in each fund/vintage.

In practice, this approach becomes very cash-intensive for these firms. Let's say XYZ Private Equity makes a 5 percent commitment of their own GP capital into each and every fund they launch. That means that for every $1 billion raised from investors, XYZ has to pony up and invest $50 million of their own cash. If they launch a new fund every two to three years, and each fund is larger than the last, these firms can easily run into a cash crunch—especially since it can take five to ten years for each fund to fully liquidate and return the rewards back to investors (including the firm's GP). Ironically, they become victims of their own success. **The better the firm does—i.e., the more funds they raise—the more capital they have to come up with. Enter GP stakes.**

When a firm sells a minority-interest GP stake, there is a clear "use of proceeds" established. That means the firm is committed to doing something specific with the proceeds from selling the GP stake. Most typically, the proceeds are used to help fund the customary "GP commitments" to the funds they manage.

Thus, investing in GP stakes is never a cash-out-and-sit-on-the-beach-sipping-piña-coladas situation. These investments are structured with alignment to add fuel to a rocket already in orbit. The GP stake investor wins by owning a piece of a high-quality operating business, and the firm wins by bringing in much needed capital that will help accelerate the growth in enterprise value.

Despite good reasons as to why an asset management firm might sell a piece, **the world of GP stakes is relatively small.** After all, the universe of high-quality private asset managers is very limited, and the percentage of

their firms they are willing to sell averages about 18 percent.* A *Forbes* article†
from 2022 explains it well:

> *Opportunities are rare—even within the institutional space. Access*
> *for retail investors will likely always be extremely rare—at best—*
> *but can be invaluable as a financial vehicle: affording performance*
> *that is not only uncorrelated, but generates unmatched absolute*
> *risk-adjusted performance. Nothing else comes even close.*

The author is spot-on. GP stakes are indeed rare and always finite in capacity. **Moreover, access to GP stakes in a business is generally limited
to investors who have long-standing relationships with said firm, as the
management teams are understandably cautious as to who they want
as their minority partners.** One thing is for certain, as the world of private
asset management continues to grow, there will undoubtedly be more high-
quality firms that will be selling a minority interest.

**For individuals who want to access a portfolio of GP stakes, there
are only a handful of vehicles available.** If you are looking for more information on GP stakes, feel free to reach out to our team by visiting us at
www.WhyGPStakes.com.

ADDING MORE VALUE THAN ANYONE ELSE

I have lived my life, both personally and professionally, with one core guiding principle: Do more for others than anyone would ever expect. **Add
more value than anyone could possibly imagine, and you will have
raving fans, not just satisfied clients.** If you have been to any of my live
events, where we spend twelve-plus hours a day in full immersion, you
know this to be true. When interviewing the most successful investors in
the world, there is an important distinction between the traders and the
private equity folks. Traders are looking for arbitrage. They are looking to

---

*http:/arc.hhs.se/download.aspx?MediumId=4842
†https:/www.forbes.com/sites/forbesfinancecouncil/2022/11/18/gp-stakes-what
-you-should-know-about-designer-financial-structures/?sh=3957bbbd57a2

create "alpha," or added returns, by buying and selling assets at the right exact time.

Private equity folks take a different approach, one that is more aligned with my life philosophy. They aim to buy good businesses and make them better. Once they buy a business, they look for all of the ways in which they can add value to the company. Whether that means taking advantage of economies of scale, bringing in new leadership, improving supply chain procurement, implementing stronger best practices etc. . . . In the early days of private equity, it is true that there were ruthless takeovers of distressed companies, but the industry has evolved in the many decades since. **The very best in the world today are looking to grow good businesses.** This was exemplified in the interview with Robert Smith of Vista Equity Partners, which you'll find in Chapter 10. His firm has spent more than two decades creating a playbook for all of the companies they acquire. The playbook is a proven set of systems and tools that will undoubtedly add value to any company lucky enough to become part of the Vista ecosystem. This is why I have a kinship with the incredible souls we have interviewed for this book. They truly care about the businesses and the employees they partner with. They are brilliant at engineering added value, and they are rewarded handsomely for doing so—as are their investors.

Now it's time to jump into the exciting world of professional sports ownership. **These conglomerates have outperformed the S&P 500 over the last decade and are incredibly resilient during difficult economic times.** But until recent rule changes, ownership was limited to the biggest billionaires. **Then, the game changed!** Turn the page, and let's discover another uncorrelated investment and the power of professional sports ownership . . .

CHAPTER 3

PRO SPORTS OWNERSHIP

SWINGING FOR THE FENCES

"Sports have the power to change the world. It has the power to inspire, the power to unite people in a way that little else does."
—Nelson Mandela

In March of 2012, the Los Angeles Dodgers made headlines by selling for an eye-popping record price of $2 billion. The most recent comparable sale was that of the storied Chicago Cubs, which went for "just" $850 million. The new Dodgers ownership group included my dear friend and partner Peter Guber (co-owner of the Golden State Warriors and LAFC, the Los Angeles Football Club), Mark Walter (CEO of financial powerhouse Guggenheim Partners), and NBA hall-of-famer Magic Johnson.

Most economists expected the Dodgers sale price to be closer to $1 billion. On the surface, $2 billion seemed well outside the ballpark of reality, and the experts took immediate issue with it. Andrew Zimbalis, an acclaimed sports economist and college professor, scoffed at the sale, saying: "Keep in mind, in addition to the price, the new ownership group will have to invest something in the neighborhood of $300 million to refurbishing Dodger Stadium and that price does not include $150 million for the surrounding real estate. At the end of the day, you have to question this deal."

Mark Rosentraub, a professor of Sports Management at the University of Michigan, didn't hold back in his scathing criticism, saying: "It's the craziest deal ever; it makes no sense. [The price] is over $800 million more than what pencils out for a profitable investment for a baseball team. If making money doesn't count, this is a great move."

Having had a front row seat to Peter's brilliance in business for the past thirty years, I knew there had to be more to the story. First, a little background: Peter is the former CEO of Sony Pictures and founder of Mandalay Entertainment. **His legendary movies include** *Midnight Express*, *Rain Man*, *Batman*, *The Color Purple*, *Gorillas in the Mist*, *Terminator 2*, *Groundhog Day*, *City Slickers*, *A Few Good Men*, **and many more!** In addition to being cinematic classics (receiving a cumulative fifty Academy Award nominations), **his films have grossed more than $3 billion worldwide.**

I reached out to Peter and asked what he was cooking up. Why would he be willing to pay such an astronomical price? He said, "Tony, I don't want to spoil the surprise. Just wait till you hear the upcoming announcement in the news and then give me a call." I don't know what I'd expected; of course, a legendary movie producer would leave me with a cliffhanger!

The sports economists and various talking heads were served a giant slice of humble pie as they read the press release. . . .

"Dodgers and Time Warner agree to more than $7 billion TV deal."*

This was the largest TV deal in sports history—even more eye-popping when you remember it was solely for the *local television* rights and the formation of a new regional Dodgers Network. **A $2 billion acquisition for $7 billion in expected revenue less than one year after the purchase.** The world of sports was floored. In the decade that followed, the Dodgers became a baseball powerhouse, delivering their home city a World Series title in 2020, their first in more than thirty years.

VANITY OR VALUE

For much of the last century, a sports franchise was the ultimate vanity purchase. Any billionaire can buy a plane or a yacht, but there are only thirty (or thirty-two) sports teams in each of the major leagues (NBA, MLB, NFL,

*https://www.cbssports.com/mlb/news/report-dodgers-time-warner-agree-to-more-than-7-billion-tv-deal/

NHL, and MLS). As we will uncover here, there have been relatively recent rule changes (as of late 2019), that have opened the door for very specific types of investment funds to buy a minority stake in not only one but numerous teams. Whether you are a sports fan or not, these global businesses have some unique characteristics that make them extremely attractive as part of one's Holy Grail strategy.

That said, a sports team is more than a trophy asset. There's something much deeper and more meaningful about it. Owning a team means owning a place in our culture. Sports transcends color or creed. It transcends our borders. It transcends socioeconomic status. It binds us together with friends and family. It gives us a tribe to root for as they go to "battle" on the field. Sports give us reprieve from the daily grind. A chance to win no matter how hard our day has been. **With winners and losers, triumphs and tragedies, sports are an undeniable part of the heartbeat of humanity.** They also happen to be incredibly lucrative.

Through much of the twentieth century, sports were almost exclusively an in-person live event business. Revenue from ticket sales and concessions were the main drivers of value. But media revenue was always important, even from the earliest days. **In 1897, the first "sale" of broadcast rights took place.** The baseball teams got Western Union to offer free telegrams for their traveling players in exchange for allowing their games to be telegrammed into saloons. Western Union ultimately started paying teams for telegram rights. Patrons in saloons nationwide waited with bated breath to see the updated scores posted every mid inning. Many team owners were worried that telegrams would decrease ticket sales, but in reality, the media got the assist in exploding baseball's popularity. The forever marriage between sports and media was solidified.

After telegrams, radio and newspaper coverage became integral to sports and their fanatics. People from all walks of life huddled around radios to listen to the crackled sounds of their favorite team in the heat of battle. **Then, on August 26, 1939, came the first televised baseball game.** Announcer Red Barber called a game between the Cincinnati Reds and the Brooklyn Dodgers. **This was at a time when there were only about four hundred television sets in the entire New York area! In 1946, just seven years later, the New York Yankees became the first team in history to** sell their local television broadcast rights, for $75,000, or about $1.14 million in today's dollars. By this time, the number of TV sets in U.S. homes had grown to eight thousand. This rapidly increased to 45 million homes by 1960!

In 1979, a channel entirely dedicated to sports was launched. Many predicted its failure, but ESPN gained immediate traction. Twenty-four seven coverage shifted sports into another gear. **Fast-forward to 2002, and the media rights for baseball exceeded "gate revenue" for the first time in history.***

The last two decades have seen an explosion of technology, all of which has added fuel to the sports business fire. High-speed internet, social media, smartphones, and streaming services have shrunk the globe and brought unprecedented accessibility to nearly any game, anywhere. Sports has evolved from a ragtag business of hot dogs and ticket stubs to a global content production and distribution machine.

MONEYBALL

Sports as an "asset class" is a relatively new concept. Only since the early 2000s have leagues and their teams grown into sophisticated global enterprises. Before we look under the hood of these multifaceted empires, let's explore their performance from an investor's point of view.

Between 2012 and 2022, the S&P 500 returned approximately 11 percent annually. The Russell 2000 (an index comprised of small cap stocks) returned 8 percent annually. Over the same period, **the big four leagues (NBA, MLB, NFL, and NHL) combined generated a staggering 18 percent compounded return (See chart on page 39).** What's more, there is very little leverage used (per league policy), so these returns are not "juiced up" in any way.

Even more interesting is the fact that the performance of sports franchises seems to have very little correlation with the public markets. (For the investment wonks, the correlation was 0.14 between 2000 and 2022.) **Low leverage and low correlation are a very attractive one-two punch for any Holy Grail portfolio.**

*https:/eh.net/encyclopedia/the-economic-history-of-major-league-baseball/

ANNUALIZED RETURN FROM 2012–2022

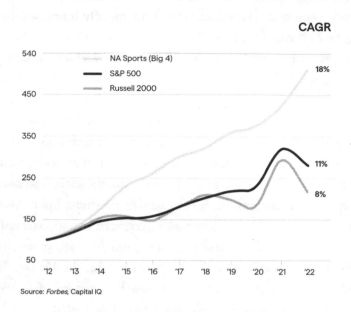

CAGR

NA Sports (Big 4)
S&P 500
Russell 2000

18%

11%

8%

Source: *Forbes*, Capital IQ

Let's dive a little deeper . . .

Between 2002 and 2021, the average price for an NBA team rose 1057 percent! By comparison, the S&P 500 returned a total of 458 percent over that period. Moreover, 2023 was a blockbuster year for record-breaking NBA transactions . . .

- **The Phoenix Suns sold for a record $4 billion to my friend and mortgage mogul Mat Ishbia.**
- **Milwaukee Bucks owner Marc Lasry sold a minority stake that put a $3.5 billion value on the team.**
- **Michael Jordan sold his majority stake in the Charlotte Hornets for $3 billion (while still holding on to a small minority position!). This was more than ten times his original investment of $275 million, made in 2010.**

Other leagues have also offered great returns (based on previous and current sale prices). **Major League Baseball teams generated an average total return of 669 percent between 2002 and 2021, and the NHL generated**

467 percent over the same period. North American Major League Soccer, the new kid on the block, is now considered the fifth major league and hit a major milestone in 2023 with its first $1 billion valuation, for the LAFC (Los Angeles Football Club).* Full disclosure: We (Peter Guber and Tony) were founding investors in the launch of LAFC, and we are so proud of the team winning the 2022 MLS Cup in Hollywood fashion with a penalty kick shootout!

As we enter an era of higher inflation, wealth preservation and purchasing power are the name of the game. In this regard, sports franchises seem to be highly defensive investments. (Yes, we plan on using as many sports analogies as possible in this chapter.) Looking to history, we can see that sports have thrived during other inflationary periods, like the 1970s and early 1980s. During the stretch from 1968 to 1982, the S&P 500 generated a 7 percent annualized return, while the enterprise value of the Big 4 teams grew at a 16 percent annualized growth rate. **Case in point: in August of 2022, the Denver Broncos were sold for a North American sports franchise record of $4.65 billion during the fastest interest rate hiking cycle in U.S. history.**

Bottom line, over the past hundred years, these leagues have survived pandemics, lockouts, world wars, player strikes, depressions, recessions, and everything in between. They are incredibly durable assets. The leagues and their teams are evolving before our eyes, and the opportunity to partake is finally open to investors like us.

> *"I don't know which SAAS (software as a service) company*
> *will be around in 5 years, but I know that 50 years from*
> *now, there will be a World Series in October."*
> —Ian Charles, Arctos Sports Partners

MULTIPLE STREAMS OF INCOME

When looking at a sports team as an investment, there are two main revenue categories: league revenue and team revenue. Let's break these

---

*https://bleacherreport.com/articles/10063920-lafc-tops-forbes-list-of-mls-team-values-1st-billionbillionbillion-dollar-franchise

down and explore why teams have such economic resiliency, making them great assets to own in a Holy Grail portfolio. (And don't worry, I will explain how we can get access in the pages ahead.)

1. Teams Receive a Portion of League Revenue—The leagues have always been responsible for negotiating the national (and international) broadcast rights and sponsorships (i.e., the deep voice that tells you "The Ford F-150 is the official truck of the NFL"). **League revenues are divided equally between all the teams, so they work together to extract the highest possible price for the broadcast rights and sponsorship.** And recent changes in consumer behavior have given the leagues more leverage. **Networks and their advertisers are becoming increasingly desperate as "cord cutting" is eroding their ability to reach their target customers via cable television. In other words, the number of people watching cable is dropping. Live sports are the only broadcasts that buck this trend. Sports are easily the highest-rated programs on all networks. As a result, advertisers covet sports programming because live TV is nearly the only place where large audiences will be willing to watch ads. In 2019, ninety-two of the top one hundred highest-rated programs on TV were sporting events.*** The leagues know this. And they've leveraged this dynamic into massive media rights contracts that drive revenue to the leagues. **A second driving force is the increasing popularity of North American sports throughout the rest of the world,** from Europe to China. The NFL will have a record five regular season games on European soil during the 2023 season. The NBA schedule now includes games in Mexico City, Japan, and Paris. North American sports are also going viral worldwide on social media; **the NBA recently surpassed more than 75 million followers on Instagram, and 70 percent of those followers are located outside of the United States.**

*https:/www.sportsbusinessjournal.com/Journal/Issues/2021/01/11/Media/Top-100 .aspx

The third driving force behind surging league revenues is the streaming wars. Apple, Amazon, Netflix, and YouTube are battling it out to become the dominant streaming player, and all of them covet the rights to live sports. **Not only do sports attract viewers, they also require very low production cost relative to coming up with the latest binge-worthy series. You don't need actors, you don't need an expensive set, you just set up the cameras and go.** The cumulative annual broadcast rights for the Big 5 leagues totaled $7.6 Billion in 2014.**It is estimated that this figure will be $16.6 billion in 2024.** As the streaming wars wage on, sports will easily be the biggest beneficiary.

2. Teams Generate Their Own Revenue—In addition to their sizeable annual revenue share from the league, each team has numerous other ancillary revenue sources that they keep for themselves. As you will see, beers and butts in seats are only two pieces of this profitable pie . . .

    Local Media—Local television has a ratings problem. They are victims of market disruption that is attacking from all angles (streaming, YouTube, social media, etc.). Frankly, sports are a lifeline for these antiquated local networks. **Compared to typical programming, sports generate two to four times the ratings. And since every team retains the revenue from selling their local media rights, this can be quite lucrative. (Just think back to that $7 billion deal for the local LA Dodgers Network.)** Many teams have followed LA's lead by creating their own local networks or partnering in joint ownership deals with local television networks.

    Real Estate—**Many sports teams own their venue and pick up all the additional revenue from concerts, events, e-sports, and more.** Brilliantly, many teams have also bought up much of the surrounding real estate. **The neighborhood around a stadium or ballpark where there can be hundreds of events annually is a fun and energetic environment for young professionals with disposable income.** From parking garages to hotels to apartments to retail, the teams are quickly becoming vertically integrated to capture as much of the peripheral revenue as possible.

Licensing/Sponsorships—When I (Christopher) walk around the Astros ballpark in Houston, I marvel at the number of local sponsorships. Signs of local businesses are plastered everywhere, including the name of the stadium itself, "Minute Maid Park." Local restaurants, breweries, and coffee shops are included in many venues and receive massive credibility by being the official "fill in the blank" for their local team. This team connection lends to measurable brand loyalty.

Tickets/Concessions—Last time I went to a game, I saw people paying $12 for a hot dog. The line was twenty people deep and nobody complained about the price. **These teams have perfected the science of sales to a captive audience who seem not to mind—or are at least willing to accept—the astronomical prices.** In 2008, New York Yankees and Dallas Cowboys owner Jerry Jones announced a joint venture called Legends Hospitality. They realized their teams were so good at maximizing food, beverage, and merchandise sales that they should offer their management services and strategies to other venues/teams around the globe. They leverage economies of scale, sophisticated logistics tools, and consumer behavior data analytics to lead teams and their venues into the twenty-first century. **The point is that these teams operate at the highest level of retail sales expertise and know exactly how to get all the juice out of the proverbial orange.** Today, the company has clients across the NFL, MLB, and the NBA, and they've also expanded to UFC (Ultimate Fighting), Wimbledon, and numerous Premier League Soccer venues.

Luxury Boxes and Suites—For decades, luxury boxes have provided high-margin foundational income streams for sports team. My friends Peter Guber and Joe Lacob, and our partners at the Golden State Warriors, broke the mold with their recently opened state-of-the-art sports and entertainment arena, the Chase Center. This $1.4 billion work of art sits right on Mission Bay and incorporates eleven acres of shops, restaurants, and bars, as well as a five-acre waterfront park. The contemporary venue is as nice as any five-star hotel and creates an elevated, dare I say luxurious, experience. With over two hundred live events and games per year, they have created a cash cow. Their luxury suites go for as much as $2.5 million per year and require a minimum contract commitment of ten years. Silicon Valley tech companies and Venture Capital firms fought tooth and nail to get their hands on a finite number of suites, making it the hottest ticket in town. From valet parking to suites catered with champagne and sushi buffets, teams are leaning into elevated VIP experiences that command much higher ticket prices.

Gambling—In 2018, the Supreme Court ended a ban on the expansion of the sports gambling industry. Whereas **sports gambling was once confined to the sports books of Vegas, as of August 2023 it is now legal in thirty-five states.** By all accounts, this is a modern-day gold rush. **In 2021, sports gambling doubled, with over $57 billion wagered.*** From TV commercials to endorsements to jersey patch sponsors, the increased advertising income from sports betting companies has added significant revenue for leagues and teams alike. While I am personally apprehensive about the societal implications of legalized gambling, the ship has sailed, and gambling will only become an increasingly inextricable part of professional sports.

A SEAT IN THE OWNER'S BOX

Becoming an owner in a professional sports team is no small feat. First and foremost, the league will vet you from every angle. Are you a moral risk? A headline risk? A financial risk? For many years, the league required owners to be individuals. They had once allowed institutions and media companies (e.g., Disney owning the Anaheim Mighty Ducks), but such firms proved unreliable as owners due to issues in their primary businesses and frequent

*https://www.americangaming.org/new/2021-commercial-gaming-revenue-shatters-industry-record-reaches-53b/

turnover among their management. So, for many years, ownership was limited to mega-wealthy captains of industry like Steve Balmer (Microsoft), Dan Gilbert (Rocket Mortgage), Joe Lacob (Kleiner Perkins), Charles Johnson (Franklin Templeton), and so forth.

Then, in 2019, Major League Baseball changed their policy. They cleverly realized that their teams, these platforms, had evolved into highly sophisticated enterprises with valuations beyond what even the wealthiest of the wealthy might be willing to pay. **Furthermore, while most teams had a single controlling owner, there were numerous smaller individual owners/investors who were along for the ride but didn't have any operational control. These individuals, many of whom were older, needed a path to liquidity, either for diversification reasons or estate planning.**

So MLB passed a new rule to allow certain types of investment funds to purchase a minority stake in a team so long as a long list of criteria were met and, most importantly, so long as the firms avoided conflicts of interest. Initially, many expected this rule change to open the floodgates for private equity firms who, for the reasons outlined in this chapter, would love an opportunity to invest. **However, numerous hurdles made many firms ineligible. For example, they were prohibited from owning any other businesses that had a conflict (e.g., sports gambling or sports agency).** Heck, many of the biggest moguls in private equity already had a personal stake in a team, thus disqualifying their firms immediately. When the dust settled, only a handful of private equity firms remained eligible. Those firms have since raised and deployed billions in capital to buy minority interests across all major sports leagues (with the NFL being the last remaining to open its doors to fund investors).

Today, qualified individual investors now have a path to ownership in professional sports. Instead of investing in a single team, some of these pooled vehicles hold a diversified basket of numerous teams across all the eligible major leagues **(MLB, the NBA, the NHL, MLS, and the Premier League).** *Bloomberg* **reported that the Fenway Sports Group (which owns the Boston Red Sox, the Pittsburgh Penguins, Liverpool), the Sacramento Kings, the Golden State Warriors, and the Tampa Bay Lightning (NHL) are just a few of the organizations that have brought**

on a private equity investor.[*] And according to PitchBook, more than a third of Europe's Big 5 soccer leagues are now backed by private equity.[†]

Holding numerous teams, across multiple leagues and geographies, creates significant uncorrelated diversification. And as a bonus, owning a share of a team can offer tax benefits as depreciation or amortization may flow through to investors in the fund. Now we have a better understanding of why many of the world's wealthiest own sports teams. They aren't just a trophy investment. In fact, after many decades in alternative investments, I would consider pro sports ownership an absolute all-star with an incredible stat line: a globally diverse, noncorrelated investment that has proven to be durable over a century.

To learn more about accessing these opportunities, you can visit **www.WhyProSports.com.**

LEADERS IN LENDING

As we shift gears to the world of private credit, you will likely feel a second bolt of lightning. Most investors only use traditional bonds when it comes to the fixed income portion of their portfolio. But you aren't most investors! Like Neo in *The Matrix*, you are now seeing the alternative reality. **This is where the smart money has been using private credit for decades as a safer and less volatile way to generate double-digit income returns.**

So let's dive in and discover why private credit is poised for massive growth as interest rates rise and banks tighten their lending appetites . . .

[*]https:/www.bloomberg.com/news/articles/2022-03-24/private-equity-funds -encroach-on-sports-owners-box
[†]https:/pitchbook.com/news/articles/european-soccer-us-private-market-capital

CHAPTER 4

PRIVATE CREDIT

LEADERS IN LENDING

"As fewer companies have gone public in recent years, the number of private companies has grown commensurately, providing a larger pool of private firms looking for access to capital."
—CNBC, *Demystifying Private Credit,* June 21, 2023*

In 2022, trillions in value were eviscerated as the value of bonds collapsed. Like tens of millions of Americans, you may have felt the sting in your portfolio. **And yet, while the traditional investor was losing sleep holding publicly traded bonds, the smart money was once again living in an alternative reality. They were generating healthy returns with the "fixed income" part of their portfolio while suffering minimal or no losses.** Welcome to the world of private credit.

For those unfamiliar, private credit is a way for established businesses to borrow money without using a bank. **For the investors like us, whose capital is being lent, this can generate two to three times the income return of traditional bonds and can serve as another noncorrelated income strategy in our Holy Grail portfolio. Why is creating a stable income stream so important?**

The ultra-wealthy are fully aware that assets will fluctuate in value. **But you cannot "spend" assets. You spend cash.** When markets drop, lots of people quickly become asset heavy and cash poor. They do not want to sell

---

*https://www.cnbc.com/2023/06/21/op-ed-demystifying-private-credit-amid-a-frozen-ipo-market.html

their assets when the market is down, but they can become forced to if they don't have sufficient income/liquidity. **This is why I live by the mantra** *"income is the outcome."* **Building a critical mass of assets that pay you a handsome income stream gives you the crucial stability you need to survive an economic winter.**

<u>**In the pages ahead, we explore how private credit has grown from just**</u> <u>**$42 billion in assets under management in the year 2000 to over $1.5**</u> <u>**trillion today!***</u> **As banks continue to clam up and tighten their lending purse strings, the industry is expected to grow to over $2.3 trillion by 2027.** Ahead, we will explain how investors can take advantage of private credit, but first, let's go back in time and discover why private credit became a favorite smart money strategy.

SHIFTING WINDS

"The 60/40 Portfolio Is Delivering Its Worst Returns in a Century"
—*Wall Street Journal*, October 14, 2022

For many decades, a time-tested strategy for most ordinary investors has been the 60/40 portfolio (60 percent stocks, 40 percent bonds). Aside from providing income, or yield, bonds have historically served to cushion a portfolio in years when stocks are down. **But in 2022, the cushion was yanked out from under investors and they landed flat on their behinds.** Stocks and bonds *both* plummeted as interest rates rose and the economy began to slow down. Stocks and bonds moving in lockstep, also known as correlation, is exactly what you DON'T want in bear markets. **And 2022 was the first year in history when stocks and bonds both went down by the same magnitude (-22 percent annualized by October 31 of 2022).**[†] **The seven largest stocks in the S&P 500 went down an average of 46**

*https://www.bloomberg.com/news/articles/2019-09-22/how-private-credit-soared -to-fuel-private-equity-boom-quicktake
†Data as of October 31, 2022. Using S&P500 and Barclays U.S. Aggregate for bonds. Assuming yearly rebalancing *2022 return corresponds to annualized YTD return.

L.LIPSCHITZ
INVESTMENT
COUNSELOR

*" You have a balanced investment portfolio.
Everything you own is losing money equally. "*

percent. **Put it all together, and the 60/40 strategy experienced one of its worst performances in nearly a hundred years.* Since then, stocks and bonds have become even more correlated, not less.** *Bloomberg* reported that **"bonds are a useless hedge for stock losses as correlation jumps."†**

Prior to COVID, investors hunting for yield were forced to take bigger risks as they waded into deeper and more dangerous waters. **With such low interest rates, and such low income returns on traditional bonds, many investors were tempted into buying riskier, higher yielding junk bonds, cleverly re-branded as "high-yield" bonds.** But don't let the name fool you: These so-called high yield bonds were paying a measly 3.97 percent in

---

*https://www.wsj.com/livecoverage/stock-market-news-today-2022-10-14/card/the
-60-40-portfolio-is-delivering-worst-returns-in-a-century-yrOrYOfkthrBQhSbf5By
†https://www.bloomberg.com/news/articles/2023-08-02/bonds-are-useless-hedge
-for-stock-losses-as-correlation-jumps

the summer of 2021. **Contrast this with private credit, which was paying 9 percent income during the same year.***

For sophisticated investors there was an uneasiness when it came to low-yielding junk bonds and how they had proliferated into the portfolios of ordinary investors. Like a dog sensing an earthquake minutes before the tremors, those who were paying attention knew something was not right. At that point in time, interest rates had nowhere to go but up, which meant the price of lower-quality junk bonds would then collapse. The risk-reward ratio was so out of whack that we knew the winds would eventually shift. And shift they did.

On November 9 of 2021, *Bloomberg* wrote . . .

"U.S Junk Bonds Set $432 Billion Record"†

Not even a year later, on October 22 of
2022, the same outlet wrote . . .

"Global Junk Bond Sales Drop Most Ever With No Signs of Recovery."‡

While bond values were collapsing with rising rates, many of the biggest institutions were enjoying the benefits of private credit. Instead of losing, their income payments from private credit were steadily rising along with interest rates.

THE ALTERNATIVE REALITY STRIKES AGAIN

> *"A bank is a place where they lend you an umbrella in fair weather and ask for it back when it begins to rain."*
> —Robert Frost

---

*https://www.forbes.com/sites/forbesfinancecouncil/2023/03/30/private-credit-investing-current-opportunities-and-risks/?sh=368627993821
†https://www.bloomberg.com/news/articles/2021-11-09/u-s-junk-bonds-set-432-billion-record-in-rush-to-beat-rates#xj4y7vzkg
‡https://www.bloomberg.com/news/articles/2022-10-24/global-junk-bond-sales-drop-most-ever-with-no-signs-of-recovery

"How would you like to dabble in some very
high quality junk bonds?"

For decades, the deepest pockets of smart money have invested massive
sums in "non-bank" lenders that generate much higher returns than
traditional bonds. This is the world of private credit. Private equity is
to public equities what private credit is to bonds.

While big businesses like Amazon, Google, and Tesla have no problem
securing loans from big banks or selling publicly traded bonds to raise capital, there is a huge swath of middle-market companies that have to look
elsewhere. But we're not talking about your local hardware store or florist
borrowing money to make payroll. According to the Corporate Finance Institute, **U.S. middle-market companies have between $100 million and
$3 billion in revenue, with anywhere between one hundred and twenty-
five hundred employees. Believe it or not, there are over two hundred
thousand companies in the United States that fit this category!**

We all know that when it comes to lending, banks have extremely tight
fists. If you have ever bought a home, you are all too familiar with the financial prostate exam required. But loans are a necessity for successful businesses, which rely heavily on them to fund operations. They have to pay all
sorts of bills up front—rent, payroll, inventory—and wait a bit for the revenue to come in. But bank loans aren't always available, or sufficient. **After**

the 2008 global financial crisis, banks were further handcuffed by regulators, diminishing their ability to issue loans, and many companies were left with one option to keep the cash flowing: private credit.

The recent boom in private equity has poured even more fuel on the private credit fire. When a private equity firm buys a company, they will often use some form of leverage (like an individual putting a mortgage on a new house). Where does that leverage come from? By now you won't be surprised to learn that a very large percentage of these mergers and acquisitions are financed by private credit firms.

THE 3 PILLARS OF PRIVATE CREDIT

It's worth repeating that just twenty-three years ago, the world of private credit topped $42 billion in total loans. After enduring the Internet Bubble and Great Financial Crisis, the evaporation of bank loan availability has resulted in a private credit boom. At the end of 2022, the global private credit market exceeded $1.5 trillion. Research firm Preqin estimates the industry will grow to over $2.3 trillion by 2027 as traditional banks further retrench.

This trend only looks likely to accelerate. In early 2023, Silicon Valley Bank collapsed nearly overnight. Numerous other regional banks followed suit. The rapid rise in interest rates had caused a collapse in their bond portfolios. Private credit firms don't face the same risks (as explained ahead). This is why many firms see a "golden moment" in this space in light of bank failures.* Moreover, regional banks account for close to 80 percent of commercial real estate loans, and with vacant office buildings piling up, we could see a major calamity when those loans come due in coming years and defaults begin to domino. All of this points to the continued use of private credit firms who are unbound by many of the constraints of traditional banks.

One thing is clear: Private credit is solidifying its position as a dominant force for middle-market companies' lending needs. These firms

*https:/pitchbook.com/news/articles/blackstone-first-quarter-earnings-private -credit-pe

are incredibly cautious but willing to lend if the risk-reward ratio makes sense. They are fast, flexible, and creative with when, where, and how they lend. The result is often a much better risk-reward situation for investors like you and me who are putting up our capital. Let's explore the three pillars of private credit, and why private credit has grown to be a sought-after asset class from an investor's point of view:

1. Higher Rates of Return—Private credit offers substantially better rates of return (aka higher yields) than other debt instruments and has **proven its ability to do so in both low and high interest rate environments.** From 2015 to 2021, when interest rates were held at historic lows, private credit still managed double-digit returns! **As you can see in the figure below, in 2021–22, private credit loans (aka direct lending) provided more than double the yields of junk bonds, and often with better protections.**

2. Private Credit Typically Has Less Interest Rate Risk—Loans made to private companies usually have floating rates that adjust with market rates. So when interest rates rise, so do the payments made by the borrower. Private credit usually makes it hard for borrowers to lock in low fixed rates for extended periods, which serves

DIRECT LENDING: HISTORICALLY HIGHER RETURNS

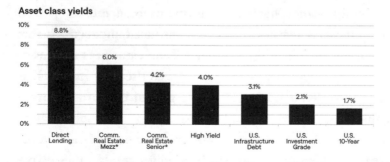

Asset class yields

Source: BofA Securities, Bloomberg Finance L.P., Clarkson, Cliffwater, Drewry Maritime Consultants, Federal Reserve, FTSE, MSCI, NCREIF, FactSet, Wells Fargo, J.P. Morgan Asset Management. *Commercial real estate (CRE) yields are as of September 30, 2021. CRE - mezzanine yield is derived from a J.P. Morgan survey and U.S. Treasuries of a similar duration. CRE - senior yield is sourced from the Gilberto-Levy Performance Aggregate Index (unlevered); U.S. high yield: Bloomberg US Aggregate Credit - Corporate - High Yield; U.S. infrastructure debt: iBoxx USD Infrastructure Index capturing USD infrastructure debt bond issuance over USD500 million; U.S. 10-year: Bloomberg U.S. 10-year Treasury yield; U.S. investment grade: Bloomberg U.S. Corporate Investment Grade. Data is based on availability as of May 31, 2022.

as great protection for the lender/investors, even as they reap rewards in the form of higher returns. **This design can be very meaningful during periods of high inflation, and it is precisely why hundreds of billions are pouring into private credit despite intense inflationary headwinds.**

3. Private Credit Can Provide Stability Through Difficult Markets and Has Experienced Low Default Rates—Private credit portfolios have proven that they can weather storms quite well. **In the eighteen-year period from June of 2004 through June of 2022, which included both the Global Financial Crisis and the COVID pandemic, loss rates for private credit loans averaged around -1 percent of loans per year, a number most banks would envy.** Furthermore, a study of the period between 1998 and 2018 showed that **the worst five-year period for private credit still produced positive returns for investors. Why?** There are really two main reasons:

First, because private credit lenders often hold their own loans (as opposed to selling them off to third parties), **they truly have their own money at risk.** This incentivizes them to adhere to strict credit research and underwriting standards—and they do. These lenders can be very picky about who they lend to, and they often choose only the highest-quality borrowers. **They can also be choosey about which *types* of companies they lend to, granting loans only to businesses in the more recession-proof industries (e.g., consumer staples, healthcare, infrastructure, etc.).**

The second appealing feature of these loans is the protections that the lender can build in. When private credit firms issue loans to companies, the transactions are typically structured as "senior secured loans." **This simply means that the lender is first in line to get paid back in the event the company has trouble.** Private credit firms are also extremely creative, and they often include specific covenants, protections, and collateral requirements that give them a high degree of confidence in making sure they do not lose money.

Remember Buffett's #1 rule of investing? DON'T LOSE MONEY! **You can see in the figure below that even in its absolute worst five-year**

HISTORICALLY CONSISTENT PERFORMANCE

Lowest 5-Year Annualized Performance (1995–2022)

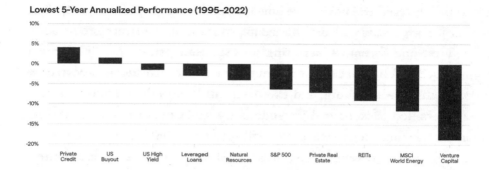

Source: Burgiss. Private Credit=Burgiss US Private Debt Funds Index. US Buyout=Burgiss US Buyout Funds Index. US High Yield=ICE BofA US High Yield Index. Leveraged Loans=Credit Suisse Leveraged Loan Index. Natural Resources=Burgiss US Natural Resouces Funds Index. S&P 500=S&P 500 Total Return Index. Private Real Estate=Burgiss US Real Estate Funds Index. REITs=S&P United States REITs. MSCI World Energy Total Return. Venture Capital=Burgiss US Venture Capital Funds Index. All data is taken from sources believed to bereliable but cannot be guaranteed.
PAST PERFORMANCE IS NOT NECESSARILY INDICATIVE OF FUTURE RESULTS.

period, private credit still made money! **Pretty impressive when you stack it up against other asset classes.**

FROM CONCEPT TO EXECUTION

> *"Nobody ever mastered any skill except through intensive, persistent and intelligent practice."*
> —Norman Vincent Peale

By now it should be clear why the biggest institutional investors find solace in their private credit investments. **They understand that income is the outcome! To recap, these are the three primary reasons why the smart money has diversified into private credit for consistent income.**

1. Low correlation to public markets (think Holy Grail)
2. Attractive risk-adjusted returns with floating rate protections as interest rates rise
3. Strong lender protections against default (e.g., senior position to be paid back first)

So now that we understand private credit conceptually, what is the best strategy for an investor wanting to allocate a portion of their portfolio to private credit? While there is no one-size-fits-all, we can certainly share our perspective, as we have invested in private credit for decades.

First and foremost, selecting an excellent private credit manager is crucial. Why? Because each manager must have deep expertise in sourcing, underwriting, and executing on hundreds of loans to create a diversified basket for their underlying investors. The success of these loans is highly contingent on the skill set of their underwriters, which the best firms have developed over decades. **In Part 2 of this book, we interview David Golub of Golub Capital. David is one of the best performing private credit managers in the world, with more than $60 billion in assets under management and a consistently stellar track record.**

There are numerous categories and subcategories of private credit that we do not need to dive into here; however, the chart below shows the impressive, industry-wide, average returns **(CAGR = compound annual growth rate)** of different private credit strategies across different geographies.

Our firm's philosophy is never to bet on just one horse in one race. We prefer to build partnerships with managers across multiple private credit strategies that create immense diversification across numerous types of loans, with varying risk profiles, across various sectors and

PRIVATE DEBT HISTORIC AND FORECAST PERFORMANCE

Performance	CAGR (2015–2021)	CAGR (2018–2021)
Private debt	9.37%	11.44%
Private debt—direct lending	6.83%	7.98%
Private debt—distressed debt	9.18%	12.64%
Private Debt—other	11.74%	14.28%
North America—private debt	8.92%	12.09%
Europe—private debt	9.88%	9.62%
APAC—private debt	10.09%	11.42%
Rest of World—private debt	13.44%	16.26%
Diversified multi-regional private debt	14.29%	21.30%

Source: PREQUIN

geographies. In short, we do not want to feel turbulence in case one specific strategy has a higher than normal default rate. Having multiple partners and multiple lending strategies helps smooth out the ride and create more predictable returns.

Is there a downside to private credit? The tradeoff in private credit is liquidity. While you still receive your monthly or quarterly income payments, it usually takes three to five years to fully harvest your investment—a relatively long time compared to bonds, which can be sold at the click of a button. This is because private credit lenders normally hold the loans they make to maturity. But that is precisely what also provides the predictability that investors have grown to really appreciate from this asset class.

To learn more about the specifics of private credit, you can visit our informational page: **www.WhyPrivateCredit.com.**

As we turn the page, we dive into one of the most important aspects of our ability to survive and thrive on this plane . . . energy! We are in the midst of an energy revolution, turning toward a combination of renewables (wind, solar, etc.) and new innovative technologies that can reduce or eliminate carbon from traditional fossil fuel burning. **With the biggest institutions and world governments throwing their weight behind this category, there is tremendous opportunity for investors.**

CHAPTER 5

ENERGY

THE POWER OF OUR LIVES (PART ONE)

"Energy is the key to human progress."
—John F. Kennedy

A Quick Note: The topic of energy is robust to say the least! As a result, we have dedicated two chapters to adequately cover it. In Chapter 5, we will set the stage and get an understanding of our current global energy situation. In Chapter 6, we will cover some of the investment opportunities that are unfolding as the world embarks on a multitrillion-dollar energy revolution.

SHARED PROSPERITY

The story of human progress is a story of energy. Prior to our ability to efficiently harness energy, we lived brutally short lives of survival. We spent our time hunting, gathering, and lighting fires to keep us warm and cook our food. This was our way of life for millennia. Aside from the elites, the vast majority were poor, illiterate, uneducated, diseased, and malnourished. Both then and now, these are the plagues of a population without energy.

Once we figured out how to harness energy, life on this planet began a steady march toward progress. Not perfection, but progress. Life became much easier when we invented new methods of heating, lighting, and transportation. The transition from wood to coal single-handedly launched the Industrial Revolution. The steam engine transformed travel and trade in one fell swoop. In the 1890s, Nikola Tesla developed AC power generation and dazzled the world when he used it to power a hundred thousand lights at the Chicago World's Fair. **Fewer than forty years later, American house-holds were filled with electric appliances, tools our ancestors would have only dreamt of.**

In 1990, nearly 1.9 billion people (35 percent of the world population) lived in extreme poverty, defined as living on less than $2 per day. Today, just a few decades later, this figure has fallen to 782 million people (or 10 percent of the world population). World Bank Group president Jim Yong Kim said, *"Over the last 25 years, more than a billion people have lifted themselves out of extreme poverty, and the global poverty rate is now lower than it has ever been in recorded history. This is one of the greatest human achievements of our time."* This great feat would have never been possible without access to energy. **Energy is the rope by which the poor can pull themselves up; it is also the rope that we, in the developed world, must let down. It is the foundation for employment, education, food security, clean water, basic healthcare, internet access, entrepreneurship, global trade, and shared prosperity. Energy is the precursor for industry; and just as our bodies need oxygen, industry needs energy.**

Today, we have two important realities to contend with:

First, we are experiencing an energy revolution wherein renewable sources of clean(er) energy are taking over market share from less clean energy sources. This trend is going to continue, but, according to numerous experts we interviewed, traditional fossil fuels will likely never be fully replaced. This may come as a shock if you were thinking society would flip a switch and rid itself of fossil fuels. This is certainly how it sounds when renewables are discussed in the media. However, as we will cover later in the chapter, the more likely outcome is that technological innovation will make existing fossil fuels much cleaner and greener. In fact, technologies that can do just that already exist, but it will take time for them to scale.

Second, the growing world population, and the billions of people in emerging economies like China and India, will need *all* forms of energy to meet ever increasing demand. Case in point, China currently generates 63 percent of its electricity from coal. That's down from 77 percent in 2000,* but coal in China isn't going anywhere any time soon. The Climate Action

*https:/www.eia.gov/todayinenergy/detail.php?id=53959

Tracker reported that coal production [in China] reached record levels in 2022 for the second year running. And while the entire world retired 187 gigawatts of coal plants between 2017 and 2022, the Chinese have added 113 gigawatts of new coal-powered plants in the last two years alone.* The Paris Climate Accords notwithstanding, China has recently permitted 180 new coal mines to be built and at the time of this writing is permitting two new power plants per week.† In February of 2023, the Center for Research on Energy and Clean Air reported that *"the coal power capacity starting construction in China was six times as large as that in all of the rest of the world combined."*

The fact is, India and China, with nearly 3 billion people combined, are going through their own Industrial Revolution with no intention of slowing down. They are keenly aware that energy drives industry and that industry will usher hundreds of millions from poverty into the middle class. President Xi Jinping says climate goals *"can't be detached from reality"* nor come at the expense of Chinese energy and food security.

NET ELECTRICITY GENERATION IN CHINA BY FUEL TYPE (2000–2020)

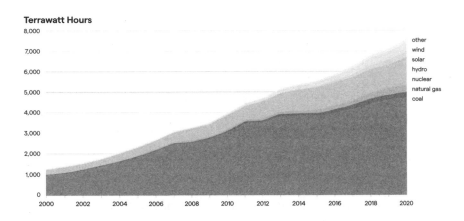

Data Source: U.S. Energy Information Administration, International Energy Statistics

*https://www.wsj.com/articles/john-kerry-china-climate-economy-xi-jinping-bei
jing-e50b9ef4?mod=hp_trending_now_opn_pos1
†https://energyandcleanair.org/publication/china-permits-two-new-coal-power
-plants-per-week-in-2022/

SEPARATING FACTS FROM FEELINGS

Upon hearing the words "energy transition," one might naturally think that we are switching from fossil fuels to renewables. Nothing could be further from the truth. Modern man has always been "transitioning" to different forms of energy, which is why the word "transition" is an unfortunate misnomer. Energy expert Wil VanLoh, whom you will hear from in Part 2 of the book, believes that energy "addition" would be a more apt term. Why? VanLoh explained that when we look at history, we can see that it takes a very long time for new energy sources to be adopted, and that they have never fully replaced the previously dominant forms of energy. He laid out the data showing that we are currently undergoing the fifth energy addition/transition in modern history. Let's take a look . . .

1. In the mid-1800s we began transitioning from wood to coal. It took fifty years for coal to reach 35 percent of global energy market share. While coal has lost market share (as a percentage) relative to other energy sources, **in 2022 we used more coal than EVER in history.** Coal remains the largest source of energy for electricity and is vital to the production of concrete, steel, paper, and more.

   In the early 1900s, following the production of Henry Ford's first Model T, we began transitioning from coal to oil. It took fifty years for oil to reach 25 percent of global energy market share. **In 2023, we are on track to use more oil than any year in history, with 2024 projected to be even higher.***

2. In 1938, the U.S. passed the "Natural Gas Act" to regulate the transition from oil to natural gas. It took natural gas fifty years to reach 25 percent of global energy market share, and as with oil, **2023 will mark another year of record demand, with 2024 demand expected to grow as well.**†

*https://www.reuters.com/business/energy/opec-upbeat-over-2024-oil-demand-outlook-despite-headwinds-2023-07-13/
†https://www.iea.org/reports/gas-2020/2021-2025-rebound-and-beyond

The 1960s saw the beginning of the proliferation of nuclear power. Nuclear peaked out in 1977 with roughly 5 percent of global energy market share, but it looks poised to make a serious comeback. (More on that later!)

Around 2010, society began the move toward wind, solar, and other renewables. Today, after thirteen years and nearly $1 trillion invested, **these renewable sources provide just 3 percent of the world's energy needs.**

Given the choice, we all want cleaner forms of energy, and we can surely get there with innovation. But we also need to understand just how much time it takes for new sources to gain substantial market share. And this, my friend, presents tremendous investment opportunity.

EXPONENTIAL DEMAND

When we look at the future, experts foresee two unavoidable variables that will impact energy demand . . .

1. Population Growth—The global population has grown from 2.5 billion in 1950 to more than 8 billion today. The International Monetary Fund (IMF) predicts that the global population will continue to surge, reaching 9.7 billion by 2050.*
2. Middle-Class Growth—As the world marches forward, **a combination of technology, advances in healthcare, and access to energy will propel billions from relative poverty into the middle class.** People who earn more, spend more. And they undoubtedly use more energy.

Point being, we aren't dealing with a static amount of energy usage; we are dealing with ever-increasing demand. The world's population currently uses about **100 million barrels of oil per day,** and that number is only expected to grow. **By 2050, most experts believe that the total global energy demand will increase by roughly 50 percent.** This is a reasonable estimate considering demand grew by 50 percent between 1990 and 2020.

*https://www.imf.org/en/Publications/fandd/issues/2020/03/infographic-global-population-trends-picture

State-owned oil company Saudi Aramco is one of the greatest beneficiaries of this ever-increasing demand. **They ranked #2 on the Fortune Global 500 largest companies in the world, with revenues of $604 billion in 2022.*** These revenue numbers dwarf Amazon (#4 on the list) and Apple (#8) and could put the company in the top spot (over Walmart) as soon as next year if they continue to grow at the current pace.

As Mark Twain said, *"history doesn't repeat itself, but it rhymes."* When we look to the future, most experts absolutely predict that renewables will grow as a percentage of our global energy supply. Renewables will gain market share—as new energy sources always have during periods of energy addition—but will likely never replace existing fossil fuel energy sources. Quite the opposite in fact. **According to the U.S. Energy and Information Administration (EIA), the use of natural gas, coal, oil, nuclear, and renewables will ALL expand to meet demand by 2050.** (See chart below.)

Every year, I (Tony) host an intimate financial event for my foundation's largest donors. We gather to hear from a who's who of financial experts, former presidents, policy-makers, and more. Much like this book, we sit at a proverbial table of titans to gain wisdom about the future and how they can capitalize.

GLOBAL PRIMARY ENERGY CONSUMPTION BY ENERGY SOURCE (2010–2050)

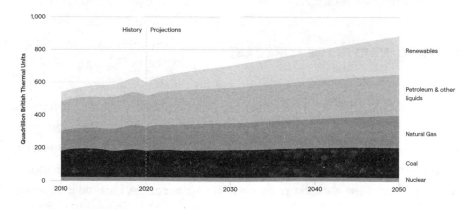

Source: U.S. Energy Information Administration, International Energy Outlook 2021 Reference case
Note: Petroleum and other liquids includes biofuels.

*https://fortune.com/2023/08/01/saudi-aramco-profitable-oil-company-trillions/

Jamie Dimon is the CEO of J.P. Morgan, the world's largest bank and a company that has committed to net-zero emissions by 2050. He graciously accepted my invitation to the event, and much of our discussion was devoted to the future of energy. To suggest he is a proponent of the green energy movement is an understatement. He shared with me how **J. P. Morgan established a clean energy allocation that is on track to finance $1.1 trillion in clean energy projects by 2030! He is also pressuring Congress to expedite the permitting of green energy technologies. And yet, Dimon explained to the audience, he may have been early in his desire to switch energy sources:** *"The lesson that was learned from Ukraine is that we need cheap, reliable, safe, secure energy, of which 80 percent comes from oil and gas. And that number's going to be very high for ten or twenty years."* Driving oil and natural gas prices higher is a punitive measure that is actually making matters worse by forcing nations to switch their coal plants back on. In a letter to J.P. Morgan's shareholders Dimon wrote *"using (natural) gas to diminish coal consumption is an actionable way to reduce CO_2 emissions expeditiously."*

For those who may cringe at the thought of more fossil fuels in the interim, not to worry. **There are countless billions pouring into carbon capture (and storage) technologies that, although not yet totally scalable, will make the use of fossil fuels far greener.** We will highlight a couple of exciting breakthroughs in Chapter 6.

Let's drill down a bit . . .

SUN AND WIND IN THE FORECAST

Wind and solar are the core technologies for renewable energy generation, but they face significant headwinds . . . pun intended. First and foremost, there are winners and losers from a geographic perspective. The wind must blow *intensely* if you want to use wind power. The sun must shine *intensely* if you want solar. Partly cloudy skies with a light breeze ain't going to cut it. To be clear, I am not talking about home solar panels, I am talking about industrial-strength solar fields that can power a grid.

In the U.S., there are huge swaths of land rich in howling wind (the middle of the country) and scorching sunshine (the Southwest). But that's not the case for most of the world. In fact, the vast majority of the world is considered unsuitable for industrial-strength wind, solar, or both. Most of the world's cities with populations over 1 million are not ideally suited for industrial-strength, renewable power generation. Thus, any solar or wind farms that power them must be placed far away, and transmission lines have to be built to transport the electricity. This is less than ideal and incredibly expensive when compared to other available sources. I don't mean to take the wind out of anyone's sails, but at the end of the day, there is a consensus among experts that solar and wind have very real limitations at scale. Among other reasons, this is why China and India are doubling down on nuclear.

NUCLEAR POWER

Only three nuclear reactors have come online in the United States over the past three decades, partly because the horrors of Three Mile Island, Chernobyl, and Fukushima left an indelible impression on a generation. While nuclear disasters are intolerable, it is also important to balance the memory and lessons of these disasters against new, safer nuclear technologies and the environmental impact of all other types of energy. From burning coal to mining critical minerals for electric cars, nearly all forms of energy have their dirty downsides. As the wise Thomas Sowell once said, *"There are no solutions, only tradeoffs."* This certainly applies here, as nuclear is still the cleanest, densest form of energy known to man. From a technology perspective, many of the reactors in use today are using decades-old technology, and the accidents that occurred were all relics of history. To be fair, we must look at today's technology and safety standards to judge nuclear. This is where small modular reactors (SMRs) come into play.

After decades of innovation, experts believe that SMRs hold great promise. About the size of a small commercial airplane these reactors are tiny compared to the massive traditional reactors you probably imagine when you hear the words "nuclear power." **They are far safer and have numerous fail-safes in place to avoid a catastrophe.** Unlike traditional reactors, which can take a decade to build, SMRs can be quickly built and assembled in a factory and delivered by truck to their final destination. This allows them to be placed in isolated areas and sites with limited access to water. **If** units like these become ubiquitous, we are talking about cheap, green energy for huge portions of the global population.

In 2022, the first U.S.-based small modular reactor was approved by regulators for construction in Idaho. There are now multiple companies developing incredibly efficient SMRs that will produce as much electricity as older, much larger, reactors—**and they'll do it with just 1 percent of the land that other renewables (wind, solar, hydro) would require to produce the same amount of electricity!**

There are numerous companies in the race to create next-generation nuclear technologies (including SMRs), which is important because as a global community, we are way behind the curve. If we are serious about getting to "net-zero," most experts believe that nuclear will need to be a major part of the solution. And yet nuclear tends to be divisive due to the tension between its potential dangers and the fact that it is the greenest form of energy we can produce. Case in point: For years, environmental groups pushed to shut down the Indian Point nuclear reactor, which supplied nearly 25 percent of New York City's power. They argued that it could be replaced by renewables like wind and solar. In 2021, the plant was shuttered, and the unintended consequences began to stack up. The state reported that since the closing, 89 percent of its electricity now comes from natural gas and oil, up from 77 percent the previous year when both of Indian Point's reactors were running.* Certainly not the outcome that environmentalists had in mind.

This anti-nuclear position also backfired in Germany. By 2022, they had retired all their nuclear plants. Exacerbated by the war with Ukraine and the elimination of Russian natural gas, the Germans have had to resort to reigniting their coal plants, replacing green nuclear energy with dirty energy. Then, in another desperate move, they disassembled a large wind farm to expand their coal mining operations!†

Many nuclear proponents suggest that Germany should have looked to their French neighbors who get 70 percent of their energy from nuclear.

---

*https://www.lohud.com/story/news/2022/07/22/new-york-fossil-fuels-increase-after-indian-point-nuclear-plant-shutdown/65379172007/
†https://www.theguardian.com/world/2022/oct/26/german-windfarm-coalmine-keyenberg-turbines-climate

WHO IS BUILDING NUCLEAR REACTORS?
Top 10 countries by nuclear capacity under construction

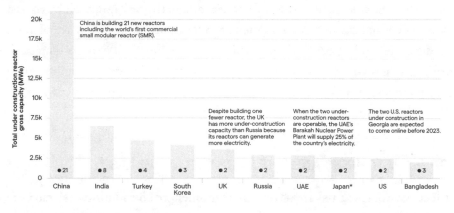

China is building 21 new reactors including the world's first commercial small modular reactor (SMR).

Despite building one fewer reactor, the UK has more under-construction capacity than Russia because its reactors can generate more electricity.

When the two under-construction reactors are operable, the UAE's Barakah Nuclear Power Plant will supply 25% of the country's electricity.

The two U.S. reactors under construction in Georgia are expected to come online before 2023.

● Reactor Under Construction   Reactor Under Construction

Source: World Nuclear Association

Instead of closing down plants, France has six new reactors coming online before 2050. The French have also pioneered an incredible strategy for recycling nuclear waste and maximizing its useful life span.

In April 2023, Finland switched on a new nuclear plant. **The plant was so effective at creating an abundance of affordable, green energy that prices dropped below zero for a short period!** Now the country can use as much energy as it pleases and know that it's nearly 100 percent green. China and India also understand that nuclear is a vital part of their own green future. Aside from growing energy demands, both countries acknowledge that they are facing major air quality and pollution issues. As the world presses forward with ESG commitments, China and India have made abundantly clear their need to balance their environmental concerns with their growing economy. They have indicated they will do this by going nuclear, and China is easily winning the race. Bolstered by deep government pockets and the absence of obstructionists, China is currently building twenty-one nuclear plants. In addition, they are investing half a trillion dollars to build 150 reactors in the next fifteen years!* This pace of expansion is unlike anything the world has seen.

*https://www.bloomberg.com/news/features/2021-11-02/china-climate-goals-hinge
-on-440-billion-nuclear-power-plan-to-rival-u-s

India is also moving at warp speed, currently building an impressive eight nuclear plants. Even oil-rich Saudi Arabia has plans to build sixteen reactors over the next two decades. Contrast this with the U.S., which has just two under construction. U.S. regulators need to move swiftly if we plan on leading the nuclear technology revolution. Most experts believe that environmentalists and politicians need to be looking at this technology through a modern lens. We don't judge the safety of cars based on models built in the 1950s. The same should hold true for nuclear power!

GREEN MACHINES AND THE RACE FOR MINERALS

Electric vehicles (EVs) are having their moment in the spotlight. With Tesla leading the way, every car manufacturer has jumped into the EV revolution. But while electric cars are greener on the road, it's undeniable that producing them is incredibly taxing on the environment. The same is true of wind turbines and solar panels. The reality is that "green machines" must be manufactured using traditional sources of energy. Oil, natural gas, and coal are needed to produce the necessary concrete, steel, and plastics. **For example, the energy equivalent of one hundred barrels of oil is required to fabricate a single EV battery that can store the equivalent of one barrel of oil.** Then we have the vast amount of critical minerals that are needed for batteries, solar panels, transformers, generators, and other inner workings of these green machines. The process of finding, mining, refining, and transporting these minerals is not at all green. Consider these facts . . .

- Nearly five hundred thousand pounds of earth are dug up and processed to create just one one-thousand-pound EV battery. This mining is often done with heavy, diesel-burning equipment.
- A standard EV battery contains about 25 pounds of lithium, 30 pounds of cobalt, 60 pounds of nickel, 110 pounds of graphite, and 90 pounds of copper.
- An EV battery contains one thousand times more cobalt than a smartphone.
- By 2030, more than 10 million tons of batteries will become garbage each year.

"Naturally, there's a trade-off for its exceptional fuel economy."

To be clear, electric vehicles, wind farms, and solar panels are indeed an important part of renewables. But the entire supply chain needs to be de-carbonizing if we are going to be intellectually honest. China has the most EVs in the world, but most of them are charged using electricity from coal. Can we really consider coal-powered cars "green"?

The bigger point I am making is that we need to separate fact from fiction, marketing from reality. We all want clean energy and to take care of our planet. And yet we must digest some difficult realities. One of those realities is the control of critical minerals by often adversarial countries.

TOTAL(ITARIAN) CONTROL

In the early 2000s, China saw the writing on the wall. They could see that the world was committing to greener technologies and knew that every one of those green machines would require critical minerals. Without substantial deposits in their own country, the Chinese government spent hundreds of billions to lock up control of numerous mining operations around the world. Notably, they flexed their power (and wallets) with the sometimes corrupt governments of Africa, a continent rich in natural resources. The Congo was China's primary conquest.

Cobalt is used in nearly every smartphone, tablet, laptop, and EV, to give batteries stability and keep them from overheating. The Democratic Republic of Congo has more cobalt deposits than the rest of the world combined. In fact, nearly 70 percent of the world's known supply is buried in the Congo's shallow red earth, where its easily accessible. (Somewhat ironic, considering that, according to the World Bank, only 19 percent of the population in the Congo has access to electricity.*)

It is estimated that fifteen of the nineteen major mines in the Congo are controlled, either directly or indirectly, by China. Some of them are the size of a European city! Most disturbing are the human rights abuses taking place. The Congo has a sad history of exploitation and slavery dating back to the late 1800s. Around 1890, there was a "bicycle craze" as millions of people around the world began to ride. Believe it or not, the earliest bikes had steel and/or wooden wheels—so it was a big deal when, in 1888, inventor John Dunlop patented a new form of pneumatic rubber tire. And his invention really took off when automobiles entered the scene. Demand for rubber exploded, and the Congo just so happened to have rubber trees as far as the eye could see. Under the colonial oppression of Belgian King Leopold II, untold numbers of Congolese villagers were forced into slavery as deforestation ravaged their lands. The Congo became the world's largest rubber exporter, and yet the people remained impoverished. Published in 1899, Joseph Conrad's famous novel *Heart of Darkness* documented the horrific tragedy of a population stripped of their freedom and a land devoured for commercial purposes.

Today, the Congo is being ravaged once again—not for rubber, but for cobalt. Around the world, tech companies buying the cobalt are often told by wholesalers that the supply chain is clean. This turns out to be untrue for most of the mining operations. Thanks to the courageous work of investigative journalists like Siddharth Kara (author of *Cobalt Red: How the Blood of the Congo is Powering Our Lives*), we now know what the bottom of our supply chain really looks like. Many of the mines are run on the backs of

*https://www.trade.gov/country-commercial-guides/democratic-republic-congo
-energy#:~:text=Despite%20millions%20of%20dollars%20of,one%20percent%20
in%20rural%20areas

modern-day slaves. Under the eye of armed militia, men, women, and children dig endlessly for cobalt. They scavenge with sticks, pickaxes, shovels, and rebar, all the while being exposed to toxic carcinogens. For twelve hours a day, hundreds of thousands of Congolese toil in the heat to make a dollar or two. Just enough to barely survive.

So proponents of the electrification of everything must also grapple with the true meaning of ESG: Environmental, Social, and Governance. Does each letter carry the same value? If the environment is being destroyed in the Congo (and elsewhere) while hundreds of thousands of natives are enslaved, could one possibly argue that the end justifies the means? Ultimately, big tech will need to wake up and address these issues in unison. **Their purchasing power can demand reform so workers can be paid and treated fairly.** We also must keep working on newer technologies that may not need some of these critical minerals. For example, solid-state batteries and other cobalt-free batteries are being implemented. Tesla is now using cobalt-free batteries in 50 percent of their cars and has indicated they want to completely remove cobalt from their products. Hats off to Elon, but other issues remain.

THE RUSSIA-CHINA BLOC

Russia, a country flush with natural resources, including substantial reserves of critical minerals, has joined forced with China in a mutually beneficial relationship. For example, while China has brought hundreds of billions to Africa, Russia has installed the muscle with paid mercenaries. These are the enforcers hired by governments to keep the populations in check.

Obviously, this China-Russia bloc is giving pause to world leaders who can see that the two have an iron fist of control around our mineral supply. Meanwhile, other not-so-friendly regimes also have a level of control of critical minerals. Consider China, Russia, Iran, Kazakhstan, North Korea, and Venezuela. These six totalitarian regimes have dominant control over the minerals (see chart below) we require for cell phones, tablets, EV batteries, solar panels, windmills, and more. This brings up a host of questions. *How do we secure a safe and reliable supply chain? How do we ensure human rights are prioritized? How will we satisfy increasing demand for critical minerals if environmental policies keep us from mining in our own country?* These

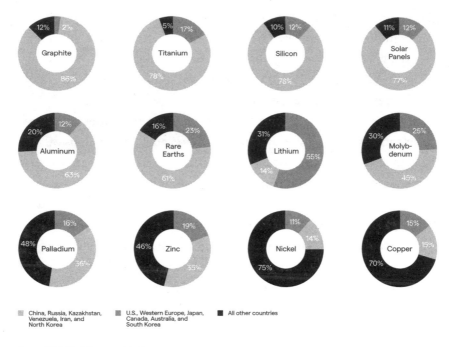

Source: USGS, World Nuclear and Statista

are questions that do not yet have great answers but will undoubtedly need to be navigated.

AN ELECTRIFIED WORLD

In 2022, California mandated that by 2035 all new vehicles sold in the state must be zero emissions (electric, hydrogen, etc.).* Ironically, not long after the announcement, California had a heat wave and pleaded with people to avoid charging their electric vehicles for fear of overloading the aging electrical grid. This begs the honest question . . . Can California's grid handle a fifteen-to-thirtyfold increase in electric cars? **It's estimated that the state will need to triple their power generation in the next decade to do so.** To put that into perspective, California is generating nearly the same amount

*https://ww2.arb.ca.gov/news/california-moves-accelerate-100-new-zero-emission -vehicle-sales-2035

of power as they did thirteen years ago.* Even a small increase is challenging enough, and this is likely why the energy commission has not released any plans on how it might go about this monumental task.

Elon Musk, founder of Tesla (the largest EV manufacturer in the world), has been quite vocal about his concern that there is "insufficient energy" for the U.S.'s goals and that we could reach a shortage in as little as two years. He predicts that our electricity demand is going to triple by 2045 and most recently shared his concerns at a conference with the nation's largest utilities. When you consider that demand has historically only increased 2 to 3 percent per year, it's easy to see why the power companies are woefully underprepared for the coming surge.

While California and twelve other states are legislating this EV mandate, the rest of the world seems intent on pushing for a similar outcome. The United Nations target of zero net emissions, known as the 2050 net-zero goal, states *"The Net Zero Emissions Scenario sees an electric car fleet of over 300 million in 2030 and electric cars accounting for 60% of new car sales."* Every manufacturer is rapidly creating new electrified versions of existing models, from the Ford F-150 Lightning truck to the upcoming electric Corvette.

NEW EV CAR PRODUCTION TARGETS

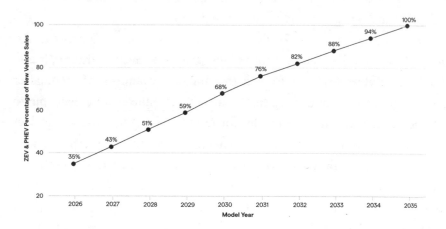

*https://www.energy.ca.gov/data-reports/energy-almanac/california-electricity -data/2021-total-system-electric-generation

Currently, there are roughly 2.5 million electric and hybrid vehicles out of a total of 290 million cars on the road (less than 1 percent) in the United States. The total number of electric cars in the entire world is 16.8 million out of roughly 1.44 billion total cars (also about 1 percent). **So with a goal of 300 million zero-emissions cars by 2030, we are talking about an unprecedented level of demand for the critical minerals needed.** Is that even doable? The challenges for such lofty goals are very real indeed.

Let's start with a glance at history. **No extractive industry (oil, gas, gold, iron ore, etc.) has EVER been able to increase global supply production by 100 percent in a single decade.** Mining is expensive, laborious, time-consuming, and a regulatory nightmare, particularly in developed nations where human rights and environmental impact studies are prioritized. A newly discovered deposit can often take many years to come online and actually start producing the raw materials needed.

Setting aside the trillions in required investment, environmental experts believe that mining the critical minerals required to produce 300 million zero-emissions vehicles may put an extraordinary burden on planet earth. When you add in the mega wind farms, industrial storage batteries, and thousands of acres of solar panels, the amount of minerals required to reach a goal of *"net-zero by 2030"* is staggering. The figure below shows the exponential demand for the various minerals required.

Take lithium for example. It's estimated that we will need eighteen times more lithium than the current amount being mined today. But lithium is not the only mineral we will need for constructing our green tech. We will need two times more copper, seventeen times more graphite, and eleven times more nickel than we currently produce today.*

Again, we have never in history been able to double the supply of any extractive mineral within a ten-year span. "Dig faster" does not seem like a viable plan.

When I discuss this *"never before in history"* scenario with energy experts, there is almost unanimous consensus that this an impossible feat. A noble goal? Yes. Great talking point for politicians? Sure. **But we must take into**

*IEA Critical Mineral Outlook

CURRENT VS FUTURE DEMAND FROM CLEAN ENERGY USES (OF TONS)

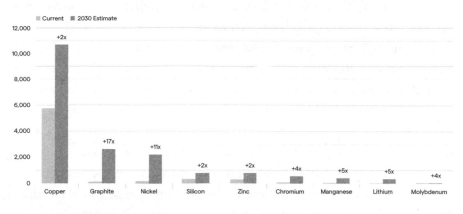

Source: IEA Critical Minerals Outlook

account the realities of what the earth will yield for us and what other costs, both human and environmental, will be incurred.

Now, depending on your presuppositions, many of the facts I have laid out thus far might be hard to digest. I think we would all love to flip a green switch and decarbonize our planet. Numerous experts and I actually believe this is possible with new innovations over the long haul. But in the interim, there will be numerous investment opportunities in an asset class where rising demand seems inevitable.

WHO DRANK ALL THE MILK?

Back when my son was living at home, I would often open the refrigerator door to find a near-empty milk carton in the fridge. It seemed like no matter how much milk we bought, the container always dwindled faster than we could replace it. Living with a teenage boy in your house is analogous to our current energy situation. Bear with me here.

Energy, like the milk within a specific carton, is finite and must be replaced. Now think of an oil or natural gas reservoir. Once we pop the top, it contains a certain amount we can extract before it is dry. **Energy companies and their investors must spend hundreds of billions, in advance, to explore and bring new projects online just to keep up with the world's current thirst.**

But what happens when we dramatically stop spending to generate new production? What happens when we fail to replace our supply for the current and growing demand? We may all find out sooner than later.

In June of 2014, oil prices surged to $107 a barrel. Then, in a dramatic turn of events, prices plunged to $44 just six months later. These rapid losses were devastating, and the biggest energy companies tightened the reins on spending as they licked their wounds. Around the same time, the ESG movement began to really gain steam. With noble goals, they unfortunately put out some incredibly unrealistic timelines. Instead of looking for innovative technology to make oil/gas/coal cleaner, the movement focused on ending fossil fuels, an aim that was even echoed by then presidential candidate Biden, who promised, *"I guarantee you. We're going to end fossil fuel."*

Energy companies were between a rock and a hard place. Institutional investors that had historically funded exploration of new replacement energy sources were pressured to avoid fossil fuel investments like the plague. CEOs of big energy were also under tremendous pressure. They were being told by board members and large shareholders, both explicitly and implicitly, NOT to spend so much on new replacement energy projects. Instead, they were encouraged to return their excess cash to investors either through dividends or share buybacks. **Thus, investments in discovering and extracting new supply dropped by nearly 50 percent in subsequent years.** To put it into perspective, before 2014, the major oil companies invested about $700 billion per year in replacement energy. Since 2014, they have spent only about $300 to $350 billion globally.

Critics argue that less spending on new "upstream" projects is a good thing. A green thing. But in reality, experts believe that it could be setting us up for a chain reaction of higher energy prices, higher food prices, and less national security. This was Jamie Dimon's earlier point regarding the unintended consequences of short-term moves that could actually inhibit everyone's long-term net-zero goals.

SEVEN SAUDI ARABIAS

As mentioned before, the world's energy use shakes out to about **100 million barrels (or barrel equivalents) per day.** To put that into perspective, a football stadium would hold about 2 million barrels. That total use equates to fifty football stadiums' worth of oil EVERY DAY. **That adds up to 36.5 billion barrels every year just to keep our world's economic engine running. Population growth and economic expansion mean demand is expected to grow by 1–2 percent, or 365–700 million barrels, per year.**

But how much do we deplete the existing supply each year? How much does the proverbial milk carton go down? This is the trillion-dollar question . . .

The global "supply decline rate" is 7–8 percent per year. This means that existing fossil fuel reservoirs and deposits are losing 7–8 percent of their total finite capacity per year. **That's 7–8 million barrels of daily supply that we need to replace EACH AND EVERY year just to keep pace with current demand, not to mention attempting to meet the future growth of demand. Wil VanLoh is the founder of Quantum Energy Partners, one of the largest private energy investors in the world. He framed the current situation best: "This is the equivalent of needing to find seven new Saudi Arabias' worth of energy production in the next twenty years."** Simply put, by slowing our replacement energy spending over the past decade, we find ourselves behind the eight ball. VanLoh also believes that the lack of replacement spending over the past several years is just now beginning to show up in prices.

Bottom line: Depleting finite projects with not enough spending to replace them is a recipe for constrained supply, higher energy prices, higher food prices, and higher consumer prices.

TIME TO PLACE OUR BETS

Now that we have parsed fact from fiction, we can see that there will be tremendous opportunity in the years ahead. In fact, many of the experts I speak to believe that we may be entering a Golden Age for energy investing. For fossil fuels, there will be shrinking supply and increased demand, likely leading to increased prices. For wind, solar, and nuclear, there will be accelerated adoption and trillions invested in innovative companies. And finally, for green technology, there are numerous decarbonization innovations coming online that will likely allow us to continue to use fossil fuels in a much greener way!

Let's explore these opportunities in Part Two! . . .

CHAPTER 6

ENERGY

THE POWER OF OUR LIVES (PART TWO)

*"Energy can neither be created or destroyed, it can
only be changed from one form to another."*
—Albert Einstein

ENERGY FOR ALL

It should not be contentious to say that less pollution is better for this beautiful planet we share. We should all be striving for greener solutions through heavy investment into renewables as well as through innovation within traditional fossil fuels (i.e., carbon capture).

Yet, as laid out in Part One, experts agree that we are living with the tension of two undeniable realities . . .

1. Demand for all forms of energy will continue to grow, fossil fuels included.
2. The burning of coal, natural gas, and oil creates a significant and impactful amount of CO_2 in the earth's atmosphere, and we should reduce it using the ***best means possible***.

The "best means possible" is where experts have major disagreements. In March of 2023, the U.N. secretary general called for "ceasing all licensing or funding of new oil and gas" as well as "stopping any expansion of existing oil and gas reserves."

While we all may want 100 percent green energy yesterday, the world is like a giant neighborhood. We need all nations to cooperate and work together. But not everyone is singing from the same sheet of music; that is, everyone has a vastly different time frame for achieving carbon neutrality. It is a delicate balance of not harming the environment while also not harming people and their ability to make a living, cook food, secure transportation, and so forth.

China, India, and many other developing nations know that flipping the off switch on fossil fuels is entirely unfeasible. Experts warn that drastic measures would send the world into a catastrophic global depression where hundreds of millions might die of starvation. Jamie Dimon of J.P. Morgan reiterated in a congressional hearing that "stopping oil and gas funding would be a road to hell for America." Remember, it takes approximately 36 billion barrels of oil per year to keep our global economic machine running, which means we can't pull the plug abruptly.

So is this really humanity's binary choice? Be destroyed by the U.N.'s prophecy of a *"climate change time bomb"* or cease using all fossil fuels immediately and be relegated to a life of green poverty? Most experts believe that a balanced point of view is what is needed. We need to strive to find innovative solutions that can keep the world on its current path of population growth and the eradication of extreme poverty worldwide. **We must deliver the cleanest energy possible to as many people as possible to drive global economic growth and food security. And we must do so in a cost-effective way.** Innovation has always been and will always be the answer to these types of problems. **As the saying goes, the Stone Age didn't end because they ran out of stones.**

THE WORLD'S FIRST NEAR ZERO-EMISSIONS NATURAL GAS PLANT

Rodney Allam is a chemical engineer who, at eighty-two years young, prefers to do his calculations on graph paper with a pencil and standard calculator. As the chief inventor at 8 Rivers, Allam attempts to look at energy problems quite differently. His unique approach has earned him numerous patents as well as the distinguished Global Energy Award (2012).

While most are trying to figure out how to capture and sequester carbon dioxide, Allam wondered if we could use it to our advantage. In 2013, he patented a revolutionary method for capturing nearly 97 percent of the carbon dioxide that is created by the burning of natural gas. Here is how it works . . .

In today's standard method, natural gas is burned to generate heat. The heat generates steam, which spins a turbine. A spinning turbine equals electricity. This process accounts for about 40 percent of the electricity generated in the U.S. The problem is that the by-product of burning the gas is carbon dioxide that is emitted into the atmosphere. The same is true with coal, although coal is significantly dirtier.

Allam wondered if instead of using steam to power the turbine, he could capture and compress the CO_2 and use *that* to spin the turbine. What if he could create a closed loop system in which most of the CO_2 would never be emitted to the atmosphere? If it worked, it would create nearly zero-emission natural gas! Over time, he refined his calculations and ultimately patented his incredible innovation. Then it was time to move from paper to plant. Working with a company called NetPower, Allam set out to complete a proof of concept and build the first near-zero-emissions natural gas power plant. They fired up the test facility in 2018, and after a few years of testing and refinement, they successfully connected it to the Texas power grid! Now they are working on building their first full-scale plant in West Texas. *(Disclosure: To be clear, we are NOT investors in NetPower at the time of this writing.)*

While NetPower is currently at the front of the pack, this type of innovation story is happening all over the world. There are literally hundreds of innovative companies with potential or proven solutions that accomplish carbon capture (and storage). From giant CO_2-sucking fans to take it right out of the air, to companies that pump excess carbon into underground rock formations for storage, they are at various stages of development (and feasibility), but the broader point is clear . . . according to experts, it will likely be innovation that will get us to net-zero, not the complete elimination of fossil fuels. In the meantime, there will be numerous investment opportunities as the world wrestles with reality vs. rhetoric. Let's drill down . . .

"OIL THAT IS, BLACK GOLD. TEXAS TEA!"

If you ask one hundred people who is the largest energy producer in the world, many will guess Saudi Arabia. But many would be wrong. **The United States is the world's largest oil and gas producer. We produce about 22 percent of the world's supply, with Russia (15 percent) and Saudi Arabia (9 percent) in second and third place.* Not only are we the largest, but we are also the cleanest (relatively speaking). Case in point, U.S. natural gas is about 30 percent cleaner than Russian natural gas.**[†] The same is true for oil. Have you ever seen a flame that is constantly burning at the top of an oil rig? This was a common sight for us Texans once upon a time. This burning flame is the result of a practice called flaring, which burns off the excess methane gas created when drilling for oil. **Methane is a far more potent greenhouse gas than CO_2,** which makes flaring quite filthy. This is why the U.S. has been leading the charge to end the practice and has reduced flaring intensity by 46 percent while still growing production.[‡] Unfortunately, countries with less environmental regulation have increased flaring over the past decade. **For example, Venezuela has eighteen times the flaring emissions when compared to the U.S. Point being, not all energy is created equal.** The U.S. has the most stringent regulation and environmental impact laws.

Aside from working to generate the cleanest versions of our fossil fuels, **our energy independence and standing as the world largest producer gives us a tremendous advantage in terms of economic security, food security, and national security.** For the past few decades, our world has become increasingly interdependent. Often for the sake of profits, the West has exported jobs in exchange for cheaper products. **We have also exported**

---

*https://www.washingtonpost.com/climate-environment/2022/10/08/us-is-worlds-largest-oil-producer-why-youre-going-pay-more-gas-anyway/#:~:text="We%27re%20the%20world%27s%20largest,100%20million%20barrels%20per%20day.

[†]https://clearpath.org/our-take/where-american-gas-goes-other-clean-energy-can-follow/

[‡]https://thedocs.worldbank.org/en/doc/1692f2ba2bd6408db82db9eb3894a789-0400072022/original/2022-Global-Gas-Flaring-Tracker-Report.pdf

emissions by allowing developing countries with cheap labor to pollute their own air and water while making the products we purchase. We tend to forget that if climate change is a global issue, polluting other countries doesn't solve the problem. We all live in a global "cul-de-sac," and pollution has no borders.

Then, along came COVID. If nothing else, the COVID pandemic pulled back the curtain on the fragility of our global economic machine. We learned quickly that our supply chains are almost entirely outside of our country, and thus, outside of our control. From pharmaceuticals to furniture, we could not get what we needed—anyone who has tried to buy a car over the past few years will know exactly what I'm talking about. Empty store shelves gave us all an eerie feeling. We took for granted that re-stocking would never be an issue . . . until it was.

After this wakeup call, countries have already begun to *onshore* critical elements of their supply chain and bring industry home. From food to microchips to equipment manufacturing, this de-globalization will require domestic energy. Countries with energy independence are positioned to thrive. And those with excess energy beyond their domestic needs will be dominant forces with the ability to be a "net exporter" to allies.

While the American energy industry has been persona non grata as of late (for all the reasons laid out in Part One), American energy stands to become critically important to our nation's prosperity in the decades ahead. We will have an incredible advantage as we lead the way in both in the implementation of renewables and innovative solutions for greener fossil fuels.

Let's explore a handful of themes where experts believe opportunity will emerge. Please note that many of these themes can be accessed in both public markets and private markets (for those that qualify). **Energy is notoriously volatile, so proceed with caution. Case in point, CAZ Investments never invests directly in energy without a strategic partner that has boots on the ground, decades of experience, and a proven track record.**

OPPORTUNITIES FOR INVESTMENT IN ENERGY AHEAD

1. Private Equity—**Approximately ten years ago, just 15 percent of the oil rigs operating in the U.S. were considered private equity–funded, with the balance owned by the big publicly traded companies. Today, more than 50 percent of the rigs running are private equity–backed.** They generate relatively predictable cash flows, and more conservative firms will also often pay for a hedge against falling prices, which effectively locks in profits. That said, private equity energy firms are still experiencing reluctance from institutional investors, which means that well-positioned investors can get greater access to quality opportunities than ever before. **Later in the book, we will glean some wisdom from two of the more successful energy investors in the world: Bob Zorich, cofounder of EnCap Investments and Wil VanLoh, of Quantum Energy Partners. Both firms have outstanding multi-decade-long track records.**

2. Undervalued Publicly Traded Oil and Gas Companies—In 2016, the S&P 1500 oil and gas exploration companies were trading at thirteen times their EBITDA, which is a fancy acronym for profits (EBITDA: Earnings Before Interest, Taxes, Depreciation, and Amortization). **At the time, this multiple was higher than the financial, industrial, and healthcare segments.** Despite the oil and gas sector's rebounding financial performance, they have fallen out of favor for the reasons previously discussed and now trade at a paltry 4.7 times EBITDA. Based on the realities laid out in this book, many energy experts believe this to be one of the more undervalued asset classes in the world today.

3. Refineries—In June of 2022, an article popped up in my inbox. **Mike Wirth, the CEO of Chevron was being interviewed by *Bloomberg* and dropped a bomb.* Noting that no new refineries have been built in the U.S. since the 1970s, he grimly**

*https:/seekingalpha.com/news/3845705-no-new-refineries-likely-ever-built-again-in-the-us-chevron-ceo-warns

forecast, *"My personal view is that there will never be a new refinery built in the United States."*

Against the backdrop of rising demand and growing populations, this could present a disaster for consumer prices but also a good opportunity for investors. Refineries play a critical role by turning crude oil into products like gasoline, diesel, and jet fuel. **More than 4 million diesel-powered freight trucks keep our stores stocked and Amazon packages coming each day. There are more than 22 million flights each year that require immense amounts of jet fuel. When airlines pay more for fuel, you pay more to fly. When truckers pay more to fill their tanks, you pay more at the register.**

In April of 2022, when some California refineries shut down for seasonal maintenance, gas prices jumped to near-record levels. What happens if or when such shutdowns become permanent? According to Laura Sanicola at *Reuters, "Since the onset of the global pandemic, the US has lost nearly 1 million barrels per day of oil refining capacity, with more set to be shuttered in the next few years."* In 2022, the *Washington Post* reported that *"five refineries have shut down in the past two years, reducing the nation's refining capacity by 5%."* **Five percent may seem small, but it was enough to send a supply shock wave through the system. As gas prices skyrocketed, a desperate U.S. government called on refineries to increase supply, but they were already running at near peak capacity.**

So now the obvious question. **Why in the world would we be shutting down refineries in the face of increasing demand?**

Historically, refineries are boom-and-bust businesses. They make a boatload of profits when prices surge and take significant losses when prices collapse. Now, with decades-old equipment, refineries are staring down the barrel at two bullets. **First, it requires billions to modernize these aging refineries, and it can take a decade to complete the renovation. Second, refiners are having a hard time raising capital for these renovations in the current environment, so some have simply chosen to scrap their facility and sell the valuable real estate to developers.** As we continue to lose refining capacity, we could see significant price increases as demand continues to grow.

4. Liquefaction—**Cheap, reliable, and relatively clean natural gas can be a powerful tool for decarbonization. Between 2009 and 2015, the U.S. reduced its emissions more than the next eight countries combined—all because of natural gas. Transporting natural gas is where it gets tricky. Standard natural gas can be moved in pipelines, but those take ages to construct and are geographically constrained to wherever the pipes go. Enter liquefied natural gas, or "LNG" for short. Natural gas can be liquefied when cooled to -260 degrees Fahrenheit. Once liquefied, it can be transported in cargo ships and trucks equipped with sophisticated cryogenic storage. Then, once it reaches its final destination, it is reheated and turned back into gas form. It's a pretty incredible innovation when you stop and think about it. But here's the issue: There is no new liquefaction capacity coming online in the near future.** We simply don't have enough facilities that can accomplish this complex task to keep pace with demand. In early 2023, the Federal Energy Regulatory Commission reported that *"tight LNG supply contributed to rising international prices, which reached record levels."* **Are you starting to see a theme here?** When reality collides with the wishful thinking of bad policy, prices tend to surge.

   Consider that at the time of this writing, Europe is paying six to ten times higher gas prices than it was a year ago because 40 percent of its natural gas used to come from Russia. That valve is quite literally closed now due to sanctions and the damage to the Nord Stream Pipeline. **According to Reuters, the U.S. is poised to become the world's largest LNG producer in 2023, just ahead of Australia.* We will have a distinct advantage, but the question of liquefaction capacity still remains.**

5. Private Credit for the Energy Industry—As we covered previously,

---

*https://www.reuters.com/business/energy/us-poised-regain-crown-worlds-top-lng-exporter-2023-01-04/

private credit has stepped in to lend money to companies when banks cannot or will not. Some of these companies are oil and gas companies. **Many banks have signed "net-zero pledges," which is a self-imposed proclamation limiting their lending to fossil fuels companies. While some banks are still lending discriminately, it is not nearly enough to keep pace with the billions of required capital. Once again, this creates opportunity for savvy investors in a very capital-intensive industry.**

CREATING A NET-ZERO WORLD WITH CLEAN CARBON TECHNOLOGIES

Imagine the best of all worlds . . . **If we could convert the already abundant resources of oil, coal, and natural gas to 100 percent net-zero green energy, we could have a cleaner planet while simultaneously providing billions of global citizens with the energy they need—not only citizens in developed nations, but also those in emerging nations that need cheap and abundant energy to power their economy and pull themselves out of poverty.**

One company in which I (Tony) am personally involved is Omnigen Global. **Their mind-blowing technology, which revolves around hydrogen, is poised to change the game. Although it's not currently a public company or available to invest in, it can give you a sense of the kind of groundbreaking innovation that many companies around the world are striving for in order to guide humanity to clean and cheap energy.**

When it comes to green energy, hydrogen is considered by many experts to be the "Holy Grail." **When hydrogen burns, the only byproduct is water vapor! However, creating, storing, and transporting hydrogen is expensive, with a current market cost in the range of $10,000 per ton. Compare that to the current cost of coal, which is about $100 per ton. That said, hydrogen has been commercially generated since 1783 and is now crucial for manufacturing everything from steel to semiconductors to fertilizer.**

There are three main methods for producing hydrogen and, as you'll see, not all hydrogen is created equal.

- Steam Reformation: Natural gas is reacted with steam to produce hydrogen. This is the cheapest method, but it produces significant greenhouse gases.
- Water Hydrolysis: Water is split into hydrogen and oxygen using electricity. However, the source of electricity can be both dirty and expensive—sometimes up to 2.5 times more expensive than the value of the hydrogen created.
- Pyrolysis: Fossil fuel (or biomass) is heated to high temperatures (1500–1800 degrees Fahrenheit) to produce hydrogen. Previous forms of this technology are much too expensive to be commercially viable, and they still generate a significant amount of carbon waste product and greenhouse emissions.

Since there are varying levels of environmental friendliness, there are universal color assignments applied based on how the hydrogen is made. For example, "Blue" and "Grey" hydrogen are made with natural gas but still release significant emissions when produced. "Green" hydrogen, considered the most environmentally friendly, is made with renewable energy sources, but isn't truly green at all. For example, if solar power is used to create the electricity, we know that the manufacturing of those panels has a substantial carbon footprint. **The solar panel manufacturing process requires the mining and transportation of critical minerals (dominated by China), the use and disposal of hazardous caustic chemicals, and dirty industrial furnaces. The panels will eventually fail over time and could ultimately end up in a landfill.** The *Harvard Business Review* estimates that retired solar panels could total 78 million tons of waste by 2050 because recycling them is not yet cost-effective.*

As I mentioned above, transporting hydrogen is a monumental and costly feat. **While coal can be shoveled onto a train or ship, hydrogen must be cooled to -253 Celsius—just twenty degrees warmer than absolute zero, at which all matter is essentially motionless! Then it must be highly pressurized to more than 10,000 psi. Even after all that, more than 10 percent is typically lost from leakage during transport.** The

*https:/hbr.org/2021/06/the-dark-side-of-solar-power

sophistication and cost of this process, from end to end, presents very real challenges to the broad use of hydrogen for the globe's energy needs. That was until a couple of brilliant material scientists started asking better questions. Ask better questions, get better answers.

What if we could use our existing power plants to generate clean and abundant hydrogen? Since those power plants are already connected to the grid, the massive costs from cooling, pressurization, and sophisticated transportation wouldn't be required.

In addition, what if we could utilize existing fossil fuels (coal, oil, and natural gas) to generate hydrogen in an entirely green way—i.e., with no CO_2 released whatsoever—thereby delivering the abundant clean energy that the world desperately needs and demands?

What if we could deliver truly green hydrogen, what the inventors call "Quantum Hydrogen," at the same price as today's traditional energy sources?

Like all great pioneers that came before, these scientists viewed the "impossible" from a different angle. They started from the belief that there must be a solution, while the "experts" stood by, arms folded, rooted in their skepticism. Truth be told, I was also skeptical until I visited one of the largest coal distribution plants in Pennsylvania that, for many years, has been doing the seemingly impossible. There I met Simon Hodson, founder of Omnigen Global, who had invited me to witness the technology in action with my own eyes. As a material scientist, Simon holds a staggering 140 issued patents.* For example, he developed some of the strongest concrete in the world and licensed his technology for use in the construction of New York's Freedom Tower. Simon was also instrumental in pioneering advancements in horizontal drilling. Horizontal drilling is the primary reason why the U.S. became a dominant force in global energy (from what was known as the Shale Revolution).

Simon also introduced me to his partner, Dr. Nansen Saleri, another brilliant scientist from the field of energy. For nearly a decade, Dr. Saleri was head of reservoir management for Saudi Aramco, the most profitable company in history. During his time there, Dr. Saleri was the chief architect

*https:/patents.justia.com/inventor/simon-k-hodson

for optimizing output from Ghawar, the world's largest oil field, and also pioneered AI-driven smart technology in this field. Together, Simon and Dr. Saleri have worked to bring this technology to light.

I had spoken to Simon and Dr. Saleri numerous times by Zoom, but seeing is believing. I walked into the nondescript metal building where Omnigen had been testing and refining their novel technologies for four years (in partnership with Consol Energy, a company that generates the coal and natural gas for nearly one-third of the electricity used in the U.S.).*

I put on ear protection before stepping inside the building, as the sound was deafening. The door swung open and there stood what Simon calls "Quantum Reformers." These three-story-tall systems can break down coal, oil, or natural gas at 5,500 degrees Fahrenheit (and with zero oxygen prevalent). That's about half of the temperature of the surface of the sun! Their major breakthrough was figuring out a way to keep the system itself from disintegrating at such temperatures—as any engineer could tell you, that's no easy feat. This is part of their proprietary twist on a process called Pulse Pyrolysis. Other Pulse Pyrolysis systems exist, but none can perform at these temperatures, do it without generating carbon waste products, or do it in a cost-effective manner.

When inserted into the Quantum Reformer, fossil fuel is instantly vaporized by the extreme temperature. This separates the fossil fuel into its individual elemental parts (carbon and hydrogen). The "Quantum Hydrogen" is then captured in near pure form and directed right into the power plant for green electricity generation. No transportation needed! **The most amazing part is that Omnigen believes they can accomplish this with no incremental cost to the electricity after the plant has been converted! Said another way, they believe they can produce hydrogen approximately 90 percent less expensive than that produced by other methods.**

But what happens to the carbon? **The carbon is captured (or sequestered) and turned into high-quality graphite!** Thousands of pounds of graphite flakes come out the other end of the equipment as it cools. Said another way, the "waste" by-product of the process is a valuable critical mineral.

Graphite is used in everything from solid state to batteries to nuclear

*https://www.consolenergy.com/about/

reactors. **As electric vehicle popularity has grown, the cost of graphite has surged more than 50 percent since 2020.** As we learned in the last chapter, China controls 86 percent of the world's graphite. **Unlocking the ability for everyone else to create huge amounts of low-cost graphite will be critical for supply chain issues and the worlds' goals for electrification.** Case in point, Tesla and other EV manufacturers are desperately trying to secure graphite from sources other than China, both for supply chain diversification and to make sure that buyers get the U.S. tax credits (which they become ineligible for if manufacturers secure minerals from "foreign entities of concern," China included).*

The high-grade graphite created by this process is composed of a high percentage of graphene. **Graphene is an incredible material that is just one atom thick, two hundred times stronger than steel, light as paper, and conducts electricity better than copper!** Scientists at MIT were recently experimenting with layers of graphene and figured out that if layered at a "magic angle," graphene turns into a superconductor—a rare class of materials able to conduct electricity with no energy loss and zero heat![†]

Previously, graphene has been prohibitively expensive, with prices running as high as $200,000 per ton! If it were cheaper, it would be used ubiquitously for its superior characteristics. However, the fact that high-grade graphite is effectively a by-product of the Omnigen process could dramatically drive down the cost. Once this happens, Omnigen believes that abundant graphene supply will become significantly more viable, perhaps even unleashing its own wave of exciting new innovations.

At the time of this writing, Omnigen Global has purchased a large coal-powered plant in West Virginia that it will be retrofitting. They are under contract with numerous others. For some perspective, there are approximately 225 coal-fired power plants in the U.S. and more than 1,100 in China (where two new power plants are being permitted every week). Many of the coal plants in the U.S. are struggling to stay alive, with potential shutdowns looming (despite the hard to swallow fact that we need this electricity to power our homes and businesses). Thousands of jobs at the newly

---

*https:/www.ft.com/content/46e5c98e-f9cd-4e88-8cd5-23427522c093
[†]https:/news.mit.edu/2022/superconducting-graphene-family-0708

acquired plant will now be saved. A true godsend for those workers and their families.

The U.S. regulatory environment, along with lack of capital investment, is accelerating the closure of U.S. coal plants that currently generate 25 percent of the nation's electricity. Thousands of jobs and the families they support are at risk. **But why close these crucial energy sources (that are already connected to the grid) if we can convert them into net-zero green power–generating machines?** And how about the thousands of coal plants worldwide, particularly those in developing nations that have no intent to close their doors? While I am thrilled to be a part of this particular company, this technology will likely be one of the many game-changing innovations that we will need to power our planet to net-zero. Naturally, we are very hopeful that Omnigen will be able to accomplish everything they believe they can, as it would be game-changing. Time will tell if the science and technology will scale for widespread use, but rest assured we will be rooting for them!

TECHNOLOGY DRIVES ABUNDANCE

In 1973, I was a thirteen-year-old eighth grader. In just a few short years, I would be able to get my driver's license and have my first taste of freedom. Then came the Arab Oil Embargo. Fuel shortages meant a rationing program where you could only get gas on days that corresponded to the last number on your license plate. Lines at gas stations often stretched for miles, and the scarcity created a palpable tension. My friends and I wondered if we would ever get to drive a car as experts prophesied a world which would soon go dark. I can still remember that gut-wrenching anxiety.

My eighth-grade shop teacher was a man in his mid sixties who could best be described as a bit of a curmudgeon. One day, he read a doom-and-gloom speech from renowned scientist Thomas Huxley about the end of our world as we know it. Huxley discussed how the *"oil supply is diminishing, and it is not improbable that there is a day in the not too distant future when it will be entirely exhausted."* My stomach sank. I would never drive a car. I figured I may as well start saving for a horse.

Then the teacher asked a classmate to come up the front of the room and read aloud the date on the speech. He shuffled to the front, squinted at the small print, and with a puzzled look read, "1868?" **The speech was about the diminishing supply of *whale oil*** before the turn of the century.

In dramatic fashion, the teacher reminded the class that **necessity is the mother of invention. When humanity hits a roadblock, we figure out a way forward. We always have and always will. There will always be solutions when people care enough. When humanity focuses its collective brain power toward innovation, nothing is impossible. As we know, humans went on to invent petroleum and vegetable oils to replace the whale oil. Then came coal, natural gas, nuclear, wind, solar, and more.**

I have never forgotten that powerful moment when the wisdom of my levelheaded teacher prevailed. We can never forget that scarcity is eliminated with technology. It is technology that drives abundance. This has been proven throughout history, over and over again. And yet purveyors of doomsday theories, who fail to recall history, seem to be the loudest voices. Unfortunately, fear sells.

As an example, in the 1968 book *The Population Bomb*, author Paul Ehrlich warned of coming mass worldwide starvation due to arrive in the 1970s. He couldn't have been more wrong. Then, in 1981, the *New York Times* wrote an article entitled "The Coming Famine." The author wrote, *"The world is on the brink of a food crisis"* and *"the population explosion is outpacing food production, and the result will be widespread starvation."*

Fast-forward to today, and according to the United Nations, the number of undernourished people in the world has fallen from 1.9 billion in 1990 to 821 million in 2019. That's a 50 percent decrease! This was entirely driven by innovation and new technologies. Sure, we must do a better job at distribution and supply chain waste, but with time, technology will help mitigate those issues as well.

TIME TO LEAD

During challenging times, leaders maintain a committed capacity to envision something better. If you are reading this book, it's my bet you are a leader. A leader of a company, your community, your church, your family, or even just yourself. **In my experience, there are three mandates of a true leader.**

First, **leaders see things as they are, not worse than they are.** Many people default to seeing things as worse than they really are. Some of these folks call themselves skeptics, but in reality, they are scared. It takes no courage to sit back and view the world through a lens of cynicism, waiting for the worst to happen.

Second, **leaders see things as better than they are,** the potential of how things *could* be. Leaders don't lie to themselves about the current situation, but they must have a vision. **As the wisdom of Proverbs says,** *"Where there is no vision, the people will perish."*

And finally, **leaders make it the way they see it.** They make their vision a reality with courage and hard work. Fortunately, there are people all over the world, folks like Simon and Dr. Saleri, who are laser-focused on solutions to support our energy needs while also taking care of the planet we have so graciously been entrusted with. Solutions are here, and more are coming! Remember that when you read the next "whale oil" headline.

In the meantime, the realities of our energy demands will create tremendous opportunities for investors. Energy may certainly find itself as part of your own personal Holy Grail portfolio.

As already mentioned, in Part 2 of this book, we will hear from Wil Van-Loh of Quantum Energy and Bob Zorich of EnCap Investments, two of the largest private energy investors in the world. They will share their vision and ideas for how one can take advantage of our current climate (no pun intended).

For more information on energy and the items we covered here, feel free to visit **www.WhyEnergyNow.com.**

BETTING ON THE OUTLIERS

Now let's take a look at venture capital, a subset of private equity that is willing and able to take gigantic risks on early stage companies in order to bring about massive change and disrupt the status quo. In fact, many venture firms are investing in breakthrough green technologies that we discussed in this chapter. Venture firms have some serious intestinal fortitude, knowing that the vast majority of the companies they invest in will likely fail. But the ones that survive could very well be the next Google or Tesla. Let's turn the page and dive into this exciting segment, which is the tip of the spear for global innovation.

CHAPTER 7

VENTURE CAPITAL AND DISRUPTIVE TECHNOLOGY

"Technology is a force that converts scarcity into
abundance, over and over again."
—Peter Diamandis

In 1996, Vinod Khosla saw a highly improbable opportunity. The internet was just beginning to take root, and Juniper Networks was a startup with a bold prediction. The founders believed that if high-speed internet was the future, everyone would need to buy the necessary equipment (IP routers). This was at a time when everyone used dial-up, Google did not yet exist, and there were fewer than one hundred thousand websites worldwide. (Today there are over 2 billion websites and growing.)

The founders of Juniper Networks had approached Khosla for a significant venture investment. He began his due diligence, and every major telecommunications company he spoke to said they didn't really see the need for ubiquitous high-speed internet access. **Undeterred and, like all great VCs, something of a contrarian, Khosla knew it is not always smart to listen to the customer.** As Henry Ford famously said, "If I would have asked them what they wanted, they would have said faster horses." **Khosla trusted his instincts, believing that high-speed internet was the way of the future and that telecommunications companies would ultimately need to buy a whole heck of a lot of Juniper's equipment.**

Khosla and his partners at the venture capital firm Kleiner Perkins plunked $4 million into the startup. **That single investment returned $7 billion in**

profits for their investors. To this day, it remains one the most successful investments in venture capital history. **Returns like this are few are far between, but the hunt for high-risk/high-reward opportunities is the business of venture capital in a nutshell.**

As a quick refresher, venture capital is a subset of private equity. But whereas traditional private equity tends to focus on established companies with significant revenue and profits—i.e., good companies that can be made better—venture capital usually focuses on early stage private companies that might have little to no revenue, but big potential to disrupt the status quo down the line. **However, investing in startup companies, which are prone to failure, is a high-risk endeavor. It is often said that about one in ten venture investments survives.** But the one that does survive, if truly a home run, offsets all the other losers and then some. **Stomaching this level of risk isn't everyone's idea of a good time. Most high-net-worth individuals have an average of 1–5 percent of their portfolio in venture capital.** Some certainly have more, but others choose to avoid it altogether as it sometimes requires nerves of steel.

As a rule of thumb, Khosla looks to generate a minimum of ten to fifty times his original investment. He is looking for moonshot companies that face enormous odds but will, if successful, reshape the future (and produce a substantial return on his investment). His extraordinary track record, both as an entrepreneur and a venture capitalist, has earned him a place among the Forbes 400 wealthiest individuals, a far cry from his humble roots in rural India.

RENTING MAGAZINES

The son of an army officer, Khosla grew up at a time when technology was only available to the elites. He still didn't have a TV or telephone in his home when he left for university. Instead, he would rent magazines and get inspired by innovative entrepreneurs on the other side of the globe. He was deeply moved by the story of Andy Grove, a Hungarian immigrant who moved to Silicon Valley to join the founding team of Intel. The company went on to become one of the biggest chip makers in the world.

At age thirty, just two years out of Stanford Business School, Khosla founded Sun Microsystems with investments from Kleiner Perkins and Sequoia, both landmark Silicon Valley venture firms. The company took off like a rocket, and within five years, Sun Microsystems had over $1 billion in annual sales! Khosla ultimately decided that managing a company was not as exciting as helping find, fund, and foster the next disruptive technology. He became a partner at Kleiner Perkins, where he made some extraordinary investments in small startups like Amazon, Google, and Twitter.

In 2004 Khosla decided that he only wanted to invest his own personal fortune and created Khosla Ventures to do so. His mission was to help companies with bold ideas in healthcare, infrastructure, robotics, transportation, augmented reality, and artificial intelligence. In 2009, he decided to let certain outside investors come alongside him, although he remains the largest investor. Talk about alignment!

To say Khosla Ventures has done well is quite the understatement. They are consistently recognized as one of the top performers in Venture Capital and have helped build over forty unicorns. (A unicorn is a startup that goes from zero to a billion or more in valuation.) They were early investors in companies many of us use every day: Affirm, Instacart, DoorDash, Stripe, Opendoor, Impossible (foods), and OpenAI (the company behind ChatGPT). Another notable Khosla Ventures investment was Square. Jack Dorsey (founder of Twitter) approached Khosla with a new idea to disrupt the antiquated credit card processing industry. He had just four employees at the time. Today, the company has a valuation north of $40 billion.

Later in the book we have the privilege of sitting down with Vinod Khosla for an interview. Full disclosure: We are big fans of Khosla, and CAZ Investments has a strategic investment relationship with the firm.

IT'S NOT ALL UNICORNS AND RAINBOWS

Although Vinod Khosla is a success story worth highlighting, the overall performance of venture capital has been choppy and less predictable. According to Preqin, there are 5,048 venture capital funds in the market globally. This adds up to a very saturated market, and for every Khosla Ventures, there are dozens of firms that perform quite poorly. Although the world tends to glamorize the many successes of venture investing, we can't gloss over the many epic failures. Because of its somewhat speculative nature, venture as an industry is often guilty of jumping on the latest trends and buying into hype. FOMO (fear of missing out) is quite prevalent when there is a race to be on the cutting edge. WeWork is perhaps one of the best examples of a company that capitalized on the herd mentality within venture capital. The company would lease office space, make it trendy inside, and rent desks to younger folks that loved a coworking environment. But instead of valuing it as the real estate business it was, the charismatic founder marketed WeWork as the *"world's first physical social network."* Venture firms clamored to get a piece of the company at each fundraising round. It was a frenzy, and WeWork became one of the largest renters of commercial space in the country, with over 11 million square feet to pay for.

Flying too close to the sun, the company's valuations soared to a preposterous $47 billion prior to their filing to go public. When Wall Street finally got a look under the hood, their financials told a story of a company with an entirely unsustainable business model that was bleeding cash. Ultimately, WeWork's financial prospects imploded. In November of 2023, the company filed for bankruptcy, sending shock waves through the industry. The company has a total valuation of just under $100 million, leaving behind it a wake of capital destruction.

When it comes to venture capital, the disparity between the all-stars and "the rest" is extremely large. **Between 2004 and 2016, the top 10 percent of venture capital firms generated returns of 34 percent annually.** This was the golden age, the era that gave us the invention of the iPhone, YouTube, Uber, and hundreds of other disruptive tech companies. **The bottom 10 percent of venture firms lost money during this period, with average returns of -6.50 percent. The middle of the pack did not do much better than traditional stocks. The NASDAQ 100, which consists of the largest one hundred tech stocks, generated returns of just over 10 percent annualized; the median return for venture firms was just over 12 percent (see figure below). Let's not sugarcoat it: Mediocre returns like those are not worth the tradeoff of having your money locked up in a fund for a decade.**

It's no accident that the same VC firms seem to appear at the top of the performance lists each and every year, both in terms of the number

Returns for Venture Firms (2004–2016)	Annualized Returns
Top Decile	34.60%
Top Quartile	22.40%
Median IRR	12.15%
Bottom Quartile	3.36%
Bottom Decile	-6.50%

Source: Cambridge and Associates

of successful companies they have invested in, as well the returns generated from the companies they have exited. I attribute this to a unique dynamic I call the "flywheel of success."

THE FLYWHEEL OF SUCCESS

If you are investing in a strategy where you expect to lose nine out of ten times, you need a few things to be successful . . .

1. Deep Pockets—Diversifying across lots of different companies requires very deep pockets. Individual investors who bet on their brother-in-law's tech startup have horrific odds compared to the professionals who allocate their portfolio across numerous companies.
2. Longevity—The most successful venture firms have numerous vehicles and launch new funds every two to four years (as a new vintage). This gives them diversification across market cycles. Spreading their investments out over time also improves the odds of one of their funds containing the next Facebook, SpaceX, or Salesforce.
3. Deal Flow—Startup entrepreneurs inevitably aim to secure investments from the best venture capital firms, who can provide

invaluable wisdom and guidance in addition to funding. When a top-tier firm makes an investment, it sends a message of confidence to the marketplace, which helps entrepreneurs raise capital, hire talent, and win customers. Therefore, the top venture firms are *invited* to invest in hot startups; the less successful firms must go deal hunting, resulting in adverse selection and poor performance relative to their peers.

The smart money knows this "flywheel" dynamic well, which is why the wealthiest investors (and institutions) almost exclusively invest with the top-tier firms. In 2022, approximately 73 percent of all new capital raised went to experienced venture capital firms that have successfully created and managed a minimum of four fund vehicles (aka vintages) in their history.

Naturally, the burning question is: **How in the world does an individual investor get access to top-tier venture capital firms?**

Top-tier venture firms will often have a "stated" minimum of $10–25 million for prospective investors. Even this is a bit misleading, though, as top firms are typically oversubscribed, meaning no new investors are allowed in—even those with giant checkbooks. Therefore, the only route for most investors is to partner with firms like ours, which have existing relationships in place. Individuals, and their advisors, can leverage our buying power and long-standing relationships. And by locking arms with our clients as one single investor, we're able to negotiate the best fees and other benefits, such as priority position to invest directly in some of the VC's winners (also called co-investment opportunities). In fairness, we are not the only firm that takes this approach, so as an investor, I would look at two important criteria before jumping in with a firm . . .

1. Are the total "all in" fees reasonable when you add the cost of the venture capital manager and the partnership that is providing access. Top-tier venture capital managers get paid well, but the organization providing you with access should be getting some preferential treatment because of their purchasing power.
2. Is there an alignment of interests? Do the access provider and its shareholders have their own personal capital at risk? Or are you

using an access "platform" that could care less how the investment performs?

The next logical question: **Is now the right time for you to invest in venture capital?**

DRY POWDER

As I write this, venture capital is experiencing a harsh winter. The tech sector has been hit hard in both public and private markets. Certain venture funds will experience rough waters ahead as their portfolio companies struggle to survive. And yet, spring always follows winter. A bull market follows a bear market. This season of austerity has created a return to healthy investing practices. In an environment where valuations are more reasonable, companies will be more prudent with their purse strings.

Many of today's biggest and best venture firms have an incredibly optimistic outlook. **First of all, the global venture community has hundreds of billions in cash (aka dry powder) ready to invest when the right opportunities come along.** Second, companies these days are waiting longer to go public, which means there is more time for value creation. This means better returns for investors as well. **Get this . . . since 2008, the average time for a company to go from launch to IPO has doubled to almost ten years.**

ACCELERATION OF INNOVATION

As we look to the horizon, **we see that we are heading into the greatest acceleration of innovation in the history of humanity,** and venture capitalists are the tip of spear. They take massive risks, and sometimes they lose big. But when they win, they win big, all while funding the next generation of life-changing innovation. Imagine a world without smartphones, personal computers, or the internet. **Companies like Apple, Amazon, Zoom, Tesla, Spotify, Airbnb, Facebook, Twitter, and SpaceX were all funded by venture capital.** There are hundreds more that have transformed our daily lives, all thanks to the bold risk-takers in venture capital.

Today, we are on the cusp of more groundbreaking, life-altering innovation. From artificial intelligence (AI), to robotics, to 3D printing, to astonishing advances in precision healthcare, the future is bright for mankind. Let's take a moment to highlight just a few of the incredible innovations that will birth thousands of new companies and create massive increases in quality of life around the world.

- Artificial Intelligence (AI)—The fastest-growing internet application in history is NOT Facebook, Instagram, or Twitter. It is in fact, ChatGPT, an AI platform in which we are investors. Within a few months of its launch, ChatGPT garnered 100 million users. *Forbes* describes ChatGPT as a *"clever ask-me-anything tool [that] has been the go-to-resource for advice on just about any topic it's been trained on and can complete complex tasks like debugging code, doing research and writing articles in an endearing human-like tone."* You are likely already using it or one of its competitors (e.g., Google's Bard).

  As those of us in the knowledge and service economies can already see, AI will make people more productive than ever. However, there is a legitimate fear that certain jobs could be eliminated as a result. While the debate is contentious on both sides, those at greatest risk are those who do not lean in and use AI to augment their work and become more efficient. The traditionalists who dig their heels in and cling to the ways of old are most at risk of becoming obsolete.

  Experts believe that doctors, lawyers, medical researchers, screenwriters, and computer programmers are just a few of the professionals that will be able to move faster than ever. AI will also be able to assist teachers. **Khan Academy, the popular free online education platform, recently launched Khanmingo, described as a "world class AI tutor for anyone, anywhere." Their technology powers an infinitely scalable solution of AI tutoring while also acting as a teacher's assistant for traditional education environments. Since high-quality education is the great equalizer, this could be wonderful for society as a whole.**

We are in the early stages of AI, but its force as a disruptive, yet incredibly helpful, technology is already clear. It will likely become as integral to our lives as the smartphone.

AI has already taken the world of venture capital by storm. **The *New York Times* writes that the "gold rush into startups working on 'generative' artificial intelligence has escalated into a no-holds-barred deal-making mania."** As we now know, the vast majority of these startups will be dismal failures, but the next Google, Apple, or Facebook is likely being created by two people in a garage at this very moment. This is where venture capitalists can usher in the next wave of innovation with their willingness to take risky bets on startups with the possibility of a gigantic asymmetric upside.

- Healthcare Advances and Precision Therapies—Neuralink, a breakthrough company cofounded by Elon Musk, has surgically installed a coin-sized brain-computer interface that "uses thousands of small electrodes embedded in the brain to read signals emitted by neurons and transmit them to a computer." This technological innovation has far-reaching implications. **The company's first goal is to successfully restore someone's vision, even if they were born blind! Next, they will work toward restoring motor function in paralyzed patients. Musk believes the implant could also help address other neurological disorders, like Parkinson's, Alzheimer's, and tinnitus.** This is truly the stuff of science fiction made real, and it has the potential to dramatically improve the quality of life for millions around the world.

Dr. David Sinclair, a leading Harvard geneticist, has answered a hotly debated question: *What drives aging?* **In 2023, he and his team demonstrated their ability to speed up or even reverse aging in cells and restore signs of youth in mice.** *Time* magazine explained that *"reversibility (of the cells) makes a strong case for the fact that the main drivers of aging aren't mutations to the DNA, but miscues in the epigenetic instructions that somehow go awry."** Sinclair

---

*https:/time.com/6246864/reverse-aging-scientists-discover-milestone/

and his team have figured out a way to reboot cells, erase their corrupted instruction files, and restore their proper function. What does this mean for you and me? By reversing the aging process in cells, we will one day be able to rejuvenate the body and halt diseases related to aging (Alzheimer's, heart disease, etc.). In one amazing example, Sinclair has successfully restored vision in blind mice by rejuvenating the nerves in their eyes through gene therapy. Next up? Testing in humans.

At the third annual "Human Genome Editing" conference, doctors shared incredible stories of people undergoing experimental treatments using CRISPR, a tool for editing or modifying genes. These patients had tried everything, and CRISPR was their last resort. Alyssa, a teenager in the UK who had an aggressive form of leukemia that did not respond to chemotherapy or a bone marrow transplant, was months from death when she decided to try CRISPR. Doctors were able to modify healthy T-cells from a donor so they would not be rejected by Alyssa's body and could freely attack her cancer. Ten months after the treatment her cancer was undetectable. She is back to living a normal teenage life.

While we could highlight countless other technologies, Tony recently published a *New York Times* bestseller titled **Life Force: How New Breakthroughs in Precision Medicine Can Transform the Quality of Your Life & Those You Love**. He interviewed more than 150 of the world's top medical minds about the latest research and amazing advancements in precision medicine. We highly recommend reading it, as it will greatly impact your health and that of your loved ones!

- Supersonic Travel—Although one can appreciate the expediency of modern air travel, sitting on a plane for hours on end can be a literal pain in the butt. Both of us are constantly on the road, so when someone declares New York to London in ninety minutes a realistic possibility, we get excited!

This is the aim of Hermeus, a startup backed by the U.S. government and elite venture capital firms, including Khosla and Founders Fund, that is building a fleet of supersonic

aircraft not far from the world's busiest airport in Atlanta, Georgia. The company intends to build planes capable of Mach 5 (3,850 mph), **a speed five times faster than any commercial aircraft today and twice as fast as the now-decommissioned Concorde.** As an added bonus, the view will also be incredible, as the planes will fly at ninety thousand feet, the highest attainable altitude before crossing the threshold of space. Imagine looking out and seeing the curvature of the earth with barely enough time to enjoy a bag of peanuts before beginning your descent. **Hermeus will be testing an autonomous plane in 2023 and hopes to have a passenger-ready plane by 2029!**

- 3D Printing and Robotics—Owning a home is a wonderful privilege. Unfortunately, for 1.6 billion people, that is currently an unattainable goal. The solution? Affordable and durable 3D-printed homes. Much like toothpaste squeezed from a tube, these homes are created by a giant printer that squirts out layer upon layer of thin, specialized concrete to create flawless, fortified walls. The homes not only look very cool, they're also wind, water, mold, and termite resistant. **This is a game changer for countries where hurricanes, typhoons, and floods quickly wipe out poorly constructed shacks at great peril to the families within.** This profound technology is being pioneered by ICON, a company Tony personally partnered with to build nearly one hundred homes in a Mexican community. ICON is now building on a large scale, beginning with a master planned community in Texas that will feature a 3D-printed spa, pool, community center, and more. (Full disclosure: CAZ Investments was a seed investor in ICON.)

  In construction and beyond, 3D printing will transform many aspects of manufacturing as we know it. One can now precision 3D print extremely complex objects using hundreds of different materials from titanium to carbon fiber. Researchers have even begun 3D printing human organs made of living human cells—equipped with blood vessels and all!

  Like 3D printing, robotics has recently taken the world by storm, and Amazon is the perfect case study. Amazon's high-tech warehouses are staffed by a mixture of humans and robots working symbiotically. Robots self-navigate around warehouses to grab whatever you ordered so it can be packaged and shipped to your doorstep. These robots can pick and place over one thousand items per hour. **It is no wonder that Amazon now manufactures their own robots and currently has over 520,000 working 24/7.** We have seen estimates that the robotics sector could compound revenue at more than an 80 percent annual rate for the next decade.

FEARLESS FUEL

A true strength of capitalism is that venture investors are willing to take massive risks on visionaries that will improve the quality of life for everyone, not only in America but around the world. Karl Marx never sat in a self-driving car! We are lucky enough to be alive when the tempo of transformation is faster than at any other time in human history.

Venture is on the front lines of almost all technological progress. With billions in cash waiting to be deployed by venture firms, we can only imagine what advances will be funded and come to market in the years ahead.

Undoubtedly, there will be some big winners and big losers. **If you decide to invest in venture, *who* you invest with means everything.** The amount you invest should also be relatively minimal. As we mentioned earlier, even ultra-high-net-worth individuals are only willing to risk an average of 1–5 percent of their portfolios in this category. But whether you choose to invest in venture or not, we will all be the beneficiaries of its successes! For more information on venture investing, please visit www.WhyVentureNow.com.

KEEPING IT REAL

Wow, we have come a long way! We have now covered numerous alternative investing strategies, many of which could be a part of our personalized Holy Grail portfolio. But we cannot leave out the largest asset class of them all, one with a total value exceeding $300 trillion! Turn the page, and let's explore the world of real estate!

CHAPTER 8

REAL ESTATE

THE WORLD'S BIGGEST ASSET

"Buy land. They aren't making any more."
—Mark Twain

Real estate is the undisputed behemoth of alternative investments and is the oldest and largest asset class. It is likely a part of most Holy Grail portfolios whether it be a residential home, investment properties, or both.

With 7.9 billion people on earth, *residential* **real estate is naturally the largest category, with a global value of $258 trillion!*** Everyone needs a place to live regardless of the economy, interest rates, etc. And North America represents nearly 20 percent of the world's total real estate value despite holding just 7 percent of the world's population.

Agricultural land is the second largest category, with a total value exceeding $35 trillion. *Commercial* real estate runs a close third, with an estimated global value of $32.6 trillion.

There are numerous subcategories of real estate, from self-storage to hotels to life sciences to timber. On the whole, and over many decades, real estate performance has generated conservative mid-single-digit to low-double-digit returns. But the use of leverage has allowed for substantially higher returns—coupled with substantially higher risk! Of course, returns are very dependent on location, the local economy, the amount of leverage (loan-to-value levels), and numerous other factors.

*https://www.savills.com/impacts/market-trends/the-total-value-of-global-real-es tate.html

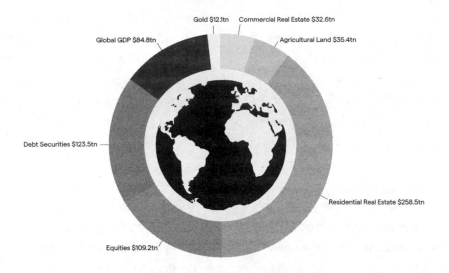

Gold $12.1tn   Commercial Real Estate $32.6tn

Global GDP $84.8tn   Agricultural Land $35.4tn

Debt Securities $123.5tn

Residential Real Estate $258.5tn

Equities $109.2tn

Real estate is the also an asset class that, for U.S. investors, offers government-sanctioned tax avoidance. As a refresher, taxpaying real estate investors receive the benefit of "depreciation," which means the cash flows from real estate income can often be sheltered from some or all taxation. Also, investors can avoid paying taxes on any increase in value when their property is sold by exercising the option of buying more property and rolling over the gains as equity in the new investment. This is called a 1031 exchange. Done over and over again, this can create a perpetual deferral of taxation.

To take it a step further, some investors can ultimately wipe out taxes on ALL their accumulated gains with some clever, and entirely legal, estate planning (particularly in the U.S.). Many of the preeminent real estate families know this tactic quite well. You should talk to your own tax advisor before using this strategy, but here is how it generally works . . .

As you buy and sell investment properties over your lifetime, you continually roll your appreciated equity gains into your next property purchase using a 1031 exchange.* Assuming current tax law holds, when you pass away, your heirs will inherit your property and receive a "step-up" in their cost basis. This means that the value of the property at the time of death

*This applies to U.S. taxpayers only and you should consult with a licensed tax practitioner.

becomes the new "floor" by which future gains will be calculated. Translation: All of the previous gains that compounded and accumulated over the course of your lifetime are eliminated, and your heirs can now choose to sell the appreciated properties with ZERO tax. **Tax-efficient income, potentially unlimited tax deferral, and tax avoidance of all capital gains (upon death) are precisely why many of the nation's wealthiest families are real estate dynasties.**

THE TIDE IS GOING OUT

For the past forty years, real estate investors have had tremendous wind at their backs. In 1981, the ten-year treasury was paying just under 16 percent interest. As interest rates fell for four straight decades, nearly all asset prices went up. Real estate was no exception (aside from the Global Financial Crisis, which had some unique dynamics that we will unpack in a bit).

In 2021, real estate was reaching a fever pitch as rates were flirting with darn near free. Unexpectedly, in the middle of the COVID pandemic, real estate produced the strongest returns since before the 2008 financial crisis (see figure on page 109). Residential real estate led the way as low inventory caused prospective homebuyers to literally form lines around the block. All cash offers, short time frames to close, no contingencies . . . these were the hallmarks of the buying frenzy.

Apartment investors were also gleeful as rents increased as fast as at any time in recent history. Industrial real estate came in a strong second, as consumer spending was fast and loose. **Self-storage facilities were sold out from the surge of people moving throughout the country. Real estate prices quickly became irrationally high, with disciplined investors left scratching their heads.**

But then, the tide turned.

The trillions of excess money printed by the government began to slosh around in the system. Inflation turned out to not be "transitory"—in fact, it was here to crash the party. The Fed began hiking rates and real estate has since felt the effects. **The lesson: While hard assets can be incredibly valuable, they can also turn quickly when their price is extremely sensitive to interest rates.**

REAL ESTATE VALUES SURGE (2021*)

Self-Storage	57.6%
Residential	45.8%
Industrial	45.4%
Retail	41.9%
Diversified	20.5%
Infrastructure	18.6%
Timber	16.4%
Office	13.4%
Retail	41.9%
Healthcare	7.7%
Lodging/Resorts	6.3%

Source: PREQUIN

As we write this, we are in the middle of a highly tumultuous real estate market, and charting a course in high seas is quite difficult. What we know for sure is that the long trend of sinking interest rates has reversed course, and as a result we are starting to see fractures within certain categories of real estate. Some segments of real estate are weathering the storm much better. **For this chapter, we will look at COMMERCIAL and RESIDENTIAL separately, as they are very different animals.**

COMMERCIAL REAL ESTATE

For decades, many have considered San Francisco the crown jewel of California, a once-gorgeous city, home to some of the world's most expensive real estate and finest restaurants. Buoyed by the explosive growth of tech companies, San Francisco was continuously ranked in the top ten most expensive cities in the world in which to live.

For companies that called San Francisco home, an office address on California Street was a coveted sign of success. As the *Wall Street Journal* reported, "The corridor runs through the heart of the city's financial district and is lined with offices for banks and other companies that help fuel the global tech economy." At 350 California Street stands a gorgeous twenty-two-story glass-and-stone tower that once housed hundreds of Union Bank employees. In 2019, the building was valued at $300 million. Today, less than four years later, the building is 70 percent vacant and droves of drug addicts and homeless loiter outside. **In early 2023, the building sold for roughly $60 million, an unprecedented 80 percent drop in value (and far less than it would cost to build today).**

According to the *San Francisco Chronicle*, the city has an "astounding 18.4 million square feet of vacant [office] space—enough to house 92,000 employees or the equivalent of 13 Salesforce towers." And it is not just San Francisco that is experiencing a commercial real estate crisis. Real estate firm Cushman and Wakefield reported that "as much as 330 million square feet of U.S. office space could become vacant and unused by 2030 due to remote and hybrid work. When added to another 740 million square feet of space that will become vacant from 'natural' causes, the total is around 1 billion square feet of unused office space building up over the next seven years."*

As we look to the future, there will be some pain and equity destruction, but like all market cycles, it will give way to some extraordinary investment opportunities. **That said, we can't treat this current downturn like those of the past.** The pandemic has introduced new risks and dynamics for us to consider when it comes to real estate investing.

RISKY BUSINESS

In decades past, we would look at commercial real estate through a standard economic lens. Real estate cycles typically coincided with the overall economy: A recession meant fewer jobs; fewer jobs meant less occupied office space; fewer jobs also meant less spending on shopping (retail) and less travel (hospitality). Historically, these downturns have predictably given way to a recovery and a new cycle begins. These traditional cycles will likely continue

---

*https:/www.cushmanwakefield.com/en/united-states/insights/obsolescence-equals -opportunity

in a broad sense, but there are some new "post-pandemic" risks we must incorporate into our typical understanding of real estate cycles.

- Obsolescence Risk—During the pandemic, we all discovered that Zoom was pretty darn effective for keeping some companies running with remote employees. Many of those companies quickly did the math and realized that remote workers could create huge cost savings by reducing the need for expensive office space. **Hence, the recent phenomenon of empty urban skyscrapers dubbed "*Zombie Towers.*"** This new dynamic of remote or hybrid work has also created what some experts are calling *obsolescence risk*. Commercial real estate buyers must ask themselves if the property they want to purchase is still viable. And beyond that, if it will be viable in ten years or fifteen years or twenty. Are traditional office buildings becoming obsolete? If so, will the surrounding retail and restaurants suffer as collateral damage? How will people choose to live, work, and shop five to ten years from now? Nobody yet knows

OFFICE VACANCIES CONTINUE TO CLIMB

Percentage of all office space that is vacant

Source: JLL

the answers, but some commercial building owners refuse to sit on their hands while they wait to find out. In Boston, for example, *Fortune* magazine reported that the "housing market shortage is so acute, and the office glut is so big that [the city] will offer 75% tax breaks on office-to-residential conversions."* Some commercial buildings are converting to apartments; others are converting to data centers. All in hopes of staving off foreclosure.

Artificial intelligence is another new risk that could affect the value of commercial real estate as it makes certain jobs obsolete or, at minimum, reduces the number of people (and thus office space) required to get the job done. In May of 2023, the CEO of Chegg, an online tutoring and exam prep company, announced that Chat-GPT was having an impact on its ability to gain new customers. **Why pay for a tutor when AI can help you with your algebra homework for free? After his comments, Chegg's stock plummeted 49 percent in a single day due to fears that the company might be a canary in the coal mine of the knowledge economy.**

In fairness, some argue that AI will create a new genre of company and that a rising field of AI-based businesses will emerge to fill empty offices. This is indeed already happening to some degree, but these companies tend to have very low head counts and no need for large amounts of office space. Midjourney, the most popular AI image creation tool, has over 15 million users, nine figures in revenue, and a team of under twenty people!† Our friend Peter Diamandis, a futurist, tweeted a prediction that with AI, "we will see the first 3 person, billion-dollar company in the next year!"

So what other obsolescence risks lie ahead? How will these disruptive trends play out when it comes to commercial real estate? The truth is, we simply do not fully know yet, thus we must proceed with caution.

*https:/fortune.com/2023/07/13/boston-housing-market-shortage-commerical-real-office-glut-pilot-program/
†https:/www.forbes.com/companies/midjourney/?sh=6d4292edf049

1. Geographic/Political Risk—As remote or hybrid work became a viable option for many, our country experienced a huge wave of internal migration. Large numbers of people fled expensive cities. **Not surprisingly, they chose states with lower tax rates, lower costs of living, and higher quality of life. California was the biggest loser in this reshuffling. Between April 2020 and July 2022, more than half a million people left California, taking with them more than $50 billion in total income. New York City lost 468,200 residents, nearly 5.7 percent of its population,* a loss reflected in high vacancy rates.** The billions lost in state income tax revenue has added to already steep deficits, raising conversation of even higher tax rates for those left behind. This vicious cycle could push even more people to pull the plug and move. California is so fearful of further exodus that they are discussing an "exit tax," which would confiscate a percentage of the total wealth of people leaving the state.† Reminds me of the classic Eagles song "Hotel California," where you can check out, but you can never leave.

   Like individuals, numerous companies have also relocated, to more business-friendly states with lower cost of employment. Stanford University reported that more than 352 major corporations have left California, including 11 Fortune 1000s. Charles Schwab, CBRE, and Oracle are just a few of the many titans that moved their headquarters from California to Texas.‡ This is bolstering the job markets of these more business-friendly states. **In 2023, the *Wall Street Journal* named Nashville, Tennessee, the**

*https:/www.foxbusiness.com/lifestyle/new-york-city-lost-nearly-half-million-resi dents-since-start-covid-pandemic
†https:/www.wsj.com/articles/the-hotel-california-wealth-tax-high-taxes-res ident-flight-new-jersey-massachusetts-new-york-texas-florida-utah-tennessee -cost-of-living-education-crime-silicon-valley-south-c39602ac?cx_testId=3&cx _testVariant=cx_171&cx_artPos=3&mod=WTRN#cxrecs_s
‡https:/www.concordia.edu/blog/19-corporations-and-businesses-fleeing-california -for-texas.html

#1 job market in the country.* The income tax–free Music City has quickly become an economic powerhouse. Florida and Texas have also seen explosive growth. So will these migratory trends continue? Only time will tell; however, we must take note as real estate values, both commercial and residential, are highly dependent on location as well as city and state level policies.

2. Interest Rates and Unintended Consequences—As we have mentioned, we've just lived through the fastest interest rate hike in history. This is going to have some harsh unintended consequences that will ripple through all the various categories of real estate, but none will take it on the chin like commercial real estate. While high vacancy is problematic, it is the trillions in loans on these buildings that could create a banking catastrophe. There is a fast-approaching debt wall. Approximately $2.5 trillion in commercial real estate loans will mature by 2028, with $1.5 trillion coming due by 2025. Barring some major government intervention, it's likely that many owners will be unable to refinance, or will be so underwater that it will be best to let the bank foreclose. This is happening already. According to *Bloomberg*, "In New York and London, owners of gleaming office towers are walking away from their debt rather than pouring good money after bad. The landlords of San Francisco's largest mall have abandoned it."[†] Banks will be left holding the proverbial bag, forced to sell these properties at deep discounts and write down the loans. To be fair, there are a few bright spots. When we interviewed Barry Sternlicht (Chapter 22), founder of real estate giant Starwood Capital, he explained that smaller, boutique buildings with world-class amenities are still filling up. They often house high-margin, low–head count firms like hedge funds, local law firms, AI companies, etc.

*https://www.wsj.com/articles/sunbelt-cities-nashville-and-austin-are-nations
-hottest-job-markets-5a454a53
†https://www.bloomberg.com/news/articles/2023-06-23/commercial-real-estate
-reset-is-causing-distress-from-san-francisco-to-hong-kong?srnd=premium

MASSIVE QUANTITY OF REAL ESTATE DEBT MATURING, NEEDING REFINANCING

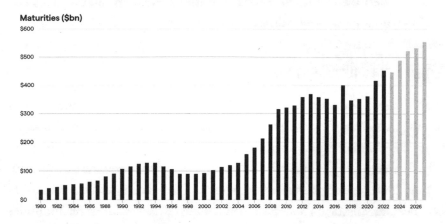

Maturities ($bn)

Source: TREPP Morgan Stanley Research Credit Daily Shot

As a result of the coming loan predicament for banks and tenants (see figure above), Morgan Stanley predicts a 40 percent drop in the value of retail and office space, which is unlike anything we have experienced in modern history.* As borrowers default, the banks will write down these loans, creating severe losses. This could ultimately lead to a banking crisis. **Even more concerning, 70 percent of commercial loans are held by regional banks, which have recently seen a string of failures, from Silicon Valley Bank to First Republic to Signature Bank.**

As values plummet, there is a tremendous amount of smart money chomping at the bit for deals. Several funds specializing in distressed real estate have recently been established and are on the prowl. Their thinking is in line with a principle made famous by the late Sir John Templeton (founder of Templeton Funds and brilliant contrarian investor): "Buy when there is blood in the streets." For investors, there will be a major opportunity to buy at deep discounts as this story unfolds.

*https:/www.bloomberg.com/news/articles/2023-04-08/a-1-5-trillion-wall-of-debt -is-looming-for-us-commercial-properties

All things considered, a significant amount of commercial real estate seems headed for a cliff, but the residential real estate market is sending different signals. Let's dive a little deeper . . .

RESIDENTIAL REAL ESTATE

As we entered the second year of the pandemic, the housing market was redlining. It was early 2022, prices were surging and buyers were desperate to purchase something . . . anything!

At first glance, one might be quick to assume that we are flirting with another 2008 residential real estate bubble. The fear-mongering media has been beating this drum for quite some time. Below is a list of headlines from articles written by MSNBC's senior real estate correspondent; taken together, they demonstrate just how wrong one can be when attempting to predict the market.

"Housing Today: A bubble larger than 2006."—October 2015

"We're in a new housing bubble."—August 2016

"It's better to rent than to buy in today's housing market."—September 2018

"The housing market is about to shift in a bad way for home buyers."—July 2019

"Next year will be hard on the housing market, especially in big cities."—December 2019

"Housing boom is over as new home sales fall." —July 2021

In the years between the first and last of these headlines, the average home price swelled from $300,000 to $523,000, and buyers were able to lock in the lowest mortgage rates in history. Today, we have even more talking heads beating the "crash is coming" drum. And while prices are most certainly softening, the data seem to be telling a different story.

HOUSING PERFORMANCE THROUGH RECESSIONS

S&P Case-Shiller U.S. National House Price Index
— Index   Recessions

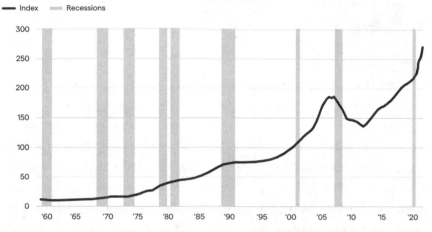

Looking at history, one would think that a recession would guarantee a decline in home prices. **However, since 1960, we have had nine recessions, and residential real estate prices only dropped during one of those—the Great Recession.** As I write this, we are flirting with another recession (the most recent being in 2020), and residential prices have indeed come down. The thirty-year mortgage rate is now above 8 percent, the highest rate seen in over twenty years. This has undoubtedly caused prices to soften. But will they keep dropping? Has demand completely dried up? Do we have too much inventory? Let's unpack the facts.

SUPPLY VS. DEMAND MATTERS

In a perfect world, the demand for new homes would line up exactly with the number of new houses being built (aka the number of "completions"). This would create a perfect supply-and-demand balance. Unfortunately, this is not how builders think. They simply make hay while the sun is shining.

Economics 101 tells us that when we have excess supply and low demand, prices will crash. For example, between 2004 and 2005, builders began building more homes than had ever been built in history. Nearly

Household Formations and New Home Completions

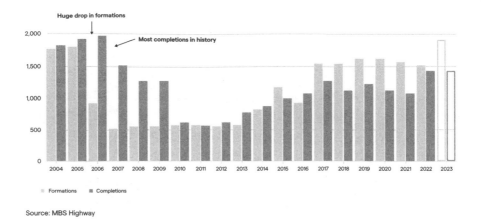

Source: MBS Highway

4 million new homes were built in just two years (see figure above). But after several years of incredible demand, the number of buyers began to dwindle. Even with all the speculators looking to flip homes for a quick buck, there still wasn't enough demand to balance the millions of excess homes for sale.

To make matters worse, we also know that during the period leading up the Great Recession, banks were being wildly irresponsible with their lending practices. No income verification, no down payment, no problem. If you could fog a mirror, you could get a loan. In the famous film *The Big Short*, a hedge fund manager visits Florida to try and decipher the insanity of the housing market. **He is introduced to a "dancer" who has five houses and a condo (with multiple loans on each house). And yes, it's a true story!**

So what's different about today? How do we know we aren't in for another collapse? It always goes back to Economics 101: supply and demand.

LOW ON INVENTORY

Home builders (and banks) learned some very painful lessons in the early 2000s. When you look at the figure below, which shows new housing inventory today, you'll see we are far below historical averages. **Consider this . . . peak inventory in 2007 was an eye-popping 4 million homes for sale.**

EXISTING HOME INVENTORY

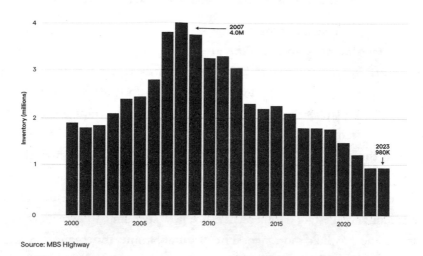

Source: MBS Highway

Today, 980,000 homes are for sale, a forty-year low.* Adding to the inventory challenge, nearly 40 percent of those are already under contract, meaning that the more accurate number of active listings, as of April 2023, is just 563,000.

That's barely more than half a million homes for sale across the entire United States—the lowest number since we began tracking this statistic back in the early eighties.[†] According to Realtor.com, in September 2022, the gap between formations (those needing homes) and completions (homes coming to market) stood at 5.8 million homes.[‡] Adding to the inventory challenge, builders are pumping the brakes on starting new homes as the cost of materials and labor has surged with inflation and rates have risen dramatically.

*https:/fred.stlouisfed.org/series/ACTLISCOUUS
[†]https:/tradingeconomics.com/united-states/total-housing-inventory#:
~:text=Total%20Housing%20Inventory%20in%20the%20United%20States%20
averaged%202287.13%20Thousands,United%20States%20Total%20Housing%20
Inventory.
[‡]https:/www.realtor.com/research/us-housing-supply-gap-nov-2022/#:
~:text=Between%20January%20and%20September%202022,single%2Dfamily%20
homes%20were%20completed.

AMERICAN HOMEOWNERS ARE EQUITY RICH

Another unique dynamic in today's market is the vast amount of equity the typical homeowner has. **In 2008, the average homeowner had just 19 percent equity in their home, making them highly leveraged and suscep-tible to price swings that could quickly put them underwater and into foreclosure. Today, as a result of larger down payment requirements and appreciation from years past, the average home buyer has 58 percent equity in their home!** Moreover, many of these buyers locked in a histori-cally low rate, making them unlikely to move anytime soon, as a new home would require a higher payment. To be clear, it's not all unicorns and rainbows for residential real estate. Homeowners are now spending 40 percent of their gross income on their mortgage. **The median home mortgage payment is now at a record high of $2,322/month not including taxes, insurance etc. This "debt-to-income" ratio is alarmingly high and even higher than 2008.** Coupled with the fact that credit card debt is also at an all-time high, there are rough waters ahead. Will this confluence of factors result in a major price drop in residential real estate? Time will tell. With such low inventory, the market might surprise us with **somewhat steady housing prices or even moderate growth in higher demand areas, particularly if mortgage rates come down from here. Bottom line: investors proceed with caution.**

"I think you can really picture yourself stuggling to make payments here."

WHAT ABOUT APARTMENTS?

Although apartments (a.k.a. multifamily) are in the residential category, they are a very different animal than homes. Multifamily investing has had a great run over the past decade or so. Rents have been steadily rising for many years, making investors quite happy. That said, apartments are beginning to show signs of weakness in certain geographies, particularly where developers have overbuilt. **Meanwhile, a perfect storm of rising interest rates, falling rents, increased evictions, and rising insurance premiums and property taxes is brewing.** The severity of the storm is highly dependent on the local market.

Many apartment owners (which are often syndicated ownership groups) got greedy and chose not to fix their interest rate for a long period, opting instead for "floating rate" debt to maximize returns when rates were low. Not surprisingly, higher returns meant higher performance fees for the managers. **Now that rates are rising sharply, those owners/ operators undoubtedly regret their decision. The adjustable-rate loans have come back to bite them as their carrying costs have skyrocketed. In August of 2023, the** *Wall Street Journal* **reported that** "the sudden surge in debt costs last year now threatens to wipe out many multifamily owners across the country. Apartment-building values fell 14% for the year ended in June after rising 25% the previous year."

Take Jay Gajavelli, for example. An Indian immigrant and former IT worker, Gajavelli made headlines in the *Wall Street Journal* by selling extraordinary returns to investors.* **Over the past decade, Gajavelli accumulated over seven thousand apartment units across the sunbelt. He pitched "double your money" returns to potential investors in his YouTube videos, which raised millions from individuals.** It worked until it didn't. Gajavelli used floating rate loans to buy his inventory, and when interest rates began to rise rapidly, it was too late for him to refinance. Bank lending had all but dried up. **Eventually, he was unable to afford the increasing payments, and thus far, he has returned three thousand units to the**

*https://www.wsj.com/articles/a-housing-bust-comes-for-thousands-of-small-time -investors-3934beb3

US MULTIFAMILY BUILDING VALUES DECLINE
Prices are down after a rapid climb in recent years, an index by MSCI shows

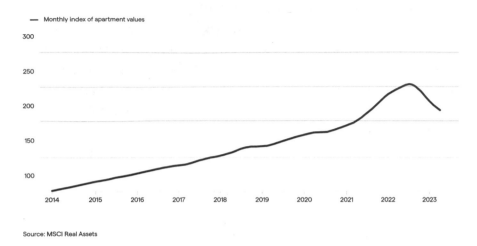

Source: MSCI Real Assets

bank in foreclosure. His investors, meanwhile, lost 100 percent of their investment—not because the apartments were bad properties, but because the owner/operator chose to take on more risk than necessary and unsophisticated investors were none the wiser.

It's not only the unsophisticated who are feeling the pain. Blackstone, one the world's largest institutions, opted to default on eleven Manhattan apartment buildings. The *Wall Street Journal* reported that "Veritas Investments, one of San Francisco's largest landlords, and partners defaulted on debt backing 95 rental buildings during the past year. It stands to lose more than one-third of its San Francisco portfolio as a result."*

IS OPPORTUNITY KNOCKING?

For those who like to buy things on sale, certain categories of real estate will become extremely attractive over the next few years. **We anticipate major discounts in commercial and multifamily real estate as sellers (and banks) are forced to unload their properties. Buyers will need to pick**

*https://www.wsj.com/articles/a-real-estate-haven-turns-perilous-with-roughly-1-trillion-coming-due-74d20528?mod=hp_lead_pos2

their spots wisely and be able to answer the tough questions regarding viability. That said, experts we interviewed believe that there will be severe dislocations in the market that will create tremendous buying opportunities that we have not seen in nearly two decades.

Private credit is a different method through which individual investors can get exposure to real estate. Bank lending has all but evaporated, but both commercial and residential owners will still need access to capital, and in the absence of banks, many will turn to a subset of private credit (in some cases known as "hard money" lenders). These non-bank lenders will lend short-term capital against an equity position when a borrower needs quick cash. **This can generate very handsome returns for the lender, with very strong protections in place if the borrower defaults.** As an investor, real estate lending could be a great addition to a Holy Grail portfolio as a way to generate portfolio income.

We will leave you with a few words of wisdom for real estate investors in today's landscape . . .

1. Seek Out the Experts—Investing in real estate is best done by sophisticated professional investors who understand the nuances of geographies and leverage and have a long-term track record of successfully navigating down-market cycles. History is littered with stories of unsophisticated real estate investors who got too far over their skis and tumbled into bankruptcy.

2. Diversify—Investing with a top-tier manager can give you a diversified portfolio of numerous properties versus betting on one or two. The same is true with private credit, so that you can invest in a portfolio of loans versus just lending to one or two borrowers.

3. Be Patient—We will see tremendous deal flow and many discounted opportunities in the years to come. Pick your spots carefully and don't jump at the first thing you see.

EVERYONE LOVES A DEAL!

Everyone loves a deal! So what happens when an investor in a private equity fund decides that they would like get their cash out early? Well, since private equity (and venture capital, for that matter) is generally illiquid, the investor is left with one choice: sell their position in the fund to another investor. **This is known as a "secondary" transaction, and for a savvy investor, it can represent an opportunity to get a great asset at a discount with a shortened timeline to getting their money back.** Let's explore!

CHAPTER 9

SECONDARIES

EVERYONE LOVES A SALE!

*"Anyone who tells you that money can't buy
happiness, doesn't know where to shop."*
—Bo Derek

We sure have come a long way and with just one strategy left to cover! So far, we have done a deep dive on six alternative investment strategies that one could consider as part of a Holy Grail portfolio design.

As we now know, Dalio's approach is to utilize eight to twelve uncorrelated investment strategies. When coupled with traditional stocks, bonds, and other more liquid investments, there are plenty of options for one to consider. That's a good thing, of course, as it goes without saying that not all strategies are right for everyone, and it's always a good idea to consult a professional advisor.

In truth, there is an entire universe of alternative investments that our research team continuously monitors and tracks.

In this final "mini-chapter," we will visit a small corner of the world of alternative investments where there are opportunities to get great discounts on high-quality investment assets. After all, who doesn't love a good deal?

THE GREAT DISCOUNT

The new, highly sought-after Ferrari F8 has a window sticker of $350,000. The cars are scarce and nearly impossible to find unless you are willing to pay more than sticker! Now imagine walking by a showroom and a sparkling red brand-new one was discounted by 25–50 percent off. **Would you pull the trigger? I sure hope so!** Everyone loves a good deal. Funny enough, this phenomenon seems to apply to everything but investments. **When stocks are 10 percent, 20 percent, or even 50 percent off their high, typical investors avoid them like the plague, and if they own them, they are likely willing to sell them to avoid further pain.**

But not everyone who sells when the market is down is having an emotional breakdown. In fact, some of the most disciplined investors in the world, the smart institutional money, are at certain times *required* to sell some of their investment holdings. Why in the world would they be "required" to sell quality investments?

Let's dive in and explore how these unique situations can give us investors (the buyers) a significant advantage . . .

OUT OF BALANCE

The most disciplined investors typically have a clear asset allocation plan: a fixed percentage they want to maintain in each type of investment (e.g., 30 percent in stocks, 20 percent in bonds, 40 percent in private equity, and so on). However, because markets fluctuate, the value of their holdings is never static, making their asset allocation target a moving one.

In 2022, the public markets took a tumble and nearly everyone felt the pain. Stocks, bonds, and real estate fell in unison, so there were very few places to hide. The biggest institutional investors in the world (endowments, sovereign wealth funds, pension plans, etc.) were left shell-shocked as their portfolios experienced their worst performance since the Great Recession. Pile on the invasion of Ukraine, rapid inflation, and persistent supply chain issues, and the world of institutional portfolio management was left battered, bruised, and confused. **How did these massive institutional investors respond? They took significant steps to get back into balance. Let me explain . . .**

First, let's talk Portfolio Management 101 for a quick second. Say you have $1 million invested in stocks and bonds, with a target allocation of 60 percent stocks and 40 percent bonds. You would strive to maintain that industry standard 60-40 allocation. If your stocks go up in value and your bonds drop

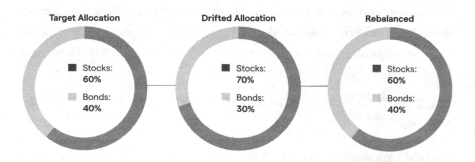

or stay flat, your percentages have now "drifted" from their intended target. You may end up with 70 percent in stocks and only 30 percent in bonds, for instance, as illustrated by the figure above. In such cases, it's time to rebalance, like replacing an unevenly worn tire that's causing your car to vibrate. For a disciplined investor in the above situation, **this would mean selling some stocks and buying some bonds in order to get back to their 60-40 target.**

In 2022, almost every institutional portfolio on the planet experienced the equivalent of three unbalanced tires that nearly shook the doors off. While stocks and bonds both dropped significantly, many of these portfolios' alternative investments (private equity, private credit, etc.) fared much better. **This meant their alternatives now represented a MUCH higher percentage of the portfolios' intended—and often required— asset allocation target.** For portfolio managers, this is less than ideal and *requires* them to take action.

ONE MAN'S TIMING IS ANOTHER MAN'S TREASURE

In today's current landscape, we know that there are hundreds of billions of dollars invested in high-quality *private equity, private credit, and private real estate* **assets, many of which have significantly grown in value in recent years. Now they will have to be sold to help these institutions rebalance their portfolios.** This is because most major institutions have a self-governing mandate to course correct and rebalance when necessary. **And if the people running those portfolios do not take action to get back in balance, they get . . . fired!** Therefore, it is not an option they might pursue; it is a move of self-preservation that they MUST pursue.

But now the obvious questions . . . **What happens when you are invested in something *illiquid* like private equity?** How does one go about selling an *illiquid* investment? **Enter the world of secondary transactions.**

EARLY BIRD GETS THE WORM BUT THE SECOND MOUSE GETS THE CHEESE

In a traditional private equity fund, investors will wait five to ten years before the fund is liquidated and their capital is returned. So if an investor wants or needs to liquidate their position early, the only way they can achieve this is by selling their position to another interested investor who would simply take their spot. This is called an *"LP-led secondary,"* as it's initiated by the limited partner.

In today's world, finding another interested investor to whom you can sell your position is quite easy. There are numerous investment funds whose sole purpose is to buy secondaries from existing investors (limited partners). In fact, in 2021, the secondary market transaction volume totaled an incredible $134 billion (up from $60 billion in 2020). Many experts believe this category will grow to $500 billion in short order.

So why have secondaries become increasingly popular as an "asset class within an asset class"? We can break the appeal down into three major benefits . . .

And why is liquidity so important to you?

1. A Discount—In a private equity investment, there is an existing quarterly valuation of your investment (sometimes called the net asset value, or "mark" for short). If an investor wants to sell their position, they are often going to have to sell their position at a discount relative to its current value. This means the buyer is already "in the money" and has a buffer by which the portfolio would have to drop in order to lose money. For example, if the current value is $100, the buyer and seller might agree on a price somewhere between 70 to 90 cents on the dollar. **The seller gets their needed liquidity, and the buyer gets a deal. Win-win.**

2. Shorter Timelines—Since it typically takes five to ten years before investors in a private equity fund get all their money back, including the profits, buying a secondary position can drastically cut down on the time it takes to return your capital. **For example, if the seller is already five years into a ten-year fund, the buyer may be cutting their "wait" time in half.** This helps eliminate the J-Curve, which we spoke about earlier. The J-Curve (shown in figure below) simply shows how investors in a private equity fund are deploying their capital into investment assets for the first many years, and once those dollars are fully deployed, only then do they start to grow. Much like planting seeds for a future harvest, it takes time for growth.

3. Visibility—When a private equity manager starts a fund and you invest right away, you are betting on their experience and track record. **This is often called "blank check" risk.** On day 1, you do not yet know what companies they will purchase in the fund, how they will perform, etc. However, by the time you're buying a secondary, the fund will usually have invested its capital, so you can see exactly what investments are owned, how they are performing, and so on. . . . **This *"information edge"* is key for experienced secondary investors who can pick and choose which secondary investments they want to buy, managed by which managers, and so forth . . .**

WHY DO INVESTORS LIKE INVESTING IN SECONDARIES?

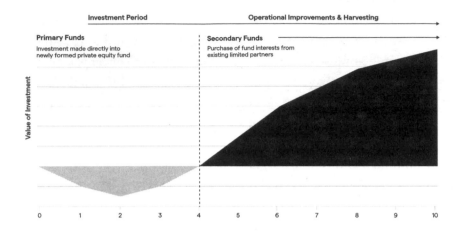

Source: CAZ Investments. This chart is for illustrative purposes only and does not represent past or projected performance of an actual investment. There is no guarantee any future performance will match this illustration

THAT'S A KEEPER

Following the global financial crisis, private equity managers found themselves in an interesting position. As mentioned, most private equity funds are set up as ten-year "closed end" funds that are required to wind down, which simply means they sell the companies and send the money back to the investors. But at the time, the managers had portfolios of some great companies that, as the economy recovered, were starting to really hit their stride. The managers knew it would be foolish to sell such great companies at that point even though the fund effectively mandated that they do so. It was time for an innovative solution.

This created a large wave of what we call "GP-led secondaries." **Instead of selling all of the companies in their fund at the end of the ten-year fund cycle, managers instead created the equivalent of an "overtime" period, in which they hand-selected one or more companies they wanted to hang on to and moved them into a new fund called a *"continuation vehicle."*** Then, they gave their investors (the LPs) two options:

1. The LP can choose to cash out at the current value and NOT participate in the overtime period. If someone chooses to cash out, this creates room for a new investor to come aboard.

2. The LP can choose to stay on board and "roll" their existing investment into the new *continuation vehicle*, which allows them to participate in the ongoing upside potential. **This is presented as an option but not an obligation.** The fund manager (GP) will typically create an alignment of interests by rolling over their personal investment and performance fees to the assets that are continuing. **They are ultimately showing their investors that they have such strong conviction in the underlying companies that they want more time to maximize the value for all parties.**

It is no surprise that "GP-led secondaries" have grown to be nearly half of the entire secondary market. The typical ten-year timeline of closed-end funds is somewhat arbitrary, and it rarely lines up to the optimal business life cycles of the underlying companies. The GP-led secondary has evolved into a valued portfolio management tool with the goal of maximizing everyone's returns. **Bottom line: Nobody wants to sell great companies too early.**

So where is the opportunity for investors like us? The good news is, for the foreseeable future, we are going to be in a buyer's market. **There simply is not enough capital to buy the number of available secondaries. Thus, sellers will likely entertain higher discounts, and we can be more discriminating in picking only the highest quality holdings.**

One can also surmise that buying secondaries requires immense sophistication. The buyer needs to be able to fully understand the asset they are buying, which requires substantial due diligence. Therefore, we would recommend the following . . .

1. Select a manager/fund that has a proven track record of successfully buying and exiting secondary positions. They should have strong relationships with the fund managers, so they are on a short list of buyers that the fund managers want to work with.

2. Invest in a fund that has numerous secondaries so that you get

diversification across a variety of managers and their underlying portfolios. Ideally, the fund is also invested in secondaries across various asset classes (e.g., private equity secondaries, energy secondaries, real estate secondaries, etc.).

3. Invest with a manager that has their own personal capital at stake to achieve maximum alignment!

For more information on investing in secondaries and to watch key interviews with experts in the space, visit **www.WhySecondaries.com.**

TIME FOR THE TITANS

Wow, we have covered some serious ground so far! Our hope is that you now feel empowered to consider how the strategies we've discussed can become part of your personal Holy Grail strategy. **Next, we have the incredible opportunity to hear directly from the "masters of the financial universe."** These are some of the most brilliant minds in the world of private equity, private credit, real estate, venture capital, and beyond. Although past performance is no guarantee of the future, many of those we will hear from have generated compounded returns of north of 20 percent annually. These titans, many of whom are self-made billionaires, have tremendous insight, and it was a privilege to be able to extract as much of their wisdom as possible to bring to these pages. Part 2 of this book contains the "boiled down" versions of these interviews, many of which ran two to three hours in length!

You can find additional insights and resources on our website:
www.TheHolyGrailofInvesting.com.

PART 2

AT THE TABLE OF
TITANS

CHAPTER 10

ROBERT F. SMITH

FOUNDER AND CEO OF VISTA EQUITY PARTNERS

Accolades: Listed by *Forbes* as one of the Top 100 Greatest Living Business Minds. Member of the philanthropic Giving Pledge. The wealthiest African American in the U.S.

Total Asset Under Management (as of August 2023): $100 billion+

Area of Focus: Enterprise software

HIGHLIGHTS

- Completed over six hundred private equity transactions, representing nearly $300 billion in transaction value since inception.
- Vista's ecosystem spans more than eighty companies with more than ninety thousand employees active in over 180 countries.
- Named as a Top Founder-Friendly Investor by *Inc.* magazine four years in a row.
- In 2017, Robert was named one of the 100 Greatest Living Business Minds by *Forbes*.
- *Time* magazine 100 Most Influential People 2020.

ROBERT:

Good to meet you, Tony! I was just telling Christopher that I get to talk to very interesting people all the time. And I shared with my wife (that I was having this interview) and this was the only one she was actually excited about! She said, "Oh my god, he is the best person you can talk to." So she's a fan.

TONY:

I'm glad to hear that! Also, I'd love to meet you in person if there's ever a chance to do that. But I want to be respectful of your time, so thank you for joining us. We really appreciate it.

ROBERT:

Thank you. Happy to be a part of this journey with you guys.

TONY:

Robert, you're a legend in this business, but I don't know if many people know your origin story. Would you mind sharing a little about that with us? How did you end up in this position?

ROBERT:

I come at this as a child of two schoolteachers in Denver, Colorado. While it was a segregated community, I always felt loved and cared for by the members of my community, which extended beyond my parents. And I think what this does is give you a sense of security and an ability to wonder—have an intellectual curiosity that you can indulge in. So, an important part of my origin story is having a regular chance to explore and learn. My father educated me in opera and classical music. My mother took us to the library every Saturday morning. We'd check out eight to ten books and she'd check out fifteen and we'd read them that week. And then we'd do it again the next week. The music and the books created a sense of wonder about the world outside the little community that I grew up in. And a curiosity about solving problems.

Fast-forward to high school and we were being introduced to computers.

My generation were digital immigrants, not digital natives. But I had this learned curiosity. I said to my teacher, "How does this thing work?"

And my teacher said, "Well, it runs on this thing called a microprocessor."

I said, "Well, how does a microprocessor work?"

My teacher said, "It's run by things called transistors."

And I said, "Who invented that?"

And my teacher said, "It's this place called Bell Laboratories."

So, I went down to our little career center and asked if there was a Bell Laboratories here in Colorado. This nice woman told me there is one in Brighton. I picked up the phone and called them, and said, "I'm interested in an internship working on computers," and the human resources person just kind of chuckled. She told me that they have internships for students who are between their junior and senior year of college. She told me to call when I was a junior in college. So, I called her the next day and the next, and she stopped taking my calls. For two weeks, I called every day and left a message. And then every Monday. I did this from about February until June. She called me back in June and said, "A student from MIT didn't show up. We have a space in the program." Then she told me I'd just need to come down for an interview.

I had one Sunday suit and I put that thing on the next day and put $2 of gas in my '69 Plymouth Satellite. I drove out there and I got a job at Bell Laboratories. I worked there basically throughout college, and the beautiful thing about that was that I discovered the joy of solving problems. Today, I like to say my real role is creating elegant solutions to complex problems. That's what Vista is. So, a lot of my origin story has to do with people who excited my imagination. People who sparked my curiosity, gave me some freedom to explore, expand, make mistakes, and ask questions. But who also took the time to unpack solution sets and help me become learned in specific technologies and sciences and mathematics that inform the way that I now invest and the way that I've built Vista.

So, a lot of my origin story has to do with people who excited my imagination. People who sparked my curiosity, gave me some freedom to explore, expand, make mistakes, and ask questions.

TONY:

As you recall that path, who are some of the most important people that shaped you? And how did you go from Bell to Vista Equity Partners?

ROBERT:

I watched my dad form a civics association in Denver. We used to get a lot of snow during the year. And of course, as a kid you celebrated because you had snow days. Well, what I eventually realized was that those were the same days my parents could not go to work because, in the black neighborhood, they didn't plow the street. So, it'd be three, four days, and then the city would put one stripe down the middle of the road, and my dad would make my brother and me dig out a path from the car to that one stripe so he could get to work. And then the bus would eventually come down and we'd get on the bus and go to school. We'd get to the white neighborhood, and guess what? The streets were not only plowed, they were also dry, which means they were plowed days ago. I saw my dad take initiative and say, we need to help people understand that if our community can't get to work, we can't feed our families. And this diminishes the standard of the whole city. He eventually got the city to plow our community's streets.

My parents leaned into their positions and used them to make positive civic changes. They helped launch the Head Start program in Colorado. And my mother wrote a $25 check to the United Negro College Fund every month for over fifty years.

Besides my parents, I was really impacted by a guy by the name of Vic Hauser, who was my first mentor at Bell Labs. I walked into Bell Labs as a teenager, all excited, and he pulls out this semiconductor to an operational amplifier. He says, "This thing is failing in our Merlin systems. Your job is to figure out why it's failing. And that's going to be your summer project. You have the full resources of Bell Labs at your disposal. Library's down the hall. I'm here. You can ask me any question you want. Good luck."

And then he turns his chair around. So, I'm thinking, man, that's pretty rude. But I walked myself down to the library to look up what an operational amplifier is. I studied the description and then I went back to Vic's office and said, okay, here's what I understand about operational amplifiers. And he turned his chair around, and for the next two hours, he started unpacking how it all works, what it is, what it's supposed to do, and what it isn't currently doing. We did that every day.

TONY:

That's beautiful.

ROBERT:

And so, what he did was he helped me discover the joy of figuring things out. He didn't give me the answer. He forced me to ask the questions and to do the research. In doing so he was reinforcing what my parents had been teaching me all along.

And so, what he did was he helped me discover the joy of figuring things out. He didn't give me the answer. He forced me to ask the questions and to do the research. In doing so he was reinforcing what my parents had been teaching me all along.

TONY:

Robert, what an incredible family you have. I honor them so much, and so many people in the world have benefited from the foundation they gave you and that you expanded on. If you don't mind, what made you finally decide to go out on your own? And what made you decide to focus on enterprise software?

ROBERT:

I'll tell you the funny story about that. So, I worked for six years as a chemical engineer. I loved it, Tony. I didn't think there was a more noble pursuit than to come up with an idea that no one else in the history of humankind had ever come up with. I was working at Goodyear Tire and Rubber, and thoroughly enjoying what I was doing, and then we had a takeover attempt by this guy, Sir James Goldsmith. So, I'm like, what's that all about? It ultimately inspired me to go get an advanced degree.

I did well—top student after the first year. And then I was asked to come back for the summer graduation to receive a first-year award. There was a keynote speaker, a guy by the name of John Utendahl. Six-foot-eight, big, tall, handsome investment banker. So, they gave me my award and he gave his keynote address and afterward he called me over and asked me if I'd ever thought about a career in investment banking. I said, I don't really understand what investment bankers do. So, he invited me to his office for a thirty-minute lunch and we went two hours. At the end of that, he picked up the phone and called all these black guys on Wall Street and tells them they should really meet me. I'm a scientist at heart, so I ended up talking to not only those guys, but to over a hundred people. I needed to understand. Eventually, I figured out that the only part of the business I liked was mergers and acquisitions. Building sustainable infrastructure through a process that's long living and that you can tune. At the time, there were six firms that did it. Goldman Sachs was the only one that had a teamwork structure.

Eventually, I got asked to be what's called the business unit manager, working for a guy by the name of Mac Hill. Brilliant M&A guy. But then Gene [Sykes] calls me to see if I'd like to work with him, and he is the only partner I hadn't worked with. I tell Mac, and he says, "Robert, let me tell you. I'm really, really good. Gene is out-of-this-world good. If you have a chance, go work with Gene."

So, Gene tells me he's thinking about starting a tech group. I said, "Only if you commit to spending time mentoring me in San Francisco." He said, "Deal." And in spring 1997, I became Goldman's first M&A banker on the ground, focused on technology.

TONY:

Wow.

ROBERT:

Now I was there in the hinterlands, i.e., away from New York City. You have nobody really helping you. So, I had to build a team and a plan. And the good news is you don't have a whole bunch of people over you. If you get on a deal in New York, you had four to five partners, who you never met, who were signing their name to your deal. But out in San Francisco, I didn't have that. So now, all of a sudden, I get to be one of the principal people working on these deals with little oversight. I had Apple. I had a little company called Microsoft. Little company called Texas Instruments. Little company called eBay. Little company called Hewlett Packard. Little company called Yahoo. This is '97, '98, '99.

Now, here's what got interesting. I started looking at these companies and the landscape of technology and I said, you know what? There is no one doing private equity in enterprise software. Why is that? If you think about it, it's the most productive tool introduced in the business economy in the last fifty years. As an engineer, I really started to understand the impact of introducing computing power to a business environment. It has an exponential return. When I was an engineer and I got done implementing what was called a programmable logic controller, Honeywell TDC 3000, into a plant for Goodyear Tire and Rubber, there was a considerable increase in productivity. This is from a plant that was built in the forties. So, with computing power, your waste goes down, your productivity goes up. That's just by putting in digital control systems. That's what enterprise software does.

Now, go put that dynamic in an insurance company and process an insurance claim. Go put it in at a bank and process a transaction. Go put it in an automobile dealership or mortgage company and process a loan. This is the level of productivity that enterprise software has infused into the entire world.

This level of productivity makes enterprise software extremely sticky for its customers. So now you have a long-term sustainable relationship with thousands of customers. Relationships that aren't measured in quarters or years; they're measured in decades. With a 95 percent gross margin product that you build once and sell as many times as you want. Negative working capital, no inventory. That's the elegant solution to a complex problem.

With a 95 percent gross margin product that you build once and sell as many times as you want. Negative working capital, no inventory. That's the elegant solution to a complex problem.

TONY:

Marc Benioff is one of my dearest friends, and he left Oracle after going to five of my events in a row. He'd be in the front row every day. I love the man so much. I'll never forget, he came up to me after an event and he said, "You've convinced me."

I said, "Well, I've not even talked to you."

He says, "No, but I've been to five events in a row. You've convinced me that I'm leaving Oracle. I'm going to start this thing called Salesforce. Tony, we're going to change business. We're going to do a hundred million in business."

Salesforce does what . . . $33 billion now? So, I've been on that figuring-it-out journey with him, watching that business take off, and it's just been incredible to see. It's so interesting to me the correlation between his path and yours. The shared intellectual curiosity and drive to find solutions to problems. I feel the same hunger in you today that you had as a young boy. Tell me this: What was the day like when you said, okay, I'm going on my own?

ROBERT:

At this stage, I'd been working with technology companies and enterprise software companies for years. I'd seen hundreds of these software companies and guess what? They all were making it up. I'm serious. How do you price software? Back then, you made it up. Somebody was sitting there and saying, "Well, okay, I've got about two years of R&D in this, and I got a bunch of computer programmers and computer hardware so I should probably sell this to that client for, I don't know, $80,000. Sure. Why not?" Seemed like a lot of money for something with a value you didn't really comprehend. But when I thought about this software, I thought, you might have one client that it saves $3 million a year and another client that saves $30 million. There was much greater value, and few people saw it.

So, what happened was, in advising and making recommendations for my clients, I realized the commonality and I said to myself, if you don't do this, someone will figure this out.

So Tony, what you do is you help inspire people to become their best selves using best practices. Marc Benioff internalized it his way and went out and did that. Similarly, we have built and continuously refine a whole set of best practices that help to accelerate the corporate maturity of the companies we buy. Since founding Vista, we have completed over six hundred transactions.

The other piece is that most software businesses are still founder-led. And most of these founders are running the biggest business that they've ever run. So, most of them are trying to figure it out, because they've never done this before, right? What do I do tomorrow to take this business that's

$100 million to $200 million, or $200 million to $400 million? So, part of our magic at Vista is that we have built an ecosystem where these executives and their direct reports can get together and learn from each other. It's kind of like Young Presidents Organization on steroids. **So, if you're a CTO of a $30 million software company, you're sitting next to a CTO of a $300 million software company being taught by a CTO of a $3 billion software company. We're creating a shared learning ecosystem where these executives can operate in a penalty-free environment.**

CHRISTOPHER:

Robert, you're talking about something Tony talks about extensively, which is that proximity is power. You share and help implement all of these best practices into these companies, but then you provide proximity to other entrepreneurs implementing the same best practices.

ROBERT:

Right, and the big advantage is that you can help them, in many cases, prevent mistakes that they would otherwise make, without that support.

TONY:

You can feel it vibrate from you, Robert. You emanate all of that, which is so beautiful. Tell me, where is the greatest opportunity for investors today in this sector in your mind? And where does AI play a role?

ROBERT:

Great, great question. I believe the best opportunity to invest is of course with Vista. No question. Hands down. And I sincerely mean it.

Why? Because we know how to bring institutionalization to the operation of these enterprise software companies. I am better off rolling as much as I can with you and then giving you and your team the tools to make the changes. As I mentioned, we accelerate the corporate maturity of enterprise software companies through sustainable infrastructure so these businesses can grow at scale, profitably. If you build infrastructure in these businesses, your CEOs get quiet time. They don't have to deal with the contract administration process. They don't have to deal with the services process because you have built systems that self-correct and self-tune and reduce noise. And so now your CEOs can think about what it is that they can go do to advance the business.

TONY:

They get to work *on* the business instead of *in* the business, which is what makes you CEO in the first place. So, tell me about what you see as the opportunity investing in this category now. We've seen the SaaS development; now we're seeing AI enter the picture. Tell us where you think the greatest opportunity is today from your perspective.

ROBERT:

So, 2010 through, call it 2013 or 2014, only about 15 percent of companies were what I call cloud native. SaaS being the business model. Today we're probably closer to 40 to 50 percent.

TONY:

Really? There's still that much growth in the market?

ROBERT:

Yes. There's a whole lot you have to convert and tune. Remember, there's a hundred thousand software companies and you probably recognize 250 of them. But the newer companies are now cloud native, so they're coming up from the bottom. But there's a middle with a whole bunch of clients that are either on-premises or hybrid and are trying to become cloud native.

The U.S. has always been the bellwether of opportunity in computing. But we distributed computing power throughout the 2000s. So now this computing power sits everywhere. And so, every economy, every industry is digitizing in one shape, form, or another. In many cases they buy U.S. source software, UK source software, but in some cases, they're trying to figure it out on their own. In fact, five of the largest economies don't have an enterprise software layer.

TONY:

Really? Who doesn't have one?

ROBERT:

China doesn't have an enterprise software layer. All their software sits in state-owned enterprises or private-owned enterprises. Japan, all the software sits in the *keiretsus* for the most part. Korea, all of it sits in the *chaebols* or the family-run businesses. India, same deal. So, there's a massive opportunity to establish enterprise software layers.

Still, the best opportunities for enterprise software are in the U.S. And what we can do is implement all forms of catalytic technologies across our platform because of our ecosystem—things like machine learning, robotic process automation, and a little thing called artificial intelligence. So, I still believe that enterprise software, on a risk-adjusted basis, is the best place to invest any form of capital, either equity or debt. You just have to put it in a place that makes sure it is evolving in utilizing these catalytic activities.

CHRISTOPHER:

Robert, when we look at enterprise software itself, we saw this massive increase in valuations. We've seen a significant correction in valuations back to more of a normal average, if you will. When you think about this, what has happened over the last couple of years that you did not expect?

ROBERT:

What I did not expect is that people would just flood that market and believe that trees would grow to the sky. You guys remember . . . '97, '98, '99, 2000, NASDAQ is going to 10,000, dotcoms, all that stuff. There was no real infrastructure to support those valuations and, of course, sure enough it didn't last. So, when you start flooding the market with free money, I thought people would be a little more thoughtful about it and wait for these valuations to come down, as opposed to paying a premium off a fifty-two-week high to take these companies private that are growing 3 to 5 percent at 30 percent or 40 percent EBITDA margins. There's not much further to go with that business unless you believe there's always a greater fool who will take you out of it.

CHRISTOPHER:

What's fascinating about that, Robert, is that many of the same people who were so excited and enthusiastic about paying those exceedingly high multiples now think enterprise software is a bad investment. Now that multiples have come down by 50 to 70 percent, they don't want any. The psychology is just fascinating to watch. Many people cannot accept the fact that there were great businesses just trading at wrong valuations.

ROBERT:

Fear begets opportunity. We continue to believe investing in enterprise software companies is the best use of capital anywhere in the financial markets.

CHRISTOPHER:

When you think about how investors are not seeing the opportunity set the way that they used to, how would you coach investors to look at enterprise software differently today, if at all, then they did in the past?

ROBERT:

It's a great question. If you look at it domestically, there's a couple macroeconomic factors that are going to influence this. First of all, in the U.S. you actually have, call it, a wage inflationary environment. So, employers have to figure out ways to drive efficiencies. Enterprise software is the most productive tool to do that. So, the consumption dynamic of enterprise software is going to continue to be robust.

If you add up all the Vista companies, it's over $25 billion in revenues. Sometimes a little bigger than Benioff, sometimes a little smaller. Across the entire enterprise, I'm looking at high teens growth rates. Even in this economy. That's the resiliency of it. We actually measure the ROI of the products that we sell to the customers. It's 640 percent. I don't know of any investment in the world that you get a 640 percent return on except software. So whatever business you're in . . . if you're in automobile repair, if you're in fast food, if you're in hotel management, your next best dollar is probably spent buying more software. The key is to figure out what software is going to be consumed in that environment.

TONY:

What are most investors getting wrong when they look at the industry?

ROBERT:

Some people will say, Robert, if you're not investing in software, what would you look at? If you are a long-term investor, you have to really understand what businesses are going to be sustainable in the context of sustaining human life. Right? And sustaining human prosperity.

CHRISTOPHER:

That's a good pivot there. Let's give you the opportunity to talk to the world for five minutes. What would you want the world to know today?

ROBERT:

I would like the world to know that there really is value in liberating the human spirit. And what I mean by that is providing the substratum of opportunity to all people. That doesn't mean everybody's entitled to a house. The substratum of opportunity is education, nutrition, and access to opportunity. Now, if people choose not to take it, that's fine. But to exclude people for different reasons, I think is a fallacy of mankind.

TONY:

Robert, I know we're kindred spirits in our value systems, that's for sure. The concept of this book is related to an interview I did years ago with Ray Dalio. I asked, what is the single most important investing principle if you had to give only one? The Holy Grail for him is finding eight to twelve uncorrelated investments because that guarantees an 80 percent risk reduction and an increase in return. Part of why we did this book was to show the general public that alternative investments are so important. High-net-worth people usually have 45 percent of their assets in alternatives. They're in private credit. They're in private equity. They're in private real estate. What would be the Holy Grail of Investing from your perspective?

ROBERT:

I'm going to first say that Ray has it exactly right—if you are a portfolio manager, managing a portfolio of a group of assets. I have the unique task to manage a portfolio of assets in alternatives and private equity. My answer for that is make sure the critical factors for success are under your control.

Give us an example, if you don't mind.

ROBERT:

So, a critical factor for success in enterprise software is something like talent and talent development. Do I just run around and try to find a bunch of headhunters who can find talent? No. I've got a whole talent management system that we juxtapose against the top performers for over thirty years across our enterprise to say, this is what a profile of a really good entry-level developer looks like. This is the profile of a great services person. This is a profile of a top salesperson. So, we can interview 450,000 people a year to find 25,000 that fit. That is a critical factor for success. That's under our control.

Another critical factor for success under our control is pricing dynamics. Understanding what is the ROI of the product that we are selling to our customers. And how can we capture that economic rent? How can we do it systemically? Well, you have to create a deal desk so that your salespeople aren't just running around with the sales sheets, saying, "Oh, they have forty-five employees. Here's the price. Oh, they have five hundred employees, here's the price." No, you sit down, and you build these ROI calculators and say, here's the value of that product to that customer. Sell it to them at that price. That's a critical factor of success. That's under our control.

Managing your cost, managing your go-to market, managing your most important resource, which is your people, your contract administration processes, all those. You can control those.

I can't control what the multiples are in the marketplace. But I can control if I want to make these companies grow and be more profitable. Even if I just make them grow and be more profitable, I can return capital through cash flows because I don't have capital expenditures in the world of software. So worst case, I'm making money on cash flow.

CHRISTOPHER:

You had a great group of mentors, you had a great construct before you started the firm, but what are a few things that you wish somebody would've told you before you started your firm?

ROBERT:

That's a good question. So, at the highest level, it would be to create a construct where I would have the ability to keep companies longer.

The way the world of private equity is constructed is that you have to buy a company, you have to, in our case, improve it, and then you have to sell it. Benioff picked one industry, in essence, and can hold it forever. And it can just grow. We have done over 130 transactions in the past two years because part of what I have to do is return capital. I wish I had figured out a construct where I could keep companies longer in the ecosystem.

CHRISTOPHER:

The private equity world is shortsighted in that regard. And it's actually in their best interest to just compound money and value and growth over decades. Not just over quarters.

ROBERT:

Exactly. So, it's the nature of the U.S. pension plan system to need money back. I get that. But there should be certain exceptions, certain businesses, where you sell the company and the LPs come back and say, okay Robert, now put it back to work. I've built some beautiful recycle models with certain clients and now they automatically recycle a certain amount. If you need the money back, you have it back. If not, we'll recycle it.

CHRISTOPHER:

I think the industry will continue to try to do that.

One of the amazing things I've witnessed in the time we've worked together, is the amount of growth that you've had as a business. Very few private equity firms, or even private alternative asset management firms in general, are able to scale the way that Vista has scaled. Why is it that some firms just cannot get from $3 billion to $30 billion or, like you, over a hundred billion AUM? What holds them back?

ROBERT:

I will give you three reasons. And I'm going to give you a contrast of what I know enables us to scale. First is a model. The model of the investment team, the value creation team, and the management teams and how we work together in that construct. Why is that important? I don't like any single point of failure. I'm an engineer, right?

So many of these firms, they build their firms based on the personality of a person or the "talented investor." And you look at many of those talented investors, they've got loss ratios that are well higher, but they just had some bigger wins. To me, investing isn't, I made a bunch of money on a couple things, I lost some on others, and I bring it together and it's pretty good on average. I look at the loss ratio. That's what I think about. So why [else] do some people not scale? Because they end up in the moral hazard problem, where they have bifurcated returns and some years it's great and some years it isn't. And some of them have built their organizations as a second point. Their organizations are too centric on one person as opposed to a system.

And I guess the third thing is the culture of the organization. We have a 95 percent retention rate of VPs and above. We have only two managing directors or above who didn't start as an analyst or an associate. This way you can build culture. And by the way, we have a gender parity firm and nearly 40 percent people of color too. What that does is give you the ability to build people and train and teach and mentor and develop and make sure they have a place where they can be their unique and authentic best self in the construct of an organization. That is going to enable them to be successful. I don't know what everybody else is doing, but that's what we do.

CHRISTOPHER:

It's a unique thing that you should be very proud of. There's no one that's going to be perfect, but it's best to try to find the people that are as close to perfect as possible. They have an edge, if you will.

ROBERT:

And part of that edge is evaluating. Is it . . . they've just got one big slugger out there and they're living and dying by that slugger? Or are they building teams, farm teams, and giving them experience and places to grow? I tell my teams all the time: There are two management styles, two ways to grow you. You can create constructs for people to grow in and you can create vacuums for them to fill. You, as a manager, have to decide what a person needs. Sometimes it's a construct where you need to be informed and learn. [Or] there's a vacuum that I need you to fill with your best self and what you've learned. It takes a lot of management overhead to do that. But if you don't consciously do that, then you have an organization that can't make decisions and can't grow without the leader.

CHRISTOPHER:

I think that's exactly what I see more than anything else. We now have GP stakes in over sixty different firms. We've gotten to know that all of them are really good at what they do, otherwise we wouldn't be there. But when we look at the differences, what I see more than anything else is talent-driven shops versus management-led shops. Neither one is a totally right or wrong answer, right? But the scalability comes from having that level of management that enables the talent to be talent and allows management to be management and allows everybody to, as you put it, become their best version of their best self.

ROBERT:

Perfectly said. That's exactly right.

TONY:

To finish that thought up, I'd like to know when you're looking at that management—which is really leadership if it's effective, right—what do you think are the most important qualities? What are the most important ingredients that you're looking for in an individual to be a true leader in your organization who can produce results and continue to grow to those higher levels?

ROBERT:

That's a great question. The majority of investors at Vista come in as analysts and associates, and part of what I'm looking for is are they naturally curious? Do they have an open mind to learn? You know this, Tony. We're in the transformation business. We have to find people who are nimble in their thinking, open-minded in their approach to life, and actually have intellectual curiosity that, you have seen from their past, they will really run things down. They're going to go figure it all the way out and say: Here's the source code to why this is the way it is. I guess you could say, I look for what I learned at the very beginning of my career at Bell Labs, what I was taught by my parents—the joy of figuring things out.

CHAPTER 11

RAMZI MUSALLAM

CEO OF VERITAS CAPITAL

Accolades: #280 on the *Forbes* 400 World's Wealthiest
Total Asset Under Management (as of August 2023): $45 Billion
Area of Focus: Veritas Capital specializes in acquiring companies in heavily regulated industries such as healthcare, national security, and education.

HIGHLIGHTS

- Veritas's portfolio companies are generating over $25 billion of annual revenue as of June 2023.
- Portfolio companies are employing over 120,000 people as of June 2023.
- In June 2023, Veritas was 2023 winner of the North America Top Performing Buyout Fund Manager Award from Preqin.
- 2022 marked Veritas's tenth consecutive year among Preqin's Most Consistent Top Performing Fund Managers.
- In February 2023, Veritas ranked #2 worldwide "in terms of aggregate performance based on all buyout funds raised between 2009 and 2018" by HEC Paris and Dow Jones.

- In August 2023, Ramzi Musallam was named one of the 21 Private Equity Power Players by *Fortune*.

TONY:

Ramzi, I know you don't do very many interviews, so we're really honored to have you. You've got an unbelievable track record. Many people know that. I don't think most people know the story of what you've gone through. You've been in the business twenty-six years. In 1997, as I understand it, you joined Veritas. Five years later, you lose your friend and partner, and you could have lost the entire business. And not a single investor left the firm. You've taken [Veritas] from $2 billion to $45 billion and have generated extraordinary returns. I'd really love it if you wouldn't mind sharing with us just a little bit about your origin story.

RAMZI:

Well, I'll give you the high level and then please interrupt with any questions. The background in terms of how we started it all is while I was at business school, I got an amazing opportunity. At the time, Jay Pritzker was the patriarch of the Pritzker family. It wasn't fifteen different fiefdoms as it is today; it was controlled entirely by him. And I basically, through a lot of perseverance at getting to know his assistant pretty well, finally connected with him. After a short conversation, he said, "Look, I have an opportunity I want you to take a look at. This is potentially of interest for me. Meet with the management team and then come back and tell me what you think."

Long story short, I came back, I sat down with him and his two right-hand people, and I provided them with my perspective on the potential investment opportunity. He hired me then and there. My mindset has always been entrepreneurial. My father came to this country and built a business. My brother's now on his third startup. So, I have that entrepreneurial mindset of being an owner, so to speak.

But the reason I bring all that up is that [while working for Jay] I was introduced to Bob McKeon, the gentleman you referred to who passed away. He was investing at the time with a group of former executives, the CEOs of Fortune 500 companies who provided a little bit of capital doing relatively small generalist deals. He and I got to know each other, and we decided to raise a fund. That's when I decided to come back to New York. I left Jay after an amazing eighteen-month experience working for him while I was in grad school. Truly transformational as it relates to my professional life.

Bob and I started to raise our fund and it was a generalist fund, no focus. And it was a small fund, $175 million. It took us eighteen months. And what happened, is that there were three transactions, three investments that Bob had been invested in prior to the fund that morphed into fund investments—a steel manufacturer, an auto components manufacturer, and a ship repair business. So, nothing to do with what we're doing today. I always say it's better to be lucky than good. I was fortunate enough, I was lucky. And the firm took advantage of the next opportunity to come.

A friend had introduced us to an opportunity down in Huntsville, Alabama. It was a defense technology business, at one time a part of Chrysler. We had never invested in that ecosystem. I went down there, and I started to learn a lot about that opportunity and the ecosystem they were a part of. Long story short, that became the cornerstone to our first investment in what we call today the intersection of technology and government—in that case, defense. That company was Integrated Defense Technologies. We built it, we repositioned it, we grew it, took it public, and then sold it. **That is the genesis of the focus today—investing in technology and technology-enabled businesses in government-influenced markets.** The three most active areas for us are national security/defense, healthcare, and education. [Early on] it became apparent to me that we were rudderless as an investment firm. We were a generalist and didn't have any raison d'être. We needed to focus. We were an investor, but without any specialized knowledge or strategic position in a marketplace. So, in October of 1998, we bought that company and consummated that deal. And since that point, we've focused strictly on this overarching technology market.

Carlyle started off in the defense world in the late 1980s, under Frank Carlucci. But by the late 1990s, [they] had moved into what they are today—a very large, successful, overarching investment firm. So, we were the only ones, and we feel like we're still the only ones with this unique focus. That really was the genesis of the track record that we have today, which we're very proud of. We're investing out of Fund VIII right now and the thrust really is that performance volatility has been almost nonexistent. Our loss ratio is less than one-half of 1 percent over the last quarter century.

TONY:

If I did my homework right, I saw there was only one deal you lost money on over these last ten to twelve years.

RAMZI:

We learned a lot more from that one than any other. We learned a lot about what we could have done better. Even in the context of the overarching returns, we don't want [our investors] up at night worrying about the returns and the volatility therein.

Going back to what happened because you highlighted it. [Bob] and I were key persons in the fund. He passed away. Very tragic for me personally. I obviously was close to him. But from a professional standpoint, our LPs (limited partners) understood how the deals were getting done since inception and what we were doing to add value to our portfolio companies. So, when we did go through that, we had 100 percent of our LPs decide that they wanted to continue with us. That was unprecedented but, from my perspective, expected. That was my mindset.

TONY:

That's incredible. Did you personally go out and talk to them?

RAMZI:

I and my partners did. We went out and met with everybody. And we did this under, quite frankly, a very difficult circumstance. I actually had our first meeting the day after he had passed away. And he had unfortunately taken his own life so it was very sudden. It was very difficult. But I felt I had a responsibility not only to our firm, but to the portfolio companies, the employees, and our investors to make sure that we could optimize their returns over the long term. So, I and two other partners from the firm started meeting with everybody right away.

Several people have said that some of your LPs were most impressed that, in the middle of this—you were personally shaken by it obviously—you somehow found the center to stay focused. That made them believe that whatever you'd face financially in the future, you'd be able to do that as well. It says so much about your character.

Well, thank you. I think one of the things that you have to be able to do in the world we live in is compartmentalize. There is a greater good. I felt as if I had the sense of responsibility to everybody to make sure that we could continue doing what we were doing and do it at the best and optimal level. There was a clear modus operandi to achieve the greater good.

From a day-to-day standpoint, people internally didn't see a difference because I had been effectively running the business anyway. So, it wasn't something that they noticed as being different. But obviously, there was a big difference. And from an LP standpoint, as I said, he was one of the key people. So, it was challenging. Fortunately, we have an amazing team. Culture really is everything. You don't differentiate yourself in the world we live in by the widgets you make. It's by the people and how you define who you are and how you maintain that culture as you grow. We have the right people in the right places and a culture of openness and collaboration. From my perspective, unlike any other. That is what I'm most proud of—this is everlasting.

We've gone from $2 billion to $45 billion over the course of the last ten years, yet our culture is the same. And that's something I take a lot of pride in. It ties to that entrepreneurial mindset that I feel like I have, that I was brought up with. A number of the other partners have similar backgrounds, very entrepreneurial, which is not typical in private equity. We are truly strategic in the markets we engage in. It's very rare that we don't know more than the management teams that we work with relative to the markets that we're focused in, whether it's healthcare technology, education technology, or a national security and defense technology. We've immersed ourselves in these markets for more than a quarter of a century. I believe we understand the levers of value better than anybody. And we continue to build on that IP. That's what we make. We generate IP and build on it. Now for over twenty-five years.

When you think about government and technology, government is at the forefront of all the complexities that we face, technology-driven and otherwise. So, if you can actually stay close to what government is seeing—what issues we are being confronted with, what complexities, what challenges, and how can technology and technology-oriented businesses help face those challenges. I call it tip of the spear internally. We have maintained that position, being at the tip of the spear. We are viewed as a custodian of national assets, quite frankly, whether it is in healthcare, education, or national security. I have the highest-level security clearance any individual can have. It's an onerous process sitting through polygraphs in intelligence agency bunkers and being vetted regularly, relative to your activities. But it's a function of being strategic in the marketplace and being able to bring that perspective to add value to what our portfolio companies care most about—our customers. That thrust has been consistent for us. It hasn't changed or wavered. And that's very important as you grow in private equity. Our first fund was $175 million. Our second fund was only $150 million. Our most recent fund was $11 billion. Now we have $45 billion of assets under management.

TONY:

That's really amazing. You've certainly aligned yourself with the biggest buyer of tech in the world, as you've said, at the forefront of the world economy. It's so smart. I'm surprised no one else has done that, but you own it at this stage.

RAMZI:

If you look at the mix of our portfolio, about 60 to 65 percent is sales to government agencies. A third to 40 percent is revenue from commercial entities. The element that's so important, which I found out during our first investment, is that the government is the largest investor in technology by multiples, relative to the VC community or otherwise. What I've learned and appreciated, which we've now really focused in on, is that the government would invest in these companies through what's called customer-funded R&D programs. Yet, these companies would retain the IP and have the ability to utilize that IP to drive opportunities not only in core markets they're engaged in, but especially into ancillary and adjacencies that they target in both commercial and government marketplaces.

So, a large part of what's on your iPhone has been developed through collaboration with the government, from Siri on. The algorithms which serve as the backbone for Google, developed by the government. Tesla technology, self-automation technology, developed by the government. It's not only the funding, which, again, represents hundreds of billions of dollars a year, but it's also the collaboration with folks within government to drive and develop those technologies. We gleaned on to that early and we utilized and leveraged that to the benefit of our customers for our portfolio companies.

TONY:

You mentioned earlier that culture is everything. And that's been consistent with every single person we've interviewed who's been the best in the business, like yourself. I'd love to hear, if you don't mind sharing, a little bit about your upbringing and how that has affected your way of developing relationships and the culture that you've built at Veritas.

RAMZI:

It is really so important to me personally and I think to the firm as well. I was born in Jordan. And I am Middle Eastern by descent. I have a Palestinian and a Lebanese background. My father had immigrated to this country to go to college. First person in his family to do so, did it on his own, didn't know anybody here. Took a boat from Italy to the United States. First night in the United States, stayed at the YMCA, went to take a shower, and everything he owned was stolen. And no cell phones back then. So, he didn't have anybody here. He still found himself a way to get to University of Missouri to ultimately get a Civil Engineering degree. And from there, he had various jobs—including the Department of Transportation and the Army Corps of Engineers.

He was working in various parts around the world when I was born in Jordan. And then, we moved to Jeddah, Saudi Arabia, first and then we went to Mbeya, Tanzania, where I was homeschooled because we were in the middle of a rural area. We then went back to Riyadh, Saudi Arabia, where I was in grade school. I think that is so important from a couple standpoints. Immersing myself in different cultures at such an early age was eye-opening to me. Living in rural Mbeya, and then living in, at the time, a very different environment in Riyadh than it is today. It allowed me to see how others live and be more empathetic to issues that we face across the globe. After that, my dad decided he wanted to start his own business, and he felt there was no better place to start his own business than the United States of America. So, we came to the United States. This gave me a firsthand view of someone who is very entrepreneurial, who said, "Look, I've learned a lot. I've developed skill sets and I'm going to now take a risk and do something that we all dream about doing in terms of starting my own company." And he obviously risked everything to do that.

That had a very significant impact on how I think about things and how I am as a person. Our culture here, as I mentioned a little bit earlier, is very entrepreneurial. So, when I talk to our team, I say, "Each one of you is an owner." You can leverage all the resources we have, all the knowledge we have, all the IP we have, and it's incumbent upon you to think like that. Take initiatives, take risks. I'm all for taking risks as long as you think through the parameters of those risks and drive opportunities for the firm therein.

So, the people that we attract are people who are very entrepreneurial in the way they think about things. And that culture is critical. We all are aligned in the same way, obviously, in the way we work in terms of the incentives and strategic objectives. But importantly, we also are aligned in the way we think and operate with one another to get to the end goal of making something bigger and better. And that I think comes from the ability to see things early on, building businesses and being part of different environments in Africa and the Middle East.

TONY:

What did you learn from your father or from your upbringing about dealing with disappointment or dealing with failure?

RAMZI:

We have a class of interns who are finishing up the summer here. **I tell them the most important [thing] is to learn from failures, because if you don't have failures, you won't succeed.** I firmly believe that. If you don't go through the hardships, you won't understand what success even means. How do you do that? You learn from your mistakes. We sit down after successful investments, and we talk about how we could have done things better. Where did we miss? What did we miss? Because even when you have a successful investment outcome for our investors, you could have done better.

There are certain things that you've missed. I always think about optimizing that intellectual property, and so, we've codified that. It's important that we institutionalize it for future folks who join Veritas and understand the playbook [on] what mistakes we made and how we could have done things better.

And here's something very unique, digressing a little bit, but important to the point that we're trying to make in terms of differentiating ourselves. This may sound unorthodox to an investor in our fund, [but] first and foremost, I don't look at the financial results of our businesses first. I look at the strategic transformation of those businesses first. So, for the first two years after every investment we make, we think about these core technologies and where we can invest in additional research and development, additional sales and marketing, to not only further penetrate the core markets we're in with this capability, but also move them into adjacencies that can drive their presence in new markets that they weren't engaged in when we acquired the businesses. How do we make them more strategic in the ecosystem? Move them up the proverbial food chain? We gauge that success, and that happens over the first two years.

So, when you look at some of the investments we make, a lot of times, expenditures are going through the roof. We're making a lot of changes relative to management teams, executives, bringing in new talent, trying to open the aperture, so to speak. So, there's a lot of, in some cases, volatility in that regard. But then, what you see is these companies become very disruptive in their ecosystems. They become very agile, so that they can actually take those capabilities, that technology, and move into targeted adjacencies that we ourselves identify as strategic. And that's a very important part of the reason that we're able to generate the types of returns over that twenty-five-year period. It's by no accident that close to seven out of ten of our exits are sales to strategics.

I always say the litmus test, if we are truly making our companies more important in those ecosystems, is that we should open the eyes of strategics in those markets.

CHRISTOPHER:

What you're talking about there is something that's such a common theme that Tony and I have had the blessing to hear from so many fantastic investors. It's consistent application of a playbook to a particular area, to a particular sector, and making a repeatable process.

When you think about investment today in government technology, what are the greatest opportunities you're seeing?

RAMZI:

That's a great question. Look, there's a reason that we're focused in the areas we're focused. It is somewhat personal for me too, at least from the context that we're making a difference for citizens, not only in the United States, but across the world. I can't think of three more important areas to focus in on, relative to our daily lives, than our own education, our own healthcare, and protection of citizens across the globe. Those are the three areas that we are focused on, and we'll continue to focus on that. And these are multitrillion-dollar markets. There's ample opportunity to find clear-cut opportunities for outsize returns as we do what we say we're going to do, making our companies more important to their customers, which is the target for each and every one of our investments.

I'll give you an example. Shortly after 9/11, many, many, many of us experienced a personal loss. One of my best friends from college was on the first plane from Boston to LA that hit the World Trade Center. It changed all of our lives. At that point, we had invested in that defense technology business that I mentioned, but we were looking at a lot of different areas. That really, quite frankly, left an imprint on me, and it became very personal for me to really try to understand how the private sector could support initiatives to help protect people across the globe.

So, I started meeting with a number of folks within the intelligence apparatus, senior-level folks. And it became apparent after sitting down with a number of those, and one of whom was the head of the CIA and NSA—the only person in our country's history to run both. And it became apparent that one of the biggest vulnerabilities we faced globally was what they referred to back then as DPIA, data protection/information assurance. And the vulnerability was strategic in nature. Back in '01 and '02, there were sensitivities to what we were engaged in at a government level. But the vulnerabilities also transcended into the private sector and the commercial markets. So, as an investor, that led us to really think about opportunities in cybersecurity way before anyone started thinking about it from a private equity standpoint.

And that market itself is significant. It's very, very large. Today, the topic du jour is artificial intelligence, ChatGPT, etc. The government's been at the forefront of artificial intelligence.

We started investing in AI businesses in 2010. For example, one of our companies back then was taking exabytes of unstructured data and satellite imagery, in real time, providing analytics to high-level cabinet members, including the president of the United States, upon which critical decisions were made.

When we think about our three core areas, I don't want to stray. One of the things that some firms have done in the private equity world is stray from what they do best. When they want to grow, they move into new areas. If you asked me how to build a retail operation or a consumer products business or a transportation company, I have no idea. I mean, throw a dart against the wall. But if you tell us to build a business in the ecosystems I've highlighted, we have a good sense of what matters, where to invest, and what markets to engage in. So, when we think about the future, I can't think of more important areas than healthcare, tech, education tech, and obviously global security technology.

CHRISTOPHER:

It's fascinating because the world obviously has changed so much in the last twenty-four to thirty-six months from a technology standpoint. Because of the volatility that we've had over the last couple of years in technology in general, and all over the general marketplace, what's happened that you did expect to occur and what has happened that you didn't expect to occur?

RAMZI:

I think volatility lends itself to opportunity, but I also think it lends itself to, quite frankly, separating the cream from the rest. Challenging environments are important from that standpoint. We have a fiduciary obligation to provide the best returns to our investors—the pensioners, the family offices, the insurance companies, whoever they may be. That's the Holy Grail for us.

We've worked through wars across the globe, the Great Recession, government shutdowns, sequestrations, continuing resolutions, a lot of chaos in the White House, however you want to qualify that. And what we've been experiencing now in the broader economy is something that everybody should have anticipated based on the environment, at least the macroeconomic environment that we had been experiencing prior to the rates and the volatility. So, I anticipate, again, the dispersion between the best performers, those who have a raison d'être, and the rest to become larger. I think that's what you're going to see.

There's a lot more focus on top performers. And there's a lot of demand for access to managers that are top performers based on the uniqueness of their strategy and application of that strategy over a long period of time.

CHRISTOPHER:

Because your strategy is very unique, I'm curious what investors get wrong when they look at technology that is engaged with the government. I have to assume people just really don't get the story until you explain it to them.

RAMZI:

Yeah, we've got the scars to prove it. It's not easy. It's a very unique marketplace. [But] this is not a monolithic entity. There are over a thousand different government agencies. But the way that the government procures products, goods, and services is very different than the commercial market. Unfortunately, while I have a lot of respect for a lot of very successful private equity firms, some have tried to come in and come out of these markets. Unless you immerse yourself full-time, especially in an area like this, it's very difficult to do so, unless you've built that IP. The IP is critical because it's not only to help understand what the businesses are. It's to help you know how to grow a business selling to government agencies. How do you grow it organically at double-digit rates? Well, you've got to make sure that you hear what the customers say, and you understand how to sell to those customers and make sure that you're satisfying each and every one of their objectives. And, quite frankly, working with them to think about the next five, ten years in terms of where things will be so that you can satisfy even those future requirements.

TONY:

You mentioned the Holy Grail of Investing for you. The book title is *The Holy Grail of Investing*. And it came from ten, fifteen years ago when I met with Ray Dalio. I interviewed Warren Buffett, Ray Dalio, the cadre there—more macro investors and so forth. And Ray and I became good friends. One of the early questions I asked him was, "If you had to codify the single most important principle of your investing, do you know what it would be?" And he said the Holy Grail of Investing is having eight to twelve uncorrelated investments. For you, there's a different way of looking at things, obviously. What's the Holy Grail of Investing for you with Veritas?

RAMZI:

What I would say, especially in the world that we live in, [is that] data is coming at us from all angles. We look at over a thousand investment opportunities every year. And we have a concentrated approach. What are the ones that we want to move forward with? And what are we going to do to transform and reposition those companies?

That's not driven by attractiveness of company. That's not driven by value. It's driven by [whether] our playbook applies to the opportunity that we see in front of us. We pass on a lot of great companies. We pass on great companies that are actually valued appropriately. But if one doesn't tie into that strategic level of immersion that I mentioned and reorientation and repositioning, we're going to pass. We see a lot of data. [But] out of all that you see, take the three most important things, and understand those to the nth degree and how you can apply them relative to strategic investment. That's much harder done than said.

It's really being able to discern what are the three or four most important things, simplistically. And then, expounding on those to drive value for us, in our model, strategically reorienting these companies so that they can move up the food chain, become more important to their customers, and take their core and move it into new adjacencies. If we can do that right, we have a high chance of getting the types of returns that we've been able to generate.

Growing large investment firms is obviously a lot more than just great performance. What do you think has been the primary reason for your success? You exploded. So, there's a fulcrum point in which your business was good, and then it went to great. What was the fulcrum point? What is that factor that has caused this explosion of growth and results?

RAMZI:

I'd say the first one was when we made that first investment in that company in 1998 and integrated and decided that we needed to focus. We also have continuity. There are folks here who have been with us since the beginning, and that continuity is very important. The ability for us to chart our own course, so to speak, and go after things that maybe we couldn't or wouldn't have been able to prior, just opened up the opportunity.

As I said earlier, one of the biggest things is I firmly believe that you'll have opportunities over the course of your lifetime; you've just got to be very prepared and eager, anxious, aggressive, relative to tackling and taking advantage of the opportunity. I'd say that was a clear opportunity that, from a market standpoint, surprised a lot of people. But I'd say [to them], stay tuned because there's a lot more to come. But it isn't only the growth in AUM.

I don't look at that. Yes, AUM has gone from $2 billion to $45 billion. Our returns, which defy the "laws" of private equity, have generally increased as our funds have gotten larger. So, fund six, as an example, which is a 2018 vintage, is the top performing fund according to Preqin. I know it sounds simple, but when you are strategic, you build on that IP. We're smarter today than we were last year. We should get better. That's our collective mindset.

That's the expectation. That's part of the culture. When I talk to people here, we talk about [how] the next fund, which we'll start raising shortly, should be our best performing fund. That's the expectation.

CHRISTOPHER:

You obviously took over under very difficult circumstances. What are a few things that you wish somebody would've told you before you took over the reins?

RAMZI:

I'd say, day-to-day it was no different for me. I and the team in place were running the investments prior and post. At the end of the day, no one could predict what's going to happen. **There are two words I live by: compassion and passion. Obviously, be compassionate, as I mentioned earlier in the background that I have. But also, passion. I love building businesses, whether it's our own or portfolio companies. You got to have that passion because ultimately that's the true test.** It's not about anything other than that. They are by-products of your success, but it's really about what you really love to do. And I can't think about anything more interesting from a day-to-day standpoint than the areas we invest in and the people we interact with within Washington. But I don't think there's anything specific that has surprised me, negatively, at least.

CHRISTOPHER:

Is there anything that, with the benefit of hindsight, you would've liked to have done differently in the business?

RAMZI:

There are always some things. People are everything for us. We take a lot of pride in developing people because, first and foremost, we are fiduciaries to our investors. We need to be the best and therefore our people need to be the best. So, can we do a better job in developing people, and mentoring people, which we look at all the time. And in some cases, you've got to make those harder decisions sooner rather than later.

One of the biggest failures comes when you hang on to someone longer than you should have. When the decision was obviously already made, but you just, for whatever reason, don't make those changes, whether it's internal of Veritas or executives or whatever the case may be. You learn from those. You want to give people ample opportunity, but you should also act when you know for a fact that things aren't going as they should.

TONY:

Building on that, when you think about the universe of investment talent, what do you believe are the most important key traits that separate the highest performers from good performers?

RAMZI:

We have our own analytics to assess that. But I'd say it's an art in terms of what we do, more than a science. For me, there's the capability side, the IQ side, which you can easily assess. But more important is the EQ side. We are in a people business. We're talking to owners. We're talking to investors. We're talking to management teams. We're working internally amongst different folks. The ability to assimilate across those levels, the ability to articulate and really understand the person you're speaking to, that art of listening, the ability to assess and judge—how do you really assess all that?

Ultimately, you don't until they're within the firm. But we look for those type of traits and those type of experiences to help us make those decisions. Because if you're coming to Veritas, you're not going to have your hand held. You're going to leverage a great platform. You're going to work with tremendously successful people, exciting people. But at the end of the day, we're looking for people who have that [entrepreneurial] mindset. And then, ultimately, passion. I mean, this is a hard business. People work long hours. You've got to understand that and appreciate that. And you've got to be in it for the right reasons. The right reason is you want to make a difference.

TONY:

The work feeds their psyche then, because it's a deeper meaning, as you said. It's not just the surface meaning.

RAMZI:

Exactly.

TONY:

And you lead by example in that area.

RAMZI:

I try.

TONY:

We really have enormous respect for what you've built here and you're just a delightful human being as well. Your father must—I know he's passed—be so damn proud.

RAMZI:

He's watching over me.

CHAPTER 12

VINOD KHOSLA

FOUNDER OF KHOSLA VENTURES

Accolades: Turned a $4 million investment in Juniper Networks into $7 billion in profits. Early investor in Open AI. Member of the philanthropic Giving Pledge.
Total Asset Under Management (as of August 2023): $15 billion
Area of Focus: Disruptive technologies in healthcare, sustainability, fintech, and AI

HIGHLIGHTS

- Vinod Khosla cofounded Sun Microsystems in 1982, which created the Java programming language, and was later acquired by Oracle for $7.4 billion.
- Through his career, Mr. Khosla has been an early investor in Google, LinkedIn, Nest, DeepMind, Instacart, DoorDash, Impossible Foods, Affirm, among many others.
- Among his many honors, Mr. Khosla has been named as one of the top tech investors in 2023 by *Forbes*, the world's greenest billionaire, and has won the National Medal of Technology.

TONY:

Vinod, I don't know if you remember but we met once when I spoke at TED back in the days when it was still down there in Monterey. I had that little interaction with the vice president, and you and a group from Kleiner Perkins invited me to dinner that night to discuss what had happened that day. I've been a fan of yours ever since, to say the least.

VINOD:

Yes! TED is of these places that has the right kinds of people. I hate to admit it, but I've gone to every main TED since 1986.

TONY:

Holy cow. You've seen a lot during that time. You're extraordinary. I'd just love if you'd share with us a little bit of your origin story about how you went from living in India with the excitement of what was happening in Silicon Valley, to being turned down multiple times by Stanford, to getting $300,000 in seed capital and building Sun Microsystems to a billion in a few years, to making those investments we know about, like the $3 million investment in Juniper that brought almost $7 billion to Kleiner Perkins. How do you go from starting there in India to one of the most respected and most successful VCs in the world?

VINOD:

I grew up in an extremely conservative household. My dad was orphaned when he was three. He lived with various other families and then at fifteen or sixteen he got recruited into the British Army. At sixteen, he was fighting in Egypt. So, the best thing that ever happened to him growing up was being a part of the army. He was never going to have to worry about a job. So, he wanted me to join the Indian Army at sixteen. That was his vision for me. I was the exact opposite. I wanted to take risks.

TONY:

Is that the way you were wired or was there something that helped to trigger that? What created the contrast?

VINOD:

I did get wired that way. [My dad] didn't think doing engineering and going to college was a good idea. **I was more focused on, what are the problems I see and are there creative ways to solve them?** By the way, I didn't know a single person in business. We always only lived in army areas. So, the equivalent of an army base. They were called containments, which were areas where only army people lived. So, I'd never known anybody in business or anybody in technology, never ran into anybody, but was curious. And when I read about Andy Grove starting Intel, I said, that'd be cool to start your own company and do something technically hard. That's why after my graduate degree in biomedical engineering, I decided I'd come to Silicon Valley. **And even though Stanford turned me down twice, I had to fight my way back in. I kept telling them they were making a mistake.**

TONY:

Third time's the charm. That's awesome.

VINOD:

Well, the real story is that I'm always looking for creative solutions. They turned me down the first time, and I was unhappy. So, I argued with them, and they said, you have to have at least two years of work experience, which means you sort of go away. So, what I did is I got two full-time jobs the next year. And I had two years of work experience in one year, and I applied again. And they turned me down again, and I argued with them. I said I had two years of experience. So, just to not have me bother them, they actually moved me from rejected to the wait list. And then I kept bugging them. They only admitted me three or four days before classes started in the business school because somebody else had canceled.

As the story goes, I was friends with everybody in the admissions office—other than the admissions director, who just hated my guts. One of the women in the office called me three or four days before classes started and said, somebody's dropping out of the class. I called the admissions director and said, "Hey, you have a slot. I'm available." I was three weeks into the business school at Carnegie Mellon already. This woman [in admissions] put me up in her living room because I had no place to go. I left Pittsburgh on twenty-four hours' notice because I didn't see why not.

CHRISTOPHER:

Persistence is an amazing thing.

TONY:

Every person we've interviewed in this context has something in their story where their level of persistence was crazy. And that's part of why they are where they are. So how did you go to Sun Microsystems? And then tell us a little about Kleiner Perkins and how that came about.

VINOD:

When I was in business school, I'd already decided I'd start a company. The story is that I was going to get married, and I had no job. So, I was going to do a startup. Then I ran into some guy who knew somebody who was thinking of starting something, and I contacted him. I said, "You can keep your job at Intel. I'll be the first full-time employee, so I'll take the risk."

Two years into it, I realized that what we were building, which was a CAD tool for electrical engineers, needed a platform company. I immediately decided Sun (Microsystems) was the platform company we needed to start. And that's how Sun started as the platform company on which the Daisy application was to be built. That's how I got going. And then Kleiner Perkins was my investor.

TONY:

They gave you $300,000? Is that true? And you turned it into a billion-dollar business in five years?

VINOD:

So, the first $300,000 came from a guy who I was working with to fund my first company, Daisy Systems. When I left Daisy to start Sun Microsystems, literally on one paragraph, he wrote me a $300,000 check because I'd tried to support him during the Daisy thing. He got screwed by one of the founders, but we kept a good relationship. Right after that, Kleiner Perkins invested in

Sun, and John Doerr came on my board. That's how I ended up working at Kleiner Perkins.

TONY:

Unbelievable success there. Tell us a little bit about why you made that move [to start Khosla Ventures] and what it's meant to you at this stage.

VINOD:

I like small groups and KPCB got too big for me. In forty years, I've never called myself a venture capitalist. I always say I'm a venture assistant. This idea you work with the founders to help them realize their dreams is what I enjoy doing and why most of my peers have retired because they were doing a job and then they retired. I'm doing a passion. So, I don't see retiring until my health doesn't allow me to continue.

In forty years, I've never called myself a venture capitalist. I always say I'm a venture assistant. This idea you work with the founders to help them realize their dreams is what I enjoy doing.

TONY:

That's beautiful. Who has been the most important person that helped to shape your success?

VINOD:

I would say I've never really had a mentor. I would say the person who's influenced me the most is John Doer, because I argued with him the most. We worked together for twenty years. We worked together at Sun, then we worked for twenty years at Kleiner Perkins. Most people would say we never agreed. **So, people always thought we would never keep working together because we always argued about everything. But what I learned from him was a critical thing. We'd always argue about what the questions were that were important. We developed a really great mutual respect, which was based on vigorous debate.**

TONY:

Finding the right questions, even though you might have different views of them, to uncover what's really needed.

VINOD:

My view was it hurts the entrepreneur if you're too polite with them. Frankly, if you say all the good things, but don't say things you're concerned about, the entrepreneur likes you more. But they don't get helped as much because they're not focusing on the weak links in their chain.

CHRISTOPHER:

It's interesting because I've heard from a number of people that what changed from 2019 to 2021 was that entrepreneurs were so courted by those in the venture space that they were told whatever they wanted to hear. And so there were not enough critical questions being asked to allow these businesses to be run in a more productive way.

VINOD:

Capital efficiency went through the window because a lot of money was available, and everybody was saying polite things.

CHRISTOPHER:

Where's the greatest opportunity for investors—as a venture assistant, as you put it?

VINOD:

Our focus is on much deeper technology that makes a large difference. Our view is if you do that then the returns will be a good side effect of building a large business as opposed to focusing on the return. I don't think I've seen an IRR calculation in our firm in the last fifteen years. We just don't do it. We're probably the only investment firm that never does an IRR calculation. **The focus is: Can we build something substantial? And if you do, then everything sort of takes care of itself. It's a very different philosophy than optimizing the transaction.**

CHRISTOPHER:

With that in mind, and knowing that you've seen so many different cycles of technology and biotechnology, is the greatest opportunity today artificial intelligence?

VINOD:

I think I've long believed in AI as a game changer. I just didn't know when it would explode. **We invested in OpenAI four or five years ago because that was the thesis I first wrote about in 2012.** There are some famous blogs that I got criticized for. Almost everybody agrees with me ten years later. So, AI is definitely one of those opportunities. But my view is, and I always look at the contrarian view, I actually believe if you look at twenty, twenty-five years from now, and look back at the early 2020s, as sad as they were, the two best things that happened to the planet were Ukraine and COVID. Why? Ukraine started a path to energy independence. There was no chance Germany was going to say, we are not going to use Russian gas. They didn't even think that was possible. And literally a year and a half later, they have now declared they have no Russian gas being used in Germany. So, what I'm leading to is that the energy transition will now happen because of Ukraine. And because of that, all of the climate technologies have become much more important and much more invigorated. We did the IRA Act, which has a lot of incentives for these climate transition technologies and infrastructure technologies. The Europeans had to compete with us, so they have their own act, which is equally impressive. All that really opens up a new era of climate-related investing.

And then what COVID did was two things. First, it proved we can develop a vaccine ten times faster than we thought we could. There were new models like remote work in enterprises. There was new consumer entertainment. There were all new sets of assumptions. But the biggest thing was not only every government, but every company is now committed to getting out of China from a single point of dependence. The world's labor was in China. The world's steel was in China. The world's rare materials were in China. **So, all supply chains and all material concentration will move out of China. That opens up a whole set of new opportunities.** So, I would say COVID started this sort of independence from China, which will mostly develop on technologies that can be cost-effective without needing to be in China. And so, the COVID axis, which is what I call the supply chain axis, and the Ukraine axis, which is the energy axis, and then AI for everything else. Those three things dramatically changed venture capital for the next fifteen years. There'll still be enterprise apps and internet apps and progress in bio technologies. We do a lot of that, and we feel like we are uniquely positioned to have an advantage in those areas because we have such a deep technical bench.

CHRISTOPHER:

What has happened over the last couple years in the world of venture that you did expect to happen and that you did not expect to happen?

VINOD:

I would say mostly that these swings, I expected them to be more moderated. It's more euphoria about AI than is warranted. Not in the impact it's going to have, but in the valuations. They make no sense at all. We've looked at almost all the billion-dollar valuations [and they] make no sense to us. You have to have real revenue to get to a return on a billion-dollar initial valuation ten years later. So, I would say we are seeing that swing in AI without enough diligence to say what will have a differentiated advantage. I jokingly say the batch of Y Combinator companies that started in January, most of them, like 60 percent were doing AI. Half of them were obsoleted by developments in the three months of the launch because ChatGPT came in. **It took TikTok almost a year to get to a hundred million users. That was the fastest ever. It took ChatGPT sixty days to get to a hundred million users. Nobody in their remote mind would've assumed revenue can grow this fast on anything, anywhere.** That was a phenomenon—how fast it happened—that surprised me.

TONY:

The title of the book we're working on is *The Holy Grail of Investing*, which sounds over the top, but it's really about finding the Holy Grail—the most important investment principle—of each of the greatest leaders that we've talked with. What's the Holy Grail of Investing for you in?

VINOD:

I would put it this way. You can have different Holy Grails for different people or, I like to say, different styles of investing. You have to know what you want to do and what you're good at, and then stay true to that. To me that's the basic principle. There are many ways to do venture well, and being conservative and shooting for lots of two-to-three-times returns results in really good IRR. We focus much more on the fundamentals. So, when the crypto thing happened, we just couldn't figure out where the meat was. We said, the blockchain is really valuable, but speculating in crypto is just not a long-term sustainable strategy. If you want to get money out of China, it makes a lot of sense to be on the blockchain. If you want to not be in Argentinian pesos, it makes a lot of sense. But what we did is a company like Helium, which uses the blockchain to build a real communications network. Now they're building a 5G cellular network using the blockchain. So, we always focused on real applications of blockchain. It doesn't happen overnight. But our focus is: Where can technology play a large role and where can it have large economic impact? If that's true, then we get the right team, and it builds a company, and if you build a big company, then you'll get fine returns. That's a very different principle than optimizing IRRs. I'd rather have solid ten-year returns than high two-year returns.

TONY:

So, you're looking for the long term. You're looking for not the two-times or three-times return; you're looking for the ten-, twenty-, or a hundred-times return by building something that has lasting value, that you see will really shift the world in some way.

VINOD:

You got it. So, when Pinterest went public, the *Wall Street Journal* did an article on the all-time best venture returns. And Juniper came up. It was a 2,500-times return. I was at Kleiner then, on a $4 million investment or something—I forget the exact numbers. We made $7 billion as distributed. Like, off the charts. But here's the thing . . . we believed in making that change happen. I actually consider this one of the most significant business achievements in my life. We made the change happen. It wasn't the return, even though it was $7 billion. I wanted the world to be TCP/IP, and no telecom carrier in the U.S. or in Europe was planning on TCP/IP as the public network. Every telecom carrier has that today, but there were zero that planned on that. If you look in 1996, every Goldman Sachs report only talked about ATM as the backbone of the internet. And I believed in TCP/IP. **I said, I don't care what the customers think; we'll build the right thing, and they will come. And that's what happened.** I don't believe TCP/IP would've happened if we hadn't done it. As weird as that sounds.

CHRISTOPHER:

It's consistent with what Henry Ford talked about. If you asked his customers, they wanted a faster horse instead of actually creating something that they absolutely needed. They just didn't realize it.

VINOD:

Right. Look at the press in 1996, every single plan for every telco was based on ATM technology. You take somebody like Cisco, which was the dominant player in TCP/IP; they bought StrataCom in 1995, because every customer wanted ATM. And their CTO told me they'd never do TCP/IP for the public network. Never. I said, fine, we'll do it. And that's why we got the return. We just built what we thought would be valuable to the world. It's very much our style.

Same thing happened when we did Impossible [Foods]. We said plant proteins, it saves the planet; it can taste better than meat. Nobody believed it. So, we took the long view and it's the only plant protein company that's growing today.

CHRISTOPHER:

Vinod, you obviously you think differently than the vast majority of the venture community. What do you look for the most in the people that you're going to hire at Khosla, that allows you to know that they're different than the average person that you might consider?

VINOD:

Both in our entrepreneurs and who we hire, the single most important factor is not what they know, but their rate of learning. What rate can they learn at, which is a very hard thing to judge when you're interviewing somebody. But the rate of learning is way more important than what you know, or what experience you have.

CHAPTER 13

MICHAEL B. KIM

FOUNDER AND CHAIRMAN OF MBK PARTNERS

Accolades: The Godfather of Asian Private Equity and wealthiest man in South Korea

Total Asset Under Management (as of August 2023): $25.6 billion

Area of Focus: North Asia markets: China, Japan, and Korea. Financial services, consumer media, and telecommunications.

HIGHLIGHTS

- MBK Partners is the largest private equity manager in North Asia, with $25.6 billion in assets under management.
- Top-decile returns performance for every active fund—"The Most Consistently Top-Performing Buyout Fund Manager(s)," 2019, by *Institutional Investor*.
- Michael B. Kim was ranked as one of "The 50 Most Influential People in the World" in 2015 by *Bloomberg*.

TONY:

Michael, as I understand it, you wanted to be a writer to start with and, somehow, you went from that to becoming the "Godfather of Asian private equity" and the richest person in Korea—the one who kind of rescued the country during tough economic times. How did that all come about? Would you mind sharing with us a little bit of your origin story?

MICHAEL:

I'm a bit of an accidental investor, but I think you'll find many of the people in my field are. I grew up in in Seoul, South Korea, thinking I'd be a writer or maybe a professor. I went to junior high school in the U.S. Didn't speak a word of English. My father was kind of old-fashioned. He said, "If you want to learn English, read." So that's what I did. I started learning English by reading books. When I told him I needed help with my oral English, his response, of course, was, "Read books out loud . . ." But reading books really is at the heart of my formative education. I fell in love with books, novels especially but also history, philosophy, science books. I went on to major in English at a liberal arts college—Haverford. Upon graduation, I was set to go to graduate school when I saw all the whip-smart kids around me applying to something called Wall Street. I had no idea what that was, but it sounded cool, so I thought I'd try it. One of the Goldman Sachs co-chairmen, John Whitehead, was a Haverford alum, and while Haverford is not a clubby place, there are so few of us in that sector that I think he took a flyer on me.

So I started as a banker at Goldman Sachs, back in '86. Worked like crazy for two years and then went back to get my MBA at Harvard Business School. I swore I'd never go back to Wall Street, and of course, upon graduation, went right back to Goldman Sachs.

TONY:

And how did you go from that to going back home to be a part of the Asian crisis? What was that transition like?

MICHAEL:

That was an inflection point in my career. I was sent out by Goldman to its Hong Kong office. It was a tiny team back then, trying to cover one-third of the world's population in Asia. I got recruited to be Salomon Brothers' COO for Asia at a young age. Then in '97 the Asia Financial Crisis hit. Korea was one of the hardest hit countries. I helped to lead the sovereign rescue not because I had any experience in sovereign restructurings—I just happened to be one of the few senior Asians in the company around at that time. People in the West probably have only faint memories of this crisis in '97–'98. But it was cataclysmic. Half of Asia was ready to collapse—Thailand, Indonesia, and, most urgently, Korea. We led the restructuring of Korea's balance sheet. We led the sovereign bond offering to get $4 billion in much needed new dollars into the country. And I guess this, in hindsight, helped me make a name for myself. From there I got recruited by David Rubenstein at Carlyle, who just wouldn't take no for an answer. And so, just as I went to Wall Street on a lark, I decided to try out this thing called private equity. I joined as president of Carlyle Asia in 1999, based in Hong Kong. And I was there for a very constructive and educational six and a half years before branching out on my own.

TONY:

What made you finally decide to branch out on your own at that stage?

MICHAEL:

I had this vision of creating an Asian private equity group owned and operated by Asians. Some people called it a hallucination. My view was that all the players in Asia at that time were global PE firms with a flag in Asia, and they were doing "pan-Asia" coverage. I will tell you pan-Asia is a false concept. It's some Western cartographer's imagination of Asia. Asia is much too large and its markets much too fragmented to treat as one monolithic market, and to try to scale. So, our concept, our strategic insight, was to focus on a sub-region. For us: China, Japan, Korea—North Asia, whose three countries constitute one of the largest economic blocs in the world. In terms of GDP, numbers two, three, and ten. That's larger than the EU and larger than the U.S. And importantly, we thought these three countries were scalable because of several millennia of shared history, some of it not so friendly, and shared culture, customs, and, today, economic trade flows and business practices.

CHRISTOPHER:

Michael, you obviously have a different perspective because of where your company is based. What is it that investors are missing right now, and what is the greatest opportunity for investors in North Asia?

MICHAEL:

I don't think investors are "missing" Asia. They understand China is big. They understand India is a big opportunity. Three billion in population between the two countries. **But I think the pitfall that many Western investors have when they're seeking to invest in Asia is looking through a Western-centric lens.** Yes, Asia is getting "Americanized," and a lot of the finance, including alternative investments, driving the development of the Asian markets was developed in the U.S. But the American way is not the only way; the American financial model is not "the end of history," as Francis Fukuyama said of the U.S. liberal democracy–free market capitalist system. This way of thinking is false, it's immoral, and it's dangerous.

You have to accept that Asia is different. Asia is also not monolithic. You need to treat each market, at least the subregions, differently from the rest of this vast area. American capital is smart, it's sharp, but it's also inward looking, thinking things should be done the American way. That the American way of finance is transferred well. There's a lot of culture sharing between America and Europe. Asia is not another Europe.

TONY:

What differences stand out most that Americans are probably missing?

MICHAEL:

It starts with the big things—the infrastructure, the regulatory environment, policy-making imperatives. Governments play an important role in in North Asia, and you have to accept that. I was trained at Harvard Business School and Goldman Sachs, so I'm a believer in laissez-faire, a free market system with as little regulation as possible. For anyone with that kind of education and training, Asia is a culture shock. Asia has a very strong and active, some would say intrusive, ministry of finance or ministry of industry and trade. You can tie back the role of these ministries to the Confucian tradition of civil servants, who assumed the role of guides and guards of society. These ministries see themselves as performing the same role. I've heard a policymaker, a government official, refer to himself as the invisible hand that Adam Smith talked about in free markets. Yes, I have a slightly different take on that. But that's the role they play. And you have to work with them if you're going to do business in Asia.

So, it starts from those things and goes to the way business groups are structured. In Korea and Japan, they have these large conglomerates. In Korea, the family-owned conglomerates control 80 percent of Korean industry. So, you have to learn to deal with these family-owned conglomerates who are now on their third generation in succession of ownership.

I mentioned the small things. **The business customs in Asia are different. The tips I was given when I was going for my Goldman interview—give 'em a firm handshake, smile, look 'em straight at the eye—all those things are considered disrespectful in Asia.** You want to be humble, and you want to keep a respectful distance while conveying your character to the person you're engaging with. I know that's maybe a difficult lesson to impart, but you start with the premise: Things in Asia are just different. If you can keep your mind open to that, you'll gain much more traction in your dealings with Asians.

TONY:

With your proximity to the leaders that you've grown up with, and with your understanding of the East and West, what do you think are the greatest opportunities for investors in Asia right now? And what is the focus of MBK Partners?

MICHAEL:

The answers to the two-part question converge. Because we practice what we preach, we think the biggest opportunity in Asia is in alternative assets. And we think it's in North Asia because of the scale I talked about, but also because of demographics. **Demographics really is destiny.** If you look at our markets, particularly Japan and Korea, which are the most bona fide buyout markets in Asia today, and sizeable, what you see is not just large economies with ready-to-play buyout candidates; you also see huge consumption markets. People think of Japan as an export-oriented country. But over two-thirds of its GDP comes from domestic consumption. **People tend to forget that Japan had been the second wealthiest country in the world after the U.S. for four decades before being surpassed by China. And its GDP per capita income is still much higher than any other Asian country. So, there's a country of vast wealth.**

Another demographic theme I'd point out is the rapidly graying population. Japan is the world's grayest population. Thirty-five percent of its population is over sixty-five years old. Guess which country is number two in silver quotient. It's Korea. And China, unbelievably, is catching up rapidly, after six decades of a one-child policy. So, this rapidly aging population has important implications for our investment strategy. We do a lot of healthcare. We went through a period where we did a lot of investing into leisure and entertainment. We owned Universal Studios in Japan. We used to own Accordia Golf, the largest chain of public golf courses in Japan. We still own the largest chain of public golf courses in Korea, called GolfZon. But we have moved from entertainment and leisure to healthcare and, in particular, elderly healthcare. We are now the owner of the largest elderly nursing care franchise in Japan. In Korea, we own a company called Osstem Implant, which is the largest dental implant provider in the world. So, we play demographic themes along with the growth that is inherent and, I think, the most attractive part of Asia.

One last statistic: The rise of China is the economic/financial story of our generation. I won't go into all the statistics you're probably already familiar with, but I'll cite you a couple. **McKinsey estimated, I think it was three years ago, that a billion Chinese would be joining the middle class in the next ten years. So, in seven years, we're going to have a billion new consumers. That's unprecedented in human history.** You may be surprised to learn that the portion of China's GDP attributable to domestic consumption is now larger than that portion attributable to exports. So, it's become a domestic consumption giant in its own right.

On the domestic consumption point, we own the number one and number two rental car operators in China. And our thesis boils down to this pair of statistics. There are 450 million driver's licenses in China but only 270 million license plates. And issuance of license plates is slowing down even further as the government tries to control emissions. So, there are 180 million drivers who are looking for cars. That's the kind of scale you just don't see. That's the booming consumption opportunity for managers like us.

TONY:

You're getting in front of a tidal wave of consumption, looking to improve the companies that you purchase, and then let it move from there. It's wild.

CHRISTOPHER:

You know, we talk a lot as a firm about investing with tailwinds. Those are tsunamis of epic proportion! What has happened that you didn't expect in the China market?

MICHAEL:

The political turn that the Chinese leadership has taken over the last couple years has taken a lot of investors, including me, by surprise. I saw China's rise from the ground up. I've been in Asia now for thirty years. I saw the way it developed. When I first came out to Asia back in '93, China and India were at about the same level of economic development. If you look at what's happened, China has done none of it by accident. They have the smartest, strategic-thinking leadership, the invisible hand, the ministries I referred to earlier. You're talking about the best and brightest out of a talent pool of 1.4 billion.

My view, watching all this happen in real time, was that the market growth will continue unabated because the Chinese leadership has brought economic prosperity to its 1.4 billion people for the first time in one and a half centuries. Why do anything to jeopardize that? But what you saw the last couple years showed the growing pains of a country and an economy that is going through an experiment unprecedented in history. And we're so used to the China boom story that we're surprised when it takes a step back, right? They're trying to pair a Communist-based political system with a command economy with important elements of a U.S. free market system. No one's ever done that, at least not successfully. China had been successful in doing that, in executing on that experiment for over two decades, and while I always advised our investors that it would not be a linear trajectory, I expect it to return to that path of success.

I think the leadership in China felt compelled to project China's emerging power and show the rest of the world that it is now not an American hegemony, but a bipolar world where China and the U.S. coexist somewhat as peers, but also as rivals ideologically, militarily, and economically. What we witnessed over the last year and a half, two years, I think, are the by-products of that projection of China's emerging power. And so, you've had this unfortunate stalemate. It's not good for anyone: not for the citizens of the two countries, and certainly not for the rest of the global economy, which has seen the adverse impacts of this kind of ongoing trade war. **My conviction—and I bet my career on it—is that China will resume its economic and financial market liberalization drive.** Once you open the doors to market liberalization, you can't close them.

TONY:

The driving force then is really the consumers of the country, meaning the citizens themselves, as long as they're prosperous. And if they're not, that creates instability. Is that the essence of it?

MICHAEL:

Exactly. I think you nailed it. Something that wasn't reported widely in the West is that when president Xi implemented this zero COVID lockdown for the second half of last year, it engendered a great deal of resistance from the people. It was the first time I saw my friends and colleagues in China very anxious and some angry, not so much about the curtailed individual freedoms but about the inability to just feed their family. They couldn't go out to the local grocery to buy food for dinner. To President Xi's credit, he sensed the growing anger among his people, and he made the extraordinary step of reversing his decision and lifting the lockdown. That's been a boon for the economy, but I think it's also an important gesture to his people, that he has their interests at heart. So the social-political covenant is restored. I think he and the leadership of China will resume its drive for economic prosperity and financial liberalization. **To summarize: Economics will trump politics.**

TONY:

Yes, and economics comes down to the quality of the life of your people, right? And you have a very large population there. If they're not happy, the politics will change.

Ray Dalio's a dear friend of mine and when I first interviewed him about a decade ago, I asked him, What is the single most important investment principle of your life? And he said, Tony, I can tell you very clearly. He said the Holy Grail of Investing is finding eight to twelve uncorrelated investments that you can bet on. I know that he's a macro investor. Obviously, private equity is a different type of investment, but what would you say is your idea of the Holy Grail of Investing?

MICHAEL:

Ray Dalio is not only a macro guy; he's a hedge fund manager. So, yes, I think his way of looking at things is a little bit different from ours. It's a bit of an oversimplification, but hedge funds seek alpha. **In private equity, we create alpha. And the way we create alpha after buying a company is by rolling up our sleeves to do the hard work to create value.** So, the Holy Grail is value creation. At MBK Partners, we buy good companies, and we make them better. So, fundamentals of the business are absolutely critical. I think every GP in our space will agree with that. The U.S. model of value creation is the blueprint. But in Asia, you have to adapt to the local conditions and the local way of doing things. The senior prime minister of Singapore, Lee Kwan Yew, was famous for saying that we in Asia need to adopt our own Asian form of democracy. You can't just take the American form of liberal democracy and transplant it to Singapore or Korea or Japan and expect it to flourish.

Conditions are different, right? You can't pluck a plant from California and expect it to flourish in Singapore, where you have different soil conditions, different sunlight—even the water is different. You have to adapt it to local conditions. And in the same way, I think you have to do your value creation in a localized Asian way.

One of the tools in a private equity manager's toolbox for value creation is cost savings. And there are many different ways to do that. What I used to do at my former firm was to cut wages. There are a lot of companies, if not almost all companies, that have fat, right? Layoffs in Asia are anywhere from discouraged, to prohibited in Korea. It's illegal to fire people. You can't have layoffs in Japan. It's discouraged. If you're a manager and you have to lay off your employees, you haven't managed very well, you haven't done your job well. So, through both cultural discouragement and some legal restrictions, we have to find other ways to capture cost savings. And we do that by getting better at procurement or consolidating back office and doing a lot of synergistic things with our sister portfolio companies. It's harder work, but we think it's the right way to do it because it's the Asian way to do it. So, there are different ways to get at value creation, but I think the Holy Grail is creating value in your business after you acquire it.

TONY:

So, there's more focus on, I assume, top line growth as well, not just the cost cutting?

MICHAEL:

Of course. Each market is different, but in the case of China and Korea, which are high-growth GDPs, the top line growth is a little bit easier. Japan is more like the U.S.—even more challenging than the U.S. Its GDP is going to grow one and a half percent, and that's cause for a celebration this year. So, the easy top line growth is a little bit different in Japan, but it's doable because of what a great fundamentals market Japan is—the best pool of mid-cap companies in the world, after the U.S. It has, I think, the most talented managerial pool in the world. And of course, it's a borrowers' paradise. You can get five-to-seven-year senior debt to support your equity in an acquisition at 2.5 percent to 3 percent, all in cost. If you can't make returns with that kind of leverage, you shouldn't be investing.

TONY:

I love your answer because in, in my own life, I'm fortunate enough to have about 111 companies of my own. We do about $7 billion in business across the different companies. Everything we do in every industry is find a way to do more for others than anybody else—add more value. And that is what I love about private equity. So, a big factor, I assume, would be having a certain amount of control over who's the CEO over a variety of factors. Is that true for you? How important is control for your organization to be able to add that value?

MICHAEL:

Control is not just helpful, but, in my experience, vital to value creation. And we can define control for you. It's control over, exactly as you pointed out, the CEO. We have to have the flexibility to hire the best CEO in her field and the ability to replace her if we're wrong. So, the CEO and top management. We have to control the board. We have to have control over the business plan, dividend policy, capital expenditure policy, capital raising, and M&A. **If we have control over those seven factors, that constitutes control, and that enables us to do real value creation.** You have to have those levers of control post investment.

TONY:

You're managing about $30 billion, if I understand correctly. As the businesses get bigger, keeping [your own company's] culture alive becomes more difficult. Tell us a little bit about how you've made your decisions. You're the biggest in all of Asia. You're the "Godfather of Private Equity in Asia." It's an amazing title to have associated to you. But when it happens, people tend to throw money at you. So how have you decided about taking money versus not? How do you manage that in your mind so that you can still be as effective as you guys have been?

MICHAEL:

We want to be right-sized. On your last point, we have always left money on the table during our fundraises. I'm focused on moving the needle on returns. The reality is—not many managers like to admit this—but the reality is that the larger your fund, the tougher it is to really generate outsized returns. So, we have been focused on returns and that has served us well over the long term.

My first day of orientation at Goldman Sachs, this guy, I think he was one of the partners, came up on the stage and told us to be "long-term greedy." There's a lot packed into that simple statement. You don't want to go for the biggest bang or the largest bucks, short-term. You want to build long-term relationships. Of course, we're about returns and of course we're about wealth creation for our investors. But you do it over the long term on the basis of long-term relationships. So, we have grown steadily. Yes, we are the largest independent manager in Asia, but we have done that in the right way over the last eighteen years. I think that's the only way you build the franchise.

A vital point, one of the key contributors to that steady growth, is culture building. We have been blessed with extraordinary stability on the staff. We have the lowest turnover in Asia. Of course, we compensate our people well. But a bigger part of it is, I like to think, the cultural ethos we built. I mentioned our mission of being the preeminent Asian GP, owned and operated by Asians. And our shared vision of being an agent of change in Asia. So, there's a sense of shared mission. Everyone at our firm has bought into that mission. That sense of shared mission is tied together by culture. Culture is everything. That was one of the great takeaways from my years at Goldman Sachs. **It's a little bit corny, but we have this thing called the "TIE" ethos: Teamwork, Integrity, and Excellence. Those are the three themes that bind the firm together.** And for us, it's important to have the sense of one firm, because we operate across three different markets, three different countries, and three different cultures. I think that sense of culture, that we're doing something special and that we're all in it together as a team, is what has sustained us and led to some great stability.

TONY:

That's beautiful. Every business has a point in which it's doing well. If the business is truly extraordinary, if it goes from good to great, there's some fulcrum point. Can you pinpoint that in your own business? What was the trigger that really took it to another level?

MICHAEL:

I'm not sure there was one inflection point or fulcrum. When I started MBK Partners, I had done private equity investing at a global firm, as I mentioned. And that was a very valuable trial and error. We tried everything in Asia. We tried different products. Every country and market in Asia, I traveled to and tried. So, that gave me a good sense of what's doable and what's not doable. I had the benefit of that experience, particularly the unsuccessful experiences, to calibrate our strategy.

TONY:

That makes sense.

CHRISTOPHER:

We started our firm in 2001, and I always think about all the things that I wish somebody would've told me before I started the firm that I had to learn the hard way. What are some of the things that you wish somebody would've told you before you started your firm in 2005?

MICHAEL:

In my case, the demands of leadership. **Leadership demands sacrifice. People think if you're born a leader, people will just follow. My experience is kind of the opposite. People follow leaders who take care of others and who are seen to be making sacrifices.** The Koreans have this concept called *jeong*, which means, literally, giving a piece of your heart. And I think that's what comes across. Words are cheap. If you can embody that concept of *jeong* and share a piece of your heart with your employees, that's the way they're going to follow you.

TONY:

What do you believe separates the highest peak performers from their peers? And, as a subset of that question, I'd like to bring it back to the very beginning and say: Why did [Goldman Sachs] pick you when you didn't even know what Wall Street was?

MICHAEL:

The first answer is that when I hire, I look for people with different perspectives, people who can bring a fresh perspective on how to approach a problem. Our business is solving problems with an unrelenting focus on excellence. Yes, a high IQ is a prerequisite. But that's what sociologists would call a necessary-but-not-sufficient condition. There are a lot of bright people in our field. And many of them have a strong work ethic. I think the sufficient condition is a willingness to learn and improve. If I look at the people among the senior ranks in our firm, they're not the ones who were the highest performers as associates. They're the ones who improved with time and effort.

The Japanese refer to something called *kaizen*, meaning continual innovation—a commitment to continual improvement. I think the highest performers have that sense of *kaizen*, and in case they forget it, we remind them through continual training.

In my case, I'm not sure what the Goldman Sachs interviewer saw in me. I'd like to think he saw that even though I didn't know finance, he recognized that knowledge is interdisciplinary. It's all related. And he saw that I was different in my perspective but got a sense of my willingness to learn and maybe a little bit of a spark that aspired to excellence. And I guess he was right about my being different. I published my novel, *Offerings*, in 2001, after working on it, on and off, for over eighteen years—thanks to my day job. I gather there aren't many novels out there written by a Wall Street insider.

TONY:

Michael, I'm most struck obviously by who you are as a man, as a leader, the quality of your values. But one of them that really comes across and you can't fake is your humility. And a big part of that, I think, comes from someone who has great gratitude in their life. I know it's a part of the culture that you're in, but I think it's such an admirable quality that so rarely is seen, unfortunately, in people that are very successful in financial terms. I'm curious, how do you cultivate that humility, that depth of caring, that depth of appreciation?

MICHAEL:

I do feel blessed. I think you inculcate in your colleagues the sense of humility or gratitude by living it and showing it. I'd like to think that the people around me in the office every day see the humility, which comes from a sense of gratitude, which comes from this recognition that there are a lot of smart people out there, there are a lot of hardworking people, and I happened to be in the right place at the right time. Call it luck, call it strategic positioning, but I happened to be someone with a little bit of international finance experience right at the peak of the Asia financial crisis. I happen to be Korean. If all those things didn't fall together, I don't know where my career would be. If I were born on a farm in North Korea, I'm pretty sure I wouldn't be where I am today.

TONY:

We're privileged to be right alongside you as general partners, investors with you. But to get a chance to meet you personally and to hear your entire philosophy, the level of humility, and yet the level of strength that you bring to the table has been a true privilege. You've shared so much solid information here that can help shape the quality of someone's life and the quality of their investing. And I think those two go together.

MICHAEL:

Couldn't agree more. **There's a lot of discussion these days about finding the right work-life balance. What I seek is not so much a balance, which implies a trade-off, as a *work-life harmony*. You can harmonize work with your personal life for mutual benefit to both sides.** Having a good, rewarding experience at work enhances, not detracts from, a good personal life.

TONY:

You talked about failure as one of the biggest keys to investing because nothing replaces experience. What was the phrase you gave about investing?

MICHAEL:

Investors are born; great investors are *made*.

CHAPTER 14

WIL VANLOH

FOUNDER AND CEO OF QUANTUM CAPITAL GROUP

Accolades: One of the largest and most successful private equity firms focused on energy investing, including both oil and gas as well as renewable energy and climate tech

Total Asset Under Management (as of August 2023): $22 billion

Area of Focus: Sustainable energy solutions for the modern world

HIGHLIGHTS

- Founded in 1998, Quantum Capital Group ("Quantum") is one of the leading and largest providers of capital to the global energy and climate tech industries, managing in excess of $22 billion across its various private equity, structured capital, private credit, and venture capital platforms.

- Quantum has differentiated itself by fully integrating technical, operational, and digital expertise into its investment decision-making and operational value-add, hands-on partnership with the companies in which it invests.

TONY:

You've got a storied career to say the least—twenty-five years in business. You've been able to be incredibly successful and take care of your investors through all that time. Would you mind sharing with us how this all came about, to build this extraordinary organization that you've built today?

WIL:

I grew up in a small town in central Texas, and both my parents had very lower-middle-income jobs. As I grew up, I didn't know I was poor, but I was poor. I wanted to play football in college, and Texas Christian University had a great football program back in the mid 1980s, when I was starting to look at colleges. I was fortunate enough to have an opportunity to go play there, but I got injured in the summer after my freshman year and my dad told me the only way I could stay is if I got a job and paid for most of my tuition and expenses. So, I started three or four businesses in college and made enough money to graduate almost debt-free from a private school.

While I was at TCU, I took a fascinating course on value investing that was based on Benjamin Graham and David Dodd's seminal book on that topic, *Security Analysis*, and I fell in love with the idea of becoming an investor. As I started exploring different career paths, **I realized that there are two types of investors: those that buy public stocks, and they are generally people that keep their heads down and crunch numbers, and those that buy private companies, and they are people that get involved with those companies they buy and help them improve their businesses.** Given that I was an entrepreneur at heart, and I loved to solve problems and interact with people, the latter sounded much better to me.

During my senior year, I was invited to join the Educational Investment Fund, an actual pool of about $1 million in capital that was set up for students to be able to make investments in the stock market. We researched stocks and then made investment recommendation to a student-led investment committee. And if the committee approved your investment recommendation, the fund would buy the stock. This experience further solidified my passion for investing and identifying companies that have a competitive advantage. A couple of my professors, Dr. Chuck Becker and Dr. Stan Block, suggested that I could further my investing skill set by going to Wall Street and working in investment banking.

I was fortunate to ultimately secure an analyst position with Kidder Peabody in their energy investment banking group, but after a few years of working ninety to a hundred hours per week, I made the decision that if I am going to work that hard, I am going to start my own investment bank. And so, when I was twenty-four, I launched Windrock Capital with Toby Neugebauer, one of my analyst colleagues from Kidder. What we really wanted to do was be principal investors, but we needed to build a track record as investors, so our strategy was to find great companies and go raise capital for them and re-invest most of our fees back into the companies for which we raised the capital.

I figured two years of working for a Wall Street investment bank made me an expert on financing oil and gas and midstream companies—right? Wrong. What I did know was how to create a financial model in Excel and how to put a pitchbook and an offering memorandum together, and I had pretty good sales skills from all those businesses that I started and marketed back in college. This was back in the early 1990s when the energy industry had been decimated from the price crash in the mid 1980s. I think 90 percent of the companies in business in 1984 were out of business by 1994, when we started Windrock Capital. And the ones that were left, they were left for a reason—because they were exceptional at something; they had some competitive advantage. The launch of our investment bank benefited from a combination of a solid foundational skillset we learned on Wall Street, the hard work ethic of a couple young and hungry entrepreneurs, and good timing. Getting into energy in the early 1990s proved to be exceptional timing, because the entrepreneurs that were still in business were still alive because they were great at what they did, and there wasn't very much money, and we had a skill set for finding capital for those great entrepreneurs. You put those things together and you can make some exceptional returns.

We spent the next five years raising money for companies, getting paid fees for doing so, and then reinvesting 75 to 80 percent of our fees back into the companies for which we raised money. After we built an investment track record, we approached A. V. Jones, a "legendary oil man turned venture capitalist" as people affectionately called him, to partner with us in raising a private equity fund. He had the experience, credibility, and capital, and we had the vision, budding private equity skills, and lots of passion and drive. Fundraising went really slow for the first year as LPs were skeptical about investing in a first-time fund raised by two guys that had not turned thirty yet, and a sixty-year-old oil man that had no formal experience in private equity. Fortunately, we met Vic Romley and Alan Hsia at Union Bank of Switzerland and they wrapped their credibility around us and introduced us to some of their LP clients in the energy private capital space. They helped us land General Motors' pension fund as our lead investor, and within a few months six other blue chip institutional LPs followed their lead and gave us $100 million to start Quantum Energy Partners in 1998.

TONY:

The first billionaire I ever met, when I was twenty years old, I asked him what the secret to his success was, and he said, I overserve underserviced markets. And I said, what does that mean? Because he sold bolts and screws and things that really didn't have much of a differentiation. He said, well, I sell them in Africa. I sell them in parts of Asia where no one goes. If I go to New York, I go to the bowels of the hospital, and I find the guy that orders everything that nobody services. And I overservice him. If I remember correctly, you went to Midland, you went to the places New York bankers weren't going to in those days. Is that true?

WIL:

That's exactly right. We went to the places that were one extra stop on Southwest Airlines. Southwest Airlines flew from Dallas to Houston and maybe to New Orleans. But they didn't go to Midland, Tulsa, or Shreveport directly. As you said, we found underserviced markets and overserviced them—we went to the places that were hard to get to, where the Wall Street banks wouldn't often go. And in those markets, we found some great entrepreneurs who had not been called on by many bankers offering them capital in a very long time.

TONY:

I'm curious to know, who is one of the most important people in your life that really helped to shape your business success and who you are today?

WIL:

It's hard to put my finger on exactly one person. I am a big believer in learning everything you can from other people's mistakes, so I am a voracious reader, which means I have learned a lot of things from a lot of people. **That said, the two people that I give most credit to making me who I am today are my mom and my dad. I am grateful for the hard work ethic they taught me and the value system they instilled in me: that you treat people like you want to be treated, and that no matter how much you want something, you always put other people's interests before your own.**

My dad was a civil servant for the U.S. government, and my mom was a schoolteacher who tried to become an entrepreneur. She failed miserably. My parents had very little savings. What little they had, they used for my mom to open a clothing store so she could literally put clothes on her four kids' backs. This was a bad reason to start a business, and after a few years, it drained all their savings and they nearly had to declare bankruptcy. But my family got through it, and despite the outcome of the clothing business failure, I always admired my mom's ambition and willingness to bet on herself. The example she set by taking a chance and starting a business inspired me and gave me the confidence to go out and try something on my own.

TONY:

Tell us a little bit about A.V. Jones. What role did he play in your life?

WIL:

A.V. was a mentor to me, but he was much more than just a mentor. He was a friend, a business partner, and most importantly, an encourager. He was the most positive person I've ever known and one of the few people that I've met in my business career that you literally could not find one person that would say something bad about him. He was humble and treated everyone with kindness and respect even though he was also a larger-than-life guy who achieved extraordinary business success. He gave us credibility by putting his name, reputation, and capital behind us and helped us build valuable relationships in the industry, given his outstanding reputation.

I remember A.V. telling me many times that "everybody thinks I was an amazing entrepreneur, and while I was a good entrepreneur, where I made my real money was picking the right people to back in business and then supporting them any way I could." That was why A.V. never tried to tell us how to run the business or what investments to make or not to make, but rather he asked some questions, offered to make introductions when he could, and encouraged us to go figure things out ourselves. **He was an amazing partner and Quantum wouldn't be the firm it is today without A.V.'s vision and generosity to back two young guys who had an insatiable curiosity and desire to learn and just didn't know how to take no for an answer.**

TONY:

So interesting because so many people as investors, when they start out, they think, I have to be the entrepreneur. But as you said, you can find somebody who's a greater entrepreneur and earn a great return if you can provide the capital for them. Let's make the shift now to where you see the greatest opportunities in this energy evolution. I'd love to hear where you see the greatest opportunity for investors. And can you give us a sense of how your business has done over the years?

WIL:

We currently manage more than $22 billion of capital and have been in business for twenty-five years. Despite tremendous volatility in commodity prices and capital markets over that time period, we are proud that **every fund we've ever raised has made money for investors and that our returns have been consistent and surpassed our expectations.**

I'm big on identifying risks that you can manage and areas where you can remove volatility. Supply and demand of energy fluctuates quite a bit over time which creates volatility in commodity prices. When you have an industry that's very volatile and you mix that volatility with financial leverage, it's a perfect formula for losing money eventually. Therefore, commodity price volatility and financial leverage are two risks that we are fixated on actively managing by aggressively hedging commodity prices in the futures markets and using modest financial leverage in the capital structures of the companies we build. If you do these two things consistently, then you can really focus on making your money through margin expansion—meaning driving down capital and operating costs and increasing revenues—which is the best way to make money in any industry.

So, what we try to do is isolate and mitigate the variables that can take us out in a down market. Being unhedged and using lots of debt may make you look really smart in an up market, but sooner or later prices will fall, and like that proverbial poker player that stayed too long at the table, you're going to lose all your money. The problem with the oil and gas sector is that it attracts very optimistic people. You must be optimistic to spend billions of dollars drilling wells ten thousand to fifteen thousand feet below the earth's surface and another ten thousand or fifteen thousand feet horizontally. We know that to be successful in this business, Quantum must not only be a risk taker, but also a risk mitigator.

TONY:

I've had the privilege of interviewing fifty of the wealthiest investors in history, the Ray Dalios, Carl Icahns, the Warren Buffetts, etc. They all have very different investment strategies, but the one thing they all seem to push for is asymmetrical risk-reward. Tell us about the industry right now as a whole. What is the greatest opportunity today and what's causing that opportunity to show up from your perspective?

WIL:

I think the greatest investment opportunity at scale in the world today is in the energy industry, specifically in the oil and gas sector, and to a lesser extent, the energy transition sector. I don't think there's a close second to oil and gas. It's not the most popular answer. Over the past two or three years many investors have been very fixated, for good reasons, on the climate. We need to be very focused on that, and we need to be doing everything we can to address changes in the climate and support efforts to achieve net-zero emissions. **But we also must be very focused on making sure the world has reliable, affordable, and abundant energy, because without it, the modern world doesn't work, and poor countries won't be able to raise their people out of poverty.**

A group of first world countries such as most of the countries in Europe, the U.S., Australia, Japan, South Korea, and a few others have become very focused on the energy transition. Christopher, you refer to it as the energy evolution and I like to think of it as the emissions transition. Energy evolution or emissions transition are much better names than energy transition because when most people think of the word "transition," they think of moving away from one thing and towards another thing; however, the truth is, the world has never displaced any form of energy, rather it has developed new sources of energy which were added to the existing energy mix in order to supply growing energy demand. **Unfortunately, most of what we hear about in the media is how renewables and EVs will take over the world and we won't need oil, gas, or coal in the not-to-distant future. Nothing could be further from the truth. Even with the massive investment going into wind and solar over the past decade, the world still only gets about 4 percent of its energy from wind and solar and 80 percent from fossil fuels.**

TONY:

The oil and gas sector was the best returning sector in the stock market last year. The S&P was down about 20 percent while the oil and gas sector was up.

WIL:

Exactly. **The public oil and gas sector was up about 86 percent in 2021 and 48 percent in 2022, which compares very favorably to the approximately positive 27 percent and negative 20 percent returns delivered by the S&P 500 in the corresponding time periods.**

TONY:

And yet the financing for oil and gas has really shrunk. So, is that part of the opportunity? Because we are going to have another 2 billion people in the next twenty to thirty years on the planet. We're going to need 50 percent more energy by 2050 than today if I understand correctly.

WIL:

Let's start by looking back to Thanksgiving 2014, when oil prices had been moving between $85 and $100 a barrel for several years. At the time, demand was falling but OPEC made the decision not to cut production. The price of oil then started to fall, and it ultimately bottomed at around $20. So, it went from roughly $85 to $100 dollars a barrel down to about $20 a barrel over about three years and created a massive financial shock to the balance sheets and income statements of oil and gas companies. Up until that time, investors had been throwing money at oil and gas companies focused on the shale revolution. The industry was spending hundreds of billions of dollars per year trying to figure out the technology to economically unlock the shales, where to drill, and how to drill and complete shale wells—all of which required a tremendous amount of experimentation and capital to figure out. During the decade between 2010 and 2020, the oil and gas sector wrote off about $350 billion of capital. To put that in context, that was approximately 55 percent of all the write-downs and write-offs in the S&P 500 in that decade. Public investors finally realized that the industry was solely focused on growing production and adding reserves, but it was not focused on making money. And that was true, but public investors didn't appreciate that finding and producing this massive shale resource required a wave of capital destruction to figure it out—no different than the destruction of capital that happened during the dotcom boom and bust, which birthed companies like Google, Amazon, and Facebook several decades ago.

There is however a silver lining to the massive capital destruction that happened in the oil and gas sector—during the decade of the 2010s, the U.S. grew oil production by about 180 percent and natural gas production by about 100 percent, which resulted in the U.S. going from being the biggest importer of oil in the world to being a net exporter of oil and becoming one of the largest global exporters of natural gas. We became energy independent, and what that did geopolitically and economically for the United States of America is nothing short of one of the greatest success stories in American history.

When the party finally ended, many public investors decided the oil and gas space was not investable because oil and gas companies were not responsible stewards of capital, and thus they decided to sell their positions and exit the sector. There was however a much smaller number of public investors that were still willing to consider investing in oil and gas and they forced a new model upon the industry that looked something like the following—companies should spend 30 percent to 50 percent of their cash flow to reinvest in their businesses and send the other 50 percent to 70 percent back to investors through share buybacks and dividends, companies should limit their production growth to low, single-digit percentages, and companies should deleverage their balance sheets.

The same destruction of capital was happening with private companies too, and thus LPs started materially slowing their commitments to private equity and private debt funds. Five years ago, there was probably $90 to $100 billion of dry powder in the oil and gas private equity and private debt space. Today there is more like $15 to $20 billion. More than half of all GPs that were active in the space five years ago are either out of business or can't raise a new fund because their returns were so poor. Banks have also meaningfully reduced their lending to the oil and gas sector.

In summary, the amount of public and private capital available to the oil and gas sector has shrunk dramatically from just a few years ago. Oil and gas are a depleting resource, so they need constant reinvestment to replace produced reserves. That investment over the past eight or nine years has averaged about 50 percent of what it should have been to replace that production. Global population will grow meaningfully as will the number of people entering the middle class between now and 2050, thus materially increasing the demand for all forms of energy, including oil and gas. **There is a huge mismatch between future global demand for oil and gas and the world's ability to supply that oil and gas, and this mismatch will likely result in meaningfully higher oil and gas prices over the next decade.**

CHRISTOPHER:

Talk about what people are not expecting over the next three years. And what should they be expecting? And then, for investors who are willing to be involved in all aspects of energy, where are we at over the next ten years?

WIL:

I think a lot of people expect that we're going to wake up in a few years and we won't need hydrocarbons anymore, that wind and solar will create all the energy we need, and all cars will be powered by batteries. This could not be further from the truth. Quite frankly, it's an incredibly dangerous way of thinking, not only because it is not possible, but also because it would jeopardize America's energy independence and put many Western countries in a disadvantaged geopolitical and financial position relative to China.

J.P. Morgan's CEO Jamie Dimon periodically comes to Houston to visit with their energy clients, of which Quantum is one of their largest credit exposures. A few years ago, I asked Jamie about how committed J.P. Morgan was to continue lending to the oil and gas sector, and I think his response pretty well sums up why the world needs to be very careful about starving the oil and gas sector of capital. He responded, and I paraphrase, that the price of energy affects almost every other sector in the economy, so **if energy prices are low, that creates tailwinds for most other sectors, and if energy prices are high, that creates headwinds for most other sectors.**

If we care about economic prosperity, if we care about the environment, we must have affordable and abundant energy so that we have the profits to reinvest in making this energy evolution happen.

If we care about economic prosperity, if we care about the environment, we must have affordable and abundant energy so that we have the profits to reinvest in making this energy evolution happen.

It is my strong belief that oil and gas is going to be used in very significant quantities, probably greater quantities than it's used today, a decade from now. I will go even further and say that I expect oil and gas will continue to be used in quantities close to that which it's used today, even two or three decades from now. So, we're going to need a lot of oil and gas to support demand and we're not investing enough in it.

Fortunately, wind and solar will continue to become an increasingly larger share of the overall energy mix, but the world needs to recognize that energy additions take a long time. The greatest market share penetration that any energy addition has ever made in its first fifty years was coal, which got to 35 percent market after its first half a century of use. For context, wind and solar are at only 4 percent after a little over ten years since the massive investments in this space began. We expect the world is going to invest more in wind and solar power, battery storage, and electrification of transportation, than it has in any sector in the history of the world, and probably by multiples. And that's going to create unbelievable opportunities to make investments.

But anytime the opportunity set increases at an incredibly rapid pace, and you have managers who haven't invested in that space before investing capital, and management teams who have never run these kinds of businesses before receiving capital, it's also a formula to destroy a lot of money. On one hand, it may be the single greatest investment opportunity, in terms of capital deployment, the world has ever seen, and on the other hand, there may be more capital destroyed in the energy transition than in any other industry in the history of capitalism.

CHRISTOPHER:

The opportunity is certainly there, as are the risks that we have to navigate through. In recent years, what has happened that you expected to happen, and what has happened that you didn't expect to happen?

WIL:

We certainly did not expect Russia to go into Ukraine. That event refocused the Western world back on the facts, instead of feelings and desires, regarding the energy transition. Before Russia went into Ukraine it was challenging to get certain institutions to sit down and talk to us about investing in oil and gas because they were either against investing in the sector for ESG reasons or they were afraid the world would not be using much oil and gas in a few years and thus the oil and gas assets we bought would have no terminal value. Most of those institutions are now engaging in discussions with us because the facts are overwhelmingly in favor of oil and gas having a long runway and being a great place to generate strong investment returns over the next decade. We didn't expect that conversation to shift so rapidly.

I also didn't expect the U.S. government to pass a landmark piece of legislation like the Inflation Reduction Act (IRA), which earmarks almost $400 billion of federal funding and tax credits to stimulate investment in the energy transition. The IRA is much bigger than its nameplate amount because it automatically keeps renewing until certain targets are achieved.

The IRA does a lot to completely change the economics not only for renewable energy, battery storage, electric vehicles, hydrogen, and nuclear, but also for carbon capture and storage (CCS). CCS is essentially decarbonizing hydrocarbons, meaning the CO_2 created when oil, gas, or coal is burned to generate energy is captured and then permanently stored or sequestered in underground reservoirs. **Natural gas turbines can turn on in a matter of minutes, which means they are baseload energy, and with a carbon capture device hooked up to that gas turbine, it turns what is considered by many to be dirty energy into baseload clean energy.** This is very different than solar and wind energy which are not baseload, because the sun doesn't always shine and the wind doesn't always blow. The world must primarily use baseload energy to run smoothly as energy demand fluctuates materially at different times during the day and night, and the world needs energy when it needs energy, not when the energy is available.

TONY:

What's different about nuclear today? Would you just take a moment and share that and what the opportunity might be there as well?

WIL:

The new generation nuclear power plants use a very different reactor technology than what was used in Three Mile Island, Fukushima, and Chernobyl, which were three nuclear power plants where accidents occurred that turned much of the world against nuclear power. The new reactors are much safer, and are generally not prone to having the reactor core meltdown that people are so worried about. Additionally, we now have what are called SMRs, or small modular reactors, which are nuclear power plants that are much smaller than utility scale nuclear power plants, so they can be built in a factory instead of onsite. SMRs can thus be built much quicker and cheaper than the old utility scale nuclear power plants. SMRs can also be built on a much smaller scale which means they can be used in a lot more applications. And the icing on the cake is that some of the SMR designs use the spent fuel from the existing nuclear reactor fleet as their fuel source which means they are essentially providing a solution regarding what to do with the nuclear waste generated from our existing fleet of nuclear power plants. Historically, one of the other big knocks on nuclear power is that it is very expensive. SMRs will likely defy this trend as they can be built in factories, and next generation utility scale power plants can defy this trend if we can remove the bureaucracy from the regulatory approval process and deploy them at scale.

TONY:

So, what are most investors getting wrong right now in the energy sector, from your perspective?

WIL:

One big thing that most investors are getting wrong is assuming this energy evolution is going to happen a lot faster than it likely will. Additionally, many investors are convincing themselves that they can make high returns in the energy transition space, when in fact, many companies operating in the energy transition sector don't make any money today and have no real apparent path to getting to profitability. And for the companies that are making money today, most of them are generating very low returns. Lastly, many investors are also underestimating the amount of risk they are accepting. As a result, the risk-adjusted returns on many opportunities in the energy transition space are very unfavorable to investors.

CHRISTOPHER:

If you had the attention of the world and you could tell them one thing to take away, what would it be?

WIL:

That is a very profound question. If I could grab the attention of the ten most important leaders in the free world, I would tell them this—be very careful what you ask for. The energy evolution is an amazingly important and noble cause, and humanity must pursue it. The prosperity we've achieved in the West over the last forty years has been made possible by two primary things: offshoring manufacturing to the country that can do it the cheapest and reducing the cost of capital to the lowest levels in history. Both these trends are likely to reverse over the next decade and that is going to create immense challenges for the West.

Part of the offshoring megatrend has included offshoring the essential components of the renewable energy transition. Essentially, in order to make wind turbines, solar panels, lithium ion batteries and electric vehicles, you have to mine minerals (like copper, lithium, cobalt, silicon, zinc, and a number of other critical minerals and rare earths), then you have to refine and process those minerals, and then you have to use those minerals to manufacture the turbines, panels and batteries. The West has offshored most of the mining, refining, and processing, and manufacturing of these essential inputs for the energy transition, to many countries around the world. The country that's taken the biggest advantage of this offshoring trend is China, as they started strategically thinking about this renewable energy transition that was coming more than a decade ago. **China has a stranglehold on all key inputs for the energy transition—their market share ranges from 30 percent to 60 percent on mining for various critical minerals, from 40 percent to 70 percent for refining and processing for various critical minerals, and from 60 percent to 80 percent for the manufacturing capacity for wind, solar, and lithium-ion batters.**

Think about the power that Saudi Arabia was able to exercise over oil prices over the last thirty or forty years and they only controlled 10 percent of the world supply. OPEC, which comprised thirteen countries, in total controlled about 30 percent of global oil supply. When they acted in concert, they could bring the world to its knees. Today, China controls four to eight times the amount of market share in each of the key areas necessary for the energy transition than Saudi controls in oil. Russia's war on Ukraine was a wake-up call to the West regarding the overwhelming importance of energy security, and for the U.S., Europe, and our allies to have energy security we must control our own supply chains.

Building our own supply chains for the energy transition in mining, refining and processing, and manufacturing will take decades, not years, and will require trillions of dollars of investment and a massively streamlined regulatory environment. On one hand, this represents the single greatest opportunity to bring high-paying jobs back to the U.S., but on the other hand, this represents the single greatest vulnerability to the United States from an economic and national security perspective if we fail to get our act together and execute.

TONY:

I want to come back to one thing before we talk about your business a little bit. I want to really emphasize these investments, because you've got this scarcity of capital and demand that's growing even more with the larger population in third world countries wanting more of this energy. A lot of us have had the mindset of, okay, we're going to embrace ESG. You look at Europe and they've reduced their domestic production of natural gas by 30 percent or 35 percent, and all that supply shortfall was being made up by Russia before they invaded Ukraine. We know what the challenge is there. Can you just comment a little further about that aspect of things and is it really as true as it seems that in order to have sustainability, hydrocarbons are the real answer—carbon capture for them—so that we have that baseload power available throughout the world and we still protect the environment? Is that the case? And what do you see as the political impact of pushing things offshore to other countries?

WIL:

It's the classic tale of two cities right here, or a tale of two continents. Europe went down the path that wind and solar should replace everything and hydrocarbons are bad. And, as I mentioned earlier, the U.S. went just the opposite direction. We went from being the largest importer to one of the largest exporters. And in doing so, not only did we become energy independent, but also, just think about the jobs, the taxes, the national security benefits of that.

I think there are a lot of good things that come with ESG. This is where I try to work as a bipartisan statesman, if you will, to bring people together on progressing toward sustainability, because I think the right and the left really get this issue wrong. Many people on the left think renewables, batteries and EVs are the answer, but they haven't taken the time to put the enormity of this transformation into perspective and understand the herculean challenges and obstacles that must be overcome to get there. They essentially have blind faith and think somehow it will just miraculously happen.

Many people on the right deny that the climate is changing, and that mankind might have something to do with the changes. Many also believe that the ESG movement is nothing more than liberal values being pushed down our throats, and so they just summarily reject both climate change and the ESG movement without considering the implications of doing so. And the truth is, like most things in life, when you really peel the onion back a few layers and you ask enough questions, you realize the truth is probably somewhere in between. I think that's the case here.

Do we have a climate issue going on right now? Yes. We can debate how much of that is caused by man and how much is just nature being nature. It doesn't really matter; it's not a risk we can afford to ignore. And oh, by the way, there's a lot of good that comes out of cleaning up hydrocarbons. We get much cleaner air. People are a lot healthier. They live longer lives. It smells better. That's what I say to my friends on the right.

And to my friends on the left I point out that energy transitions take decades, not years, and that there are many structural challenges to the energy transition that we must contend with and that if what they really want is clean energy, that we can provide that through a process known as carbon capture and storage. I also point out that we have an entire infrastructure system built out in the U.S. and globally to supply this energy, transport and store it, and then use it, so all we have to do is add on the CCS technology and build out the infrastructure to store the CO_2. **In summary, natural gas and coal, combined with CCS technology, can deliver baseload (remember, wind and solar are intermittent energy) power that is as clean or cleaner than wind and solar power, and the U.S. has a massive domestic supply of both.**

Many don't realize that more people die every day in third world countries from breathing carcinogens released from burning dung and wood to cook food in their homes than have died in the history of mankind from all the nuclear power plant accidents which have ever happened. Many people have an irrational fear of nuclear, but nuclear must be a significant part of the solution if we are serious about providing clean, baseload energy. China has plans to build at least 150 new nuclear reactors in the next fifteen years, which is almost double the number of reactors in operation in the U.S. today. Even our friends in the Middle East are embracing nuclear. They have hundreds of years of oil and gas supply and yet they want to build nuclear power plants because they want to get to net-zero and export another kind of energy. **Nuclear is going to become increasingly relevant, and it's**

not dangerous. Hydrocarbons can be decarbonized, and wind and solar are really good forms of energy. We need as much of them as we can get. And for the math to add up, we must have all the above. And, if we don't, it's a dark, dire future for humanity.

One more important point I'd like to make—my family foundation does a lot of work in the southern part of Africa, where I have seen the horrible implications of energy poverty. **There's probably a billion people on the continent of Africa who live in abject energy poverty. They don't have energy, and it takes energy, lots of it, to move up the economic prosperity ladder. They cook with wood or cow dung, and the carcinogens they breath in from doing so kill millions of people a year. That's not fair— those people deserve access to energy and thus we're going to need all forms of energy to supply the modern world with the energy it needs to sustain itself and the developing world with the energy it needs to improve its quality of life.**

TONY:

And it's got to be at a price people can afford, because, in those countries, that's an even bigger issue. So, carbon capture and storage sounds like it's one of the ultimate solutions. We need all these forms of energy, as you said, but that one would allow us to use hydrocarbons in a way that wouldn't have a negative impact on the environment. Let me shift a little bit for a moment to your firm because the size and growth of your firm is pretty historic and growing a large investment firm takes a lot more than just having great investments. Aside from strong performance, what will you say is the primary reason for the success of your business?

WIL:

I'd say two things. Our people and our culture. In any industry, any business, people are your most valuable asset. Humans are the only aspects of any business that can cause the future to change. They can come up with innovative ideas. They can out hustle the competition. They can do things in new ways that haven't been done before. So, we are and have always been focused on hiring the absolute best people in all the different disciplines necessary to run a world-class energy investment firm.

We also focus on maintaining a strong culture. Unfortunately, Wall Street investment firms in general are known to be sharp elbowed places that attract very talented, successful people, but a lot of times, also very individualistic people. It's an industry where, if you're really good, you can make a lot of money and achieve a lot of fame for yourself. And the problem is that you can have teams that become dominated by one or two franchise players. But individuals don't win championships, teams do. The best investment firms are very collegial. Teamwork is at the core of what we do because it takes a lot of people with many different areas of expertise, working in concert, to execute our business well.

My background was in finance, so when we started the firm, I knew we needed to go out and partner with operating and technical experts. And, twenty-five years later, we have a firm where more than one-third of our investment team has either technical, operating, or digital backgrounds, and they are all fully integrated members of the overall investment team. Every person on our team understands the unique value or skill set that every other member on our team brings to the team. We have this philosophy that we win as a team and we lose as a team, but we're always a team first. I think it's made us an enduring franchise.

TONY:

As you look at the history in your company, what would you say was the real fulcrum point that allowed you to go from good to great?

WIL:

I think for us it was a confluence of two things. In the beginning, we had all the ingredients, but we didn't have the scale. And without the scale, it was truly impossible to attract the world-class talent in some of the critical skill sets we needed. Our firm was founded in 1998, but when the shale industry took off about a decade later, I realized the world had really changed. The capital intensity of the companies we were backing increased by literally adding a zero. We used to write $10, $20, $30 million checks—all of a sudden, we needed write a $100, $200, $300 million checks. This was because shale wells cost about ten times more to drill than a conventional well. Shale wells also have about ten to twenty times more recoverable hydrocarbons. So, the scale changed. And when that happened, the fund sizes that we were raising increased a lot, providing us with the revenue to then go out and hire more of the best, world-class people. That was the inflection point for Quantum.

It's a dynamic world we live in. The only constant is change. No matter how well you think you have planned, things change, often very materially. Thus, it is important to be quick on your feet and able to realize that something has changed, and then have the will and courage to make mid-course corrections and adjustments to end up getting to where you're trying to go.

CHRISTOPHER:

You and I have something in common in that we both started our businesses at very young ages. What are a few things that you wish somebody would've told you before you started your business in your late twenties?

WIL:

Starting a business is the most exciting thing you'll probably ever do, and the most terrifying thing you'll ever do. So, do it while you're young. Also, don't be afraid of failure. You are going to fail, so fail quickly, learn from your mistakes, make adjustments, and try again. Most people are afraid to admit they've failed because they think it makes them look weak or bad, so they cover up their failure or don't admit they failed and keep doing the wrong thing over and over. I call that pride, and it is the single largest contributor to most people's inability to achieve greatness. You have to put failure in its proper perspective—most people see it as a negative—I see it as a positive, meaning, failure is successfully figuring out another way not to do something and puts me one step closer to figuring out the right way to do something.

The other thing I'd say is have fun. Life is so short. We're here for a very short period of time. Do it with people that you love being around. Buffett says he does business with people he likes, admires, and trusts. That may be the sagest advice I ever got—to do business with people that you like, admire, and trust.

CHRISTOPHER:

Indeed. When you think about Quantum's history, what is something that you would've done differently if you had it to do over again?

WIL:

In the early days, we were probably too conservative, too afraid of failure. I think being young, we were very fearful that if we made a big mistake, we might not ever raise another fund. You know the old saying that a master tailor measures three times and cuts once? We probably measured eight or nine times before we cut. We may have made the most perfectly tailored suit, but by the time we finished it, our suit size had changed—so in hindsight, I wish I would have been a little more willing to take the advice I now give on appropriately embracing failure.

CHRISTOPHER:

What do you think are the biggest difference makers for why firms are able to scale and why they're not?

WIL:

It goes back to the people in your organization. As you scale and you do bigger deals, the complexity increases, the managing of those businesses and operations increases, and it requires a different skillset. **Therefore, you must hire curious people, who have high integrity, a voracious work ethic, and an insatiable desire to keep learning. They may be really good at what they do today, but they have to also want to keep getting better and be committed to being lifelong learners.**

What I look for is people that have above average intelligence, that are hungry and have a strong work ethic, and are honest. And when I find those three things, I know we can teach those kinds of people everything they need to know.

One big mistake I see a lot of founders and senior partners of investment firms making is they hog too much of the economics for themselves. And that's the best way to ensure that your best people go somewhere else. We have a program at Quantum where every single employee across the firm participates in the carried interest we earn as the general partner of our funds, either directly or through an employee pool. Everybody therefore thinks like an owner. And the only way you can foster this mindset is by compensating your team and treating them well.

There are levels of intelligence and there are different types of intelligence, right? Musical intelligence, book intelligence, street intelligence. What separates those highest performers from the peers? Is there anything we've not mentioned?

WIL:

Self-awareness, humility, and great communication skills would be three attributes that separate those highest performers from their peers. We were built to interact with other human beings. Getting along, building relationships, and communicating are skillsets that are critical to being a great private equity or private credit investor. I think that to be good at doing these things you must be self-aware and humble. You also must have a reasonably high EQ. And so, we look very hard for that. **Emotional intelligence is often much more important to being a successful investor than being smarter than everyone else.** The relationships we make and the people's lives we touch and influence are what continue to effectively live on after we are gone. When you build an organization with people that possess these skills, you will not only have an amazing culture, but you will also generate great returns for your investors.

TONY:

Yes. When I was interviewing Warren Buffett, I asked him what was the best investment he ever made. I thought he was going to say Coca-Cola or Geico. He said it was Dale Carnegie, because if he hadn't learned to communicate, everything else wouldn't have happened.

CHAPTER 15

IAN CHARLES

FOUNDER OF ARCTOS SPORTS PARTNERS

Accolades: A pioneer in creating the industry's first sell-side advisor for private equity secondaries

Total Asset Under Management (as of August 2023): $6 billion

Area of focus: Professional sports (MLB, NBA, MLS, NHL, Premier League)

HIGHLIGHTS

- In 2002, Ian Charles cofounded Cogent Partners, the first secondary market sell-side advisory firm, which was later sold for nearly $100 million. Cogent is widely recognized for transforming the private equity secondary market by providing institutional-grade advisory services while providing unprecedented deal flow.
- Mr. Charles later went on to cofound Arctos Partners, the first institutional platform to pursue a global, multi-league, multi-franchise sports investment strategy.
- Arctos was the first firm to be approved to purchase multiple franchises across all eligible U.S. sports leagues, and their 2020 equity

investment into the Fenway Sports Group marked the first ever fund investment into a professional sports team by a private equity firm.

- Arctos's debut fund was the largest first-time private equity fund ever raised at close to $2.9 billion, and the firm was included in the 2023 *Sports Illustrated* Power List, which marks the fifty most influential figures in sports.

TONY:

Ian, what you've built is amazing. I understand you're not a sports fan, and yet you've put together the most amazing thing I've ever seen in sports. So, can you give us a little bit of background of how this all came together?

IAN:

If I go back to where it started. First and foremost, I've been an entrepreneur since I was probably thirteen or fourteen years old. I'm also a nerd and my first job just happened to be at a private equity fund of funds, learning the asset class at a very high level making primary fund investments and equity co-investments. Back then private equity was much more illiquid than it is today. If you were invested in a private equity fund, you were kind of stuck there for ten to fifteen years. If you needed or wanted to get out, there were only four or five firms in the world that would give the option to buy you out, and they would take a significant pound of flesh to provide you with liquidity. The market for private equity fund liquidity is known as the secondaries market.

The discounts in private equity secondaries used to be substantial. I was really young and really naïve, and I had a couple of colleagues who were also young, and we were all a bit naïve, I guess. We thought we could help these sellers, and our idea was to start the industry's very first advisor in the secondaries market, helping institutional investors sell their funds. That business was hugely successful and really transformed liquidity for private equity globally and created all the infrastructure that powers the global secondaries market today. Helping start that firm and my role there really launched my professional opportunity as an entrepreneur in illiquidity.

From there, I joined one of the original buyers in the secondary industry, and for fifteen years I helped them create competitive advantages, hone their strategy, and create other products to unlock liquidity in other illiquid markets. One of the markets I spent some time looking at was the professional sports market in North America.

North American sports assets, like Major League Baseball and the National Basketball Association, was a big, growing market, with a lot of minority ownership and no access to institutional capital. The sports market looked a lot like private equity twenty years ago. But when I started to study the sports industry, we realized none of the North American leagues allowed institutional capital. It was prohibited by the leagues, which are, in effect, the regulators. Sports was a really interesting asset class, because it was mathematically very difficult to replicate the risk/return characteristics of predominantly North American sports. These are very unique businesses. But if the regulator doesn't allow you to invest, you're not allowed to invest. That prohibition on institutional capital changed in 2019. Major League Baseball was the first North American league to open up its ownership architecture for institutional investment, but only to a very specific kind of fund that requires unique architecture, an onerous approval process, and there are a bunch of investing conflicts that have to be managed by any new entrant. But we identified the opportunity to be the first mover in this space. **I knew enough about this market to know that a bunch of finance geeks weren't going to be successful on their own. You really needed to partner with people that were accepted by this industry, had strong reputations in this industry and operating experience in sports.** So, our founding team has a blend of backgrounds that look like mine, or they look like my partner David O'Connor's—everybody calls him Doc—where they have decades building, running, and leading important parts of the sports and live entertainment ecosystem. Together with our founding colleagues, we built the first firm designed to provide value-added growth capital and liquidity solutions to North American sports teams and ownership groups. It has been an unbelievable experience. But, for me, the origin really started twenty-five years ago, helping create liquidity solutions in other illiquid markets and understanding kind of repeatable patterns that appear in illiquid investments and in building businesses in alternative assets. When you marry that up with Doc's experience as an operator and entrepreneur in sports and live entertainment, that gave us an opportunity to build something pretty special, and since our founding we've tried really hard not to blow that opportunity.

TONY:

Give us of a feeling of what came out of that, because you guys didn't enter in with just capital. You really have this massive added value that you bring to these sports entities that are now really media companies. Maybe you can give a little bit of what the benefit of that is and how it is that you serve them.

IAN:

What's really interesting is that when we started the firm, if you had asked me that question, I would've said, look, to be honest, I don't know. I don't know what we're going to be allowed to do in that area. Because the leagues hadn't really set the rules. We didn't know what the leagues would allow, or what owners were going to be receptive to [or] where they were going to want or need help. Over the last three years, as our firm has grown its reputation, scale, asset portfolio, and data, we have continued to invest in our own capabilities, our team, and in our data systems to build a proprietary data science and applied research business, which we call Arctos Insights, and a value creation program, which we call the Arctos Operating Platform. What we've done is we've built a whole suite of services around data, analytics, and value-add. I guarantee you, if you ask me this question in six months, the answer will be a little bit different. And in a year, better be a lot different. We're constantly evaluating our customers' needs. Because we have two sets of customers, the owners that we've partnered with and the investors who have entrusted us with their capital. The feedback loop we have with the owners, leagues, and club executives is a constant part of our process. **So today we help them with acquisitions, buying other franchises, real estate, live entertainment complexes, investing in technology, and improving their venues. We're helping them in areas like digital engagement, data science, and machine learning.** We're a huge data shop. We've built an applied research business where we provide really important business content and analytics to the owners in our portfolio. International expansion is a really important topic for owners as they want to take these brands and grow them to a global audience and fan base. Some of them have no idea how to do that. We just opened our London office because our teams want to grow internationally. We want to have boots on the ground, resources, and a playbook that they can just grab and tap into in order to accelerate the growth of their business and grow their brand internationally.

So, it's a constantly evolving, deep set of capabilities, and this is an industry that really hasn't had a chance to partner with an institutional resource like us. So, there's a lot of low-hanging fruit. There's a lot of repeatable pattern recognition. **What one team needs, probably fifteen other teams in the same league need. We are able to invest centrally in these capabilities because we know that we can spread the cost of that investment across six, seven, sometimes twenty platforms.**

TONY:

Peter Guber is one of my dearest friends, and I know you've done multiple deals with him, obviously between the Warriors and the Dodgers. But what about the investors themselves? What advantages are there? This idea of this legal monopoly, the impact on inflation, and the fact that these teams, like in the NBA, own one-thirtieth of all the revenues. I mean, most of these things, investors have no clue about.

IAN:

Peter is incredible. He sees just about everything a little earlier than the rest of us, but you are right. What you're hitting on is a very unique feature of North American sports assets. This isn't true in European football or other kinds of sports ecosystem opportunities. Every North American team owns an equal share of the global business that is their league, and the league is a global intellectual property and a kind of brand management business. The leagues sell media rights, data rights, and sponsorship at the national and international level. The leagues have their own overhead and cost structure, but then they generate dividends, and they pay them out annually in equal proportions to their owners. So, it doesn't matter if you're in the smallest market or the biggest market, you get the same dividend distribution. It also doesn't matter if you finish in last place or first place, you get the same payment. The ownership stake in the league and the aggregate revenue that comes from long-term, diversified contracts with annual payment escalators create this really stable, durable asset that everyone in the league owns.

The leagues and owners don't like to call the local license a monopoly, but it functions like one. A sports franchise owner has a protected geographic region, just like the franchisor of a restaurant chain—no one is allowed to compete with you in your geographic zone for revenue around your sport. **The fandom around these brands is generational and these are important assets in their communities, so your customer acquisition cost is essentially zero. These businesses are communal, they're shared experiences across generations, across political parties—they are the only asset that has those characteristics today.** Owners can then use that local license to expand into real estate and build a live entertainment complex, digital distribution, and marketing direct to your consumer. We find that local platform activity interesting. **If you are doing it right, this is a platform for you to be a civic leader, but also compound your wealth in an uncorrelated way with very little leverage, very little geopolitical risk, no currency risk.** When you combine the ownership stake in the league with the local license, a North American club provides a nice "portfolio effect," has all of these really unique attributes that are hard to find and replicate. For our fund, because we provide liquidity to minority owners when they want out, and provide growth capital to owners that have a big vision, we're able to come into partnership with great owners in great markets who have unbelievable brands and ideas, and do that at a really attractive entry point.

TONY:

And you've done so much to add value. Then you've got this inflation hedge with both the real estate and also the pricing power because as you said, these people are fanatics; they're tried-and-true in that area. Tell us a little bit more about you for a moment. Who's been the most important person or one of the most important people in your life that shaped your growth, your success, and your career or life path?

IAN:

This is going to be super cheesy, and Christopher might make fun of me down the road, but it's true. I always tell people I met my wife when I was thirteen years old. She didn't know I existed until I was probably sixteen; she was too cool and too beautiful to pay attention to me! We grew up in the same small town. We made a bet on each other. Despite both of our parents forbidding us from going to college together, we outfoxed them a little bit and ended up going to school together. If it wasn't for my wife, Jamie, I never would've taken that first risk as an entrepreneur starting the secondary advisory business. She was a special education teacher, and I was working as an analyst at this fund of funds business. If not for her paycheck, her faith in me, and her encouragement, I wouldn't have had the courage to leave my job and try to start the business.

TONY:

Wow.

IAN:

Fast-forward almost twenty years later, and she knew that I was longing for something different professionally. She knew that I had this itch to be an entrepreneur again. **I think we all probably put way too much of our career into our self-worth and personal identity. I know I certainly have many, many times. The idea of leaving a great job and an important role, you have a bit of an identity crisis, right? It's scary.** But Jamie knew me better than I knew myself. She knew I have this drive to try and build something. She also knew if I ever made that leap, I wanted to use the name Arctos and that the name had connectivity to our roots in Alaska and to the bear. She knew those things. My Christmas gift from Jamie in 2018 was a crystal bear and a note that just said: "I think it's time." Five months later Major League Baseball changed their ownership rules. She's always believed in me. She's always encouraged me. She's lifted me up and supported me when I didn't even know I needed it. So, she would, without a doubt, be the answer to that question.

CHRISTOPHER:

The thing that's so amazing for a lot of us men is, if we would do more of what our wife thinks we should do, we would be much better off and much happier.

IAN:

We'd be happier. No doubt.

CHRISTOPHER:

Let's talk about sports a little bit. So obviously we talked about the attributes of sports that are very different than most of the other investments that are out there. As you know, but for the benefit of everyone else, it took about eighteen months for us to have a good conversation and for us to understand the business model before we did our partnership together. And it's something that just, candidly, took me a long time to figure out. When you think about the opportunity set, what do you feel like the opportunity is? What are the real interesting opportunities for investors in the world of professional sports or sports in general?

IAN:

We are laser-focused on helping North American owners unlock all of the potential of the assets that they have right in front of them. Sometimes it's that simple. Sometimes you've got something so special in front of you that has so many growth nodes and opportunities to unlock that the best thing to do is just focus and help them. So, over the next three or four years, it's all about live entertainment, improving the fan experience, media rights becoming more valuable as you go from a linear system to a streaming system. It's about helping these brands grow internationally. And it's about creating that direct connectivity with the customer.

As an example, if you're a season ticket owner with the Astros and you can't go to the game, you may decide to sell that ticket on one of these ticket exchanges. Let's say I buy it, but then Jamie (my wife) reminds me we have a scheduling conflict (which happens a lot by the way). I can then choose to put that ticket up on another exchange and Tony may buy it from me.

Right now, the team doesn't know who I am (the first buyer of the ticker), and they don't know who Tony is (the next buyer), even though Tony brought his family to the game. Soon, the team will know exactly who owned that ticket throughout the entire value chain. The team will be able to market to all three of us directly for future sales, and on this particular transaction, the team will be able to participate in the gain along the way. So, if your ticket has a face value of $200, but Tony bought it for $600, right now the team just gets $200, but soon they'll be able to take a portion of that profit along the chain. That simple change unlocks 30 to 50 percent upside in just the ticketing revenue. There are so many near-term opportunities to help owners monetize and grow these incredible local brands, improve the fan experience, and participate in owning one of the most important kinds of content over the next twenty years. That's what we're laser focused on.

CHRISTOPHER:

As we went through our diligence on sports in general, what finally got me over the edge and made me a believer was the resiliency of the revenues. I don't think most investors fully appreciate how predictable and how consistent these revenue streams are. So, when you think about what's transpired, you've been spot-on with your projections of what was going to happen in professional sports. But there have been things over the last couple of years that have happened that you didn't expect. First, what are the things you expected to happen that have occurred? And then, what happened that you just didn't expect to occur in the last couple of years?

IAN:

Oh, man, that's a great question. When we started this thing and started talking to people, in March and April of 2020, there were no games. I had no idea when there would ever be games again.

TONY:

Did that provide discounts for you in terms of purchases at that time?

IAN:

What it did is provide me with anxiety. But we knew sports would come back and we were confident that sports as an industry, with its history of innovation, that sports would likely be an early recovery industry. We didn't know what the recovery would look like and we didn't know how strong the demand curve would be. It felt like it might be very regional. The snapback, the rebound, has been much stronger than our base case assumptions. As an example, the **NBA regular season gates closed two weeks ago—number** one season ever for total attendance. So, the speed and strength of that recovery is one thing that has surprised me.

CHRISTOPHER:

So that leads to the next question. There's a lot of investors that get sports wrong, and they don't understand it. But what is it that you hear the most where people are really misunderstanding the business of sports?

IAN:

I think they don't understand the valuation framework of these businesses. **On the revenue side you already noted the stability, predictability, and the durability of the revenue streams in North American sports are really unusual. They're more akin to infrastructure assets**—fifteen-year contracts on your stadium naming rights, five-to-ten-year contracts on your media rights at a national level, seven-to-twenty-year contracts at the local level for regional sports rights. That predictability is not well understood, but it is really valuable in a world of uncertainty.

The valuation environment in sports is also one that has been remarkably stable over the last fifteen years. Remember what I said earlier, institutional capital was never allowed to come into this space.

Another thing that the leagues are very, very protective of in North America is they don't let you use a lot of leverage on these businesses. For almost my entire career, the cost of capital has been getting lower and lower every year. When we started Arctos, there was about $18 trillion of sovereign debt that had a negative yield. If you're an institutional investor, that repricing of risk across asset classes made it really hard for you to achieve your actuarial returns or your personal return targets. As a result, you had to go out of the risk curve to achieve your return targets or just sit things out in cash earning no return and hope that things improved. Sitting on cash is really hard for most investors to do because of benchmarking and career risk. So, most investors felt compelled to put more into riskier and riskier strategies. As an unprecedented amount of global liquidity washed around the globe looking for things to buy, if it tried to invest in North American sports, the leagues prohibited that investment and the wave of liquidity bounced off and went in search of another opportunity. League debt limitations made it nearly impossible to use a lot of cheap leverage to buy a sports team, and institutions couldn't flood the market with capital. They weren't allowed to.

As a result, the valuation expansion that you had in so many sectors over more than a decade, it didn't happen in sports. In fact, sports and hydrocarbons are the only industries we've identified that had P/E (price to earnings) multiple compression from 2011 to 2021 because the combination of earnings growth and revenue growth in sports was higher than valuation growth. So, in this big unwind, this big repricing of risk over the last eighteen months, sectors that had their valuation metrics swollen from cheap debt and lower cost of capital have all seen valuation compression that has hurt returns.

TONY:

Haven't the returns been greater than the S&P and greater than the Russell 2000 on these four core sports organizations that you've invested in?

IAN:

What's interesting is the answer to that is yes, but more importantly in very different environments. So, the most accommodating decade of my career would've been 2011 to 2021. If you were invested in venture capital or leveraged buyout funds, you would've gotten like a 17 percent to a 20 percent return over a decade. Which is amazing. Public markets would've given you about a 10 to 11 percent return, which is also historically very, very attractive. Sports gave you 18 percent with no skill, just buying the broad market at no discount. But that was a pretty easy market environment, right? Just about everything worked. When the cost of money is falling every year, assets just become worth more if you just hold them. But in a totally different environment, the mid-1960s to the mid-1980s was a very different environment, with very high volatility and persistently high inflation. The 60/40 portfolio, that every investor kind of banks on, didn't work.

For twenty years (mid sixties to mid eighties), your compounded return from the S&P 500 was about 4 percent with inflation an average of 7 percent. So, you destroyed real wealth for twenty years if you were long equities. North American sports during that time frame, mid sixties to mid eighties, gave you a 16 percent [compounded return]. **It's been remarkably** resilient in its outperformance. It has very low volatility for a lot of really nerdy mathematical reasons. It's got a lower negative correlation to other asset classes. And again, you don't have a lot of leverage. So, you don't have the whipsaw of global liquidity impacting valuations like you do in other sectors. It's a really, really hard thing to find these characteristics.

TONY:

It ties into our next question. You know, Ray Dalio is a good friend of mine, and I asked him what the single most important investment principle was, and he called it the Holy Grail. And the title of this book is based on him. One of the reasons, obviously, that we're partners with you in this area is because it's such a non-correlated investment, on top of everything else you just talked about. But what would you say is the Holy Grail of Investing from your perspective?

IAN:

I talked to Ray about our strategy about a year ago. It was a fascinating discussion—he cut right to the lack of correlation. He actually flipped it into a slightly different mathematical construct and we started to talk about the cost to carry, because sports teams used to cost you money every year to own them via operating losses and capital calls. But that cash flow characteristic has changed over the last fifteen years. The cost of carry has flipped and that change has produced a big fundamental change on valuations in North America.

My entire career, I've been trained and sought advice and mentorship from successful and wise practitioners in illiquid markets. And **for me, the Holy Grail of a strong fundamental value investment philosophy is an intrinsic value arbitrage. Howard Marks and other value investors call it the margin of safety. Investing in things that are non-obvious, which means they are likely less competitive, at an attractive margin of safety in partnership with management teams and owners you believe in— if you do that while building a diversified portfolio of opportunities with these attributes, you will outperform the market because of that margin of safety and because of the performance of the people you've backed.**

TONY:

One of the questions I throw at people is this: If you had the world's attention for five minutes, what would you want to tell them?

IAN:

Oh man. If I had the world's attention for five minutes, what would I tell them? I'd probably tell them everything is going to be okay.

TONY:

That's great. I agree with you. But also tell me why?

IAN:

I think a lot of people are scared today, insecure. I think a lot of people are lonely. I don't think people have meaningful connections or as many meaningful interactions as we all need. **I would tell people, especially men, to reach out to other people that they respect and tell them they're doing a great job and that you love them. If you're friends with somebody and they're a good dad, tell them they're a good dad. Or if you think they are a great partner/spouse, tell them. Tell them that they are a great friend and how much you appreciate them.** I would tell people it's going to be okay.

CHRISTOPHER:

That's a beautiful thing.

TONY:

Beautiful. Let's talk about the investment business itself. You know, growing a large investment firm is a lot more than just having great investments. What do you think has been the primary reason for your success in your business?

IAN:

I think the edge that we have during the three years we've been building this thing is the people that we have here. We're very, very selective on who gets to come and be on this journey with us, and we've set some real parameters and filters around that process. We have six core values that are really important to us. One of the things that we talked a lot about as a founding group is, **if we're lucky enough to have success, there's going to be a lot of "shiny things" along the way. It's going to be really important to know when we want to reach down and pick one up, and when we need to keep on running and not get distracted.** So, we have these defined terms—our passion and our niche, from Gino Wickman's book *Traction*—they keep us focused. The core values . . . there's a lot of discussion around the value of diversity. **We are uncompromising in diversity; we want absolutely no diversity in values. If you are not aligned with our values, this is not the right place for you.**

TONY:

Do you mind sharing those six values with us? I'd love to hear that.

IAN:

Servant leadership, trust, teamwork, insights, character, and excellence. After our founding team spent a bunch of time with each other, starting to build the business, we actually hit the pause button and gave everybody a day off with a homework project. The homework project was, when we come back here tomorrow, you have to bring the two things you love about everybody here.

TONY:

That's great.

IAN:

Eight founders—that means you're getting feedback from seven people. There's a little bit of overlap and redundancy, so you're getting eight to ten things about each person. We went through this [list], trimming and consolidating, and at the end of that process there was this shared DNA. And so, our six core values are the shared core attributes of our founding team that we all loved in each other and that we are inspired to be more like in each other.

TONY:

That's beautiful. That's really beautiful. Thank you for sharing that. That's something any organization could grab and run with. What would you say would be the fulcrum point in your business that really allowed you to leap forward, you know, from good to great?

IAN:

So, about a year into it, it was easy to look around and be like, holy shit, this is incredible. But we actually had the opposite feeling. It was like, oh my gosh, we're going to blow it. How do we make sure we don't screw this up? Always having this imposter syndrome anxiety. **The one thing I know is that, in a year, our process won't look like it does today. The services we offer our owners will be different. The way we use data will be different. The kinds of data that we collect and analyze will be different. We have to make sure our people are comfortable challenging the way we think. We have to constantly reinvest and reevaluate and be totally fine ripping something up and saying, "That worked really well two years ago but stop talking about that because it doesn't matter tomorrow."** So, I think for us, about a year into it, we stepped back and said, okay, we have a chance to do something really special here. How do we define our right to win?

What are the best firms excelling at? And what does that look like? What did José and Behdad do at Clearlake? What did Robert (Smith) do at Vista? Robert dominated in his sector early, but then he doubled down and built the Vista playbook. He and his team keep reinvesting in this seemingly insurmountable intellectual property stack. We have to do that in sports. So, one of the things we did is we just stepped back and said, look at all these firms that we admire. And there are so many of them. What have they done that made them special? And what could we do in our industry to replicate some of those attributes?

CHRISTOPHER:

What are the few things that you wish you would've done differently when you started the firm?

IAN:

I wish I would've grabbed a couple of machine learning engineers, because when we started the firm three years ago, most people couldn't spell AI. Data science has been a big part of our business plan from the very beginning, but

I wish we would've over-indexed into that area. I know we're leading in that area. I know we're innovating and we're using data science in ways that most managers haven't even started to think about. But I wish we would've really doubled down on that early.

CHRISTOPHER:

Why are most investment firms and the vast majority of private asset management firms unable to scale?

IAN:

Well, first of all, some asset management firms shouldn't scale. Some, what they do really well just doesn't scale. And if they try, they will move away from their circle of competence, they will leave the market position where they have a right to win. I think the areas that firms can really excel at are pretty well documented: You can be an industry specialist or a country-specific expert. There are big macro/competency areas where you can dominate, like credit or infrastructure, but then there are organizational things you can dominate and excel at too. Culture, people . . . actually, a really easy thing to win in our industry is just treating people like they're human beings and that this might not be the only place they work their entire career. Just giving them grace and investing in them. You can win on organizational health and talent density. You can win in organizational management and people. If you have proprietary deal flow, real actual proprietary deal flow—where you have the luxury of being a hunter or a gatherer. Just harvesting whatever bountiful season presents itself, that is truly very rare. Originating differently, pricing risk differently, managing risk differently, managing the liquidity and monetization of your portfolio differently. Those are all areas where you can build core competencies and differentiation. Most great firms are really good at four or five of those things. But you have to know where, why, and how you have a right to win. And you have to have the confidence and humility to pressure test those conclusions regularly.

CHRISTOPHER:

It's fascinating to see exactly what you described, not only how hard it is to have those key attributes among the founding group, but also to make sure that persists through the generational transfers that occur inevitably over time. Some do it exceedingly well and some obviously don't.

IAN:

That is the biggest risk, in my opinion, in private markets—that generational transition. Investors don't understand how to underwrite it. A lot of times they're scared to ask about it. Those are hard questions to ask, but they are the most important questions. You have to be curious about how each firm is working, again "what is their right to win?" that's working, and you have to have the courage to double click and go deep into those topics because if the people you're backing aren't there in three or four years, the franchise has real risk.

TONY:

I love your language and thought process around the right to win. You do these things that earn the right to win. That's a very different way of looking at things than most people do, Ian. Speaking of investment talent, what do you believe are the key traits that separate the highest performers from their peers in your mind?

IAN:

Well, I do want to give credit where credit is due. The "right to win" is something that my friend Hugh MacArthur taught me, and he's been helping managing partners at private equity firms understand their right to win for a long time. What are the key traits to separate the highest performers from their peers? I actually think this is pretty simple. If you have a compelling strategy and thesis that has been vetted and supported by very sophisticated institutional investors and attracts capital, and **you do what you say you're going to do, and you do it with good human beings who are really talented, and you keep investing in those people and investing in your process, I think that's what the highest performing firms do.** They identify, defend, and grow their right to win.

CHAPTER 16

DAVID SACKS

COFOUNDER OF CRAFT VENTURES

Accolades: Cohost of the *All In* podcast and original member of the PayPal "mafia" with Elon Musk and Peter Thiel
Total Asset Under Management (as of August 2023): $3 billion
Area of focus: Enterprise and consumer technology

HIGHLIGHTS

- David Sacks has invested in over twenty unicorns, including Affirm, Airbnb, Eventbrite, Facebook, Houzz, Lyft, Palantir, Postmates, Slack, SpaceX, Twitter, and Uber.
- David began his career as founding COO and product leader at PayPal and then founder/CEO of Yammer, which he sold to Microsoft for $1.2 billion.
- He founded Craft Ventures in 2017 and now has $3 billion AUM across six funds. Portfolio companies include SpaceX, Reddit, Boring Company, ClickUp, SentiLink, OpenPhone, Vanta, Neuralink, Replit, and Sourcegraph.

TONY:

With all you've done in your life from PayPal to being an early investor in Facebook, Airbnb, and SpaceX—it's mind-boggling what you've accomplished and you're still a force of nature, not only in technology and as an investor, but also in politics to a great extent. And we're big fans of your podcast. Tell us a little bit about your origin story. How did this all come to be?

DAVID:

My family moved to America from South Africa when I was five years old. We became citizens when I was ten, and I grew up mainly in Memphis, Tennessee. I went to Stanford and graduated in 1994. That time period was around the birth of the internet in Silicon Valley. 1995 was an important year—the year that Netscape IPO'd. It was the first commercial browser for the internet. Unfortunately, I had graduated the year before and gone off to law school. It wasn't until 1999 that I came back to Silicon Valley. A friend of mine from Stanford, Peter Thiel, was starting a company. We talked a lot about what he was doing, and I eventually decided to join up with him. That company ended up becoming PayPal. So that was how I got into technology. Since then, I've mostly been involved in founding and investing in technology startups.

TONY:

And the type of startups you've been part of are some of the biggest in history. What's been your secret sauce in identifying these types of opportunities?

DAVID:

There are a few things I look for. One I call the product hook. **What is that simple, repeatable transaction or interaction at the heart of your product that users will want to do over and over again?** At PayPal, it was entering someone's email address and a dollar amount, and sending them money very easily. With Uber, you put a destination on a map and a car comes to pick you up. Google is the simplest of all. It's just that search box—a very simple interaction that users want to engage in over and over again. I think a lot of companies miss this because they think that if they keep layering on more and more features and adding more and more complexity, they can solve the problem of product-market fit. But if you can't get users to do something simple, it's very hard to get them to do something complicated. You want to start with something simple that users embrace and then layer complexity on top of it.

The other big thing that I look for is some sort of innovation on distribution. I call it the distribution trick—something unique that the company is doing to find users or buyers. At PayPal, we invented a lot of these tricks. Users could email money to someone who wasn't even a user yet. We embedded PayPal payment buttons inside of eBay auctions, bootstrapping off their platform. We gave people sign-up and referral bonuses. There are a lot of these tricks that PayPal pioneered that made the product go viral. If you look at other companies that have grown explosively fast, they're usually innovating on distribution, which is to say, reaching users in a new way. The reason that's important is that the world is so crowded that just building a good product is not a guarantee that you'll be successful. We wish it would be, but it's a big internet out there, and you need to find a way to reach your users in a cost-effective way, or they may never find you no matter how good your product is.

TONY:

You've had such an amazing group of friends, some of which are the most influential people in the world in tech. Who had the most influence on your life? And how did they help shape you in positive ways?

DAVID:

In terms of my business career, I was very lucky to work with two great founders in my first startup: Peter Thiel and Elon Musk. Those were the two CEOs I worked for as either head of product or COO. Getting to work with both of them was a great learning experience for me. They have very different styles as CEO. Elon is very hands-on, very involved in every part of the business, especially the product. And Peter is more of a delegator and focuses on big strategic issues. Both styles obviously have their merits and can work. When I founded Yammer after PayPal, I felt like I was able to take the best techniques that I had learned from both of them.

TONY:

Would you say you fall in the middle [of their styles]? Or do you strategically use one or the other depending on the situation?

DAVID:

I fall in the middle. Elon is incredibly hands-on with every part of the business. If you look at his org chart, he has a lot of reports because he keeps things very flat. I had a more conventional org chart. I liked to work through my executives, but there were two areas where I was more hands-on. One was the product. You can't fully delegate that if you're the one with the product vision. The other is that when a functional area was going well, I would give my executives more latitude, but if it wasn't going well, I would breathe down their neck until we fixed it. For example, if sales was hitting their numbers, I would mostly leave them alone, but if they were missing, they would really feel my presence and there would be a lot more inspections. You want to be hands-on where you think you have a special advantage or skill set or, certainly, if anything's going wrong. But you can trust your executives to operate more independently when they've demonstrated success in doing that.

CHRISTOPHER:

It's a fine balance to walk there. When you look at technology today, it's changing a lot. What are the greatest opportunities for investors?

DAVID:

The great thing about Silicon Valley is that there's been a platform shift roughly every decade. If you go back all the way to the eighties, the personal computer replaced the mainframe. Then in the nineties, we had the birth of the internet, and computing moved from on-premise to the cloud, or from the desktop to the cloud. Then we had the launch of social in the early 2000s. We had the birth of mobile in the late 2000s. **Now the big platform shift is to AI.** It always seems to happen about once a decade. It is a little bit of a I to say that AI is the big wave, but I think it is, and we're just at the beginning of this cycle. There's going to be a tremendous amount of opportunity for new as well as existing companies.

TONY:

If you look at AI right now, it's very much like the [early] days of the internet. There are a zillion companies forming and many of them are not going to be around long. When you look specifically at AI [companies], what are the ones that pull your attention?

DAVID:

There are a couple of things we're going to look for. One is a founder who has vision, tenacity, and creativity. Someone who really understands the space—AI is fairly technical, so founders who are able to combine a technical aptitude with a vision for where the space is going have a better chance at success. The people bet is even more important at this super early stage.

The other thing we'll look for are ideas that we think fit where the market's going or what the market wants. **We think there's a market opportunity in what have broadly been called "copilots" for professionals. We think there's going to be a copilot for doctors, a copilot for lawyers. Pretty much every profession you can think of, every job function you can think of, there's going to be an AI copilot to help that person do their job.** We think that will create a lot of opportunities for founders who can go deep in a particular area—they understand the job requirements and they understand AI, and they can match those two things together.

CHRISTOPHER:

What has happened in the last couple of years that you expected to happen, and what has happened that you didn't expect to happen?

DAVID:

Silicon Valley is going through a huge reset right now. We had the popping of the biggest asset bubble since the dotcom crash in 2000. In hindsight, the Fed's zero-interest rate policies, or "ZIRP," going back all the way to 2008, had a lot more impact than people wanted to admit. It had a big impact on the amount of capital that came into the industry. There was all this free money sloshing around looking for a return.

The conventional wisdom about VC, roughly a decade or two ago, was that it wasn't a business that scaled. It's not like public market investing where you can just invest billions and billions of dollars or even hundreds of billions of dollars very easily. It's very much a business where VCs are working hand-in-hand with founders. It's just never been an asset class that's capable of putting a ton of money to work. That was the conventional understanding. What happened was that during this zero-interest rate period, a lot of new money came into the industry.

A lot of public market investors came in thinking: We've seen how well these startups do when they go public, so we'll just invest in the last private round before they go public. They looked at the numbers and it appeared there was an arbitrage there. So they started investing in the last private round. Then they realized: Wait a second, the guys who are investing in the second-to-last private round are getting marked up by us, so there's an arbitrage there too. **They started using that logic, and they worked all the way down the stack, without necessarily having the expertise to evaluate early stage startups.** You can imagine the result of this. Money flooded into startups, and it drove valuations sky high. But as interest rates have gone up, liquidity has gone down, and there's been a popping of that bubble. So, the industry is going through a big reset right now.

The way that capital markets behavior translated into startup behavior is that a lot of founders thought money would always be available, that they could always raise a new round at a higher valuation. Money grew on trees, and founders got lax in their spending. I think founders lost focus on the idea of ever getting to profitability; it was all just about top-line revenue. The whole mentality was to grow regardless of how inefficient that growth was, regardless of how unprofitable it was. In their defense, founders felt like they had to play the game that was on the field. That game was that if you didn't show the most top-line growth and your competitor did, they would raise all the money and they'd be able to buy up the rest of the market. **You saw this dynamic in the whole Uber versus Lyft battle where they were both raising huge amounts of money and deploying it inefficiently but they felt trapped in a prisoner's dilemma—as long as there was an investor willing to fund the other guy, then you had to play the same game. This dynamic trained these companies to be very inefficient.**

Now that capital is not as available as it used to be, founders and startups have had to become much more efficient. We've gone from a situation where the only focus was on growth to one in which there's a more balanced focus. Founders have to think about the efficiency of growth, as reflected in metrics like burn, margins, and unit economics.

That's been a huge change in the industry because these bad behaviors built up over roughly fifteen years. There's an old saying that the market is an escalator on the way up and an elevator on the way down, and we just took the elevator down. It's been a rude awakening for a lot of VCs and founders.

CHRISTOPHER:

So, what are investors getting wrong today when they're thinking about technology and specifically growth and venture capital? What are they not seeing that they should be?

DAVID:

That's tough. We are in the midst of this big reset, and people are waking up to capital being much less available than it was in the past. The last decade or so was a very unusual period. I think we're going to be in a much more capital-constrained environment moving forward. Everyone's going to have to adjust their behavior accordingly.

CHRISTOPHER:

Do you think the valuations have fully begun to adjust for that or is it still further to go?

DAVID:

It's a good question. I would say that the valuation adjustments are happening in a somewhat uneven way. In a lot of areas, the adjustment has occurred and it's appropriate. But whenever an area gets hot in VC land, the valuations go crazy. For example, even though we're excited about AI, we are a bit concerned about how crazy some of the valuations are getting. We're starting to see companies with no revenue be valued at hundreds of millions of dollars. We've even seen some unicorn valuations without any revenue yet. We're back to multiples of a hundred times ARR (Annual Recurring Revenue) for hot AI companies. So, in that sense, VCs never seem to learn the lesson. Or they forget it when an area gets hot.

I'm a big believer in AI and believe it is going to create a lot of opportunity. The problem is that you still have a bit of a mania going on in some VC circles, so it's hard to find AI companies that are both promising and reasonably valued. We look for both.

TONY:

I met Ray Dalio about fourteen years ago and we became friends, and I asked him, "What's the single most important investment principle that guides you?" That's what this book is about—the Holy Grail of Investing. Ray told me at the time that it was finding eight to twelve uncorrelated investments because it reduces your risk by 80 percent and increases your upside. It is such a simple principle. What would be the Holy Grail of Investing for you?

DAVID:

Well, it's interesting. The type of investing I do is like the opposite of what he's doing. He's a macro investor, and I'm the most micro investor you can find. Not only am I investing in private companies, I'm investing in the earliest stage of private companies. I'm investing in the companies that just got started—many of which we know statistically aren't going to work out. The hope is that one or two do work out and can return the entire fund and then some. In my business, you're always looking for that power law company. The power law states that the most valuable investment in any given portfolio will generate the majority of the returns for that portfolio. So, it's almost the opposite of Ray's investing strategy.

I would not recommend this for the average investor. This is not a good way to construct a portfolio for the average investor. This is one asset class within what would be a balanced portfolio. Maybe you have a few percent of your portfolio in private companies, and then within that bucket you have this power law dynamic. We're always looking for that power law company. You can tell from what we've talked about today that I'm very much in the weeds when it comes to product. How is the product being distributed? How is it going to market? What is the founder's vision?

What are the intangible qualities the founder has that could make this an outlier company? It's very micro. The most important thing for startups is if you can find one that is catching fire. That's really the trick—to find something that's at the inflection point of the hockey stick.

We've developed our own understanding of what metrics are important for software startups. We look at not just their annually recurring revenue (ARR) and growth rates. We look at their customer acquisition costs. We have various metrics of capital efficiency. We talk to customers on our own. We try to make sure that the product actually is loved and is being referred by customers to others. We're always trying to look for signals that the company's taking off.

TONY:

And if you can find the right timing with those signals, you're then using the expertise of your decades of experience to help them grow. This is kind of a silly question for you because you have the world's attention in so many different ways but, if you have the world's attention for five minutes, what would you want people to know?

DAVID:

One of the themes I keep coming back to on my podcast is that the world that's emerging right now is a multipolar world. That's different from the world around 1990 when the Berlin Wall fell and the Soviet Union broke up. America was the only superpower left. Now we're in a world, roughly thirty years later, where a number of countries are becoming powerful and innovating with technology. Back in the late nineties when I got to Silicon Valley, there was really only one Silicon Valley, one epicenter for technology in the world, and that was true for a long time. Now you see that technology centers have sprouted up all over the world.

Innovation is hard. Often you need geniuses to achieve breakthroughs. But once a breakthrough occurs, anyone can copy it. Catching up is a lot easier than breaking new ground. And there are a lot of parts of the world that are catching up to the United States. I think that's going to require us to think about the world in a different way.

I'm a believer in American exceptionalism, but what that means to me is that we should try to set a good example rather than impose our values on everyone else. If we do a good job and create an attractive model, other people will want to copy us. But a heavy-handed approach is going to be fiercely resisted across the world. If we don't adapt our thinking to allow for the rise of others, the result will be a great deal of conflict.

TONY:

In order to build Craft Ventures into a great firm, it takes more than just great investments. What aside from strong performance has been a primary reason for the success of your business? And what was the fulcrum point of your business, if there is one, that allowed you jump from good to great?

DAVID:

The question for us is: Why would a founder want to have Craft on his or her cap table? When Ray Dalio or Warren Buffett decide they're going to buy Apple, they don't need the permission of the company. They can just go out in the public market and buy it. Apple doesn't really know or care if I own a share of their stock. They're agnostic on that question. But founders really know who's on their cap table and they care a lot. And so, we have to create a value proposition for them in the same way they have to create a value proposition for their customers.

We've spent a lot of time figuring out how to be helpful to startups. Obviously, it starts with the fact that I've been in their shoes before. I've created companies, and my partners at Craft all have operating experience and/ or founding experience—they know what it's like to be on that journey. By specializing in SaaS, we can cultivate and share a lot of expertise and best practices relevant for SaaS founders. We created a tool called SaaSGrid that shows founders all the key metrics they should be looking at for their business; they just connect their data sources, and the charts and dashboards appear automatically. Finally, we have our platform team—operating partners who are specialists in areas where most startups need expertise they can't yet afford: recruiting, marketing, PR, InfoSec, legal, government relations, and the like. Whenever one of our portfolio companies needs help, there's an expert with decades of experience to help them. We focus a lot on the question: How are we going to add value to our founders?

TONY:

And, as you said, you're not somebody looking from the outside in. You're somebody who's been on the inside yourself. It's fantastic.

DAVID:

We're trying to build the VC firm that we wish we had when we were founders.

CHRISTOPHER:

With that in mind, what are some things that you wish you would've known or that somebody would've told you, before you started the firm?

DAVID:

I wish I had known how much Fed policy was going to impact our world! Maybe in a completely well-functioning economy, you wouldn't have to worry that much about it. But we're living in a time of great distortions. Fed policy swung very rapidly from a zero-interest rate policy to the fastest rate-tightening cycle ever—from zero to 5.5 percent in one year. You just can't underestimate the trickle-down effects of that; not only has it reduced capital availability and valuations, but it's also created a software recession. Tech companies are doing layoffs, and as they lay off employees, they buy less software because software is generally sold on a seat basis. The cycle feeds on itself. I think we've probably bottomed out and now we're seeing new opportunities with AI, but there has been a major recession in software for the last year or two.

CHRISTOPHER:

One of the greatest concerns right now in the marketplace is higher inflation for longer. Do you think that the reset has happened enough to where people will just go back to building businesses? Or do you think it continues to ripple?

DAVID:

Right now the market seems to believe that inflation is largely a solved problem, that you'll have inflation in the 2.5 to 3 percent range at the end of the year, and that there's a good chance we'll get rate cuts next year. The market is starting to price in this scenario, so if inflation rebounds and we don't get rate cuts, then there is downside risk to current price levels. That will trickle down to private markets because the public markets are our exit comps.

That's what we saw in 2022. When the Fed raised interest rates, the public markets crashed, especially growth stocks, and then it worked its way down to the private markets. The private markets take their cue from what's happening in the public markets. But right now, people think we've bottomed out and these problems are on their way to being solved, albeit things are not going back to the way they used to be during the heady days of ZIRP (zero interest rate policy).

CHRISTOPHER:

One of the things that I'd love to hear your feedback on is that as AI becomes more prevalent throughout the business community and disrupts and eliminates bodies and jobs, as it does that, it feels like it would also reduce the number of licenses [or the] number of seats, which would have an impact on software. Does that spiral because of the secular trend of AI? Or is this more cyclical [and] tied to the softness of the economy?

TONY:

Or is it just replaced by AI software sales of some sort?

DAVID:

I think we're still a ways away from AI that can completely replace human job functions. The category that is showing the most promise right now are these copilots. I think that is the right way to look at it. It's a human working with AI to be more productive than they otherwise could have been, or to do their job faster or in a higher quality way. It's about humans gaining leverage through productivity tools. Does that wipe out tons of jobs? I am skeptical of that. First of all, we're going to get a lot of new software companies creating new products. Those products have to be sold; they have to be marketed. So, first, we will have an explosion of company creation in order to create the AI tools we're talking about. That's one part of it.

The second part is that the customers of this AI software can now get more done. It lowers the startup cost for a founder to create a company. We have the famous story of Mark Zuckerberg creating the first version of Facebook in his dorm room at Harvard. He had the ability to code the first version himself. A lot of founders or would-be-founders don't have that ability. But now, thanks to AI tools, they're going to be able to do more of it themselves. So, there'll be more people who can get started creating more companies.

The history of innovation is that as we make humans more productive, it makes our species richer. It doesn't put people out of work. We always find new things for them to do. As long as people are adaptive and are willing to be in a constant process of learning, I think it will be beneficial.

The history of innovation is that as we make humans more productive, it makes our species richer. It doesn't put people out of work. We always find new things for them to do.

TONY:

A lot of people have a very daunting view of the future. There are always challenges, obviously, but it bothers me when I see young people talking about not having kids because they think the whole world's going to end in twelve years, which we all know is not true. There are plenty of challenges, but I'm curious: Where do you see the world going?

DAVID:

One of the reasons I'm excited to be in tech is that I think it has consistently delivered the most progress for people. Even as our politics become more dysfunctional or divisive, and so many parts of our society aren't working, technological progress is still working and does deliver a better future for people.

I've seen it over the course of my career. Over the last three decades, I've seen that technology keeps becoming a bigger and bigger part of our economy and of our way of doing things. It creates products that make our lives better and more convenient, helps cure diseases, helps us get the information we need, the learning we need. The real key is to have as many people benefit from it and be included in it as possible. That goes back to what we were talking about with learning; you need people to see learning as a continuous process throughout their lives as opposed to a degree that gets stamped.

CHRISTOPHER:

It is a great tie-in to a question we've asked everybody. When you're looking for people to join your team, what are the key characteristics? What makes them stand out?

DAVID:

In an investor, you want somebody who is scrappy and sniffs out opportunity. The funny term we have for this is a truffle pig—those pigs they train to find truffles. I don't know how they do it, but these pigs go rooting around in the dirt and somehow they dig up these valuable truffles. Good investors are like that.

CHAPTER 17

MICHAEL REES

COFOUNDER OF DYAL CAPITAL, COFOUNDER AND COPRESIDENT OF BLUE OWL

Accolades: The market leader in GP stakes
Total Asset Under Management (as of August 2023): $150 billion
Area of focus: GP stakes

HIGHLIGHTS

- The largest investor in GP stakes, with a market share of approximately 60 percent in terms of fund capital raised for GP stakes over the last twelve years.
- The firm has a market share of nearly 90 percent for GP stake deals done with an investment size in excess of $600 million.
- Mr. Rees is cofounder and copresident of Blue Owl, which manages $150 billion and was formed in 2021 when his Dyal Capital merged with Owl Rock Capital.

CHRISTOPHER:

As a way to set the table, why don't you tell us your origin story—how you ended up in your current position.

MICHAEL:

I started my financial services career at Lehman Brothers, and somewhat serendipitously I was the fourth teammate to join the strategy group. And if you rank ordered the performance of the major groups at Lehman, fixed income was the bellwether, then equities, then investment banking, and then asset management. And so the first person hired into the group had the option to pick to be on the fixed income team. And the last one on the list was somewhat stuck with a nascent, sort of white-sheet-of-paper investment management division. And so I guess I was the one who got stuck with it. It kind of felt like I got the short end of the stick. It was a total build project; with the goal being that Lehman was going to try to grow rapidly into investment management to have a division on par with Goldman Sachs or Merrill Lynch.

At the time, hedge funds were the talk of the town. It was 2000, 2001, and hedge fund performance coming out of that time frame was pretty strong, and large hedge fund businesses were being built. The question was, should we buy one of these? We sat back and talked about it—part of the reason we decided not to is that no hedge fund that escaped Wall Street wanted to come back and be a part of a big firm. Also, we thought that these were highly entrepreneurial investors that were creating these businesses, and we wanted them to be highly aligned with them, not controlling them within the walls of a twenty-thousand-person organization. We asked, does buying a hundred percent of their business take away their motivation?

So, we came up with this crazy idea (at least it was crazy at the time): Let's just buy 20 percent of a few hedge funds instead of buying 100 percent of one. The rest is history for me. I've done close to ninety minority stake transactions over the twenty-two years since we sat back and came up with this strategy. You know, my life falls under the adage when you're a hammer, everything looks like a nail. **Everything I look at daily, every business I think about, I ask myself, "Could we buy 20 percent of this? Is it a great**

business run by smart people, and would aligning myself with them be a smart idea?" That was the beginning, and it has been a great run since the beginning.

And then as time moved forward, I had a real love for this space and I wanted to set up my own team—Neuberger Berman was a great place to do that. We spun the investment management business out of the aftermath of the Lehman bankruptcy, and starting building this minority stakes business at Neuberger. From its inception, the firm had this multi-product platform where each group had its own investment authority, and each team had the financial upside that came with building its own successful pod. We were able to convince investors that investing in minority stakes in alternative firms was a good thing to do. That signaled the start of the Dyal business within Neuberger. And we grew it quite rapidly. **Now we have about a 60 percent market share of all of the investment capital ever raised in the minority stake space. And when you look at just the larger deals, our market share is close to 90 percent for deals above $600 million.** So that origin story dates back to getting the short end of the stick at Lehman Brothers when I joined. And, luckily, I did.

CHRISTOPHER:

It's a great example of how life is happening for us and not to us, for those that take the opportunity and run with it. It's a fascinating fifteen-to-twenty-year run. Who was the most important person in your life, that shaped your success, and how did they shape that success?

MICHAEL:

It's a little cliché but my father and mother. I work with my brother and have for twenty years. It's been a familial approach to what we're doing. But, coming from Pittsburgh, largely a blue-collar town, my father was a salesman, my mother was a nurse. **They instilled in us as kids that this world is about hard work. It's about looking people in the eye. It's about a firm handshake.** The financial services and "Wall Street" industry has a lot of personalities, a lot of egos. And one of the things I hear a lot and that I'm really proud of is that myself, my brother, and the rest of the team have that humble, personable, Pittsburgh approach to the business. One based on trusted relationships where our word is our bond. We're the kind of people that you want to do business with as a partner for a long time.

CHRISTOPHER:

When we think about minority stakes, otherwise known as GP stakes, where's the greatest opportunity for investors right now?

MICHAEL:

We are still really strong believers in private assets and the markets at large. We still see a lot of incremental allocation to alternatives. We do see a rising tide and a long-term trend towards private alternative investments (buyout, growth, private credit, real estate). It will not be a straight line, but if you look at the global allocation of pensions, sovereign wealth funds, and individuals to these strategies, you see a lot of upside. But I guess your question is: Where is it most acute and where is the real interesting aspect of it?

We're believers in the consolidation trend of industries. It happens in nearly every industry we have studied. Here we are in the soft drink market with two main producers. Over time, the industry consolidates because there is power in scale. And I just think we're on a long-term trend that benefits the bigger businesses in the industry. That was a soft tailwind that was working to the benefit of the bigger firms from 2015 to 2021.

But 2022 and 2023 has really turned the soft tailwind into a really powerful tailwind. Hence why we're really focused now on truly scaled players that have the benefits of a global reach to investors in the Middle East, in Asia, possibly retail, and with networks like yours. And so, we think brand name is important, stability is important, and we think these types of investors put preference in a safe pair of hands. All of those things typically benefit established players that have been building a business over time with strong cornerstones and brand recognition. Our phrase, "the big get bigger and the strong get stronger," has been something we've believed in now for eight years. And the last eighteen months has really strengthened that belief.

CHRISTOPHER:

Do you think the outlook over the next three years is different from the next ten years, or do you think it's more of the same?

MICHAEL:

Private markets move at a slow, almost glacial pace. I think a lot of what is beneficial about private markets is that you have time on your side, and you can outlive the acute moves in the public equity and fixed income markets. So, three years is a blink of the eye in the private markets. So, I think more of the same and continued consolidation at the top, and growth. I do think the next ten years are going to be extremely strong for private markets. But I don't really see any acute trends that will change dramatically over the three-to-ten-year window.

CHRISTOPHER:

What has happened recently in the GP stake landscape that you expected to happen, and what has surprised you?

MICHAEL:

I don't know if a lot happened that surprised us in the last couple years. We haven't seen a dramatic shift in the performance of our managers from a fund perspective, owning what we believe are long-term, stable businesses. You know, you hear all of the investment chatter about software, and how amazing mission-critical software is because you get three-to-five-year contracts that have net retention rates near a hundred percent. That's all good and software will drive the economy. **That being said, I believe that private equity and the private markets are even better. Owning stakes in the GP of private market firms is a fantastic business where you see layering and layering of revenue streams just like in software.** That is the common model. Growth happens quite nicely as you layer fund after fund after fund.

I like software. I think a lot of our partners invest in software, but I'll take the private equity business and the private markets business all day long. I think high-quality, mission-critical private market firms are meant for times like this. **Whether it is COVID, whether it's the banking crisis of late, or just the overall rising inflation and interest rate environments that we've seen for the last two years. The private markets firms and the strategies they employ are built to weather that storm and be quite stable.**

CHRISTOPHER:

You've talked to many investors about GP stakes over the last eight years, particularly as Dyal has grown so dramatically. What is it that you see that investors typically get wrong about the space, or that they miss when they're evaluating GP stakes and the opportunity set there?

MICHAEL:

The phrase that bothers me the most, that I don't think I'll ever get over, is the term "cash out." People assume that the money we invest in a GP stake goes right into the pocket of the ownership group. And then, if they want to take it one step further, it goes into a fancy boat or a fancy car. **What really sparked the GP stakes industry and has created such strong growth is that when you look at a private markets firm, particularly a successful one, it consumes capital. There's a window of time during that growth trend of a firm when it needs incremental capital.** And so, most of the capital, the vast majority of the capital that we invest in GP stakes has nothing to do with the "cash out." It has everything to do with supporting the growth of these best-in-class firms. And one of the unique things that we hypothesized would be the case, and has turned out, is that the firms that want to do a deal are the ones that perform the best. Some investors say, "You're going to get adverse selection. You're only going to get called by the people that are nervous and not doing well, and they're going to try to sell you something." What we've seen empirically is the exact opposite. **It's that the firms that are doing the best and see the highest potential and opportunity in front of them—they are the ones that need the growth capital. If you're not growing, you don't need growth capital.**

CHRISTOPHER:

It's interesting because so many people do think that it's an exit strategy for these folks when in reality it's a growth engine for people as the primary motivation for these transactions.

MICHAEL:

Yes. Every investor knows that a tech company that's growing and developing its business needs to go through an A round, a B round, a C round, a

D round. That's sort of what the venture and growth market is all about. It surprises me that it's taken a lot of education over time to convince investors out there that a private markets business, a successful GP, would be the exact same thing. They need capital to fund their growth. And I'm happy to be the C, D, and E round for a lot of these really good firms.

CHRISTOPHER:

It's a very different way to frame the conversation because every business that wants to grow is going to consume capital at some point. And there are different places they can get it. But if the capital is not only available, but also is strategic and can add value to them, that is absolutely the best kind of growth capital one can access. So, if you had the attention of the world for five minutes to talk about anything that you think the world should be focused on, what would it be?

MICHAEL:

Well, as this banking situation plays out, I'm sort of in the minority that is thinking it's not over and maybe not even really getting started. I know this puts a line in the sand from a timing perspective, so we'll be able to judge if I was right or wrong, but I remember acutely being at Lehman Brothers. Bear Stearns happened six months before, and, you know, the situation we saw in 2007 and 2008 evolved over a twelve-to-eighteen-month window. I'm very hopeful that that isn't the case. But I think there are several more shoes to drop in the situation that was caused by a rapid increase in interest rates and unprecedented government liquidity being pumped into the system during COVID and, most likely, a liability and funding mismatch across a lot of midsized banking balance sheets. Hopefully I'm wrong, but if I could have the world's attention, at least the policymakers' attention for five minutes, I would say act quickly, powerfully, and convincingly, because there's nothing worse than a financial crisis that's caused by confidence.

CHRISTOPHER:

We had the initial big earthquake that got everybody's attention. The after-shocks can also be very problematic if they're not managed.

When you look at growing a large investment firm, what's been the primary reason for the success of Dyal?

MICHAEL:

The one thing that irks me from time to time when I meet with a private markets firm, or any investment firm for that matter, is the sentence: "I'm just going to focus on great returns, and everything else at my business will work itself out." I surprisingly have heard it hundreds of times over the last twenty years. The frequency is not going down. I think it couldn't be more wrong. This manner of thinking ignores all of the other aspects that go into making a great firm and a firm great. Investing (and doing it well) is certainly fundamental. But there's a lot more to a successful firm.

It's hard to have a batting average of a thousand. You're not going to get everything right all the time. What's been important at Dyal and Blue Owl is a focus on the whole business. Client service and client relationships are at the very top of the list of things that really take focus, making sure that you're not just coming around asking for money every few years, making sure you're trying to help investors to solve their problems. Maybe this comes in the form of a new product, maybe with advice in something you're seeing throughout the industry. To me, investment performance is very important. But how you run the rest of the business, how you interact with your clients are critical parts of building a money management business. We all saw what happened at the end of the nineties, when most hedge funds had no business but for the investing aspect. They were return generators; reporting was bad, client interactions were bad, operations not great. And it did cause problems over time. What we've seen is that a lot of the better firms over the last twenty years have decided to make their firm into a real business. They've decided to think about all aspects of their game and try to instill best practices across them.

CHRISTOPHER:

When you think about the growth of Dyal, what was the fulcrum point? What was that seminal event, if you will?

MICHAEL:

We intentionally had a focus on midsize hedge funds as our target for our early two funds. And those continue to perform well. But as we moved into fund three, we decided to launch a much bigger fund, not focusing on midsize private markets firms, but focusing on the larger best-in-class brand names. And when you're out there marketing a story, there are some investors that are willing to believe a story, but more investors want to see where the proof is in the pudding. The ability to raise capital for our private markets fund with investments with Vista, EnCap, Starwood, and Silver Lake, to come out of the gate with those great partners, really set the table and really put us in a great position. And that was certainly an inflection point for us. It showed the market and the Investor group that you can partner with really high-quality, best-in-class firms (which was doubted at the time) and that these investments should make for a better-than-average growth investment.

CHRISTOPHER:

What are a few things you wish somebody would've told you before you started your firm?

MICHAEL:

I guess it never hurts to reiterate that it's never easy. I think if it ever got to a point where it was easy, you'd know something was wrong. You really have to improve your game, month after month, fund after fund, whatever it is. And you have to earn your investors' trust on a continuous basis. That's probably something everybody should have written somewhere in their office. It's not going to get any easier. But it gets more enjoyable. And it's great to have a team that's worked together and collaborated for a long time.

CHRISTOPHER:

If you could do anything differently in your business with the benefit of hindsight, what would you have done differently? Or what would you advise someone else to do differently than you did?

MICHAEL:

I think even though we've grown very rapidly and have created a leadership position in this space, we really grew in a very methodical way. We didn't hire that second person until we had enough revenue to pay for that person. And the fund size we targeted was just enough to execute our strategy. From the beginning, we took a very cautious approach to growth. We were able to, knock on wood, stay slightly ahead of the competition. And we continue to feel really good about our competitive position.

But what you hear and what you see across the tech and venture world is that much of the growth in innovation comes from people in their twenties who have nothing to lose and who go at it a thousand percent, not a hundred percent. And so, maybe in our early stages we put 110 percent into this idea and grew it very methodically and consistently. Who knows where we would be if we would've gone a lot harder and a lot faster and really expanded the opportunity set.

I do think one of the hardest things in our industry is to find innovation out of the professional crowd that is in my age bracket because that group has a much larger focus on downside, and maybe there's more innovation coming out of the "young and ignorant" (that I certainly was) in one's twenties or early thirties and having nothing to lose. That's maybe an attribute that should be celebrated more.

CHRISTOPHER:

What is the primary reason that you believe most investment firms don't scale?

MICHAEL:

At the core, there are very low barriers to entry into the investment space overall, and that applies to alternative asset management as well. You can get someone to back you for your first deal or maybe even for your first fund. So we will always have a very wide base to the industry pyramid and a lot of new entrants. However, it's an industry where that first five-year window has a percentage of success that is very low. I do think if you can clear that hurdle . . . and get to a point where you have a high-quality group of core investors, and a process that has some consistency and experience to it, the moat starts getting deeper and wider.

We don't really focus on what happens when a firm scales that first $100 million fund to get to the $300 million. That's not my area of expertise, but that's where the weeding out happens. I think it's rare that a large-scale firm can't weather a tough market or soft period and get to the other side. For smaller firms, getting to the other side means ten, fifteen years. It's one of those industries that weeds you out quickly—chews you up and spits you out. But if you can break through that barrier, it's a pretty accommodating and stable industry if you build a solid foundation.

CHRISTOPHER:

It is unique in that regard. As you think about talent—obviously you've hired a lot of people over the years and Dyal and Blue Owl have grown quite dramatically—what are the key traits that you look for that separate the highest performers from their peers?

MICHAEL:

I think it differs dramatically depending on what type of firm it is and what the core objective of that firm or group happens to be. The question I try to ask is: What's the goal, and what's the best person that fits that organization? There are firms where you want to be full of graduates from Wharton and Harvard and Yale and Stanford. We happen to have a nice cross-section of Big 10 and Big East graduates. It's just a different type of hiring and team approach. We've found that the success of our teammates has really been driven by that ability to engender a partnership mentality and confidence with investors and with our GP stakes partners. It's not about being the smartest person in the room. It's about being a good partner to the person on the other side of the table. Granted you have to be smart and highly motivated, but school pedigree doesn't drive success for us.

> **It's not about being the smartest person in the room. It's about being a good partner to the person on the other side of the table.**

CHRISTOPHER:

That's a really good way to look at it. It is very idiosyncratic based on the business and the personalities of that business and the people that will thrive and be fulfilled while working in that particular business.

TONY:

Michael, as you know, we're writing a book with an audacious title: *The Holy Grail of Investing*. It's a phrase Ray Dalio used to describe to me his most important principle in investing. What you've built over the years is amazing, and we're so proud and excited to be partners with you in GP stakes. When you look at investment, what would you say the most important principle, the Holy Grail, is?

MICHAEL:

As it relates to private investment with a human capital firm, it really is as simple as partnering with good people. I know that sounds trivial, and maybe shallow, but when you are looking to establish a relationship that you can't get out of and you really are thinking about your investment as permanent, you don't have the luxury of bickering, fighting, and getting divorced. So, we've found across fifty-eight different investments, fifty-five of them have been with good people. And we spend 90 percent of our time dealing with the three that have, you know, more challenging individuals.

This [Holy Grail] is not just about our relationships with them. It also means that when they are doing deals in their space, they're treating their other constituents with the same congeniality and partnership that we look for. So, we certainly benefit on the point-to-point relationship, but it also permeates all of their underlying investments. It surprises me that we've seen that phenomenon (that the success of our deal is a function of the "goodness" of the partner) really play out with almost a perfect correlation from the very beginning in this GP stakes business—but that's the truth.

TONY:

We all know the right people can take a terrible company and make it strong. How do you make those choices? What are some of the criteria you look for to know a company is going to be the right relationship?

MICHAEL:

The process of getting to know an organization can be long. It's been upwards of seven or eight years to get to know a firm and to help them through the process. Or it can be as short as four or five months. But you just really get the sense, when you get into the nitty-gritty of the negotiation, about whether the counterparty is viewing everything as a zero-sum game and just trying to win as many points as possible, or whether they're willing to take a view of the issues from both sides of the table. And that's the easiest lens to look through. If a partner is going to sit down and say, "I understand why these three things are important to you, and I'd like you to understand why these other three things are important to me," well, that is the kind of dialogue that really, really works and foreshadows behavior over the next decade or two.

In most cases, a firm that succeeded in getting to the size and scale that we're looking at is going to have that type of human capital within its walls. Every once in a while, though, you get too far down the path, and you realize this person is just arguing for every nickel and dime. It's a pretty good litmus test to really understand what the future's going to look like if you look at the term sheet negotiation as a predictor of the future.

TONY:

Even though it's simple, it's super helpful. If someone is trying to maximize every single dollar, they are not going be playing for the long term with anybody else, much less you. It makes total sense.

CHRISTOPHER:

One of the things that's really interesting about Dyal is how diversified they are. How do you look at the mixture between private equity, between buyout, between private credit, between real estate, technology, etc.?

MICHAEL:

We are fortunate enough to be investing in a great industry. And those that have gotten to the more premium end have built really nice businesses. And our goal is to really try to partner with those firms that are truly specialized in what they do. They are the best at X. Generalization, we think, is sort of a race for mediocrity. I don't think we have a view of whether an upstream energy manager is going to do better than a technology manager, but we want to be partnered with the best one of each. And having that type of diversification has certainly helped. There's a bit of a winner's curse in GP stake investing, and that means that the better a firm does, typically, the faster it grows and the more likely it is to need growth capital.

There's a bit of a winner's curse in GP stake investing, and that means that the better a firm does, typically, the faster it grows and the more likely it is to need growth capital.

So, we're fortunate that we don't get a lot of phone calls from firms that are mediocre. We seem to only get phone calls from the good ones. And we can really try to understand and determine who's really special in the area in which they operate. There are a few really good generalists, but where you see your really high-quality firms that we believe have longevity is where they truly do something that's differentiated and specialized. And that's obvious in a lot of industries.

TONY:

Having interviewed several of the players for the book here, many of which are partners through you, you really see that in a Vista, for example. You see the level of specialization that [Robert has] in SaaS. It's mind boggling. When you look at the world we are in now, how do you think private equity is affected by rising interest rates, after forty-five years of slowly dropping interest rates? Does that affect it in a significant way, and does it affect your partners?

MICHAEL:

Tony, it's funny you mentioned the number forty-five. I was going to bring it up in my response. There are a handful of private equity firms that have been around between forty-five and fifty years, and they have generated tremendous returns for investors and generated tremendous wealth for their owners in so many different interest-rate environments. That spans the seventies, eighties, nineties. And we're still at historic lows of overall interest rates when you measure it over that period. Now, that being the case, there are a lot of investments that were made when rates were low, and rates have ramped quite quickly. And so that may put some strain on those recent investments. But measured over a longer arc, we still have accommodating rates and there is still a lot of growth out there.

In general, depending on what multiple you want to pay and how you want to think about your terminal value, you can make money with interest rates where they are today. It's just going to take a different type of value creation approach and it's certainly going to take a different valuation paradigm. **It doesn't have to be an era of free money to make a good return. It was certainly easy from 2009 to about 2020 to sort of just throw darts at the wall and a lot of things worked. I think over this next phase we'll certainly see a separation of high-quality firms from the rest**.

On the flip side, private credit is just slowly chipping away at the market share that banks had in lending. And there are a lot of reasons why it's better to work with a private lender that understands your business's needs and is willing to work with you through the good times and bad. Doesn't mean they're always going to give you a break, but they're going to want to see you do well. And that flexibility that a private direct lender brings to the buyout space is one that's going to continue to gain market share. **We've seen a lot of really talented people leave banks over the last decade or two, and a lot of them ended up in direct lending at private credit managers.** And I think they've just built a better mousetrap. We certainly are honored here at Blue Owl to have one of the best mousetraps out there. Overall, as an industry, we're only at a market share of about 9 percent or 10 percent. So, there's a lot of room to grow for private credit, and that makes up a meaningful part of our investment program.

TONY:

Last question, what gives you the most personal satisfaction in your life at this stage? I'm curious.

MICHAEL:

Oh, man. It's all about the team, and Christopher has been fortunate to get to know a number of the folks on the Blue Owl team. And I am honored each compensation season by the reactions that I get from the vast majority of the team here, which is appreciation for the financial wealth that we can all create together, but also a recognition that most of them would come in and do it for free. When you hear that, that people are willing to work their butts off for all this time, all because they love the camaraderie, they love the sport . . . well, that's the best feeling you can have as a business leader. So that's why I certainly come in each day to partner with great folks like my colleagues here at Blue Owl, like Christopher and the team at CAZ, and like a lot of our great stakeholders.

TONY:

I'm going to ask you one more since you've walked me right into it. So how do you build that culture? Is it coming back to the first principle used for investing—finding the right people?

MICHAEL:

There's not a great answer to it, but it's the good old-fashioned Pittsburgh airport test when you're interviewing. Getting to know an individual that you're going to spend a lot of time with, and it won't all be poring over spreadsheets. [Instead], there's a lot of time in airports and in cars where you have to feel a connection and a trust. That's what we look for. I think this group that we've assembled is truly special in the way they interact with each other and the type of friends that we've all come to be.

CHAPTER 18

BILL FORD

CEO OF GENERAL ATLANTIC

Accolades: Member of the Council on Foreign Relations, McKinsey Advisory Council, and chair of Rockefeller University
Total Asset Under Management (as of August 2023): $77 billion
Area of Focus: Consumer, financial services, life sciences, and healthcare

HIGHLIGHTS

- As of July 2023, GA has invested over $55B in more than 500 companies across multiple stages of growth. We have $77B of assets under management across more than 215+ current portfolio companies and deploy $8–9 billion in capital annually with ~60% invested outside the U.S.
- We are now active in six global sectors and five major geographies with a team of 272 investment professionals working across 16 global locations.
- General Atlantic is currently ranked ninth in Private Equity International's PEI 300 ranking of the largest private equity firms in the world, thanks in large part to Mr. Ford's leadership.

TONY:

So, we're working on a new book and I'm doing my third in the series. We've been interviewing the best investors in the world, and you guys obviously have to be near the top with your track record. What you've done at General Atlantic is just unbelievable. We wanted to start out, if we could, and just ask if you'd share with us a little bit about your origin story, how you ended up in this position, and the development and expansion of General Atlantic over these years since you began.

BILL:

Thank you, Tony. This is our forty-third year. We started in 1980 as a family office, and for our first decade, we were primarily managing capital for an individual named Chuck Feeney, who was a self-made entrepreneur from New Jersey.

TONY:

The same Chuck Feeney that was giving all his money away? I interviewed him. He is extraordinary.

BILL:

You probably interviewed him, Tony, because he is considered the father of the Giving Pledge. Warren Buffett and Bill Gates will tell you that because Chuck invented this idea of giving while living, he was very focused on giving back and ultimately made it his life's work. When we started General Atlantic in 1980, Chuck had already built significant wealth and was receiving strong cashflows from the Duty Free Shoppers business. At this point, Chuck then hired two people out of McKinsey—Steve Denning, our founder, and another professional named Ed Cohen. These two started the firm and, for ten years, we only had one investor: Chuck Feeney. He was building wealth for himself and also for what became the Atlantic Philanthropies.

Then, around 1990, Chuck had a life event and decided to leave the company entirely—exit operations, exit leadership—and commit himself fully to philanthropy for the balance of his life. He decided to put all of his money into the Atlantic Philanthropies and then give that money away during his lifetime. With this in mind, Chuck encouraged General Atlantic to go out and find other investors. That was 1990; I joined in 1991.

We then began a process of becoming a more institutionalized firm by adding other clients, starting with wealthy families, before moving into endowments and foundations, and then moving into institutions with large capital pools like insurance companies, sovereign wealth funds, and pension funds. But, as mentioned, our starting point was Chuck, who sold the Duty Free Shoppers business to Louis Vuitton in 1997 for $3.7 billion. Between that and what we compounded for him, he ultimately gave away about $10 billion during his lifetime. So, Chuck lived up to his idea of giving while living and that journey led to our style of investing and the firm's culture. [Chuck] cared about two things. One was philanthropy, and specifically, compounding his capital so he could give more back. The second was a conviction about entrepreneurs. **He had a deep belief that entrepreneurs were going to change the world for the better. So, the firm was built on the ethos of supporting entrepreneurs and helping add value to their efforts to build new companies and do more philanthropy.**

We still carry these ideas forward. Today, we continue to focus our efforts on giving back as a firm, while maintaining a passion for backing entrepreneurs. We invest across many sectors around the world, not just in technology in the U.S.—but what drives our investment program is a strategy called growth equity, which is essentially trying to identify companies that have made it past the venture capital stage and need help growing fast. By identifying the right entrepreneurs and companies, and participating in that growth, you can generate outstanding returns for your investors.

Over the period of thirty-plus years, General Atlantic has become truly global. We're in the U.S., Europe, India, China, Southeast Asia and Latin America, with about 60 percent of our portfolio outside the U.S. One of the greatest journeys for me personally has been working and building relationships around the world. We've always been ahead of the curve when it comes to seeing where innovation is going, and then built our human capital to capitalize on it. So, now we're nearly 560 people with sixteen global locations across five regions, investing about $8 to $9 billion a year in growth equity.

TONY:

Who's been the most important person in shaping your success in life? And what did you learn or pull from them that shaped you?

BILL:

That's a great question, Tony. Steve Denning and Chuck Feeney were hugely influential. As mentioned, Steve is the founder of General Atlantic, and the one who hired me. Many of our firm's core values come directly from him, as Steve was a values-driven person. After I took over the firm as CEO, Steve went on to become the chairman of the board of Stanford University and did that for a decade. He was a great mentor, and I learned a lot from him.

Chuck also shaped who I became, because he was this incredible man who did something that nobody does, right? At the time, Chuck was one of the wealthiest men in the world. He created an industry, travel retail, had the winning company, and was a brilliant entrepreneur. To pivot from that to a full stop and commit himself completely to philanthropy at fifty-five years old, and ultimately give all his money away, is remarkable. You don't meet many people like that. He was very impactful.

Finally, the last big influence has been all the entrepreneurs I've gotten to work with—people like yourself. Entrepreneurs are the most interesting people in the world. They see the world differently. They've been told about fifty times that their idea won't work, and they somehow persevere. They're people you could inherently learn from. I think about all the entrepreneurs I've worked with over the years and there are a lot that come to mind. For example, Larry Fink, Jamie Dimon, and James Gorman—those three I put in a category of mentors and people I deeply admire as leaders, who helped me grow and become successful.

Entrepreneurs are the most interesting people in the world. They see the world differently. They've been told about fifty times that their idea won't work, and they somehow persevere.

CHRISTOPHER:

That is a great group to be associated with in so many ways. Let's transition a little bit to the investment side. Your firm does more sectors now than many others, but it all fits in the bucket of growth equity. In the world of growth equity right now, in this economic cycle that we're dealing with, where do you see the greatest opportunity that people aren't paying enough attention to?

BILL:

I think three big themes are going to shape the investment environment in the next few decades and shape our opportunity set. One is the continued expansion of what I call the global digital economy. We've been seeing this happen for years, more and more industries, parts of the economy, and geographies are being fundamentally impacted by technology. We are in the midst of the fourth wave of computing that I've witnessed in my career. When I started, we were in the era of mainframe or centralized computing, in the eighties. We saw the advent of personal computing. Now, we are in the advent of artificial intelligence. This will reshape the computing landscape, the technology landscape, and will open up many possibilities for investment.

The second major investment theme is life sciences. **We are in a golden moment of biology and life sciences innovation, based on what we know about the genome and cell biology. AI supercharges all this innovation because of what it does for drug discovery. You're going to see a real acceleration in human therapeutics.** We know healthcare access is a huge issue, especially in emerging markets, but we need to rethink our healthcare systems to create more efficiency, more access, and better outcomes. So, while there's [investment opportunity in] life sciences, it's also a very large industry that needs disruption, change, and innovation. This is where AI can play an important role.

The third theme is energy transition. I look at a world that uses 110 million barrels of oil a day, and that number will eventually increase to 180 million barrels of oil a day. One, carbon can't even meet the energy needs of the world over the next two or three decades. And two, we need to work our way down from 110 [million barrels] to use cleaner sources of energy. The amount of innovation and investment that's going to be required to do that is going to be massive. It could be climate technology. It could be green energy generation. It could be carbon capture. Whatever it is, we need to think about the idea of shifting the energy base from carbon to non-carbon and dealing with climate problems.

TONY:

You say these are themes for decades, not themes for a couple of years.

BILL:

Yes, multi-decades. Themes that can have exceptional growth, can generate exceptional investment returns.

CHRISTOPHER:

We refer to it as wind at our back versus wind in our face.

BILL:

We want tailwinds, and these tailwinds will create opportunities for new entrants to come into the market and create value. If we have our human capital focused on that, we should be able to find good opportunities.

CHRISTOPHER:

What has happened that you expected to happen, and that you did not expect to happen, in the last eighteen to twenty-four months?

BILL:

The biggest major shift in the environment has to be U.S.-China relations. We've operated in a world where the integration of China into the global economy has been a tailwind and has been a net positive for global growth. Now, we're in a world where U.S. and China relations are going to be much more challenged, leading to a fundamental shift in the investment environment. It has implications for global trade. It has implications for innovation. It has implications for global investors.

CHRISTOPHER:

Related to that, what do you think investors are getting wrong today, where they're just not positioned correctly?

BILL:

I think many investors are underestimating the innovation that's going to come from technology, life sciences, and healthcare. It's very easy to underestimate the amount of prospective innovation that will keep coming and how long these trends will last—and I think life sciences and the tech space are the best examples of this. A year ago, no one would have had any expectations about how impactful AI was going to become, and how quickly it would become impactful. I think we're underestimating the impact of that on the investment environment and the investment opportunity set.

CHRISTOPHER:

Goes back to that old line: People overestimate what can be done in two years and underestimate what can be done in ten.

BILL:

That is perfectly said. Another thing is that it is easy to quantify what jobs may be lost from this technology shift, but it's very difficult to identify exactly what jobs will be created. I believe this is a moment where many people don't fully appreciate what positives will come from these developments.

Now, on the negative side as investors, we're moving from a world that was oversupplied relative to demand, which meant low inflation, and entering a world where demand exceeds supply. We might have fundamental inflation for a period of time, or, at least, we've run out of a deflationary capacity. I think that's a shift in the investment environment that's going to be with us for a while, and investors have to recalibrate. At some point the music ends on the two decades of easy money that we've had. Now, we're back in a world where we have a real rate of interest. We now have a reasonably high nominal rate of interest. We have a real discount rate for future cash flows that we didn't have before. Those are the big headwinds and big changes that make innovation more valuable because innovation is growth, and growth can outrun some of that.

TONY:

Ray Dalio is obviously a macro investor; it's not the same. But when he talks about his Holy Grail, meaning the ultimate principle he uses in the environment you're describing. When you're going to invest in companies, when you're looking for great entrepreneurs, what is your Holy Grail of investing?

BILL:

I want to go back to what you just said, Tony. We are micro investors operating in a macro context. We think about how big the market that this company is trying to serve is, and how fast it's going to grow. But we [also] think about how it is structured and whether there will be an attractive profit pool at the end. We're right into the micro of that. And, what's been the Holy Grail? It really comes down to three things. One, I just talked about, is market. Two, is it a big enough prize? Is it a business model that can yield high levels of profitability over time? Sometimes you can build a business in a great market, but the business model is fundamentally a 20 percent gross margin industry with 1 percent or 2 percent profit margins. You can build it, but you're not going to generate a very large profit. We actually do business model training with our teams about which ones are fundamentally attractive versus fundamentally unattractive. And the third is people and management. We call it management but it's really the quality of the entrepreneur. Is this the kind of individual or leader who can actually make something happen, overcome adversity and attract followership to build a team? Every time we're looking at our micro-opportunity, we're looking at those three variables in depth.

TONY:

You said you train your people to look at these business models. These are the attractive ones. Some are not so attractive. What are some of the criteria that you look at besides, obviously, margin in that area? And then, secondly, same thing on the people side. How do you know if it's the right leadership or the right entrepreneur?

BILL:

We look at pricing power, capital intensity, and high gross margins. Capital intensity creates a fundamental investment risk. You need more of it; it dilutes your equity base. It is usually a fixed cost that can't be managed, so we have a tendency to like low capital intensity businesses better. And pricing power. If you have pricing power, it usually goes hand in hand with higher gross margins and higher operating margins. The worst thing to be in is a commodity business where you have no pricing power and you're capital intensive. **So, we love those two things: pricing power combined with low capital intensity leads to high gross margins, high barriers to entry, and then ultimately high profit margins.**

And then, [for] people we do a lot of things. We do formal management assessments with other companies. We invest in understanding what got them to where they are, what's motivating them for what they want to accomplish, and what is in their background that they've actually accomplished that indicates they'll be able to accomplish the challenges ahead of them. And then there's always the intrinsic aspect. The one comment I've heard over the years that always resonates with me is that the best people are ambitious for the company and not as ambitious for themselves.

TONY:

I love that.

BILL:

That said, you should never take ego out of the equation—you need that. But some people are in it for themselves and what they can get out of it, whether that be wealth, power, or notoriety. Others are ambitious to really solve a hard problem. To me, that means ambition for the company, and what motivates them. They will let few things stand in their way to get to the outcome.

TONY:

That is so simple and so clear. These criteria are fantastic.

CHRISTOPHER:

Let's shift back to a little bit about your business side. Growing a large investment firm takes a lot more than just making great investments. So beyond strong performance, what's been the primary reason for the success of the business? And what was the real fulcrum in your business that allowed you to take the leap from good to great?

BILL:

The three things that have led to our success include our focus on talent, culture, and process. At the end of the day, we must have great people. If we aren't absolutely committed to being a talent driven organization, we will lose. So, we have a relentless focus on talent and human capital, and developing our people as best we can.

Second is culture. This is hard to develop and build, and it's easy to lose. So, having the people and a commitment to maintaining a culture—not just talking about it, but living it—is vital.

Finally, as I mentioned, you can't grow without process. Whether it's an investment committee process or portfolio committee process, you have to pay attention to implementing the right processes to allow the organization to remain effective and do what it does.

One other thing is that you can't get talent and culture without liberally sharing the economics. If the senior professionals keep too much of the economics, they will not be able to attract and retain the next generation of great people. It's remarkable how many organizations do not follow that, and they will lose their way on talent and culture as a result.

My predecessor, Steve Denning, would always be on the side of taking less, giving more, and that's allowed us to attract great people. People want to stay; they want to build a career here.

CHRISTOPHER:

You grew up through the organization and then took over the helm of the organization. What's something that you wish somebody would've told you before you took the role that you have now?

BILL:

I'm good with numbers and financials. I think I'm pretty good on strategy. I think I'm good on selling and communicating. And then, you very quickly realize [success] comes down to people. **All the joys of the job are about people, and all of its challenges have to do with people.** No one explicitly told me about that, and I had to learn from experience. If you're an empathetic, caring person, it's hard. It should never feel easy, and it isn't easy.

CHRISTOPHER:

You know, it's fascinating to me to watch why some firms scale and get large, like General Atlantic has become, and others have not. As somebody who's built a firm the way that you have, over a long period of time, why do you think some firms are able to scale and others are not able to scale?

BILL:

I think it has to do with sharing the economics, but there are other important considerations as well. It's also about sharing responsibility and decision-making. Some of the best investors are great individual investors, but they want to control the decision-making. If you build a firm around that—a small cadre of people who are excellent investors—you're obviously going to be limiting your scale to what they're able to do. I can think of many firms that had tremendous ten- or twenty-year runs around a set of individuals or an individual, and then ultimately started to peter out because they could not scale beyond that group. And that might be because of the [lack of shared] economics, but maybe more than that.

TONY:

You talked earlier about your relentless focus on talent that picks up on this as well. I'd love to go a little deeper on that. When you think about the universe of investment talent, what do you think are the key traits that separate those peak performers from their peers?

BILL:

That's hard to pinpoint, Tony. It's the hardest thing to do, and it's why you need time to let people grow and evolve. At the end of the day, it's a wonderful blend of IQ and EQ that make great talent. People must be smart and highly motivated to succeed. You have to have a little bit of that insecurity as well, but good talent will be able to manage their ego in a way where they can synthesize this information, be strong listeners, and make good decisions. Let me try to make that more tangible. Take somebody who says, "I really want to do this investment because I believe in my gut this is a 3x outcome. I'm convicted [*sic*] about it, and I'm convicted [*sic*] for the right reasons."

Someone's going to put their ego aside, use their intellect, and get to a point where they can say, "I have the ability to bring all this information and all this uncertainty together and still have conviction and push it through an investment committee." For me, it's been hard to figure out who gets to that place, but you start to see it as the years go on.

TONY:

It actually reflects what you look at with the entrepreneurs as well, right? You're looking for the value system: Is it me, me, me? Or is it something larger than me that I'm invested in? Which is consistent with the entire culture that starts all the way back with your founders, So that's really beautiful. Just one last question. I'm just curious, when you look around and see people that have entered the business and they have that sense of absolute mission versus those that don't, where do you think that comes from? I know it's different for everybody, but underneath it all, is there a pattern you notice?

BILL:

It's hard [because] you're always making decisions under uncertainty. You never have all the information. If you come here and say, "I want to do this because I want to be really rich and I want to be a great private equity executive," you're probably going to fail all the way. If [instead] you love competing and you say, "I really want to find great investments, I want to learn my craft and be really, really good at it." And if you're intellectually curious, so meeting people, learning new things, and seeing new markets motivates you. If you're that kind of person, then this is the most fun business in the world because it's always changing. It's never static, never the same. It involves people, and you are always learning something.

When we first started, private equity was a backwater. No one knew what it was. We didn't even have a name for it. People came into it because they loved investing and they loved, in our case, company-building and working with entrepreneurs. We're a $11 trillion industry and I worry about people coming in and saying, this is the winning job. That actually scares me as a recruiter. I want [people who] say, I want it because I love this. Then I know they can get passionate about it and acquire the right skills.

CHAPTER 19

TONY FLORENCE

CO-PRESIDENT OF NEA

Accolades: Founded over forty years ago, NEA was one of the original Silicon Valley venture firms with notable early stage investments in Slack, Airbnb, and Stripe.
Total Asset Under Management (as of August 2023): $25 billion
Area of Focus: Technology and healthcare

HIGHLIGHTS

- NEA's assets under management have more than doubled over the last decade, totaling more than $25 billion as of March 31, 2023.
- The firm's investments across the spectrum of technology and healthcare have resulted in more than 270 IPOs and 450-plus mergers and acquisitions.
- NEA has helped build more than one hundred companies valued at $1 billion or more.
- The firm's portfolio companies have generated over $550 billion in cumulative market value.

TONY ROBBINS:

You have a seventeen-year storied career at NEA, and you've basically taken this technology division to another level. You've taken some big companies public, and you've sold some. How did you come to be in this position—the grandfather of all these venture firms?

TONY FLORENCE:

Well, my origins date back to Pittsburgh, Pennsylvania. And a lot of what I feel is behind what I focus on today was built back then. I developed a passion for a couple of things but one of them is certainly just having a very long-term perspective on people and recognizing that people can change in so many ways. It really gets back to entrepreneurship and the core fundamentals of what we do here. **Most of us had a combination of other people helping create some luck for us and then [we] have created our own luck with that.**

I had the good fortune to work with NEA for a long time when I was running tech banking at Morgan Stanley—another place that was foundational for me. The origin was that I really wanted to go work with young companies and help them on their decade-, two-decade-, three-decade-long journey and try to play a small role in helping people fulfill their visions and dreams, and the network effect that would have. And so, I started in that journey a long time ago and, as you've done and Christopher has done, it's just one day after the other.

TONY ROBBINS:

Tell us a little about a company like, let's say, a Casper or a Jet.com, that I know you guys sold to Walmart. Tell us what you saw in the beginning, how you look at a company like that, how you decide to make the investments. I'd love to hear some of the criteria that you look through.

TONY FLORENCE:

I tell you, Jet is a great example. That starts with a founder named Marc Lore. Marc was my first investment at NEA back in 2009. And to me, this is the hidden gem, the most fun and rewarding part of what I get to do. I'm going to be working with Marc till I end up not working anymore. I'm on my third company with Marc; I invested in Diapers.com with Marc originally, which became Quidsi. We sold that company to Amazon, and I had a front-row seat to a founder that built a business [that] started in his garage literally reselling diapers. He was a dad that was frustrated going to CVS and [them] being out of stock.

When I met Marc, and he told me the original reasons why he built that business, I knew that he would not stop until it was successful. It didn't matter what was in front of him. **And so, one of the key things that we look for is that level of endurance and obsession that it's not for the money and it's not for any recognition.** For Marc, in that particular case, it started with his passion and obsession as a customer and his wife's frustration, but then it became: How can I help every mom in the country?

I remember, I left my first meeting with Marc, and I called my partner. I said, "I've got my first investment. You guys are going to hate it but I'm just telling you this guy's going to win. He's selling 10 percent gross margin products on the internet, and he is going to beat Amazon." Six years later, Jeff Bezos was calling him, threatening him one minute, and the next minute, sweet-talking him into coming (into) to the company. And then I had the board of Walmart calling me saying, "Hey, why don't you guys sell to us?" And so, **I realized that a guy from New Jersey who started an idea in his garage around selling diapers online built something that had relevance for the two largest retailers in the country: Amazon and Walmart.**

This little idea built to half a billion dollars (in sales) and hundreds of employees and hundreds of thousands of customers that loved that a mom didn't have to go to the store anymore and could get stuff delivered tomorrow. I learned a lot from Marc around the power of that high-frequency customer relationship. If you win that, the rest is easy. For every two moms that came in, one never came back and the other came back twenty-six times.

We sold that for $3.5 billion. Lots of details in that story, but Marc was the central figure and the reason. I'm on my third company with Marc now, called Wonder, which I think in a decade will be his biggest company.

So, if I can have one of those in a career, let alone a couple, that's the fun thing. I think one of the best things about being an investor and being a founder and an entrepreneur is you have to be a good steward of risk and opportunity. And so, in Marc and many of the other founders I've worked with, they lean into risk, but they'll listen to data and to the market and to people and feedback, and they're happy to evolve their thinking and what they do along the way.

TONY ROBBINS:

You've seen so much in the e-commerce space. I read an article where you described two different types of people: the person that's there to solve the problem like Marc, and the person who really just sees how to streamline or maximize. Where does Casper [mattresses] fall in that as just an example? I'm curious of that story as an example. And then, I'd love to know along the way who really influenced you the most?

TONY FLORENCE:

I think Casper was a little bit of a different story. There was an efficiency story that took shape there where they collapsed the distribution chain and then, ultimately, the middleman. That's the power of the internet ultimately. There's a streamlining of distribution and they happen to get lucky with a little bit of a marketing twist. They had a bed in a box that created a viral video and that caught fire and helped them break out of a pack, if you will.

And so, there was a little bit of luck involved, a little bit of ingenuity, a little bit of the we can do it better than they can, but I think that business model really spoke to me because everybody in the country has to buy a mattress. It's a problem and an experience that everybody's been through to certain degrees, and there's nobody that would rate that as a positive experience. And so, at a minimum, you had a market that everybody could understand and an experience that everybody either was neutral on or didn't like.

And so, a couple young kids, literally, somebody from University of Texas and a few others that he brought along the way, had an idea that you could collapse that whole supply chain and distribution chain and make it efficient. And you could actually get (a mattress) delivered in a box to your house instead of having it be delivered or [driven] on the roof of the car. And they developed a brand around it. You had an internet-based company that used marketing to effectively build a really big business.

We try to help pull out a vision. Hopefully, it's crystallized a little bit and we help along the way in small ways to amplify the things that they need to realize the vision. These guys wanted to build something unique, and they did.

TONY ROBBINS:

Who influenced *you* the most along the way? What did you learn from that person? Maybe there have been more than one, I'm sure, in your life, but who would stand out for you?

TONY FLORENCE:

Well, nothing starts and stops without your grandmother and mother. So, for me, it's the two of them. I was raised by both my mom and grandmother, and then by my wife. So, I think that I would probably say that I've hit my stride more than even I expected just because of their collective support and steadfastness. I've [also] been very lucky to have a lot of mentors along the way both at NEA and outside of NEA. And the founders that I work with are the ones that I draw inspiration from every day.

I was talking with one of them this morning and it just got me really energized, really excited. I was like, "Okay, let's go figure this out." And so, to some extent, it's a daily thing to get energized in this business. At this point in my life, I look for inspiration and little snippets along the way, not for something dramatic. I've got a great foundation from my family and that's what centers me. Everything else is just gravy at this point.

CHRISTOPHER:

NEA is called both a venture firm and a growth firm. Obviously, you now have capital to deploy. What do you see as the greatest opportunities?

TONY FLORENCE:

There's no doubt that when we realize our fullest potential on behalf of our limited partners, we do two things really well. One is that we get in early to a company and we can help them over a decade or two decades. Some of our best companies that are $50 billion market caps didn't start out that way. They started out with a $5 million (investment) check and a couple people. So, that's really where we can participate in the most value creation and we've architected ourselves to be able to do that at every stage along the way with the same level of passion around risk and opportunity that we had ten years ago when we first got involved in the company. That's what commitment means from NEA.

On a Sunday, when I get a phone call, even if I've been working with this company for a decade, it's as if nothing else matters and it's all in at the same level of effort that I had from the beginning. Today, we're very lucky that we can pick points in time in a company's development where we can take advantage of those things. So, at the earliest stages, we're seeing dramatic opportunities in AI and what we see in software development. So, we were leaning in heavily in early stage and mid-stage investments there. And then, at the growth stage, we're waiting for that opportunity to really accelerate but we're starting to see real value in growth-stage development companies.

These are businesses that are established, their risk has been removed from the business model, and they just need capital to grow. **And we've been in an environment where that's been very difficult for young companies to get capital and so we're just starting to see the pricing dynamics become much more favorable.**

CHRISTOPHER:

Well, we had the opportunity at breakfast when you came down and spoke at our Themes event in January to debrief on what happened in the world that was 2022. What happened recently in the world of venture and growth that you really did not expect to happen as you look back post COVID through today? What's happened that you really did expect?

TONY FLORENCE:

The thing that jumps to the top of my head is we had a credit crisis in tech with SVB that nobody would have predicted. Fortunately, we got ahead of it and pulled our capital out of SVB before there was an issue. But I think the speed at which a large public company like that collapsed was probably the biggest surprise of the year for us. It seems like it was a long time ago. The other thing that's interesting is the market snapped back pretty quickly, so that's been a big surprise.

I think the second is that the public markets have recovered so quickly, particularly with the large-cap tech companies. We thought we'd be in a more prolonged environment of malaise, and we'd have a more difficult interest rate environment. And the economy has been a little stronger, and more buoyant than we expected.

CHRISTOPHER:

That leads to the next question. What are investors getting wrong when they're looking at venture and growth right now? What is it that they're just not either fully appreciating the risk of or fully appreciating the opportunity of?

TONY FLORENCE:

Well, **I think crises create opportunity and so there's been a liquidity and a capital market, and an interest rate crisis created.** And so, this is the time where you want to be leaning in on secondaries and things that are nontraditional. We are trying to do that as we think about our business in the secondaries and in credit and other places. The second thing I'd say is that innovation does not stop. People who are founding companies today, they're not as worried about the Fed and about the recession as the three of us may think.

And so, **you have to be time-diversified in venture capital and early stage investments, especially, and you have to have the right duration outlook.** There are companies being created last year, this year, next year, that, ten years from now, we're going to look back and [say], "Wow, that was an amazing time to be investing in venture capital." So, I think what's happened in our business is that it's become a little more cyclical than it should be because these are long-duration assets. It takes a long time to build a company and you can't time when the next Marc Lore walks in with a great idea that's going to take eight years to build. But when he does, it's going to be an amazing outcome for your LPs.

So, you have to manage that with the environment. We closed a big fund in February. **We believe it's a good time, a healthy time, to be responsible but to be investing. And I think that's sometimes hard for limited partners to understand because, when it's scary and raining outside, sometimes that's the best time to have a long-term outlook.**

CHRISTOPHER:

If somebody gave you a bucket of money and said, "I don't want it back for twenty years, twenty-five years, thirty years, would you be excited about that? Would you be afraid about that? You talked about how long it takes for these businesses to build, but the typical LP structure of having to return capital is the nature of the industry that we operate in. Yet, it feels like permanent capital would be such a better solution in the world of venture and growth.

TONY FLORENCE:

There's no doubt about it, and I think that a bit of the Holy Grail for a lot of investment firms is to have more permanent capital. That's why a lot of firms have gone public. We are always in search of that long-duration partner. We've got a few. We have not taken advantage of it just because we've got traditional structures. But we are absolutely trying to think through what the right balance is.

Again, every dollar that we take, we take with extreme levels of accountability and responsibility and so you'd have to have the right expectation with that. I think the industry, over time, will continue to mature. I think we feel the same way about venture and growth.

Our fund life is twelve years, which is much longer than a traditional fund. Typically, these funds are eight years, maybe ten, so we are on the longer side because of that exact reason. But the good news is that it hasn't kept us from trying to maximize value for our limited partners.

TONY ROBBINS:

You bring up the Holy Grail. That's the title of this book, *The Holy Grail of Investing*. Ray Dalio is a good friend of mine, I was interviewing him, digging in with him, and I said, "What's the single most important investment principle that guides your decision-making?" And his answer that he called the Holy Grail was that you should have eight to twelve uncorrelated investments. I'm curious, what do you perceive to be the Holy Grail of Investing as you look at it through your lens?

TONY FLORENCE:

Well, it is, and it isn't, Tony, just to be direct. Anybody that's in our business that hasn't read everything that Ray Dalio has written or that you've written about him is probably shortchanging himself. We're lucky that we get to read that stuff. Our firm was founded forty-five years ago with a hundred-year vision, and it always had a couple key things. One is that it always had tech and healthcare. So, by definition, we have uncorrelated investing activities just by nature of that. We have diversification that's probably more similar to what Ray is saying. We also dynamically allocate capital, which is another one of his principles, within a fund structure, based on an environment. **We might over-allocate to certain areas or under-allocate to other areas, and we have that flexibility carved into what we do.** Then, we have time diversification.

What's nice about what we do is that I'll make an investment today, but I have seven to eight years of investment decisions to make on that company. So, I have lots of time diversification to see what technology cycles have played out. The original idea and the original product or technology that we invested in, is it still relevant today? We lean into that.

And then, lastly, I would say that, because of our scale, we take small bets that are very uncorrelated, that are more futuristic, that may not be in classic social media or e-commerce or AI today, but they may be in a robotics or automation company that has nothing to do with 95 percent of our portfolio but, if it works, could be super special. Or we take a small bet in an area of life sciences like CRISPR. Back when we invested in CRISPR technology, it was so crazy but yet that was against the grain on everything that had been done in life sciences. And so, we have the ability to have these small experiments, but in small investments that don't risk a lot of capital but provide that nice level of diversification that you're talking about.

TONY ROBBINS:

You've worked with so many entrepreneurs over the years. If you had to come up with one, two, or three principles that you think make entrepreneurs successful across the board, what would stand out to you?

TONY FLORENCE:

I hate to be repetitive, but I would say one is that they're obsessed with what they're doing. **They obsess over the opportunity, and they obsess over the risk. Both of those are important.** Number two, they have a very clear vision for themselves that they can go and build around, recruit around. That's very, very important and they're able to communicate it. And the third is that they have something inside of them that you know is working for you twenty-four hours a day. It's not just the obsessed part but it's a belief that this has to happen; there's a reason that they exist.

When I was talking to Marc yesterday about his new company, he's literally like, "Tony, there are millions of people that need this," and he actually believes in his heart that what he's doing is an important thing and it has nothing to do with a scoreboard.

TONY ROBBINS:

Growing a large investment firm requires a lot more than just making great investments or [having] great performance. What do you think has been the primary reason for the success of your firm over, what, forty-five years? And was there a fulcrum point in your business where it allowed the company to really take off?

TONY FLORENCE:

I think, like everything, it gets back to we're a human capital organization. So, everything is about the people and the team. If you look at NEA, most people that join here end up retiring from here. Most of our partners have been here for fifteen, twenty years. It is a very, very tight culture based on teamwork, trust, and excellence, and we try to live that every day. We obsess over this stuff. Everything that we do has to reinforce the teamwork, trust, and excellence of our culture. And when we see things that are not aligned with that, we [remove] it really quickly, whether it's a person or behavior. And we try to structure the way we do things, the way we work, the way we credit, the way we incentivize people, all to reinforce those key parts of the culture.

The second thing I'd say is that we have a concept of shared outcomes. **At the end of the day, we're just a small part of a company's journey and a founder's journey,** and we have a whole team. So, on average, eight to ten people at NEA will touch a company and that's really important. If you talk to a founder of ours, they might say some nice things about one partner, but what we really want them to do is talk about NEA. What we really want them to do is talk about how all the people at NEA love what they do and leaned in and had enthusiasm. That shared outcome concept is so vital.

The last thing is that we have a long-term focus on relationships. So, we have some of our limited partners that have been with us for thirty years.

TONY ROBBINS:

Wow.

TONY FLORENCE:

When you can sit there and work with somebody over one or two or three decades, that's something to really treasure and be proud of. So, we take that approach to founders [too]. That long-term approach to relationships matters.

CHRISTOPHER:

What are a few things that, before you took the reins, you wish somebody would've told you?

TONY FLORENCE:

I don't think somebody could have said this, but I feel very privileged, way more privileged to be doing what I get to do today than I thought I would. I get to work with great people. It's a hard business to get right in; there's a lot of decisions every day that add up to the long-term. And so, the long-term consequences of our decisions are what we debate the most. It's very easy to make a quick decision in what we do. What's hard is to make those decisions in the context of what this could mean for when we're not here.

And so, the basic tenets of what you would want somebody to be thinking for you is how we try to manage the firm. We're all aggressive. We're all type A people. We are all competitive, but sometimes you have to be measured and thoughtful in the way you make real decisions that can seem very small in the moment and very easy to make but have long-term implications. That's something that we spent a lot of time with, and [at the beginning] I probably didn't appreciate it as much.

CHRISTOPHER:

It goes back to what you said earlier which is that the firm was started forty-five years ago with a hundred-year horizon. That's such a beautiful way to look at it. If you could do anything over in your business with the benefit of hindsight, what would you do differently?

TONY FLORENCE:

I come from a bit of a nothing background in Pittsburgh and a conservative background from Morgan Stanley and so I obsess over not losing money. That's the thing, you don't want to lose money as an investor. But you got to take risk. In our business, I would say that we probably could [have taken] some more risk at certain points in time. So, if I look back to 2008 and '09, I wish we had probably taken a little more risk back in those days when we probably had a position of strength like we do now. I would say, right after COVID, things happened so quickly but there was a moment, a six-to-twelve-month moment, where there was an enormous amount of opportunity created.

In hindsight, we haven't made a lot of mistakes and we haven't stubbed our toe. But there were a bunch of things that I knew were great investments in those time periods [and] I just said now's not the right time to step on the gas because you just don't know. It's very easy in hindsight to say what I'm saying but, yeah, I wish we had done a few of those.

CHRISTOPHER:

We make the best decision we can with the information that's available to us at that point in time. You all have built what is a very unusual business which is a venture and growth business that has lasted for a very long time and gotten to enormous size and scale. What are the reasons why you believe most investment firms cannot scale or don't make that step to that long-term business?

TONY FLORENCE:

It's so funny, two weeks ago I had a dinner in New York with eleven or twelve PE and hedge fund heads or CEOs. We were all talking about this a little bit. I think it comes back to [that] there's a lot of psychology involved in being financial entrepreneurs. At the end of the day, an investment firm is typically run by financial entrepreneurs and it's hard to get aligned. You have personalities and people's lives change. We actually track the firms that were in a great position but didn't survive because we want to be humbly reminded of the fact that company X in 1996, '97, '98, and '99 were the best firms in our industry and they're nowhere today.

Why is that?

It's because, typically, the partners didn't get along, they had misalignment, they didn't have the long-term objectives right, and frankly, I think they didn't really want to sacrifice for scale. You got to really have a vision for what you want to be ten, fifteen, twenty years, and they're more in the moment. Just like building a company, you have to have a vision for scale, and you have to be able to put the pieces in place and be willing to continue to do that even when it's not obvious. A lot of venture firms have avoided scale. It's a very comfortable business to have four people around the table and they don't want to bring on partners and have the complications of making decisions and accountability. You have to really be willing to give back into the firm and the team more than you get—that's the bottom line.

TONY ROBBINS:

Tony, when you think about the universe of investment talent out there, what do you believe are some of the key traits that separate the highest performers from their peers? Because the building of the business really comes down to the people, right?

TONY FLORENCE:

You have to have a great investment team and you have to always be restocking the bench. In our business, we obsess over performance, so we take that very seriously on an annual basis and we try to make sure that we are hiring better people than we have today always and pushing ourselves. And I think you have to balance being willing to give people a lot of autonomy. You have to always balance that because you have to give people enough room to grow. Because we've been a growing firm, we've always had enough opportunity for people and creating that opportunity is really important to attract some of the best people.

TONY ROBBINS:

So, you're looking out for people that have their own sense of vision, the people that can build those same types of trusting relationships, the people that can balance the risk versus opportunity, those basic fundamentals that you talked about earlier then. Is that right, Tony?

TONY FLORENCE:

Yeah, absolutely. And I think, when you're recruiting people, you want people that are going to make you better, going to make the firm better, and going to bring something incremental. It could be a different type of background. It could be a different way of thinking; it could be a different level of ambition. Those things are good, and you have to be willing to take a little bit of that personal risk with people because that's important to continue to stay fresh.

CHAPTER 20

BOB ZORICH

COFOUNDER OF ENCAP INVESTMENTS

Accolades: EnCap is one of the top ten energy investors in the U.S. Zorich is a member of the Independent Petroleum Association of America and also serves on the board of several Houston charities, including the WorkFaith Connection and the Hope and Healing Center.
Total Asset Under Management (as of August 2023): $40 billion
Area of focus: Growth capital for independent energy companies

HIGHLIGHTS

- Zorich and his partners have successfully raised and managed $40 billion across twenty-four funds, attracting the trust and support of over 350 institutional investors from around the globe.
- Having an unwavering commitment to identifying and nurturing talent, EnCap has backed over 275 startup energy companies throughout their history.
- These teams used experience and focus to create billions of value for investors and were key instigators to the shale revolution.

CHRISTOPHER:

To get started, please tell us your origin story, how you ended up where you are, and a little bit about the business.

BOB:

I grew up in the Bay Area in what became the Silicon Valley. Born and raised there. Steve Jobs was five years behind me in high school, same high school, Wozniak one year behind. My dad was not an engineer, but a lot of other people's dads were. So, it was a competitive environment and was something I likely benefited from. Anyway, I went to college at UC Santa Barbara, got my undergraduate degree in economics, and met and married my current wife of fifty-one years. We moved to Phoenix, where I received my master's from Thunderbird and then we moved to Dallas, where I joined the Energy Department of Republic National Bank of Dallas in 1974. So, you know, about fifty years in the business. So, energy was not anything I knew anything about, but it was really the premier place within the bank to operate. Instead of participating in New York–originated loans, we were one of the leaders in energy financing. And one of the things I quickly learned about oil and gas is that it is difficult for those outside of oil and gas to understand. It is a very nuanced field. Engineers can ascribe a value to a property, but if you don't know what assumptions were used to generate the value number then you cannot understand the qualitative importance of the value ascribed.

Fast-forward, I went to London and I did some things with the bank—big North Sea financings—and I gained some confidence in myself and the ability to compete against very smart people. I also learned, when I went to London, that working for myself and getting up every day, and getting to go do things that would change the outcome of my life was fun. Harrowing at times, but fun. This experience caused me to embrace the concept of leaving the bank when that opportunity arose in the early 1980s. One of my best friends at Republic and I left the bank together to form a startup oil company in 1981.

We did that for five or six years in the early eighties, during a period of time when prices were going down. But we got to learn a lot more about oil and gas and about all of the technical and operational details that allow one to evaluate risk and values. If you recall, the oil market crashed in 1986 and we sold our company. We had five tiers of preferred stock, so we learned a lot about capitalization, capital structure, risk, bank debt, and so forth. At that point, I had almost fifteen years of experience in investing in and managing oil and gas risk. I moved to Houston to work for a money manager who managed pension fund money. They had a mezzanine debt product that was oil and gas related. In the middle of the crisis, I started my job with them. By 1988, it appeared to me that they were too narrowly focused on expensive debt. Mentioned that to my boss and my boss said that he wanted to continue focusing on the mezzanine product. While grateful for the opportunity, my desire to follow my instincts led me to think about doing something else. Discussed the opportunity to bring oil and gas financial product to the institutional community with my former oil company partner, and we decided to discuss the idea with two other top oil and gas Republic Bank friends, and the concept of EnCap was born. So that partnership has endured now for thirty-five years. **The real simple concept, Christopher, was to use our experience and contacts to deliver high-quality oil and gas investment product to the institutions.** So that's what we did.

CHRISTOPHER:

It's interesting because when you think about EnCap, you are oil and gas people who are really, really good at finance as opposed to finance people who think they're going to be good at oil and gas. I think that's been a real edge that EnCap has brought to the equation for a long time. Going back a little bit, who is the most important person that shaped your success, and how did they do that?

BOB:

You know, I've given a little bit of thought to that over time. **I really attribute my success to my partners and our collective character. You know, working hard, showing up, treating others as you want to be treated, and doing the right thing has driven all of us.** Maybe ultimately the attribution should go to our parents who raised us. Also, my wife is clearly responsible for helping support me in all the time and work it took to make EnCap a success. Without my partners, I wouldn't be as successful. So, I think when it comes to character, once you decide you're going to be in a certain lane, then you want to work with other people that also want to be in that lane. Looking back after thirty-five years I can only be grateful for the fate that brought us all together.

CHRISTOPHER:

What's the greatest opportunity for investors when they're looking at energy, you know, as we move forward from 2023 and beyond?

BOB:

Today, you've got this overlay—the world policymakers have decided that there's a weather model that indicates that too much CO_2 in the air will eventually superheat the earth. At least that's the summary thesis. There is some evidence that 600 million years ago, there was a lot of CO_2 in the atmosphere and the earth was very warm. Of course, a lot of things have happened over the 600 million years. I've read a lot about modeling, and because models have limited variables relative to the real world, they tend to overlook certain variables which can cause the outcomes to be quite different from the model. Econometrics and weather modeling are two good examples of being interesting but unreliable. So basing decisions and policies on an imperfect model creates an opportunity today. Simply put, we are not being efficient with the dollars we are investing relative to the impacting energy output. If you think about energy as though it were food and you are trying to feed the world, you need to invest in high-calorie food to be most efficient. You have to eat many pounds of kale for every pound of protein to get the same calorie intake. Similarly with energy, oil, gas, coal, and nuclear are your protein-equivalent dense fuels. Wood, solar, and wind are the kale low-density equivalents. Our policies are directing our capital toward low-density answers and away from high-density solutions. The result will be a train wreck as we will find ourselves short of the energy required to fuel the world's energy demand. **This makes this period unique and will result in unusual low-risk high-return investment opportunities when the policymakers wake up to the need for energy-dense solutions.**

Our policies are directing our capital toward low-density answers and away from high-density solutions. The result will be a train wreck as we will find ourselves short of the energy required to fuel the world's energy demand.

CHRISTOPHER:

I would say that probably pretty close to 99 percent of people would never think about an energy investor today not being involved in the exploration side, but rather focusing on the engineering side. In this day and age, we just have to figure out how to get to it, as you put it. And so that's a very different risk-reward than what the vast majority of people realize is going on in the actual deployment of capital. And so, when you think about that train wreck, as you put it, of potentially underinvesting in fossil fuels, overinvesting in renewables, not getting enough yield from the renewables to offset the decline that's inevitable in fossil fuels, is that a three-year problem? Is it ten years?

BOB:

I think it is very apparent that it's happening. I don't think it's even close to being a mystery. But the combination of social media, the real media, wishful thinking, uninformed policymakers, and so on, they all kind of come together to create this misadventure that we're on. And it's obvious. It's going to happen. When does the Western world wake up to that? Hopefully three years but maybe ten?

Every country will be impacted differently by this train wreck. Those with energy resources—the U.S., Canada, Australia, Russia—will be in better shape; those without—China, Europe, Africa—will be at a disadvantage. Other non-energy issues will also create complications with energy maybe being the catalyst of a totally changed landscape.

TONY:

So, when you think about the last five, six, seven years, the energy world has changed a lot. But what has happened that you really expected to happen? And what has happened that you really didn't expect to happen?

BOB:

I think the failure of the European experiment, so quickly, it surprised me. You know, the failure of Europe's various decisions, whether they're stopping all nuclear, relying on Russian gas, building windmills, or building solar in Northern Europe. I lived in Northern Europe for three and a half years—I bet we saw the sun three weeks a year. Things like that have amazed me. And then the failure of the same policymakers anywhere in the world wanting to learn from that error is equally astounding. Most people in our industry kind of shake our heads at this and think it's obvious. There's a guy in Missouri who runs a co-op, an energy co-op, and he said exactly the truth: which is you cannot count on renewables as part of your baseload capacity. Because the wind may not blow, and the sun may not shine. So, if your people need energy 24/7 or some component of it, you can't rely on it. And if you're in charge of that process, and you're given a mandate that you use renewable first, it flips the logic. It's all turned upside down, unfortunately.

CHRISTOPHER:

You've been in the industry obviously for a long, long time. What has happened that you've expected to happen?

BOB:

Well, the success of the shales was very predictive. It's an interesting world we live in because there's always somebody saying something negative about everything. And yet, when you know your space, you can have confidence that what you're doing makes sense. And even though the oil industry was castigated for making a lot of bad investments, the truth of the matter is they made a lot of investments that were generally very good. What wasn't good was stability of pricing and cost structure. But when prices go up, cost structure will eventually go up, and that takes away a lot of the margin that was originally forecast by companies who bought the leases.

In our case, we tried to be very prudent about land prices paid and we only used leverage modestly against proven production-related cash flow. But we were not perfect. The bottom line is that the industry was by and large not irresponsible, but twenty-twenty hindsight measured by changing variables can make many industries look fragile from time to time, particularly those who used debt in any meaningful way.

CHRISTOPHER:

When you talk to investors now, people who are actually looking at the industry and considering making investments in the industry, what are they getting wrong when they think about investing in energy today?

BOB:

Honestly, there are so few of them, I don't think any of them are getting it wrong. I think a lot of people are staying away from fossil fuels because of their board and/or their committees. Some of them have come back and have continued to invest in things that make sense. EnCap is the top-performing fund in many of our investors' portfolios because we're returning a lot of cash and they can see it. But their boss can't go to committee with a fossil fuel investment for political reasons. Eventually, I believe this will change.

CHRISTOPHER:

So, switch gears just a little bit. If you had the attention of the world for five minutes, what would you tell them about the ramifications of not investing properly in traditional energy along with renewable or green energy?

BOB:

I think the message would involve focusing on fundamental truths and believing what your own brain tells you will happen relative to fundamentals. The importance of density relative to energy solutions is one of those fundamentals. The importance of energy relative to human flourishing. **We need policies that promote energy for human flourishing that also cause respect for the environment we live in.** This is a world problem and not a Western problem. **There are 7 billion folks who are not part of the West and they need energy and solutions to make it work for the world and they are capital constrained.**

CHRISTOPHER:

So, aside from the strong performance, which obviously you have had, what's been the primary reason for the success of EnCap?

BOB:

I'd say we're adaptable. I don't think any of the four of us could have accomplished what we accomplished just on our own. I think the strength of the rope with four strands to it is the reason for our success. And the ability to stay together and not cut each other's strand over that period of time has been highly beneficial for all of us and the success of EnCap.

TONY:

What was the fulcrum point that allowed your business to take the leap from a good business to a great business and really accelerate the growth?

BOB:

Well, without a track record, you can't establish yourself in this business. So, we built the track record of safe, consistent, solid returns in our early years. That was important. But then, staying within our focus area has also been important. **The exogenous events that include the shale revolution and our quick adaptability to that new set of economics and opportunity was one critical fulcrum point.** Others, who approached the business with a less technically driven decision process were slower to adapt. It allowed us to be very successful and grow substantially during that period.

CHRISTOPHER:

What are a few things you wish somebody would've told you before you started your firm?

BOB:

You know, it's honestly nothing because it would've robbed us of the joy of discovery. **I think you need to be tested by mistakes and learn from them and embrace them.** So, I'm happy our partnership got to search for the best practices as the opportunities unfolded. Maybe our common credit backgrounds made this process a lot easier to reach agreement on decisions along the way.

CHRISTOPHER:

None of us like going through what we go through in our path to growth, but when we look back with hindsight, usually we look back and go, you know, I'm glad I went through that because it made me stronger, made me wiser, made me realize different things. How would you have done things differently with the benefit of hindsight?

BOB:

I think with the objective being to finish strong, I'm perfectly happy the way it worked. Were there ways to make more money? Sure. Were there ways to do this or that, but those would've involved sacrifice on the family side, or a sacrifice within the partnership? It's hard to second-guess. You know, when the whole turns out in a complete baked cake that tastes good, it's hard to second-guess.

CHRISTOPHER:

Why do you think most firms are not able to scale?

BOB:

I go back to the adaptability thing. We saw many people struggle with shales because the technology was more complicated. Our partnership embraced involvement because the technical risk was actually lower. I think having a partnership, which I mentioned earlier, gave EnCap four different points of view on what was best and safe. And I think that's healthy. And the one thing you do learn is nobody's point of view is flawless. So, there are flaws, but I think you avert the biggest mistakes when you have more than one point of view to consider.

CHRISTOPHER:

You know, when you are talking about people, obviously people are a complicated animal, and so partnerships are complicated. What are those traits that separate the highest performers from their peer group?

BOB:

The character piece is number one. Everybody can perform differently yet still fit into the team, so to speak, if they have character. **We all showed up, worked hard, and were curious and able to defend our point of view within our boundaries of providing a safe, solid return on investment.** We had individual thoughts but a common goal of providing safe and sound investments to our institutional clients.

TONY:

Bob, one time I was speaking at one of the J.P. Morgan summits that they do for about 250 people and they're all billionaires. Ray Dalio was [speaking] right before me and he said that the Holy Grail of Investing is finding eight to twelve uncorrelated investments you believe in that will reduce your risk by 80 percent. There is no more important principle to him. That's part of the thesis of the book. We'd love to know what is the Holy Grail of Investing in your view, after decades of investing in the energy sector?

BOB:

You know, Tony, we view our investing much like we view our lives. You have to stick with values in order to be happy long-term. For us, what that means is reducing risk relative to what we're trying to accomplish. If you think about real estate, you think about your apartments full of people. They're paying you checks every month. That is pretty safe. If you think about oil and gas, the equivalent of that are wells that have been drilled and are producing and have a cash flow stream. And there are other methods even to protect against the rent payments, if you will, such as hedging that can reduce your risk. The other extreme would be exploration. You're going to a place where no well has been drilled before. And you can assume you're going to have a 10 percent chance of success if you're lucky and have used the best science available. We've always stayed away from those kinds of things. We don't like to fret about those kinds of risks. And so that's really been our Holy Grail, if you want to call it that. It is to establish some values around risk and around what we're trying to do. They can be operational, price, or production related. As you watch the facts unfold, you establish where you are and where you are not going to step with the business.

TONY:

So, one of the ways you've done that is by partnering with mature companies and then agreeing on that growth plan. Asymmetrical risk-reward is everybody's dream, obviously. But the way you do that is by reducing the risk as much as possible. I understand exploration. My hat's off to the people that can do that. I would be quite uncomfortable with a 10 percent chance of success in something.

BOB:

We actually partnered with lean but mature and seasoned management teams who were likely trained at mature companies. **We always tried to only partner with seasoned teams that viewed risk like we did.** Our capital was only released in quantity into situations where the growth had a high probability of success. That kept us primarily in the area of developing already proven concepts.

CHRISTOPHER:

The interesting thing about what Bob is describing, Tony, is how it fits with so many of the other concepts that we've talked about. While [EnCap] is not going out and doing real estate, credit, etc., inside of their space the same rules still apply—eight to twelve non-correlated asset streams, which in their particular case could be different basins in different parts of the country. It could be drilling in different areas of depth. It could be infrastructure versus upstream. All of these don't necessarily correlate to each other.

BOB:

The basic premise that supported the formation of EnCap is that oil and gas is complicated to invest in. An example would be understanding shale production. The big concept is that you had large geographic areas where there was a lot of oil in place, and simply by cracking the rock, you can get more oil or gas out. If you understood the dynamics of the reservoir and the history of the rock, you could then begin to understand which areas were going to give up economic quantities and which areas were not. There were ways to minimize risk and, at same time, apply reasonably proven technology to get economic returns. If you take that story to Wall Street, and you're going as somebody who needs their money not as somebody who is protecting their money, then there's a misalignment of interest. The guy with the gifted tongue possibly wins and the investor possibly loses. When that happens enough times, people start to stay away from the industry, and it gains a reputation for being high risk when, in fact, if you are deep in the weeds within the industry, you can understand the difference between the risk profile of different assets and different opportunities and assist the institutions you represent by keeping the risk profile low on the investment.

TONY:

You've certainly ridden decades of ups and downs that the industry goes through. And you've obviously had to manage your risk incredibly well to do as well as you've done on $40 billion of investment. I'm curious, what's your view of the most promising green energy? So much green energy has been promoted and yet doesn't seem to be ready for prime time. You guys have made investments in that area, if I understand correctly. What's your mindset?

BOB:

Our investment targets in that space are in areas where something is going to be safe, proven, but economically disruptive. We're not in the business to make a 3 to 4 percent rate of return on a piece of contracted infrastructure. So, we hired experts in that area that had been in the power business for a long time to be our investment staff. Their view was that batteries were the most disruptive space. Simply put, if you can place a battery in an area where existing infrastructure already exists, you have all the things you need to be able to disperse the energy from those batteries out into the grid in a very cost-effective way. **You can power the batteries up during low-cost times and dispatch power very similar to gas storage when prices go up.** That is one example of how we think about making a solid returning yet safe investment in the green space. And our first energy transition fund looks like it's going to be a very high rate of return over a four-year period. Good quality deals and management teams. Our second fund is going to be focused similarly but will include different opportunities.

You know, the Inflation Reduction Act doesn't mean a thing in terms of inflation reduction. But it is going to change the economic landscape. You can't deny the fact that subsidy is going to influence investment activity. When the volume of that subsidy is put into the marketplace, there's going to be a lot of money spent in a lot of directions and some of it will not turn out very well. **Our focus will be on areas with established proven management and technologies where the application can be implemented with a reliable economic benefit.**

CHAPTER 21

DAVID GOLUB

FOUNDER OF GOLUB CAPITAL

Accolades: Awarded "Lender of the Decade" by *Private Debt Investor* magazine
Total Asset Under Management (as of August 2023): $60 billion
Area of Focus: Private credit lending

HIGHLIGHTS

- David Golub has been named by *Private Debt Investor* as one of the thirty top change-makers driving the evolution and growth of the private credit asset class.
- Golub Capital has received numerous accolades, including the prestigious PDI Lender of the Decade, Americas, award in 2023 and has also been recognized as Lender of the Year in the Americas in 2015, 2016, 2018, 2021, and 2022.
- Mr. Golub has invested in over one thousand companies and has been a contributor to the *Wall Street Journal*, the *New York Times*, and *Bloomberg Businessweek*.

- Mr. Golub created the "Golub Capital Altman Index," which has become a key, widely anticipated measure of performance in middle-market private companies.

CHRISTOPHER:

How did you end up where you are today, leading one of the largest private credit firms in the world?

DAVID:

I love telling Golub Capital's origin story. Flash back a few decades and imagine the Golub family dinner table. My brother Lawrence is eleven, and I am nine. Mom and Dad are talking about psychotherapy. Again. By way of background, both my parents were psychotherapists. Just imagine how desperate my brother and I were to change the subject. So we did what kids normally do—we came up with a business plan to create a middle-market lending firm.

Okay, that's a tall tale. The only true part is that my parents were both psychotherapists. The truth of how Golub Capital came to be is really a story about serendipity and path-dependency.

I started my career as a private equity investor. My brother started as an investment banker and later as a private equity investor. **In the late 1990s, we both had the same insight, which was that the private equity industry was going to continue to grow and prosper. And with that growth, we saw a huge opportunity to create a lending business to serve private equity sponsors.** What happened after that included a lot of luck. The financial crisis distracted a bunch of lenders that were less careful about underwriting and financing than we were. And, as much as we had high hopes in the 1990s about how much the private equity industry was going to grow, it has grown much more than anybody expected. So, the Golub Capital origin story is like a lot of origin stories. It's one that started with a good idea—the idea of creating a partnership-oriented specialty lender to private equity–backed companies. **But how we got to be as big as we are today— that's as much a story about surprises, coincidences, and luck as it is a story about great design.**

TONY:

Along the way, who is the most important person in your life that shaped your success and how did they influence you?

DAVID:

I've had a lot of mentors who've been really important to me. My mentors have been critical in my development as a leader and in the success of my firm. One of my mentors was Jay Fishman. Jay was my first boss when I came out of business school and started my career at what was then Shearson Lehman American Express. Jay later went on to become chairman and CEO of Travelers. Jay taught me many things, but the most important was how to be a good leader and how to be kind at the same time. **Learn everybody's name, even the building staff. Go out of your way to be there for employees who get into difficulties. And be careful what you ask your people to do.** Jay had an aphorism about this. He said, "Be careful what you ask your people to do, because they'll do it."

One of the tricks in life is to learn from other people's mistakes in addition to your own. And one of the reasons I think mentors can be so valuable is, often, they can share with you wisdom that comes from decisions they wish they'd made differently.

CHRISTOPHER:

And many times they also have observed other people make mistakes, right? There's a lot of shared collective wisdom across their ecosystem and their network that they developed over time. Let's pivot to the investment world for a minute, and let's talk about private credit, and let's talk about the world that you operate in every day. Where is the greatest opportunity for investors who are looking at private credit today?

DAVID:

To answer your question, I need to start with a bit of a philosophy statement about how I approach investing and how we as a firm approach investing. Some people think investing is different from other businesses. They believe good investors are geniuses. Think Warren Buffett or Bill Ackman. I think those kinds of individuals are extremely rare. **I think good investing**

businesses don't rely on a genius behind the curtain. Instead, good investing businesses are like other good businesses in the sense that they have some identifiable and really compelling sources of competitive advantage. So, in our business, the key to success is having a set of competitive advantages that give us an ability to produce consistent premium returns over time.

What kinds of advantages am I talking about? Let me tell you about several. First, we're big believers in relationships. We work with the same core group of about two hundred private equity firms over and over again. They represent a very small subset of the private equity universe, but they're 90 percent of our business every year. They like working with us—repeatedly—because they like our capabilities and our approach. We can help them with a wide array of their financing needs. We can do small transactions and large transactions. We have deep expertise across a variety of different industries. We can help their companies grow by providing more financing for acquisitions or capital spending programs. We can add value to their diligence processes. We're win-win oriented—so, if there's a hiccup, if there's a bump in the road, we're going to be very solution-oriented with them and not try to hold them up. Another example: We can give them solutions that they can't easily find elsewhere. We were a pioneer in the development of what's called one-stop, or unitranche, loans. It's a way of financing companies that makes it much easier to do acquisitions than the traditional multilayer capital structure that's very hard to manage.

Those are some examples of ways in which we come to the table with a distinctive approach. And that distinctive approach in turn makes us a compelling partner to our customers.

CHRISTOPHER:

So, you know the industry's changed here in the last year pretty dramatically simply because of the change in the interest rate regime. When people think about credit, they think about that as a negative. Just for the benefit of the audience, would you mind talking through why rising interest rates is less of an issue or even a positive for a private credit firm such as Golub.

DAVID:

Sure. **We've been big beneficiaries of rising rates.** We lend on a floating-rate basis; we earn a spread over a base rate called SOFR. So, a typical loan that we would make in today's environment would be SOFR (secured overnight financing rate) plus 6 percent. And SOFR today is about 5 percent. To your point, Christopher, a little over a year ago, SOFR was at roughly 1 percent. **So, where a typical loan that we were holding a year and a half ago would be paying us 7 percent, that same loan to that same borrower today would be paying us 11 percent.** That's good for our investors. The flip side is that borrowers have to pay a higher amount in interest expense, and that puts more pressure on them. It eats into their margin of safety. At some level of interest rates, the balance shifts from this being good for investors to being bad for investors because borrowers can't afford to pay the higher rates—but that's not where we are today.

CHRISTOPHER:

I think investors of all levels of sophistication failed to anticipate the rising rate regime and how it would change the perspective of different asset classes. It's one of the things that made us very, very optimistic about private credit as an asset class and particularly about acquiring stakes in firms that are in the private credit world because of the benefit that they are deriving from the higher rates. As you said, credit quality is still very important, and the ability to avoid defaults and those kinds of things. As we think out over the next three to ten years, what would you say is your outlook for private credit as an industry, and specifically, what impact could interest rates have over that period of time?

DAVID:

I think there's an important contrast between the short-term outlook and the medium- to long-term outlook. Start with the short-term outlook. We're in a bit of a strange time right now. We've been through this very rapid increase in interest rates. We are seeing this very rapid decline in inflation. The economy's a bit muddling. Equity values have dropped significantly. And as a consequence of that panoply of factors, and the uncertainty associated with them, we're seeing a slowdown in deal activity. Private equity firms are having trouble reaching agreement with sellers on price. Some private equity firms are putting off selling because they think things will be better in the future. So, right now we're seeing a favorable environment for the kind of lending that we do, but not as many new transactions as we'd like—the food is good, but the portions are small.

Now, let's take the longer-term view. While I can't tell you exactly when deal activity is going to speed up, I think it's very clearly a question of "when"—not "if." Looking out over the next three to seven years, our business has three fundamental tailwinds. The first tailwind is that the private equity ecosystem is going to grow significantly. We know that because there's about $2 trillion today of committed-but-uninvested capital in the private equity ecosystem. And that "dry powder" has a time fuse on it. Private equity firms have to use it over the course of the coming several years, or they lose access to it. I've been in this business for thirty years. I know that when you have that combination of factors, the capital's going to get used.

The first tailwind is that the private equity ecosystem is going to grow significantly. We know that because there's about $2 trillion today of committed-but-uninvested capital in the private equity ecosystem. And that "dry powder" has a time fuse on it. Private equity firms have to use it over the course of the coming several years, or they lose access to it.

The second factor is that historically the private equity ecosystem has looked for debt capital from both private credit players like Golub Capital and from the liquid credit market. **Over the last few years, the private credit market has been taking share from the liquid credit market, and I think that trend is likely to continue.** There are a variety of different reasons for this. One of the really important reasons is that the private credit industry's gotten big. And so, it's capable now of providing solutions for much larger companies than it used to be able to provide solutions for. In 2019, it was unusual to find a $500 million private credit deal. In 2023, we have had a $5 billion private credit deal. So, the second tailwind is that we're gaining (market) share.

The third tailwind is within the private credit industry. If you look at who's winning and who's not winning within the private credit industry, the winners are the larger players—those with scale, the capacity to provide a wide variety of different solutions, deep expertise across a range of industries, long track records of reliability. Again, this is predictable. If you imagine yourself as the CEO of a leading private equity firm, you too would choose to work with the largest, most scaled private credit players. So, the third big tailwind means that we and a couple of other large players are going to gain share within our industry.

CHRISTOPHER:

When you think about what's happened with the interest rate cycle, when you think about what's happened within the industry as a whole, what has happened recently that you did not expect to occur, and what has happened that you really expected to occur?

DAVID:

I'm going to start with what I didn't expect, although maybe I should have expected it. **One of the most consistent patterns in the history of finance is that banks make big mistakes.** Not every bank and not every year. In hindsight, I should not have been surprised that some banks were unprepared for the steep increase in interest rates we've seen since early 2022.

Something that does not surprise me is the continued outperformance of private equity. I've got a different take on this phenomenon than I've heard from many others. My take is that private equity competes very well against the two other principal forms of business ownership. The first of those is being publicly owned. Anyone who has served as an executive, board member, or advisor of a public company knows how challenged the public model has become. There is a heavy cost and regulatory burden, and unless you're a very large company, you don't get good research analyst coverage, you don't have good liquidity in your shares, and you don't get a strong valuation. **Being public for all but very large companies is a very flawed model.**

The second form of ownership is family ownership. This can be good for the entrepreneur-founder, but then things get difficult. Imagine an entrepreneur creates a company. The entrepreneur makes all the decisions—governance is simple! Maybe even one generation later this works because the entrepreneur only has a couple of kids and the kids all agree about how to operate the company. But as the group gets larger, maybe a third generation, it gets very difficult to maintain consensus among the owners. You need to navigate compensation for family members when some family members want to work in the business, and others don't. Some maybe want liquidity, and some don't want liquidity. It is just very, very challenging.

So, my take on the success of private equity is for many businesses it's just a better ownership model than either public ownership or family ownership. I think we're likely to see private equity continue to expand.

CHRISTOPHER:

There's so much press around some of the higher-profile transactions that either have worked or not worked over time in the private equity world. There's very little, and certainly not enough coverage in my opinion, of all the hundreds and hundreds of success stories where companies have been able to be improved dramatically. And so, it's a really interesting perspective to hear you say that related to private equity.

When investors are trying to decide where they should allocate assets, what are they getting wrong when they think about private credit?

DAVID:

I think what some investors get wrong about private credit is that they underestimate the incentives for mediocrity at big brand-name asset management firms. It's hard to be great at many different investment strategies. **Instead of focusing on giant firms with well-known brands, I suggest focusing on managers with clear, identifiable sources of edge.** Who has a proven track record in that niche? Who has competitive advantages that will enable them to sustain that track record over time? In many cases, figuring this out is not very complicated, but my experience is that often investors flock to a well-known name instead of doing the work.

CHRISTOPHER:

Let's pivot a little bit and give you the opportunity to talk to the world. If you had the attention of the world for a few minutes, what would you tell them?

DAVID:

I'm a giant believer in the impact of nonprofits. **We may be a polarized country politically, but I think almost all of us can agree that thriving, effective nonprofits have a hugely positive impact on American life.** So, my message, Christopher, is really simple: Get involved in a local nonprofit. Pick something that you're passionate about. It could promoting music and the arts, it could be serving the unhoused, it could be combating drug addiction—any of a variety of different things. I'd encourage everybody to find a nonprofit that they want to get involved with. I think you'll find it to be life-transforming.

TONY:

You talked a lot about having a clearly defined niche, and edge is the word you used. What else would you say has been important for the success of Golub Capital?

DAVID:

Success in business is complicated, but I tell you that every successful business I've gotten close to over time has had some core principles that are reflected in everything that they do. We've got two core principles. The first we already talked about—investing's hard, but it's not different from any other business. You can't rely on a genius sitting in the corner. You can't rely on a proprietary model. **You've got to figure out a set of competitive advantages, and you got to nurture those advantages over time so that you can outcompete your competition.** The second principle that underlies our business is that relationships matter. We're old-fashioned. We don't believe in the modern Wall Street mantra that everybody's a counterparty. We think good businesses work with the same parties over and over again. They work with the same suppliers, with the same customers, with the same investors. And they do that because they're able to develop a compelling value proposition for each of these groups so that each of these groups wants to work with that company, over and over again.

These two principles are very guiding. They have led us to sustain a very narrow mission: to be best at sponsored finance. We're not trying to be best at real estate. We're not trying to be best at oil extraction. We're trying to be best at making loans to companies that are controlled by private equity firms.

And we also have a very clear culture that, again, goes with the two core principles. Our culture is defined by two words: gold standard. And what we mean by gold standard is that we treat all our partners the way we would want to be treated if we were on the other side of the table.

CHRISTOPHER:

You've had a fantastic, long career at Golub Capital. But there are always things that we learn along the way that are sometimes less pleasant. What are some things that you wish you had been told before you started the business to spare you some of those less pleasant learning experiences?

DAVID:

That's a really long list. We've made a ton of mistakes over the years. **One of the things I have learned is the value of process and investment infrastructure. The non-glamorous parts of a business often don't get enough attention.** In lending, that's a mistake. We learned early that this was an area that we needed to really focus on, and it's become one of our core strengths. But I wish somebody had told me that at the beginning.

CHRISTOPHER:

It is inevitably the blocking and tackling that goes on behind the scenes that enables the business to prosper and to be successful. If you could do anything over in your business with the benefit of hindsight, what would you do differently?

DAVID:

You know, I don't mean to duck the question, but I feel very fortunate. There's not a lot I regret. There are things we could have done better; I'm sure I could name ten of them. They're not that important. I feel very lucky to have gotten right the important things—and a lot of those revolve around people. We have a phenomenal team.

CHRISTOPHER:

You and your brother and the rest of the team at Golub Capital have stayed very true to your niche and skill set. And it's interesting because there's a school of thought that the way that you scale a business in the investment world is by having lots of different offerings and lots of different verticals and lots of different segments. And there's been firms that have done that very, very successfully. You have chosen to do that in a very narrow focus. Very few firms with that narrow focus have been able to scale. What are the primary reasons that you think most investment firms are not able to get to that scale?

DAVID:

I think you make a really important point. If you think about most investing businesses, the challenge of scaling is that you need to go to your next best idea. Imagine for example, that you are a long-only equity manager, and somebody gives you $100 million. You do a great job with it, and then the next year, instead of having a hundred million to invest, you've got more investors, and you've got a billion dollars to invest. So, you've got to go from building a portfolio with your top twenty best ideas to one with your top one hundred best ideas. And your one hundredth best idea probably isn't as good as your twentieth best idea. What this illustrates is that most investment businesses aren't scalable because, fundamentally, the investment strategy isn't scalable.

Contrast that with our business. Our growth has actually put us in a position to be a more valuable partner to our private equity firm clients. It's the opposite of my long-only equity manager. **Growth doesn't diminish returns. Growth enhances our competitive advantages by enabling us to do more for our private equity firm clients.** I'd argue our growth has enhanced our capacity to sustain our track record of premium returns over time.

CHRISTOPHER:

It's really interesting the way that you describe it because what happens to most firms is that they, in the name of growth, end up having to sacrifice quality or sacrifice the level of work and diligence. When you think about the universe of talent in the investment business, what do you believe are the key traits that separate the highest performers from their peers?

DAVID:

I think there are a couple of different models to think about talent in the investing space. There's absolutely a set of investment firms where stars are critically important—where you need Michael Jordan. That's not how we operate. **For us, success is a team sport. No one's great at everything. Everybody's better in a collaborative setting.** So, what we're focused on all the time, micro level, macro level, in managing the firm is making sure we've got the right mix of people, and making sure that we are providing development opportunities to all of our folks so they can continue to grow over time. And we're able to measure our success in doing that in a couple of different ways. We can measure our success with our investors through our returns. We can measure our success with private equity sponsors through repeat business. We can measure our success with our financing partners through their desire to continue to work with us. And we can measure success with our team by looking at engagement survey data and retention stats. And in this era, when we've all read about the extraordinary growth of resignations during COVID or, more recently, all the articles about quiet quitting, I think you can tell an enormous amount about a company by looking at whether those phenomena are hitting the company. I'd argue that if you find a company that has high levels of engagement and low levels of attrition, you have probably found a winner. I think at the end of the day, while all of the strategy issues that we talked about over the course of our discussion are really important, if you don't have the right team, nothing else matters.

CHRISTOPHER:

We talk a lot about different businesses and the dynamics of the leadership. In your case, you've got your brother that you have worked with during the entirety of the business. And I don't know too many brothers that have built businesses as successfully as the Golub brothers have.

TONY:

And stayed together for that many decades as well. That's an art by itself.

DAVID:

Hey, we have passionate disagreements. It's not all a symphony of peace and happiness. But one of the great things about working with my brother has been that we can have passionate disagreements, and we both know we're going to wake up the next morning and we're still going to be brothers and we're still going to be best friends and we're still going to be business partners.

TONY:

David, the title of the book is *The Holy Grail of Investing*, which sounds over the top. But the reason is that when I did my first book, I interviewed fifty of the best financial investors in the world. When I talked to Ray Dalio, he said that the Holy Grail of investing is finding eight to twelve uncorrelated investments that I feel strongly about. So, the whole book is about all these alternative investment opportunities to help you fill that out. But we'd really like to ask you from your perspective, David, what is the Holy Grail of Investing for you?

DAVID:

My perspective, Tony, is that investing really isn't different from other businesses. If we turned around your question and we asked what makes a great business, I think there'd be enormous agreement around that answer. We'd talk about competitive advantages and ways in which the business has a moat around it, which makes it hard to compete with. For me, in our niche, which is lending to private equity–backed companies, it's all about our competitive advantages. **By nurturing those competitive advantages, we're able to continue to produce consistent premium returns.**

Now, Ray Dalio is a genius, and he can figure out, well, these are the ideas for the moment that are particularly attractive. I'm not a genius. My business does not rely on genius to produce really good, consistent returns year over year. What we need to do is continue to benefit from and to nurture these core competitive advantages. **This is what I would describe as the Holy Grail: You want to invest alongside managers who have a business and not just a fund—managers who benefit from some sustainable source of competitive advantages.**

TONY:

It's very similar to Vista with Robert [Smith]. The same mindset of knowing more about it than anybody else in the industry. Having all that specialization, having the ongoing clients that come back to him again and again. You both have done unbelievably well in different industries. One more quick question for you. I was with Sheikh Tahnoon recently, and he was being advised by all these people financially. One of them was a gentleman from SoftBank and he was saying to him that now is the time for private credit. He was promoting private credit over private equity even. And he gave all his reasons for it and so forth. I'm curious, why private credit now, why is it even more important than ever before from your perspective? Why should investors be considering it?

DAVID:

If you think about what changed in July 2022, we saw interest rates go up. We saw growth slow down. So, both of these are factors that are very significant headwinds for many different asset classes. For equities, for example, you're simultaneously taking down net income because you've got a higher expense and you are putting pressure on multiples. **Traditional fixed income performs terribly in a rising rate context. By contrast, our business has tailwinds.** We have a growing private equity ecosystem. **Rising rates result in higher profits (so long as we control credit losses). The banks are out of our market and not coming back.** Scale is a major source of competitive advantage. There a lot of reasons for optimism.

I think that lies at the core of your colleague's argument. And I think he's right; there are unusual opportunities right now in private credit with the right managers. But I'd still advise caution. You can make mistakes in any asset class. Maybe I'm going to sound like a credit guy, but I think if anybody ever tells you: "This asset class is fail safe"—hold your wallet!

CHAPTER 22

BARRY STERNLICHT

COFOUNDER, CHAIRMAN, AND CEO OF STARWOOD CAPITAL

Accolades: Starwood was one of the world's largest public hotel companies (they have since merged their hotel holdings with Marriot). They are also one of the largest multifamily owners, one of the largest public REITs, and one of the largest owners and operators of single family home rentals.
Total Asset Under Management (as of August 2023): $115 billion
Area of focus: Global real estate—all real estate asset classes across thirty countries

HIGHLIGHTS

- Barry Sternlicht is the cofounder, chairman, and CEO of Starwood Capital Group, which was founded in 1991.
- Starwood currently has $115 billion of assets under management and has invested over $240 billion over the last thirty years across all major real estate asset classes.
- Starwood's investments include market leaders in residential, hotels, office, industrial, and retail.
- The firm was founded during the depths of the savings and loan

crisis and now has five thousand employees across sixteen global offices.

- Mr. Sternlicht is on the board of directors of the Estée Lauder Companies, Baccarat Crystal, the Robin Hood Foundation, Dreamland Community Theater, the Juvenile Diabetes Research Foundation's National Leadership Advocacy Program, and the Business Committee for the Arts.

TONY:

Barry, tell us a little bit about your journey, how you go from [borrowing] $20 million to, if I understand correctly, $115 billion AUM today. That's quite a journey. Tell us a little bit about your origin story, if you would, just to give people an orientation.

BARRY:

Thanks, Tony. Sure. My mom was a schoolteacher, and my dad was an engineer, and he came to the country after World War II. During the war, he fought with the Czech partisans. So, I think probably the most defining thing about my career and my life is that my worst day was better than his best day, growing up in a war. I always like to keep that in perspective. We really are blessed. And he so loved this country, and the opportunities it presented which said, you can do anything if you work hard and commit.

We were middle class. We lived in a small home in Long Island, and moved when I was five to Connecticut. My mom taught while her three boys went to school. I went to public high school, a class of two thousand kids. And then I was told I could go to college, but it had to be within driving distance of the house. So, I went to Brown because I wasn't really a math guy. My selection process was the best college where I didn't have to take a math course. People know me as a finance wizard, and the secret is I'm not. I just know how to use a calculator really well, have a good memory, and as an artist in high school, I think with both my left and right brain. So, I majored in something called Law and Society. I called that "Lost in Society" because I was somebody who knew a lot of things, but not a lot of about anything. When I graduated, I had three jobs in two years coming out of school, and my last job was actually as an arbitrage trader on Wall Street. My father, being who he was, said, "Do you want to look at a little green screen for the rest of your life?" So, even though I was making good money, I decided if I could get in, I would further my education and go to business school. I applied to only two, and I got into Harvard and I still don't know how.

I thought I'd last five minutes when they found out I couldn't add and subtract. But I survived that, and did pretty well. I've always been good at talking, and half your grade is class participation! I took a job in Chicago working for a real estate firm called JMB because I got a call from a friend who was an alum of JMB. I was choosing between there or working on Wall Street at Goldman Sachs, which was the only job I could get. But I really liked design. I liked art, I liked architecture. I liked travel and people. So real estate, as a principal, seemed like a good place to start. JMB hired me and I rose rapidly at the firm. I was a pretty creative guy.

There was a finance professor at HBS (Harvard Business School) who taught Entrepreneurial Finance. I didn't take the course, but I was told to go to his last class, so, I did. And the professor said a couple things. He said, "Be careful what you ask for, because you may achieve it." That has been an interesting motto that I've thought about my whole career. And then he said, **"Find the freight trains in your life and get on them instead of in front of them."** I actually think about both of these all the time. You know, luck is when preparation meets opportunity. You create your own luck. You set the table to get lucky. And, I think you have to have chips on the table to be successful and play the game.

It's no skill to say no to everything. You have to take risks and you're going to fail. I think the most important milestones of my early career were the worst deals I did, because of how much I learned from those. My son just graduated from HBS last week and I was telling him that the most exciting part about investing and learning is that I actually approach every investment like I'm stupid. I think about what could go wrong—worry about the downside, and the upside will take care of itself. So, in investing, you try to take the right risks and never cross the line on ethics, ever. I think that among other things, that has been the reason Starwood Capital Group has been so successful. We've always put our investors first, and we've always done the right thing, even when they didn't know we were doing the right thing. We have the same fee structure in our funds today that we had in 1991. Investors get their money back, a return on their money, and then we participate. As my father said, "If you do the right thing, you can always feel good when you look in the mirror every morning."

So, in my career, I'd say the pivotal moment was that I got let go when I was thirty-one. I was working at JMB. I was the wunderkind. I was in Chicago. Then the savings and loans crisis hit, and I was let go. It was shocking. I took the bus to apply for unemployment benefits. But I was very close with the man who ran JMB, who was on the Forbes 400, and I was worth about $8,000. But we were good friends. I was at his house with his wife and his kids. I skied with him. He gave me a million dollars to start my firm. With two other families, we had our first fund of $21 million. That's where we started. We couldn't afford anything. We had no credit—we couldn't even get a fax machine. We borrowed offices from the AMA in Chicago. We even borrowed their employees and had them sit on our side of the building so that we could look more robust than we were. It's been quite a ride.

We first bought a bunch of apartments. I sold them to Sam Zell, and we tripled our investors' money in eighteen months. And then myself and my partner, who was a friend from business school, split and I went east. I took advantage of a really odd-looking public company that I tripped over and merged a bunch of assets that we owned with that company, and changed its name to Starwood Lodging. It had an $8 million market cap at the time [and] $200 million of debt. We bought a bunch of the debt, and then we merged and took control of the company. From there, Starwood started doing lots of deals. We bought Westin Hotels for $5 billion. And then we bought ITT Sheraton for $14 billion. We were a $7 billion company buying a $14 billion company, bidding against Hilton Worldwide. **All of a sudden, in three years, we were the world's largest hotel company measured by cash flow.**

TONY:

Wow, how did you outsmart them with that little bit of capital?

BARRY:

We always treated our public shareholders like they were our partners. So, Fidelity owned 10 percent of the company. I knew all those guys. We needed their support. We made a stock offer for ITT. Our stock was trading at a relatively huge multiple at the time. And Hilton made a cash offer. They weren't trading at the multiple we were because we were growing so much faster. Normally, the acquirer's stock falls after a takeover offer, but the portfolio manager of Fidelity's real estate group said, "Starwood stock is worth more than cash." When we announced the deal, our stock was $53 a share. And after we announced it, our stock went to $60. So, that offer was worth even more than our first offer, and then we threw in some cash. Hilton offered basically $81 a share in cash. We were $84, but it was stock and $30 in cash. The shareholders voted for us.

TONY:

And you were thirty-eight years old at the time?

BARRY:

I was thirty-eight. Sometimes youth and innocence can mean stupidity and, you know, you have to figure it out in full view of the public.

CHRISTOPHER:

It goes back to your point from your professor, which is to be careful what you wish for. You might get it. You had 120,000 employees all of a sudden.

BARRY:

And then I had three of everything. I had three CFOs. I had three chief counsels. I had three heads of IT, and [it was] like, eeny, meeny, miny, moe. So, I went out and got some help. I had people evaluate the team, and it was a bouncy ride. So, my day job became running Starwood Hotels, and I ran it for ten years. It was the best of times and the worst of times. In the media's eye, I was a genius and an idiot. I didn't really like the publicity that much. I'm a sensitive guy. And the press, you know, they loved me. And they hated me.

TONY:

You had some really interesting comments [in Miami] at the J.P. Morgan conference saying hospitality is going crazy. We've all seen it. The prices are going nuts. Everybody was cooped up for COVID. Tell us your view of the real estate market today and how your firm is looking at it.

BARRY:

Historically, it's the real estate industry that causes crashes. You know, '07, '08, the housing industry, the ninja loans, selling loans with derivatives, all this stuff was toxic waste. I was not a home builder, but we were instrumental as an industry in nearly taking down the entire world's banking system. You could borrow 110 percent of the purchase price of an asset, and it got silly aggressive. One of the other key factors when you invest in real estate is that it's not really a great idea to buy a property when debt is more expensive than the yield on the property. We call that negative leverage. [If] you're borrowing 9 percent and paying a 6 percent yield for a property, you're in the hole from the start. This was the market in 2007–2008. Of course, that wasn't the case in 2020, and 2021, no bank was really that aggressive lending after '07, '08. They kind of learned their lessons, and for a while, there was positive leverage in every asset class.

So, in late '21, the Fed said, you know, we can control inflation and rates will be "lower longer." As you know, the Treasury printed $6 trillion during COVID, and there were no goods on the shelves. The supply chain broke. Everybody ran to buy not only their groceries, but their golf carts, their vacation homes, their couches, their desks. With no supply, prices went bananas, used car prices went crazy, and inflation took off. When inflation hit the real estate world, the rents and apartments rose like 20 percent in our markets in 2021–2022. In forty years, I've never seen anything like that. It was insane. But then the government finally caught on and raised interest rates in a straight line, the fastest in history. So, basically, real estate got blindsided. However, the fundamentals remain okay. If you look at the real estate asset classes, the residential business is strong. Apartments across the nation are 95 percent occupied. Rents are rising, not 20 percent, but nationally like 4 percent, and that's a very healthy market. Normally, pre-pandemic, we'd be happy with the 4 percent increase in rents. With single family—they're not building as many single-family homes; people can't afford a new house right now because the mortgage is too expensive. There's a wave of new apartment supply finishing, but there will be nothing behind it. In the aggregate between single family and multi, Powell's policy will create an even bigger deficit of housing units. So, there'll be pressure on both home prices and apartment rents whenever we get out of whatever it is we're in right now.

And, as you know, the hotel market took off, especially the resort market, immediately when the pandemic began to clear. People went on vacation and worked from anywhere but the office. And that market has been really strong. Both occupancy and the rates. In the beginning, I was like, "Well, the airline ticket was very cheap." Now the airline ticket's really expensive and people are still traveling. It's actually one of the conundrums. I'm scratching my head. I don't understand it really, how these room rates are staying this high all over the world.

TONY:

Is it that there's this amount of money that's still in the economy from all the money that was shoved into people's pockets? And it was going to run out, if I understood it correctly, in October of this year. Is that still happening?

BARRY:

I think those Americans—the ones we have heard about that didn't have an extra $400 in their savings account, and then got several thousand dollars from the government—I think they're out of excess savings, or close to it right now. And they're on their credit cards. Credit card debt is through the moon and beyond. I'm watching delinquencies at Bank of America. They're saying they're normal, but I don't think they'll stay normal. Now, the reason all this is okay at the moment is that people are still employed. People are spending money they may not have, but they have a job, and they feel secure in their job. So, if the Fed actually gets what they want, which is to get the unemployment rate up and wage growth to slow, that could unwind a lot of things.

The one thing I'm talking to our clients about is the American "virtual" office.

TONY:

That's what I want to know. We're now complaining about working three days a week at the office. [People are] willing to go to work around the world, except here. It's crazy.

BARRY:

Oh, it's crazy. **You know, everyone's in their offices in the Middle East. I was in a building in Dubai yesterday that's as busy as can be. It's like you're in Manhattan pre-pandemic. And then Europe and Asia, Tokyo in particular, not only are people in the office, but the vacancy rates are really low. In most of the major cities of Germany, office vacancy rates are below 5 percent. That compares to 25 percent in San Francisco and above 20 percent in New York City.**

So, there's a couple issues in the U.S. One is this: We're delighted to work from Jackson Hole, and we'll work from the beach, and we'll work from wherever we are. And it was led by the tech companies, which are our biggest companies, the biggest component of the S&P 500. What they do, everybody notices. But now, Amazon, in their new headquarters in Virginia asked everyone to come back to work four days a week. Last week, Google said, we want to see you back in the office. Every CEO is going to fire the people who stay home, first. They're not even being subtle about it. All the CEOs are in the office, but nobody's in the office with them. When I started my career, when the boss was in the office on Saturday, guess who went to the office on Saturday? I might be playing a game on my computer, but I wanted him to see that I was there. It's a different generation, and I think their grit is defined differently.

TONY:

Where do you see it going? Do you think this is a ten-year period or this is a two-year period before people start to change lifestyle?

BARRY:

If you look at what's happened in office since the pandemic, there's been like a hundred million square feet leased in buildings built since 2015, and a hundred million square feet vacant in older buildings. So, there's been a shift in demand. People want really nice buildings that attract their employees to come back. I built a building in Miami, and we leased the whole thing in the pandemic. It's a hundred percent leased. There was no leasing broker. My team just did it. And we started out at $52 rents and the last rent was $95. So, there are parts of the country where office is doing fine—Nashville, Tennessee, Austin, Texas, even the Atlantas and the Raleighs are doing okay.

And then there's the derivatives of office. Life sciences are booming, data centers are booming. They're not really office, but people are converting office buildings to data centers. So, it's another use. Much like the retail business where the good malls are continuing to stay occupied and thriving, and the bad malls kind of went the way of the dodo bird. So, you're going to see the office markets kind of bifurcate. Really good buildings will be full, with good tenants. But there's a new assault coming to the office markets. And that's AI. AI is going after skilled workers like lawyers and accountants and also advertising agencies. And it's going to be really interesting to see because these are major users of office space, right? Who's going to backfill that space? Where's the demand going to come from? It's going to be a very stressful time for the office asset class for a couple of years. **The Fed can fix all this, by the way. Lowering interest rates would give people time to refinance and cover. Nobody knows what the proper price is for an office building today— you can't get financing.** And if you get financing, they're going to charge you like 10 percent for it. You might have bought that really nice building and a 6 percent yield. So technically you're, well you're not solvent.

CHRISTOPHER:

Barry, you talked about a couple of themes that a lot of investors know are coming. They don't know the magnitude. They don't know what's going fix it. They don't know how long it's going to last. From your perspective, what are most investors getting wrong right now when they look at real estate?

BARRY:

First, what I'm thinking about myself is the long term. Like, what industries won't be impacted by AI. And when I say won't be impacted, [I mean] the demand will stay in place. How you choose to get to your hotel or how you choose a house may change, but the demand for residential will be solid. I think investors tend to throw the baby out with the bathwater. That's what we look for. We look for the babies that are being thrown out with the bathwater. We look for the really good office building with a really good tenant roster, and we can buy it at a price that's way below replacement cost. We'll buy it with all equity or mostly equity, we'll put a tiny little loan on it, and then rates will come down and we'll refinance it. Investors know that in the history of the United States, the interest curve has never stayed inverted forever. It's never happened. It'll never happen. Short-term rates will come down.

TONY:

Investors have to marry the property and date the rate.

BARRY:

Exactly. And what you look for are great assets with the wrong balance sheet. Then you can fix the balance sheet. Or find a really distressed seller, and there are a lot of distressed people right now. There's a lot of distress, and you don't see it until the loan matures. So, the loans are maturing every month, and it's going to be a minefield for years and everything will be helped if rates come down. Right now, there's a lot of fear and anxiety in the market. But there's [also] a lot of dry powder. So, it'll work out.

And some of us will be bold and buy stuff, and people will think we're nuts, and we'll know that in the future they may be the best purchases of our lifetime. **I think if you pick the right markets, and you pay attention, real estate is the most practical application of common sense there is. It is not genius, but you have to be completely objective. Do not fall in love with anything.** People get it wrong. They get emotional. They don't pay attention to the details. And it is the physical real estate that matters.

There is one thing I'd say though: real estate's a little like the stock market. I don't know who said this, but the markets can be irrational longer than you and I can be solvent. That applies to real estate too. So, sometimes the flow of funds overwhelms fundamentals. Like if Europeans decide that they don't care what the yield is on that building in Greensboro, South Carolina, or Charleston or Murfreesboro or Orlando. They want New York or they want DC. They're never going to get fired for buying a beautiful office building on Park Avenue in New York. So regardless of what the fundamentals are, you can't find a buyer. I've had to learn to really watch capital flows, as well as fundamentals. And it's so true in anything you invest in, right?

TONY:

One of the reasons we wrote this book is that Ray Dalio became a friend of mine over the last few years, and when I first met him, one of the questions

I asked him was: What's the single most important principle in investing? He's a macro trader, obviously, but what's the most important principle that guides all your decision-making? He turned to me, and he said, "You mean, the Holy Grail of Investing?' Then he said, Holy Grail investing is finding eight to twelve uncorrelated return streams or investments that you really believe in because it reduces your risk by 80 percent. So, one of the reasons we wrote this book is to show people alternatives and their impact so that they can get those eight to twelve. So, I'm curious, in your business, what is the Holy Grail of Investing?

BARRY:

Good question, A couple things come to mind. One, I asked a friend who's very successful in the hedge fund world, I said, what was your worst investment? And he said, selling my winners early. When you have something that's really working for you, ride it. But, conscious that every day you hold it, you've bought it again. It's human nature to think if you haven't sold it, you haven't made any money. You sell your gains, and you hold on to your losses hoping they get better. That is a terrible strategy in the stock market, and a terrible strategy in real estate.

It's human nature to think if you haven't sold it, you haven't made any money. You sell your gains, and you hold on to your losses hoping they get better. That is a terrible strategy in the stock market, and a terrible strategy in real estate.

We owned a business called Intown Suites. It's a budget hotel company and charges $350 a week, not per day. We were making a couple of hundred million dollars a year in cash flow. And after debt service, it was a hundred million dollars of free cash flow. So, I'm like, why would I ever sell this? There's no new supply, no competition. Nobody can build anything profitably and charge $350 a week. So, we held it an extra couple years and made an extra half a billion dollars. We just sold it last year.

I'd say the other thing in real estate is that it's really important to think about what could be there, as opposed to what is there today. And then be really objective about your competitive set. Like, what are you competing against, and how can I you make this property better? So, I'll use Post Properties as an example. It was a really nice apartment company based in Atlanta. We owned an apartment building right next to a Post property, built the same year. They were physical clones. If you looked at their property, it was beautiful. Their landscaping was fantastic. They ran four (percentage) points higher occupancy, and $150 higher rent than us because it just looked better. That's what I call common sense. The only time I yelled at a GM in ten years at Starwood Hotels was when I walked into a W in Chicago, and the plants were dead at the front door. First impressions matter. You can't put dead flowers into a spreadsheet.

There's a company I worked for in my summer of business school called Arvida Davis. They built some of the greatest resort communities in Florida—Boca, West Boca, Longboat Key, Sawgrass, a whole bunch of really successful master-planned communities. They spent, I think it was, $15,000 a house on landscaping when everyone else was spending $5,000. Not very complicated. They sold their houses faster and at higher prices, and had an incredible return on investment. But that's just the application of common sense. The most overused term in real estate is below replacement cost. Well, if it's twenty years old or thirty, it's a product that's not relevant today, it doesn't matter what you pay for it! People get trapped in that catchall phrase. I say it's "relevant replacement cost." I was in Saudi Arabia a couple days ago and I was saying that our goal if we continue to play in the office markets will be to "act like the Saudis." We're going to buy that beautiful Park Avenue office building that somebody paid, you know, $1,200 a foot for, and we'll buy it for $200 a foot and rent it for $20 a foot, net. I'll be full because I'm now the lowest cost of supply. If you can buy it really cheaply, you can destabilize the market. You can rent to that competitive advantage and fill your building and everyone else can't match you because they didn't buy the building for $200 a foot.

TONY:

I started working with Paul Tudor Jones twenty-five years ago, and one of the first lessons he gave me, he said, let me show you this stock. And he shows me that it's growing and growing and growing. He asks, "What do you do?"

And I said, "Well, I'm not the professional investor, but I'd keep going." And he says, "That's exactly what I try to teach. Almost everybody sells." Then he said that one of the reasons Warren Buffett is as rich as he is, is that he hates paying taxes. So, he hangs on to things forever. How do you know when you have the wins though? When do you sell? I'm curious about your principle for that. You've got something that's a winner—when do you sell?

BARRY:

We try to sell, if you see a ton of new supply coming into a market or an asset category. If we think there's going to be a shift in capital flows, like people will lose interest in one thing and go into something else. I think, when you're running a fund, you have to look at the whole fund and then you look at: What are the best things I can ride and what is just a trade? Second, there's always a buyer for great assets.

I'm in Dubai and we opened a Baccarat Residence here. They sold all the penthouses first. All of them. Seven. Went instantly. My friend had an apartment in, what is it, 59th Street, the new building in New York City, the beautiful, incredible residential tower. He bought his apartment for $95 million. We were convinced he was going to lose $50 million on it. He never finished it. He put it on the market. A buyer from China came and paid him $200 million for it. He was just hoping to get his money out. **There's always a buyer for great assets.**

THE TRUE HOLY GRAIL

"For where your treasure is, there your heart will be also."
Matthew 6:21

Like a marathon runner finally crossing the finish line, I hope you have a sense of satisfaction and fulfillment after taking in the content of this book. We have covered a lot of ground, and my deepest personal desire is that the wisdom, strategies, and insights herein become foundational in your pursuit of financial freedom (as they have for me and my family). More important, I want to remind you of a core truth: **Knowledge is not power, it's potential power. Execution trumps knowledge every day of the week.** My original mentor, Jim Rohn, used to say, "Don't let your learning lead to knowledge. You will become a fool. Let your learning lead to action!"

So how will you build *your* Holy Grail portfolio? As Dalio taught us early on, which 8–12 twelve uncorrelated strategies might you consider implementing to maximize upside and reduce risk by up to 80 percent? What steps can you immediately take on your financial freedom journey? **Which begs the question: What is financial freedom for you?**

When I interviewed the late Sir John Templeton, one of the first great international investors to become a billionaire, I asked him, "What's the secret to wealth?" He said, "Tony, it's what you teach." I laughed and said, "I teach a lot of things. Which thing?"

With a big smile on his face, he replied, "Gratitude! You know, Tony, we've both met people who have a billion dollars, and they live in state of frustration and anger. They're miserable. So they're truly poor. And we both know people who seemingly have nothing, yet they're grateful for the breath of life, for everything. So they're rich beyond compare."

In our hearts we all know that it's not money that makes us rich. As I'm sure you've found, the greatest treasures are never financial. It's those moments of grace when we appreciate the perfection and beauty of it all. It's those moments when we feel something eternal and invincible inside us, the core of our spirit. It's the loving warmth of our relationships with family and friends. It's laughter. It's finding meaningful work. It's the capacity to learn and grow, to share and serve. **This is the true Holy Grail.**

For me (Tony), it's also the joy of helping people break through their limits and seeing them light up as they remember who they really are and what they're capable of achieving. It's the delight of seeing their lives become a celebration instead of a battle. It's the magical feeling that somehow I've played a role in the awakening of a marvelous and unique human being. It's appreciating that everything I've gone through has served not only me but others—that even the deepest pain I've experienced has led to something beautiful. In fact, there can be no greater gift than for your life to have meaning beyond yourself. This is the ultimate game changer. Find something to serve, a cause you can be passionate about that's greater than yourself, and this will make you wealthy. Nothing enriches us like helping others.

The second tip I got from Sir John Templeton was the importance of tithing, or taking a portion of what you have—regardless how small—and giving it to others in need. Templeton shared that he had never met anyone who had faithfully given ten percent of their income for more than a decade that didn't also become abundantly wealthy. And the tithe doesn't need to be a church. It could be charity, your community, or anything that makes a positive impact in the world.

This psychological shift from scarcity to abundance makes you truly wealthy and brings you a glorious sense of freedom. In making this shift, you're training your brain to recognize that there's so much more available for you to give, to appreciate, and to love. And remember: It's not just money that you can donate. You can also give your time, your talent, your love, your compassion, and your heart.

I often hear people say that they will give when they become wealthy. This is a farce. A childhood friend of mine was recently on a flight. The gentleman next to him was reading *Life Force*, my recent book on the future of regenerative medicine and precision health. They struck up a conversation, and the gentleman had nothing but positive things to say about the book and recognized that all the proceeds from the book were being donated. Despite loving the book, he brushed off the donation, saying, "but he is rich, so he can afford it." My friend smiled and decided to reveal our friendship of more than forty-five years. He told the man that I had been donating since I was a broke teenager and recalled many moments where I would dig in my pockets for five or ten dollars to give to a homeless man even though I had less than a hundred dollars to my name.

Here is what I know: Waiting until you're wealthy to donate is a massive mistake, because you will rob yourself of the fulfillment you deserve and will likely never become generous. And if a person won't give a dime out of a dollar they will never give a hundred thousand out of a million or ten million out of a hundred million.

As an aside, I want to thank you for purchasing this book, as 100 percent of the proceeds will be provided to Feeding America. I was fed when I was eleven years old, and my family often struggled to put food on the table. It changed the course of my life and started me on a journey to provide meals to those in need. We already reached our goal of 1 billion meals served, and I am now working on a global 100 Billion Meal challenge!

Having said all this, I want you to know that my daily prayer is to be a blessing in the lives of all those I meet. If you make the tools and principles in this book a part of your core, you'll be able to receive—and give—more than you could ever imagine. As this extraordinary abundance flows to and from you, you will feel truly blessed—and become a greater blessing in the lives of others. This is what it feels like to possess real wealth.

I'm thankful that you've allowed us the privilege of spending this time with you. I know that the titans we interviewed are also grateful to be a part of your story. I sincerely hope that the contents of this book have been helpful to you on your journey. Perhaps someday our paths will cross, and I'll have the privilege of hearing the story of how this book has helped you accelerate the building of the life you desire and deserve.

Please return to these pages whenever you need a reminder of who you really are and all that you can create. Remember that you are more than the moment. You are more than your economics. You are more than any challenging time you may face.

God bless you, and LIVE WITH PASSION!

Continue the journey with us! While a book is a snapshot in time, we will be providing ongoing education and resources with our podcast, newsletter and more . . .

www.TheHolyGrailofInvesting.com

ACKNOWLEDGMENTS

TONY ROBBINS

As I reflect on over four and half decades of my mission, so many incredible human beings have been with me along the way. I'd like briefly to express my deep gratitude to those who have touched this particular project.

First, my family, of course. This begins and ends with my wife, Bonnie Pearl—my Sage. I love you. I give thanks for the grace that breathes our love and our life. To my dearest daughter, Violet Pearl—the incredible gift that God brought into our lives in an unexpected and beautiful way. To Mary B., my right hand, best friend, and co-mother of our little Violet. To my son, Josh, without whom this book wouldn't have been possible. You have done some serious heavy lifting to bring this book to fruition, and I am forever grateful for how much fun it is to work with my son on such an impactful project.

To my dear friend and partner Christopher Zook and the entire team at CAZ Investments. I am forever grateful for our partnership and for the wisdom and insights you bring to the table day in and day out. This book will be a part of your legacy of impact. To Ajay Gupta, my brother from another mother, and partner in our joint family office, Robbins Gupta Holdings. Thank you for your never-ending friendship, loyalty, and late-night strategy sessions!

My deepest thanks, respect, and admiration for those who shared their precious time and life's work in our interview sessions. Specifically, to the thirteen brilliant minds that generously contributed their wisdom from decades of experience for the benefit of our readers. To Robert F. Smith, Vinod Khosla, Michael Rees, Barry Sternlicht, Michael B. Kim, Bill Ford, Bob Zorich, Ian Charles, David Golub, Wil VanLoh, David Sacks, Tony Florence, and Ramzi Musallam.

A special thanks to my dear friend Ray Dalio, whose core principle of the Holy Grail of Investing inspired both the title and mission of this book.

Thanks again to all my partners at Simon & Schuster, especially CEO Jonathan Karp. And my incredible agent and dear friend of forty years, Jan Miller.

To my core team at Robbins Research International—all of our fiercely loyal and mission-driven executive staff—I count my blessings for you every day.

To the folks at Tiny Wins for their brilliant visual design and execution.

My life has been powerfully shaped by deep friendships with four brilliant men. To my role models Peter Guber, Marc Benioff, Paul Tudor Jones, and Steve Wynn.

Of course, the mission of this book is to serve not only those who will be reading. And so my deepest thanks to everyone at the Anthony Robbins Foundation and our strategic partners, namely, Claire Babineaux-Fontenot.

And Dan Nesbit at Feeding America for helping us coordinate our next 1 Billion Meals Challenge!

To the grace that has guided this entire process, and to all those friends and teachers along the path of my life—too many to mention, some famous and some unknown, whose insights, strategies, example, love, and caring are the shoulders I have had the honor to stand on. On this day, I give thanks to you all, and I continue my never-ending quest to each day be a blessing in the lives of all those I have the privilege to meet, love, and serve.

CHRISTOPHER ZOOK

From beginning to end, the entire project of producing this book has been surreal. Three decades ago, I began listening to Tony Robbins's coaching when the only mode of communication was through a cassette tape. If someone had told me then that thirty-plus years later Tony and I would co-author a book together, I am not sure what I would have said. Yet I also know God has a wonderful way of uniting people at just the right time. Tony, words cannot express the impact you have had on my life, from a young man listening to your teachings to a seasoned investor now operating a company with a worldwide footprint. I will be forever grateful for the partnership and friendship that has developed over the past years, and I look forward to what the future holds.

Josh Robbins, this book would not have been possible without the heavy lifting you did from beginning to end. You are extremely talented and a joy to work with. I am honored to call you friend.

Ajay Gupta, I am thankful for our friendship and the extent to which you support our team, and specifically me. Your joyful spirit brings a smile to my day.

To the CAZ Investments team, I thank God for you daily, and this firm, our firm, would not be where it is today without each of you. Everyone on our team has had an impact and I would like to give a special thank-you to Matt, Clark, Mark, Steve, Lucia, Isaiah, and Heather for everything they have done to put us on the map. We would not be where we are today without your Herculean work. And to Bailey and Kirk, who went above and beyond to keep the whirlwind at bay so I could dedicate the time needed for this project.

I send my endless thanks to the shareholders of CAZ. You are the ones who took a chance on a young man with a dream. I will forever be grateful.

To my mom, Dee; mother-in-law, Winona; sister, Kimberly; and extended family, each of you has breathed life into me in different ways. I am the man I am today because of what you have meant to my life.

I send my love to my son and daughter-in-law, Christopher and Cecelia, who are always there to share in our excitement and provide encouragement. And to Christopher III (Tripp), my first grandchild, you bring light to each day. It is the three of you I often think of when I remember why I go through the daily grind and stress. You are my motivation.

Above all others, and with deep, abiding love, I want to thank my wife, Lisa. You are my best friend, my high school sweetheart, and my cheerleader. When needed, you set me straight, and when I am too hard on myself, you make me laugh. Outside of God, the only reason I can soar is because you have always believed in me. I cannot imagine what my life would have been like without you. You are my greatest gift.

NOTES

CHAPTER ONE: THE SEARCH FOR THE HOLY GRAIL

5   *Private Credit, an alternative to bonds*: Moriah Costa, "Private or Public: Investing in Private Credit vs Bonds," *MoneyMade*, October 18, 2022.

7   *The G.O.A.T. For those who aren't familiar, Ray is the founder of Bridgewater*: Bridgewater Associated, LP, Berkshire Hathaway Inc., June 30, 2023.

7   *Their "Pure Alpha" fund has averaged over 11 percent*: Carolina Mandl, "Bridgewater's flagship fund posts gains of 32% through June," Reuters, July 5, 2022.

8   *In August of 2023, a Bloomberg headline*: Ye Xie, "Bonds Are Useless Hedge for Stock Losses as Correlation Jumps," *Bloomberg*, August 2, 2023.

8   *Between 2010 and 2020, REITs had an 80 percent positive correlation with the S&P 500*: Roger Wohlner, "REITs: Still a Viable Investment?," *Investopedia*, September 22, 2021.

9   *A Georgetown University study found that "crypto assets followed the market's lead"*: Hannah Zhang, "Crypto Is Becoming More Correlated to Stocks—And It's Your Fault," *Institutional Investor*, February 9, 2023.

9   *"The same is true for almost a quarter (25%) of those ages 75 to 84"*: Anne Tergesen, "America's Retirees Are Investing More Like 30-Year-Olds," *Wall Street Journal*, July 4, 2023.

12   *Ultra-high-net-worth families (those with over $30 million)*: Henry H. McVey, *KKR Blog*, May 10, 2017.

13   *On a global level, private equity outperformed public markets*: Caryn Slotsky, "Global ex US PE/VC Benchmark Commentary: Calendar Year 2021," Cambridge Associates LLC, August 2022.

13   *As you can see in the figure below, as an entire asset class, private euity produced average annual returns of 14.2 percent*: Caryn Slotsky, "US PE/VC Benchmark Commentary: First Half 2021," Cambridge Associates, January 2022.

14   *In all three cases, the "peak to trough" declines of the S&P 500 were far steeper*: "Current benchmark statistics," Cambridge Associates, Q1, 2023.

14   *Case in point, in 2021, on the heels of the pandemic and a global supply chain crisis*:

"McKinsey Global Private Markets Review: Private markets turn down the volume," McKinsey & Company, March 21, 2023.

14   *This is just slightly below the stellar performance of 33 percent in year 2020*: "A year of disruption in the private markets: McKinsey Global Private Markets Review 2021," McKinsey & Company, April 5, 2021.

15   *Private equity heavyweight Bain Capital wrote*: Hugh MacArthur et al., "The Private Equity Market in 2021: The Allure of Growth," Global Private Equity Report, Bain & Company, March 7, 2022.

15   *In fact, according to the* Financial Times: Robin Wigglesworth, "US has fewer listed public companies than China," *Financial Times*, October 6, 2019.

15   *In fact, back in 2009, 81 percent of public companies were profitable*: "Share of companies that were profitable after their IPO in the United States from 2008 to 2021," Statista, June 30, 2022.

15   *When you look at the total value of all publicly traded companies globally*: "2021 Preqin Global Private Equity & Venture Capital Report," Preqin Ltd., February 4, 2021.

16   *Numerous studies have shown that adding private equity to a typical stock-and-bond portfolio*: Anthony Tutrone, "Private Equity and Your Portfolio," Neuberger Berman Global Insights, January 2019.

16   *In addition to the many trillions already flowing into private markets*: Austin Ramsey, "Private Equity Firms Are Winning the Fight for Your 401(k)," *Bloomberg Law*, January 31, 2022.

18   *A story in the* Wall Street Journal *summed it up*: Miriam Gottfried, "Buying Stakes in Private-Equity Firms, Not Just Their Funds, Pays Big," *Wall Street Journal*, November 18, 2018.

21   *The firm has grown to be one of the top 200 allocators*: "April 2022 Global Markets Snapshot," PitchBook News & Analysis, May 3, 2022.

CHAPTER TWO: GP STAKES: A PIECE OF THE ACTION

25   *"More than a quarter of the wealthiest people in America"*: Rachel Sandler, "Nearly Half of America's Richest Billionaires Have Fortunes in These Two Industries," *Forbes*, October 26, 2021.

27   *For the investment nerds like us*: Author's note: In typical private equity investing, the J-Curve means investors in a fund initially show "losses" while their capital is being put to work to buy assets in the fund. This is followed by a reversal once the gains start to materialize, creating a J-like curve on a graph.

33   *After all, the universe of high-quality private asset managers is very limited*: Erik Fogelstrom and Jonatan Gustafsson, "GP Stakes in Private Equity: An Empirical Analysis of Minority Stakes in Private Equity Firms," MSc Thesis in Finance, Stockholm School of Economics, Spring 2020.

33   *A* Forbes *article from 2022 explains it well*: Benjamin Summers, "GP Stakes:

What You Should Know About Designer Financial Structures," *Forbes*, November 18, 2022.

CHAPTER THREE: PRO SPORTS OWNERSHIP: SWINGING FOR THE FENCES

36 *The sports economists and various talking heads*: Dayn Perry, "Report: Dodgers, Time Warner agree to more than $7 billion TV deal," CBSSports.com, January 22, 2013.

38 *Fast-forward to 2002*: Michael Haupert, "The Economic History of Major League Baseball," EH.net (Economic History Association), 2007.

40 *North American Major League Soccer*: Joseph Zucker, "LAFC Tops Forbes List of MLS Team Values; 1st Billion Dollar Franchise," Bleacher Report, February 2, 2023.

41 *In 2019, ninety-two of the top one hundred highest-rated programs on TV*: Austin Karp and John Ourand, "Politics aside, sports still dominated the list of the 100 most-viewed programs of 2020," *Sports Business Journal*, January 11, 2021.

44 *By all accounts, this is a modern-day gold rush*: News release, "2021 Commercial Gaming Revenue Shatters Industry Record, Reaches $53B," American Gaming Association, February 15, 2022.

46 Bloomberg *reported that the Fenway Sports Group*: Alex Wittenberg et al., "Private Equity Funds Are Pushing Deeper Into Pro Sports," *Bloomberg*, March 24, 2022.

46 *And according to PitchBook, more than a third of Europe's Big 5 soccer leagues*: Marie Kemplay, "US private capital scores big in European soccer," PitchBook, August 3, 2023.

CHAPTER FOUR: PRIVATE CREDIT: LEADERS IN LENDING

47 *"As fewer companies have gone public in recent years"*: Stacy Francis, "Op-ed: Demystifying private credit amid a frozen IPO market," CNBC, June 21, 2023.

48 *In the pages ahead, we explore how private credit has grown*: Kelsey Butler, "How Private Credit Soared to Fuel Private Equity Boom," *Bloomberg*, September 22, 2019.

49 *Put it all together*: Akane Otani, "The 60/40 Portfolio Is Delivering Its Worst Returns in a Century," *Wall Street Journal*, October 14, 2022.

49 Bloomberg *reported that "bonds are a useless hedge"*: Ye Xie, "Bonds Are Useless Hedge for Stock Losses as Correlation Jumps," *Bloomberg*, August 2, 2023.

50 *Contrast this with private credit*: Jeffrey Bartel, "Private Credit Investing: Current Opportunities and Risks," *Forbes*, March 30, 2023.

50 *On November 9 of 2021*, Bloomberg *wrote*: Paula Seligson, "U.S. Junk Bonds Set $432 Billion Record in Rush to Beat Rates," *Bloomberg*, November 9, 2021.

50 *Not even a year later, on October 22 of 2022*: Giulia Morpurgo et al., "Global Junk-Bond Sales Drop Most Ever With No Signs of Recovery," *Bloomberg*, October 24, 2022.

52 *This is why many firms see a "golden moment"*: Jessica Hamlin, "Blackstone sees a 'golden moment' in private credit after bank failures," PitchBook, April 20, 2023.

CHAPTER FIVE: ENERGY: THE POWER OF OUR LIVES (PART ONE)

59 *That's down from 77 percent in 2000*: "China increased electricity generation annually from 2000 to 2020," U.S. Energy Information Administration (EIA), September 22, 2022.

60 *And while the entire world retired 187 gigawatts of coal plants*: Editorial, "John Kerry Tilts at Chinese Coal Plants," *Wall Street Journal*, July 17, 2023.

60 *The Paris Climate Accords*: "China permits two new coal power plants per week in 2022," Centre for Research on Energy and Clean Air (CREA)," February 2023.

61 *In 2023, we are on track to use more oil*: Alex Lawler, "OPEC sees 2.2% oil demand growth in 2024 despite headwinds," Reuters, July 13, 2023.

61 *It took natural gas fifty years to reach 25 percent of global energy market share*: "2021–2025: Rebound and beyond," International Energy Agency (AEA), 2020.

62 *The International Monetary Fund (IMF) predicts*: Neil Ruiz et al., "Coming of Age," International Monetary Fund, March 2020.

63 *They ranked #2 on the Fortune Global 500 largest companies*: Vivienne Walt, "Saudi Arabia has the most profitable company in the history of the world, and $3.2 trillion to invest by 2030. Who will say no to that tidal wave of cash?" *Fortune*, August 1, 2023.

66 *The state reported that since the closing*: Thomas Zambito, "NY's fossil fuel use soared after Indian Point plant closure; officials sound the alarm," *Journal News* and lohud.com, July 22, 2022.

66 *Then, in another desperate move*: Philip Oltermann, "Stop dismantling German windfarm to expand coalmine, say authorities," *Guardian*, October 26, 2022.

67 *In addition, they are investing half a trillion dollars*: Dan Murtaugh and Krystal Chia, "China's Climate Goals Hinge on a $440 Billion Nuclear Buildout," *Bloomberg*, November 2, 2021.

70 *Somewhat ironic, considering that*: "Democratic Republic of the Congo—Country Commercial Guide," International Trade Administration, December 14, 2022.

72 *In 2022, California mandated that by 2035*: "California moves to accelerate to 100% new zero-emission vehicle sales by 2035," California Air Resources Board, CA.gov, August 25, 2022.

73 *To put that into perspective*: "2021 Total System Electric Generation," California Energy Commission, accessed on August 27, 2023.

74 *We will need two times more copper*: "Critical minerals market sees unprecedented growth as clean energy demand drives strong increase in investment," International Energy Agency, July 11, 2023.

CHAPTER SIX: ENERGY: THE POWER OF OUR LIVES (PART TWO)

81 *We produce about 22 percent of the world's energy*: Shannon Osaka, "The U.S. is the world's largest oil producer. You'll still pay more for gas," *Washington Post*, October 8, 2022.

81 *Case in point, U.S. natural gas is about 30 percent cleaner*: Matthew Mailloux, "Where American Gas Goes, Other Clean Energy Can Follow," ClearPath, June 16, 2022.

81 *This is why the U.S. has been leading the charge*: "2022 Global Gas Flaring Tracker Report," The World Bank, 2022.

83 *Mike Wirth, the CEO of Chevron*: Carl Surran, "No new refineries ever built again in the U.S., Chevron CEO warns," Seeking Alpha, June 3, 2022.

85 *According to Reuters, the U.S. is poised to become the world's largest LNG producer*: Scott Disavino, "U.S. poised to regain crown as world's top LNG exporter," Reuters, January 4, 2023.

87 *The* Harvard Business Review *estimates that retired solar panels*: Atalay Atasu et al., "The Dark Side of Solar Power," *Harvard Business Review*, June 18, 2021.

88 *As a material scientist, Simon holds a staggering 140 issued patents*: "Patents by Inventor Simon K. Hodson," JUSTIA Patents, Filed from 1990–1995; Patent dates from 1992–1997, accessed August 27, 2023.

89 *He walked into the nondescript metal building*: "Operating with Ethics and Integrity; a proud history of responsibility," Consol Energy, accessed August 27, 2023.

90 *Case in point, Tesla and other EV manufacturers*: Mirza Shehnaz, "Tesla supplier warns of graphite supply risk in 'opaque' market," *Financial Times*, November 20, 2022.

90 *Scientists at MIT were recently experimenting*: Jennifer Chu, "Physicists discover a 'family' of robust, superconducting grapheme structures," press release, MIT News, July 8, 2022.

CHAPTER SEVEN: VENTURE CAPITAL: INNOVATION AND DISRUPTIVE TECHNOLOGY

102 Time *magazine explained that*: Alice Park, "Scientists Have Reached a Key Milestone in Learning How to Reverse Aging," *Time*, January 12, 2023.

CHAPTER EIGHT: REAL ESTATE: THE WORLD'S BIGGEST ASSET

106 *With 7.9 billion people on earth*: Paul Tostevin, "The total value of global real estate," Savills, September 2021.

110 *When added to another 740 million square feet of space*: "Obsolescence Equals Opportunity," Report, Cushman & Wakefield, accessed on August 27, 2023.

112 Fortune *magazine reported that the "housing market shortage is so acute"*: Alena Botros, "Housing market shortage is so acute and the office glut is so big that Boston will offer 75% tax breaks on office-to-residential conversions," *Fortune*, July 13, 2023.

112 *Midjourney, the most popular AI image creation tool*: "Profile, Midjourney Company Stats," *Forbes*, accessed August 27, 2023.

113   *New York City lost 468,200 residents*: Elizabeth Pritchett, "New York City has lost nearly half a million residents since start of COVID pandemic," FoxBusiness, May 19, 2023.

113   *California is so fearful of further exodus*: Arthur Laffer and Stephen Moore, "'The 'Hotel California' Wealth Tax," *Wall Street Journal Opinion*, March 5, 2023.

113   *Charles Schwab, CBRE, and Oracle are just a few of the many titans*: "19 Corporations & Businesses Fleeing California for Texas," blog entry, Concordia University Texas, June 16, 2021.

114   *In 2023, the* Wall Street Journal *named Nashville, Tennessee*: Sarah Chaney Cambon and Danny Dougherty, "Sunbelt Cities Nashville and Austin Are Nation's Hottest Job Markets," *Wall Street Journal*, April 1, 2023.

114   *The landlords of San Francisco's largest mall*: Natalie Wong et al., "The World's Empty Office Buildings Have Become a Debt Time Bomb," *Bloomberg*, June 23, 2023.

115   *As a result of the coming loan predicament for banks and tenants*: Neil Callanan, "A $1.5 Trillion Wall of Debt Is Looming for US Commercial Properties," *Bloomberg*, April 8, 2023.

119   *Today, 980,000 homes are for sale, a forty-year low*: "Housing Inventory: Active Listing Count in the United States," FRED Economic Resource, updated August 8, 2023.

119   *That's barely more than half a million homes for sale*: "United States Total Housing Inventory," Trading Economics, July, 2023.

119   *According to Realtor.com, in September 2022*: Hannah Jones, "Data, Economic Coverage, Housing Supply," Realtor.com, November 21, 2022.

121   *An Indian immigrant and former IT worker*: Will Parker et al., "A Housing Bust Comes for Thousands of Small-Time Investors," *Wall Street Journal*, May 23, 2023.

122   *The* Wall Street Journal *reported that*: Konrad Putzier and Will Parker, "A Real-Estate Haven Turns Perilous With Roughly $1 Trillion Coming Due," *Wall Street Journal*, August 7, 2023.

INDEX

ABOUT THE AUTHORS

TONY

TONY ROBBINS is an entrepreneur, #1 *NY Times* bestselling author, philanthropist, and the nation's #1 life & business strategist. He has empowered more than 50 million people from 100 countries around the world through his audio programs, educational videos, and live seminars. For more than four and a half decades, millions of people have enjoyed the warmth, humor, and transformational power of Tony's business and personal development events.

Mr. Robbins is the author of six international bestsellers, including the 2014 *New York Times* #1 financial bestseller *MONEY: Master the Game* and *UNSHAKEABLE: Your Financial Freedom Playbook* (2017). His most recent book, *LIFE FORCE: How New Breakthroughs in Precision Medicine Can Transform the Quality of Your Life and Those You Love*, was released in February 2022.

Mr. Robbins is involved in more than 100 privately held businesses with combined sales exceeding $6 billion a year. He has been honored by Accenture as one of the "Top 50 Business Intellectuals in the World," by Harvard Business Press as one of the "Top 200 Business Gurus," and by American Express as one of the "Top Six Business Leaders in the World." *Fortune* magazine's cover article named him the "CEO Whisperer," and he has been named in the Top 50 of *Worth* magazine's 100 most powerful people in global finance for three consecutive years.

Mr. Robbins is a leader called upon by leaders. He has worked with four U.S. presidents, top entertainers—from Aerosmith to Green Day, Usher, and Pitbull, and athletes and sports teams, including tennis great Serena Williams, UFC champion Conor McGregor, and the NBA's Golden State Warriors. Business leaders and financial moguls from Salesforce.com founder Marc Benioff to Ray Dalio of Bridgewater Associates have tapped him for personal coaching.

Mr. Robbins is a leading philanthropist. Through his partnership with Feeding America, Mr. Robbins has provided more than one billion meals through his "1 Billion Meals" challenge, which was completed ahead of schedule. He is now working on a global "100 Billion Meal Challenge." Through the Tony Robbins Foundation, he has also awarded more than 2,000 grants and other resources to health and human services organizations, implemented a life-changing curriculum in 1,700-plus correctional facilities and gathered thousands of young leaders from around the world with its youth programs.

CHRISTOPHER

CHRISTOPHER ZOOK is the Founder, Chairman, and Chief Investment Officer of CAZ Investments (www.CAZInvestments.com). He has more than 30 years of experience investing in both traditional and alternative asset classes. Zook was recently honored with the Texas Alternative Investments Association's (TAIA) Lifetime Achievement Award in recognition of his contributions to, and sustained support of, the industry in Texas. He is a regular contributor to major media outlets, including CNBC, Fox Business, and Bloomberg.

In 2001, Zook founded CAZ Investments with one aim: to curate unique and exclusive investment opportunities for a network of investors—investments that most individuals would not otherwise have access to, as they are typically accessible only by major institutional investors. Fast-forward 23 years and CAZ Investments has more than 3,000 high-net-worth families (and numerous investment advisors) across the globe that have chosen to lock arms and invest as a unified front. Collectively, CAZ Investments is the equivalent of a large institutional investor, with superior access and buying power.

The mission of CAZ Investments is to lead with alignment. Zook and the shareholders invest their own personal capital first so that clients can rest assured that the correct incentives are in place.

Prior to starting CAZ Investments in 2001, Zook served in senior leadership positions with Oppenheimer, Prudential Securities, Lehman Brothers, and Paine Webber. Zook is actively involved in public policy and frequently serves as a resource to state and local officials. In 2019, Zook was appointed by the Texas governor to serve on the State of Texas Pension Review Board, where he serves as Chair of the Investment Committee. He also recently served two terms as a member of the Greater Houston Partner¬ship's Executive Committee and is past president of numerous charitable organizations. He is a graduate of Texas Tech University, where he was recently honored as a Distinguished Alumnus.

Zook is a lifelong Houstonian, and his greatest joy comes from being married to his high school sweetheart and from spending time with his son, daughter-in-law, and grandson.